MW00815170

THIS BIBLE BELONGS TO:

GIVEN BY:

DATE:

OCCASION:

"Strengthen yourselves so that you will live
here on earth doing what God wants."
—1 PETER 4:2

ALIGN

THE COMPLETE NEW TESTAMENT FOR MEN

NCV

NEW CENTURY VERSION®

WWW.MYFAITHANDLIFE.COM

NELSON BIBLES

A Division of Thomas Nelson Publishers

Since 1798

Align: The Complete New Testament for Men

Copyright © 2005 by Thomas Nelson, Inc.

The Holy Bible, New Century Version®.

Copyright © 2005 by Thomas Nelson, Inc. All rights reserved.

The Publisher is hereby pleased to grant permission for the *New Century Version* to be quoted or reprinted without written permission with the following qualifications: (1) up to and including one thousand (1,000) verses may be quoted, except: (a) the verses being quoted may not comprise as much as 50 percent of the work in which they are quoted, and/or (b) the verses quoted may not comprise an entire book of the Bible when quoted; (2) all NCV quotations must conform accurately to the NCV text.

Quotations from this Bible may be identified in written form with the abbreviation (NCV) in less formal documents, such as bulletins, newsletters, curriculum, media pieces, posters, transparencies, and where space is limited.

A proper credit line must appear on the title or copyright page of any work quoting from the *New Century Version*, as follows:

"Scriptures quoted from *The Holy Bible, New Century Version*®, copyright © 2005 by Thomas Nelson, Inc. Used by permission."

Quotations of more than 1,000 verses, or other permission requests, must be approved by Thomas Nelson, Inc., in writing in advance of use.

All excerpts used by permission.

The preliminary research and development of the *New Century Version* was done by the World Bible Translation Center, Inc., Fort Worth, TX 76182.

For media inquiries, contact Thomas Nelson, Inc., at:

P.O. Box 141000
Nashville, TN 37214-1000
1-800-251-4000

Managing Editor: Sean Fowlds
Cover Design: Anderson Thomas Design
Interior Design: Anderson Thomas Design
Contributors: Sean Fowlds, Dennis Hensley, Jeremy Roe, Ken Walker, Michael Warden, Terry Whalin, Marcus Yoars

All rights reserved.

Printed in the United States of America

1 2 3 4 5 6 7 8 9 10 --- 11 10 09 08 07 06 05

Introduction »

Getting properly aligned makes the journey smoother.

Align. One definition of the word is "to be in or come into precise adjustment or correct relative position." Namely, the person we are to come into precise adjustment or correct relative position to is Jesus Christ. He is our ultimate example of manhood, the one we are to align our lives with in spirit, soul, and body. Studying his life gives us the premier model upon which to pattern our relationships, homes, families, careers, businesses, and identities.

At its core, the New Testament is the action-packed story of the birth, life, death, burial, resurrection, and ascension of the founder of Christianity. In an effort to capture the meaning of the man and his message for contemporary audiences, this version of the New Testament is based on the *New Century Version* of the Bible. The text is incredibly reader-friendly, and its format is that of a magazine to further enhance your reading experience. Specifically designed to speak to every area of a man's life, it is called *Align*.

People Skills equips us to improve the interpersonal relationships in our lives. From communication techniques to conflict resolution to anger management, all and more is covered here.

If you're like most guys, you've craved the equivalent of an owner's manual for the women in your life, so we've done you the favor of creating one. It's called **For Men Only**, and it deals with issues like communicating in her language and understanding what makes her tick...and ticked off.

For fitness buffs and wannabes alike, **Get Fit** offers multiple tips for getting strengthened and toned through a range of activities, including swimming, biking, surfing, running, skiing, and kayaking.

Sexcess addresses the desires, needs, and problem areas of male sexuality and gives helpful suggestions for experiencing success with the opposite sex. Hot topics include resisting temptation, controlling your sex drive, and dealing with lust.

Many guys struggle with the management of money, so we've compiled useful guidelines for getting ahead without cutting corners in the feature called **The Bottom Line**. Whether it's budgeting, tithing, buying insurance, making investments, establishing savings, or paying taxes, you'll learn lots here.

Modern men interface with all sorts of technology, from high-tech computers to low-tech appliances. For extra help dealing with it all, there is **Tech Support**, our savvy guide to managing multiple media tools.

Whether or not you're a do-it-yourselfer, it helps to learn some simple cost-cutting methods for saving cash around the house. **Survival Guide** offers handy hints and how-to advice for handling such household chores as fixing leaky toilets and building outdoor decks.

Get Aligned offers practical insights from selected scriptures to help you center your priorities and maintain your focus on what really matters. From conquering complacency to learning to lead, help is here for the asking.

Whether you are a veteran traveler on the Christian voyage or a relative newcomer to the pilgrimage of faith, getting properly aligned will make your journey go much smoother. Wherever you are on your odyssey, *Align* will help you get to your destination with the tools needed for dealing with the potholes, as well as the pleasures, of life. As you follow Christ, be willing to make adjustments as necessary, and remember to schedule time for preventative measures, such as routine maintenance, along the highway of life.

> **"*Align.* One definition of the word is 'to be in or come into precise adjustment or correct relative position.'"**

{ Table of Contents }

>> Features

SURVIVAL GUIDE

GET FIT

TECH SUPPORT

>> Features (CONTINUED)

A note about the
New Century Version® »»

God never intended the Bible to be too difficult for his people. To make sure God's message was clear, the authors of the Bible recorded God's word in familiar everyday language. These books brought a message that the original readers could understand. These first readers knew that God spoke through these books. Down through the centuries, many people wanted a Bible so badly that they copied different Bible books by hand!

Today, now that the Bible is readily available, many Christians do not regularly read it. Many feel that the Bible is too hard to understand or irrelevant to life.

The *New Century Version* captures the clear and simple message that the very first readers understood. This version presents the Bible as God intended it: clear and dynamic.

A team of scholars from the World Bible Translation Center worked together with twenty-one other experienced Bible scholars from all over the world to translate the text directly from the best available Greek and Hebrew texts. You can trust that this Bible accurately presents God's Word as it came to us in the original languages.

Translators kept sentences short and simple. They avoided difficult words and worked to make the text easier to read. They used modern terms for places and measurements. And they put figures of speech and idiomatic expressions ("he was gathered to his people") in language that even children understand ("he died").

Following the tradition of other English versions, the *New Century Version* indicates the divine name, *Yahweh*, by putting LORD, and sometimes GOD, in capital letters. This distinguishes it from *Adonai*, another Hebrew word that is translated Lord.

We acknowledge the infallibility of God's Word and yet our own frailty. We pray that God will use this Bible to help you understand his rich truth for yourself. To God be the glory.

From the Editors of *Align: The Complete New Testament for Men*

THE GOSPEL ACCORDING TO Matthew

AUTHOR: MATTHEW
DATE WRITTEN: A.D. 45–70

RECEIVING A LETTER WITH THE RETURN address of the Internal Revenue Service typically makes your heart race a little. Whether or not you've done anything wrong, suddenly you have to respond directly to the tax agency. Tax collectors are generally unpopular during any era of history, but that was especially so during the reign of the Roman Empire. The public tax collector was the very last person someone would want as a friend.

Matthew was one of those despised tax collectors, yet Jesus Christ called him to leave everything and follow him as one of the chosen apostles. And as a result of his writing, the Gospel of Matthew records the life of Christ from his unique perspective. Throughout his account, Matthew tells stories that emphasize how Jesus fulfilled the prophecies of the Old Testament.

Keenly aware of his audience, Matthew knew many Jews were looking for their Messiah. So, he begins by tracing the ancestors of Jesus back to the line of David and telling about Jesus' birth and early years, including his escape to Egypt as a child. The stories from Matthew reveal Jesus as the Messiah while introducing the kingdom of God to readers.

The Family History of Jesus

1 This is the family history of Jesus Christ. He came from the family of David, and David came from the family of Abraham. [2]Abraham was the father[*] of Isaac.

Isaac was the father of Jacob.

Jacob was the father of Judah and his brothers.

[3]Judah was the father of Perez and Zerah.

(Their mother was Tamar.)

Perez was the father of Hezron.

Hezron was the father of Ram.

[4]Ram was the father of Amminadab.

Amminadab was the father of Nahshon.

Nahshon was the father of Salmon.

[5]Salmon was the father of Boaz.

(Boaz's mother was Rahab.)

Boaz was the father of Obed.

(Obed's mother was Ruth.)

Obed was the father of Jesse.

[6]Jesse was the father of King David.

David was the father of Solomon.

(Solomon's mother had been Uriah's wife.)

[7]Solomon was the father of Rehoboam.

Rehoboam was the father of Abijah.

Abijah was the father of Asa.[*]

[8]Asa was the father of Jehoshaphat.

Jehoshaphat was the father of Jehoram.

Jehoram was the ancestor of Uzziah.

[9]Uzziah was the father of Jotham.

Jotham was the father of Ahaz.

Ahaz was the father of Hezekiah.

[10]Hezekiah was the father of Manasseh.

Manasseh was the father of Amon.

Amon was the father of Josiah.

[11]Josiah was the grandfather of Jehoiachin[*] and his brothers.

(This was at the time that the people were taken to Babylon.)

[12]After they were taken to Babylon:

Jehoiachin was the father of Shealtiel.

Shealtiel was the grandfather of Zerubbabel.

[13]Zerubbabel was the father of Abiud.

Abiud was the father of Eliakim.

Eliakim was the father of Azor.

[14]Azor was the father of Zadok.

Zadok was the father of Akim.

Akim was the father of Eliud.

[15]Eliud was the father of Eleazar.

Eleazar was the father of Matthan.

Matthan was the father of Jacob.

[16]Jacob was the father of Joseph.

Joseph was the husband of Mary,

and Mary was the mother of Jesus.

Jesus is called the Christ.

[17]So there were fourteen generations from Abraham to David. And there were fourteen generations from David until the people were taken to Babylon. And there were fourteen generations from the time when the people were taken to Babylon until Christ was born.

The Birth of Jesus Christ

[18]This is how the birth of Jesus Christ came about. His mother Mary was engaged[*] to marry Joseph, but before they married, she learned she was pregnant by the power of the Holy Spirit. [19]Because Mary's husband, Joseph, was a good man, he did not want to disgrace her in public, so he planned to divorce her secretly.

Q: If Jesus was the Son of God, why did he call himself the Son of Man?

A: The phrase "Son of Man" is a reference to Jesus' humanity, not a denial of his deity. By becoming a man, Jesus did not cease being God. The incarnation of Christ did not involve the subtraction of deity, but the addition of humanity (Luke 9:22; John 3:13).

Principles: BAPTISM

Baptism is a ceremony that publicly acknowledges a person's faith in Jesus Christ. Jesus demonstrated its importance in Matthew 3:13–15 when he went to the Jordan River to be baptized by John. When John protested that he should be baptized instead, Jesus replied, "We should do all things that are God's will." Likewise, when those who responded to Peter's preaching asked what they should do afterward, he replied, "Change your heart and lives and be baptized…" (Acts 2:38). However, even this outward ceremony isn't as important as the change that takes place in a person's heart.

>> **1:2 father** "Father" in Jewish lists of ancestors can sometimes mean grandfather or more distant relative. **1:7 Asa** Some Greek copies read "Asaph," another name for Asa (see 1 Chronicles 3:10). **1:11 Jehoiachin** The Greek reads "Jeconiah," another name for Jehoiachin (see 2 Kings 24:6 and 1 Chronicles 3:16). **1:18 engaged** For the Jewish people an engagement was a lasting agreement, which could only be broken by a divorce. If a bride-to-be was unfaithful, it was considered adultery, and she could be put to death.

▶Get Aligned

Matthew 2:12

THE WISE MEN WERE SMART. They were schooled individuals. The original Greek term indicates they were an elite class of astronomers. However, all the intelligence in the world couldn't guide them through the trap Herod had set for them. He wanted Jesus dead before the reported messiah could threaten his rulership. Yet he feigned adoration of Christ, asking the easterners to reveal the child's location so he, too, could worship him.

Consumed with the historical events surrounding them, the wise men were probably oblivious to Herod's real intentions. For all their wisdom, they lacked discernment—until God spoke to them. In fact, the Lord intervened with divine wisdom several times within the context of this verse. His holy guidance was literally life-saving for those to whom he spoke.

It's no different today. Hearing God's voice is essential to the Christian walk. Discerning good from evil is a fundamental tool for believers, but it still requires divine intervention more than knowledge or intellect. When you're facing a tough decision, the Father is waiting with guidance for your life. Likewise, when the path seems clear, it's just as crucial to listen for his direction.

the prophet: [23]"The virgin will be pregnant. She will have a son, and they will name him Immanuel,'" which means "God is with us."

[24]When Joseph woke up, he did what the Lord's angel had told him to do. Joseph took Mary as his wife, [25]but he did not have sexual relations with her until she gave birth to the son. And Joseph named him Jesus.

Wise Men Come to Visit Jesus

2 Jesus was born in the town of Bethlehem in Judea during the time when Herod was king. When Jesus was born, some wise men from the east came to Jerusalem. [2]They asked, "Where is the baby who was born to be the king of the Jews? We saw his star in the east and have come to worship him."

[3]When King Herod heard this, he was troubled, as were all the people in Jerusalem. [4]Herod called a meeting of all the leading priests and teachers of the law and asked them where the Christ would be born. [5]They answered, "In the town of Bethlehem in Judea. The prophet wrote about this in the Scriptures:

[6]"But you, Bethlehem, in the land of Judah,
    are not just an insignificant village in Judah.
 A ruler will come from you
    who will be like a shepherd for my people Israel.' "   *Micah 5:2*

[7]Then Herod had a secret meeting with the wise men and learned from them the exact time they first saw the star. [8]He sent the wise men to Bethlehem, saying, "Look carefully for the child. When you find him, come tell me so I can worship him too."

[9]After the wise men heard the king, they left. The star that they had seen in the east went before them until it stopped above the place where the child was. [10]When the wise men saw the star, they were filled with joy. [11]They came to the house where the child was and saw him with his mother, Mary, and they bowed down and worshiped him. They opened their gifts and gave him treasures of gold, frankincense, and myrrh. [12]But God warned the wise men in a dream not to go back to Herod, so they returned to their own country by a different way.

[20]While Joseph thought about these things, an angel of the Lord came to him in a dream. The angel said, "Joseph, descendant of David, don't be afraid to take Mary as your wife, because the baby in her is from the Holy Spirit. [21]She will give birth to a son, and you will name him Jesus,[a] because he will save his people from their sins." [22]All this happened to bring about what the Lord had said through

▶ Survival Guide

AIR CONDITIONING: COOL IDEAS

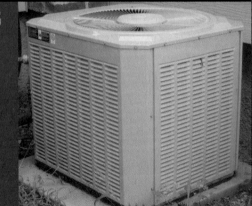

Nearly two-thirds of American homes have air conditioning, but not all use it properly. Pick the right size for the area you're cooling. Whether too large or too small, the wrong unit can waste electricity and spell poor results. Clean or replace the filter regularly, as well as the condenser coils and fins. Don't overcool; you can save up to three percent on utility costs for every degree you raise the thermostat in warm weather. And don't fear sweat. Those glands are God's way of cooling us down.

>> **1:21 Jesus** The name "Jesus" means "salvation."   **1:23 "The virgin ... Immanuel"** Quotation from Isaiah 7:14.

Jesus' Parents Take Him to Egypt

[13]After they left, an angel of the Lord came to Joseph in a dream and said, "Get up! Take the child and his mother and escape to Egypt, because Herod is starting to look for the child so he can kill him. Stay in Egypt until I tell you to return."

[14]So Joseph got up and left for Egypt during the night with the child and his mother. [15]And Joseph stayed in Egypt until Herod died. This happened to bring about what the Lord had said through the prophet: "I called my son out of Egypt."[n]

Herod Kills the Baby Boys

[16]When Herod saw that the wise men had tricked him, he was furious. So he gave an order to kill all the baby boys in Bethlehem and in the surrounding area who were two years old or younger. This was in keeping with the time he learned from the wise men. [17]So what God had said through the prophet Jeremiah came true:

[18]"A voice was heard in Ramah
　　of painful crying and deep sadness:
Rachel crying for her children.
　　She refused to be comforted,
　　because her children are dead."

Jeremiah 31:15

Joseph and Mary Return

[19]After Herod died, an angel of the Lord spoke to Joseph in a dream while he was in Egypt. [20]The angel said, "Get up! Take the child and his mother and go to the land of Israel, because the people who were trying to kill the child are now dead."

[21]So Joseph took the child and his mother and went to Israel. [22]But he heard that Archelaus was now king in Judea since his father Herod had died. So Joseph was afraid to go there. After being

<< TechSupport >>

HANDHELD DEVICES

When it comes to electronic calendars and planning tools, there are a wide variety of choices. From personal digital assistants to handhelds, there is a style for everyone. Instead of lugging around a separate address book, calendar, and cell phone, consider the latest combination of handhelds. They pack cell phone functionality into the compact electronic handheld format, including an address book and calendar. They even synchronize with your home or work computer. Install an electronic Bible program, and you'll have instant access to the ultimate guide for your life.

Change >> Your WORLD

ADVANCING CHURCHES IN MISSIONS COMMITMENT

One of the last commandments from Jesus Christ was to preach the Good News throughout the world. With specific interest in missions, on the decline in the early seventies, Advancing Churches in Missions Commitment (ACMC) was started so the local church could mobilize its limited resources to evangelize the world for Christ. The group holds seminars to educate individuals regarding how they can touch their world spiritually, physically, and emotionally. The quarterly publication *Mobilizer* includes practical resources, such as books, videos, and other materials to help believers of every age become involved in missions.

To change your world, visit www.acmc.org.

warned in a dream, he went to the area of Galilee, [23]to a town called Nazareth, and lived there. And so what God had said through the prophets came true: "He will be called a Nazarene."[n]

The Work of John the Baptist

3 About that time John the Baptist began preaching in the desert area of Judea. [2]John said, "Change your hearts and lives because the kingdom of heaven is near." [3]John the Baptist is the one Isaiah the prophet was talking about when he said:

"This is a voice of one
　　who calls out in the desert:
'Prepare the way for the Lord.
　　Make the road straight for him.' "

Isaiah 40:3

[4]John's clothes were made from camel's hair, and he wore a leather belt around his waist. For food, he ate locusts and wild honey. [5]Many people came from Jerusalem and Judea and all the area around the

>> **2:15** "I called … Egypt." Quotation from Hosea 11:1.　**2:23** **Nazarene** A person from the town of Nazareth. Matthew may be referring to Isaiah 11:1, where the Hebrew word translated "branch" sounds like "Nazarene."

5

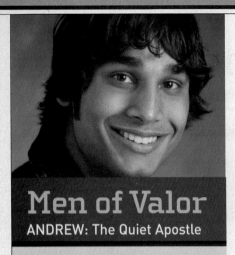

Men of Valor

ANDREW: The Quiet Apostle

Not much is written about Peter's brother, but there are signs of his faithfulness and service. According to John 1:35–42, Andrew was the first one to follow Christ, and he was alongside Christ at key events. After Jesus performed a miracle of exorcism, he went to Andrew and Peter's home. Andrew was one of four followers whom Christ told about end-time events. When Christ fed five thousand people, Andrew found the boy with five loaves and two fish, which Jesus miraculously multiplied. Andrew was present when the apostles gathered after Christ rose into heaven. This follower is proof that quiet and humble people can play a valuable role in God's service.

Jordan River to hear John. [6]They confessed their sins, and he baptized them in the Jordan River.

[7]Many of the Pharisees and Sadducees came to the place where John was baptizing people. When John saw them, he said, "You are snakes! Who warned you to run away from God's coming punishment? [8]Do the things that show you really have changed your hearts and lives. [9]And don't think you can say to yourselves, 'Abraham is our father.' I tell you that God could make children for Abraham from these rocks. [10]The ax is now ready to cut down the trees, and every tree that does not produce good fruit will be cut down and thrown into the fire."

[11]"I baptize you with water to show that your hearts and lives have changed. But there is one coming after me who is greater than I am, whose sandals I am not good enough to carry. He will baptize you with the Holy Spirit and fire. [12]He will come ready to clean the grain, separating the good grain from the chaff. He will put the good part of the grain into his barn, but he will burn the chaff with a fire that cannot be put out."[n]

Jesus Is Baptized by John

[13]At that time Jesus came from Galilee to the Jordan River and wanted John to baptize him. [14]But John tried to stop him, saying, "Why do you come to me to be baptized? I need to be baptized by you!"

[15]Jesus answered, "Let it be this way for now. We should do all things that are God's will." So John agreed to baptize Jesus.

[16]As soon as Jesus was baptized, he came up out of the water. Then heaven opened, and he saw God's Spirit coming down on him like a dove. [17]And a voice from heaven said, "This is my Son, whom I love, and I am very pleased with him."

The Temptation of Jesus

4 Then the Spirit led Jesus into the desert to be tempted by the devil. [2]Jesus fasted for forty days and nights. After this, he was very hungry. [3]The devil came to Jesus to tempt him, saying, "If you are the Son of God, tell these rocks to become bread."

[4]Jesus answered, "It is written in the Scriptures, 'A person lives not on bread alone, but by everything God says.' "[n]

[5]Then the devil led Jesus to the holy city of Jerusalem and put him on a high place of the Temple. [6]The devil said, "If you are the Son of God, jump down, because it is written in the Scriptures:

'He has put his angels in charge of you.
    They will catch you in their hands
so that you will not hit your foot on a
    rock.' "   Psalm 91:11–12

[7]Jesus answered him, "It also says in the Scriptures, 'Do not test the Lord your God.' "[n]

[8]Then the devil led Jesus to the top of a very high mountain and showed him all the kingdoms of the world and all their splendor. [9]The devil said, "If you will bow down and worship me, I will give you all these things."

[10]Jesus said to the devil, "Go away from me, Satan! It is written in the Scriptures, 'You must worship the Lord your God and serve only him.' "[n]

[11]So the devil left Jesus, and angels came and took care of him.

Jesus Begins Work in Galilee

[12]When Jesus heard that John had been put in prison, he went back to Galilee. [13]He left Nazareth and went to live in Capernaum, a town near Lake Galilee, in the area near Zebulun and Naphtali. [14]Jesus did this to bring about what the prophet Isaiah had said:

[15]"Land of Zebulun and land of Naphtali
    along the sea,
beyond the Jordan River.
    This is Galilee where the non-Jewish
        people live.
[16]These people who live in darkness
    will see a great light.
They live in a place covered with the
        shadows of death,
    but a light will shine on them."
                              Isaiah 9:1–2

Jesus Chooses Some Followers

[17]From that time Jesus began to preach, saying, "Change your hearts and lives, because the kingdom of heaven is near."

[18]As Jesus was walking by Lake Galilee, he saw two brothers, Simon (called Peter) and his brother Andrew. They were throwing a net into the lake because they were fishermen. [19]Jesus said, "Come follow me, and I will

FACTOIDS!

Ten times more people suffer from major depression now than in 1945. [American Psychological Association Monitor]

>> **3:10 The ax ... fire.** This means that God is ready to punish his people who do not obey him.   **3:12 He will ... out.** This means that Jesus will come to separate good people from bad people, saving the good and punishing the bad.   **4:4 'A person ... says.'** Quotation from Deuteronomy 8:3.   **4:7 'Do ... God.'** Quotation from Deuteronomy 6:16.   **4:10 'You ... him.'** Quotation from Deuteronomy 6:13.

Q: Where did God come from?

A: The Bible makes it clear that God is eternal, with no beginning or end. He exists outside of the dimension we call time. In fact, he is the creator of time. Therefore, he is not limited or defined by it. He is timeless (John 1:1–3).

make you fish for people." ²⁰So Simon and Andrew immediately left their nets and followed him.

²¹As Jesus continued walking by Lake Galilee, he saw two other brothers, James and John, the sons of Zebedee. They were in a boat with their father Zebedee, mending their nets. Jesus told them to come with him. ²²Immediately they left the boat and their father, and they followed Jesus.

Jesus Teaches and Heals People

²³Jesus went everywhere in Galilee, teaching in the synagogues, preaching the Good News about the kingdom of heaven, and healing all the people's diseases and sicknesses. ²⁴The news about Jesus spread all over Syria, and people brought all the sick to him. They were suffering from different kinds of diseases. Some were in great pain, some had demons, some were epileptics," and some were paralyzed. Jesus healed all of them. ²⁵Many people from Galilee, the Ten Towns," Jerusalem, Judea, and the land across the Jordan River followed him.

Jesus Teaches the People

5 When Jesus saw the crowds, he went up on a hill and sat down. His followers came to him, ²and he began to teach them, saying:

>> live the life

Matthew 5:9

The Principle > **Become a peacemaker.**

Practicing It > **Think about how you can promote peace in your community. Become a peacemaker by supporting people, causes, or organizations that promote peace around the world.**

³"They are blessed who realize their spiritual poverty,
for the kingdom of heaven belongs to them.
⁴They are blessed who grieve,
for God will comfort them.
⁵They are blessed who are humble,
for the whole earth will be theirs.
⁶They are blessed who hunger and thirst after justice,
for they will be satisfied.
⁷They are blessed who show mercy to others,
for God will show mercy to them.
⁸They are blessed whose thoughts are pure,
for they will see God.
⁹They are blessed who work for peace,
for they will be called God's children.
¹⁰They are blessed who are persecuted for doing good,
for the kingdom of heaven belongs to them.
¹¹"People will insult you and hurt you. They will lie and say all kinds of evil things about you because you follow me. But when they do,

Get Fit

EATING BREAKFAST Your body needs fuel to run at its peak. If you skip breakfast because you feel you don't have time to eat, your energy will plummet. And if you skip the morning meal regularly, you're setting up a chain reaction in your body that can lead to low blood sugar, headaches, sleep problems, and unwanted weight gain. Research shows that breakfast eaters not only feel better mentally and physically compared with guys who skip breakfast, but they also tend to enjoy a healthier lifestyle and are better at dealing with depression and emotional stress. Starting your day with feeding on the Word of God will keep you spiritually fit, also.

>> **4:24 epileptics** People with a disease that causes them sometimes to lose control of their bodies and maybe faint, shake strongly, or not be able to move. **4:25 Ten Towns** In Greek, called "Decapolis." It was an area east of Lake Galilee that once had ten main towns.

People Skills

Nonverbal Communication

Communication research suggests that up to 80 percent of all communication is nonverbal. To enjoy success relating to other people, it is vital to know exactly what your body language is saying. To gain insight into your own nonverbal cues, take a few moments to imagine your typical day projected onto a screen as a silent movie. As you watch the movie, notice what messages your body language is communicating to the people you encounter. Are those the messages you want to communicate? Think about how you might change your body language to better reflect the message you want to send to others. Pray also for personal insight.

you will be blessed. [12]Rejoice and be glad, because you have a great reward waiting for you in heaven. People did the same evil things to the prophets who lived before you.

You Are Like Salt and Light

[13]"You are the salt of the earth. But if the salt loses its salty taste, it cannot be made salty again. It is good for nothing, except to be thrown out and walked on.

[14]"You are the light that gives light to the world. A city that is built on a hill cannot be hidden. [15]And people don't hide a light under a bowl. They put it on a lampstand so the light shines for all the people in the house. [16]In the same way, you should be a light for other people. Live so that they will see the good things you do and will praise your Father in heaven.

The Importance of the Law

[17]"Don't think that I have come to destroy the law of Moses or the teaching of the prophets. I have not come to destroy them but to bring about what they said. [18]I tell you the truth, nothing will disappear from the law until heaven and earth are gone. Not even the smallest letter or the smallest part of a letter will be lost until everything has happened. [19]Whoever refuses to obey any command and teaches other people not to obey that command will be the least important in the kingdom of heaven. But whoever obeys the commands and teaches other people to obey them will be great in the kingdom of heaven. [20]I tell you that if you are no more obedient than the teachers of the law and the Pharisees, you will never enter the kingdom of heaven.

Jesus Teaches About Anger

[21]"You have heard that it was said to our people long ago, 'You must not murder anyone.'[n] Anyone who murders another will be judged.' [22]But I tell you, if you are angry with a brother or sister,[n] you will be judged. If you say bad things to a brother or sister, you will be judged by the council. And if you call someone a fool, you will be in danger of the fire of hell.

[23]"So when you offer your gift to God at the altar, and you remember that your brother or sister has something against you, [24]leave your gift there at the altar. Go and make peace with that person, and then come and offer your gift.

[25]"If your enemy is taking you to court, become friends quickly, before you go to court. Otherwise, your enemy might turn you over to the judge, and the judge might give you to a guard to put you in jail. [26]I tell you the truth, you will not leave there until you have paid everything you owe.

Jesus Teaches About Sexual Sin

[27]"You have heard that it was said, 'You must not be guilty of adultery.'[n] [28]But I tell you that if anyone looks at a woman and wants to sin sexually with her, in his mind he has already done that sin with the woman. [29]If your right eye causes you to sin, take it out and throw it away. It is better to lose one part of your body than to have your whole body thrown into hell. [30]If your right hand causes you to sin, cut it off and throw it away. It is better to lose one part of your body than for your whole body to go into hell.

Jesus Teaches About Divorce

[31]"It was also said, 'Anyone who divorces his wife must give her a written divorce paper.'[n] [32]But I tell you that anyone who divorces his wife forces her to be guilty of adultery. The only reason for a man to divorce his wife is if she has sexual relations with another man. And anyone who marries that divorced woman is guilty of adultery.

> **FACT-OIDS!** The presidential salary has grown from George Washington's $25,000 in 1789 to George W. Bush's $400,000 in 2005. [Library of Congress]

▶▶ 5:21 'You . . . anyone.' Quotation from Exodus 20:13; Deuteronomy 5:17. 5:22 sister Some Greek copies continue, "without a reason." 5:27 'You . . . adultery.' Quotation from Exodus 20:14; Deuteronomy 5:18. 5:31 'Anyone . . . divorce paper.' Quotation from Deuteronomy 24:1.

>> live the life

Matthew 5:37

The Principle > Honor your word.

Practicing It > An important part of being a man of God is being a man of your word. People need to know that when you say yes, they can trust that you mean it. Don't go back on your words. If you say you'll do something, do it.

Make Promises Carefully

33"You have heard that it was said to our people long ago, 'Don't break your promises, but keep the promises you make to the Lord.'" 34But I tell you, never swear an oath. Don't swear an oath using the name of heaven, because heaven is God's throne. 35Don't swear an oath using the name of the earth, because the earth belongs to God. Don't swear an oath using the name of Jerusalem, because that is the city of the great King. 36Don't even swear by your own head, because you cannot make one hair on your head become white or black. 37Say only yes if you mean yes, and no if you mean no. If you say more than yes or no, it is from the Evil One.

Don't Fight Back

38"You have heard that it was said, 'An eye for an eye, and a tooth for a tooth.'" 39But I tell you, don't stand up against an evil person. If someone slaps you on the right cheek, turn to him the other cheek also. 40If someone wants to sue you in court and take your shirt, let him have your coat also. 41If someone forces you to go with him one mile, go with him two miles. 42If a person asks you for something,

(▷) Get Aligned

Matthew 5:22

THIS PASSAGE DESCRIBES some harsh punishments for what seem to be minor issues. Getting angry? Saying bad things? Calling someone a fool? Surely such acts aren't worthy of being judged as deserving the fire of hell.

Not so fast. Jesus' teaching about God's kingdom turned the Mosaic Law upside down. It infuriated the scribes and Pharisees who took great pride in following those regulations exactly. The Lord's purpose was not to disregard the system God had established; it was to show how serious an issue judging others is to the Father. Getting angry with someone for no reason, talking about him behind his back, calling him a fool—these are all actions of self-elevation. Whether you realize it or not, you're playing the role of the ultimate judge when you attack a person's character. Only God determines the fool from the wise man.

Does this mean if you've ever called someone a fool or criticized a person you're going to hell? No, but it does mean you should put more stock in how you act toward others. When it comes to lashing out against someone, remember that God knows your thoughts, he sees your actions, and he hears your words. He's the judge, not you.

give it to him. Don't refuse to give to someone who wants to borrow from you.

Love All People

43"You have heard that it was said, 'Love your neighbor" and hate your enemies.' 44But I say to you, love your enemies. Pray for

→ The Bottom Line

Bankruptcy: Counting the Cost

IF YOU'VE MAXIMIZED your credit cards, owe more on your cars than they're worth, and are always staggering to the next payday, bankruptcy may sound like the solution. But in Luke 14:28, Jesus advised readers that before doing something, it is wise to count the cost. Not only does new federal legislation make it tougher to wipe out debts, things like student loans, alimony, and child support might never be canceled. Other financial and psychological costs, such as filing fees, attorneys' billing time, and damage to your credit record can be steep. In the short run, fiscal lifestyle adjustments may be tough, but they pay off in the end.

>> **5:33** 'Don't ... Lord.' This refers to Leviticus 19:12; Numbers 30:2; Deuteronomy 23:21.   **5:38** 'An eye ... tooth.' Quotation from Exodus 21:24; Leviticus 24:20; Deuteronomy 19:21.   **5:43** 'Love your neighbor' Quotation from Leviticus 19:18.

FOR Men Only

LISTENING   Men are often good talkers, but not such good listeners. Yet women value a listening ear as much, if not more, than smooth talk. One way to show a woman you value her is to maintain good eye contact while she is speaking. Not the creepy stare-down, mind you, just attentive watchfulness that says, "I care as you share." Don't use your time spent listening only to think of what to say next. Whereas hearing merely involves the processing of sounds, listening means paying attention to what is said. Smooth talkers are a dime a dozen, but good listeners are few and far between.

those who hurt you." ⁴⁵If you do this, you will be true children of your Father in heaven. He causes the sun to rise on good people and on evil people, and he sends rain to those who do right and to those who do wrong. ⁴⁶If you love only the people who love you, you will get no reward. Even the tax collectors do that. ⁴⁷And if you are nice only to your friends, you are no better than other people. Even those who don't know God are nice to their friends. ⁴⁸So you must be perfect, just as your Father in heaven is perfect.

Jesus Teaches About Giving

6 "Be careful! When you do good things, don't do them in front of people to be seen by them. If you do that, you will have no reward from your Father in heaven.

>> live the life

Matthew 5:39–42

The Principle > **Go the extra mile.**

Practicing It > **Let God's Word stretch you beyond your comfort zone. If you do, you'll experience the presence of Christ and the power of the Good News in new and deeper ways.**

²"When you give to the poor, don't be like the hypocrites. They blow trumpets in the synagogues and on the streets so that people will see them and honor them. I tell you the truth, those hypocrites already have their full reward. ³So when you give to the poor, don't let anyone know what you are doing. ⁴Your giving should be done in secret. Your Father can see what is done in secret, and he will reward you.

Jesus Teaches About Prayer

⁵"When you pray, don't be like the hypocrites. They love to stand in the synagogues and on the street corners and pray so people will see them. I tell you the truth, they already have their full reward. ⁶When you pray, you should go into your room and close the door and pray to your Father who cannot be seen. Your Father can see what is done in secret, and he will reward you.

⁷"And when you pray, don't be like those people who don't know God. They continue saying things that mean nothing, thinking that God will hear them because of their many words. ⁸Don't be like them, because your Father knows the things you need before you ask him. ⁹So when you pray, you should pray like this:

'Our Father in heaven,
may your name always be kept holy.
¹⁰May your kingdom come
and what you want be done,
    here on earth as it is in heaven.
¹¹Give us the food we need for each day.
¹²Forgive us for our sins,
    just as we have forgiven those who sinned against us.
¹³And do not cause us to be tempted,
    but save us from the Evil One.'
        [The kingdom, the
        power, and the glory
        are yours forever.
        Amen.]"

¹⁴Yes, if you forgive others for their sins, your Father in heaven will also forgive you for your sins. ¹⁵But if you don't forgive others, your Father in heaven will not forgive your sins.

Jesus Teaches About Worship

¹⁶"When you fast," don't put on a sad face like the hypocrites. They make their faces look sad to show people they are fasting. I tell you the truth, those hypocrites already have their full reward. ¹⁷So when you fast, comb your hair

Q: How can a loving God send anyone to hell?

A: The truth is that God doesn't send anyone to hell. He gives all people free will to choose where they will spend eternity (1 Corinthians 6:9–10; Galatians 5:19–21).

>> 5:44 **you** Some Greek copies continue, "Bless those who curse you, do good to those who hate you." Compare Luke 6:28.   6:13 **The … Amen.** Some Greek copies do not contain the bracketed text.
6:16 **fast** The people would give up eating for a special time of prayer and worship to God. It was also done to show sadness and disappointment.

and wash your face. [18]Then people will not know that you are fasting, but your Father, whom you cannot see, will see you. Your Father sees what is done in secret, and he will reward you.

God Is More Important than Money

[19]"Don't store treasures for yourselves here on earth where moths and rust will destroy them and thieves can break in and steal them. [20]But store your treasures in heaven where they cannot be destroyed by moths or rust and where thieves cannot break in and steal them. [21]Your heart will be where your treasure is.

[22]"The eye is a light for the body. If your eyes are good, your whole body will be full of light. [23]But if your eyes are evil, your whole body will be full of darkness. And if the only light you have is really darkness, then you have the worst darkness.

[24]"No one can serve two masters. The person will hate one master and love the other, or will follow one master and refuse to follow the other. You cannot serve both God and worldly riches.

Don't Worry

[25]"So I tell you, don't worry about the food or drink you need to live, or about the clothes you need for your body. Life is more than food, and the body is more than

THINK ABOUT IT Matthew 6:33–34

NO MATTER HOW MUCH MONEY YOU MAKE, you are likely to wonder if it is enough at times. If money woes hit too close to home, you may even worry about whether or not you'll be able to pay the bills, much less save for retirement and other future expenses.

As Jesus was speaking to the crowds gathered for what has become known as the Sermon on the Mount, he recognized that worry was frequently a part of people's daily lives. Much like today, people often worried about what to eat, drink, or wear. Yet Christ addressed people's deepest concerns and cares with words of comfort and compassion.

If your greatest goal is to do what God wants, then you don't need to worry. As a Christian, your source is God, and his limitless resources are at your disposal. If your priorities are aligned properly, you can trust God to provide for your every need, just as he has promised he will do. As you seek the will of God, he will meet your needs according to his abundant supply.

clothes. [26]Look at the birds in the air. They don't plant or harvest or store food in barns, but your heavenly Father feeds them. And you know that you are worth much more than the birds. [27]You cannot add any time to your life by worrying about it.

[28]"And why do you worry about clothes? Look at how the lilies in the field grow. They don't work or make clothes for themselves. [29]But I tell you that even Solomon with his riches was not dressed as beautifully as one of these flowers. [30]God clothes the grass in

 # Survival Guide

BATHROOM REMODELING: RETURN ON INVESTMENT

Home remodeling experts say remodeling your bathroom is probably the best return on investment, since it needs fewer repairs and offers more décor style than any other room. However, before running out to hire a contractor, think about things you can do yourself. You can handle tasks like laying new tile, installing shelves or mirrors, replacing light fixtures or faucets, and painting the walls. Most hardware stores can offer advice if needed. Being a good steward by saving money wherever possible is a scriptural principle.

>> live the life

Matthew 6:6

The Principle > **Pray to God in private.**

Practicing It > **Start a prayer journal. Record your daily prayer requests in your journal, leaving room after each one to add comments later. Every few weeks, go back through the entries and record how God has answered your prayers.**

the field, which is alive today but tomorrow is thrown into the fire. So you can be even more sure that God will clothe you. Don't have so little faith! [31]Don't worry and say, 'What will we eat?' or 'What will we drink?' or 'What will we wear?' [32]The people who don't know God keep trying to get these things, and your Father in heaven knows you need them. [33]Seek first God's kingdom and what God wants. Then all your other needs will be met as well. [34]So don't worry about tomorrow, because tomorrow will have its own worries. Each day has enough trouble of its own.

⏵ Get Aligned

Matthew 7:9—11

DADS CAN BE SOFTIES WHEN IT comes to giving their kids gifts. We want the best for our children. Whether we're compensating for our own childhood lack or we're simply generous by nature, it doesn't make much difference once we see our children tearing off the wrapping paper and screaming their approval. Fathers love to give to their children.

Our innate desire to please our kids is no fluke; it is God-given. In fact, it exemplifies our heavenly Father. Those who grew up with little may have a hard time believing God desires to shower them

with gifts, but it's true nonetheless. Whereas monetary blessing is part of God's plan for our lives, what's more important to God than our material wealth is our spiritual wealth.

When it comes to giving you eternal gifts—gifts that really matter—your Father is no miser. James 1:17 says, "Every good action and every perfect gift is from God." Reflect upon all the good things that have happened to you lately and count all the blessings in your life. God is generous when it comes to giving; all we need to do is ask.

Be Careful About Judging Others

7 "Don't judge others, or you will be judged. [2]You will be judged in the same way that you judge others, and the amount you give to others will be given to you. [3]"Why do you notice the little piece of dust in your friend's eye, but you don't notice the big piece of wood in your own eye? [4]How can you say to your friend, 'Let me take that little piece of dust out of your eye'? Look at yourself! You still have that big piece of wood in your own eye. [5]You hypocrite! First, take the wood out of your own eye. Then you will see clearly to take the dust out of your friend's eye.

[6]"Don't give holy things to dogs, and don't throw your pearls before pigs. Pigs will only trample on them, and dogs will turn to attack you.

Ask God for What You Need

[7]"Ask, and God will give to you. Search, and you will find. Knock, and the door will open for you. [8]Yes, everyone who asks will receive. Everyone who searches will find. And everyone who knocks will have the door opened. [9]"If your children ask for bread, which of you would give them a stone? [10]Or if your children ask for a fish, would you give them a snake? [11]Even though you are bad, you know how to give good gifts to your children. How much more your heavenly Father will give good things to those who ask him!

The Most Important Rule

[12]"Do to others what you want them to do to you. This is the meaning of the law of Moses and the teaching of the prophets.

The Way to Heaven Is Hard

[13]"Enter through the narrow gate. The gate is wide and the road is wide that leads to hell, and many people enter through that gate. [14]But the gate is small and the road is narrow that leads to true life. Only a few people find that road.

People Know You by Your Actions

[15]"Be careful of false prophets. They come to you looking gentle like sheep, but they are really dangerous like wolves. [16]You will know

Q: How do I know if I'm a Christian?

A: You can be confident that you are a Christian if you have proclaimed your trust in Jesus as the one who paid the ultimate price for your sin, you believe that he has forgiven you, and you have committed your life to following his will (Romans 10:9; 1 John 1:9).

these people by what they do. Grapes don't come from thornbushes, and figs don't come from thorny weeds. ¹⁷In the same way, every good tree produces good fruit, but a bad tree produces bad fruit. ¹⁸A good tree cannot produce bad fruit, and a bad tree cannot produce good fruit. ¹⁹Every tree that does not produce good fruit is cut down and thrown into the fire. ²⁰In the same way, you will know these false prophets by what they do.

²¹"Not all those who say 'You are our Lord' will enter the kingdom of heaven. The only people who will enter the kingdom of heaven are those who do what my Father in heaven wants. ²²On the last day many people will say to me, 'Lord, Lord, we spoke for you, and through you we forced out demons and did many miracles.' ²³Then I will tell them clearly, 'Get away from me, you who do evil. I never knew you.'

Two Kinds of People

²⁴"Everyone who hears my words and obeys them is like a wise man who built his house on rock. ²⁵It rained hard, the floods came, and the winds blew and hit that house. But it did not fall, because it was built on rock. ²⁶Everyone who hears my words and does not obey them is like a foolish man who built his house on sand. ²⁷It rained hard, the floods came, and the winds blew and hit that house, and it fell with a big crash."

²⁸When Jesus finished saying these things, the people were amazed at his teaching, ²⁹because he did not teach like their teachers of the law. He taught like a person who had authority.

Jesus Heals a Sick Man

8 When Jesus came down from the hill, great crowds followed him. ²Then a man with a skin disease came to Jesus. The man bowed down before him and said, "Lord, you can heal me if you will."

³Jesus reached out his hand and touched the man and said, "I will. Be healed!" And immediately the man was healed from his disease. ⁴Then Jesus said to him, "Don't tell anyone about this. But go and show yourself to the priest" and offer the gift Moses

THINK ABOUT IT Matthew 7:24–27

WHETHER YOU BUILD A HOUSE OR BUY AN EXISTING ONE, you probably realize how important it is to establish a good foundation underneath the house so that it can support the structure being built. Shoddy groundwork invariably leads to poor stability.

Jesus identified two different kinds of people in the world as he told this parable about the wise man and the foolish man. He described the wise man as one who built his house on the rock. Though the rains and the winds came, the house stood firm. On the other hand, Jesus described the foolish man as one who built his house on the sand. When the rains came and the winds blew, they destroyed the home.

As Jesus portrayed the two types of people, he also personalized the parable. "Everyone who hears my words and obeys them is like a wise man," he said. When we obey the promises in the Bible, then we are choosing godly wisdom to build our lives upon, and our lives will stand the test of time.

The Bottom Line

Starting a Business: Seek Advice

PERHAPS YOU'VE INVENTED a gadget you are sure will fatten your wallet. Before setting up your own business, this wisdom from Proverbs 20:18 will help: "Get advice if you want your plans to work." Ask others who have been there. Many entrepreneurs can share stories of going years without a vacation, working harder for themselves than they ever did for someone else, and fretting about survival. As an alternative, you may want to set your business up at home, working at night or on weekends to determine whether it can be a full-time venture for you.

8:4 show…priest The Law of Moses said a priest must say when a Jewish person with a skin disease was well.

commanded[b] for people who are made well. This will show the people what I have done."

Jesus Heals a Soldier's Servant

[5]When Jesus entered the city of Capernaum, an army officer came to him, begging for help. [6]The officer said, "Lord, my servant is at home in bed. He can't move his body and is in much pain."

[7]Jesus said to the officer, "I will go and heal him."

[8]The officer answered, "Lord, I am not worthy for you to come into my house. You only need to command it, and my servant will be healed. [9]I, too, am a man under the authority of others, and I have soldiers under my command. I tell one soldier, 'Go,' and he goes. I tell another soldier, 'Come,' and he comes. I say to my servant, 'Do this,' and my servant does it."

[10]When Jesus heard this, he was amazed. He said to those who were following him, "I tell you the truth, this is the greatest faith I have found, even in Israel. [11]Many people will come from the east and from the west and will sit and eat with Abraham, Isaac, and Jacob in the kingdom of heaven. [12]But those people who should be in the kingdom will be thrown outside into the darkness, where people will cry and grind their teeth with pain."

[13]Then Jesus said to the officer, "Go home. Your servant will be healed just as you believed he would." And his servant was healed that same hour.

Jesus Heals Many People

[14]When Jesus went to Peter's house, he saw that Peter's mother-in-law was sick in bed with a fever. [15]Jesus touched her hand, and the fever left her. Then she stood up and began to serve Jesus.

[16]That evening people brought to Jesus many who had demons. Jesus spoke and the demons left them, and he healed all the sick. [17]He did these things to bring about what Isaiah the prophet had said:

> "He took our suffering on him
> and carried our diseases." *Isaiah 53:4*

People Want to Follow Jesus

[18]When Jesus saw the crowd around him, he told his followers to go to the other side of the lake. [19]Then a teacher of the law came to Jesus and said, "Teacher, I will follow you any place you go."

[20]Jesus said to him, "The foxes have holes to live in, and the birds have nests, but the Son of Man has no place to rest his head."

[21]Another man, one of Jesus' followers, said to him, "Lord, first let me go and bury my father."

[22]But Jesus told him, "Follow me, and let the people who are dead bury their own dead."

Jesus Calms a Storm

[23]Jesus got into a boat, and his followers went with him. [24]A great storm arose on the lake so that waves covered the boat, but Jesus was sleeping. [25]His followers went to him and woke him, saying, "Lord, save us! We will drown!"

[26]Jesus answered, "Why are you afraid? You don't have enough faith." Then Jesus got up and gave a command to the wind and the waves, and it became completely calm.

[27]The men were amazed and said, "What kind of man is this? Even the wind and the waves obey him!"

Jesus Heals Two Men with Demons

[28]When Jesus arrived at the other side of the lake in the area of the Gadarene[c] people, two men who had demons in them met him. These men lived in the burial caves and were so dangerous that people could not use the road by those caves. [29]They shouted, "What do you want with us, Son of God? Did you come here to torture us before the right time?"

[30]Near that place there was a large herd of pigs feeding. [31]The demons begged Jesus, "If you make us leave these men, please send us into that herd of pigs."

[32]Jesus said to them, "Go!" So the demons left the men and went into the pigs. Then the whole herd rushed down the hill into the lake and were drowned. [33]The herdsmen ran away and went into town, where they told about all of this and what had happened to the men who had demons. [34]Then the whole town went out to see Jesus. When they saw him, they begged him to leave their area.

Q: What does it mean to repent?

A: The word "repent" literally means to stop, turn around, and go in the opposite direction. When the Bible talks about repenting from sin, it is referring to more than simply stopping a bad behavior. It involves a change of heart and life (Matthew 3:2; Luke 13:3).

>> live the life

Matthew 8:26

The Principle > Strengthen your faith.

Practicing It > Consider the one area of your life where you struggle most with trusting God. Think of one or two things you can begin to do today to strengthen your faith in those areas of your life.

 8:4 Moses commanded Read about this in Leviticus 14:1–32.   **8:28 Gadarene** From Gadara, an area southeast of Lake Galilee. The exact location is uncertain and some Greek copies read "Gergesene"; others read "Gerasene."

Jesus Heals a Paralyzed Man

9 Jesus got into a boat and went back across the lake to his own town. ²Some people brought to Jesus a man who was paralyzed and lying on a mat. When Jesus saw the faith of these people, he said to the paralyzed man, "Be encouraged, young man. Your sins are forgiven."

³Some of the teachers of the law said to themselves, "This man speaks as if he were God. That is blasphemy!"ⁿ

⁴Knowing their thoughts, Jesus said, "Why are you thinking evil thoughts? ⁵Which is easier: to say, 'Your sins are forgiven,' or to tell him, 'Stand up and walk'? ⁶But I will prove to you that the Son of Man has authority on earth to forgive sins." Then Jesus said to the paralyzed man, "Stand up, take your mat, and go home." ⁷And the man stood up and went home. ⁸When the people saw this, they were amazed and praised God for giving power like this to human beings.

Jesus Chooses Matthew

⁹When Jesus was leaving, he saw a man named Matthew sitting in the tax collector's booth. Jesus said to him, "Follow me," and he stood up and followed Jesus.

¹⁰As Jesus was having dinner at Matthew's house, many tax collectors and "sinners" came and ate with Jesus and his followers. ¹¹When the Pharisees saw this, they asked Jesus' followers, "Why does your teacher eat with tax collectors and sinners?"

¹²When Jesus heard them, he said, "It is not the healthy people who need a doctor, but the sick. ¹³Go and learn what this means: 'I want kindness more than I want animal sacrifices.'ⁿ I did not come to invite good people but to invite sinners."

Jesus' Followers Are Criticized

¹⁴Then the followers of Johnⁿ came to Jesus and said, "Why do we and the Pharisees often fastⁿ for a certain time, but your followers don't?"

¹⁵Jesus answered, "The friends of the bridegroom are not sad while he is with them. But the time will come when the bridegroom will be taken from them, and then they will fast.

¹⁶"No one sews a patch of unshrunk cloth over a hole in an old coat. If he does, the patch will shrink and pull away from the coat, making the hole worse. ¹⁷Also, people never pour new wine into old leather bags. Otherwise, the bags will break, the wine will spill, and the wine bags will be ruined. But people always pour new wine into new wine bags. Then both will continue to be good."

Jesus Gives Life to a Dead Girl and Heals a Sick Woman

¹⁸While Jesus was saying these things, a leader of the synagogue came to him. He bowed down before Jesus and said, "My daughter has just died. But if you come and lay your hand on her, she will live again." ¹⁹So Jesus and his followers stood up and went with the leader.

²⁰Then a woman who had been bleeding for twelve years came behind Jesus and touched the edge of his coat. ²¹She was thinking, "If I can just touch his clothes, I will be healed."

²²Jesus turned and saw the woman and said, "Be encouraged, dear woman. You are made well because you believed." And the woman was healed from that moment on.

²³Jesus continued along with the leader and went into his house. There he saw the funeral musicians and many people crying. ²⁴Jesus said, "Go away. The girl is not dead, only asleep." But the people laughed at him. ²⁵After the crowd had been thrown out of the house, Jesus went into the girl's room and took hold of her hand, and she stood up. ²⁶The news about this spread all around the area.

Jesus Heals More People

²⁷When Jesus was leaving there, two blind men followed him. They cried out, "Have mercy on us, Son of David!"

²⁸After Jesus went inside, the blind men went with him. He asked the men, "Do you believe that I can make you see again?"

They answered, "Yes, Lord."

²⁹Then Jesus touched their eyes and said, "Because you believe I can make you see again, it will happen." ³⁰Then the men were able to see. But Jesus warned them strongly, saying, "Don't tell anyone about this." ³¹But the blind men left and spread the news about Jesus all around that area.

³²When the two men were leaving, some people brought another man to Jesus. This man could not talk because he had a demon in him. ³³After Jesus forced the demon to leave the man, he was able to speak. The crowd was amazed and said, "We have never seen anything like this in Israel."

³⁴But the Pharisees said, "The prince of

▶ Sexcess:
THE ART OF ROMANCE

While the act of sex itself is often top-of-mind for men, the art of romance is what is on women's radar screen. The number one way to win the heart of a woman is to woo her with romance. And try to think outside the box...of chocolates, that is. While the obligatory sweets, perfume, and flowers are all fine gifts at times, women want to know that you put some thought into your gift giving. The type of gift that keeps on giving is one that demonstrates your affection for your beloved in a tangible *and* personal way.

 9:3 blasphemy Saying things against God or not showing respect for God.   **9:13 'I want ... sacrifices.'** Quotation from Hosea 6:6.   **9:14 John** John the Baptist, who preached to people about Christ's coming (Matthew 3, Luke 3).   **9:14 fast** The people would give up eating for a special time of prayer and worship to God. It was also done to show sadness and disappointment.

+ Ten Ways to Romance Your Sweetheart

1. Give her flowers for no reason.
2. Do chores around the house.
3. Fix her a nice dinner.
4. Encourage her to dream.
5. Speak her love language.
6. Take care of her when she is sick.
7. Compliment her in front of others.
8. Send her a thoughtful card.
9. Treat her to a massage.
10. Pray and worship together.

demons is the one that gives him power to force demons out."

[35]Jesus traveled through all the towns and villages, teaching in their synagogues, preaching the Good News about the kingdom, and healing all kinds of diseases and sicknesses. [36]When he saw the crowds, he felt sorry for them because they were hurting and helpless, like sheep without a shepherd. [37]Jesus said to his followers, "There are many people to harvest but only a few workers to help harvest them. [38]Pray to the Lord, who owns the harvest, that he will send more workers to gather his harvest."

Jesus Sends Out His Apostles

10 Jesus called his twelve followers together and gave them authority to drive out evil spirits and to heal every kind of disease and sickness. [2]These are the names of the twelve apostles: Simon (also called Peter) and his brother Andrew; James son of Zebedee, and his brother John; [3]Philip and Bartholomew; Thomas and Matthew, the tax collector; James son of Alphaeus, and Thaddaeus; [4]Simon the Zealot and Judas Iscariot, who turned against Jesus.

[5]Jesus sent out these twelve men with the following order: "Don't go to the non-Jewish people or to any town where the Samaritans live. [6]But go to the people of Israel, who are like lost sheep. [7]When you go, preach this: 'The kingdom of heaven is near.' [8]Heal the sick, raise the dead to life again, heal those who have skin diseases, and force demons out of people. I give you these powers freely, so help other people freely. [9]Don't carry any money with you—gold or silver or copper. [10]Don't carry a bag or extra clothes or sandals or a walking stick. Workers should be given what they need.

[11]"When you enter a city or town, find some worthy person there and stay in that home until you leave. [12]When you enter that home,

Q: What is sin?

A: The word "sin" literally means to "miss the mark"— as in an archer who misses a target. In the biblical context, the "mark" or target is God's holiness. We were born into sin as human beings, and only the blood of Jesus can wash it away (Romans 3:23–25).

Get Fit

WATCHING YOUR WAISTLINE   Obesity is at an all-time high in the United States, and the epidemic is getting worse. Those who are overweight or obese have increased risks for diseases and conditions, such as diabetes, high blood pressure, heart disease, and stroke. God calls each of us to take care of our bodies, and one key to maintaining a healthy weight is regular physical activity. If you're already active, make it a priority to stay that way. If you're not currently active, you can start now. Just don't try to turn your life around all at once. If you make changes in small, controllable increments, you'll be more likely to reach your goals and stay with them.

>> 9:37–38 "There are … harvest." As a farmer sends workers to harvest the grain, Jesus sends his followers to bring people to God.

say, 'Peace be with you.' ¹³If the people there welcome you, let your peace stay there. But if they don't welcome you, take back the peace you wished for them. ¹⁴And if a home or town refuses to welcome you or listen to you, leave that place and shake its dust off your feet." ¹⁵I tell you the truth, on the Judgment Day it will be better for the towns of Sodom and Gomorrah⁰ than for the people of that town.

Jesus Warns His Apostles

¹⁶"Listen, I am sending you out like sheep among wolves. So be as clever as snakes and as innocent as doves. ¹⁷Be careful of people, because they will arrest you and take you to court and whip you in their synagogues. ¹⁸Because of me you will be taken to stand before governors and kings, and you will tell them and the non-Jewish people about me. ¹⁹When you are arrested, don't worry about what to say or how to say it. At that time you will be given the things to say. ²⁰It will not really be you speaking but the Spirit of your Father speaking through you.

²¹"Brothers will give their own brothers to be killed, and fathers will give their own children to be killed. Children will fight against their own parents and have them put to death. ²²All people will hate you because you follow me, but those people who keep their faith until the end will be saved. ²³When you are treated badly in one city, run to another city. I tell you the truth, you will not finish

Fear God, Not People

²⁶"So don't be afraid of those people, because everything that is hidden will be shown. Everything that is secret will be made known. ²⁷I tell you these things in the dark, but I want you to tell them in the light. What you hear whispered in your ear you should shout from the housetops. ²⁸Don't be afraid of people, who can kill the body but cannot kill the soul. The only one you should fear is the one who can destroy the soul and the body in hell. ²⁹Two sparrows cost only a penny, but not even one of them can die without your Father's knowing it. ³⁰God even knows how many hairs are on your head. ³¹So don't be afraid. You are worth much more than many sparrows.

Tell People About Your Faith

³²"All those who stand before others and say they believe in me, I will say before my Father in heaven that they belong to me. ³³But all who stand before others and say they do not believe in me, I will say before my Father in heaven that they do not belong to me.

³⁴"Don't think that I came to bring peace to the earth. I did not come to bring peace, but a sword. ³⁵I have come so that

'a son will be against his father,
    a daughter will be against her mother,
a daughter-in-law will be against her
        mother-in-law.

Men of Valor
APOLLOS: A Wise Apostle

Apollos is immortalized as a knowledgeable man and a good speaker in Acts 18:24–28. He traveled to Greece and, in discussions with other Jews, proved from the Scriptures that Jesus was the Christ. Such skill resulted in Apollos becoming a follower and even developing his own "following." This surfaced in 1 Corinthians 3:4–6, where Paul referred to disputes among Christians who were claiming different allegiances, some to Paul and others to Apollos. Paul rebuked them, pointing out that Christ died for all. While it wasn't Apollos's fault that some followed him, his story reminds Christians their allegiance belongs to Christ, not a man or a denomination.

FACT-OIDS!

In the 1984 presidential election, President Ronald Reagan carried 49 states, with history's largest-ever percentage of both the popular and electoral vote. [Infoplease.com]

going through all the cities of Israel before the Son of Man comes.

²⁴"A student is not better than his teacher, and a servant is not better than his master. ²⁵A student should be satisfied to become like his teacher; a servant should be satisfied to become like his master. If the head of the family is called Beelzebul, then the other members of the family will be called worse names!

³⁶   A person's enemies will be members of
        his own family.'   *Micah 7:6*
³⁷"Those who love their father or mother more than they love me are not worthy to be my followers. Those who love their son or daughter more than they love me are not worthy to be my followers. ³⁸Whoever is not willing to carry the cross and follow me is not worthy of me. ³⁹Those who try to hold on to their lives will give up true life. Those who

give up their lives for me will hold on to true life. ⁴⁰Whoever accepts you also accepts me, and whoever accepts me also accepts the One who sent me. ⁴¹Whoever meets a prophet and accepts him will receive the reward of a prophet. And whoever accepts a good person because that person is good will receive the reward of a good person. ⁴²Those who give one of these little ones a cup of cold water because they are my followers will truly get their reward."

>> 10:14 **shake … feet** A warning. It showed that they had rejected these people.   10:15 **Sodom and Gomorrah** Two cities that God destroyed because the people were so evil.

Jesus and John the Baptist

11 After Jesus finished telling these things to his twelve followers, he left there and went to the towns in Galilee to teach and preach.

²John the Baptist was in prison, but he heard about what the Christ was doing. So John sent some of his followers to Jesus. ³They asked him, "Are you the One who is to come, or should we wait for someone else?"

⁴Jesus answered them, "Go tell John what you hear and see: ⁵The blind can see, the crippled can walk, and people with skin diseases are healed. The deaf can hear, the dead are raised to life, and the Good News is preached to the poor. ⁶Those who do not stumble in their faith because of me are blessed."

⁷As John's followers were leaving, Jesus began talking to the people about John. Jesus said, "What did you go out into the desert to see? A reed" blown by the wind? ⁸What did you go out to see? A man dressed in fine clothes? No, those who wear fine clothes live in kings' palaces. ⁹So why did you go out? To see a prophet? Yes, and I tell you, John is more than a prophet. ¹⁰This was written about him:

'I will send my messenger ahead of you,
    who will prepare the way for you.'   *Malachi 3:1*

¹¹I tell you the truth, John the Baptist is greater than any other person ever born, but even the least important person in the kingdom of heaven is greater than John. ¹²Since the time John the Baptist came until now, the kingdom of heaven has been going forward in strength, and people have been trying to take it by force. ¹³All the prophets and the law of Moses told about what would happen until the time John came. ¹⁴And if you will believe what they said, you will believe that John is Elijah, whom they said would come. ¹⁵Let those with ears use them and listen!

¹⁶"What can I say about the people of this time? What are they like? They are like children sitting in the marketplace, who call out to each other,

¹⁷'We played music for you, but you did not dance;
    we sang a sad song, but you did not cry.'

¹⁸John came and did not eat or drink like other people. So people say, 'He has a demon.' ¹⁹The Son of Man came, eating and drinking, and people say, 'Look at him! He eats too much and drinks too much wine, and he is a friend of tax collectors and sinners.' But wisdom is proved to be right by what she does."

Jesus Warns Unbelievers

²⁰Then Jesus criticized the cities where he did most of his miracles, because the people did not change their lives and stop sinning. ²¹He said, "How terrible for you, Korazin! How terrible for you, Bethsaida! If the same miracles I did in you had happened in Tyre and Sidon," those people would have changed their lives a long time ago. They would have worn rough cloth and put ashes on themselves to show they had changed. ²²But I tell you, on the Judgment Day it will be better for Tyre and Sidon than for you. ²³And you, Capernaum," will you be lifted up to heaven? No, you will be thrown down to the depths. If the miracles I did in you had happened in Sodom," its people would have stopped sinning, and it would still be a city today. ²⁴But I tell you, on the Judgment Day it will be better for Sodom than for you."

Jesus Offers Rest to People

²⁵At that time Jesus said, "I praise you, Father, Lord of heaven and earth, because you have hidden these things from the people who are wise and smart. But you have shown them to those who are like little children. ²⁶Yes, Father, this is what you really wanted.

²⁷"My Father has given me all things. No one knows the Son, except the Father. And no one knows the Father, except the Son and those whom the Son chooses to tell.

²⁸"Come to me, all of you who are tired and have heavy loads, and I will give you rest. ²⁹Accept my teachings and learn from me, because I am gentle and humble in spirit, and you will find rest for your lives. ³⁰The burden that I ask you to accept is easy; the load I give you to carry is light."

Jesus Is Lord of the Sabbath

12 At that time Jesus was walking through some fields of grain on a Sabbath day. His followers were hungry, so they began to pick the grain and eat it. ²When the Pharisees saw this, they said to Jesus, "Look! Your followers are doing what is unlawful to do on the Sabbath day."

▶Get Aligned
Matthew 11:25

INTELLIGENCE IS A WONDERFUL THING. God gave us the ability to expand our minds through learning, to grow in understanding, and to increase our intellects. However, knowledge also can be dangerous. Like athleticism, wealth, good looks, and charisma, knowledge can easily become an obstacle in pursuing God. If we've got life all figured out, why would we need God? If we can reduce spirituality to a science, why should we rely on faith?

For all the good of intelligence, it doesn't get us one step closer to God. Jesus used children to show who really saw and understood the kingdom of God. In fact, he said the Father had chosen to hide his truths from the "wise and smart." Why give divine understanding to the simple and not the brilliant? Because a child doesn't process what he believes through layers of intellectual filters. He doesn't even base his faith on experience. He simply accepts.

Jesus occasionally reiterated the need for us to be childlike in our faith. In God's eyes, a child often knows more of what really matters than an adult. Don't let head knowledge keep you from the joyous experience of knowing God, simply and freely as a child.

 11:7 **reed** It means that John was not ordinary or weak like grass blown by the wind.   11:21 **Tyre and Sidon** Towns where wicked people lived.   11:21, 23 **Korazin ... Bethsaida ... Capernaum** Towns by Lake Galilee where Jesus preached to the people.   11:23 **Sodom** A city that God destroyed because the people were so evil.

18

[3]Jesus answered, "Have you not read what David did when he and the people with him were hungry? [4]He went into God's house, and he and those with him ate the holy bread, which was lawful only for priests to eat. [5]And have you not read in the law of Moses that on every Sabbath day the priests in the Temple break this law about the Sabbath day? But the priests are not wrong for doing that. [6]I tell you that there is something here that is greater than the Temple. [7]The Scripture says, 'I want kindness more than I want animal sacrifices.'" You don't really know what those words mean. If you understood them, you would not judge those who have done nothing wrong.

[8]"So the Son of Man is Lord of the Sabbath day."

Jesus Heals a Man's Hand

[9]Jesus left there and went into their synagogue, [10]where there was a man with a crippled hand. They were looking for a reason to accuse Jesus, so they asked him, "Is it right to heal on the Sabbath day?"

[11]Jesus answered, "If any of you has a sheep, and it falls into a ditch on the Sabbath day, you will help it out of the ditch. [12]Surely a human being is more important than a sheep. So it is lawful to do good things on the Sabbath day."

[13]Then Jesus said to the man with the crippled hand, "Hold out your hand." The man held out his hand, and it became well again, like the other hand. [14]But the Pharisees left and made plans to kill Jesus.

Jesus Is God's Chosen Servant

[15]Jesus knew what the Pharisees were doing, so he left that place. Many people followed him, and he healed all who were sick. [16]But Jesus warned the people not to tell who he was. [17]He did these things to bring about what Isaiah the prophet had said:

[18]"Here is my servant whom I have chosen.
  I love him, and I am pleased with him.
 I will put my Spirit upon him,
   and he will tell of my justice to all people.
[19]He will not argue or cry out;
   no one will hear his voice in the streets.

>> live the life

Matthew 11:28–30

The Principle > Take time for rest.

Practicing It > Make a personal commitment not to work on your day of worship, even on chores or other duties around the house. Instead, spend the time playing with your kids, talking with your wife, or spending quiet time in prayer and worship.

Change >> Your WORLD

BIBLE LEAGUE

Many people in other countries are unaware of the privilege of picking up a Bible and reading it. Since the early 1930s, the Bible League has been dedicated to giving the Scriptures to people around the world. More than simply providing the Bibles, the Bible League is actively involved in evangelism, discipleship, and church growth. In more than fifty countries, it works with local churches to train Christians to help them reach the lost for Christ. During 2004, the Bible League trained Christians who established 4,047 new congregations in previously unreached communities. There are numerous ways to volunteer, and you can even donate your old Bibles to the cause.

To change your world, visit www.bibleleague.org.

[20]He will not break a crushed blade of grass
   or put out even a weak flame
 until he makes justice win the victory.
[21]   In him will the non-Jewish people find hope."   *Isaiah 42:1–4*

Jesus' Power Is from God

[22]Then some people brought to Jesus a man who was blind and could not talk, because he had a demon. Jesus healed the man so that he could talk and see. [23]All the people were amazed and said, "Perhaps this man is the Son of David!"

[24]When the Pharisees heard this, they said, "Jesus uses the power of Beelzebul, the ruler of demons, to force demons out of people."

[25]Jesus knew what the Pharisees were thinking, so he said to them, "Every kingdom that is divided against itself will be destroyed. And any city or family that is divided against itself will not continue. [26]And if Satan forces out himself, then Satan is divided against himself, and his kingdom will not continue. [27]You say that I use the

---

>> 12:7 'I ... sacrifices.' Quotation from Hosea 6:6.   12:10 Is it right ... day? It was against Jewish Law to work on the Sabbath day.

→ The Bottom Line

Buying a Car: Shop Smart

TOO MANY CAR BUYERS get hung up on monthly payments when the primary issue is cost. Whether buying outright or with a trade, the price tag, less the down payment, determines your monthly payment. Get strapped with one too high, and you could ultimately lose the car. If your financing term lasts five years or more, after awhile you may discover you owe more on the car than it's worth. Cars depreciate quickly, so consider a used one instead of a new model. Don't let a car drive you to the poor house as life speeds past.

power of Beelzebul to force out demons. If that is true, then what power do your people use to force out demons? So they will be your judges. [28]But if I use the power of God's Spirit to force out demons, then the kingdom of God has come to you.

[29]"If anyone wants to enter a strong person's house and steal his things, he must first tie up the strong person. Then he can steal the things from the house.

[30]"Whoever is not with me is against me. Whoever does not work with me is working against me. [31]So I tell you, people can be forgiven for every sin and everything they say against God. But whoever speaks against the Holy Spirit will not be forgiven. [32]Anyone who speaks against the Son of Man can be forgiven, but anyone who speaks against the Holy Spirit will not be forgiven, now or in the future.

People Know You by Your Words

[33]"If you want good fruit, you must make the tree good. If your tree is not good, it will have bad fruit. A tree is known by the kind of fruit it produces. [34]You snakes! You are evil people, so how can you say anything good? The mouth speaks the things that are in the heart. [35]Good people have good things in their hearts, and so they say good things. But evil people have evil in their hearts, so they say evil things. [36]And I tell you that on the Judgment Day people will be responsible for every careless thing they have said. [37]The words you have said will be used to judge you. Some of your words will prove you right, but some of your words will prove you guilty."

The People Ask for a Miracle

[38]Then some of the Pharisees and teachers of the law answered Jesus, saying, "Teacher, we want to see you work a miracle as a sign." [39]Jesus answered, "Evil and sinful people are the ones who want to see a miracle for a sign. But no sign will be given to them, except the sign of the prophet Jonah. [40]Jonah was in the stomach of the big fish for three days and three nights. In the same way, the Son of Man will be in the grave three days and three nights. [41]On the Judgment Day the people from Nineveh" will stand up with you people who live now, and they will show that you are guilty. When Jonah preached to them, they were sorry and changed their lives. And I tell you that someone greater than Jonah is here. [42]On the Judgment Day, the Queen of the South" will stand up with you people who live today. She will show that you are guilty, because she came from far away to listen to Solomon's wise teaching. And I tell you that someone greater than Solomon is here.

People Today Are Full of Evil

[43]"When an evil spirit comes out of a person, it travels through dry places, looking for a place to rest, but it doesn't find it. [44]So the spirit says, 'I will go back to the house I left.' When the spirit comes back, it finds the house still empty, swept clean, and made neat. [45]Then the evil spirit goes out and brings seven other spirits even more evil than it is, and they go in and live there. So the person has even more trouble than before. It is the same way with the evil people who live today."

Q: Why does God allow suffering?

A: Suffering exists in the world as a direct consequence of our free will as human beings. When humans first sinned against God, we brought suffering and death into the world. Though God did not create suffering, he allows it to exist (Matthew 4:24; 1 Peter 1:6–7).

12:41 Nineveh The city where Jonah preached to warn the people. Read Jonah 3.   **12:42 Queen of the South** The Queen of Sheba. She traveled a thousand miles to learn God's wisdom from Solomon. Read 1 Kings 10:1–13.

Jesus' True Family

⁴⁶While Jesus was talking to the people, his mother and brothers stood outside, trying to find a way to talk to him. ⁴⁷Someone told Jesus, "Your mother and brothers are standing outside, and they want to talk to you."ⁿ

⁴⁸He answered, "Who is my mother? Who are my brothers?" ⁴⁹Then he pointed to his followers and said, "Here are my mother and my brothers. ⁵⁰My true brother and sister and mother are those who do what my Father in heaven wants."

A Story About Planting Seed

13 That same day Jesus went out of the house and sat by the lake. ²Large crowds gathered around him, so he got into a boat and sat down, while the people stood on the shore. ³Then Jesus used stories to teach them many things. He said: "A farmer went out to plant his seed. ⁴While he was planting, some seed fell by the road, and the birds came and ate it all up. ⁵Some seed fell on rocky ground, where there wasn't much dirt. That seed grew very fast, because the ground was not deep. ⁶But when the sun rose, the plants dried up, because they did not have deep roots. ⁷Some other seed fell among thorny weeds, which grew and choked the good plants. ⁸Some other seed fell on good ground where it grew and produced a crop. Some plants made a hundred times more, some made sixty times more, and some made thirty times more. ⁹Let those with ears use them and listen."

Why Jesus Used Stories to Teach

¹⁰The followers came to Jesus and asked, "Why do you use stories to teach the people?"

¹¹Jesus answered, "You have been chosen to know the secrets about the kingdom of heaven, but others cannot know these secrets. ¹²Those who have understanding will be given more, and they will have all they need. But those who do not have understanding, even what they have will be taken away from them. ¹³This is why I use stories to teach the people: They see, but they don't really see. They hear, but they don't really hear or understand. ¹⁴So they show that the things Isaiah said about them are true:

'You will listen and listen, but you will
        not understand.
    You will look and look, but you will
        not learn.
¹⁵For the minds of these people have
        become stubborn.
    They do not hear with their ears,
    and they have closed their eyes.
Otherwise they might really
        understand
    what they see with their eyes
    and hear with their ears.

People Skills

Reflective Listening

The next time you find yourself arguing with someone, try a simple technique to cool tempers and resolve the conflict more quickly. It's called reflective listening, and it's an easy skill to learn. First, listen to what the other person is saying. Then before you respond, repeat back to him or her what you heard that person say, using your own words, before asking him or her to verify that you've understood correctly. It can be as simple as this: "It sounds like you think I'm being unfair about this. Is that right?" It is an effective way to defuse an argument and help the other person feel heard.

Deal With It: *Busyness

IF WE ARE NOT CAREFUL, we can start to brag about our busyness as if it were a badge of courage. But activity is not the same as productivity. One of the keys to maximizing our personal and professional effectiveness is to discern between good ideas and God ideas. The way to do that is to weigh the demands on our time in light of the eternal versus the temporal. Long-term vision helps give us short-term perspective. As the old saying goes, "No one ever said on his deathbed he wished he had spent more time at the office."

▶▶ 12:47 Someone...you." Some Greek copies do not have verse 47.

21

FOR Men Only

CONVERSATION One of the most attractive qualities to women is a man's ability to carry on an intelligent conversation. By that, we're not talking about sports and the weather. An intelligent conversation is simply one that engages the mind and involves some degree of depth beyond just the facts. If you don't already do so, try to stay abreast of current events, either by subscribing to a daily newspaper or reading online news sites. Also, visit your local library or neighborhood bookstore periodically to read about the latest trends, in addition to what interests you personally. Remember, it's not only librarians who find a well-read man attractive.

They might really understand in their minds
and come back to me and be healed.'
Isaiah 6:9–10

[16]But you are blessed, because you see with your eyes and hear with your ears. [17]I tell you the truth, many prophets and good people wanted to see the things that you now see, but they did not see them. And they wanted to hear the things that you now hear, but they did not hear them.

Jesus Explains the Seed Story

[18]"So listen to the meaning of that story about the farmer. [19]What is the seed that fell by the road? That seed is like the person who hears the message about the kingdom but does not understand it. The Evil One comes and takes away what was planted in that person's heart. [20]And what is the seed that fell on rocky ground? That seed is like the person who hears the teaching and quickly accepts it with joy. [21]But he does not let the teaching go deep into his life, so he keeps it only a short time. When trouble or persecution comes because of the teaching he accepted, he quickly gives up. [22]And what is the seed that fell among the thorny weeds? That seed is like the person who hears the teaching but lets worries about this life and the temptation of wealth stop that teaching from growing. So the teaching does not produce fruit" in that person's life. [23]But what is the seed that

fell on the good ground? That seed is like the person who hears the teaching and understands it. That person grows and produces fruit, sometimes a hundred times more, sometimes sixty times more, and sometimes thirty times more."

A Story About Wheat and Weeds

[24]Then Jesus told them another story: "The kingdom of heaven is like a man who planted good seed in his field. [25]That night, when everyone was asleep, his enemy came and planted weeds among the wheat and then left. [26]Later, the wheat sprouted and the heads of grain grew, but the weeds also grew. [27]Then the man's servants came to him and said, 'You planted good seed in your field. Where did the weeds come from?' [28]The man answered, 'An enemy planted weeds.' The servants asked, 'Do you want us to pull up the weeds?' [29]The man answered, 'No, because when you pull up the weeds, you might also pull up the wheat. [30]Let the weeds and the wheat grow together until the harvest time. At harvest time I will tell the workers, "First gather the weeds and tie them together to be burned. Then gather the wheat and bring it to my barn." ' "

Stories of Mustard Seed and Yeast

[31]Then Jesus told another story: "The kingdom of heaven is like a mustard seed that a man planted in his field. [32]That seed is the smallest of all seeds, but when it grows, it is one of the largest garden plants. It becomes big enough for the wild birds to come and build nests in its branches."

[33]Then Jesus told another story: "The kingdom of heaven is like yeast that a woman took and hid in a large tub of flour until it made all the dough rise."

[34]Jesus used stories to tell all these things to the people; he always used stories to teach them. [35]This is as the prophet said:

"I will speak using stories;
I will tell things that have been secret since the world was
made."
Psalm 78:2

Jesus Explains About the Weeds

[36]Then Jesus left the crowd and went into the house. His followers came to him and said, "Explain to us the meaning of the story about the weeds in the field."

[37]Jesus answered, "The man who planted the good seed in the field is the Son of Man. [38]The field is the world, and the good seed are all of God's children who belong to the kingdom. The weeds are those people who belong to the Evil One. [39]And the enemy who planted the bad seed is the devil. The harvest time is the end of the age, and the workers who gather are God's angels.

[40]"Just as the weeds are pulled up and burned in the fire, so it will be at the end of the age. [41]The Son of Man will send out his angels, and they will gather out of his kingdom all who cause sin and all who do

---

▶▶ **13:22 produce fruit** To produce fruit means to have in your life the good things God wants.

evil. [42]The angels will throw them into the blazing furnace, where the people will cry and grind their teeth with pain. [43]Then the good people will shine like the sun in the kingdom of their Father. Let those with ears use them and listen.

Stories of a Treasure and a Pearl

[44]"The kingdom of heaven is like a treasure hidden in a field. One day a man found the treasure, and then he hid it in the field again. He was so happy that he went and sold everything he owned to buy that field.

[45]"Also, the kingdom of heaven is like a man looking for fine pearls. [46]When he found a very valuable pearl, he went and sold everything he had and bought it.

A Story of a Fishing Net

[47]"Also, the kingdom of heaven is like a net that was put into the lake and caught many different kinds of fish. [48]When it was full, the fishermen pulled the net to the shore. They sat down and put all the good fish in baskets and threw away the bad fish. [49]It will be this way at the end of the age. The angels will come and separate the evil people from the good people. [50]The angels will throw the evil people into the blazing furnace, where people will cry and grind their teeth with pain."

[51]Jesus asked his followers, "Do you understand all these things?"

They answered, "Yes, we understand."

[52]Then Jesus said to them, "So every teacher of the law who has been taught about the kingdom of heaven is like the owner of a house. He brings out both new things and old things he has saved."

Jesus Goes to His Hometown

[53]When Jesus finished teaching with these stories, he left there. [54]He went to his hometown and taught the people in the synagogue, and they were amazed. They said, "Where did this man get this wisdom and this power to do miracles? [55]He is just the son of a carpenter. His mother is Mary, and his brothers are James, Joseph, Simon, and Judas. [56]And all his sisters are here with us. Where then does this man get all these things?" [57]So the people were upset with Jesus.

But Jesus said to them, "A prophet is honored everywhere except in his hometown and in his own home."

[58]So he did not do many miracles there because they had no faith.

How John the Baptist Was Killed

14 At that time Herod, the ruler of Galilee, heard the reports about Jesus. [2]So he said to his servants, "Jesus is John the Baptist, who has risen from the dead. That is why he can work these miracles."

[3]Sometime before this, Herod had arrested John, tied him up, and put him into prison. Herod did this because of Herodias, who had been the wife of Philip, Herod's brother. [4]John had been telling Herod, "It is not lawful for you to be married to Herodias." [5]Herod wanted to kill John, but he was afraid of the people, because they believed John was a prophet.

[6]On Herod's birthday, the daughter of Herodias danced for Herod

Q: What are angels?

A: Angels are intelligent beings created by God to glorify and serve him in heaven, as well as to do his bidding on earth. Angels are not the glorified spirits of dead humans; rather, they are a completely separate type of created being (Luke 2:10,13; Acts 12:7–19).

Survival Guide
STARTING A FIRE: HOT IDEAS

Hebrews 1:7 says God makes his angels like flames of fire. If you're in the woods and are all thumbs when it comes to starting a fire, you might feel like praying for an angel. But here are some practical tips. Gather dry sticks and twigs for kindling. Bring along old newspapers to help start the fire, or try adding a few lumps of charcoal or starter logs used in fireplaces. Avoid dousing the fire with lighter fluid, though. You want a campfire, not a bonfire.

and his guests, and she pleased him. [7]So he promised with an oath to give her anything she wanted. [8]Herodias told her daughter what to ask for, so she said to Herod, "Give me the head of John the Baptist here on a platter." [9]Although King Herod was very sad, he had made a promise, and his dinner guests had heard him. So Herod ordered that what she asked for be done. [10]He sent soldiers to the prison to cut off John's head. [11]And they brought it on a platter and gave it to the girl, and she took it to her mother. [12]John's followers came and got his body and buried it. Then they went and told Jesus.

More than Five Thousand Fed

[13]When Jesus heard what had happened to John, he left in a boat and went to a lonely place by himself. But the crowds heard about it and followed him on foot from the towns. [14]When he arrived, he saw a great crowd waiting. He felt sorry for them and healed those who were sick.

[15]When it was evening, his followers came to him and said, "No one lives in this place, and it is already late. Send the people away so they can go to the towns and buy food for themselves."

[16]But Jesus answered, "They don't need to go away. You give them something to eat."

[17]They said to him, "But we have only five loaves of bread and two fish."

[18]Jesus said, "Bring the bread and the fish to me." [19]Then he told the people to sit down on the grass. He took the five loaves and the two fish and, looking to heaven, he thanked God for the food. Jesus divided the bread and gave it to his followers, who gave it to the people. [20]All the people ate and were satisfied. Then the followers filled twelve baskets with the leftover pieces of food. [21]There were about five thousand men there who ate, not counting women and children.

FACT-OIDS! Fifty-six percent of all adults reported owning a DVD player in 2003, compared to only 18% in 2000. [Barna.org]

Jesus Walks on the Water

[22]Immediately Jesus told his followers to get into the boat and go ahead of him across the lake. He stayed there to send the people home. [23]After he had sent them away, he went by himself up into the hills to pray. It was late, and Jesus was there alone. [24]By this time, the boat was already far away from land. It was being hit by waves, because the wind was blowing against it.

[25]Between three and six o'clock in the morning, Jesus came to them, walking on the water. [26]When his followers saw him walking on the water, they were afraid. They said, "It's a ghost!" and cried out in fear. [27]But Jesus quickly spoke to them, "Have courage! It is I. Do not be afraid."

[28]Peter said, "Lord, if it is really you, then command me to come to you on the water."

[29]Jesus said, "Come."

And Peter left the boat and walked on the water to Jesus. [30]But when Peter saw the wind and the waves, he became afraid and began to sink. He shouted, "Lord, save me!"

[31]Immediately Jesus reached out his hand and caught Peter. Jesus said, "Your faith is small. Why did you doubt?"

[32]After they got into the boat, the wind became calm. [33]Then those who were in the boat worshiped Jesus and said, "Truly you are the Son of God!"

[34]When they had crossed the lake, they came to shore at Gennesaret. [35]When the people there recognized Jesus, they told people all around there that Jesus had come, and they brought all their sick to him. [36]They begged Jesus to let them touch just the edge of his coat, and all who touched it were healed.

Get Fit

GETTING ACTIVE The majority of American men do not get enough physical activity to provide health benefits. For adults, thirty minutes of moderate physical activity on most days of the week is recommended. It doesn't take a lot of time or money, but it does take commitment. Start slowly, work up to a satisfactory level, and don't overdo it. Staying active is less about the drudgery of forced discipline and more about creating an active lifestyle that you genuinely enjoy. To achieve lasting change, try out different fun ways to stay in shape and feel good, such as getting involved in tennis, biking, swimming, hiking, or jogging. The more you can get out and enjoy nature, the better off you'll be.

TheFinalScore »

VINCE LOMBARDI: Mastering the Fundamentals

VINCE LOMBARDI. HIS NAME ADORNS THE TROPHY awarded to each Super Bowl championship team. When this little-known assistant coach from New York joined Green Bay, he told the Packers, "I have never been on a losing team, gentlemen, and I do not intend to start now!"

The statement proved prophetic. Lombardi led the team to a winning record the next season en route to five league championships in nine years, including the first two Super Bowls. He would later coach the Washington Redskins to a winning season before cancer claimed his life at 57.

A legendary taskmaster, Lombardi was famous for opening summer training camp with the simple statement: "Gentlemen, this is a football." Such attention to detail characterized Lombardi's teams. He knew that mastering the basics like blocking

and tackling preceded any great triumph, together with such qualities as character, determination, commitment, and sacrifice.

Lombardi used to ask, "Unless a man believes in himself and puts everything he has into it—his mind, his body, his heart—what's life worth to him?" For anyone tempted to quit amid tough battles, he reminded them, "It's not whether you get knocked down, it's whether you get up."

Such words can inspire us on a spiritual level. Just as Lombardi believed in mastering the fundamentals, we also must remember principles when life hands us its inevitable setbacks and disappointments. Such qualities as prayer, Bible study, and enduring faith in God's promises can lift us to even greater victories than those found on a football field.

> "He reminded them, 'It's not whether you get knocked down, it's whether you get up.'"

Obey God's Law

15 Then some Pharisees and teachers of the law came to Jesus from Jerusalem. They asked him, [2]"Why don't your followers obey the unwritten laws which have been handed down to us? They don't wash their hands before they eat."

[3]Jesus answered, "And why do you refuse to obey God's command so that you can follow your own teachings? [4]God said, 'Honor your father and your mother,'" and 'Anyone who says cruel things to his father or mother must be put to death.'" [5]But you say a person can tell his father or mother, 'I have something I could use to help you, but I have given it to God already.' [6]You teach that person not to honor his father or his mother. You rejected what God said for the sake of your own rules. [7]You are hypocrites! Isaiah was right when he said about you:

[8]"These people show honor to me with
    words,
  but their hearts are far from me.
[9]Their worship of me is worthless.
  The things they teach are nothing but
    human rules.'"   *Isaiah 29:13*

[10]After Jesus called the crowd to him, he said, "Listen and understand what I am saying. [11]It is not what people put into their mouths that makes them unclean. It is what comes out of their mouths that makes them unclean."

[12]Then his followers came to him and asked, "Do you know that the Pharisees are angry because of what you said?"

[13]Jesus answered, "Every plant that my Father in heaven has not planted himself will be pulled up by the roots. [14]Stay away from the Pharisees; they are blind leaders." And if a blind person leads a blind person, both will fall into a ditch."

[15]Peter said, "Explain the example to us."

[16]Jesus said, "Do you still not understand? [17]Surely you know that all the food that enters the mouth goes into the stomach and then goes out of the body. [18]But what people say with their mouths comes from the way they think; these are the things that make people unclean. [19]Out of the mind come evil thoughts, murder, adultery, sexual sins, stealing, lying, and speaking evil of others.

[20]These things make people unclean; eating with unwashed hands does not make them unclean."

Jesus Helps a Non-Jewish Woman

[21]Jesus left that place and went to the area of Tyre and Sidon. [22]A Canaanite woman from that area came to Jesus and cried out, "Lord, Son of David, have mercy on me! My daughter has a demon, and she is suffering very much."

[23]But Jesus did not answer the woman. So his followers came to Jesus and begged him, "Tell the woman to go away. She is following us and shouting."

[24]Jesus answered, "God sent me only to the lost sheep, the people of Israel."

[25]Then the woman came to Jesus again and bowed before him and said, "Lord, help me!"

[26]Jesus answered, "It is not right to take the children's bread and give it to the dogs."

[27]The woman said, "Yes, Lord, but even the dogs eat the crumbs that fall from their masters' table."

[28]Then Jesus answered, "Woman, you have great faith! I will do what you asked." And at that moment the woman's daughter was healed.

Jesus Heals Many People

[29]After leaving there, Jesus went along the shore of Lake Galilee. He went up on a hill and sat there. [30]Great crowds came to Jesus, bringing with them the lame, the blind, the crippled, those who could not speak, and many others. They put them at Jesus' feet, and he healed them. [31]The crowd was amazed when they saw that people who could not speak before were now able to speak. The crippled were made strong. The lame could walk, and the blind could see. And they praised the God of Israel for this.

More than Four Thousand Fed

[32]Jesus called his followers to him and said, "I feel sorry for these people, because they have already been with me three days, and they have nothing to eat. I don't want to send them away hungry. They might faint while going home."

[33]His followers asked him, "How can we get enough bread to feed all these people? We are far away from any town."

[34]Jesus asked, "How many loaves of bread do you have?"

They answered, "Seven, and a few small fish."

[35]Jesus told the people to sit on the ground. [36]He took the seven loaves of bread and the fish and gave thanks to God. Then he divided the food and gave it to his followers, and they gave it to the people. [37]All the people ate and were satisfied. Then his followers filled seven baskets with the leftover pieces of food. [38]There were about four thousand men there who ate, besides women and

{ Book of the Month }

Margin
by Richard A. Swenson

Physician Richard Swenson has for years treated patients suffering from the pain of their modern-day lifestyles. Progress has brought the world more of everything, faster than ever. But it has also exponentially increased the pressures upon men beyond their ability to manage. Dr. Swenson's prescription? The restoration of reserves, or margin. Without reducing his advice to self-help clichés, Swenson's thorough suggestions aim to restore margin in each of the dimensions of men's lives: physical, emotional, time, and financial. Follow the good doctor's orders and you'll be on the path to a healthier lifestyle and peak performance, with energy to spare.

 15:4 'Honor...mother.' Quotation from Exodus 20:12; Deuteronomy 5:16.   **15:4** 'Anyone...death.' Quotation from Exodus 21:17.   **15:14 leaders** Some Greek copies continue, "of blind people."

26

>>January

QUOTE OF THE MONTH:
"A good plan today is better than a great plan tomorrow." —General George S. Patton

1 Celebrate **New Year's Day** by reading the Bible and praying.

2 Clean out your closet and donate some clothes to charity.

3 **Hawaii** officially became the 50th state on this day in 1959.

4

5  Memorize Mark 11:24.

6

7

8 **Elvis** has left the building, but he was born on this day in 1935.

9

10

11

12 Pray for a person of influence: Today is entrepreneur **Jeff Bezos's** birthday.

13

14 Start collecting the necessary paperwork for tax preparation.

15 Celebrate the birthday of **Martin Luther King Jr.** Honor his legacy with respect.

16

17 Pray for a person of influence: Today is boxer **Muhammad Ali's** birthday.

18

19

20 Set some new goals for yourself personally and professionally.

21 Pray for a person of influence: Today is golfer **Jack Nicklaus's** birthday.

22

23 Buy extra batteries for emergencies.

24

25 Plan a special date with your significant other.

26

27 Classical musician **Wolfgang Mozart** was born on this day in 1756.

28

29 Pray for a person of influence: Today is entertainer **Oprah Winfrey's** birthday.

30 Former president **Franklin Delano Roosevelt** was born today in 1882.

31 Do a chore around the house.

→ The Bottom Line

Leasing a Car: Ask Questions

MANY PEOPLE USE LEASING AS A WAY TO DRIVE A NEWER CAR. There are advantages, such as less money down and lower monthly payments. But before signing a lease, examine the fine print. Inquire if there is a penalty for driving beyond a certain number of miles in a year, whether or not there is a balloon payment due at the end of the lease, and if there is an early-termination charge. Failure to understand such conditions may leave you feeling shortchanged. Also, remember that after the lease ends, you will not have a car. So exercise wisdom.

children. ³⁹After sending the people home, Jesus got into the boat and went to the area of Magadan.

The Leaders Ask for a Miracle

16 The Pharisees and Sadducees came to Jesus, wanting to trick him. So they asked him to show them a miracle from God. ²Jesus answered," "At sunset you say we will have good weather, because the sky is red. ³And in the morning you say that it will be a rainy day, because the sky is dark and red. You see these signs in the sky and know what they mean. In the same way, you see the things that I am doing now, but you don't know their meaning. ⁴Evil and sinful people ask for a miracle as a sign, but they will not be given any sign, except the sign of Jonah."" Then Jesus left them and went away.

Guard Against Wrong Teachings

⁵Jesus' followers went across the lake, but they had forgotten to bring bread. ⁶Jesus said to them, "Be careful! Beware of the yeast of the Pharisees and the Sadducees."

⁷His followers discussed the meaning of this, saying, "He said this because we forgot to bring bread."

⁸Knowing what they were talking about, Jesus asked them, "Why are you talking about not having bread? Your faith is small. ⁹Do you still not understand? Remember the five loaves of bread that fed the five thousand? And remember that you filled many baskets with the leftovers? ¹⁰Or the seven loaves of bread that fed the four thousand and the many baskets you filled then also? ¹¹I was not talking to you about bread. Why don't you understand that? I am telling you to beware of the yeast of the Pharisees and the Sadducees." ¹²Then the followers understood that Jesus was not telling them to beware of the yeast used in bread but to beware of the teaching of the Pharisees and the Sadducees.

Peter Says Jesus Is the Christ

¹³When Jesus came to the area of Caesarea Philippi, he asked his followers, "Who do people say the Son of Man is?"

¹⁴They answered, "Some say you are John the Baptist. Others say you are Elijah, and still others say you are Jeremiah or one of the prophets."

¹⁵Then Jesus asked them, "And who do you say I am?"

¹⁶Simon Peter answered, "You are the Christ, the Son of the living God."

¹⁷Jesus answered, "You are blessed, Simon son of Jonah, because no person taught you that. My Father in heaven showed you who I am. ¹⁸So I tell you, you are Peter." On this rock I will build my church, and the power of death will not be able to defeat it. ¹⁹I will give you the keys of the kingdom of heaven; the things you don't allow on earth will be the things that God does not allow, and the things you allow on earth will be the things that God allows." ²⁰Then Jesus warned his followers not to tell anyone he was the Christ.

Jesus Says that He Must Die

²¹From that time on Jesus began telling his followers that he must go to Jerusalem, where the Jewish elders, the leading priests, and the teachers of the law would make him suffer many things. He told them he must be killed and then be raised from the dead on the third day.

Q: Why does God allow sickness?

A: When humanity rebelled against God, sin came into the world, and with sin came decay, disease, and death. It was not God's original plan for people to experience sickness, nor does he cause it, but healing and health are from God (1 Peter 2:24).

➤➤ **16:2–3 answered** Some Greek copies do not have the rest of verse 2 and verse 3. **16:4 sign of Jonah** Jonah's three days in the fish are like Jesus' three days in the tomb. The story about Jonah is in the Book of Jonah. **16:18 Peter** The Greek name "Peter," like the Aramaic name "Cephas," means "rock."

²²Peter took Jesus aside and told him not to talk like that. He said, "God save you from those things, Lord! Those things will never happen to you!"

²³Then Jesus said to Peter, "Go away from me, Satan!" You are not helping me! You don't care about the things of God, but only about the things people think are important."

²⁴Then Jesus said to his followers, "If people want to follow me, they must give up the things they want. They must be willing even to give up their lives to follow me. ²⁵Those who want to save their lives will give up true life, and those who give up their lives for me will have true life. ²⁶It is worthless to have the whole world if they lose their souls. They could never pay enough to buy back their souls. ²⁷The Son of Man will come again with his Father's glory and with his angels. At that time, he will reward them for what they have done. ²⁸I tell you the truth, some people standing here will see the Son of Man coming with his kingdom before they die."

Jesus Talks with Moses and Elijah

17 Six days later, Jesus took Peter, James, and John, the brother of James, up on a high mountain by themselves. ²While they watched, Jesus' appearance was changed; his face became bright like the sun, and his clothes became white as light. ³Then Moses and Elijah" appeared to them, talking with Jesus.

⁴Peter said to Jesus, "Lord, it is good that we are here. If you want, I will put up three tents here—one for you, one for Moses, and one for Elijah."

⁵While Peter was talking, a bright cloud covered them. A voice came from the cloud and said, "This is my Son, whom I love, and I am very pleased with him. Listen to him!"

⁶When his followers heard the voice, they were so frightened they fell to the ground. ⁷But Jesus went to them and touched them and said, "Stand up. Don't be afraid." ⁸When they looked up, they saw Jesus was now alone.

⁹As they were coming down the mountain, Jesus commanded them not to tell anyone about what they had seen until the Son of Man had risen from the dead.

<<TechSupport>>

PERSONAL GROOMING

Unless he sported a beard, your dad probably used to drag some type of straight razor across his stubbly face every morning. Today's electric razors include vibrating heads that coax stubborn hairs out of their follicles and lotion dispensers built in to soften and protect your skin as you shave. There just isn't any excuse for five o'clock shadows or razor burns nowadays. Just as it's easier to shave with supple skin, it's easier to hear the truth when your heart is softened.

¹⁰Then his followers asked him, "Why do the teachers of the law say that Elijah must come first?"

¹¹Jesus answered, "They are right to say that Elijah is coming and that he will make everything the way it should be. ¹²But I tell you that Elijah has already come, and they did not recognize him. They did to him whatever they wanted to do. It will be the same with the Son of Man; those same people will make the Son of Man suffer." ¹³Then the followers understood that Jesus was talking about John the Baptist.

Jesus Heals a Sick Boy

¹⁴When Jesus and his followers came back to the crowd, a man came to Jesus and bowed before him. ¹⁵The man said, "Lord, have mercy on my son. He has epilepsy" and is suffering very much, because he often falls into the fire or into the water. ¹⁶I brought him to your followers, but they could not cure him."

¹⁷Jesus answered, "You people have no faith, and your lives are all wrong. How long must I put up with you? How long must I continue to be patient with you? Bring the boy here." ¹⁸Jesus commanded the

Principles: BIBLE

The Bible is the Word of God to man, and it remains the world's best-selling book nearly two thousand years after its completion. Composed of sixty-six books in the Old and New Testaments, it is the basis of Christian preaching, instruction, and personal study. Jesus demonstrated its importance when he quoted God's Word to withstand Satan's temptations (Matthew 4:1–11). In Ephesians 6:17, Paul called God's Word the "sword of the Spirit." The Bible has such depth that many differ on how to interpret certain aspects of its commands, yet it remains the guide for wise living.

16:23 Satan Name for the devil, meaning "the enemy." Jesus means that Peter was talking like Satan. **17:3 Moses and Elijah** Two of the most important Jewish leaders in the past. God had given Moses the Law, and Elijah was an important prophet. **17:15 epilepsy** A disease that causes a person sometimes to lose control of his body and maybe faint, shake strongly, or not be able to move.

demon inside the boy. Then the demon came out, and the boy was healed from that time on.

¹⁹The followers came to Jesus when he was alone and asked, "Why couldn't we force the demon out?"

²⁰Jesus answered, "Because your faith is too small. I tell you the truth, if your faith is as big as a mustard seed, you can say to this mountain, 'Move from here to there,' and it will move. All things will be possible for you. [²¹That kind of spirit comes out only if you use prayer and fasting.]"ⁿ

Jesus Talks About His Death

²²While Jesus' followers were gathering in Galilee, he said to them, "The Son of Man will be handed over to people, ²³and they will kill him. But on the third day he will be raised from the dead." And the followers were filled with sadness.

Jesus Talks About Paying Taxes

²⁴When Jesus and his followers came to Capernaum, the men who collected the Temple tax came to Peter. They asked, "Does your teacher pay the Temple tax?"

²⁵Peter answered, "Yes, Jesus pays the tax."

Peter went into the house, but before he could speak, Jesus said to him, "What do you think? The kings of the earth collect different kinds of taxes. But who pays the taxes—the king's children or others?"

²⁶Peter answered, "Other people pay the taxes."

Jesus said to Peter, "Then the children of the king don't have to pay taxes. ²⁷But we don't want to upset these tax collectors. So go to the lake and fish. After you catch the first fish, open its mouth and you will find a coin. Take that coin and give it to the tax collectors for you and me."

<<TechSupport>>

DIGITAL MUSIC

While the practice of unauthorized music downloading is widespread and the temptation is strong to follow the trend, it is saner and safer simply to download the legal stuff off legitimate sites and spare yourself the trouble. To begin building your own collection of digital music, check out iTunes and Napster, each of which offers different approaches to online music downloads. Add a portable music device, and you will be able to synchronize with your personal computer. Choosing uplifting music can have a positive effect on your attitude and also makes it easy to integrate worship into your daily life.

Who Is the Greatest?

18 At that time the followers came to Jesus and asked, "Who is greatest in the kingdom of heaven?"

²Jesus called a little child to him and stood the child before his followers. ³Then he said, "I tell you the truth, you must change and become like little children. Otherwise, you will never enter the kingdom of heaven. ⁴The greatest person in the kingdom of heaven is the one who makes himself humble like this child.

⁵"Whoever accepts a child in my name accepts me. ⁶If one of these little children believes in me, and someone causes that child to sin, it would be better for that person to have a large stone tied around the neck and be drowned in the sea. ⁷How terrible for the people of the world because of the things that cause them to sin. Such things will happen, but how terrible for the one who causes them to happen! ⁸If your hand or your foot causes you to sin, cut it off and throw it away. It is better for you to lose part of your body and live forever than to have two hands and two feet and be thrown into the fire that burns forever. ⁹If your eye causes you to sin, take it out and throw it away. It is better for you to have only one eye and live forever than to have two eyes and be thrown into the fire of hell.

A Lost Sheep

¹⁰"Be careful. Don't think these little children are worth nothing. I tell you that they have angels in heaven who are always with my Father in heaven. [¹¹The Son of Man came to save lost people.]ⁿ

¹²"If a man has a hundred sheep but one of the sheep gets lost, he will leave the other ninety-nine on the hill and go to look for the lost sheep. ¹³I tell you the truth, if he finds it he is happier about that one sheep than about the ninety-nine that were never lost. ¹⁴In the same way, your Father in heaven does not want any of these little children to be lost.

When a Person Sins Against You

¹⁵"If your fellow believer sins against you,ⁿ go and tell him in private what he did wrong. If he listens to you, you have helped that person to be your brother or sister again. ¹⁶But if he refuses to listen, go to him again and take one or two other people with you. 'Every case may be proved by two or three witnesses.'ⁿ ¹⁷If he refuses to listen to them, tell the church. If he refuses to listen to the church, then treat him like a person who does not believe in God or like a tax collector.

¹⁸"I tell you the truth, the things you don't allow on earth will be the things God does not allow. And the things you allow on earth will be the things that God allows.

¹⁹"Also, I tell you that if two of you on earth agree about something and pray for it, it will be done for you by my Father in heaven. ²⁰This is true because if two or three people come together in my name, I am there with them."

An Unforgiving Servant

²¹Then Peter came to Jesus and asked, "Lord, when my fellow believer sins against me, how many times must I forgive him? Should I forgive him as many as seven times?"

17:21 That ... fasting. Some Greek copies do not contain the bracketed text.   **18:11 The ... people.** Some Greek copies do not contain the bracketed text.   **18:15 against you** Some Greek copies do not have "against you."   **18:16 'Every ... witnesses.'** Quotation from Deuteronomy 19:15.

²²Jesus answered, "I tell you, you must forgive him more than seven times. You must forgive him even if he wrongs you seventy times seven.

²³"The kingdom of heaven is like a king who decided to collect the money his servants owed him. ²⁴When the king began to collect his money, a servant who owed him several million dollars was brought to him. ²⁵But the servant did not have enough money to pay his master, the king. So the master ordered that everything the servant owned should be sold, even the servant's wife and children. Then the money would be used to pay the king what the servant owed.

²⁶"But the servant fell on his knees and begged, 'Be patient with me, and I will pay you everything I owe.' ²⁷The master felt sorry for his servant and told him he did not have to pay it back. Then he let the servant go free.

²⁸"Later, that same servant found another servant who owed him a few dollars. The servant grabbed him around the neck and said, 'Pay me the money you owe me!'

²⁹"The other servant fell on his knees and begged him, 'Be patient with me, and I will pay you everything I owe.'

³⁰"But the first servant refused to be patient. He threw the other servant into prison until he could pay everything he owed. ³¹When the other servants saw what had happened, they were very sorry. So they went and told their master all that had happened.

³²"Then the master called his servant in and said, 'You evil servant! Because you begged me to forget what you owed, I told you that you did not have to pay anything. ³³You should have showed mercy to that other servant, just as I showed mercy to you.' ³⁴The master was very angry and put the servant in prison to be punished until he could pay everything he owed.

³⁵"This king did what my heavenly Father will do to you if you do not forgive your brother or sister from your heart."

Jesus Teaches About Divorce

19 After Jesus said all these things, he left Galilee and went into the area of Judea on the other side of the Jordan River. ²Large crowds followed him, and he healed them there.

³Some Pharisees came to Jesus and tried to trick him. They asked, "Is it right for a man to divorce his wife for any reason he chooses?"

⁴Jesus answered, "Surely you have read in the Scriptures: When God made the world, 'he made them male and female.'ⁿ ⁵And God said, 'So a man will leave his father and mother and be united with his wife, and the two will become one body.'ⁿ ⁶So there are not two, but one. God has joined the two together, so no one should separate them."

⁷The Pharisees asked, "Why then did Moses give a command for a man to divorce his wife by giving her divorce papers?"

⁸Jesus answered, "Moses allowed you to divorce your wives because you refused to accept God's teaching, but divorce was not allowed in the beginning. ⁹I tell you that anyone who divorces his wife and marries another woman is guilty of adultery.ⁿ The only reason for a man to divorce his wife is if his wife has sexual relations with another man."

>> live the life

Matthew 19:13–15

The Principle > **Bless the needy.**

Practicing It > **Sponsor a child through a reputable Christian organization that specializes in such ministry. Write letters to your children and send special gifts to them to share with them the love of Christ.**

¹⁰The followers said to him, "If that is the only reason a man can divorce his wife, it is better not to marry."

¹¹Jesus answered, "Not everyone can accept this teaching, but God has made some able to accept it. ¹²There are different reasons why some men cannot marry. Some men were born without the ability to become fathers. Others were made that way later in life by other people. And some men have given up marriage because of the kingdom of heaven. But the person who can marry should accept this teaching about marriage."ⁿ

Jesus Welcomes Children

¹³Then the people brought their little children to Jesus so he could put his hands on themⁿ and pray for them. His followers told them to stop, ¹⁴but Jesus said, "Let the little children come to me. Don't stop them, because the kingdom of heaven belongs to people who are like these children." ¹⁵After Jesus put his hands on the children, he left there.

A Rich Young Man's Question

¹⁶A man came to Jesus and asked, "Teacher, what good thing must I do to have life forever?"

¹⁷Jesus answered, "Why do you ask me about what is good? Only God is good. But if you want to have life forever, obey the commands."

¹⁸The man asked, "Which commands?"

Jesus answered, " 'You must not murder anyone; you must not be guilty of adultery; you must not steal; you must not tell lies about your neighbor; ¹⁹honor your father and mother;ⁿ and love your neighbor as you love yourself.' "ⁿ

²⁰The young man said, "I have obeyed all these things. What else do I need to do?"

²¹Jesus answered, "If you want to be perfect, then go and sell your possessions and give the money to the poor. If you do this, you will have treasure in heaven. Then come and follow me."

²²But when the young man heard this, he left sorrowfully, because he was rich.

²³Then Jesus said to his followers, "I tell you the truth, it will be hard

---

19:4 'he made … female' Quotation from Genesis 1:27 or 5:2.   **19:5 'So … body.'** Quotation from Genesis 2:24.   **19:9 adultery** Some Greek copies continue, "And anyone who marries a divorced woman is guilty of adultery." Compare Matthew 5:32.   **19:12 But … marriage.** This may also mean, "The person who can accept this teaching about not marrying should accept it."   **19:13 put his hands on them** Showing that Jesus gave special blessings to these children.   (Matthew 19 notes cont. on p. 32.)

Change >> Your WORLD

BILLY GRAHAM EVANGELISTIC ASSOCIATION

Millions of people have started a personal relationship with Jesus Christ through the faithful ministry of the Billy Graham Evangelistic Association (BGEA). Whereas the organization was established to support the ministry of Billy Graham, it is a diverse ministry. Charged to take the Good News about Jesus Christ to as many people as possible, BGEA uses evangelistic crusades, telecasts, the Internet, radio programs, literature, and films. The Schools of Evangelism train pastors in evangelistic methods, and The Billy Graham Training Center presents seminars on Bible studies and evangelism ministry. There are multiple ways to take an active role, from prayer to spiritual guidance to evangelism.

To change your world, visit www.billygraham.org.

for a rich person to enter the kingdom of heaven. [24]Yes, I tell you that it is easier for a camel to go through the eye of a needle than for a rich person to enter the kingdom of God."

[25]When Jesus' followers heard this, they were very surprised and asked, "Then who can be saved?"

[26]Jesus looked at them and said, "For people this is impossible, but for God all things are possible."

[27]Peter said to Jesus, "Look, we have left everything and followed you. So what will we have?"

[28]Jesus said to them, "I tell you the truth, when the age to come has arrived, the Son of Man will sit on his great throne. All of you who followed me will also sit on twelve thrones, judging the twelve tribes of Israel. [29]And all those who have left houses, brothers, sisters, father, mother,[n] children, or farms to follow me will get much more than they left, and they will have life forever. [30]Many who are first now will be last in the future. And many who are last now will be first in the future.

A Story About Workers

20 "The kingdom of heaven is like a person who owned some land. One morning, he went out very early to hire some people to work in his vineyard. [2]The man agreed to pay the workers one coin[n] for working that day. Then he sent them into the vineyard to work. [3]About nine o'clock the man went to the marketplace and saw some other people standing there, doing nothing. [4]So he said to them, 'If you go and work in my vineyard, I will pay you what your work is worth.' [5]So they went to work in the vineyard. The man went out again about twelve o'clock and three o'clock and did the same thing. [6]About five o'clock the man went to the marketplace again and saw others standing there. He asked them, 'Why did you stand here all day doing nothing?' [7]They answered, 'No one gave us a job.' The man said to them, 'Then you can go and work in my vineyard.'

[8]"At the end of the day, the owner of the vineyard said to the boss of all the workers, 'Call the workers and pay them. Start with the last people I hired and end with those I hired first.'

[9]"When the workers who were hired at five o'clock came to get their pay, each received one coin. [10]When the workers who were hired first came to get their pay, they thought they would be paid more than the others. But each one of them also received one coin. [11]When they got their coin, they complained to the man who owned the land. [12]They said, 'Those people were hired last and worked only one hour. But you paid them the same as you paid us who worked hard all day in the hot sun.' [13]But the man who owned the vineyard said to one of those workers, 'Friend, I am being fair to you. You agreed to work for one coin. [14]So take your pay and go. I want to give the man who was hired last the same pay that I gave you. [15]I can do what I want with my own money. Are you jealous because I am good to those people?'

[16]"So those who are last now will someday be first, and those who are first now will someday be last."

Jesus Talks About His Own Death

[17]While Jesus was going to Jerusalem, he took his twelve followers aside privately and said to them, [18]"Look, we are going to Jerusalem. The Son of Man will be turned over to the leading priests and the teachers of the law, and they will say that he must die. [19]They will give the Son of Man to the non-Jewish people to laugh at him and beat him with whips and crucify him. But on the third day, he will be raised to life again."

A Mother Asks Jesus a Favor

[20]Then the wife of Zebedee came to Jesus with her sons. She bowed before him and asked him to do something for her.

[21]Jesus asked, "What do you want?"

She said, "Promise that one of my sons will sit at your right side and the other will sit at your left side in your kingdom."

[22]But Jesus said, "You don't understand what you are asking. Can you drink the cup that I am about to drink?"[n]

The sons answered, "Yes, we can."

[23]Jesus said to them, "You will drink from my cup. But I cannot

---

 19:19 'You ... mother.' Quotation from Exodus 20:12–16; Deuteronomy 5:16–20. **19:19** 'love ... yourself' Quotation from Leviticus 19:18. **19:29 mother** Some Greek copies continue, "or wife." **20:2 coin** A Roman denarius. One coin was the average pay for one day's work. **20:22 drink ... drink** Jesus used the idea of drinking from a cup to ask if they could accept the same terrible things that would happen to him.

choose who will sit at my right or my left; those places belong to those for whom my Father has prepared them."

[24]When the other ten followers heard this, they were angry with the two brothers.

[25]Jesus called all the followers together and said, "You know that the rulers of the non-Jewish people love to show their power over the people. And their important leaders love to use all their authority. [26]But it should not be that way among you. Whoever wants to become great among you must serve the rest of you like a servant. [27]Whoever wants to become first among you must serve the rest of you like a slave. [28]In the same way, the Son of Man did not come to be served. He came to serve others and to give his life as a ransom for many people."

Jesus Heals Two Blind Men

[29]When Jesus and his followers were leaving Jericho, a great many people followed him. [30]Two blind men sitting by the road heard that Jesus was going by, so they shouted, "Lord, Son of David, have mercy on us!"

[31]The people warned the blind men to be quiet, but they shouted even more, "Lord, Son of David, have mercy on us!"

[32]Jesus stopped and said to the blind men, "What do you want me to do for you?"

[33]They answered, "Lord, we want to see."

[34]Jesus felt sorry for the blind men and touched their eyes, and at once they could see. Then they followed Jesus.

Jesus Enters Jerusalem as a King

21 As Jesus and his followers were coming closer to Jerusalem, they stopped at Bethphage at the hill called the Mount of Olives. From there Jesus sent two of his followers [2]and said to them, "Go to the town you can see there. When you enter it, you will quickly find a donkey tied there with its colt. Untie them and bring them to me. [3]If anyone asks you why you are taking the donkeys, say that the Master needs them, and he will send them at once."

[4]This was to bring about what the prophet had said:

[5]"Tell the people of Jerusalem,
   'Your king is coming to you.
He is gentle and riding on a donkey,
   on the colt of a donkey.' "   *Isaiah 62:11; Zechariah 9:9*

[6]The followers went and did what Jesus told them to do. [7]They brought the donkey and the colt to Jesus and laid their coats on them, and Jesus sat on them. [8]Many people spread their coats on the road. Others cut branches from the trees and spread them on the road. [9]The people were walking ahead of Jesus and behind him, shouting,

"Praise[n] to the Son of David!

God bless the One who comes in the name of the Lord!
                                         Psalm 118:26

Praise to God in heaven!"

[10]When Jesus entered Jerusalem, all the city was filled with excitement. The people asked, "Who is this man?"

[11]The crowd said, "This man is Jesus, the prophet from the town of Nazareth in Galilee."

Jesus Goes to the Temple

[12]Jesus went into the Temple and threw out all the people who were buying and selling there. He turned over the tables of those who were exchanging different kinds of money, and he upset the benches of those who were selling doves. [13]Jesus said to all the people there, "It is written in the Scriptures, 'My Temple will be called a house for prayer.'[n] But you are changing it into a 'hideout for robbers.' "[n]

[14]The blind and crippled people came to Jesus in the Temple, and he healed them. [15]The leading priests and the teachers of the law saw that Jesus was doing wonderful things and that the children were praising him in the Temple, saying, "Praise[n] to the Son of David." All these things made the priests and the teachers of the law very angry.

[16]They asked Jesus, "Do you hear the things these children are saying?"

Jesus answered, "Yes. Haven't you read in the Scriptures, 'You have taught children and babies to sing praises'?"[n]

[17]Then Jesus left and went out of the city to Bethany, where he spent the night.

The Power of Faith

[18]Early the next morning, as Jesus was going back to the city, he became hungry. [19]Seeing a fig tree beside the road, Jesus went to it, but there were no figs on the tree, only leaves. So Jesus said to the tree, "You will never again have fruit." The tree immediately dried up.

[20]When his followers saw this, they were amazed. They asked, "How did the fig tree dry up so quickly?"

[21]Jesus answered, "I tell you the truth, if you have faith and do not doubt, you will be able to do what I did to this tree and even more. You will be able to say to this mountain, 'Go, fall into the sea.' And if you have faith, it will happen. [22]If you believe, you will get anything you ask for in prayer."

Leaders Doubt Jesus' Authority

[23]Jesus went to the Temple, and while he was teaching there, the leading priests and the elders of the people came to him. They said,

Q: Is looking at pornography really a sin?

A: Yes. Jesus clearly taught that all forms of sexual sin are more a matter of the heart than of any particular outward behavior. So lusting after an image of a woman is the same as lusting after a woman in real life and having sex with her (Matthew 5:28).

21:9, 15 **Praise** Literally, "Hosanna," a Hebrew word used at first in praying to God for help. At this time it was probably a shout of joy used in praising God or his Messiah.   21:13 **'My Temple ... prayer.'** Quotation from Isaiah 56:7.   21:13 **'hideout for robbers'** Quotation from Jeremiah 7:11.   21:16 **'You ... praises.'** Quotation from the Septuagint (Greek) version of Psalm 8:2.

33

<<TechSupport>>

DIGITAL PHOTOGRAPHY

Choosing a digital camera can be a complicated venture, so here is a quick primer. Unless you are an aspiring photographer, four megapixels should probably meet your needs. Choose a camera that supports widely available and low-cost storage media, such as CompactFlash or Secure Digital memory. In addition, get a camera with at least 3X optical zoom, which uses glass lenses to bring the image closer and results in a sharper image than 2X optical zoom. And, spiritually speaking, remember that you are made in the image of God, so your life ought to reflect that.

"What authority do you have to do these things? Who gave you this authority?"

²⁴Jesus answered, "I also will ask you a question. If you answer me, then I will tell you what authority I have to do these things. ²⁵Tell me: When John baptized people, did that come from God or just from other people?"

They argued about Jesus' question, saying, "If we answer, 'John's baptism was from God,' Jesus will say, 'Then why didn't you believe him?' ²⁶But if we say, 'It was from people,' we are afraid of what the crowd will do because they all believe that John was a prophet."

²⁷So they answered Jesus, "We don't know."

Jesus said to them, "Then I won't tell you what authority I have to do these things.

A Story About Two Sons

²⁸"Tell me what you think about this: A man had two sons. He went to the first son and said, 'Son, go and work today in my vineyard.' ²⁹The son answered, 'I will not go.' But later the son changed his mind and went. ³⁰Then the father went to the other son and said, 'Son, go and work today in my vineyard.' The son answered, 'Yes, sir, I will go and work,' but he did not go. ³¹Which of the two sons obeyed his father?"

The priests and leaders answered, "The first son."

Jesus said to them, "I tell you the truth, the tax collectors and the prostitutes will enter the kingdom of God before you do. ³²John came to show you the right way to live. You did not believe him, but the tax collectors and prostitutes believed him. Even after seeing this, you still refused to change your ways and believe him.

A Story About God's Son

³³"Listen to this story: There was a man who owned a vineyard. He put a wall around it and dug a hole for a winepress and built a tower.

Then he leased the land to some farmers and left for a trip. ³⁴When it was time for the grapes to be picked, he sent his servants to the farmers to get his share of the grapes. ³⁵But the farmers grabbed the servants, beat one, killed another, and then killed a third servant with stones. ³⁶So the man sent some other servants to the farmers, even more than he sent the first time. But the farmers did the same thing to the servants that they had done before. ³⁷So the man decided to send his son to the farmers. He said, 'They will respect my son.' ³⁸But when the farmers saw the son, they said to each other, 'This son will inherit the vineyard. If we kill him, it will be ours!' ³⁹Then the farmers grabbed the son, threw him out of the vineyard, and killed him. ⁴⁰So what will the owner of the vineyard do to these farmers when he comes?"

⁴¹The priests and leaders said, "He will surely kill those evil men. Then he will lease the vineyard to some other farmers who will give him his share of the crop at harvest time."

⁴²Jesus said to them, "Surely you have read this in the Scriptures:

'The stone that the builders rejected
    became the cornerstone.
The Lord did this,
    and it is wonderful to us.'
                                    Psalm 118:22–23

⁴³"So I tell you that the kingdom of God will be taken away from you and given to people who do the things God wants in his kingdom. ⁴⁴The person who falls on this stone will be broken, and on whomever that stone falls, that person will be crushed."ⁿ

⁴⁵When the leading priests and the Pharisees heard these stories, they knew Jesus was talking about them. ⁴⁶They wanted to arrest him, but they were afraid of the people, because the people believed that Jesus was a prophet.

A Story About a Wedding Feast

22 Jesus again used stories to teach them. He said, ²"The kingdom of heaven is like a king who prepared a wedding feast for his son. ³The king invited some people to the feast. When the feast was ready, the king sent his servants to tell the people, but they refused to come.

Q: What does it mean to follow the Holy Spirit?

A: The Holy Spirit of God inhabits every believer. A Christian follows the leading of the Holy Spirit by prayerfully heeding inner promptings from God in making decisions or choosing a course of action in daily life in accordance with the Bible (Galatians 5:16).

>> 21:44 **The … crushed.** Some Greek copies do not have verse 44.

⁴"Then the king sent other servants, saying, 'Tell those who have been invited that my feast is ready. I have killed my best bulls and calves for the dinner, and everything is ready. Come to the wedding feast.'

⁵"But the people refused to listen to the servants and left to do other things. One went to work in his field, and another went to his business. ⁶Some of the other people grabbed the servants, beat them, and killed them. ⁷The king was furious and sent his army to kill the murderers and burn their city.

⁸"After that, the king said to his servants, 'The wedding feast is ready. I invited those people, but they were not worthy to come. ⁹So go to the street corners and invite everyone you find to come to my feast.' ¹⁰So the servants went into the streets and gathered all the people they could find, both good and bad. And the wedding hall was filled with guests.

¹¹"When the king came in to see the guests, he saw a man who was not dressed for a wedding. ¹²The king said, 'Friend, how were you allowed to come in here? You are not

FACT- OIDS! About 36% of Americans reported owning a digital camera in 2003.   [Barna.org]

dressed for a wedding.' But the man said nothing. ¹³So the king told some servants, 'Tie this man's hands and feet. Throw him out into the darkness, where people will cry and grind their teeth with pain.'

¹⁴"Yes, many are invited, but only a few are chosen."

Is It Right to Pay Taxes or Not?

¹⁵Then the Pharisees left that place and made plans to trap Jesus in saying something wrong. ¹⁶They sent some of their own followers and some people from the group called Herodians.ⁿ They said, "Teacher, we know that you are an honest man and that you teach the truth about God's way. You are not afraid of what other people think about you, because you pay no attention to who they are. ¹⁷So tell us what you think. Is it right to pay taxes to Caesar or not?"

¹⁸But knowing that these leaders were trying to trick him, Jesus said, "You hypocrites! Why are you trying to trap me? ¹⁹Show me a coin used for paying the tax." So the men showed him a coin.ⁿ ²⁰Then Jesus asked, "Whose image and name are on the coin?"

²¹The men answered, "Caesar's."

Then Jesus said to them, "Give to Caesar the things that are Caesar's, and give to God the things that are God's."

²²When the men heard what Jesus said, they were amazed and left him and went away.

Some Sadducees Try to Trick Jesus

²³That same day some Sadducees came to Jesus and asked him a question. (Sadducees believed that people would not rise from the dead.) ²⁴They said, "Teacher, Moses said if a married man dies without having children, his brother must marry the widow and have children for him. ²⁵Once there were seven brothers among

us. The first one married and died. Since he had no children, his brother married the widow. ²⁶Then the second brother also died. The same thing happened to the third brother and all the other brothers. ²⁷Finally, the woman died. ²⁸Since all seven men had married her, when people rise from the dead, whose wife will she be?"

²⁹Jesus answered, "You don't understand, because you don't know what the Scriptures say, and you don't know about the power of God. ³⁰When people rise from the dead, they will not marry, nor will they be given to someone to marry. They will be like the angels in heaven. ³¹Surely you have read what God said to you about rising from the dead. ³²God said, 'I am the God of Abraham, the God of Isaac, and the God of Jacob.'ⁿ God is the God of the living, not the dead."

Men of Valor
AQUILA: Full-time Christian

Aquila and his wife Priscilla played vital roles in the first-century church. Banished from Rome by the emperor, this Jewish couple met Paul in Corinth. Also tentmakers by trade, they invited the apostle to stay with them. While there, Paul visited the synagogue each Sabbath day to talk about Christ. His influence touched Aquila and Priscilla, who later sailed with Paul to Syria. They parted ways in Ephesus, where the couple met Apollos. Although strong in faith, Apollos needed spiritual education, which Aquila and Priscilla provided. This enabled Apollos to present a forceful case for Christ in Greece. Later, Paul sent greetings to the church that met at their home. Aquila shows that a relationship with God continues around the clock.

³³When the people heard this, they were amazed at Jesus' teaching.

The Most Important Command

³⁴When the Pharisees learned that the Sadducees could not argue with Jesus' answers to them, the Pharisees met together. ³⁵One Pharisee, who was an expert on the law of

---

➤➤ **22:16 Herodians** A political group that followed Herod and his family.   **22:19 coin** A Roman denarius. One coin was the average pay for one day's work.   **22:32 'I am...Jacob.'** Quotation from Exodus 3:6.

▶Get Aligned

Matthew 23:3–5

JESUS HAD HAD ENOUGH. Throughout his ministry, the Pharisees relentlessly tried to frame him. They wanted the so-called dangerous teacher out of the picture so he couldn't influence the masses, and they persisted in trying to find a charge against Jesus. As such, after yet another round of being grilled by the Pharisees, the Sadducees, and the teachers of the law, it was time for Jesus to reveal the truth about these men.

His acerbic rant about these Jewish leaders could be titled, "What *Not* To Do." It's a list of the things God detests. Beyond the religious details he mentions, there is his underlying point: Hypocrisy has no place in the life of a true believer.

There's a reason why Jesus spoke so harshly to those in the Temple. The church is God's living body, his chosen family of believers. As Christians, we are actually his representation to a world that's quick to point fingers at our inconsistencies. Jesus was passionate about proving to his followers that our faith must be lived out with more than mere words and rituals. It must be authentic, meaningful, and alive, or else it will become just another valid target for criticism.

Moses, asked Jesus this question to test him: [36]"Teacher, which command in the law is the most important?"

[37]Jesus answered, " 'Love the Lord your God with all your heart, all your soul, and all your mind.'[n] [38]This is the first and most important command. [39]And the second command is like the first: 'Love your neighbor as you love yourself.'[n] [40]All the law and the writings of the prophets depend on these two commands."

Jesus Questions the Pharisees

[41]While the Pharisees were together, Jesus asked them, [42]"What do you think about the Christ? Whose son is he?"

They answered, "The Christ is the Son of David."

[43]Then Jesus said to them, "Then why did David call him 'Lord'? David, speaking by the power of the Holy Spirit, said,

[44]"The Lord said to my Lord,

"Sit by me at my right side,

until I put your enemies under your control.' '   *Psalm 110:1*

[45]David calls the Christ 'Lord,' so how can the Christ be his son?"

[46]None of the Pharisees could answer Jesus' question, and after that day no one was brave enough to ask him any more questions.

Jesus Accuses Some Leaders

23 Then Jesus said to the crowds and to his followers, [2]"The teachers of the law and the Pharisees have the authority to tell you what the law of Moses says. [3]So you should obey and follow whatever they tell you, but their lives are not good examples for you to follow. They tell you to do things, but they themselves don't do them. [4]They make strict rules and try to force people to obey them, but they are unwilling to help those who struggle under the weight of their rules.

[5]"They do good things so that other people will see them. They enlarge the little boxes[n] holding Scriptures that they wear, and they make their special prayer clothes very long. [6]Those Pharisees and teachers of the law love to have the most important seats at feasts and in the synagogues. [7]They love people to greet them with respect in the marketplaces, and they love to have people call them 'Teacher.'

[8]"But you must not be called 'Teacher,' because you have only one Teacher, and you are all brothers and sisters together. [9]And don't call any person on earth 'Father,' because you have one Father, who is in heaven. [10]And you should not be called 'Master,' because you have only one Master, the Christ. [11]Whoever is your servant is the greatest among you. [12]Whoever makes himself great will be made humble. Whoever makes himself humble will be made great.

[13]"How terrible for you, teachers of the law and Pharisees! You are hypocrites! You close the door for people to enter the kingdom of heaven. You yourselves don't enter, and you stop others who are trying to enter. [[14]How terrible for you, teachers of the law and Pharisees. You are hypocrites. You take away widows' houses, and you say long prayers so that people will notice you. So you will have a worse punishment.][n]

[15]"How terrible for you, teachers of the law and Pharisees! You are hypocrites! You travel across land and sea to find one person who will change to your ways. When you find that person, you make him more fit for hell than you are.

[16]"How terrible for you! You guide the people, but you are blind. You say, 'If people swear by the Temple when they make a promise, that means nothing. But if they swear by the gold that is in the Temple, they must keep that promise.' [17]You are blind fools! Which is greater: the gold or the Temple that makes that gold holy? [18]And you say, 'If people swear by the altar when they make a promise, that means nothing. But if they swear by the gift on the altar, they must keep that promise.' [19]You are blind! Which is greater: the gift or the altar that makes the gift holy? [20]The person who swears by the altar is really using the altar and also everything on the altar. [21]And the person who swears by the Temple is really using the Temple and also everything in the Temple. [22]The person who swears by heaven is also using God's throne and the One who sits on that throne.

[23]"How terrible for you, teachers of the law and Pharisees! You are hypocrites! You give to God one-tenth of everything you earn—even your mint, dill, and cumin.[n] But you don't obey the really important teachings of the law—justice, mercy, and being loyal. These are the things you should do, as well as those other things. [24]You guide the people, but you are blind! You are like a person who picks a fly out of a drink and then swallows a camel!"

[25]"How terrible for you, teachers of the law and Pharisees! You are hypocrites! You wash the outside of your cups and dishes, but inside they are full of things you got by cheating others and by pleasing only

▶▶ **22:37 'Love … mind.'** Quotation from Deuteronomy 6:5.   **22:39 'Love … yourself.'** Quotation from Leviticus 19:18.   **23:5 boxes** Small leather boxes containing four important Scriptures. Some Jews tied these to their foreheads and left arms, probably to show they were very religious.   **23:14 How … punishment.** Some Greek copies do not contain the bracketed text.   **23:23 mint, dill, and cumin** Small plants grown in gardens and used for spices. Only very religious people would be careful enough to give a tenth of these plants.

yourselves. ²⁶Pharisees, you are blind! First make the inside of the cup clean, and then the outside of the cup can be truly clean.

²⁷"How terrible for you, teachers of the law and Pharisees! You are hypocrites! You are like tombs that are painted white. Outside, those tombs look fine, but inside, they are full of the bones of dead people and all kinds of unclean things. ²⁸It is the same with you. People look at you and think you are good, but on the inside you are full of hypocrisy and evil.

²⁹"How terrible for you, teachers of the law and Pharisees! You are hypocrites! You build tombs for the prophets, and you show honor to the graves of those who lived good lives. ³⁰You say, 'If we had lived during the time of our ancestors, we would not have helped them kill the prophets.' ³¹But you give proof that you are descendants of those who murdered the prophets. ³²And you will complete the sin that your ancestors started.

³³"You are snakes! A family of poisonous snakes! How are you going to escape God's judgment? ³⁴So I tell you this: I am sending to you prophets and wise men and teachers. Some of them you will kill and crucify. Some of them you will beat in your synagogues and chase from town to town. ³⁵So you will be guilty for the death of all the good people who have been killed on earth—from the murder of that good man Abel to the murder of Zechariah* son of Berakiah, whom you murdered between the Temple and the altar. ³⁶I tell you the truth, all of these things will happen to you people who are living now.

Jesus Feels Sorry for Jerusalem

³⁷"Jerusalem, Jerusalem! You kill the prophets and stone to death those who are sent to you. Many times I wanted to gather your people as a hen gathers her chicks under her wings, but you did not let me. ³⁸Now your house will be left completely empty. ³⁹I tell you, you will not see me again until that time when you will say, 'God bless the One who comes in the name of the Lord.' "*

The Temple Will Be Destroyed

24 As Jesus left the Temple and was walking away, his followers came up to show him the Temple's buildings. ²Jesus asked, "Do you see all these buildings? I tell you the truth, not one stone will be left on another. Every stone will be thrown down to the ground."

³Later, as Jesus was sitting on the Mount of Olives, his followers came to be alone with him. They said, "Tell us, when will these things happen? And what will be the sign that it is time for you to come again and for this age to end?"

⁴Jesus answered, "Be careful that no one fools you. ⁵Many will come in my name, saying, 'I am the Christ,' and they will fool many people. ⁶You will hear about wars and stories of wars that are coming, but don't be afraid. These things must happen before the end comes. ⁷Nations will fight against other nations; kingdoms will fight against other kingdoms. There will be times when there is no food for people to eat, and there will be earthquakes in different places. ⁸These things are like the first pains when something new is about to be born.

⁹"Then people will arrest you, hand you over to be hurt, and kill you. They will hate you because you believe in me. ¹⁰At that time, many will lose their faith, and they will turn against each other and hate each other. ¹¹Many false prophets will come and cause many people to believe lies. ¹²There will be more and more evil in the world, so most people will stop showing their love for each other. ¹³But those people who keep their faith until the end will be saved. ¹⁴The Good News about God's kingdom will be preached in all the world, to every nation. Then the end will come.

¹⁵"Daniel the prophet spoke about 'a blasphemous object that brings destruction.'* You will see this standing in the holy place." (You who read this should understand what it means.) ¹⁶"At that time, the people in Judea should run away to the mountains. ¹⁷If people are on the roofs* of their houses, they must not go down to get anything out of their houses. ¹⁸If people are in the fields, they must not go back to get their coats. ¹⁹At that time, how terrible it will be for

 # Survival Guide

CAULKING WINDOWS: SEAL YOUR HOME

Small gaps around window frames that allow cold air inside can drive heating bills beyond all reason. A little caulking pays huge dividends. Hardware stores and home centers carry caulking guns and tubes. Simply clean the surface and apply the caulk in a straight line over the gap. Use your finger to smooth over any excess. After it dries, a coat of paint will improve the appearance, and lower heating bills will warm your heart.

23:24 **You…camel!** Meaning, "You worry about the smallest mistakes but commit the biggest sin." 23:35 **Abel…Zechariah** In the order of the books of the Hebrew Old Testament, the first and last men to be murdered. 23:39 **'God…Lord.'** Quotation from Psalm 118:26. 24:15 **'a blasphemous object that brings destruction'** Mentioned in Daniel 9:27; 12:11 (see also Daniel 11:31). 24:17 **roofs** In Bible times houses were built with flat roofs. The roof was used for drying things such as flax and fruit. And it was used as an extra room, as a place for worship, and as a cool place to sleep in the summer.

women who are pregnant or have nursing babies! ²⁰Pray that it will not be winter or a Sabbath day when these things happen and you have to run away, ²¹because at that time there will be much trouble. There will be more trouble than there has ever been since the beginning of the world until now, and nothing as bad will ever happen again. ²²God has decided to make that terrible time short. Otherwise, no one would go on living. But God will make that time short to help the people he has chosen. ²³At that time, someone might say to you, 'Look, there is the Christ!' Or another person might say, 'There he is!' But don't believe them. ²⁴False Christs and false prophets will come and perform great wonders and miracles. They will try to fool even the people God has chosen, if that is possible. ²⁵Now I have warned you about this before it happens.

²⁶"If people tell you, 'The Christ is in the desert,' don't go there. If they say, 'The Christ is in the inner room,' don't believe it. ²⁷When the Son of Man comes, he will be seen by everyone, like lightning flashing from the east to the west. ²⁸Wherever the dead body is, there the vultures will gather.

²⁹"Soon after the trouble of those days,
'the sun will grow dark,
   and the moon will not give its light.
The stars will fall from the sky.
   And the powers of the heavens will be shaken.'   *Isaiah 13:10; 34:4*
³⁰"At that time, the sign of the Son of Man will appear in the sky. Then all the peoples of the world will cry. They will see the Son of Man coming on clouds in the sky with great power and glory. ³¹He will use a loud trumpet to send his angels all around the earth, and they will gather his chosen people from every part of the world.

³²"Learn a lesson from the fig tree: When its branches become green and soft and new leaves appear, you know summer is near. ³³In the same way, when you see all these things happening, you will know that the time is near, ready to come. ³⁴I tell you the truth, all these things will happen while the people of this time are still living. ³⁵Earth and sky will be destroyed, but the words I have said will never be destroyed.

When Will Jesus Come Again?

³⁶"No one knows when that day or time will be, not the angels in heaven, not even the Son." Only the Father knows. ³⁷When the Son of Man comes, it will be like what happened during Noah's time. ³⁸In those days before the flood, people were eating and drinking, marrying and giving their children to be married, until the day Noah entered the boat. ³⁹They knew nothing about what was happening until the flood came and destroyed them. It will be the same when the Son of Man comes. ⁴⁰Two men will be in the field. One will be taken, and the other will be left. ⁴¹Two women will be grinding grain with a mill." One will be taken, and the other will be left.

⁴²"So always be ready, because you don't know the day your Lord will come. ⁴³Remember this: If the owner of the house knew what time of night a thief was coming, the owner would watch and not let the thief break in. ⁴⁴So you also must be ready, because the Son of Man will come at a time you don't expect him.

⁴⁵"Who is the wise and loyal servant that the master trusts to give the other servants their food at the right time? ⁴⁶When the master comes and finds the servant doing his work, the servant will be blessed. ⁴⁷I tell you the truth, the master will choose that servant to take care of everything he owns. ⁴⁸But suppose that evil servant thinks to himself, 'My master will not come back soon,' ⁴⁹and he begins to beat the other servants and eat and get drunk with others like him? ⁵⁰The master will come when that servant is not ready and is not expecting him. ⁵¹Then the master will cut him in pieces and send him away to be with the hypocrites, where people will cry and grind their teeth with pain.

A Story About Ten Bridesmaids

25 "At that time the kingdom of heaven will be like ten bridesmaids who took their lamps and went to wait for the bridegroom. ²Five of them were foolish and five were wise. ³The five foolish bridesmaids took their lamps, but they did not take more oil for the lamps to burn. ⁴The wise bridesmaids took their lamps and more oil in jars. ⁵Because the bridegroom was late, they became sleepy and went to sleep.

⁶"At midnight someone cried out, 'The bridegroom is coming! Come and meet him!' ⁷Then all the bridesmaids woke up and got their lamps ready. ⁸But the foolish ones said to the wise, 'Give us some of your oil, because our lamps are going out.' ⁹The wise bridesmaids answered, 'No, the oil we have might not be enough for all of us. Go to the people who sell oil and buy some for yourselves.'

Principles: CHURCH

Church is often thought of as a building where people gather for a worship service. However, it is much more than that. In Matthew 18:20, Jesus promised wherever two or three people decide to come together in his name, he will be with them. The New Testament portrays a church characterized by camaraderie and generosity, its members eating together in each other's homes and helping everyone with a need. The church is a group of followers who meet regularly in a particular place, as well as everyone around the world who accepts Jesus Christ as Lord and Savior.

▶▶ **24:36 not even the Son** Some Greek copies do not have this phrase.   **24:41 mill** Two large, round, flat rocks used for grinding grain to make flour.

10"So while the five foolish bridesmaids went to buy oil, the bridegroom came. The bridesmaids who were ready went in with the bridegroom to the wedding feast. Then the door was closed and locked.

11"Later the others came back and said, 'Sir, sir, open the door to let us in.' 12But the bridegroom answered, 'I tell you the truth, I don't want to know you.'

13"So always be ready, because you don't know the day or the hour the Son of Man will come.

A Story About Three Servants

14"The kingdom of heaven is like a man who was going to another place for a visit. Before he left, he called for his servants and told them to take care of his things while he was gone. 15He gave one servant five bags of gold, another servant two bags of gold, and a third servant one bag of gold, to each one as much as he could handle. Then he left. 16The servant who got five bags went quickly to invest the money and earned five more bags. 17In the same way, the servant who had two bags invested them and earned two more. 18But the servant who got one bag went out and dug a hole in the ground and hid the master's money.

19"After a long time the master came home and asked the servants what they did with his money. 20The servant who was given five bags of gold brought five more bags to the master and said, 'Master, you trusted me to care for five bags of gold, so I used your five bags to earn five more.' 21The master answered, 'You did well. You are a good and loyal servant. Because you were loyal with small things, I will let you care for much greater things. Come and share my joy with me.'

22"Then the servant who had been given two bags of gold came to the master and said, 'Master, you gave me two bags of gold to care for, so I used your two bags to earn two more.' 23The master answered, 'You did well. You are a good and loyal servant. Because you were loyal with small things, I will let you care for much greater things. Come and share my joy with me.'

24"Then the servant who had been given one bag of gold came to the master and said, 'Master, I knew that you were a hard man. You harvest things you did not plant. You gather crops where you did not sow any seed. 25So I was afraid and went and hid your money in the ground. Here is your bag of gold.' 26The master answered, 'You are a wicked and lazy servant! You say you knew that I harvest things I did not plant and that I gather crops where I did not sow any seed. 27So you should have put my gold in the

People Skills

Cultivating Curiosity

Empathy, compassion, and understanding all have their roots in basic curiosity. To be the best friend you can become, practice being curious. Rather than just listening quietly to a friend share his story, ask questions about any aspect of it that intrigues you. Don't worry that your friends will think you are being nosy. God created us as inquisitive creatures, and curiosity is a natural expression of that. Asking good questions is an effective way to deepen understanding between you and your friends and strengthen the bonds of your friendship. As the saying goes, "Inquiring minds want to know," so go ahead and ask!

▶ Sexcess:
PREPARING FOR PASSION

Passion is one of those words that means different things to different people. While it can refer to an overall attitude toward life, of course, it can also refer to the art of love. Men can get passionate about football, and women can get passionate about shopping; but if you want to experience some passion *together*, start preparing outside the bedroom. Instead of collapsing on the couch after a day at the office, offer to watch the kids while your wife relaxes with a bubble bath. Rather than delegating all the cooking, serve your sweetie some breakfast in bed and watch the sparks fly.

▶Get Aligned
Matthew 25:45

TAKING CARE OF THE "LEAST" IS A BIG DEAL TO GOD. Proverbs 19:17 says, "Being kind to the poor is like lending to the LORD; he will reward you for what you have done." The parable of the sheep and the goats in this chapter makes it clear that Christian love involves reaching out to those to whom Christ came to offer hope. In fact, Jesus equates our service to those in need with serving him. That means even the smallest step we take to help others is noted by God and is credited to our account.

The problem is, it's easy to feel like we've done our job after cutting that big check to a relief charity or preparing a Christmas bundle for an inner-city family. Whereas those are wonderful acts of service, our job as Christ's hands and feet is never a one-time effort. We are called to reach out to the least for as long as we're alive.

Who are the "least" in your world? Whether it's a widow in your neighborhood, a low-income family at church, or a homeless guy downtown, pray that God would help you be faithful in lending to him by reaching out to those in need.

bank. Then, when I came home, I would have received my gold back with interest.'

28"So the master told his other servants, 'Take the bag of gold from that servant and give it to the servant who has ten bags of gold. 29Those who have much will get more, and they will have much more than they need. But those who do not have much will have everything taken away from them.' 30Then the master said, 'Throw that useless servant outside, into the darkness where people will cry and grind their teeth with pain.'

The King Will Judge All People

31"The Son of Man will come again in his great glory, with all his angels. He will be King and sit on his great throne. 32All the nations of the world will be gathered before him, and he will separate them into two groups as a shepherd separates the sheep from the goats. 33The Son of Man will put the sheep on his right and the goats on his left.

34"Then the King will say to the people on his right, 'Come, my Father has given you his blessing. Receive the kingdom God has prepared for you since the world was made. 35I was hungry, and you gave me food. I was thirsty, and you gave me something to drink. I was alone and away from home, and you invited me into your house. 36I was without clothes, and you gave me something to wear. I was sick, and you cared for me. I was in prison, and you visited me.'

37"Then the good people will answer, 'Lord, when did we see you hungry and give you food, or thirsty and give you something to drink? 38When did we see you alone and away from home and invite you into our house? When did we see you without clothes and give you something to wear? 39When did we see you sick or in prison and care for you?'

40"Then the King will answer, 'I tell you the truth, anything you did for even the least of my people here, you also did for me.'

41"Then the King will say to those on his left, 'Go away from me. You will be punished. Go into the fire that burns forever that was prepared for the devil and his angels. 42I was hungry, and you gave me nothing to eat. I was thirsty, and you gave me nothing to drink. 43I was alone and away from home, and you did not invite me into your house. I was without clothes, and you gave me nothing to wear. I was sick and in prison, and you did not care for me.'

44"Then those people will answer, 'Lord, when did we see you hungry or thirsty or alone and away from home or without clothes or sick or in prison? When did we see these things and not help you?'

45"Then the King will answer, 'I tell you the truth, anything you refused to do for even the least of my people here, you refused to do for me.'

46"These people will go off to be punished forever, but the good people will go to live forever."

The Plan to Kill Jesus

26 After Jesus finished saying all these things, he told his followers, 2"You know that the day after tomorrow is the day of the Passover Feast. On that day the Son of Man will be given to his enemies to be crucified."

3Then the leading priests and the elders had a meeting at the palace of the high priest, named Caiaphas. 4At the meeting, they planned to set a trap to arrest Jesus and kill him. 5But they said, "We must not do it during the feast, because the people might cause a riot."

Perfume for Jesus' Burial

6Jesus was in Bethany at the house of Simon, who had a skin disease. 7While Jesus was there, a woman approached him with an alabaster jar filled with expensive

Q: What does it mean to lay down our lives as a "living sacrifice" to God?

A: By calling us to be a "living sacrifice," God is not commanding us to die for him by sacrificing our lives literally, but rather to live for him by choosing to follow his will in all things over our own (Romans 12:1).

perfume. She poured this perfume on Jesus' head while he was eating.

⁸His followers were upset when they saw the woman do this. They asked, "Why waste that perfume? ⁹It could have been sold for a great deal of money and the money given to the poor."

¹⁰Knowing what had happened, Jesus said, "Why are you troubling this woman? She did an excellent thing for me. ¹¹You will always have the poor with you, but you will not always have me. ¹²This woman poured perfume on my body to prepare me for burial. ¹³I tell you the truth, wherever the Good News is preached in all the world, what this woman has done will be told, and people will remember her."

Judas Becomes an Enemy of Jesus

¹⁴Then one of the twelve apostles, Judas Iscariot, went to talk to the leading priests. ¹⁵He said, "What will you pay me for giving Jesus to you?" And they gave him thirty silver coins. ¹⁶After that, Judas watched for the best time to turn Jesus in.

Jesus Eats the Passover Meal

¹⁷On the first day of the Feast of Unleavened Bread, the followers came to Jesus. They said, "Where do you want us to prepare for you to eat the Passover meal?"

¹⁸Jesus answered, "Go into the city to a certain man and tell him, 'The Teacher says: "The chosen time is near. I will have the Passover with my followers at your house." ' " ¹⁹The followers did what Jesus told them to do, and they prepared the Passover meal.

²⁰In the evening Jesus was sitting at the table with his twelve followers. ²¹As they were eating, Jesus said, "I tell you the truth, one of you will turn against me."

²²This made the followers very sad. Each one began to say to Jesus, "Surely, Lord, I am not the one who will turn against you, am I?"

²³Jesus answered, "The man who has dipped his hand with me into the bowl is the one who will turn against me. ²⁴The Son of Man will die, just as the Scriptures say. But how terrible it will be for the person who hands the Son of Man over to be killed. It would be better for him if he had never been born."

²⁵Then Judas, who would give Jesus to his enemies, said to Jesus, "Teacher, surely I am not the one, am I?"

Jesus answered, "Yes, it is you."

The Lord's Supper

²⁶While they were eating, Jesus took some bread and thanked God for it and broke it. Then he gave it to his followers and said, "Take this bread and eat it; this is my body."

²⁷Then Jesus took a cup and thanked God for it and gave it to the followers. He said, "Every one of you drink this. ²⁸This is my blood which is the new agreement that God makes with his people. This blood is poured out for many to forgive their sins. ²⁹I tell you this: I will not drink of this fruit of the vine again until that day when I drink it new with you in my Father's kingdom."

³⁰After singing a hymn, they went out to the Mount of Olives.

Jesus' Followers Will Leave Him

³¹Jesus told his followers, "Tonight you will all stumble in your faith on account of me, because it is written in the Scriptures:

'I will kill the shepherd,
and the sheep will scatter.' *Zechariah 13:7*

³²But after I rise from the dead, I will go ahead of you into Galilee."

³³Peter said, "Everyone else may stumble in their faith because of you, but I will not."

³⁴Jesus said, "I tell you the truth, tonight before the rooster crows you will say three times that you don't know me."

³⁵But Peter said, "I will never say that I don't know you! I will even die with you!" And all the other followers said the same thing.

Jesus Prays Alone

³⁶Then Jesus went with his followers to a place called Gethsemane. He said to them, "Sit here while I go over there and pray." ³⁷He took Peter and the two sons of Zebedee with him, and he began to be very

The Bottom Line

Financial Planning: Start Small

THE GREATEST ASSET IN YOUR 20S AND 30S IS TIME. Despite lower pay as you start your career, you should start planning for the future. If saddled with student loans, credit card debt, and other financial obligations, pay off the loan with the highest interest rate first. Take advantage of any 401(k) at work or open an IRA at a bank or other financial institution. Even small amounts of money can multiply when invested for thirty to forty years. By adequately saving for the future, you will be able to sufficiently meet your needs, as well as those of the ones you love.

>> 26:28 **new** Some Greek copies do not have this word. Compare Luke 22:20.   26:29 **fruit of the vine** Product of the grapevine; this may also be translated "wine."

sad and troubled. [38]He said to them, "My heart is full of sorrow, to the point of death. Stay here and watch with me."

[39]After walking a little farther away from them, Jesus fell to the ground and prayed, "My Father, if it is possible, do not give me this cup[n] of suffering. But do what you want, not what I want." [40]Then Jesus went back to his followers and found them asleep. He said to Peter, "You men could not stay awake with me for one hour? [41]Stay awake and pray for strength against temptation. The spirit wants to do what is right, but the body is weak."

[42]Then Jesus went away a second time and prayed, "My Father, if it is not possible for this painful thing to be taken from me, and if I must do it, I pray that what you want will be done."

[43]Then he went back to his followers, and again he found them asleep, because their eyes were heavy. [44]So Jesus left them and went away and prayed a third time, saying the same thing.

[45]Then Jesus went back to his followers and said, "Are you still sleeping and resting? The time has come for the Son of Man to be handed over to sinful people. [46]Get up, we must go. Look, here comes the man who has turned against me."

Jesus Is Arrested

[47]While Jesus was still speaking, Judas, one of the twelve apostles, came up. With him were many people carrying swords and clubs who had been sent from the leading priests and the Jewish elders of the people. [48]Judas had planned to give them a signal, saying, "The man I kiss is Jesus. Arrest him." [49]At once Judas went to Jesus and said, "Greetings, Teacher!" and kissed him.

[50]Jesus answered, "Friend, do what you came to do."

Then the people came and grabbed Jesus and arrested him. [51]When that happened, one of Jesus' followers reached for his sword and pulled it out. He struck the servant of the high priest and cut off his ear.

[52]Jesus said to the man, "Put your sword back in its place. All who use swords will be killed with swords. [53]Surely you know I could ask my Father, and he would give me more than twelve armies of angels. [54]But it must happen this way to bring about what the Scriptures say."

[55]Then Jesus said to the crowd, "You came to get me with swords and clubs as if I were a criminal. Every day I sat in the Temple teaching, and you did not arrest me there. [56]But all these things have happened so that it will come about as the prophets wrote." Then all of Jesus' followers left him and ran away.

Jesus Before the Leaders

[57]Those people who arrested Jesus led him to the house of Caiaphas, the high priest, where the teachers of the law and the elders were gathered. [58]Peter followed far behind to the courtyard of the high priest's house, and he sat down with the guards to see what would happen to Jesus.

[59]The leading priests and the whole Jewish council tried to find something false against Jesus so they could kill him. [60]Many people came and told lies about him, but the council could find no real reason to kill him. Then two people came and said, [61]"This man said, 'I can destroy the Temple of God and build it again in three days.'"

[62]Then the high priest stood up and said to Jesus, "Aren't you going to answer? Don't you have something to say about their charges against you?" [63]But Jesus said nothing.

Again the high priest said to Jesus, "I command you by the power of the living God: Tell us if you are the Christ, the Son of God."

[64]Jesus answered, "Those are your words. But I tell you, in the future you will see the Son of Man sitting at the right hand of God, the

Q: Why is there hypocrisy in the church?

A: The church is made up of imperfect people. Sometimes some of them try to hide their imperfections by pretending to be something they're not. The point to remember is that the church is not for the faultless, but the forgiven (Romans 10:10).

▶ Get Aligned

Matthew 26:43

JESUS' FOLLOWERS FAILED MISERABLY in the single task Jesus gave them here. All they had to do was stay awake while he prayed. Obviously, it was a traumatic night. In Luke 22:45, Luke points out that they fell asleep "because of their sadness." Still, they allowed emotional and physical distress to get in the way of remaining loyal to Jesus' charge.

We've all failed the Lord more than we'd like to admit. But the key to rebounding from such disappointment is to remind ourselves of God's perspective regarding our faith. In Matthew 25:21, Jesus explains the starting place for every believer who desires to be used by God. Like moving up a corporate ladder, we begin with the "small things," tasks that seem inconsequential, mundane, and even pointless.

The truth is, however, that no assignment is trivial in God's eyes. He's just as interested in your heart's response as he is in the task you've been given. Your goal ought to be to please him and only him, whether that's through cleaning bathrooms or leading worship at church. He's looking for those who will be faithful with the small, so he can entrust them with even greater tasks.

▶▶ **26:39 cup** Jesus is talking about the terrible things that will happen to him. Accepting these things will be very hard, like drinking a cup of something bitter.

Powerful One, and coming on clouds in the sky."

[65] When the high priest heard this, he tore his clothes and said, "This man has said things that are against God! We don't need any more witnesses; you all heard him say these things against God. [66] What do you think?"

The people answered, "He should die."

[67] Then the people there spat in Jesus' face and beat him with their fists. Others slapped him. [68] They said, "Prove to us that you are a prophet, you Christ! Tell us who hit you!"

Peter Says He Doesn't Know Jesus

[69] At that time, as Peter was sitting in the courtyard, a servant girl came to him and said, "You also were with Jesus of Galilee."

[70] But Peter said to all the people there that he was never with Jesus. He said, "I don't know what you are talking about."

[71] When he left the courtyard and was at the gate, another girl saw him. She said to the people there, "This man was with Jesus of Nazareth."

[72] Again, Peter said he was never with him, saying, "I swear I don't know this man Jesus!"

[73] A short time later, some people standing there went to Peter and said, "Surely you are one of those who followed Jesus. The way you talk shows it."

[74] Then Peter began to place a curse on himself and swear, "I don't know the man." At once, a rooster crowed. [75] And Peter remembered what Jesus had told him: "Before the rooster crows, you will say three times that you don't know me." Then Peter went outside and cried painfully.

Jesus Is Taken to Pilate

27 Early the next morning, all the leading priests and elders of the people decided that Jesus should die. [2] They tied him, led him away, and turned him over to Pilate, the governor.

Judas Kills Himself

[3] Judas, the one who had given Jesus to his enemies, saw that they had decided to kill Jesus. Then he was very sorry for what he had done. So he took the thirty silver coins back to the priests and the leaders, [4] saying, "I sinned; I handed over to you an innocent man."

The leaders answered, "What is that to us? That's your problem, not ours."

[5] So Judas threw the money into the Temple. Then he went off and hanged himself.

[6] The leading priests picked up the silver coins in the Temple and said, "Our law does not allow us to keep this money with the Temple money, because it has paid for a man's death." [7] So they decided to use the coins to buy Potter's Field as a place to bury strangers who died in Jerusalem. [8] That is why that field is still called the Field of Blood. [9] So what Jeremiah the prophet had said came true: "They took thirty silver coins. That is how little the Israelites thought he was worth. [10] They used those thirty silver coins to buy the potter's field, as the Lord commanded me."[n]

Pilate Questions Jesus

[11] Jesus stood before Pilate the governor, and Pilate asked him, "Are you the king of the Jews?"

Jesus answered, "Those are your words."

[12] When the leading priests and the elders accused Jesus, he said nothing.

[13] So Pilate said to Jesus, "Don't you hear them accusing you of all these things?"

[14] But Jesus said nothing in answer to Pilate, and Pilate was very surprised at this.

Pilate Tries to Free Jesus

[15] Every year at the time of Passover the governor would free one prisoner whom the people chose. [16] At that time there was a man in prison, named Barabbas,[n] who was known to be very bad. [17] When the people gathered at Pilate's house, Pilate said, "Whom do you want me to set free: Barabbas[n] or Jesus who is called the Christ?" [18] Pilate knew that they turned Jesus in to him because they were jealous.

Get Fit

ABSTAINING FROM TOBACCO Health concerns associated with tobacco use are too serious to ignore. Smoking significantly increases your risk of cancer and lung disease, and it triples the risk of dying from heart disease among those who are middle-aged. If you are using tobacco either through smoking or chewing, make the commitment to quit. It's not only a good decision for your health and a great way to honor God with your body, but it's also one of the most loving choices you can make for the people who love you. After all, they want you to be around to enjoy life with them for a long time to come.

▶▶ 27:9–10 "They…commanded me." See Zechariah 11:12–13 and Jeremiah 32:6–9.   27:16–17 Barabbas Some Greek copies read "Jesus Barabbas."

[19]While Pilate was sitting there on the judge's seat, his wife sent this message to him: "Don't do anything to that man, because he is innocent. Today I had a dream about him, and it troubled me very much."

[20]But the leading priests and elders convinced the crowd to ask for Barabbas to be freed and for Jesus to be killed.

[21]Pilate said, "I have Barabbas and Jesus. Which do you want me to set free for you?"

The people answered, "Barabbas."

[22]Pilate asked, "So what should I do with Jesus, the one called the Christ?"

They all answered, "Crucify him!"

[23]Pilate asked, "Why? What wrong has he done?"

But they shouted louder, "Crucify him!"

[24]When Pilate saw that he could do nothing about this and that a riot was starting, he took some water and washed his hands[n] in front of the crowd. Then he said, "I am not guilty of this man's death. You are the ones who are causing it!"

[25]All the people answered, "We and our children will be responsible for his death."

[26]Then he set Barabbas free. But Jesus was beaten with whips and handed over to the soldiers to be crucified.

[27]The governor's soldiers took Jesus into the governor's palace, and they all gathered around him. [28]They took off his clothes and put a red robe on him. [29]Using thorny branches, they made a crown, put it on his head, and put a stick in his right hand. Then the soldiers bowed before Jesus and made fun of him, saying, "Hail, King of the Jews!" [30]They spat on Jesus. Then they took his stick and began to beat him on the head. [31]After they finished, the soldiers took off the robe and put his own clothes on him again. Then they led him away to be crucified.

Jesus Is Crucified

[32]As the soldiers were going out of the city with Jesus, they forced a man from Cyrene, named Simon, to carry the cross for Jesus. [33]They all came to the place called Golgotha, which means the Place of the Skull. [34]The soldiers gave Jesus wine mixed with gall[n] to drink. He tasted the wine but refused to drink it. [35]When the soldiers had crucified him, they threw lots to decide who would get his clothes."[n] [36]The soldiers sat there and continued watching him. [37]They put a sign above Jesus' head with a charge against him. It said: THIS IS JESUS, THE KING OF THE JEWS. [38]Two robbers were crucified beside Jesus, one on the right and the other on the left. [39]People walked by and insulted Jesus and shook their heads, [40]saying, "You said you could destroy the Temple and build it again in three days. So save yourself! Come down from that cross if you are really the Son of God!"

[41]The leading priests, the teachers of the law, and the Jewish elders were also making fun of Jesus. [42]They said, "He saved others, but he can't save himself! He says he is the king of Israel! If he is the king, let him come down now from the cross. Then we will believe in him. [43]He trusts in God, so let God save him now, if God really wants him. He himself said, 'I am the Son of God.' " [44]And in the same way, the robbers who were being crucified beside Jesus also insulted him.

Jesus Dies

[45]At noon the whole country became dark, and the darkness lasted for three hours. [46]About three o'clock Jesus cried out in a loud voice, "Eli, Eli, lama sabachthani?" This means, "My God, my God, why have you abandoned me?"

[47]Some of the people standing there who heard this said, "He is calling Elijah."

[48]Quickly one of them ran and got a sponge and filled it with vinegar and tied it to a stick and gave it to Jesus to drink. [49]But the others said, "Don't bother him. We want to see if Elijah will come to save him."

[50]But Jesus cried out again in a loud voice and died.

[51]Then the curtain in the Temple[n] was torn into two pieces, from the top to the bottom. Also, the earth shook and rocks broke apart. [52]The graves opened, and many of God's people who had died were raised from the dead. [53]They came out of the graves after Jesus was raised from the dead and went into the holy city, where they appeared to many people.

[54]When the army officer and the soldiers guarding Jesus saw this earthquake and everything else that happened, they were very fright-

▶Get Aligned

Matthew 28:9-10

There are two perfect responses to encountering Jesus. First and foremost, we're to worship him. The women leaving Jesus' tomb were undoubtedly having a supernatural experience. They'd just met an angel and discovered their Lord's body was missing. Yet their confusion and excitement was insignificant when they saw their teacher face-to-face and fell at his feet.

They weren't being ritualistic or melodramatic. These women were in complete, genuine awe. Jesus had done exactly what he said he'd do, and here he was in person to prove his victory over death. There was nothing they could do but worship him. We need to respond to Jesus with the same wonder.

Obviously, Jesus deserved to be worshiped. But he didn't let the women linger in that place of adoration forever. He immediately gave them a charge: Go tell the others. It's the same task we have today. Sure, worshiping at church, in God's presence, is life changing and essential. But Jesus asks us to worship him by also telling others of what he's done. True worship is more than keeping the good news to ourselves; it's going outside our safe boundaries and spreading the news.

27:24 **washed his hands** He did this as a sign to show that he wanted no part in what the people did.   27:34 **gall** Probably a drink of wine mixed with drugs to help a person feel less pain.

▶▶ 27:35 **clothes** Some Greek copies continue, "So what God said through the prophet came true, 'They divided my clothes among them, and they threw lots for my clothing.' " See Psalm 22:18.   27:51 **curtain in the Temple** A curtain divided the Most Holy Place from the other part of the Temple. That was the special building in Jerusalem where God commanded the Jewish people to worship him.

ened and said, "He really was the Son of God!"

[55]Many women who had followed Jesus from Galilee to help him were standing at a distance from the cross, watching. [56]Mary Magdalene, and Mary the mother of James and Joseph, and the mother of James and John were there.

Jesus Is Buried

[57]That evening a rich man named Joseph, a follower of Jesus from the town of Arimathea, came to Jerusalem. [58]Joseph went to Pilate and asked to have Jesus' body. So Pilate gave orders for the soldiers to give it to Joseph. [59]Then Joseph took the body and wrapped it in a clean linen cloth. [60]He put Jesus' body in a new tomb that he had cut out of a wall of rock, and he rolled a very large stone to block the entrance of the tomb. Then Joseph went away. [61]Mary Magdalene and the other woman named Mary were sitting near the tomb.

The Tomb of Jesus Is Guarded

[62]The next day, the day after Preparation Day, the leading priests and the Pharisees went to Pilate. [63]They said, "Sir, we remember that while that liar was still alive he said, 'After three days I will rise from the dead.' [64]So give the order for the tomb to be guarded closely till the third day. Otherwise, his followers might come and steal the body and tell people that he has risen from the dead. That lie would be even worse than the first one."

[65]Pilate said, "Take some soldiers and go guard the tomb the best way you know." [66]So they all went to the tomb and made it safe from thieves by sealing the stone in the entrance and putting soldiers there to guard it.

Jesus Rises from the Dead

28 The day after the Sabbath day was the first day of the week. At dawn on the first day, Mary Magdalene and another woman named Mary went to look at the tomb.

[2]At that time there was a strong earthquake. An angel of the Lord came down from heaven, went to the tomb, and rolled the stone away from the entrance. Then he sat on the stone. [3]He was shining as bright as

---

THINK ABOUT IT Matthew 28:18–20

IF YOU NEED EXTRA GUIDANCE ON A PROJECT, you simply ask for a meeting with your superior and request some additional instruction. If you're a good listener, you will pay close attention to all that is said, for what is frequently the most important direction of all is saved for last.

In the final days of his resurrected life on earth, Jesus turned to his followers and gave them what has come to be called "The Great Commission." His speech to them left them with specific instructions about what to do on earth after his ascension into heaven.

Jesus gave them a powerful charge to be about the business of evangelism and discipleship: "Go and make followers of all people in the world...Teach them to obey everything that I have taught you, and I will be with you always, even until the end of this age." Jesus didn't want the apostles to forget his final words, and we shouldn't either. Ask God to guide you and give you the words to say. With his help, you, too, can succeed in carrying out his command to reach others.

---

lightning, and his clothes were white as snow. [4]The soldiers guarding the tomb shook with fear because of the angel, and they became like dead men.

[5]The angel said to the women, "Don't be afraid. I know that you are looking for Jesus, who has been crucified. [6]He is not here. He has risen from the dead as he said he would. Come and see the place where his body was. [7]And go quickly and tell his followers, 'Jesus has risen from the dead. He is going into Galilee ahead of you, and you will see him there.'" Then the angel said, "Now I have told you."

[8]The women left the tomb quickly. They were afraid, but they were also very happy. They ran to tell Jesus' followers what had happened. [9]Suddenly, Jesus met them and said, "Greetings." The women came up to him, took hold of his feet, and worshiped him. [10]Then Jesus said to them, "Don't be afraid. Go and tell my followers to go on to Galilee, and they will see me there."

The Soldiers Report to the Leaders

[11]While the women went to tell Jesus' followers, some of the soldiers who had been guarding the tomb went into the city to tell the leading priests everything that had happened. [12]Then the priests met with the elders and made a plan. They paid the soldiers a large amount of money [13]and said to them, "Tell the people that Jesus' followers came during the night and stole the body while you were asleep. [14]If the governor hears about this, we will satisfy him and save you from trouble." [15]So the soldiers kept the money and did as they were told. And that story is still spread among the people even today.

Jesus Talks to His Followers

[16]The eleven followers went to Galilee to the mountain where Jesus had told them to go. [17]On the mountain they saw Jesus and worshiped him, but some of them did not believe it was really Jesus. [18]Then Jesus came to them and said, "All power in heaven and on earth is given to me. [19]So go and make followers of all people in the world. Baptize them in the name of the Father and the Son and the Holy Spirit. [20]Teach them to obey everything that I have taught you, and I will be with you always, even until the end of this age."

THE GOSPEL ACCORDING TO Mark

AUTHOR: MARK
DATE WRITTEN: A.D. 67–68

FANS CHEER THEIR FAVORITE TEAM TO inspire them to win the game. The victors celebrate with trophies and ticker tape parades. Everyone wants to be associated with a champion, but few are willing to do what is necessary to become one. Yet, the Gospel of Mark presents a picture of Jesus Christ as one who was willing to pay the price.

With a straightforward storytelling style, Mark shows that Jesus Christ entered history not as a vanquishing conqueror, but as the servant of humankind. Written to encourage fellow believers, Mark shares stories that show Jesus came as God in the flesh. And the majority of his book is dedicated to the miracles of Jesus.

Mark presents a simple, yet vivid account of the ministry of Jesus, his torturous death, and his victorious resurrection. The stories in the Gospel of Mark present Jesus Christ as a man of action and prove that his true identity was revealed as much by what he did as by what he said. As the Book of Mark shows, Jesus came to serve, sacrifice, and save.

John Prepares for Jesus

1 This is the beginning of the Good News about Jesus Christ, the Son of God,[n] ²as the prophet Isaiah wrote:

"I will send my messenger ahead of you,
who will prepare your way."   *Malachi 3:1*

³"This is a voice of one
who calls out in the desert:
'Prepare the way for the Lord.
Make the road straight for him.'"   *Isaiah 40:3*

⁴John was baptizing people in the desert and preaching a baptism of changed hearts and lives for the forgiveness of sins. ⁵All the people from Judea and Jerusalem were going out to him. They confessed their sins and were baptized by him in the Jordan River. ⁶John wore clothes made from camel's hair, had a leather belt around his waist, and ate locusts and wild honey. ⁷This is what John preached to the people: "There is one coming after me who is greater than I; I am not good enough even to kneel down and untie his sandals. ⁸I baptize you with water, but he will baptize you with the Holy Spirit."

Jesus Is Baptized

⁹At that time Jesus came from the town of Nazareth in Galilee and was baptized by John in the Jordan River. ¹⁰Immediately, as Jesus was coming up out of the water, he saw heaven open. The Holy Spirit came down on him like a dove, ¹¹and a voice came from heaven: "You are my Son, whom I love, and I am very pleased with you."

¹²Then the Spirit sent Jesus into the desert. ¹³He was in the desert forty days and was tempted by Satan. He was with the wild animals, and the angels came and took care of him.

Jesus Chooses Some Followers

¹⁴After John was put in prison, Jesus went into Galilee, preaching the Good News from God. ¹⁵He said, "The right time has come. The kingdom of God is near. Change your hearts and lives and believe the Good News!"

¹⁶When Jesus was walking by Lake Galilee, he saw Simon[n] and his brother Andrew throwing a net into the lake because they were fishermen. ¹⁷Jesus said to them, "Come follow me, and I will make you fish for people." ¹⁸So Simon and Andrew immediately left their nets and followed him.

¹⁹Going a little farther, Jesus saw two more brothers, James and John, the sons of Zebedee. They were in a boat, mending their nets. ²⁰Jesus immediately called them, and they left their father in the boat with the hired workers and followed Jesus.

Jesus Forces Out an Evil Spirit

²¹Jesus and his followers went to Capernaum. On the Sabbath day He went to the synagogue and began to teach. ²²The people were amazed at his teaching, because he taught like a person who had authority, not like their teachers of the law. ²³Just then, a man was there in the synagogue who had an evil spirit in him. He shouted, ²⁴"Jesus of Nazareth! What do you want with us? Did you come to destroy us? I know who you are—God's Holy One!"

²⁵Jesus commanded the evil spirit, "Be quiet! Come out of the man!" ²⁶The evil spirit shook the man violently, gave a loud cry, and then came out of him.

²⁷The people were so amazed they asked each other, "What is happening here? This man is teaching something new, and with authority. He even gives commands to evil spirits, and they obey him." ²⁸And the news about Jesus spread quickly everywhere in the area of Galilee.

Jesus Heals Many People

²⁹As soon as Jesus and his followers left the synagogue, they went with James and John to the home of Simon[n] and Andrew. ³⁰Simon's mother-in-law was sick in bed with a fever, and the people told Jesus about her. ³¹So Jesus went to her bed, took her hand, and helped her up. The fever left her, and she began serving them.

³²That evening, after the sun went down, the people brought to Jesus all who were sick and had demons in them. ³³The whole town gathered at the door. ³⁴Jesus healed many who had different kinds of sicknesses, and he forced many demons to leave people. But he would not allow the demons to speak, because they knew who he was.

▶ Get Aligned

Mark 1:20

LITTLE IS KNOWN ABOUT THE TWELVE APOSTLES' lives before Jesus came along. The four apostles mentioned in this passage were all fishermen. They were uneducated, hard-working men. Their livelihood depended on the size of their daily catch. In James and John's cases, they were likely to take over their father's business once he was unable to work. So, to leave their nets and follow a complete stranger at the drop of a hat wasn't just risky or impulsive, it was downright foolish!

That's exactly how following Jesus seems at times. Resigning from a job because of a moral issue is foolishness in the world's eyes. Telling the truth, even though doing so will cost us dearly, seems absurd to a society in which everyone looks out for himself. The Christian life will always conflict with the world's way of living, yet nothing is more rewarding than forsaking everything for Jesus. Once we choose to follow him, we're never the same.

Jesus' followers went from average, mundane existences to spending every moment with the Son of God. We have that same opportunity today. But it takes the willingness to lay everything aside and follow him at all costs.

1:1 **the Son of God** Some Greek copies do not have this phrase.   1:16, 29 **Simon** Simon's other name was Peter.

Ten Ways to Get Organized

1. Create a useable filing system.
2. Start a recycling program.
3. Toss junk mail upon receipt.
4. Get rid of stuff you no longer need.
5. Eliminate clutter in your office.
6. Scan documents to limit paperwork.
7. Cancel subscriptions you do not read.
8. Shred sensitive papers before trashing.
9. Collect receipts for tax purposes.
10. Keep a list of daily goals at your desk.

Jesus Heals a Sick Man

³⁵Early the next morning, while it was still dark, Jesus woke and left the house. He went to a lonely place, where he prayed. ³⁶Simon and his friends went to look for Jesus. ³⁷When they found him, they said, "Everyone is looking for you!"

³⁸Jesus answered, "We should go to other towns around here so I can preach there too. That is the reason I came." ³⁹So he went everywhere in Galilee, preaching in the synagogues and forcing out demons.

⁴⁰A man with a skin disease came to Jesus. He fell to his knees and begged Jesus, "You can heal me if you will."

⁴¹Jesus felt sorry for the man, so he reached out his hand and touched him and said, "I will. Be healed!" ⁴²Immediately the disease left the man, and he was healed.

⁴³Jesus told the man to go away at once, but he warned him strongly, ⁴⁴"Don't tell anyone about this. But go and show yourself to the priest. And offer the gift Moses commanded for people who are made well." This will show the people what I have done." ⁴⁵The man left there, but he began to tell everyone that Jesus had healed him, and so he spread the news about Jesus. As a result, Jesus could not enter a town if people saw him. He stayed in places where nobody lived, but people came to him from everywhere.

Jesus Heals a Paralyzed Man

2 A few days later, when Jesus came back to Capernaum, the news spread that he was at home. ²Many people gathered together so that there was no room in the house, not even outside the door. And Jesus was teaching them God's message. ³Four people came, carrying a paralyzed man. ⁴Since they could not get to Jesus because of the crowd, they dug a hole in the roof right above where he was speaking. When they got through, they lowered the mat with the paralyzed man on it. ⁵When Jesus saw the faith of these people, he said to the paralyzed man, "Young man, your sins are forgiven."

⁶Some of the teachers of the law were sitting there, thinking to themselves, ⁷"Why does this man say things like that? He is speaking as if he were God. Only God can forgive sins."

⁸Jesus knew immediately what these teachers of the law were thinking. So he said to them, "Why are you thinking these things? ⁹Which is easier: to tell this paralyzed man, 'Your sins are forgiven,' or to tell him, 'Stand up. Take your mat and walk'? ¹⁰But I will prove to you that the Son of Man has authority on earth to forgive sins." So Jesus said to the paralyzed man, ¹¹"I tell you, stand up, take your mat, and go home." ¹²Immediately the paralyzed man stood up, took his mat, and walked out while everyone was watching him.

The people were amazed and praised God. They said, "We have never seen anything like this!"

Q: Is masturbation a sin?

A: The Bible doesn't specifically say whether masturbation is a sin. In fact, there is no direct reference to masturbation at all in Scripture. However, the Bible says lust and impure thoughts are sinful, and both are often associated with the act of masturbation.

<<TechSupport>>

CELL PHONES

Cell phones have come a long way in a relatively short time. Many models now come loaded with digital cameras, address books, Internet access, and instant messaging. Some phones even download and play music and offer games on the go. But don't get caught in the trap of letting your cell phone rule your life. Avoid placing it on the table in front of you when you're in meetings. Turn off the ringer when you enter a public place so you don't steal the scene every time your ring tone chimes. Courtesy is the best policy.

▶▶ 1:44 Moses...well Read about this in Leviticus 14:1–32.

[13]Jesus went to the lake again. The whole crowd followed him there, and he taught them. [14]While he was walking along, he saw a man named Levi son of Alphaeus, sitting in the tax collector's booth. Jesus said to him, "Follow me," and he stood up and followed Jesus.

[15]Later, as Jesus was having dinner at Levi's house, many tax collectors and "sinners" were eating there with Jesus and his followers. Many people like this followed Jesus. [16]When the teachers of the law who were Pharisees saw Jesus eating with the tax collectors and "sinners," they asked his followers, "Why does he eat with tax collectors and sinners?"

[17]Jesus heard this and said to them, "It is not the healthy people who need a doctor, but the sick. I did not come to invite good people but to invite sinners."

Jesus' Followers Are Criticized

[18]Now the followers of John[n] and the Pharisees often fasted[n] for a certain time. Some people came to Jesus and said, "Why do John's followers and the followers of the Pharisees often fast, but your followers don't?"

[19]Jesus answered, "The friends of the bridegroom do not fast while the bridegroom is still with them. As long as the bridegroom is with them, they cannot fast. [20]But the time will come when the bridegroom will be taken from them, and then they will fast.

[21]"No one sews a patch of unshrunk cloth over a hole in an old coat. Otherwise, the patch will shrink and pull away—the new patch will pull away from the old coat. Then the hole will be worse. [22]Also, no one ever pours new wine into old leather bags. Otherwise, the new wine will break the bags, and the wine will be ruined along with the bags. But new wine should be put into new leather bags."

Jesus Is Lord of the Sabbath

[23]One Sabbath day, as Jesus was walking through some fields of grain, his followers began to pick some grain to eat. [24]The Pharisees said to Jesus, "Why are your followers doing what is not lawful on the Sabbath day?"

[25]Jesus answered, "Have you never read what David did when he and those with him were hungry and needed food? [26]During the time of Abiathar the high priest, David went into God's house and ate the holy bread, which is lawful only for priests to eat. And David also gave some of the bread to those who were with him."

[27]Then Jesus said to the Pharisees, "The Sabbath day was made to help people; they were not made to be ruled by the Sabbath day. [28]So then, the Son of Man is Lord even of the Sabbath day."

Jesus Heals a Man's Hand

3 Another time when Jesus went into a synagogue, a man with a crippled hand was there. [2]Some people watched Jesus closely to see if he would heal the man on the Sabbath day so they could accuse him. [3]Jesus said to the man with the crippled hand, "Stand up here in the middle of everyone."

[4]Then Jesus asked the people, "Which is lawful on the Sabbath day: to do good or to do evil, to save a life or to kill?" But they said nothing to answer him.

[5]Jesus was angry as he looked at the people, and he felt very sad because they were stubborn. Then he said to the man, "Hold out

---

FACT-OIDS! On June 14, 1954, the phrase "Under God" was added to the Pledge of Allegiance. [Infoplease.com]

→ The Bottom Line

College: Start Saving Now

IF YOU ARE STILL SADDLED WITH STUDENT LOANS from college, imagine what tuition will be twenty or thirty years from now. If you have children, or expect to start a family one day, check out college savings plans, known as "529 Plans." Whereas deductions vary by state, these plans are exempt from federal income tax and are a sound way to establish long-term education savings. They include both prepaid tuition and college savings plans and have generous contribution limits. However, each plan has rules and restrictions, so investigate carefully. And while waiting for your children to mature, rear them with God's training and teaching.

>> **2:18 John** John the Baptist, who preached to the Jewish people about Christ's coming (Mark 1:4–8). **2:18 fasted** The people would give up eating for a special time of prayer and worship to God. It was also done to show sadness and disappointment.

FOR Men Only

ETIQUETTE Contrary to popular belief, etiquette is not only for women. Whereas some guys think it's funny to belch in public or cut in line, only clueless women are attracted to such men. What really gets a gal's attention is when a guy knows how to act like a gentleman. It goes far beyond simply holding the door open for a lady. Etiquette includes such commonsense attitudes as thoughtfulness, respect, and generosity. A godly guy treats women like the precious people they are. Remember, a little etiquette goes a long way toward impressing a woman and winning her affection.

your hand." The man held out his hand and it was healed. ⁶Then the Pharisees left and began making plans with the Herodians⁕ about a way to kill Jesus.

Many People Follow Jesus

⁷Jesus left with his followers for the lake, and a large crowd from Galilee followed him. ⁸Also many people came from Judea, from Jerusalem, from Idumea, from the lands across the Jordan River, and from the area of Tyre and Sidon. When they heard what Jesus was doing, many people came to him. ⁹When Jesus saw the crowds, he told his followers to get a boat ready for him to keep people from crowding against him. ¹⁰He had healed many people, so all the sick were pushing toward him to touch him. ¹¹When evil spirits saw Jesus, they fell down before him and shouted, "You are the Son of God!" ¹²But Jesus strongly warned them not to tell who he was.

Jesus Chooses His Twelve Apostles

¹³Then Jesus went up on a mountain and called to him those he wanted, and they came to him. ¹⁴Jesus chose twelve and called them apostles.⁕ He wanted them to be with him, and he wanted to send them out to preach ¹⁵and to have the authority to force demons out of people. ¹⁶These are the twelve men he chose: Simon (Jesus named him Peter), ¹⁷James and John, the sons of Zebedee (Jesus named them Boanerges, which means "Sons of Thunder"), ¹⁸Andrew, Philip, Bartholomew, Matthew, Thomas, James the son of Alphaeus, Thad-

daeus, Simon the Zealot, ¹⁹and Judas Iscariot, who later turned against Jesus.

Some People Say Jesus Has a Devil

²⁰Then Jesus went home, but again a crowd gathered. There were so many people that Jesus and his followers could not eat. ²¹When his family heard this, they went to get him because they thought he was out of his mind. ²²But the teachers of the law from Jerusalem were saying, "Beelzebul is living inside him! He uses power from the ruler of demons to force demons out of people."

²³So Jesus called the people together and taught them with stories. He said, "Satan will not force himself out of people. ²⁴A kingdom that is divided cannot continue, ²⁵and a family that is divided cannot continue. ²⁶And if Satan is against himself and fights against his own people, he cannot continue; that is the end of Satan. ²⁷No one can enter a strong person's house and steal his things unless he first ties up the strong person. Then he can steal things from the house. ²⁸I tell you the truth, all sins that people do and all the things people say against God can be forgiven. ²⁹But anyone who speaks against the Holy Spirit will never be forgiven; he is guilty of a sin that continues forever."

³⁰Jesus said this because the teachers of the law said that he had an evil spirit inside him.

Jesus' True Family

³¹Then Jesus' mother and brothers arrived. Standing outside, they sent someone in to tell him to come out. ³²Many people were sitting around Jesus, and they said to him, "Your mother and brothers⁕ are waiting for you outside."

³³Jesus asked, "Who are my mother and my brothers?" ³⁴Then he looked at those sitting around him and said, "Here are my mother and my brothers! ³⁵My true brother and sister and mother are those who do what God wants."

A Story About Planting Seed

4 Again Jesus began teaching by the lake. A great crowd

Q: What is faith?

A: Faith is the absolute confidence in God's good character and the unshakeable belief that his Word is true regardless of our circumstances or our feelings. Faith is a personal commitment to place your trust in God and to follow his plan for your life (Hebrews 11:1).

>> **3:6 Herodians** A political group that followed Herod and his family.   **3:14 and called them apostles** Some Greek copies do not have this phrase.   **3:32 brothers** Some Greek copies continue, "and sisters."

gathered around him, so he sat down in a boat near the shore. All the people stayed on the shore close to the water. ²Jesus taught them many things, using stories. He said, ³"Listen! A farmer went out to plant his seed. ⁴While he was planting, some seed fell by the road, and the birds came and ate it up. ⁵Some seed fell on rocky ground where there wasn't much dirt. That seed grew very fast, because the ground was not deep. ⁶But when the sun rose, the plants dried up because they did not have deep roots. ⁷Some other seed fell among thorny weeds, which grew and choked the good plants. So those plants did not produce a crop. ⁸Some other seed fell on good ground and began to grow. It got taller and produced a crop. Some plants made thirty times more, some made sixty times more, and some made a hundred times more."

⁹Then Jesus said, "Let those with ears use them and listen!"

Jesus Tells Why He Used Stories

¹⁰Later, when Jesus was alone, the twelve apostles and others around him asked him about the stories.

¹¹Jesus said, "You can know the secret about the kingdom of God. But to other people I tell everything by using stories ¹²so that:

'They will look and look, but they will not learn.
They will listen and listen, but they will not understand.
If they did learn and understand,
they would come back to me and be forgiven.'"   *Isaiah 6:9–10*

Jesus Explains the Seed Story

¹³Then Jesus said to his followers, "Don't you understand this story? If you don't, how will you understand any story? ¹⁴The farmer is like a person who plants God's message in people. ¹⁵Sometimes the teaching falls on the road. This is like the people who hear the teaching of God, but Satan quickly comes and takes away the teaching that was planted in them. ¹⁶Others are like the seed planted on rocky ground. They hear the teaching and quickly accept it with joy. ¹⁷But since they don't allow the teaching to go deep into their lives, they keep it only a short time. When trouble or persecution comes because of the teaching they accepted, they quickly give up. ¹⁸Others are like the seed planted among the thorny weeds. They hear the teaching, ¹⁹but the worries of this life, the temptation of wealth, and many other evil desires keep the teaching from growing and producing fruit* in their lives. ²⁰Others are like the seed planted in the good ground. They hear the teaching and accept it. Then they grow and produce fruit—sometimes thirty times more, sometimes sixty times more, and sometimes a hundred times more."

Use What You Have

²¹Then Jesus said to them, "Do you hide a lamp under a bowl or under a bed? No! You put the lamp on a lampstand. ²²Everything that is hidden will be made clear and every secret thing will be made known. ²³Let those with ears use them and listen!

²⁴"Think carefully about what you hear. The way you give to others is the way God will give to you, but God will give you even more. ²⁵Those who have understanding will be given more. But those who do not have understanding, even what they have will be taken away from them."

Jesus Uses a Story About Seed

²⁶Then Jesus said, "The kingdom of God is like someone who plants seed in the ground. ²⁷Night and day, whether the person is asleep or awake, the seed still grows, but the person does not know how it grows. ²⁸By itself the earth produces grain. First the plant grows, then the head, and then all the grain in the head. ²⁹When the grain is ready, the farmer cuts it, because this is the harvest time."

A Story About Mustard Seed

³⁰Then Jesus said, "How can I show you what the kingdom of God is like? What story can I use to explain it? ³¹The kingdom of God is like a mustard seed, the smallest seed you plant in the ground. ³²But when planted, this seed grows and becomes the largest of all garden plants. It produces large branches, and the wild birds can make nests in its shade."

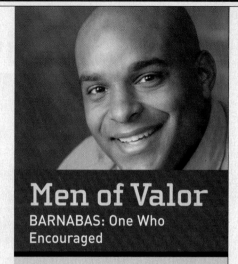

Men of Valor
BARNABAS: One Who Encouraged

Paul is the most prolific writer of the New Testament. But without Barnabas, he might have been a footnote in history. After selling a field and giving the money to the apostles, Barnabas gained credibility in the early church. Following Paul's dramatic conversion, Paul tried to join the church. Not only were the apostles afraid of Paul, the men didn't believe a zealous persecutor of Christians could actually become a genuine believer. That changed when Barnabas stepped in and took Paul to meet with church leaders. Barnabas later joined Paul on his missionary journey to Greece, breaking down barriers between Jew and Gentile. Though not as well known as Paul, Barnabas lived up to his name as "one who encourages," and as a result, we know of Paul, also.

³³Jesus used many stories like these to teach the crowd God's message—as much as they could understand. ³⁴He always used stories to teach them. But when he and his followers were alone, Jesus explained everything to them.

>> **4:19 producing fruit** To produce fruit means to have in your life the good things God wants.

Survival Guide

CONSERVING ENERGY: RESPECT THE ENVIRONMENT

Environmentalism is a hot political issue, but concern for the environment starts at home. Simple steps will not only save money but will also reduce energy usage and harmful carbon dioxide emissions. Such steps as turning down the refrigerator thermometer and the water heater thermostat, not overheating or overcooling rooms, and using energy-efficient appliances can combine to save significant amounts of energy. So can using compact fluorescent bulbs in your lamps. Caring for the earth shows respect for all of creation.

KILOWATTHOURS

Jesus Calms a Storm

[35]That evening, Jesus said to his followers, "Let's go across the lake." [36]Leaving the crowd behind, they took him in the boat just as he was. There were also other boats with them. [37]A very strong wind came up on the lake. The waves came over the sides and into the boat so that it was already full of water. [38]Jesus was at the back of the boat, sleeping with his head on a cushion. His followers woke him and said, "Teacher, don't you care that we are drowning!"

[39]Jesus stood up and commanded the wind and said to the waves, "Quiet! Be still!" Then the wind stopped, and it became completely calm.

[40]Jesus said to his followers, "Why are you afraid? Do you still have no faith?"

[41]The followers were very afraid and asked each other, "Who is this? Even the wind and the waves obey him!"

A Man with Demons Inside Him

5 Jesus and his followers went to the other side of the lake to the area of the Gerasene[n] people. [2]When Jesus got out of the boat, instantly a man with an evil spirit came to him from the burial caves. [3]This man lived in the caves, and no one could tie him up, not even with a chain. [4]Many times people had used chains to tie the man's hands and feet, but he always broke them off. No one was strong enough to control him. [5]Day and night he would wander around the burial caves and on the hills, screaming and cutting himself with stones. [6]While Jesus was still far away, the man saw him, ran to him, and fell down before him.

[7]The man shouted in a loud voice, "What do you want with me, Jesus, Son of the Most High God? I command you in God's name not to torture me!" [8]He said this because Jesus was saying to him, "You evil spirit, come out of the man."

[9]Then Jesus asked him, "What is your name?"

He answered, "My name is Legion,[n] because we are many spirits."

[10]He begged Jesus again and again not to send them out of that area. [11]A large herd of pigs was feeding on a hill near there. [12]The demons begged Jesus, "Send us into the pigs; let us go into them." [13]So Jesus allowed them to do this. The evil spirits left the man and went into the pigs. Then the herd of pigs—about two thousand of them—rushed down the hill into the lake and were drowned.

[14]The herdsmen ran away and went to the town and to the countryside, telling everyone about this. So people went out to see what had happened. [15]They came to Jesus and saw the man who used to have the many evil spirits, sitting, clothed, and in his right mind. And they were frightened. [16]The people who saw this told the others what had happened to the man who had the demons living in him, and they told about the pigs. [17]Then the people began to beg Jesus to leave their area.

[18]As Jesus was getting back into the boat, the man who was freed from the demons begged to go with him.

[19]But Jesus would not let him. He said, "Go home to your family and tell them how much the Lord has done for you and how he has had mercy on you." [20]So the man left and began to tell the people in the Ten Towns[n] about what Jesus had done for him. And everyone was amazed.

Jesus Gives Life to a Dead Girl and Heals a Sick Woman

[21]When Jesus went in the boat back to the other side of the lake, a large crowd gathered around him there. [22]A leader of the synagogue, named Jairus, came there, saw Jesus, and fell at his feet. [23]He begged Jesus, saying again and again, "My daughter is dying. Please come and put your hands on her so she will be healed and will live." [24]So Jesus went with him.

A large crowd followed Jesus and pushed very close around him. [25]Among them was a woman who had been bleeding for twelve years. [26]She had suffered very much from many doctors and had spent all

5:1 Gerasene From Gerasa, an area southeast of Lake Galilee. The exact location is uncertain and some Greek copies read "Gergesene"; others read "Gadarene." **5:9 Legion** Means very many. A legion was about five thousand men in the Roman army. **5:20 Ten Towns** In Greek, called "Decapolis." It was an area east of Lake Galilee that once had ten main towns.

the money she had, but instead of improving, she was getting worse. [27]When the woman heard about Jesus, she came up behind him in the crowd and touched his coat. [28]She thought, "If I can just touch his clothes, I will be healed." [29]Instantly her bleeding stopped, and she felt in her body that she was healed from her disease.

[30]At once Jesus felt power go out from him. So he turned around in the crowd and asked, "Who touched my clothes?"

[31]His followers said, "Look at how many people are pushing against you! And you ask, 'Who touched me?' "

[32]But Jesus continued looking around to see who had touched him. [33]The woman, knowing that she was healed, came and fell at Jesus' feet. Shaking with fear, she told him the whole truth. [34]Jesus said to her, "Dear woman, you are made well because you believed. Go in peace; be healed of your disease."

[35]While Jesus was still speaking, some people came from the house of the synagogue leader. They said, "Your daughter is dead. There is no need to bother the teacher anymore."

[36]But Jesus paid no attention to what they said. He told the synagogue leader, "Don't be afraid; just believe."

[37]Jesus let only Peter, James, and John the brother of James go with him. [38]When they came to the house of the synagogue leader, Jesus found many people there making lots of noise and crying loudly. [39]Jesus entered the house and said to them, "Why are you crying and making so much noise? The child is not dead, only asleep." [40]But they laughed at him. So, after throwing them out of the house, Jesus took the child's father and mother and his three followers into the room where the child was. [41]Taking hold of the girl's hand, he said to her, "Talitha, koum!" (This means, "Young girl, I tell you to stand up!") [42]At once the girl stood right up and began walking. (She was twelve years old.) Everyone was completely amazed. [43]Jesus gave them strict orders not to tell people about this. Then he told them to give the girl something to eat.

Jesus Goes to His Hometown

6 Jesus left there and went to his hometown, and his followers went with him. [2]On the Sabbath day he taught in the synagogue.

Change >> Your WORLD

CAMPUS CRUSADE FOR CHRIST

A simple little booklet called *The Four Spiritual Laws* has guided millions of people to a personal relationship with Jesus Christ. From humble beginnings, Campus Crusade for Christ International (CCCI) has grown into an interdenominational ministry committed to helping take the Good News of Jesus Christ to all nations. CCCI has a large umbrella of ministries reaching into different areas of campus ministry, including the Jesus Film Project, FamilyLife, Josh McDowell Ministry, Athletes in Action, and Student Venture. Each of these respected ministries is involved in education and training and can use financial and prayer support.

To change your world, visit www.ccci.org.

Many people heard him and were amazed, saying, "Where did this man get these teachings? What is this wisdom that has been given to him? And where did he get the power to do miracles? [3]He is just the carpenter, the son of Mary and the brother of James, Joseph, Judas, and Simon. And his sisters are here with us." So the people were upset with Jesus.

[4]Jesus said to them, "A prophet is honored everywhere except in his hometown and with his own people and in his own home." [5]So Jesus was not able to work any miracles there except to heal a few sick people by putting his hands on them. [6]He was amazed at how many people had no faith.

Then Jesus went to other villages in that area and taught. [7]He called his twelve followers together and got ready to send them out two by two and gave them authority over evil spirits. [8]This is what Jesus commanded them: "Take nothing for your trip except a walking stick. Take no bread, no bag, and no money in your pockets. [9]Wear sandals,

>> live the life

Mark 6:7–13

The Principle > Reach out to help others.

Practicing It > Sign up to go on a short-term mission trip with your church or with another Christian organization. Use the time to discover more about how reaching out to others can deepen your relationship with God.

▶Get Aligned

Mark 6:5

COMPLACENCY IS A SILENT KILLER IN THE CHRISTIAN LIFE. Whether you've been a believer for decades or just recently found Jesus, one of the greatest obstacles in your spiritual walk is becoming so familiar with the things of God that they become ordinary. Jesus' return to his hometown didn't elicit a joyous celebration, merely questions. His neighbors couldn't believe the man they watched grow up could do such amazing things. To them, he was simply Jesus, the quiet carpenter from down the street.

Their inability to see beyond the limitations they had placed on Jesus left them without faith. And without faith, he could do nothing for them. Even if Jesus performed miracle after miracle, they likely would have questioned their authenticity. When you don't believe in something, you'll always find a way to reason it out of existence.

If you've become complacent with God's movement in your life, consider it a red flag. It's often a sign that the author of your faith has become just another part of your life. Talk to him about your lax attitude, and ask for his help in restoring your passion for him and his holy presence.

---

but take only the clothes you are wearing. [10]When you enter a house, stay there until you leave that town. [11]If the people in a certain place refuse to welcome you or listen to you, leave that place. Shake its dust off your feet[n] as a warning to them."[n]

[12]So the followers went out and preached that people should change their hearts and lives. [13]They forced many demons out and put olive oil on many sick people and healed them.

How John the Baptist Was Killed

[14]King Herod heard about Jesus, because he was now well known. Some people said,[n] "He is John the Baptist, who has risen from the dead. That is why he can work these miracles."

[15]Others said, "He is Elijah."[n]

Other people said, "Jesus is a prophet, like the prophets who lived long ago."

[16]When Herod heard this, he said, "I killed John by cutting off his head. Now he has risen from the dead!"

[17]Herod himself had ordered his soldiers to arrest John and put him in prison in order to please his wife, Herodias. She had been the wife of Philip, Herod's brother, but then Herod had married her. [18]John had been telling Herod, "It is not lawful for you to be married to your brother's wife." [19]So Herodias hated John and wanted to kill him. But

she couldn't, [20]because Herod was afraid of John and protected him. He knew John was a good and holy man. Also, though John's preaching always bothered him, he enjoyed listening to John.

[21]Then the perfect time came for Herodias to cause John's death. On Herod's birthday, he gave a dinner party for the most important government leaders, the commanders of his army, and the most important people in Galilee. [22]When the daughter of Herodias[n] came in and danced, she pleased Herod and the people eating with him.

So King Herod said to the girl, "Ask me for anything you want, and I will give it to you." [23]He promised her, "Anything you ask for I will give to you—up to half of my kingdom."

[24]The girl went to her mother and asked, "What should I ask for?" Her mother answered, "Ask for the head of John the Baptist."

[25]At once the girl went back to the king and said to him, "I want the head of John the Baptist right now on a platter."

[26]Although the king was very sad, he had made a promise, and his dinner guests had heard it. So he did not want to refuse what she asked. [27]Immediately the king sent a soldier to bring John's head. The soldier went and cut off John's head in the prison [28]and brought it back on a platter. He gave it to the girl, and the girl gave it to her mother. [29]When John's followers heard this, they came and got John's body and put it in a tomb.

More than Five Thousand Fed

[30]The apostles gathered around Jesus and told him about all the things they had done and taught. [31]Crowds of people were coming and going so that Jesus and his followers did not even have time to eat. He said to them, "Come away by yourselves, and we will go to a lonely place to get some rest."

[32]So they went in a boat by themselves to a lonely place. [33]But many people saw them leave and recognized them. So from all the towns they ran to the place where Jesus was going, and they got there before him. [34]When he arrived, he saw a great crowd waiting. He felt sorry for them, because they were like sheep without a shepherd. So he began to teach them many things.

[35]When it was late in the day, his followers came to him and said, "No one lives in this place, and it is already very late. [36]Send the people away so they can go to the coun-

Q: Is it wrong to drink alcohol?

A: Jesus never sinned, yet he drank wine. In fact, his first recorded miracle was to turn water into wine at a wedding feast. Drinking alcohol is not condemned in the Bible, but drunkenness is. So any drinking is to be done in moderation (Luke 7:33–34; John 2:1–10).

⏩ 6:11 Shake...feet A warning. It showed that they were rejecting these people.   6:11 them Some Greek copies continue, "I tell you the truth, on the Judgment Day it will be better for the towns of Sodom and Gomorrah than for the people of that town." See Matthew 10:15.   6:14 Some people said Some Greek copies read "He said."   6:15 Elijah A great prophet who spoke for God and who lived hundreds of years before Christ. See 1 Kings 17.   6:22 When...Herodias Some Greek copies read "When his daughter Herodias."

tryside and towns around here to buy themselves something to eat."

[37]But Jesus answered, "You give them something to eat."

They said to him, "We would all have to work a month to earn enough money to buy that much bread!"

[38]Jesus asked them, "How many loaves of bread do you have? Go and see."

When they found out, they said, "Five loaves and two fish."

[39]Then Jesus told his followers to have the people sit in groups on the green grass. [40]So they sat in groups of fifty or a hundred. [41]Jesus took the five loaves and two fish and, looking up to heaven, he thanked God for the food. He divided the bread and gave it to his followers for them to give to the people. Then he divided the two fish among them all. [42]All the people ate and were satisfied. [43]The followers filled twelve baskets with the leftover pieces of bread and fish. [44]There were five thousand men who ate.

Jesus Walks on the Water

[45]Immediately Jesus told his followers to get into the boat and go ahead of him to Bethsaida across the lake. He stayed there to send the people home. [46]After sending them away, he went into the hills to pray.

[47]That night, the boat was in the middle of the lake, and Jesus was alone on the land. [48]He saw his followers struggling hard to row the boat, because the wind was blowing against them. Between three and six o'clock in the morning, Jesus came to them, walking on the water, and he wanted to walk past the boat. [49]But when they saw him walking on the water, they thought he was a ghost and cried out. [50]They all saw him and were afraid. But quickly Jesus spoke to them and said, "Have courage! It is I. Do not be afraid." [51]Then he got into the boat with them, and the wind became calm. The followers were greatly amazed. [52]They did not understand about the miracle of the five loaves, because their minds were closed.

>> live the life

Mark 6:31

The Principle > Get away for some recreation.

Practicing It > At least once a month take a weekend off to do nothing but relax and have fun. Go on a short trip with your wife, enjoy an outing with your friends, or just sit back in your favorite chair and read a good book.

[53]When they had crossed the lake, they came to shore at Gennesaret and tied the boat there. [54]When they got out of the boat, people immediately recognized Jesus. [55]They ran everywhere in that area and began to bring sick people on mats wherever they heard he was. [56]And everywhere he went—into towns, cities, or countryside—the people brought the sick to the marketplaces. They begged him to let them touch just the edge of his coat, and all who touched it were healed.

Obey God's Law

7 When some Pharisees and some teachers of the law came from Jerusalem, they gathered around Jesus. [2]They saw that some of Jesus' followers ate food with hands that were not clean, that is, they hadn't washed them. [3](The Pharisees and all the Jews never eat before washing their hands in the way required by their unwritten laws. [4]And when they buy something in the market, they never eat it until

Get Fit

CATCHING THE WAVE   More and more men are discovering the joy of surfing. It's terrific exercise, it's challenging, and it's so much fun that you don't even realize you're working hard until your exhausted body collapses on the beach. If you've ever dreamed of riding the waves for yourself, here's your chance to learn more. Surf over to www.surfing-waves.com, a comprehensive site with tips and resources that tells you everything you need to know to get started. It even shows you where to catch the right-sized waves for your skill level. An added benefit of surfing is that the ocean waves remind you of the ebb and flow of life and the vastness of God.

People Skills

Purposeful Parenting

Building a strong relationship with your kids is a lot like exercise. The more you use certain muscle groups, the stronger and healthier they become. To strengthen the bonds with your children, set up a daily practice of connecting with your kids. Try to schedule special moments with them during the day. For example, serve breakfast to them periodically, drive them to or from school regularly, read to them aloud, or check their homework each evening. If you work late, call them before they head off to bed. Parent your kids with purpose, and not only will they thank you later, but you'll thank yourself.

they wash themselves in a special way. They also follow many other unwritten laws, such as the washing of cups, pitchers, and pots.") ⁵The Pharisees and the teachers of the law said to Jesus, "Why don't your followers obey the unwritten laws which have been handed down to us? Why do your followers eat their food with hands that are not clean?"

⁶Jesus answered, "Isaiah was right when he spoke about you hypocrites. He wrote,

'These people show honor to me with
words,
but their hearts are far from me.
⁷Their worship of me is worthless.
The things they teach are nothing but
human rules.'   Isaiah 29:13

⁸You have stopped following the commands of God, and you follow only human teachings.'"

⁹Then Jesus said to them, "You cleverly ignore the commands of God so you can follow your own teachings. ¹⁰Moses said, 'Honor your father and your mother,'" and 'Anyone who says cruel things to his father or mother must be put to death.'" ¹¹But you say a person can tell his father or mother, 'I have something I could use to help you, but it is Corban—a gift to God.' ¹²You no longer let that person use that money for his father or his mother. ¹³By your own rules, which you teach people, you are rejecting what God

said. And you do many things like that." ¹⁴After Jesus called the crowd to him again, he said, "Every person should listen to me and understand what I am saying. ¹⁵There is nothing people put into their bodies that makes them unclean. People are made unclean by the things that come out of them. [¹⁶Let those with ears use them and listen.]"

¹⁷When Jesus left the people and went into the house, his followers asked him about this story. ¹⁸Jesus said, "Do you still not understand? Surely you know that nothing that enters someone from the outside can make that person unclean. ¹⁹It does not go into the mind, but into the stomach. Then it goes out of the body." (When Jesus said this, he meant that no longer was any food unclean for people to eat.)

²⁰And Jesus said, "The things that come out of people are the things that make them unclean. ²¹All these evil things begin inside people, in the mind: evil thoughts, sexual sins, stealing, murder, adultery, ²²greed, evil actions, lying, doing sinful things, jealousy, speaking evil of others, pride, and foolish living. ²³All these evil things come from inside and make people unclean."

Jesus Helps a Non-Jewish Woman

²⁴Jesus left that place and went to the area around Tyre." When he went into a house, he did not want anyone to know he was there,

⊙ Sexcess: KISSING KEYS

Kissing is one of the most intimate gestures exchanged between two people, so it should be reserved exclusively for that special someone in your life. And, believe it or not, there are ways to improve your kissing technique to give her maximum pleasure. This should go without saying, but ensure that your breath is clean. Nothing can spoil the mood quicker than a case of bad breath. Next, moisten your lips and tilt your head slightly for optimal contact. Whether you go for the French kiss or not is a matter of personal preference, both yours *and* your partner's, so keep that in mind as you get intimate.

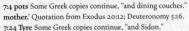

7:4 **pots** Some Greek copies continue, "and dining couches."   7:8 **teachings** Some Greek copies continue, "You wash pitchers and jugs and do many other such things."   7:10 **'Honor...**
mother.' Quotation from Exodus 20:12; Deuteronomy 5:16.   7:10 **'Anyone...death.'** Quotation from Exodus 21:17.   7:16 **Let...listen.** Some Greek copies do not contain the bracketed text.
7:24 **Tyre** Some Greek copies continue, "and Sidon."

>> live the life

Mark 6:34

The Principle > Demonstrate compassion to others.

Practicing It > Follow the example of Jesus by ministering to the people in your life with an act of compassion. Teach them what you know about learning to trust God in every area of life.

but he could not stay hidden. ²⁵A woman whose daughter had an evil spirit in her heard that he was there. So she quickly came to Jesus and fell at his feet. ²⁶She was Greek, born in Phoenicia, in Syria. She begged Jesus to force the demon out of her daughter.

²⁷Jesus told the woman, "It is not right to take the children's bread and give it to the dogs. First let the children eat all they want."

²⁸But she answered, "Yes, Lord, but even the dogs under the table can eat the children's crumbs."

²⁹Then Jesus said, "Because of your answer, you may go. The demon has left your daughter."

³⁰The woman went home and found her daughter lying in bed; the demon was gone.

Jesus Heals a Deaf Man

³¹Then Jesus left the area around Tyre and went through Sidon to Lake Galilee, to the area of the Ten Towns." ³²While he was there, some people brought a man to him who was deaf and could not talk plainly. The people begged Jesus to put his hand on the man to heal him.

³³Jesus led the man away from the crowd, by himself. He put his fingers in the man's ears and then spit and touched the man's tongue. ³⁴Looking up to heaven, he sighed and said to the man, "Ephphatha!" (This means, "Be opened.") ³⁵Instantly the man was able to hear and to use his tongue so that he spoke clearly.

³⁶Jesus commanded the people not to tell anyone about what happened. But the more he commanded them, the more they told about it. ³⁷They were completely amazed and said, "Jesus does everything well. He makes the deaf hear! And those who can't talk he makes able to speak."

More than Four Thousand People Fed

8 Another time there was a great crowd with Jesus that had nothing to eat. So Jesus called his followers and said, ²"I feel sorry for these people, because they have already been with me for three days, and they have nothing to eat. ³If I send them home hungry, they will faint on the way. Some of them live a long way from here."

⁴Jesus' followers answered, "How can we get enough bread to feed all these people? We are far away from any town."

⁵Jesus asked, "How many loaves of bread do you have?"

They answered, "Seven."

⁶Jesus told the people to sit on the ground. Then he took the seven loaves, gave thanks to God, and divided the bread. He gave the pieces to his followers to give to the people, and they did so. ⁷The followers also had a few small fish. After Jesus gave thanks for the fish, he told his followers to give them to the people also. ⁸All the people ate and were satisfied. Then his followers filled seven baskets with the leftover pieces of food. ⁹There were about four thousand people who ate. After they had eaten, Jesus sent them home. ¹⁰Then right away he got into a boat with his followers and went to the area of Dalmanutha.

The Leaders Ask for a Miracle

¹¹The Pharisees came to Jesus and began to ask him questions. Hoping to trap him, they asked Jesus for a miracle from God. ¹²Jesus sighed deeply and said, "Why do you people ask for a miracle as a sign? I tell you the truth, no sign will be given to you." ¹³Then Jesus left the Pharisees and went in the boat to the other side of the lake.

▶ Get Aligned

Mark 8:33

IF YOU'VE EVER MET SOMEONE SO FOCUSED on something that it was virtually impossible to distract him, you've witnessed single-mindedness. It's being consumed with a goal and not being satisfied until that objective is accomplished. Jesus was on a mission from God. Although he went on divine detours when he was moved by compassion for people, he never lost sight of his purpose on earth. Because of that, any obstacle in his path that threatened to veer him off course was doomed.

Consider how focused you are when it comes to the things of God. In case you haven't realized it, you have a mission. God has even equipped you with talents, abilities, and resources to get the job done. Your mission is to emulate Christ, to follow him, and to share his love with others. The details of how to walk that out may be different for each person, but the objective is the same, as is the focus required to finish the task.

There will be countless attempts to get you off track. Satan will launch personal attacks. Enemies will try to derail you. The world will undermine your efforts. However, with Christlike determination and Holy Spirit-led direction, you will succeed in your mission.

>> 7:31 **Ten Towns** In Greek, called "Decapolis." It was an area east of Lake Galilee that once had ten main towns.

Guard Against Wrong Teachings

¹⁴His followers had only one loaf of bread with them in the boat; they had forgotten to bring more. ¹⁵Jesus warned them, "Be careful! Beware of the yeast of the Pharisees and the yeast of Herod."

¹⁶His followers discussed the meaning of this, saying, "He said this because we have no bread."

¹⁷Knowing what they were talking about, Jesus asked them, "Why are you talking about not having bread? Do you still not see or understand? Are your minds closed? ¹⁸You have eyes, but you don't really see. You have ears, but you don't really listen. Remember when ¹⁹I divided five loaves of bread for the five thousand? How many baskets did you fill with leftover pieces of food?"

They answered, "Twelve."

²⁰"And when I divided seven loaves of bread for the four thousand, how many baskets did you fill with leftover pieces of food?"

They answered, "Seven."

²¹Then Jesus said to them, "Don't you understand yet?"

Jesus Heals a Blind Man

²²Jesus and his followers came to Bethsaida. There some people brought a blind man to Jesus and begged him to touch the man. ²³So Jesus took the blind man's hand and led him out of the village. Then he spit on the man's eyes and put his hands on the man and asked, "Can you see now?"

²⁴The man looked up and said, "Yes, I see people, but they look like trees walking around."

²⁵Again Jesus put his hands on the man's eyes. Then the man opened his eyes wide and they were healed, and he was able to see everything clearly. ²⁶Jesus told him to go home, saying, "Don't go into the town."ⁿ

Peter Says Jesus Is the Christ

²⁷Jesus and his followers went to the towns around Caesarea Philippi. While they were traveling, Jesus asked them, "Who do people say I am?"

²⁸They answered, "Some say you are John the Baptist. Others say you are Elijah," and others say you are one of the prophets."

²⁹Then Jesus asked, "But who do you say I am?"

Peter answered, "You are the Christ."

³⁰Jesus warned his followers not to tell anyone who he was.

³¹Then Jesus began to teach them that the Son of Man must suffer many things and that he would be rejected by the Jewish elders, the leading priests, and the teachers of the law. He told them that the Son of Man must be killed and then rise from the dead after three days. ³²Jesus told them plainly what would happen. Then Peter took Jesus aside and began to tell him not to talk like that. ³³But Jesus turned and looked at his followers. Then he told Peter not to talk that way. He said, "Go away from me, Satan!" You don't care about the things of God, but only about things people think are important."

³⁴Then Jesus called the crowd to him, along with his followers. He said, "If people want to follow me, they must give up the things they want. They must be willing even to give up their lives to follow me. ³⁵Those who want to save their lives will give up true life. But those who give up their lives for me and for the Good News will have true life. ³⁶It is worthless to have the whole world if they lose their souls. ³⁷They could never pay enough to buy back their souls. ³⁸The people who live now are living in a sinful and evil time. If people are ashamed of me and my teaching, the Son of Man will be ashamed of them when he comes with his Father's glory and with the holy angels."

9 Then Jesus said to the people, "I tell you the truth, some people standing here will see the kingdom of God come with power before they die."

Jesus Talks with Moses and Elijah

²Six days later, Jesus took Peter, James, and John up on a high mountain by themselves. While they watched, Jesus' appearance was

Q: Why did God forsake Jesus on the cross?

A: The Bible tells us that at the point of his death, Jesus took upon himself the sins of the whole world, literally becoming our sin. Because the Father is sinless and holy, he could not remain with Jesus in that state and turned away from him (2 Corinthians 5:21).

<<TechSupport>>

COMPUTER SHOPPING

If your computer is several years old, it has probably become vulnerable to viruses and is unable to take advantage of new software and wireless capabilities. It may be time to upgrade! You'll want to research both Macs and PCs to determine what will best meet your computing needs and budget restraints. No matter what you choose, be sure to get at least 40 gigabytes of hard drive space, and try to upgrade to 512 megabytes of memory. Even if you purchase the latest and greatest computer, it's likely that the technology will soon be outpaced with a newer model in a few short months. Isn't it reassuring to know that God's love never becomes obsolete?

▶▶ **8:26 town** Some Greek copies continue, "Don't even go and tell anyone in the town." **8:28 Elijah** A man who spoke for God and who lived hundreds of years before Christ. See 1 Kings 17. **8:33 Satan** Name for the devil meaning "the enemy." Jesus means that Peter was talking like Satan.

changed. ³His clothes became shining white, whiter than any person could make them. ⁴Then Elijah and Moses⁴ appeared to them, talking with Jesus.

⁵Peter said to Jesus, "Teacher, it is good that we are here. Let us make three tents—one for you, one for Moses, and one for Elijah." ⁶Peter did not know what to say, because he and the others were so frightened.

⁷Then a cloud came and covered them, and a voice came from the cloud, saying, "This is my Son, whom I love. Listen to him!"

⁸Suddenly Peter, James, and John looked around, but they saw only Jesus there alone with them.

⁹As they were coming down the mountain, Jesus commanded them not to tell anyone about what they had seen until the Son of Man had risen from the dead.

¹⁰So the followers obeyed Jesus, but they discussed what he meant about rising from the dead.

¹¹Then they asked Jesus, "Why do the teachers of the law say that Elijah must come first?"

¹²Jesus answered, "They are right to say that Elijah must come first and make everything the way it should be. But why does the Scripture say that the Son of Man will suffer much and that people will treat him as if he were nothing? ¹³I tell you that Elijah has already come. And people did to him whatever they wanted to do, just as the Scriptures said it would happen."

Jesus Heals a Sick Boy

¹⁴When Jesus, Peter, James, and John came back to the other followers, they saw a great crowd around them and the teachers of the law arguing with them. ¹⁵But as soon as the crowd saw Jesus, the people were surprised and ran to welcome him.

¹⁶Jesus asked, "What are you arguing about?"

THINK ABOUT IT Mark 9:23

IF YOU PAUSE TO CONSIDER IT, almost everyone has something in his life that is overwhelming. Maybe your neighbor is annoying the daylights out of you and there is nothing you can say to change it. Perhaps one of your family members is ill and can't seem to recover from the trauma. Each situation appears impossible and unable to be fixed.

Jesus Christ knows about the impossible situations of life. He had just been transfigured in front of his three closest followers, and when they walked down the mountain, they found a large crowd gathered around the other apostles. The men had been unable to cast out a demon from a young boy, and the father pleaded for Jesus to help.

Jesus responded, "All things are possible for the one who believes." This father wisely asked for Jesus to help increase his belief. Through the resource of prayer, God can move in the hearts of men and fix seemingly impossible situations in our lives, also. He will answer in his timing, but we have to believe all things are possible.

¹⁷A man answered, "Teacher, I brought my son to you. He has an evil spirit in him that stops him from talking. ¹⁸When the spirit attacks him, it throws him on the ground. Then my son foams at the mouth, grinds his teeth, and becomes very stiff. I asked your followers to force the evil spirit out, but they couldn't."

¹⁹Jesus answered, "You people have no faith. How long must I stay with you? How long must I put up with you? Bring the boy to me."

²⁰So the followers brought him to Jesus. As soon as the evil spirit saw Jesus, it made the boy lose control of himself, and he fell down and rolled on the ground, foaming at the mouth.

²¹Jesus asked the boy's father, "How long has this been happening?"

The father answered, "Since he was very young. ²²The spirit often throws him into a fire or into water to kill him. If you can do anything for him, please have pity on us and help us."

²³Jesus said to the father, "You said, 'If you can!' All things are possible for the one who believes."

²⁴Immediately the father cried out, "I do believe! Help me to believe more!"

²⁵When Jesus saw that a crowd was quickly gathering, he ordered the evil spirit, saying, "You spirit that makes people unable to hear or speak, I command you to come out of this boy and never enter him again!"

²⁶The evil spirit screamed and caused the boy to fall on the ground again. Then the spirit came out. The boy looked as if he were dead, and many people said, "He is dead!" ²⁷But Jesus took hold of the boy's hand and helped him to stand up.

²⁸When Jesus went into the house, his followers began asking him privately, "Why couldn't we force that evil spirit out?"

²⁹Jesus answered, "That kind of spirit can only be forced out by prayer."ⁿ

FACTOIDS! The total funds needed worldwide for unmet basic human needs—including food, clean water, shelter, and immunizations—is $80 billion. [Emptytomb.org]

9:4 **Elijah and Moses** Two of the most important Jewish leaders in the past. God had given Moses the Law, and Elijah was an important prophet. 9:29 **prayer** Some Greek copies continue, "and fasting."

Jesus Talks About His Death

[30]Then Jesus and his followers left that place and went through Galilee. He didn't want anyone to know where he was, [31]because he was teaching his followers. He said to them, "The Son of Man will be handed over to people, and they will kill him. After three days, he will rise from the dead." [32]But the followers did not understand what Jesus meant, and they were afraid to ask him.

Who Is the Greatest?

[33]Jesus and his followers went to Capernaum. When they went into a house there, he asked them, "What were you arguing about on the road?" [34]But the followers did not answer, because their argument on the road was about which one of them was the greatest.

[35]Jesus sat down and called the twelve apostles to him. He said, "Whoever wants to be the most important must be last of all and servant of all."

[36]Then Jesus took a small child and had him stand among them. Taking the child in his arms, he said, [37]"Whoever accepts a child like this in my name accepts me. And whoever accepts me accepts the One who sent me."

Anyone Not Against Us Is for Us

[38]Then John said, "Teacher, we saw someone using your name to force demons out of a person. We told him to stop, because he does not belong to our group."

[39]But Jesus said, "Don't stop him, because anyone who uses my name to do powerful things will not easily say evil things about me. [40]Whoever is not against us is with us. [41]I tell you the truth, whoever gives you a drink of water because you belong to the Christ will truly get his reward.

[42]"If one of these little children believes in me, and someone causes that child to sin, it would be better for that person to have a large stone tied around his neck and be drowned in the sea. [43]If your hand causes you to sin, cut it off. It is better for you to lose part of your body and live forever than to have two hands and go to hell, where the fire never goes out. [[44]In hell the worm does not die; the fire is never put out.]" [45]If your foot causes you to sin, cut it off. It is better for you to lose part of your body and to live forever than to have two feet and be thrown into hell. [[46]In hell the worm does not die; the fire is never put out.]" [47]If your eye causes you to sin, take it out. It is better for you to enter the kingdom of God with only one eye than to have two eyes and be thrown into hell. [48]In hell the worm does not die; the fire is never put out. [49]Every person will be salted with fire.

[50]"Salt is good, but if the salt loses its salty taste, you cannot make it salty again. So, be full of salt, and have peace with each other."

Jesus Teaches About Divorce

10 Then Jesus left that place and went into the area of Judea and across the Jordan River. Again, crowds came to him, and he taught them as he usually did.

[2]Some Pharisees came to Jesus and tried to trick him. They asked, "Is it right for a man to divorce his wife?"

Q: Is the resurrection a myth?

A: While belief in the resurrection of Christ is ultimately a matter of faith, there is substantial evidence to support its veracity. Aside from the apostles' written accounts and other historical records, there were five hundred others who witnessed it (1 Corinthians 15:6).

→ The Bottom Line

Living with Debt: Eliminate It

FROM 1999 TO 2004, AMERICANS' REVOLVING CREDIT DEBT ROSE nearly thirty-three percent, increasing to almost $800 billion. The "buy now, pay later" habit can start in college with exotic spring break trips, not to mention student loans and credit card debt. Several years later, the bills are still there—only now they include the mortgage, car payment, health insurance, and furniture. Yet Hebrews 13:5 says, "Keep your lives free from the love of money, and be satisfied with what you have." Such satisfaction saves you from worrying about how to pay for stuff long after the thrill of ownership is gone.

>> 9:44, 46 **In...out.** Some Greek copies do not contain the bracketed text.

TheFinalScore »

BOSTON MARATHON: Finishing Strong

THE ROOTS OF THE WORLD'S OLDEST RACE, THE marathon, go back nearly 2,500 years. The 20,000 runners who gather in Boston each April draw historical inspiration from the Greek soldier who ran 26 miles, 385 yards from Marathon to Athens in 490 B.C., carrying news of a Greek victory over Persia.

Running the Boston Marathon is no simple feat, calling for year-round strength training, running, and psychological preparation. On race day, careful planning is necessary to withstand the rigors of the daunting course as it weaves through the city.

The first mile begins with a 100-foot drop, more than 20 percent of the 490-foot elevation at the start. Failing to maintain a wise pace at the start can lead to problems 20.5 miles later with the appearance of Heartbreak Hill, which ascends for a half-mile. Although the course's final hill isn't an insurmountable challenge, that far into the race it becomes grueling.

While only a small fraction of the population is mentally and physically suited to run a marathon, everyone encounters the endurance test known as life. As in Boston, there will be breezy downhill stretches. Yet, challenging disappointments, crushed dreams, and disillusionment may appear—sometimes just when we thought we had conquered the course.

In Acts 20:24, the apostle Paul talked about completing a different kind of race: the work of telling others about God's grace. Keeping that goal in front of your eyes will help you focus on finishing strong.

"...disillusionment may appear—sometimes just when we thought we had conquered the course."

Survival Guide

ADDING A DECK: DO IT YOURSELF

A deck is popular for cookouts, games, and parties. It also can be an expensive addition if you hire a contractor to build one. Try doing it yourself. Many home supply stores offer kits to simplify the process, as well as classes that demonstrate how to build the deck. Experts say the primary skills needed are the ability to hammer, saw a straight line, and read a level. If you need some help, ask a friend and handyman to oversee the project. Once you build the deck, invite some neighbors over for fellowship.

³Jesus answered, "What did Moses command you to do?"

⁴They said, "Moses allowed a man to write out divorce papers and send her away.""

⁵Jesus said, "Moses wrote that command for you because you were stubborn. ⁶But when God made the world, 'he made them male and female.'" ⁷'So a man will leave his father and mother and be united with his wife," ⁸and the two will become one body.'" So there are not two, but one. ⁹God has joined the two together, so no one should separate them."

¹⁰Later, in the house, his followers asked Jesus again about the question of divorce. ¹¹He answered, "Anyone who divorces his wife and marries another woman is guilty of adultery against her. ¹²And the woman who divorces her husband and marries another man is also guilty of adultery."

Jesus Accepts Children

¹³Some people brought their little children to Jesus so he could touch them, but his followers told them to stop. ¹⁴When Jesus saw this, he was upset and said to them, "Let the little children come to me. Don't stop them, because the kingdom of God belongs to people who are like these children. ¹⁵I tell you the truth, you must accept the kingdom of God as if you were a little child, or you will never enter it." ¹⁶Then Jesus took the children in his arms, put his hands on them, and blessed them.

A Rich Young Man's Question

¹⁷As Jesus started to leave, a man ran to him and fell on his knees before Jesus. The man asked, "Good teacher, what must I do to have life forever?"

¹⁸Jesus answered, "Why do you call me good? Only God is good. ¹⁹You know the commands: 'You must not murder anyone. You must not be guilty of adultery. You must not steal. You must not tell lies about your neighbor. You must not cheat. Honor your father and mother.' ""

²⁰The man said, "Teacher, I have obeyed all these things since I was a boy."

²¹Jesus, looking at the man, loved him and said, "There is one more thing you need to do. Go and sell everything you have, and give the money to the poor, and you will have treasure in heaven. Then come and follow me."

²²He was very sad to hear Jesus say this, and he left sorrowfully, because he was rich.

²³Then Jesus looked at his followers and said, "How hard it will be for the rich to enter the kingdom of God!"

²⁴The followers were amazed at what Jesus said. But he said again, "My children, it is very hard" to enter the kingdom of God! ²⁵It is easier for a camel to go through the eye of a needle than for a rich person to enter the kingdom of God."

²⁶The followers were even more surprised and said to each other, "Then who can be saved?"

²⁷Jesus looked at them and said, "For people this is impossible, but for God all things are possible."

²⁸Peter said to Jesus, "Look, we have left everything and followed you."

²⁹Jesus said, "I tell you the truth, all those who have left houses, brothers, sisters, mother, father, children, or farms for me and for the Good News ³⁰will get more than they left. Here in this world they will have a hundred times more homes, brothers, sisters, mothers, children, and fields. And with those things, they will also suffer for their belief. But in this age they will have life forever. ³¹Many who are first now will be last in the future. And many who are last now will be first in the future."

Jesus Talks About His Death

³²As Jesus and the people with him were on the road to Jerusalem, he was leading the way. His followers were amazed, but others in the crowd who followed were afraid. Again Jesus took the twelve apostles

▶▶ 10:4 "Moses...away." Quotation from Deuteronomy 24:1.   10:6 'he made...female' Quotation from Genesis 1:27.   10:7 and...wife Some Greek copies do not have this phrase.   10:7–8 'So... body.' Quotation from Genesis 2:24.   10:19 'You...mother.' Quotation from Exodus 20:12–16; Deuteronomy 5:16–20.   10:24 hard Some Greek copies continue, "for those who trust in riches."

aside and began to tell them what was about to happen in Jerusalem. [33]He said, "Look, we are going to Jerusalem. The Son of Man will be turned over to the leading priests and the teachers of the law. They will say that he must die, and they will turn him over to the non-Jewish people, [34]who will laugh at him and spit on him. They will beat him with whips and crucify him. But on the third day, he will rise to life again."

Two Followers Ask Jesus a Favor

[35]Then James and John, sons of Zebedee, came to Jesus and said, "Teacher, we want to ask you to do something for us."

[36]Jesus asked, "What do you want me to do for you?"

[37]They answered, "Let one of us sit at your right side and one of us sit at your left side in your glory in your kingdom."

[38]Jesus said, "You don't understand what you are asking. Can you drink the cup that I must drink? And can you be baptized with the same kind of baptism that I must go through?"

[39]They answered, "Yes, we can."

Jesus said to them, "You will drink the same cup that I will drink, and you will be baptized with the same baptism that I must go through. [40]But I cannot choose who will sit at my right or my left; those places belong to those for whom they have been prepared."

[41]When the other ten followers heard this, they began to be angry with James and John.

[42]Jesus called them together and said, "The other nations have rulers. You know that those rulers love to show their power over the people, and their important leaders love to use all their authority. [43]But it should not be that way among you. Whoever wants to become great among you must serve the rest of you like a servant. [44]Whoever wants to become the first among you must serve all of you like a slave. [45]In the same way, the Son of Man did not come to be served. He came to serve others and to give his life as a ransom for many people."

Jesus Heals a Blind Man

[46]Then they came to the town of Jericho. As Jesus was leaving there with his followers and a great many people, a blind beggar named Bartimaeus son of Timaeus was sitting by the road. [47]When he heard that Jesus from Nazareth was walking by, he began to shout, "Jesus, Son of David, have mercy on me!"

[48]Many people warned the blind man to be quiet, but he shouted even more, "Son of David, have mercy on me!"

[49]Jesus stopped and said, "Tell the man to come here."

So they called the blind man, saying, "Cheer up! Get to your feet. Jesus is calling you." [50]The blind man jumped up, left his coat there, and went to Jesus.

[51]Jesus asked him, "What do you want me to do for you?"

The blind man answered, "Teacher, I want to see."

[52]Jesus said, "Go, you are healed because you believed." At once the man could see, and he followed Jesus on the road.

Jesus Enters Jerusalem as a King

11 As Jesus and his followers were coming closer to Jerusalem, they came to the towns of Bethphage and Bethany near the Mount of Olives. From there Jesus sent two of his followers [2]and said to them, "Go to the town you can see there. When you enter it, you will quickly find a colt tied, which no one has ever ridden. Untie it and bring it here to me. [3]If anyone asks you why you are doing this, tell him its Master needs the colt, and he will send it at once."

[4]The followers went into the town, found a colt tied in the street near the door of a house, and untied it. [5]Some people were standing there and asked, "What are you doing? Why are you untying that

Q: What is the kingdom of God?

A: The kingdom of God is where God's rule and reign have been established. Therefore, the kingdom of God lives in the heart of every believer. Likewise, his kingdom is present whenever Christians gather to pray, preach, or praise the Lord (Matthew 6:33).

Principles: CRUCIFIXION

The crucifixion refers to the gruesome method of Christ's death on the cross. In that era, crucifixion was the accepted method of capital punishment among Romans. In Matthew 26:2, Jesus told his followers that he would be crucified, words that soon came true after his appearance before the Roman governor Pontius Pilate. By suffering the torture and humiliation he endured on the cross, Christ proved the depth of his love for humankind. After undergoing the ultimate form of punishment, Jesus' resurrection became the miracle that verified his deity.

>> 10:38 Can you ... through? Jesus was asking if they could suffer the same terrible things that would happen to him.

Change >> YourWORLD

CHILD EVANGELISM FELLOWSHIP

Nearly half of all Americans who accept Jesus Christ as their Savior do so before the age of thirteen, and about thirty percent of the world's population is under the age of fifteen. Citing such statistics, Child Evangelism Fellowship (CEF) has made children its focus since 1917. Last year, its workers reached 5.1 million children in 155 countries. Perhaps you've seen the small wordless book they publish. It is a colorful book that can be used to share the message of Good News. For more than seventy years, CEF has brought the love of Jesus to the world by providing training, equipping, and encouragement to reach children worldwide.

To change your world, visit www.cefonline.com.

---

¹²The next day as Jesus was leaving Bethany, he became hungry. ¹³Seeing a fig tree in leaf from far away, he went to see if it had any figs on it. But he found no figs, only leaves, because it was not the right season for figs. ¹⁴So Jesus said to the tree, "May no one ever eat fruit from you again." And Jesus' followers heard him say this.

Jesus Goes to the Temple

¹⁵When Jesus returned to Jerusalem, he went into the Temple and began to throw out those who were buying and selling there. He turned over the tables of those who were exchanging different kinds of money, and he upset the benches of those who were selling doves. ¹⁶Jesus refused to allow anyone to carry goods through the Temple courts. ¹⁷Then he taught the people, saying, "It is written in the Scriptures, 'My Temple will be called a house for prayer for people from all nations.'ⁿ But you are changing God's house into a 'hideout for robbers.' "ⁿ

¹⁸The leading priests and the teachers of the law heard all this and began trying to find a way to kill Jesus. They were afraid of him, because all the people were amazed at his teaching. ¹⁹That evening, Jesus and his followersⁿ left the city.

The Power of Faith

²⁰The next morning as Jesus was passing by with his followers, they saw the fig tree dry and dead, even to the roots. ²¹Peter remembered the tree and said to Jesus, "Teacher, look! The fig tree you cursed is dry and dead!"

²²Jesus answered, "Have faith in God. ²³I tell you the truth, you can say to this mountain, 'Go, fall into the sea.' And if you have no doubts in your mind and believe that what you say will happen, God will do it for you. ²⁴So I tell you to believe that you have received the things you ask for in prayer, and God will give them to you. ²⁵When you are praying, if you are angry with someone, forgive him so that your Father in heaven will also forgive your sins. [²⁶But if you don't forgive other people, then your Father in heaven will not forgive your sins.]"ⁿ

Leaders Doubt Jesus' Authority

²⁷Jesus and his followers went again to Jerusalem. As Jesus was walking in the Temple, the leading priests, the teachers of the law,

---

colt?" ⁶The followers answered the way Jesus told them to answer, and the people let them take the colt.

⁷They brought the colt to Jesus and put their coats on it, and Jesus sat on it. ⁸Many people spread their coats on the road. Others cut branches in the fields and spread them on the road. ⁹The people were walking ahead of Jesus and behind him, shouting,

"Praise God!
God bless the One who comes in the name of the Lord!
Psalm 118:26

¹⁰God bless the kingdom of our father David!
That kingdom is coming!
Praiseⁿ to God in heaven!"

¹¹Jesus entered Jerusalem and went into the Temple. After he had looked at everything, since it was already late, he went out to Bethany with the twelve apostles.

>> live the life

Mark 11:25

The Principle > Forgive others when praying.

Practicing It > Make a list of all the people in your life who have wounded you deeply. Then prayerfully go through the list, asking God to reveal if you are harboring unforgiveness against them. If you are, make the conscious choice to forgive them.

 11:10 Praise Literally, "Hosanna," a Hebrew word used at first in praying to God for help, but at this time it was probably a shout of joy used in praising God or his Messiah.   **11:17 'My Temple … nations.'** Quotation from Isaiah 56:7.   **11:17 'hideout for robbers'** Quotation from Jeremiah 7:11.   **11:19 his followers** Some Greek copies mention only Jesus here.   **11:26 But … sins.** Some Greek copies do not contain the bracketed text.

and the elders came to him. ²⁸They said to him, "What authority do you have to do these things? Who gave you this authority?"

²⁹Jesus answered, "I will ask you one question. If you answer me, I will tell you what authority I have to do these things. ³⁰Tell me: When John baptized people, was that authority from God or just from other people?"

³¹They argued about Jesus' question, saying, "If we answer, 'John's baptism was from God,' Jesus will say, 'Then why didn't you believe him?' ³²But if we say, 'It was from other people,' the crowd will be against us." (These leaders were afraid of the people, because all the people believed that John was a prophet.)

³³So they answered Jesus, "We don't know." Jesus said to them, "Then I won't tell you what authority I have to do these things."

A Story About God's Son

12 Jesus began to use stories to teach the people. He said, "A man planted a vineyard. He put a wall around it and dug a hole for a winepress and built a tower. Then he leased the land to some farmers and left for a trip. ²When it was time for the grapes to be picked, he sent a servant to the farmers to get his share of the grapes. ³But the farmers grabbed the servant and beat him and sent him away empty-handed. ⁴Then the man sent another servant. They hit him on the head and showed no respect for him. ⁵So the man sent another servant, whom they killed. The man sent many other servants; the farmers beat some of them and killed others.

⁶"The man had one person left to send, his son whom he loved. He sent him last of all, saying, 'They will respect my son.'

⁷"But the farmers said to each other, 'This son will inherit the vineyard. If we kill him, it will be ours.' ⁸So they took the son, killed him, and threw him out of the vineyard.

⁹"So what will the owner of the vineyard do? He will come and kill those farmers and will give the vineyard to other farmers. ¹⁰Surely you have read this Scripture:

'The stone that the builders rejected became the cornerstone.

THINK ABOUT IT Mark 11:24

DOUBTS CAN ARISE AT VARIOUS points in our lives. We may doubt we will be selected for that company promotion. We may doubt our serve is adequate for that tennis tournament. Whether the issues are large or small, doubts can plague our thoughts during the day. We try to play mind games to see if we can overcome them, but the Bible suggests another resource—faith.

One day Jesus was looking for some figs from a tree, but since it was the wrong season, he didn't find any fruit. He cursed the tree and said that no one would ever eat from it again. A few days later, Jesus and his followers walked past the tree again, and it was completely dead.

Peter remembered the incident and asked about it. With his response, Jesus spoke about the need to have faith. Then he said, "So I tell you to believe that you have received the things you ask for in prayer, and God will give them to you." As this story illustrates, there is no room for doubt in the prayer of faith.

¹¹The Lord did this,
and it is wonderful to us.' "

Psalm 118:22–23

¹²The Jewish leaders knew that the story was about them. So they wanted to find a way to arrest Jesus, but they were afraid of the people. So the leaders left him and went away.

Is It Right to Pay Taxes or Not?

¹³Later, the Jewish leaders sent some Pharisees and Herodians* to Jesus to trap him in saying something wrong. ¹⁴They came to him and said, "Teacher, we know that you are an honest man. You are not afraid of what other people think about you, because you pay no attention to who they are. And you teach the truth about God's way. Tell us: Is it right to pay taxes to Caesar or not? ¹⁵Should we pay them, or not?"

But knowing what these men were really trying to do, Jesus said to them, "Why are you trying to trap me? Bring me a coin to look at." ¹⁶They gave Jesus a coin, and he asked, "Whose image and name are on the coin?"

They answered, "Caesar's."

¹⁷Then Jesus said to them, "Give to Caesar the things that are Caesar's, and give to God the things that are God's." The men were amazed at what Jesus said.

Some Sadducees Try to Trick Jesus

¹⁸Then some Sadducees came to Jesus and asked him a question. (Sadducees believed that people would not rise from the dead.) ¹⁹They said, "Teacher, Moses wrote that if a man's brother dies, leaving a wife but no children, then that man must marry the widow and have children for his brother. ²⁰Once there were seven brothers. The first brother married and died, leaving no children. ²¹So the second brother married the widow, but he also died and had no children. The same thing happened with the third brother. ²²All seven brothers married her and died, and none of the brothers had any children. Finally the woman died too.

▶▶ **12:13 Herodians** A political group that followed Herod and his family.

THINK ABOUT IT Mark 12:29–31

MANY DIFFERENT THINGS DEMAND our attention and our focus throughout the day. Our family has its demands. Our job takes a certain priority. For some of us, exercise has a place in the day. Perhaps we even have time to read a good book or listen to music.

Within the spectrum of demands, it is important to make time for our spiritual life, also. During the time of Jesus, the Jews focused on the Ten Commandments and tried to obey a multitude of other religious laws. Of course, they couldn't do it completely. No one did it without sin, except Jesus Christ. One day, a teacher of the law asked Jesus which was the greatest commandment of all.

He answered, "Love the Lord your God with all your heart, all your soul, all your mind, and all your strength." The priority for our attention is clear. As we place a premium on our love for God in every aspect of our life, then the other priorities will fall into their proper perspective and place.

34When Jesus saw that the man answered him wisely, Jesus said to him, "You are close to the kingdom of God." And after that, no one was brave enough to ask Jesus any more questions.

35As Jesus was teaching in the Temple, he asked, "Why do the teachers of the law say that the Christ is the son of David? 36David himself, speaking by the Holy Spirit, said:

'The Lord said to my Lord,
"Sit by me at my right side,
until I put your enemies under your
control." ' *Psalm 110:1*

37David himself calls the Christ 'Lord,' so how can the Christ be his son?" The large crowd listened to Jesus with pleasure.

38Jesus continued teaching and said, "Beware of the teachers of the law. They like to walk around wearing fancy clothes, and they love for people to greet them with respect in the marketplaces. 39They love to have the most important seats in the synagogues and at feasts. 40But they cheat widows and steal their houses and then try to make themselves look good by saying long prayers. They will receive a greater punishment."

True Giving

41Jesus sat near the Temple money box and watched the people put in their money. Many rich people gave large sums of money. 42Then a poor widow came and put in two small copper coins, which were only worth a few cents.

43Calling his followers to him, Jesus said, "I tell you the truth, this poor widow gave more than all those rich people. 44They gave only

23Since all seven brothers had married her, when people rise from the dead, whose wife will she be?"

24Jesus answered, "Why don't you understand? Don't you know what the Scriptures say, and don't you know about the power of God? 25When people rise from the dead, they will not marry, nor will they be given to someone to marry. They will be like the angels in heaven. 26Surely you have read what God said about people rising from the dead. In the book in which Moses wrote about the burning bush," it says that God told Moses, 'I am

Seeing that Jesus gave good answers to their questions, he asked Jesus, "Which of the commands is most important?"

29Jesus answered, "The most important command is this: 'Listen, people of Israel! The Lord our God is the only Lord. 30Love the Lord your God with all your heart, all your soul, all your mind, and all your strength.' 31The second command is this: 'Love your neighbor as you love yourself.' There are no commands more important than these."

32The man answered, "That was a good answer, Teacher. You were right when you said

"Love the Lord your God with all your heart, all your soul, all your mind, and all your strength [and] 'Love your neighbor as yourself.'" MARK 12:30-31

the God of Abraham, the God of Isaac, and the God of Jacob." 27God is the God of the living, not the dead. You Sadducees are wrong!"

The Most Important Command

28One of the teachers of the law came and heard Jesus arguing with the Sadducees.

God is the only Lord and there is no other God besides him. 33One must love God with all his heart, all his mind, and all his strength. And one must love his neighbor as he loves himself. These commands are more important than all the animals and sacrifices we offer to God."

what they did not need. This woman is very poor, but she gave all she had; she gave all she had to live on."

The Temple Will Be Destroyed

13 As Jesus was leaving the Temple, one of his followers said to him,

12:26 **burning bush** Read Exodus 3:1–12 in the Old Testament. 12:26 '**I am … Jacob.**' Quotation from Exodus 3:6. 12:30 '**Listen … strength.**' Quotation from Deuteronomy 6:4–5.
12:31 '**Love … yourself.**' Quotation from Leviticus 19:18.

66

Q: What are the "synoptic" Gospels?

A: Matthew, Mark, and Luke are sometimes called the "synoptic" Gospels. Synoptic means "with the same eye," appropriate because all three Gospels cover the same basic events in the life of Jesus. Many passages from all three books are parallel to each other.

"Look, Teacher! How beautiful the buildings are! How big the stones are!"

[2]Jesus said, "Do you see all these great buildings? Not one stone will be left on another. Every stone will be thrown down to the ground."

[3]Later, as Jesus was sitting on the Mount of Olives, opposite the Temple, he was alone with Peter, James, John, and Andrew. They asked Jesus, [4]"Tell us, when will these things happen? And what will be the sign that they are going to happen?"

[5]Jesus began to answer them, "Be careful that no one fools you. [6]Many people will come in my name, saying, 'I am the One,' and they will fool many people. [7]When you hear about wars and stories of wars that are coming, don't be afraid. These things must happen before the end comes. [8]Nations will fight against other nations, and kingdoms against other kingdoms. There will be earthquakes in different places, and there will be times when there is no food for people to eat. These things are like the first pains when something new is about to be born.

[9]"You must be careful. People will arrest you and take you to court and beat you in their synagogues. You will be forced to stand before kings and governors, to tell them about me. This will happen to you because you follow me. [10]But before these things happen, the Good News must be told to all people. [11]When you are arrested and judged, don't worry ahead of time about what you should say. Say whatever is given you to say at that time, because it will not really be you speaking; it will be the Holy Spirit.

[12]"Brothers will give their own brothers to be killed, and fathers will give their own children to be killed. Children will fight against their own parents and cause them to be put to death. [13]All people will hate you because you follow me, but those people who keep their faith until the end will be saved.

[14]"You will see 'a blasphemous object that brings destruction'[n] standing where it should not be." (You who read this should understand what it means.) "At that time, the people in Judea should run away to the mountains. [15]If people are on the roofs[n] of their houses, they must not go down or go inside to get anything out of their houses. [16]If people are in the fields, they must not go back to get their coats. [17]At that time, how terrible it will be for women who are pregnant or have nursing babies! [18]Pray that these things will not happen in winter, [19]because those days will be full of trouble. There will be more trouble than there has ever been since the beginning, when God made the world, until now, and nothing as bad will ever happen again. [20]God has decided to make that terrible time short. Otherwise, no one would go on living. But God will make that time short to help the people he has chosen. [21]At that time, someone might say to you, 'Look, there is the Christ!' Or another person might say, 'There he is!' But don't believe them. [22]False Christs and false prophets will come and perform great wonders and miracles. They will try to fool even the people God has chosen, if that is possible. [23]So be careful. I have warned you about all this before it happens.

[24]"During the days after this trouble comes,

'the sun will grow dark,
    and the moon will not give its light.
[25]The stars will fall from the sky.
    And the powers of the heavens will be shaken.'

Isaiah 13:10; 34:4

[26]"Then people will see the Son of Man coming in clouds with great power and glory. [27]Then he will send his angels all around the earth to gather his chosen people from every part of the earth and from every part of heaven.

▶ Get Aligned
Mark 13:32–35

AROUND A.D. 90, SAINT CLEMENT I SAID THE WORLD WOULD END AT ANY MOMENT. In 500, several scholars believed Armageddon would take place that year. The same prediction was made in 1000 among several groups, and later around 1500. The past century saw hundreds of so-called experts and prophets forecast a specific time of Christ's return—from the Watchtower Society to the Branch Davidians.

So far, we humans have a lousy track record when it comes to predicting the end of the world. The only thing we can be certain of is the uncertainty of this time. In verse 32 of this passage, Jesus said, "No one knows when that day or time will be, not the angels in heaven, not even the Son. Only the Father knows."

Thankfully, Jesus left us with more than a simple "your-guess-is-as-good-as-mine." His instructions are perfectly clear: Be ready. The specific time is sure to surprise everyone; but, as believers, we can stay prepared for Christ's anticipated arrival by living each day with purpose and determination. We can love, bless, and serve others as if every moment were our last.

13:14 'a blasphemous object that brings destruction' Mentioned in Daniel 9:27; 12:11 (cf. Daniel 11:31). **13:15 roofs** In Bible times houses were built with flat roofs. The roof was used for drying things such as flax and fruit. And it was used as an extra room, as a place for worship, and as a cool place to sleep in the summer.

Men of Valor
THE CENTURION: Strong Believer

Though the story of the centurion who asked Jesus to heal his servant is brief, he serves as an outstanding example of faith. A Roman commander of one hundred soldiers, this centurion loved the Jews and had built them a synagogue. Jewish elders went to see Jesus, asking him to heal the servant. But when Christ came near his home, the centurion sent messengers to tell Jesus he wasn't worthy to receive the Lord. However, since he recognized authority, he told Jesus to just give the word and his servant would be healed. Jesus replied, "I tell you the truth, this is the greatest faith I have found..." (Matthew 8:10), and granted his request. Through the centuries, the centurion's faith has stood out.

²⁸"Learn a lesson from the fig tree: When its branches become green and soft and new leaves appear, you know summer is near. ²⁹In the same way, when you see these things happening, you will know that the time is near, ready to come. ³⁰I tell you the truth, all these things will happen while the people of this time are still living. ³¹Earth and sky will be destroyed, but the words I have said will never be destroyed.

³²"No one knows when that day or time will be, not the angels in heaven, not even the Son. Only the Father knows. ³³Be careful! Always be ready," because you don't know when that time will be. ³⁴It is like a man who goes on a trip. He leaves his house and lets his servants take care of it, giving each one a special job to do. The man tells the servant guarding the door always to be watchful. ³⁵So always be ready, because you don't know when the owner of the house will come back. It might be in the evening, or at midnight, or in the morning while it is still dark, or when the sun rises. ³⁶Always be ready. Otherwise he might come back suddenly and find you sleeping. ³⁷I tell you this, and I say this to everyone: 'Be ready!' "

The Plan to Kill Jesus

14 It was now only two days before the Passover and the Feast of Unleavened Bread. The leading priests and teachers of the law were trying to find a trick to arrest Jesus and kill him. ²But they said, "We must not do it during the feast, because the people might cause a riot."

A Woman with Perfume for Jesus

³Jesus was in Bethany at the house of Simon, who had a skin disease. While Jesus was eating there, a woman approached him with an alabaster jar filled with very expensive perfume, made of pure nard. She opened the jar and poured the perfume on Jesus' head.

⁴Some who were there became upset and said to each other, "Why waste that perfume? ⁵It was worth a full year's work. It could have been sold and the money given to the poor." And they got very angry with the woman.

⁶Jesus said, "Leave her alone. Why are you troubling her? She did an excellent thing for me. ⁷You will always have the poor with you, and you can help them anytime you want. But you will not always have me. ⁸This woman did the only thing she could do for me; she poured perfume on my body to prepare me for burial. ⁹I tell you the truth, wherever the Good News is preached in all the world, what this woman has done will be told, and people will remember her."

Judas Becomes an Enemy of Jesus

¹⁰One of the twelve apostles, Judas Iscariot, went to talk to the leading priests to offer to hand Jesus over to them. ¹¹These priests were pleased about this and promised to pay Judas money. So he watched for the best time to turn Jesus in.

Jesus Eats the Passover Meal

¹²It was now the first day of the Feast of Unleavened Bread when the Passover lamb was sacrificed. Jesus' followers said to him, "Where do you want us to go and prepare for you to eat the Passover meal?"

¹³Jesus sent two of his followers and said to them, "Go into the city and a man carrying a jar of water will meet you. Follow him. ¹⁴When he goes into a house, tell the owner of the house, 'The Teacher says: "Where is my guest room in which I can eat the Passover meal with my followers?" ' ¹⁵The owner will show you a large room upstairs that is furnished and ready. Prepare the food for us there."

¹⁶So the followers left and went into the city. Everything happened as Jesus had said, so they prepared the Passover meal.

¹⁷In the evening, Jesus went to that house with the twelve. ¹⁸While they were all eating, Jesus said, "I tell you the truth, one of you will turn against me—one of you eating with me now."

¹⁹The followers were very sad to hear this. Each one began to say to Jesus, "I am not the one, am I?"

²⁰Jesus answered, "It is one of the twelve—the one who dips his bread into the bowl with me. ²¹The Son of Man will die, just as the Scriptures say. But how terrible it will be for the person who hands the Son of Man over to be killed. It would be better for him if he had never been born."

The Lord's Supper

²²While they were eating, Jesus took some bread and thanked God for it and broke it.

>> **13:33 ready** Some Greek copies continue, "and pray."

Then he gave it to his followers and said, "Take it; this is my body." [23]Then Jesus took a cup and thanked God for it and gave it to the followers, and they all drank from the cup.

[24]Then Jesus said, "This is my blood which is the new[n] agreement that God makes with his people. This blood is poured out for many. [25]I tell you the truth, I will not drink of this fruit of the vine[n] again until that day when I drink it new in the kingdom of God."

[26]After singing a hymn, they went out to the Mount of Olives.

Jesus' Followers Will Leave Him

[27]Then Jesus told the followers, "You will all stumble in your faith, because it is written in the Scriptures:

'I will kill the shepherd,
    and the sheep will scatter.'   *Zechariah 13:7*

[28]But after I rise from the dead, I will go ahead of you into Galilee."

[29]Peter said, "Everyone else may stumble in their faith, but I will not."

[30]Jesus answered, "I tell you the truth, tonight before the rooster crows twice you will say three times you don't know me."

[31]But Peter insisted, "I will never say that I don't know you! I will even die with you!" And all the other followers said the same thing.

Jesus Prays Alone

[32]Jesus and his followers went to a place called Gethsemane. He said to them, "Sit here while I pray." [33]Jesus took Peter, James, and John with him, and he began to be very sad and troubled. [34]He said to them, "My heart is full of sorrow, to the point of death. Stay here and watch."

[35]After walking a little farther away from them, Jesus fell to the ground and prayed that, if possible, he would not have this time of suffering. [36]He prayed, "Abba,[n] Father! You can do all things. Take away this cup[n] of suffering. But do what you want, not what I want."

[37]Then Jesus went back to his followers and found them asleep. He said to Peter, "Simon, are you sleeping? Couldn't you stay awake with me for one hour? [38]Stay awake and pray for strength against temptation. The spirit wants to do what is right, but the body is weak."

[39]Again Jesus went away and prayed the same thing. [40]Then he went back to his followers, and again he found them asleep, because their eyes were very heavy. And they did not know what to say to him.

[41]After Jesus prayed a third time, he went back to his followers and said to them, "Are you still sleeping and resting? That's enough. The time has come for the Son of Man to be handed over to sinful people. [42]Get up, we must go. Look, here comes the man who has turned against me."

Jesus Is Arrested

[43]At once, while Jesus was still speaking, Judas, one of the twelve apostles, came up. With him were many people carrying swords and clubs who had been sent from the leading priests, the teachers of the law, and the Jewish elders.

Q: What does the Bible say about racism?

A: The Bible makes it clear that God shows no preference toward one person over another, whether on the basis of race, gender, or any other measure. We are all equally special in God's eyes and should treat one another accordingly (Galatians 3:28).

Get Fit

GETTING CHECKED   Sometimes checkups are once a year. Other times they're more or less often. Based on your age, health history, lifestyle, and other important issues, you and your doctor can determine how often you will need to be examined and screened for certain diseases and conditions. These include high blood pressure, high cholesterol, diabetes, and cancers of the skin, prostate, and colon. You wouldn't avoid taking the car in for an oil change just because you feared something might be wrong with the engine, would you? Then don't treat your body that way. Get your scheduled health screenings to make sure everything is running smoothly. And while you're at it, study the Word to maintain your spiritual health, too.

14:24 new Some Greek copies do not have this word. Compare Luke 22:20.   **14:25 fruit of the vine** Product of the grapevine; this may also be translated "wine."   **14:36 Abba** Name that a Jewish child called his father.   **14:36 cup** Jesus is talking about the terrible things that will happen to him. Accepting these things will be very hard, like drinking a cup of something bitter.

People
Skills

Understanding Others

Conversation is not meant to be a competition, yet some men try to turn it into one. Rather than genuinely listening to what the other person is saying, they mentally jump ahead to what they want to say next. They are quick to interrupt and will even raise their voices to drown out other people so they can offer another comment. This was not the way Christ conversed with others, and it's not the way we should either. Practice giving other people the time needed to finish their thoughts before you offer a response. Follow the example of Jesus by seeking first to understand, then to be understood.

⁴⁴Judas had planned a signal for them, saying, "The man I kiss is Jesus. Arrest him and guard him while you lead him away." ⁴⁵So Judas went straight to Jesus and said, "Teacher!" and kissed him. ⁴⁶Then the people grabbed Jesus and arrested him. ⁴⁷One of his followers standing nearby pulled out his sword and struck the servant of the high priest and cut off his ear.

⁴⁸Then Jesus said, "You came to get me with swords and clubs as if I were a criminal. ⁴⁹Every day I was with you teaching in the Temple, and you did not arrest me there. But all these things have happened to make the Scriptures come true." ⁵⁰Then all of Jesus' followers left him and ran away.

⁵¹A young man, wearing only a linen cloth, was following Jesus, and the people also grabbed him. ⁵²But the cloth he was wearing came off, and he ran away naked.

Jesus Before the Leaders

⁵³The people who arrested Jesus led him to the house of the high priest, where all the leading priests, the elders, and the teachers of the law were gathered. ⁵⁴Peter followed far behind and entered the courtyard of the high priest's house. There he sat with the guards, warming himself by the fire.

⁵⁵The leading priests and the whole Jewish council tried to find something that Jesus had done wrong so they could kill him. But the council could find no proof of anything. ⁵⁶Many people came and told false things about him, but all said different things—none of them agreed.

⁵⁷Then some people stood up and lied about Jesus, saying, ⁵⁸"We heard this man say, 'I will destroy this Temple that people made. And three days later, I will build another Temple not made by people.'" ⁵⁹But even the things these people said did not agree.

⁶⁰Then the high priest stood before them and asked Jesus, "Aren't you going to answer? Don't you have something to say about their charges against you?" ⁶¹But Jesus said nothing; he did not answer.

The high priest asked Jesus another question: "Are you the Christ, the Son of the blessed God?"

⁶²Jesus answered, "I am. And in the future you will see the Son of Man sitting at the right hand of God, the Powerful One, and coming on clouds in the sky."

⁶³When the high priest heard this, he tore his clothes and said, "We don't need any more witnesses! ⁶⁴You all heard him say these things against God. What do you think?"

They all said that Jesus was guilty and should die. ⁶⁵Some of the people there began to spit at Jesus. They blindfolded him and beat him with their fists and said, "Prove you are a prophet!" Then the guards led Jesus away and beat him.

Peter Says He Doesn't Know Jesus

⁶⁶While Peter was in the courtyard, a servant girl of the high priest came there. ⁶⁷She saw Peter warming himself at the fire and looked closely at him.

Then she said, "You also were with Jesus, that man from Nazareth."

⁶⁸But Peter said that he was never with Jesus. He said, "I don't know or understand what you are talking about." Then Peter left and went toward the entrance of the courtyard. And the rooster crowed.ⁿ

⁶⁹The servant girl saw Peter there, and again she said to the people who were standing nearby, "This man is one of those who followed Jesus." ⁷⁰Again Peter said that it was not true.

A short time later, some people were standing near Peter saying, "Surely you are one of those who followed Jesus, because you are from Galilee, too."

⁷¹Then Peter began to place a curse on himself and swear, "I don't know this man you're talking about!"

⁷²At once, the rooster crowed the second time. Then Peter remembered what Jesus had told him: "Before the rooster crows twice, you will say three times that you don't know me." Then Peter lost control of himself and began to cry.

Pilate Questions Jesus

15 Very early in the morning, the leading priests, the elders, the teachers of the law, and all the Jewish council decided

---

▸▸ **14:68 And the rooster crowed.** Some Greek copies do not have this phrase.

what to do with Jesus. They tied him, led him away, and turned him over to Pilate, the governor.

²Pilate asked Jesus, "Are you the king of the Jews?"

Jesus answered, "Those are your words."

³The leading priests accused Jesus of many things. ⁴So Pilate asked Jesus another question, "You can see that they are accusing you of many things. Aren't you going to answer?"

⁵But Jesus still said nothing, so Pilate was very surprised.

Pilate Tries to Free Jesus

⁶Every year at the time of the Passover the governor would free one prisoner whom the people chose. ⁷At that time, there was a man named Barabbas in prison who was a rebel and had committed murder during a riot. ⁸The crowd came to Pilate and began to ask him to free a prisoner as he always did.

⁹So Pilate asked them, "Do you want me to free the king of the Jews?" ¹⁰Pilate knew that the leading priests had turned Jesus in to him because they were jealous. ¹¹But the leading priests had persuaded the people to ask Pilate to free Barabbas, not Jesus.

¹²Then Pilate asked the crowd again, "So what should I do with this man you call the king of the Jews?"

¹³They shouted, "Crucify him!"

¹⁴Pilate asked, "Why? What wrong has he done?"

But they shouted even louder, "Crucify him!"

¹⁵Pilate wanted to please the crowd, so he freed Barabbas for them. After having Jesus beaten with whips, he handed Jesus over to the soldiers to be crucified.

¹⁶The soldiers took Jesus into the governor's palace (called the Praetorium) and called all the other soldiers together. ¹⁷They put a purple robe on Jesus and used thorny branches to make a crown for his head. ¹⁸They began to call out to him, "Hail, King of

▶ Get Aligned
Mark 15:29–32

WHAT IS YOUR FIRST REACTION WHEN SOMEONE DOES YOU WRONG? For most men, it's the thought of retribution, payback, or revenge. When we are unjustly accused of something, not only is our instinct to prove those people wrong, we want them to eat their words, as well.

If anyone had the right to lash out at his accusers, it was Jesus. Here was the Son of God, dying for the very people who mocked him as he hung in complete shame. He could have instantly silenced every venomous word spat at him. He could have killed anyone who dared scorn him in this ultimate moment of sacrifice. The truth is, he could have saved himself and put an end to the crowd's malice. Instead, he restrained himself. He chose to take the higher path, letting truth speak for him in the end.

When is the last time you allowed God to speak for you rather than react rashly to someone's offensive words? It's difficult to hold your tongue when your mind is thinking of all the ways you could lash out at a wrongful allegation. Yet, that is exactly the restraint Christ displayed as the ultimate example we are to follow.

the Jews!" ¹⁹The soldiers beat Jesus on the head many times with a stick. They spit on him and made fun of him by bowing on their knees and worshiping him. ²⁰After they finished, the soldiers took off the purple robe and put his own clothes on him again. Then they led him out of the palace to be crucified.

Jesus Is Crucified

²¹A man named Simon from Cyrene, the father of Alexander and Rufus, was coming from the fields to the city. The soldiers forced Simon to carry the cross for Jesus. ²²They led Jesus to the place called Golgotha, which means the Place of the Skull. ²³The soldiers tried to give Jesus wine mixed with myrrh to drink, but he refused. ²⁴The soldiers crucified Jesus and divided his clothes among themselves, throwing lots to decide what each soldier would get.

²⁵It was nine o'clock in the morning when they crucified Jesus. ²⁶There was a sign with this charge against Jesus written on it: THE KING OF THE JEWS. ²⁷They also put two robbers on crosses beside Jesus, one on the right, and the other on the left. [²⁸And the Scripture came true that says, "They put him with criminals."]* ²⁹People walked by and insulted Jesus and shook their heads, saying, "You said you could destroy the Temple and build it again in three days. ³⁰So save yourself! Come down from that cross!"

‹‹ Tech Support ››

WEB SEARCH

Web search consistently ranks at the top of activities Americans pursue online. If search is the on-ramp to the information super-highway, then Google must be its sports car. If you like Google and want to try some of its more advanced features, check out Soople.com, which takes all of Google's power and puts it on one convenient page. While you're searching, check out Google Maps and click on the satellite view. As you're panning across the globe, pause and thank God for the vastness of his creation.

>> **15:28 And … criminals."** Some Greek copies do not contain the bracketed text, which quotes from Isaiah 53:12.

THINK ABOUT IT Mark 16:6–7

LIFE IS FILLED WITH SOME DISAPPOINTMENTS. Your favorite sports team loses in the play-off games. Maybe your supervisor says there is a budget reduction, and you can't make a trip that you were planning. Or you look forward to a special weekend away with your wife, but a family outing with the in-laws nixes the plans. These types of personal disappointments are temporary, and, in general, we get over them.

But imagine the sense of disappointment and disillusionment that filled the hearts of Jesus' followers after his death on the cross. For three years, the men had given up their occupations and lives to follow Jesus. Emotion also weighed on the hearts of the believers who went to Jesus' tomb to care for his body. When they looked inside the tomb, they saw a man dressed in white who said, "Don't be afraid. You are looking for Jesus from Nazareth, who has been crucified. He has risen from the dead; he is not here." Those words removed the disappointment and replaced those feelings of disillusionment with joy and hope. Our disappointments from life are temporary, but our lasting hope is in the promise of the resurrection. Jesus has risen from the dead.

[31]The leading priests and the teachers of the law were also making fun of Jesus. They said to each other, "He saved other people, but he can't save himself. [32]If he is really the Christ, the king of Israel, let him come down now from the cross. When we see this, we will believe in him." The robbers who were being crucified beside Jesus also insulted him.

Jesus Dies

[33]At noon the whole country became dark, and the darkness lasted for three hours. [34]At three o'clock Jesus cried in a loud voice, "Eloi, Eloi, lama sabachthani." This means, "My God, my God, why have you abandoned me?"

[35]When some of the people standing there heard this, they said, "Listen! He is calling Elijah."

[36]Someone there ran and got a sponge, filled it with vinegar, tied it to a stick, and gave it to Jesus to drink. He said, "We want to see if Elijah will come to take him down from the cross."

[37]Then Jesus cried in a loud voice and died.

[38]The curtain in the Temple" was torn into two pieces, from the top to the bottom. [39]When the army officer who was standing in front of the cross saw what happened when Jesus died," he said, "This man really was the Son of God!"

[40]Some women were standing at a distance from the cross, watching; among them were Mary Magdalene, Salome, and Mary the mother of James and Joseph. (James was her youngest son.) [41]These women had followed Jesus in Galilee and helped him. Many other women were also there who had come with Jesus to Jerusalem.

Jesus Is Buried

[42]This was Preparation Day. (That means the day before the Sabbath day.) That evening, [43]Joseph from Arimathea was brave enough to go to Pilate and ask for Jesus' body. Joseph, an important member of the Jewish council, was one of the people who was waiting for the kingdom of God to come. [44]Pilate was amazed that Jesus would have already died, so he called the army officer who had guarded Jesus and asked him if Jesus had already died. [45]The officer told Pilate that he was dead, so Pilate told Joseph he could have the body. [46]Joseph bought some linen cloth, took the body down from the cross, and wrapped it in the linen. He put the body in a tomb that was cut out of a wall of rock. Then he rolled a very large stone to block the entrance of the tomb. [47]And Mary Magdalene and Mary the mother of Joseph saw the place where Jesus was laid.

Jesus Rises from the Dead

16 The day after the Sabbath day, Mary Magdalene, Mary the mother of James, and Salome bought some sweet-smelling spices to put on Jesus' body. [2]Very early on that day, the first day of the week, soon after sunrise, the women were on their way to the tomb. [3]They said to each other, "Who will roll away for us the stone that covers the entrance of the tomb?"

[4]Then the women looked and saw that the stone had already been rolled away, even though it was very large. [5]The women entered the tomb and saw a young man wearing a white robe and sitting on the right side, and they were afraid.

[6]But the man said, "Don't be afraid. You are looking for Jesus from Nazareth, who has been crucified. He has risen from the dead; he is not here. Look, here is the place they laid him. [7]Now go and tell his followers and Peter, 'Jesus is going into Galilee ahead of you, and you will see him there as he told you before.'"

[8]The women were confused and shaking with fear, so they left the tomb and ran away. They did not tell anyone about what happened, because they were afraid.

Verses 9–20 are not included in some of the earliest surviving Greek copies of Mark.

 15:38 curtain in the Temple A curtain divided the Most Holy Place from the other part of the Temple. That was the special building in Jerusalem where God commanded the Jewish people to worship him.   **15:39 when Jesus died** Some Greek copies read "when Jesus cried out and died."

Some Followers See Jesus

[⁹After Jesus rose from the dead early on the first day of the week, he showed himself first to Mary Magdalene. One time in the past, he had forced seven demons out of her. ¹⁰After Mary saw Jesus, she went and told his followers, who were very sad and were crying. ¹¹But Mary told them that Jesus was alive. She said that she had seen him, but the followers did not believe her.

¹²Later, Jesus showed himself to two of his followers while they were walking in the country, but he did not look the same as before. ¹³These followers went back to the others and told them what had happened, but again, the followers did not believe them.

Jesus Talks to the Apostles

¹⁴Later Jesus showed himself to the eleven apostles while they were eating, and he criticized them because they had no faith. They were stubborn and refused to believe those who had seen him after he had risen from the dead.

¹⁵Jesus said to his followers, "Go everywhere in the world, and tell the Good News to everyone. ¹⁶Anyone who believes and is baptized will be saved, but anyone who does not believe will be punished.

¹⁷And those who believe will be able to do these things as proof: They will use my name to force out demons. They will speak in new languages." ¹⁸They will pick up snakes and drink poison without being hurt. They will touch the sick, and the sick will be healed."

¹⁹After the Lord Jesus said these things to his followers, he was carried up into heaven, and he sat at the right side of God. ²⁰The followers went everywhere in the world and told the Good News to people, and the Lord helped them. The Lord proved that the Good News they told was true by giving them power to work miracles.]

>> 16:17 **languages** This can also be translated "tongues."

THE **GOSPEL** ACCORDING TO
Luke

AUTHOR: LUKE
DATE WRITTEN: A.D. 58–63

WHEN YOU READ VARIOUS BOOKS OR
magazine articles, you quickly notice that some writers
capture your attention more than others. Maybe it's their
use of action to pull you into the story. Or perhaps their
rich characterization draws you into the material. Many
scholars have applauded the way Luke had a command of
the Greek language. Some passages include rich and ex-
tensive vocabulary, and the style of some sections approaches classical Greek, whereas other passages show a
geographical and cultural sensitivity to the audience.

Luke was probably a doctor and a Gentile, which would
make him the only non-Jewish author in the New Testa-
ment. He provides detailed descriptions about everything from the birth of Jesus to
his days as a young man in the Temple to his return to heaven. Luke presents the
life and times of Christ with an emphasis on his humanity.

The book is addressed to Theophilus, which means "one who loves God" in
Greek. Some scholars believe Theophilus was a Roman official or at least someone
of high position and wealth who served as a patron or publisher of Luke's writings.
The stories in this account emphasize Jesus' relationship with people, and a large
portion of this book is exclusive to this Gospel.

Luke Writes About Jesus' Life

1 Many have tried to report on the things that happened among us. ²They have written the same things that we learned from others—the people who saw those things from the beginning and served God by telling people his message. ³Since I myself have studied everything carefully from the beginning, most excellent[n] Theophilus, it seemed good for me to write it out for you. I arranged it in order, ⁴to help you know that what you have been taught is true.

Zechariah and Elizabeth

⁵During the time Herod ruled Judea, there was a priest named Zechariah who belonged to Abijah's group.[n] Zechariah's wife, Elizabeth, came from the family of Aaron. ⁶Zechariah and Elizabeth truly did what God said was good. They did everything the Lord commanded and were without fault in keeping his law. ⁷But they had no children, because Elizabeth could not have a baby, and both of them were very old.

⁸One day Zechariah was serving as a priest before God, because his group was on duty. ⁹According to the custom of the priests, he was chosen by lot to go into the Temple of the Lord and burn incense. ¹⁰There were a great many people outside praying at the time the incense was offered. ¹¹Then an angel of the Lord appeared to Zechariah, standing on the right side of the incense table. ¹²When he saw the angel, Zechariah

was startled and frightened. ¹³But the angel said to him, "Zechariah, don't be afraid. God has heard your prayer. Your wife, Elizabeth, will give birth to a son, and you will name him John. ¹⁴He will bring you joy and gladness, and many people will be happy because of his birth. ¹⁵John will be a great man for the Lord. He will never drink wine or beer, and even from birth, he will be

FACT-OIDS! The number of Internet pornography sites increased from 71,831 in 1998 to 1.3 million in 2003. [Ag.org]

filled with the Holy Spirit. ¹⁶He will help many people of Israel return to the Lord their God. ¹⁷He will go before the Lord in spirit and power like Elijah. He will make peace between parents and their children and will bring those who are not obeying God back to the right way of thinking, to make a people ready for the coming of the Lord."

¹⁸Zechariah said to the angel, "How can I know that what you say is true? I am an old man, and my wife is old, too."

¹⁹The angel answered him, "I am Gabriel. I stand before God, who sent me to talk to you and to tell you this good news. ²⁰Now, listen! You will not be able to speak until the day these things happen, because you did not

believe what I told you. But they will really happen."

²¹Outside, the people were still waiting for Zechariah and were surprised that he was staying so long in the Temple. ²²When Zechariah came outside, he could not speak to them, and they knew he had seen a vision in the Temple. He could only make signs to them and remained unable to speak. ²³When

his time of service at the Temple was finished, he went home.

²⁴Later, Zechariah's wife, Elizabeth, became pregnant and did not go out of her house for five months. Elizabeth said, ²⁵"Look what the Lord has done for me! My people were ashamed[n] of me, but now the Lord has taken away that shame."

An Angel Appears to Mary

²⁶During Elizabeth's sixth month of pregnancy, God sent the angel Gabriel to Nazareth, a town in Galilee, ²⁷to a virgin. She was engaged to marry a man named Joseph from the family of David. Her name was Mary. ²⁸The angel came to her and said, "Greetings! The Lord has blessed you and is with you."

The Bottom Line

Credit Cards: Paying on Time

WHETHER YOU OWE A BALANCE ON CREDIT CARDS or are struggling to pay other bills, you still need to meet payment deadlines. Paying any bill late can trigger a credit card issuer's "universal default policy." This means being late on any payment, such as a telephone bill or car loan, allows the card issuer to increase your interest rate to its highest level. That can increase minimum payments and your customary rate. If this happens, you may need to negotiate with the issuer or get a loan to pay it off.

>> 1:3 **excellent** This word was used to show respect to an important person like a king or ruler.   1:5 **Abijah's group** The Jewish priests were divided into twenty-four groups. See 1 Chronicles 24.
1:25 **ashamed** The Jewish people thought it was a disgrace for women not to have children.

²⁹But Mary was very startled by what the angel said and wondered what this greeting might mean.

³⁰The angel said to her, "Don't be afraid, Mary; God has shown you his grace. ³¹Listen! You will become pregnant and give birth to a son, and you will name him Jesus. ³²He will be great and will be called the Son of the Most High. The Lord God will give him the throne of King David, his ancestor. ³³He will rule over the people of Jacob forever, and his kingdom will never end."

³⁴Mary said to the angel, "How will this happen since I am a virgin?"

³⁵The angel said to Mary, "The Holy Spirit will come upon you, and the power of the Most High will cover you. For this reason the baby will be holy and will be called the Son of God. ³⁶Now Elizabeth, your relative, is also pregnant with a son though she is very old. Everyone thought she could not have a baby, but she has been pregnant for six months. ³⁷God can do anything!"

³⁸Mary said, "I am the servant of the Lord. Let this happen to me as you say!" Then the angel went away.

Mary Visits Elizabeth

³⁹Mary got up and went quickly to a town in the hills of Judea. ⁴⁰She came to Zechariah's house and greeted Elizabeth. ⁴¹When Elizabeth heard Mary's greeting, the unborn baby inside her jumped, and Elizabeth was filled with the Holy Spirit. ⁴²She cried out in a loud voice, "God has blessed you more than any other woman, and he has blessed the baby to which you will give birth. ⁴³Why has this good thing happened to me, that the mother of my Lord comes to me? ⁴⁴When I heard your voice, the baby inside me jumped with joy. ⁴⁵You are blessed because you believed that what the Lord said to you would really happen."

Mary Praises God

⁴⁶Then Mary said,

"My soul praises the Lord;
⁴⁷ my heart rejoices in God
    my Savior,
⁴⁸because he has shown his
    concern for his
    humble servant girl.
From now on, all people will
    say that I am blessed,
⁴⁹ because the Powerful One
    has done great things
    for me.
His name is holy.
⁵⁰God will show his mercy
    forever and ever
to those who worship and
    serve him.
⁵¹He has done mighty deeds by
    his power.
He has scattered the people
    who are proud
and think great things
    about themselves.
⁵²He has brought down rulers
    from their thrones
and raised up the humble.
⁵³He has filled the hungry with
    good things
and sent the rich away with
    nothing.
⁵⁴He has helped his servant, the
    people of Israel,
remembering to show them mercy
⁵⁵as he promised to our ancestors,
    to Abraham and to his children forever."

Q: Who is Satan?

A: At one time, Satan was known as Lucifer and was one of the most beautiful angels in heaven. However, pride entered his heart, and he began to covet the glory and worship that was God's alone, causing God to cast him out of heaven for his rebellion (Luke 10:18).

Survival Guide

DISHWASHERS: SAVING ON COSTS

If you are in the market for a new dishwasher, focus on checking out the energy-saving models. Depending on the size of the load, they can save fifty percent or more on water use. That is significant, since about eighty percent of the energy used by dishwashers goes to heat water. If yours works fine, remember that running only full loads will save money. So will using cold water for rinsing and drying dishes by air or hand. In Matthew 25:21, Jesus said those who are loyal in caring for small things will be entrusted with much greater things.

[56]Mary stayed with Elizabeth for about three months and then returned home.

The Birth of John

[57]When it was time for Elizabeth to give birth, she had a boy. [58]Her neighbors and relatives heard how good the Lord was to her, and they rejoiced with her.

[59]When the baby was eight days old, they came to circumcise him. They wanted to name him Zechariah because this was his father's name, [60]but his mother said, "No! He will be named John."

[61]The people said to Elizabeth, "But no one in your family has this name." [62]Then they made signs to his father to find out what he would like to name him.

[63]Zechariah asked for a writing tablet and wrote, "His name is John," and everyone was surprised. [64]Immediately Zechariah could talk again, and he began praising God. [65]All their neighbors became alarmed, and in all the mountains of Judea people continued talking about all these things. [66]The people who heard about them wondered, saying, "What will this child be?" because the Lord was with him.

Zechariah Praises God

[67]Then Zechariah, John's father, was filled with the Holy Spirit and prophesied:

[68]"Let us praise the Lord, the God of Israel,
   because he has come to help his people
      and has given them freedom.
[69]He has given us a powerful Savior
   from the family of God's servant David.
[70]He said that he would do this
   through his holy prophets who lived long ago:
[71]He promised he would save us from our enemies
   and from the power of all those who hate us.
[72]He said he would give mercy to our ancestors
   and that he would remember his holy promise.
[73]God promised Abraham, our father,
[74]   that he would save us from the power of our enemies
so we could serve him without fear,
[75]being holy and good before God as long as we live.

[76]"Now you, child, will be called a prophet of the Most High God.
   You will go before the Lord to prepare his way.
[77]You will make his people know that they will be saved
   by having their sins forgiven.
[78]With the loving mercy of our God,
   a new day from heaven will dawn upon us.
[79]It will shine on those who live in darkness,
   in the shadow of death.
   It will guide us into the path of peace."
[80]And so the child grew up and became strong in spirit. John lived in the desert until the time when he came out to preach to Israel.

The Birth of Jesus

2 At that time, Augustus Caesar sent an order that all people in the countries under Roman rule must list their names in a register. [2]This was the first registration;[a] it was taken while Quirinius was governor of Syria. [3]And all went to their own towns to be registered.

[4]So Joseph left Nazareth, a town in Galilee, and went to the town of Bethlehem in Judea, known as the town of David. Joseph went there because he was from the family of David. [5]Joseph registered with Mary, to whom he was engaged[b] and who was now pregnant. [6]While they were in Bethlehem, the time came for Mary to have the baby, [7]and she gave birth to her first son. Because there were no rooms left in the inn, she wrapped the baby with pieces of cloth and laid him in a feeding trough.

Shepherds Hear About Jesus

[8]That night, some shepherds were in the fields nearby watching their sheep. [9]Then an angel of the Lord stood before them. The glory of the Lord was shining around them, and they became very frightened. [10]The angel said to them, "Do not be afraid. I am bringing you good news that will be a great joy to all the people. [11]Today your Savior was born in the town of David. He is Christ, the Lord. [12]This is how you will know him: You will find a baby wrapped in pieces of cloth and lying in a feeding box."

[13]Then a very large group of angels from heaven joined the first angel, praising God and saying:

[14]"Give glory to God in heaven,
   and on earth let there be peace among
      the people who please God."[c]
[15]When the angels left them and went back to heaven, the shepherds said to each other,

{ Deal With It: *Race

WHILE THE ISSUE OF RACE has troubled people throughout time, the love of God is colorblind. Whether we realize it or not, God loves us all the same and commands us to love each other equally. As Galatians 3:28 declares, "In Christ, there is no difference between Jew and Greek, slave and free person, male and female. You are all the same in Christ Jesus." It is a sin to treat another person or group of people differently based on the color of their skin. Whatever our ethnicity, we need to adopt the attitude of God and do our part to reconcile the races.

2:2 **registration** Census. A counting of all the people and the things they own.   2:5 **engaged** For the Jewish people, an engagement was a lasting agreement. It could only be broken by divorce.
2:14 **and ... God** Some Greek copies read "and on earth let there be peace and goodwill among people."

77

"Let's go to Bethlehem. Let's see this thing that has happened which the Lord has told us about."

[16]So the shepherds went quickly and found Mary and Joseph and the baby, who was lying in a feeding trough. [17]When they had seen him, they told what the angels had said about this child. [18]Everyone was amazed at what the shepherds said to them. [19]But Mary treasured these things and continued to think about them. [20]Then the shepherds went back to their sheep, praising God and thanking him for everything they had seen and heard. It had been just as the angel had told them.

[21]When the baby was eight days old, he was circumcised and was named Jesus, the name given by the angel before the baby began to grow inside Mary.

Jesus Is Presented in the Temple

[22]When the time came for Mary and Joseph to do what the law of Moses taught about being made pure,[n] they took Jesus to Jerusalem to present him to the Lord. [23](It is written in the law of the Lord: "Every firstborn male shall be given to the Lord.")[n] [24]Mary and Joseph also went to offer a sacrifice, as the law of the Lord

FACT-OIDS! Seventy-three percent of Americans subscribe to cable television and 28% get their programming via satellite dish. [Barna.org]

says: "You must sacrifice two doves or two young pigeons."[n]

Simeon Sees Jesus

[25]In Jerusalem lived a man named Simeon who was a good man and godly. He was waiting for the time when God would take away Israel's sorrow, and the Holy Spirit was in him. [26]Simeon had been told by the Holy Spirit that he would not die before he saw the Christ promised by the Lord. [27]The Spirit led Simeon to the Temple. When Mary and Joseph brought the baby Jesus to the Temple to do what the law said they must do, [28]Simeon took the baby in his arms and thanked God:

[29]"Now, Lord, you can let me, your servant,
 die in peace as you said.
[30]With my own eyes I have seen your
 salvation,
[31] which you prepared before all people.
[32]It is a light for the non-Jewish people to
 see
 and an honor for your people, the
 Israelites."

[33]Jesus' father and mother were amazed at what Simeon had said about him. [34]Then Simeon blessed them and said to Mary, "God has chosen this child to cause the fall and rise of many in Israel. He will be a sign from God that many people will not accept [35]so that the thoughts of many will be made known. And the things that will happen will make your heart sad, too."

Anna Sees Jesus

[36]There was a prophetess, Anna, from the family of Phanuel in the tribe of Asher. Anna was very old. She had once been married for seven years. [37]Then her husband died, and she was a widow for eighty-four years. Anna never left the Temple but worshiped God, going without food and praying day and night. [38]Standing there at that time, she thanked God and spoke about Jesus to all who were waiting for God to free Jerusalem.

Joseph and Mary Return Home

[39]When Joseph and Mary had done everything the law of the Lord commanded, they went home to Nazareth, their own town in Galilee. [40]The little child grew and became strong. He was filled with wisdom, and God's goodness was upon him.

Jesus As a Boy

[41]Every year Jesus' parents went to Jerusalem for the Passover Feast. [42]When he was twelve years old, they went to the feast as they always did. [43]After the feast days were over, they started home. The boy Jesus stayed behind in Jerusalem, but his parents did not know it. [44]Thinking that Jesus was with them in the group, they traveled for a whole day. Then they began to look for him among their family and friends. [45]When they did not find him, they went back to Jerusalem to look for him there. [46]After three days they found Jesus sitting in the Temple with the teachers, listening to them and asking them questions. [47]All who heard him were amazed at his understanding and answers. [48]When Jesus' parents saw him, they were astonished. His mother said to him, "Son, why did you do this to us? Your father and I were very worried about you and have been looking for you."

[49]Jesus said to them, "Why were you looking for me? Didn't you know that I must be in my Father's house?" [50]But they did not understand the meaning of what he said.

[51]Jesus went with them to Nazareth and was obedient to them. But his mother kept in her mind all that had happened. [52]Jesus became wiser and grew physically. People liked him, and he pleased God.

The Preaching of John

3 It was the fifteenth year of the rule of Tiberius Caesar. These men were under Caesar: Pontius Pilate, the ruler of Judea; Herod, the ruler of Galilee; Philip, Herod's brother, the ruler of Iturea and Traconitis; and Lysanias, the ruler of Abilene. [2]Annas and Caiaphas were the high priests. At this time, the word of God came to John son of Zechariah in the desert. [3]He went all over the area around the Jordan River preaching a baptism of changed hearts and lives for the forgiveness of sins. [4]As it is written in the book of Isaiah the prophet:

"This is a voice of one
 who calls out in the desert:
'Prepare the way for the Lord.
 Make the road straight for him.
[5]Every valley should be filled in,
 and every mountain and hill should be
 made flat.
Roads with turns should be made
 straight,

2:22 pure The Law of Moses said that forty days after a Jewish woman gave birth to a son, she must be cleansed by a ceremony at the Temple. Read Leviticus 12:2–8. 2:23 "Every...Lord." Quotation from Exodus 13:2. 2:24 "You...pigeons." Quotation from Leviticus 12:8.

78

Q: Are there degrees of sin?

A: In a word, no. All sin misses the mark of God's holiness and divine will, and whether you miss it by a little or a lot is not the issue. Sin is sin. However, while all sin is the same before God, the human consequences for sin vary (Romans 6:23).

and rough roads should be made smooth.
⁶And all people will know about the salvation of God!' "

Isaiah 40:3—5

⁷To the crowds of people who came to be baptized by John, he said, "You are all snakes! Who warned you to run away from God's coming punishment? ⁸Do the things that show you really have changed your hearts and lives. Don't begin to say to yourselves, 'Abraham is our father.' I tell you that God could make children for Abraham from these rocks. ⁹The ax is now ready to cut down the trees, and every tree that does not produce good fruit will be cut down and thrown into the fire.'"

¹⁰The people asked John, "Then what should we do?"

¹¹John answered, "If you have two shirts, share with the person who does not have one. If you have food, share that also."

¹²Even tax collectors came to John to be baptized. They said to him, "Teacher, what should we do?"

¹³John said to them, "Don't take more taxes from people than you have been ordered to take."

¹⁴The soldiers asked John, "What about us? What should we do?"

John said to them, "Don't force people to give you money, and don't lie about them. Be satisfied with the pay you get."

¹⁵Since the people were hoping for the Christ to come, they wondered if John might be the one.

¹⁶John answered everyone, "I baptize you with water, but there is one coming who is greater than I am. I am not good enough to untie his sandals. He will baptize you with the Holy Spirit and fire. ¹⁷He will come ready to clean the grain, separating the good grain from the chaff. He will put the good part of the grain into his barn, but he will burn the chaff with a fire that cannot be put out.'" ¹⁸And John continued to preach the Good News, saying many other things to encourage the people.

¹⁹But John spoke against Herod, the governor, because of his sin with Herodias, the wife of Herod's brother, and because of the many other evil things Herod did. ²⁰So Herod did something even worse: He put John in prison.

Jesus Is Baptized by John

²¹When all the people were being baptized by John, Jesus also was baptized. While Jesus was praying, heaven opened ²²and the Holy Spirit came down on him in the form of a dove. Then a voice came from heaven, saying, "You are my Son, whom I love, and I am very pleased with you."

The Family History of Jesus

²³When Jesus began his ministry, he was about thirty years old. People thought that Jesus was Joseph's son.

Joseph was the son" of Heli.
²⁴Heli was the son of Matthat.
Matthat was the son of Levi.
Levi was the son of Melki.
Melki was the son of Jannai.
Jannai was the son of Joseph.
²⁵Joseph was the son of Mattathias.
Mattathias was the son of Amos.
Amos was the son of Nahum.
Nahum was the son of Esli.
Esli was the son of Naggai.
²⁶Naggai was the son of Maath.
Maath was the son of Mattathias.
Mattathias was the son of Semein.
Semein was the son of Josech.
Josech was the son of Joda.
²⁷Joda was the son of Joanan.

▶ Get Aligned
Luke 3:21—22

WHO WOULDN'T WANT TO HEAR his dad say how proud he is of him? A father's approval has always carried tremendous weight, whether it is regarding a tough decision or simply an assessment of character. The words of a father matter! And that's why it is so important, if you have children, to shower them with affirming words of love.

It would've been easy for God to show his endorsement of Jesus in a private way. After all, the two were in constant communication. The Father could've simply conveyed his love for his Son via the Spirit they shared. Instead, he chose to publicly voice his pleasure, proving to all those around that this was undoubtedly the Son of God.

The New Testament establishes that our faith in Jesus makes us sons of God. For men whose dads were absent or negligent, this is especially good news. Yet, for those who have godly fathers, it is an added reminder of God's goodness. Because of Jesus, God is fundamentally pleased with us. Absolutely nothing can separate us from the Father's divine pleasure in each of us as men (see Romans 8:38–39).

3:9 The ax...fire. This means that God is ready to punish his people who do not obey him. **3:17 He will...out.** This means that Jesus will come to separate good people from bad people, saving the good and punishing the bad. **3:23 son** "Son" in Jewish lists of ancestors can sometimes mean grandson or more distant relative.

FOR Men Only

HUMOR Ask any woman what characteristics she looks for and likes in a man, and more than likely, one of them will be "a sense of humor." Now it is important to distinguish between laughing *with* someone and laughing *at* him. Whereas some people's idea of humor is playing jokes on others or poking fun at their expense, genuine humor involves seeing and celebrating the lighter side of life. So whether or not you possess the timing of a comic genius, simply reveling in life and learning to laugh at your own foibles not only reveals your humanity but also a good sense of humor.

Joanan was the son of Rhesa.
Rhesa was the son of Zerubbabel.
Zerubbabel was the grandson of Shealtiel.
Shealtiel was the son of Neri.
28 Neri was the son of Melki.
Melki was the son of Addi.
Addi was the son of Cosam.
Cosam was the son of Elmadam.
Elmadam was the son of Er.
29 Er was the son of Joshua.
Joshua was the son of Eliezer.
Eliezer was the son of Jorim.
Jorim was the son of Matthat.
Matthat was the son of Levi.
30 Levi was the son of Simeon.
Simeon was the son of Judah.
Judah was the son of Joseph.
Joseph was the son of Jonam.
Jonam was the son of Eliakim.
31 Eliakim was the son of Melea.
Melea was the son of Menna.
Menna was the son of Mattatha.
Mattatha was the son of Nathan.
Nathan was the son of David.
32 David was the son of Jesse.
Jesse was the son of Obed.
Obed was the son of Boaz.
Boaz was the son of Salmon."
Salmon was the son of Nahshon.
33 Nahshon was the son of Amminadab.
Amminadab was the son of Admin.
Admin was the son of Arni.
Arni was the son of Hezron.
Hezron was the son of Perez.
Perez was the son of Judah.
34 Judah was the son of Jacob.
Jacob was the son of Isaac.
Isaac was the son of Abraham.
Abraham was the son of Terah.
Terah was the son of Nahor.
35 Nahor was the son of Serug.
Serug was the son of Reu.
Reu was the son of Peleg.
Peleg was the son of Eber.
Eber was the son of Shelah.
36 Shelah was the son of Cainan.
Cainan was the son of Arphaxad.
Arphaxad was the son of Shem.
Shem was the son of Noah.
Noah was the son of Lamech.
37 Lamech was the son of Methuselah.
Methuselah was the son of Enoch.
Enoch was the son of Jared.
Jared was the son of Mahalalel.
Mahalalel was the son of Kenan.
38 Kenan was the son of Enosh.
Enosh was the son of Seth.
Seth was the son of Adam.
Adam was the son of God.

Jesus Is Tempted by the Devil

4 Jesus, filled with the Holy Spirit, returned from the Jordan River. The Spirit led Jesus into the desert 2 where the devil tempted Jesus for forty days. Jesus ate nothing during that time, and when those days were ended, he was very hungry.

3 The devil said to Jesus, "If you are the Son of God, tell this rock to become bread."

4 Jesus answered, "It is written in the Scriptures: 'A person does not live on bread alone.' ""

5 Then the devil took Jesus and showed him all the kingdoms of the world in an instant. 6 The devil said to Jesus, "I will give you all these kingdoms and all their power and glory. It has all been given to me, and I can give it to anyone I wish. 7 If you worship me, then it will all be yours."

8 Jesus answered, "It is written in the Scriptures: 'You must worship the Lord your God and serve only him.' ""

>> **3:32 Salmon** Some Greek copies read "Sala."   **4:4 'A person...alone.'** Quotation from Deuteronomy 8:3.   **4:8 'You...him.'** Quotation from Deuteronomy 6:13.

⁹Then the devil led Jesus to Jerusalem and put him on a high place of the Temple. He said to Jesus, "If you are the Son of God, jump down. ¹⁰It is written in the Scriptures:

'He has put his angels in charge of you
  to watch over you.'   *Psalm 91:11*

¹¹It is also written:

'They will catch you in their hands
  so that you will not hit your foot on a rock.' "   *Psalm 91:12*

¹²Jesus answered, "But it also says in the Scriptures: 'Do not test the Lord your God.' "ⁿ

¹³After the devil had tempted Jesus in every way, he left him to wait until a better time.

Jesus Teaches the People

¹⁴Jesus returned to Galilee in the power of the Holy Spirit, and stories about him spread all through the area. ¹⁵He began to teach in their synagogues, and everyone praised him.

¹⁶Jesus traveled to Nazareth, where he had grown up. On the Sabbath day he went to the synagogue, as he always did, and stood up to read. ¹⁷The book of Isaiah the prophet was given to him. He opened the book and found the place where this is written:

¹⁸"The Lord has put his Spirit in me,
  because he appointed me to tell the Good News to the poor.
He has sent me to tell the captives they are free
  and to tell the blind that they can see again.   *Isaiah 61:1*
God sent me to free those who have been treated unfairly   *Isaiah 58:6*
¹⁹   and to announce the time when the Lord will show his
    kindness."   *Isaiah 61:2*

²⁰Jesus closed the book, gave it back to the assistant, and sat down. Everyone in the synagogue was watching Jesus closely. ²¹He began to say to them, "While you heard these words just now, they were coming true!"

²²All the people spoke well of Jesus and were amazed at the words of grace he spoke. They asked, "Isn't this Joseph's son?"

²³Jesus said to them, "I know that you will tell me the old saying: 'Doctor, heal yourself.' You want to say, 'We heard about the things you did in Capernaum. Do those things here in your own town!' "

²⁴Then Jesus said, "I tell you the truth, a prophet is not accepted in his hometown. ²⁵But I tell you the truth, there were many widows in Israel during the time of Elijah. It did not rain in Israel for three and one-half years, and there was no food anywhere in the whole country. ²⁶But Elijah was sent to none of those widows, only to a widow in Zarephath, a town in Sidon. ²⁷And there were many with skin diseases living in Israel during the time of the prophet Elisha. But none of them were healed, only Naaman, who was from the country of Syria."

²⁸When all the people in the synagogue heard these things, they became very angry. ²⁹They got up, forced Jesus out of town, and took him to the edge of the cliff on which the town was built. They planned to throw him off the edge, ³⁰but Jesus walked through the crowd and went on his way.

Jesus Forces Out an Evil Spirit

³¹Jesus went to Capernaum, a city in Galilee, and on the Sabbath day, he taught the people. ³²They were amazed at his teaching, because he spoke with authority. ³³In the synagogue a man who had within him an evil spirit shouted in a loud voice, ³⁴"Jesus of Nazareth! What do you want with us? Did you come to destroy us? I know who you are—God's Holy One!"

³⁵Jesus commanded the evil spirit, "Be quiet! Come out of the man!" The evil spirit threw the man down to the ground before all the people and then left the man without hurting him.

³⁶The people were amazed and said to each other, "What does this mean? With authority and power he commands evil spirits, and they come out." ³⁷And so the news about Jesus spread to every place in the whole area.

Jesus Heals Many People

³⁸Jesus left the synagogue and went to the home of Simon.ⁿ Simon's mother-in-law was sick with a high fever, and they asked Jesus to help her. ³⁹He came to her side and commanded the fever to leave. It left her, and immediately she got up and began serving them.

⁴⁰When the sun went down, the people brought those who were sick to Jesus. Putting his hands on each sick person, he healed every one of them. ⁴¹Demons came out of many people, shouting, "You are the Son of God." But Jesus commanded the demons and would not allow them to speak, because they knew Jesus was the Christ.

⁴²At daybreak, Jesus went to a lonely place, but the people looked for him. When they found him, they tried to keep him from leaving. ⁴³But Jesus said to them, "I must preach about God's kingdom to other towns, too. This is why I was sent."

⁴⁴Then he kept on preaching in the synagogues of Judea.ⁿ

Jesus' First Followers

5 One day while Jesus was standing beside Lake Galilee, many people were pressing all around him to hear the word of God. ²Jesus saw two boats at the shore of the lake. The fishermen had left

>> live the life

Luke 4:18

The Principle > Share faith in practical ways.

Practicing It > You don't just share your faith by your words, but also through your actions. Sign up with a local relief agency to serve the poor and homeless in your community. Demonstrate the Good News to them by meeting their needs in practical ways.

>> 4:12 'Do...God.' Quotation from Deuteronomy 6:16.   4:38 Simon Simon's other name was Peter.   4:44 Judea Some Greek copies read "Galilee."

81

THINK ABOUT IT Luke 5:31–32

IT IS HUMAN NATURE TO DIVIDE OURSELVES into groups, whether it is the sports clique in high school or the country club when we retire. There is nothing wrong with choosing our associates, but it becomes a concern when it consumes too much of our attention or causes us to discriminate against others.

Jesus was criticized because he associated with sinners. Even during that day, people were busy comparing themselves and striving to associate with the teachers of the law and other important people. One day Jesus told a tax collector to follow him. Tax collectors were at the bottom of the social register, yet Jesus went to his home for a meal.

The teachers of the law were critical of Jesus' choice and asked him why he associated with such people. He said, "It is not the healthy people who need a doctor, but the sick. I have not come to invite good people but sinners to change their hearts and lives." Our challenge is to break out of our comfort zones and to help others, also.

every town in Galilee and Judea and from Jerusalem were there. The Lord was giving Jesus the power to heal people. [18]Just then, some men were carrying on a mat a man who was paralyzed. They tried to bring him in and put him down before Jesus. [19]But because there were so many people there, they could not find a way in. So they went up on the roof and lowered the man on his mat through the ceiling into the middle of the crowd right before Jesus. [20]Seeing their faith, Jesus said, "Friend, your sins are forgiven."

[21]The Jewish teachers of the law and the Pharisees thought to themselves, "Who is this man who is speaking as if he were God? Only God can forgive sins."

{ Book of the Month }

them and were washing their nets. [3]Jesus got into one of the boats, the one that belonged to Simon, and asked him to push off a little from the land. Then Jesus sat down and continued to teach the people from the boat.

[4]When Jesus had finished speaking, he said to Simon, "Take the boat into deep water, and put your nets in the water to catch some fish."

[5]Simon answered, "Master, we worked hard all night trying to catch fish, and we caught nothing. But you say to put the nets in the water, so I will." [6]When the fishermen did as Jesus told them, they caught so many fish that the nets began to break. [7]They called to their partners in the other boat to come and help them. They came and filled both boats so full that they were almost sinking.

[8]When Simon Peter saw what had happened, he bowed down before Jesus and said, "Go away from me, Lord. I am a sinful man!" [9]He and the other fishermen were amazed at the many fish they caught, as were [10]James and John, the sons of Zebedee, Simon's partners.

Jesus said to Simon, "Don't be afraid. From now on you will fish for people." [11]When the men brought their boats to the shore, they left everything and followed Jesus.

Jesus Heals a Sick Man

[12]When Jesus was in one of the towns, there was a man covered with a skin disease. When he saw Jesus, he bowed before him and begged him, "Lord, you can heal me if you will."

[13]Jesus reached out his hand and touched the man and said, "I will. Be healed!" Immediately the disease disappeared. [14]Then Jesus said, "Don't tell anyone about this, but go and show yourself to the priest and offer a gift for your healing, as Moses commanded. This will show the people what I have done."

[15]But the news about Jesus spread even more. Many people came to hear Jesus and to be healed of their sicknesses, [16]but Jesus often slipped away to be alone so he could pray.

Jesus Heals a Paralyzed Man

[17]One day as Jesus was teaching the people, the Pharisees and teachers of the law from

The Five Love Languages
by Gary Chapman

Don't let the purple cover fool you—Gary Chapman's book is a key to understanding the most important relationships in a man's life. Chapman divides what he calls love languages into five types, based on the five ways people prefer to receive love: physical touch, words of affirmation, acts of service, quality time, and receiving gifts. If you crave physical touch, you probably tend to show your love that way, too. Yet, a husband who understands his wife's love language—especially if it's different from his own—communicates more effectively and gives love the way she needs to receive it.

 5:3 Simon Simon's other name was Peter. **5:14 show…priest** The Law of Moses said a priest must say when a Jewish person with a skin disease was well. **5:14 Moses commanded** Read about this in Leviticus 14:1–32.

82

>>February

QUOTE OF THE MONTH:
"Action springs not from thought, but from a readiness for responsibility."
—Dietrich Bonhoeffer

1

2
Celebrate **Groundhog Day** by watching the movie of the same name.

3

4
Attend a time management seminar.

5

6
Alan Shepard hit the first golf ball off the moon on this day in 1971.

7

8
Pray for a person of influence: Today is journalist **Ted Koppel's** birthday.

9

10
Read the **Book of Philippians** and practice praising God.

11
Go skiing with some buddies.

12

13
Pray for a person of influence: Today is musician **Peter Gabriel's** birthday.

14
Treat your significant other to a special dinner.

15

16

17
Listen to your favorite worship music.

18

19
Memorize John 10:10.

20

21

22
Pray for a person of influence: Today is politician **Ted Kennedy's** birthday.

23
Go for a brisk outdoor walk to get your blood pumping.

24
Pray for a person of influence: Today is entrepreneur **Steven Jobs's** birthday.

25

26

27

28
Get a jump on your taxes online at www.irs.gov.

²²But Jesus knew what they were thinking and said, "Why are you thinking these things? ²³Which is easier: to say, 'Your sins are forgiven,' or to say, 'Stand up and walk'? ²⁴But I will prove to you that the Son of Man has authority on earth to forgive sins." So Jesus said to the paralyzed man, "I tell you, stand up, take your mat, and go home."

²⁵At once the man stood up before them, picked up his mat, and went home, praising God. ²⁶All the people were fully amazed and began to praise God. They were filled with much respect and said, "Today we have seen amazing things!"

Levi Follows Jesus

²⁷After this, Jesus went out and saw a tax collector named Levi sitting in the tax collector's booth. Jesus said to him, "Follow me!" ²⁸So Levi got up, left everything, and followed him.

²⁹Then Levi gave a big dinner for Jesus at his house. Many tax collectors and other people were eating there, too. ³⁰But the Pharisees and the men who taught the law for the Pharisees began to complain to Jesus' followers, "Why do you eat and drink with tax collectors and sinners?"

³¹Jesus answered them, "It is not the healthy people who need a doctor, but the sick. ³²I have not come to invite good people but sinners to change their hearts and lives."

Jesus Answers a Question

³³They said to Jesus, "John's followers often fast* for a certain time and pray, just as the Pharisees do. But your followers eat and drink all the time."

³⁴Jesus said to them, "You cannot make the friends of the bridegroom fast while he is still with them. ³⁵But the time will come when the bridegroom will be taken away from them, and then they will fast."

³⁶Jesus told them this story: "No one takes cloth off a new coat to cover a hole in an old coat. Otherwise, he ruins the new coat, and the cloth from the new coat will not be the same as the old cloth. ³⁷Also, no one ever pours new wine into old leather bags. Otherwise, the new wine will break the bags, the wine will spill out, and the leather bags will be ruined. ³⁸New wine must be put into new leather bags. ³⁹No one after drinking old wine wants new wine, because he says, 'The old wine is better.'"

Jesus Is Lord over the Sabbath

6 One Sabbath day Jesus was walking through some fields of grain. His followers picked the heads of grain, rubbed them in their hands, and ate them. ²Some Pharisees said, "Why do you do what is not lawful on the Sabbath day?"

³Jesus answered, "Have you not read what David did when he and those with him were hungry? ⁴He went into God's house and took and ate the holy bread, which is lawful only for priests to eat. And he gave some to the people who were with him." ⁵Then Jesus said to the Pharisees, "The Son of Man is Lord of the Sabbath day."

Change >> Your WORLD

CHRISTIAN CAMP AND CONFERENCE ASSOCIATION

There is something life changing about going to camp each summer. At a Christian camping program, children are able to grow in their faith, and many make a first time decision at these meetings. The Christian Camp and Conference Association (CCCA) began in the late 1940s and early 1950s as an informal group to solve common problems and gather new ideas. Today, CCCA is the largest of eighteen autonomous associations on six continents and represents most major denominations and church associations. Each year, nearly eight million people are involved in the various camping programs and conferences, and tens of thousands come to Christ each year.

To change your world, visit www.cciusa.org.

Jesus Heals a Man's Hand

⁶On another Sabbath day Jesus went into the synagogue and was teaching, and a man with a crippled right hand was there. ⁷The teachers of the law and the Pharisees were watching closely to see if Jesus would heal on the Sabbath day so they could accuse him. ⁸But he knew what they were thinking, and he said to the man with the crippled hand, "Stand up here in the middle of everyone." The man got up and stood there. ⁹Then Jesus said to them, "I ask you, which is lawful on the Sabbath day: to do good or to do evil, to save a life or to destroy it?" ¹⁰Jesus looked around at all of them and said to the man, "Hold out your hand." The man held out his hand, and it was healed. ¹¹But the Pharisees and the teachers of the law were very angry and discussed with each other what they could do to Jesus.

Jesus Chooses His Apostles

¹²At that time Jesus went off to a mountain to pray, and he spent the night praying to God. ¹³The next morning, Jesus called his followers

>> 5:33 **fast** The people would give up eating for a special time of prayer and worship to God. It was also done to show sadness and disappointment.

to him and chose twelve of them, whom he named apostles: [14]Simon (Jesus named him Peter), his brother Andrew, James, John, Philip, Bartholomew, [15]Matthew, Thomas, James son of Alphaeus, Simon (called the Zealot), [16]Judas son of James, and Judas Iscariot, who later turned Jesus over to his enemies.

Jesus Teaches and Heals

[17]Jesus and the apostles came down from the mountain, and he stood on level ground. A large group of his followers was there, as well as many people from all around Judea, Jerusalem, and the seacoast cities of Tyre and Sidon. [18]They all came to hear Jesus teach and to be healed of their sicknesses, and he healed those who were troubled by evil spirits. [19]All the people were trying to touch Jesus, because power was coming from him and healing them all.

[20]Jesus looked at his followers and said,

"You people who are poor are blessed,
    because the kingdom of God belongs to you.
[21]You people who are now hungry are blessed,
    because you will be satisfied.
You people who are now crying are blessed,
    because you will laugh with joy.

[22]"People will hate you, shut you out, insult you, and say you are evil because you follow the Son of Man. But when they do, you will be blessed. [23]Be full of joy at that time, because you have a great reward in heaven. Their ancestors did the same things to the prophets.

[24]"But how terrible it will be for you who are rich,
    because you have had your easy life.
[25]How terrible it will be for you who are full now,
    because you will be hungry.
How terrible it will be for you who are laughing now,
    because you will be sad and cry.

[26]"How terrible when everyone says only good things about you, because their ancestors said the same things about the false prophets.

Love Your Enemies

[27]"But I say to you who are listening, love your enemies. Do good to those who hate you, [28]bless those who curse you, pray for those who are cruel to you. [29]If anyone slaps you on one cheek, offer him the other cheek, too. If someone takes your coat, do not stop him

from taking your shirt. [30]Give to everyone who asks you, and when someone takes something that is yours, don't ask for it back. [31]Do to others what you would want them to do to you. [32]If you love only the people who love you, what praise should you get? Even sinners love the people who love them. [33]If you do good only to those who do good to you, what praise should you get? Even sinners do that! [34]If you lend things to people, always hoping to get something back, what praise should you get? Even sinners lend to other sinners so that they can get back the same amount! [35]But love your enemies, do good to them, and lend to them without hoping to get anything back. Then you will have a great reward, and you will be children of the Most High God, because he is kind even to people who are ungrateful and full of sin. [36]Show mercy, just as your Father shows mercy.

Q: What happens after we die?

A: The Bible tells us that after you die, your spirit is carried away to appear before God for judgment. Those who have put their faith in Jesus are welcomed into heaven. Those who have not placed their faith in Christ spend eternity in hell (Matthew 25:31–46).

Look at Yourselves

[37]"Don't judge others, and you will not be judged. Don't accuse others of being guilty, and you will not be accused of being guilty. Forgive, and you will be forgiven. [38]Give, and you will receive. You will be given much. Pressed down, shaken together, and running over, it will spill into your lap. The way you give to others is the way God will give to you."

[39]Jesus told them this story: "Can a blind person lead another blind person? No! Both of them will fall into a ditch. [40]A student is not better than the teacher, but the student who has been fully trained will be like the teacher.

[41]"Why do you notice the little piece of dust in your friend's eye, but you don't notice the big piece of wood in your own eye? [42]How can you say to your friend, 'Friend, let me take that little piece of dust out of your eye' when you cannot see that big piece of wood in your own eye! You hypocrite! First, take the wood out of your own eye. Then you will see clearly to take the dust out of your friend's eye.

Two Kinds of Fruit

[43]"A good tree does not produce bad fruit, nor does a bad tree produce good fruit. [44]Each tree is known by its own fruit. People don't gather figs from thornbushes, and they don't get grapes from bushes.

>> live the life

Luke 6:27–28

The Principle > Love your enemies.

Practicing It > Think of one or two people in your life who have mistreated you or those you love. Begin to pray for them today, asking God to show you how you can extend love to them.

[45]Good people bring good things out of the good they stored in their hearts. But evil people bring evil things out of the evil they stored in their hearts. People speak the things that are in their hearts.

Two Kinds of People

[46]"Why do you call me, 'Lord, Lord,' but do not do what I say? [47]I will show you what everyone is like who comes to me and hears my words and obeys. [48]That person is like a man building a house who dug deep and laid the foundation on rock. When the floods came, the water tried to wash the house away, but it could not shake it, because the house was built well. [49]But the one who hears my words and does not obey is like a man who built his house on the ground without a foundation. When the floods came, the house quickly fell and was completely destroyed."

Jesus Heals a Soldier's Servant

7 When Jesus finished saying all these things to the people, he went to Capernaum. [2]There was an army officer who had a servant who was very important to him. The servant was so sick he was nearly dead. [3]When the officer heard about Jesus, he sent some Jewish elders to him to ask Jesus to come and heal his servant. [4]The men went to Jesus and begged him, saying, "This officer is worthy of your help. [5]He loves our people, and he built us a synagogue."

[6]So Jesus went with the men. He was getting near the officer's house when the officer sent friends to say, "Lord, don't trouble yourself, because I am not worthy to have you come into my house. [7]That is why I did not come to you myself. But you only need to command it, and my servant will be healed. [8]I, too, am a man under the authority of others, and I have soldiers under my command. I tell one soldier, 'Go,' and he goes. I tell another soldier, 'Come,' and he comes. I say to my servant, 'Do this,' and my servant does it."

[9]When Jesus heard this, he was amazed. Turning to the crowd that was following him, he said, "I tell you, this is the greatest faith I have found anywhere, even in Israel."

[10]Those who had been sent to Jesus went back to the house where they found the servant in good health.

Jesus Brings a Man Back to Life

[11]Soon afterwards Jesus went to a town called Nain, and his followers and a large crowd traveled with him. [12]When he came near the town gate, he saw a funeral. A mother, who was a widow, had lost her only son. A large crowd from the town was with the mother while her son was being carried out. [13]When the Lord saw her, he felt very sorry for her and said, "Don't cry." [14]He went up and touched the coffin, and the people who were carrying it stopped. Jesus said, "Young man, I tell you, get up!" [15]And the son sat up and began to talk. Then Jesus gave him back to his mother.

[16]All the people were amazed and began praising God, saying, "A great prophet has come to us! God has come to help his people."

[17]This news about Jesus spread through all Judea and into all the places around there.

John Asks a Question

[18]John's followers told him about all these things. He called for two of his followers [19]and sent them to the Lord to ask, "Are you the One who is to come, or should we wait for someone else?"

[20]When the men came to Jesus, they said, "John the Baptist sent us to you with this question: 'Are you the One who is to come, or should we wait for someone else?' "

[21]At that time, Jesus healed many people of their sicknesses, diseases, and evil spirits, and he gave sight to many blind people. [22]Then Jesus answered John's followers, "Go tell John what you saw and heard here. The blind can see, the crippled can walk, and people with skin diseases are healed. The deaf can hear, the dead are raised to life,

Q: What about sex before marriage?

A: God created sex as a wonderful blessing, but he has restricted its use to the protective environment of a marriage relationship. God designed sex to be the physical expression of the spiritual act of marriage in which two mates become one (1 Thessalonians 4:3).

▶ Get Aligned

Luke 7:9

IMAGINE THE PRIDE THIS OFFICER must have felt in hearing Jesus' words: "This is the greatest faith I have found anywhere." That's high praise. But what was so special about this man's faith? The answer is simple: he believed without seeing. He didn't need proof to know that Christ was who he said he was and, therefore, could instantly heal his servant. For most of his ministry, Jesus was surrounded by people who claimed to believe in him, yet doubted.

The officer had in all probability never met Jesus. Still, due to his experience with exercising authority in the army, he understood the awesome power in which Jesus walked. He knew that Jesus could merely speak the word and his servant would be well.

That's a faith we can admire. It is also one we can emulate. Though we have the Bible to prove who God is and all he has done for us, he remains unseen to our natural eye. Believing in him still requires a type of blind faith. Yet taking that step of trust always gets unbelievable results.

and the Good News is preached to the poor. ²³Those who do not stumble in their faith because of me are blessed!"

²⁴When John's followers left, Jesus began talking to the people about John: "What did you go out into the desert to see? A reed* blown by the wind? ²⁵What did you go out to see? A man dressed in fine clothes? No, people who have fine clothes and much wealth live in kings' palaces. ²⁶But what did you go out to see? A prophet? Yes, and I tell you, John is more than a prophet. ²⁷This was written about him:

'I will send my messenger ahead of you,
    who will prepare the way for you.'   *Malachi 3:1*

²⁸I tell you, John is greater than any other person ever born, but even the least important person in the kingdom of God is greater than John."

²⁹(When the people, including the tax collectors, heard this, they all agreed that God's teaching was good, because they had been baptized by John. ³⁰But the Pharisees and experts on the law refused to accept God's plan for themselves; they did not let John baptize them.)

³¹Then Jesus said, "What shall I say about the people of this time? What are they like? ³²They are like children sitting in the marketplace, calling to one another and saying,

'We played music for you, but you did not dance;
    we sang a sad song, but you did not cry.'

³³John the Baptist came and did not eat bread or drink wine, and you say, 'He has a demon in him.' ³⁴The Son of Man came eating and drinking, and you say, 'Look at him! He eats too much and drinks too much wine, and he is a friend of tax collectors and sinners!' ³⁵But wisdom is proved to be right by what it does."

A Woman Washes Jesus' Feet

³⁶One of the Pharisees asked Jesus to eat with him, so Jesus went into the Pharisee's house and sat at the table. ³⁷A sinful woman in the town learned that Jesus was eating at the Pharisee's house. So she brought an alabaster jar of perfume ³⁸and stood behind Jesus at his

<<TechSupport>>

IDENTITY THEFT

Some e-mail hoaxes are hard to spot, but they have one thing in common. They are asking for something no legitimate business would ask for, and that is your password. If you suspect that your personal identifying information has been stolen or compromised, immediately report it to the authorities and to the company that was the subject of the fraud. Meanwhile, remind yourself that when you became a Christian, you gained a new identity in Christ that supersedes your former identity.

946-0-784

feet, crying. She began to wash his feet with her tears, and she dried them with her hair, kissing them many times and rubbing them with the perfume. ³⁹When the Pharisee who asked Jesus to come to his house saw this, he thought to himself, "If Jesus were a prophet, he would know that the woman touching him is a sinner!"

⁴⁰Jesus said to the Pharisee, "Simon, I have something to say to you."

Simon said, "Teacher, tell me."

⁴¹Jesus said, "Two people owed money to the same banker. One owed five hundred coins* and the other owed fifty. ⁴²They had no money to pay what they owed, but the banker told both of them they did not have to pay him. Which person will love the banker more?"

⁴³Simon, the Pharisee, answered, "I think it would be the one who owed him the most money."

➔ The Bottom Line

Selling Your Home: Curb Appeal

WITH ONE IN EVERY FIVE AMERICANS MOVING ANNUALLY, chances are you won't live in your home forever. If you own a house and a move is in the picture, remember curb appeal is vital to a sale. And it's not just how the front looks, but the back as well. Trimming shrubbery, painting doors and shutters, cleaning windows, mowing grass, and planting flowers are all inexpensive steps that can put your house at the top of a buyer's list. Sprucing up your home's curb appeal makes a deal much more likely and a sale more favorable for you.

➤➤ **7:24 reed** It means that John was not ordinary or weak like grass blown by the wind.   **7:41 coins** Roman denarii. One coin was the average pay for one day's work.

87

Men of Valor
CLEOPAS: Good News Messenger

Cleopas and an unnamed friend of his encountered Jesus on the road from Jerusalem to Emmaus, a pivotal New Testament event depicted in Luke 24:13–35. The passage describes how the two men were discussing Christ's crucifixion when Jesus came near and walked with them, asking, "What are these things you are talking about while you walk?" After they described their efforts to find Christ at his tomb, Jesus called them "foolish" and explained everything the prophets had said about him in the Scriptures. Once he left, the men recognized they had just seen Jesus and rushed to Jerusalem to tell the apostles Christ had risen from the dead. Cleopas helped deliver history's best news.

Jesus said to Simon, "You are right." ⁴⁴Then Jesus turned toward the woman and said to Simon, "Do you see this woman? When I came into your house, you gave me no water for my feet, but she washed my feet with her tears and dried them with her hair. ⁴⁵You gave me no kiss of greeting, but she has been kissing my feet since I came in. ⁴⁶You did not put oil on my head, but she poured perfume on my feet. ⁴⁷I tell you that her many sins are forgiven, so she showed great love. But the person who is forgiven only a little will love only a little."

⁴⁸Then Jesus said to her, "Your sins are forgiven."

⁴⁹The people sitting at the table began to say among themselves, "Who is this who even forgives sins?"

⁵⁰Jesus said to the woman, "Because you believed, you are saved from your sins. Go in peace."

The Group with Jesus

8 After this, while Jesus was traveling through some cities and small towns, he preached and told the Good News about God's kingdom. The twelve apostles were with him, ²and also some women who had been healed of sicknesses and evil spirits: Mary, called Magdalene, from whom seven demons had gone out; ³Joanna, the wife of Cuza (the manager of Herod's house); Susanna; and many others. These women used their own money to help Jesus and his apostles.

A Story About Planting Seed

⁴When a great crowd was gathered, and people were coming to Jesus from every town, he told them this story:

⁵"A farmer went out to plant his seed. While he was planting, some seed fell by the road. People walked on the seed, and the birds ate it up. ⁶Some seed fell on rock, and when it began to grow, it died because it had no water. ⁷Some seed fell among thorny weeds, but the weeds grew up with it and choked the good plants. ⁸And some seed fell on good ground and grew and made a hundred times more."

As Jesus finished the story, he called out, "Let those with ears use them and listen!"

⁹Jesus' followers asked him what this story meant.

¹⁰Jesus said, "You have been chosen to know the secrets about the kingdom of God. But I use stories to speak to other people so that:

'They will look, but they may not see.
They will listen, but they may not understand.'   *Isaiah 6:9*

¹¹"This is what the story means: The seed is God's message. ¹²The seed that fell beside the road is like the people who hear God's teaching, but the devil comes and takes it away from them so they cannot believe it and be saved. ¹³The seed that fell on rock is like those who hear God's teaching and accept it gladly, but they don't allow the teaching to go deep into their lives. They believe for a while, but

⊙ Sexcess:
GETTING INTIMATE

The act of lovemaking tends to be more of a physical one for men and typically a more emotional one for women. As a result, when it is said that men fear intimacy, what is actually meant is that men have more trouble getting emotionally intimate than they do getting physically intimate. Therein lies the rub, so to speak. If we are going to truly connect with our better halves, we had better learn to share our thoughts and feelings with them, or else risk being banished to the couch until we do. Sex is the most intimate act of all, so expressing yourself verbally needn't be a big deal.

when trouble comes, they give up. ¹⁴The seed that fell among the thorny weeds is like those who hear God's teaching, but they let the worries, riches, and pleasures of this life keep them from growing and producing good fruit. ¹⁵And the seed that fell on the good ground is like those who hear God's teaching with good, honest hearts and obey it and patiently produce good fruit.

Use What You Have

¹⁶"No one after lighting a lamp covers it with a bowl or hides it under a bed. Instead, the person puts it on a lampstand so those who come in will see the light. ¹⁷Everything that is hidden will become clear, and every secret thing will be made known. ¹⁸So be careful how you listen. Those who have understanding will be given more. But those who do not have understanding, even what they think they have will be taken away from them."

Jesus' True Family

¹⁹Jesus' mother and brothers came to see him, but there was such a crowd they could not get to him. ²⁰Someone said to Jesus, "Your mother and your brothers are standing outside, wanting to see you." ²¹Jesus answered them, "My mother and my brothers are those who listen to God's teaching and obey it!"

Jesus Calms a Storm

²²One day Jesus and his followers got into a boat, and he said to them, "Let's go across the lake." And so they started across. ²³While they were sailing, Jesus fell asleep. A very strong wind blew up on the lake, causing the boat to fill with water, and they were in danger. ²⁴The followers went to Jesus and woke him, saying, "Master! Master! We will drown!"

Jesus got up and gave a command to the wind and the waves. They stopped, and it became calm. ²⁵Jesus said to his followers, "Where is your faith?"

The followers were afraid and amazed and said to each other, "Who is this that commands even the wind and the water, and they obey him?"

A Man with Demons Inside Him

²⁶Jesus and his followers sailed across the lake from Galilee to the area of the Gerasene[n] people. ²⁷When Jesus got out on the land, a man from the town who had demons inside him came to Jesus. For a long time he had worn no clothes and had lived in the burial caves, not in a house. ²⁸When he saw Jesus, he cried out and fell down before him. He said with a loud voice, "What do you want with me, Jesus, Son of the Most High God? I beg you, don't torture me!" ²⁹He said this because Jesus was commanding the evil spirit to come out of the man. Many times it had taken hold of him. Though he had been kept under guard and chained hand and foot, he had broken his chains and had been forced by the demon out into a lonely place.

³⁰Jesus asked him, "What is your name?"

He answered, "Legion,"[n] because many demons were in him. ³¹The demons begged Jesus not to send them into eternal darkness.[n] ³²A

Survival Guide

DOORS: SECURING THE ENTRY

In Matthew 7:7, Jesus said that if we seek God, he will open doors when we knock. But you don't want to open your doors to air drafts and other unwanted guests. If you can run a sheet of paper under your doorway, that means cold air, rain, dirt, and insects can slip through, too. Installing a new threshold can seal the opening and improve the door's appearance. Another solution is to attach a door bottom to seal openings. Weather-stripping around edges will also prevent outside air from entering your home.

Q: What is God like?

A: Because God is infinite, much of what he is like is beyond our finite comprehension. However, the Bible teaches that the best way to understand what God is like is to look at Jesus. Christ is the perfect representation of who God is (Hebrews 1:1-4).

8:26 **Gerasene** From Gerasa, an area southeast of Lake Galilee. The exact location is uncertain and some Greek copies read "Gadarene"; others read "Gergesene." 8:30 **Legion** Means very many. A legion was about five thousand men in the Roman army. 8:31 **eternal darkness** Literally, "the abyss," something like a pit or a hole that has no end.

large herd of pigs was feeding on a hill, and the demons begged Jesus to allow them to go into the pigs. So Jesus allowed them to do this. [33]When the demons came out of the man, they went into the pigs, and the herd ran down the hill into the lake and was drowned.

[34]When the herdsmen saw what had happened, they ran away and told about this in the town and the countryside. [35]And people went to see what had happened. When they came to Jesus, they found the man sitting at Jesus' feet, clothed and in his right mind, because the demons were gone. But the people were frightened. [36]The people who saw this happen told the others how Jesus had made the man well. [37]All the people of the Gerasene country asked Jesus to leave, because they were all very afraid. So Jesus got into the boat and went back to Galilee.

[38]The man whom Jesus had healed begged to go with him, but Jesus sent him away, saying, [39]"Go back home and tell people how much God has done for you." So the man went all over town telling how much Jesus had done for him.

Jesus Gives Life to a Dead Girl and Heals a Sick Woman

[40]When Jesus got back to Galilee, a crowd welcomed him, because everyone was waiting for him. [41]A man named Jairus, a leader of the synagogue, came to Jesus and fell at his feet, begging him to come to his house. [42]Jairus' only daughter, about twelve years old, was dying.

While Jesus was on his way to Jairus' house, the people were crowding all around him. [43]A woman was in the crowd who had been bleeding for twelve years,* but no one was able to heal her. [44]She came up behind Jesus and touched the edge of his coat, and instantly her bleeding stopped. [45]Then Jesus said, "Who touched me?"

When all the people said they had not touched him, Peter said, "Master, the people are all around you and are pushing against you."

[46]But Jesus said, "Someone did touch me, because I felt power go out from me." [47]When the woman saw she could not hide, she came forward, shaking, and fell down before Jesus. While all the people listened, she told why she had touched him and how she had been instantly healed. [48]Jesus said to her, "Dear woman, you are made well because you believed. Go in peace."

[49]While Jesus was still speaking, someone came from the house of the synagogue leader and said to him, "Your daughter is dead. Don't bother the teacher anymore."

[50]When Jesus heard this, he said to Jairus, "Don't be afraid. Just believe, and your daughter will be well."

[51]When Jesus went to the house, he let only Peter, John, James, and the girl's father and mother go inside with him. [52]All the people were crying and feeling sad because the girl was dead, but Jesus said, "Stop crying. She is not dead, only asleep."

[53]The people laughed at Jesus because they knew the girl was dead. [54]But Jesus took hold of her hand and called to her, "My child, stand up!" [55]Her spirit came back into her, and she stood up at once. Then Jesus ordered that she be given something to eat. [56]The girl's parents were amazed, but Jesus told them not to tell anyone what had happened.

Jesus Sends Out the Apostles

9 Jesus called the twelve apostles together and gave them power and authority over all demons and the ability to heal sicknesses. [2]He sent the apostles out to tell about God's kingdom and to heal the sick. [3]He said to them, "Take nothing for your trip, neither a walking stick, bag, bread, money, or extra clothes. [4]When you enter a house, stay there until it is time to leave. [5]If people do not welcome you, shake the dust off of your feet* as you leave the town, as a warning to them."

[6]So the apostles went out and traveled through all the towns, preaching the Good News and healing people everywhere.

Get Fit

EATING YOUR VEGGIES "An apple a day keeps the doctor away." There is more truth to the saying than we once thought. What you eat and drink can definitely make a difference to your health. Eating five to eight servings of fruits and vegetables a day and taking in less saturated fat can improve your health and may reduce the risk of cancer and other chronic diseases. To help increase your fruit and vegetable intake, try selecting a fruit or vegetable you don't normally buy each time you walk through your grocer's produce department. God has provided a wealth of healthy fruits and vegetables to choose from, and you might find a new favorite.

>> **8:43 years** Some Greek copies continue, "and she had spent all the money she had on doctors."   **9:5 shake…feet** A warning. It showed that they had rejected these people.

Herod Is Confused About Jesus

[7]Herod, the governor, heard about all the things that were happening and was confused, because some people said, "John the Baptist has risen from the dead." [8]Others said, "Elijah has come to us." And still others said, "One of the prophets who lived long ago has risen from the dead." [9]Herod said, "I cut off John's head, so who is this man I hear such things about?" And Herod kept trying to see Jesus.

More than Five Thousand Fed

[10]When the apostles returned, they told Jesus everything they had done. Then Jesus took them with him to a town called Bethsaida where they could be alone together. [11]But the people learned where Jesus went and followed him. He welcomed them and talked with them about God's kingdom and healed those who needed to be healed.

[12]Late in the afternoon, the twelve apostles came to Jesus and said, "Send the people away. They need to go to the towns and countryside around here and find places to sleep and something to eat, because no one lives in this place."

[13]But Jesus said to them, "You give them something to eat."

They said, "We have only five loaves of bread and two fish, unless we go buy food for all these people." [14](There were about five thousand men there.)

Jesus said to his followers, "Tell the people to sit in groups of about fifty people."

[15]So the followers did this, and all the people sat down. [16]Then Jesus took the five loaves of bread and two fish, and looking up to heaven, he thanked God for the food. Then he divided the food and gave it to the followers to give to the people. [17]They all ate and were satisfied, and what was left over was gathered up, filling twelve baskets.

Jesus Is the Christ

[18]One time when Jesus was praying alone, his followers were with him, and he asked them, "Who do the people say I am?"

[19]They answered, "Some say you are John the Baptist. Others say you are Elijah.* And others say you are one of the prophets from long ago who has come back to life."

[20]Then Jesus asked, "But who do you say I am?"

Peter answered, "You are the Christ from God."

[21]Jesus warned them not to tell anyone, saying, [22]"The Son of Man must suffer many things. He will be rejected by the Jewish elders, the leading priests, and the teachers of the law. He will be killed and after three days will be raised from the dead."

[23]Jesus said to all of them, "If people want to follow me, they must give up the things they want. They must be willing to give up their lives daily to follow me. [24]Those who want to save their lives will give up true life. But those who give up their lives for me will have true life. [25]It is worthless to have the whole world if they themselves are destroyed or lost. [26]If people are ashamed of me and my teaching, then the Son of Man will be ashamed of them when he comes in his glory and with the glory of the Father and the holy angels. [27]I tell you the truth, some people standing here will see the kingdom of God before they die."

Jesus Talks with Moses and Elijah

[28]About eight days after Jesus said these things, he took Peter, John, and James and went up on a mountain to pray. [29]While Jesus was praying, the appearance of his face changed, and his clothes became shining white. [30]Then two men, Moses and Elijah,* were talking with Jesus. [31]They appeared in heavenly glory, talking about his departure which he would soon bring about in Jerusalem. [32]Peter and the others were very sleepy, but when they awoke fully, they saw the glory of Jesus and the two men standing with him. [33]When Moses and Elijah were about to leave, Peter said to Jesus, "Master, it is good that we are here. Let us make three tents—one for you, one for Moses, and one for Elijah." (Peter did not know what he was talking about.)

[34]While he was saying these things, a cloud came and covered them, and they became afraid as the cloud covered them. [35]A voice came from the cloud, saying, "This is my Son, whom I have chosen. Listen to him!"

People Skills

Listening Closely

When arguing with someone, don't just listen to what he or she is saying; listen for the emotion between the words. For example, if your wife comes to you and starts berating you for not helping out with chores around the house, notice the feeling behind her words. Is she feeling overwhelmed or unsupported? Rather than get defensive about your own busy schedule, speak to the emotion you hear in her voice. Addressing what you hear between the lines will help her feel understood and may derail an argument before it has a chance to build. It might not seem like a big deal, but listening closely is an act of love.

>> **9:19 Elijah** A man who spoke for God and who lived hundreds of years before Christ. See 1 Kings 17. **9:30 Moses and Elijah** Two of the most important Jewish leaders in the past. God had given Moses the Law, and Elijah was an important prophet.

³⁶When the voice finished speaking, only Jesus was there. Peter, John, and James said nothing and told no one at that time what they had seen.

Jesus Heals a Sick Boy

³⁷The next day, when they came down from the mountain, a large crowd met Jesus. ³⁸A man in the crowd shouted to him, "Teacher, please come and look at my son, because he is my only child. ³⁹An evil spirit seizes my son, and suddenly he screams. It causes him to lose control of himself and foam at the mouth. The evil spirit keeps on hurting him and almost never leaves him. ⁴⁰I begged your followers to force the evil spirit out, but they could not do it."

⁴¹Jesus answered, "You people have no faith, and your lives are all wrong. How long must I stay with you and put up with you? Bring your son here."

⁴²While the boy was coming, the demon threw him on the ground and made him lose control of himself. But Jesus gave a strong command to the evil spirit and healed the boy and gave him back to his father. ⁴³All the people were amazed at the great power of God.

Jesus Talks About His Death

While everyone was wondering about all that Jesus did, he said to his followers, ⁴⁴"Don't forget what I tell you now: The Son of Man will be handed over to people." ⁴⁵But the followers did not understand what this meant; the meaning was hidden from them so they could not understand. But they were afraid to ask Jesus about it.

Who Is the Greatest?

⁴⁶Jesus' followers began to have an argument about which one of them was the greatest. ⁴⁷Jesus knew what they were thinking, so he took a little child and stood the child beside him. ⁴⁸Then Jesus said, "Whoever accepts this little child in my name accepts me. And whoever accepts me accepts the One who sent me, because whoever is least among you all is really the greatest."

Anyone Not Against Us Is for Us

⁴⁹John answered, "Master, we saw someone using your name to force demons out of people. We told him to stop, because he does not belong to our group."

⁵⁰But Jesus said to him, "Don't stop him, because whoever is not against you is for you."

A Town Rejects Jesus

⁵¹When the time was coming near for Jesus to depart, he was determined to go to Jerusalem. ⁵²He sent some messengers ahead of him, who went into a town in Samaria to make everything ready for him. ⁵³But the people there would not welcome him, because he was set on going to Jerusalem. ⁵⁴When James and John, followers of Jesus, saw this, they said, "Lord, do you want us to call fire down from heaven and destroy those people?"

⁵⁵But Jesus turned and scolded them. [And Jesus said, "You don't know what kind of spirit you belong to. ⁵⁶The Son of Man did not come to destroy the souls of people but to save them."] Then they went to another town.

Following Jesus

⁵⁷As they were going along the road, someone said to Jesus, "I will follow you any place you go."

⁵⁸Jesus said to them, "The foxes have holes to live in, and the birds have nests, but the Son of Man has no place to rest his head."

⁵⁹Jesus said to another man, "Follow me!"

But he said, "Lord, first let me go and bury my father."

⁶⁰But Jesus said to him, "Let the people who are dead bury their own dead. You must go and tell about the kingdom of God."

⁶¹Another man said, "I will follow you, Lord, but first let me go and say good-bye to my family."

Q: Did God create evil?

A: God is not the author of evil. Because God gives man free will, we have the choice to either obey his commands or reject them. But when we reject them, we are, in effect, choosing evil. It is through our rebellion against God that evil entered the world.

Principles: FAITH

Faith is trusting in what we can't experience with our five physical senses. As believers, Jesus is the object of our faith, even though we can't sense him. At its core, faith is a belief in the trustworthiness and faithfulness of God. Faith in God means living as though we actually believe he loves us and desires the best for our lives. As it states in Hebrews 11:1, "Faith means being sure of the things we hope for and knowing that something is real even if we do not see it."

9:54 **people** Some Greek copies continue "as Elijah did." 9:55–56 **And…them.** Some Greek copies do not contain the bracketed text. 10:1 **seventy-two** Some Greek copies read "seventy." 10:11 **dirt…you** A warning. It showed that they had rejected these people. 10:12 **Sodom** City that God destroyed because the people were so evil. 10:13 **Tyre and Sidon** Towns where wicked people lived. 10:13, 15 **Korazin…Bethsaida…Capernaum** Towns by Lake Galilee where Jesus preached to the people. 10:17 **seventy-two** Some Greek copies read "seventy."

[62]Jesus said, "Anyone who begins to plow a field but keeps looking back is of no use in the kingdom of God."

Jesus Sends Out the Seventy-Two

10 After this, the Lord chose seventy-two" others and sent them out in pairs ahead of him into every town and place where he planned to go. [2]He said to them, "There are a great many people to harvest, but there are only a few workers. So pray to God, who owns the harvest, that he will send more workers to help gather his harvest. [3]Go now, but listen! I am sending you out like sheep among wolves. [4]Don't carry a purse, a bag, or sandals, and don't waste time talking with people on the road. [5]Before you go into a house, say, 'Peace be with this house.' [6]If peace-loving people live there, your blessing of peace will stay with them, but if not, then your blessing will come back to you. [7]Stay in the same house, eating and drinking what the people there give you. A worker should be given his pay. Don't move from house to house. [8]If you go into a town and the people welcome you, eat what they give you. [9]Heal the sick who live there, and tell them, 'The kingdom of God is near you.' [10]But if you go into a town, and the people don't welcome you, then go into the streets and say, [11]'Even the dirt from your town that sticks to our feet we wipe off against you." But remember that the kingdom of God is near.' [12]I tell you, on the Judgment Day it will be better for the people of Sodom" than for the people of that town.

Jesus Warns Unbelievers

[13]"How terrible for you, Korazin! How terrible for you, Bethsaida! If the miracles I did in you had happened in Tyre and Sidon," those people would have changed their lives long ago. They would have worn rough cloth and put ashes on themselves to show they had changed. [14]But on the Judgment Day it will be better for Tyre and Sidon than for you. [15]And you, Capernaum," will you be lifted up to heaven? No! You will be thrown down to the depths!

[16]"Whoever listens to you listens to me, and whoever refuses to accept you refuses to accept me. And whoever refuses to accept me refuses to accept the One who sent me."

Satan Falls

[17]When the seventy-two" came back, they were very happy and said, "Lord, even the demons obeyed us when we used your name!"

[18]Jesus said, "I saw Satan fall like lightning from heaven. [19]Listen, I have given you power to walk on snakes and scorpions, power that is greater than the enemy has. So nothing will hurt you. [20]But you should not be happy because the spirits obey you but because your names are written in heaven."

Jesus Prays to the Father

[21]Then Jesus rejoiced in the Holy Spirit and said, "I praise you, Father, Lord of heaven and earth, because you have hidden these things from the people who are wise and smart. But you have shown them to those who are like little children. Yes, Father, this is what you really wanted.

>> live the life

Luke 10:33

The Principle > Help the less fortunate.

Practicing It > Volunteer at the local hospital or nursing home to spend time with people who are lonely or in need of human contact. Bring a collection of books you can read aloud to people, or just ask them to share with you their life story.

[22]"My Father has given me all things. No one knows who the Son is, except the Father. And no one knows who the Father is, except the Son and those whom the Son chooses to tell."

[23]Then Jesus turned to his followers and said privately, "You are blessed to see what you now see. [24]I tell you, many prophets and kings wanted to see what you now see, but they did not, and they wanted to hear what you now hear, but they did not."

The Good Samaritan

[25]Then an expert on the law stood up to test Jesus, saying, "Teacher, what must I do to get life forever?"

[26]Jesus said, "What is written in the law? What do you read there?"

[27]The man answered, "Love the Lord your God with all your heart, all your soul, all your strength, and all your mind.'" Also, "Love your neighbor as you love yourself.'"

[28]Jesus said to him, "Your answer is right. Do this and you will live."

[29]But the man, wanting to show the importance of his question, said to Jesus, "And who is my neighbor?"

[30]Jesus answered, "As a man was going down from Jerusalem to Jericho, some robbers attacked him. They tore off his clothes, beat him, and left him lying there, almost dead. [31]It happened that a priest was going down that road. When he saw the man, he walked by on the other side. [32]Next, a Levite" came there, and after he went over and looked at the man, he walked by on the other side of the road. [33]Then a Samaritan" traveling down the road came to where the hurt man was. When he saw the man, he felt very sorry for him. [34]The Samaritan went to him, poured olive oil and wine" on his wounds, and bandaged them. Then he put the hurt man on his own donkey and took him to an inn where he cared for him. [35]The next day, the Samaritan brought out two coins," gave them to the innkeeper, and said, 'Take care of this man. If you spend more money on him, I will pay it back to you when I come again.' "

[36]Then Jesus said, "Which one of these three men do you think was a neighbor to the man who was attacked by the robbers?"

[37]The expert on the law answered, "The one who showed him mercy."

Jesus said to him, "Then go and do what he did."

10:27 "Love...mind." Quotation from Deuteronomy 6:5.   10:27 "Love...yourself." Quotation from Leviticus 19:18.   10:32 **Levite** Levites were members of the tribe of Levi who helped the Jewish priests with their work in the Temple. Read 1 Chronicles 23:24–32.   10:33 **Samaritan** Samaritans were people from Samaria. These people were part Jewish, but the Jews did not accept them as true Jews. Samaritans and Jews disliked each other.   10:34 **olive oil and wine** Oil and wine were used like medicine to soften and clean wounds.   10:35 **coins** Roman denarii. One coin was the average pay for one day's work.

Men of Valor
CORNELIUS: Barrier Breaker

A centurion in the Roman army, Cornelius didn't seem poised to alter history. However, his belief in God, his generosity to the poor, and his continuous prayers thrust him into that role. One afternoon an angel appeared to him, told him God had heard his prayers, and then directed him to send men to bring Peter back to his home (Acts 10:3–6). Meanwhile, Peter had a vision from God that showed him that the Good News was not only for the Jews. It was intended for all people, and Peter appreciated the full impact of this once he went to Cornelius's house. No longer would the Good News be restricted, thanks to a soldier who didn't belong to the clique of his time.

Mary and Martha

³⁸While Jesus and his followers were traveling, Jesus went into a town. A woman named Martha let Jesus stay at her house. ³⁹Martha had a sister named Mary, who was sitting at Jesus' feet and listening to him teach. ⁴⁰But Martha was busy with all the work to be done. She went in and said, "Lord, don't you care that my sister has left me alone to do all the work? Tell her to help me."

⁴¹But the Lord answered her, "Martha, Martha, you are worried and upset about many things. ⁴²Only one thing is important. Mary has chosen the better thing, and it will never be taken away from her."

Jesus Teaches About Prayer

11 One time Jesus was praying in a certain place. When he finished, one of his followers said to him, "Lord, teach us to pray as John taught his followers."

²Jesus said to them, "When you pray, say:
'Father, may your name always be kept holy.
May your kingdom come.
³Give us the food we need for each day.
⁴Forgive us for our sins,
    because we forgive everyone who has done wrong to us.
And do not cause us to be tempted.' "ⁿ

Continue to Ask

⁵Then Jesus said to them, "Suppose one of you went to your friend's house at midnight and said to him, 'Friend, loan me three loaves of bread. ⁶A friend of mine has come into town to visit me, but I have nothing for him to eat.' ⁷Your friend inside the house answers, 'Don't bother me! The door is already locked, and my children and I are in bed. I cannot get up and give you anything.' ⁸I tell you, if friendship is not enough to make him get up to give you the bread, your boldness will make him get up and give you whatever you need. ⁹So I tell you, ask, and God will give to you. Search, and you will find. Knock, and the door will open for you. ¹⁰Yes, everyone who asks will receive. The one who searches will find. And everyone who knocks will have the door opened. ¹¹If your children ask forⁿ a fish, which of you would give them a snake instead? ¹²Or, if your children ask for an egg, would you give them a scorpion? ¹³Even though you are bad, you know how to give good things to your children. How much more your heavenly Father will give the Holy Spirit to those who ask him!"

Jesus' Power Is from God

¹⁴One time Jesus was sending out a demon who could not talk. When the demon came out, the man who had been unable to speak, then spoke. The people were amazed. ¹⁵But some of them said, "Jesus uses the power of Beelzebul, the ruler of demons, to force demons out of people."

¹⁶Other people, wanting to test Jesus, asked him to give them a sign from heaven. ¹⁷But knowing their thoughts, he said to them, "Every kingdom that is divided against itself will be destroyed. And a family that is divided against itself will not continue. ¹⁸So if Satan is divided against himself, his kingdom will not continue. You say that I use the power of Beelzebul to force out demons. ¹⁹But if I use the power of Beelzebul to force out demons, what power do your people use to force demons out? So they will be your judges. ²⁰But if I use the power of God to force out demons, then the kingdom of God has come to you.

²¹"When a strong person with many weapons guards his own house, his possessions are safe. ²²But when someone stronger comes and defeats him, the stronger one will take away the weapons the first man trusted and will give away the possessions.

²³"Anyone who is not with me is against me, and anyone who does not work with me is working against me.

The Empty Person

²⁴"When an evil spirit comes out of a person, it travels through dry places, looking for a place to rest. But when it finds no place, it says, 'I will go back to the house I left.' ²⁵And when it comes back, it finds that house swept clean and made neat. ²⁶Then the evil spirit goes out and brings seven other spirits more evil than it is, and they go in and live there. So the person has even more trouble than before."

People Who Are Truly Blessed

²⁷As Jesus was saying these things, a woman in the crowd called out to Jesus, "Blessed is the mother who gave birth to you and nursed you."

²⁸But Jesus said, "No, blessed are those who hear the teaching of God and obey it."

The People Want a Miracle

²⁹As the crowd grew larger, Jesus said, "The people who live today are evil. They want to

---

 11:2–4 *'Father...tempted.'* Some Greek copies include phrases from Matthew's version of this prayer (Matthew 6:9–13). **11:11 for** Some Greek copies include the phrase "for bread, which of you would give them a stone, or if they ask for ..." **11:29 sign of Jonah** Jonah's three days in the fish are like Jesus' three days in the tomb. See Matthew 12:40.

Q: Does God love everyone or just Christians?

A: God shows no favoritism when it comes to love. He loves every person on earth with the same perfect, infinite passion. However, because Christians have placed their faith in Jesus Christ, they enjoy a relationship with God that non-Christians don't (John 3:16).

see a miracle for a sign, but no sign will be given them, except the sign of Jonah." ³⁰As Jonah was a sign for those people who lived in Nineveh, the Son of Man will be a sign for the people of this time. ³¹On the Judgment Day the Queen of the South" will stand up with the people who live now. She will show they are guilty, because she came from far away to listen to Solomon's wise teaching. And I tell you that someone greater than Solomon is here. ³²On the Judgment Day the people of Nineveh will stand up with the people who live now, and they will show that you are guilty. When Jonah preached to them, they were sorry and changed their lives. And I tell you that someone greater than Jonah is here.

Be a Light for the World

³³"No one lights a lamp and puts it in a secret place or under a bowl, but on a lampstand so the people who come in can see. ³⁴Your eye is a light for the body. When your eyes are good, your whole body will be full of light. But when your eyes are evil, your whole body will be full of darkness. ³⁵So be careful not to let the light in you become darkness. ³⁶If your whole body is full of light, and none of it is dark, then you will shine bright, as when a lamp shines on you."

Jesus Accuses the Pharisees

³⁷After Jesus had finished speaking, a Pharisee asked Jesus to eat with him. So Jesus went in and sat at the table. ³⁸But the Pharisee was surprised when he saw that Jesus did not wash his hands" before the meal. ³⁹The Lord said to him, "You Pharisees clean the outside of the cup and the dish, but inside you are full of greed and evil. ⁴⁰You foolish people! The same one who made what is outside also made what is inside. ⁴¹So give what is in your dishes to the poor, and then you will be fully clean. ⁴²How terrible for you Pharisees! You give God one-tenth of even your mint, your rue, and every other plant in your garden. But you fail to be fair to others and to love God. These are the things you should do while continuing to do those other things. ⁴³How terrible for you Pharisees, because you love to have the most important seats in the synagogues, and you love to be greeted with respect in the marketplaces. ⁴⁴How terrible for you, because you are like hidden graves, which people walk on without knowing."

Jesus Talks to Experts on the Law

⁴⁵One of the experts on the law said to Jesus, "Teacher, when you say these things, you are insulting us, too."

⁴⁶Jesus answered, "How terrible for you, you experts on the law! You make strict rules that are very hard for people to obey, but you yourselves don't even try to follow those rules. ⁴⁷How terrible for you, because you build tombs for the prophets whom your ancestors killed! ⁴⁸And now you show that you approve of what your ancestors did. They killed the prophets, and you build tombs for them! ⁴⁹This is why in his wisdom God said, 'I will send prophets and apostles to them. They will kill some, and they will treat others cruelly.' ⁵⁰So you who live now will be punished for the deaths of all the prophets who were killed since the beginning of the world— ⁵¹from the killing of Abel to the killing of Zechariah," who died between the altar and the Temple. Yes, I tell you that you who are alive now will be punished for them all.

⁵²"How terrible for you, you experts on the law. You have taken away the key to learning about God. You yourselves would not learn, and you stopped others from learning, too."

⁵³When Jesus left, the teachers of the law and the Pharisees began to give him trouble, asking him questions about many things, ⁵⁴trying to catch him saying something wrong.

▶Get Aligned
Luke 11:34–35

IT IS COMMON KNOWLEDGE THAT MEN ARE MORE VISUALLY ORIENTED THAN WOMEN. One of our strongest senses is sight. Our eyes serve as the gate to our soul, permitting both good and bad to enter. The more time we spend allowing darkness in our lives, the more we're corrupting our body, soul, and spirit.

That's why pornography is so harmful. For ages, men have come up with excuse after excuse for why they feel it is okay to dabble with porn. It's *not* okay! Statistics prove otherwise. More importantly, the lives of men who view pornography, and not just the hardcore sex addicts, reveal that even the smallest dose has a negative effect.

But this passage of Scripture goes beyond sampling pornography. Lusting after someone or checking out other women when your wife or friends aren't around isn't healthful either. God desires for you to be full of light, and each moment presents the choice for us to be filled with either light or darkness. Learn to veer your eyes away from what's harmful and turn them toward the things of God.

11:31 Queen of the South The Queen of Sheba. She traveled a thousand miles to learn God's wisdom from Solomon. Read 1 Kings 10:1–3. **11:38 wash his hands** This was a Jewish religious custom that the Pharisees thought was very important. **11:51 Abel … Zechariah** In the Hebrew Old Testament, the first and last men to be murdered.

▶ Get Aligned

Luke 12:4—5

IT IS ESTIMATED THAT ALMOST 450 CHRISTIANS die on account of their faith each day. That's one death every three and a half minutes! Most of those people went to their graves fearing God more than their killers. They were willing to give up their lives because they personally knew the giver of life and thought more of him than their attackers.

Most of us don't live under such extreme circumstances. We don't have to fear being killed just for saying Jesus' name. Still, we need to ask ourselves if we hon-estly respect God more than any-thing. Do we believe that he, and he alone, holds our life in his hands?

That can be a tough issue for men. Deep in our hearts, we're afraid of losing our jobs, our families, our money, or our secu-rity. Those things all serve as buffers to our ultimate fear of dying. The more stability we have in life, the less fear we have in facing our own mortality. But as believers, fearing God should be a healthy part of our walk. Today, revere him for his righteous pu-rity.

Don't Be Like the Pharisees

12 So many thousands of people had gathered that they were stepping on each other. Jesus spoke first to his followers, saying, "Beware of the yeast of the Pharisees, because they are hyp-ocrites. ²Everything that is hidden will be shown, and everything that is secret will be made known. ³What you have said in the dark will be heard in the light, and what you have whispered in an inner room will be shouted from the housetops.

⁴"I tell you, my friends, don't be afraid of people who can kill the body but after that can do nothing more to hurt you. ⁵I will show you the one to fear. Fear the one who has the power to kill you and also to throw you into hell. Yes, this is the one you should fear.

⁶"Five sparrows are sold for only two pennies, and God does not forget any of them. ⁷But God even knows how many hairs you have on your head. Don't be afraid. You are worth much more than many sparrows.

Don't Be Ashamed of Jesus

⁸"I tell you, all those who stand before others and say they believe in me, I, the Son of Man, will say before the angels of God that they be-long to me. ⁹But all who stand before others and say they do not be-lieve in me, I will say before the angels of God that they do not belong to me.

¹⁰"Anyone who speaks against the Son of Man can be forgiven, but anyone who speaks against the Holy Spirit will not be forgiven.

¹¹"When you are brought into the synagogues before the leaders and other powerful people, don't worry about how to defend yourself or what to say. ¹²At that time the Holy Spirit will teach you what you must say."

Jesus Warns Against Selfishness

¹³Someone in the crowd said to Jesus, "Teacher, tell my brother to di-vide with me the property our father left us."

¹⁴But Jesus said to him, "Who said I should judge or decide between you?" ¹⁵Then Jesus said to them, "Be careful and guard against all kinds of greed. Life is not measured by how much one owns."

¹⁶Then Jesus told this story: "There was a rich man who had some land, which grew a good crop. ¹⁷He thought to himself, 'What will I do? I have no place to keep all my crops.' ¹⁸Then he said, 'This is what I will do: I will tear down my barns and build bigger ones, and there

➡ The Bottom Line

Establishing Reserves: Life Happens

THE CAR BREAKS DOWN. The refrigerator quits. The lawn mower dies. These things likely won't happen all at once, but life can produce some costly surprises. And not all of them will be taken care of by extended warranties or insurance coverage. That is why a cash reserve—most experts recommend at least one thousand dollars—is a good idea in case of expensive emergencies. The alternative is relying on credit, which sinks you deeper in debt. Romans 13:8 says that the only thing we should owe is love for each other.

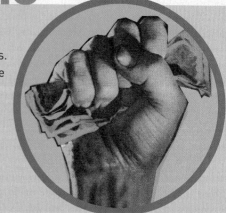

I will store all my grain and other goods. ¹⁹Then I can say to myself, "I have enough good things stored to last for many years. Rest, eat, drink, and enjoy life!" '

²⁰"But God said to him, 'Foolish man! Tonight your life will be taken from you. So who will get those things you have prepared for yourself?'

²¹"This is how it will be for those who store up things for themselves and are not rich toward God."

Don't Worry

²²Jesus said to his followers, "So I tell you, don't worry about the food you need to live, or about the clothes you need for your body. ²³Life is more than food, and the body is more than clothes. ²⁴Look at the birds. They don't plant or harvest, they don't have storerooms or barns, but God feeds them. And you are worth much more than birds. ²⁵You cannot add any time to your life by worrying about it. ²⁶If you cannot do even the little things, then why worry about the big things? ²⁷Consider how the lilies grow; they don't work or make clothes for themselves. But I tell you that even Solomon with his riches was not dressed as beautifully as one of these flowers. ²⁸God clothes the grass in the field, which is alive today but tomorrow is thrown into the fire. So how much more will God clothe you? Don't have so little faith! ²⁹Don't always think about what you

will eat or what you will drink, and don't keep worrying. ³⁰All the people in the world are trying to get these things, and your Father knows you need them. ³¹But seek God's kingdom, and all your other needs will be met as well.

THINK ABOUT IT Luke 12:35–40

WHEN YOU'RE GETTING READY FOR WORK at the beginning of the day, most likely you check the newspaper or the television or the radio for the daily weather report. What you hear will affect how warmly you dress or whether you carry an umbrella or not. Whereas the forecast may be inaccurate at times, it is wise to be prepared for the day's weather.

You probably make the same sort of preparation before a major meeting at the office. Your boss spells out the agenda and asks you to come prepared on a particular topic. If you ignore his instructions, you will look foolish and unprepared before your boss and your colleagues.

Jesus also forewarned his followers to be prepared. He used the story about the master of the home returning from a wedding and finding his servants prepared for his arrival. Any time the master returned, he found his servants prepared. More than a nice tale, Jesus applied the lesson to the day that he will return to the earth for those who know him. He said, "The Son of Man will come at a time when you don't expect him!" It is important to be prepared for his return.

Don't Trust in Money

³²"Don't fear, little flock, because your Father wants to give you the kingdom. ³³Sell your possessions and give to the poor. Get for yourselves purses that will not wear out, the treasure in heaven that never runs out,

 ## Survival Guide

DRILLS: USING THEM SAFELY

An essential part of a tool collection, a drill comes in handy for many home maintenance and repair projects. A drill is a versatile tool. Used with different attachments, it can bore holes, strip paint, install screws, and sand or polish objects. No matter what kind of drill you use, safety glasses are always a good idea when operating power equipment. Be sure you have the right bit for the type of material you're drilling, and use light, but steady pressure. Like a drill, faith comes in handy in a variety of settings and circumstances.

where thieves can't steal and moths can't destroy. ³⁴Your heart will be where your treasure is.

Always Be Ready

³⁵"Be dressed, ready for service, and have your lamps shining. ³⁶Be like servants who are waiting for their master to come home from a wedding party. When he comes and knocks, the servants immediately open the door for him. ³⁷They will be blessed when their master comes home, because he sees that they were watching for him. I tell you the truth, the master will dress himself to serve and tell the servants to sit at the table, and he will serve them. ³⁸Those servants will be blessed when he comes in and finds them still waiting, even if it is midnight or later.

³⁹"Remember this: If the owner of the house knew what time a thief was coming, he would not allow the thief to enter his house. ⁴⁰So you also must be ready, because the Son of Man will come at a time when you don't expect him!"

Who Is the Trusted Servant?

⁴¹Peter said, "Lord, did you tell this story to us or to all people?"

⁴²The Lord said, "Who is the wise and trusted servant that the master trusts to give the other servants their food at the right time? ⁴³When the master comes and finds the servant doing his work, the servant will be blessed. ⁴⁴I tell you the truth, the master will choose that servant to take care of everything he owns. ⁴⁵But suppose the servant thinks to himself, 'My master will not come back soon,' and he begins to beat the other servants, men and women, and to eat and drink and get drunk. ⁴⁶The master will come when that servant is not ready and is not expecting him. Then the master will cut him in pieces and send him away to be with the others who don't obey.

⁴⁷"The servant who knows what his master wants but is not ready, or who does not do what the master wants, will be beaten with many blows! ⁴⁸But the servant who does not know what his master wants and does things that should be punished will be beaten with few blows. From everyone who has been given much, much will be demanded. And from the one trusted with much, much more will be expected.

Jesus Causes Division

⁴⁹"I came to set fire to the world, and I wish it were already burning! ⁵⁰I have a baptism" to suffer through, and I feel very troubled until it is over. ⁵¹Do you think I came to give peace to the earth? No, I tell you, I came to divide it. ⁵²From now on, a family with five people will be divided, three against two, and two against three. ⁵³They will be divided: father against son and son against father, mother against daughter and daughter against mother, mother-in-law against daughter-in-law and daughter-in-law against mother-in-law."

Understanding the Times

⁵⁴Then Jesus said to the people, "When you see clouds coming up in the west, you say, 'It's going to rain,' and it happens. ⁵⁵When you feel the wind begin to blow from the south, you say, 'It will be a hot day,' and it happens. ⁵⁶Hypocrites! You know how to understand the appearance of the earth and sky. Why don't you understand what is happening now?

Settle Your Problems

⁵⁷"Why can't you decide for yourselves what is right? ⁵⁸If your enemy is taking you to court, try hard to settle it on the way. If you don't, your enemy might take you to the judge, and the judge might turn you over to the officer, and the officer might throw you into jail. ⁵⁹I tell you, you will not get out of there until you have paid everything you owe."

Change Your Hearts

13 At that time some people were there who told Jesus that Pilate" had killed some people from Galilee while they were worshiping. He mixed their blood with the blood of the animals they were sacrificing to God. ²Jesus answered, "Do you think this happened to them because they were more sinful than all others from

Q: Is it wrong to question God?

A: Honest questioning and heartfelt inquiry are often part of a genuine faith relationship with God. However, such inquiry becomes unfruitful if it moves from questioning God's actions to questioning his character or his love, which is unquestionable (James 1:17).

<<TechSupport>>

BACKUP SUPPORT

Don't wait for your hard drive to crash before making a backup. As they say in the hard drive recovery business, it's not a question of *if*, but *when*. Making a backup is as simple as one, two, three. One: find a backup medium, such as a portable hard drive or a DVD, if your computer can burn to DVD. Two: Decide if you're going to back up automatically or manually. Three: Make it a habit. Backing up your data is just being a good steward of the things that God has entrusted to you.

>> 12:50 I...baptism Jesus was talking about the suffering he would soon go through. 13:1 Pilate Pontius Pilate was the Roman governor of Judea from A.D. 26 to A.D. 36.

Galilee? ³No, I tell you. But unless you change your hearts and lives, you will be destroyed as they were! ⁴What about those eighteen people who died when the tower of Siloam fell on them? Do you think they were more sinful than all the others who live in Jerusalem? ⁵No, I tell you. But unless you change your hearts and lives, you will all be destroyed too!"

The Useless Tree

⁶Jesus told this story: "A man had a fig tree planted in his vineyard. He came looking for some fruit on the tree, but he found none. ⁷So the man said to his gardener, 'I have been looking for fruit on this tree for three years, but I never find any. Cut it down. Why should it waste the ground?' ⁸But the servant answered, 'Master, let the tree have one more year to produce fruit. Let me dig up the dirt around it and put on some fertilizer. ⁹If the tree produces fruit next year, good. But if not, you can cut it down.' "

Jesus Heals on the Sabbath

¹⁰Jesus was teaching in one of the synagogues on the Sabbath day. ¹¹A woman was there who, for eighteen years, had an evil spirit in her that made her crippled. Her back was always bent; she could not stand up straight. ¹²When Jesus saw her, he called her over and said, "Woman, you are free from your sickness." ¹³Jesus put his hands on her, and immediately she was able to stand up straight and began praising God.

¹⁴The synagogue leader was angry because Jesus healed on the Sabbath day. He said to the people, "There are six days when one has to work. So come to be healed on one of those days, and not on the Sabbath day."

¹⁵The Lord answered, "You hypocrites! Doesn't each of you untie your work animals and lead them to drink water every day—even on the Sabbath day? ¹⁶This woman that I healed, a daughter of Abraham, has been held by Satan for eighteen years. Surely it is not wrong for her to be freed from her sickness on a Sabbath day!" ¹⁷When Jesus said this, all of those who were criticizing him were ashamed, but the entire crowd rejoiced at all the wonderful things Jesus was doing.

Stories of Mustard Seed and Yeast

¹⁸Then Jesus said, "What is God's kingdom like? What can I compare it with? ¹⁹It is like a mustard seed that a man plants in his garden. The seed grows and becomes a tree, and the wild birds build nests in its branches."

²⁰Jesus said again, "What can I compare God's kingdom with? ²¹It is like yeast that a woman took and hid in a large tub of flour until it made all the dough rise."

The Narrow Door

²²Jesus was teaching in every town and village as he traveled toward Jerusalem. ²³Some-one said to Jesus, "Lord, will only a few people be saved?"

Jesus said, ²⁴"Try hard to enter through the narrow door, because many people will try to enter there, but they will not be able. ²⁵When the owner of the house gets up and closes the door, you can stand outside and knock on the door and say, 'Sir, open the door for us.' But he will answer, 'I don't know you or where you come from.' ²⁶Then you will say, 'We ate and drank with you, and you taught in the streets of our town.' ²⁷But he will say to you, 'I don't know you or where you come from. Go away from me, all you who do evil!'

FACT-OIDS! Americans' top favorite online destinations are e-mail, research, news and weather, and information about hobbies or social activities. [Harris Interactive]

Get Fit

REDUCING STRESS Perhaps now more than ever, job stress poses a threat to the health of men in our country. Consider your own situation: what level of stress do you typically experience each day? Chances are that it's too high. Balancing obligations to your employer and your family can be challenging. But you can protect your health by engaging in activities that help you reduce your stress at work and at home. Block out a day each week to relax. Read a book for fun. Play with a pet. Get a massage. Listen to music. Make time for church and other spiritual activities. Put relationships ahead of work. You'll reap huge dividends.

[28]You will cry and grind your teeth with pain when you see Abraham, Isaac, Jacob, and all the prophets in God's kingdom, but you yourselves thrown outside. [29]People will come from the east, west, north, and south and will sit down at the table in the kingdom of God. [30]There are those who are last now who will be first in the future. And there are those who are first now who will be last in the future."

Jesus Will Die in Jerusalem

[31]At that time some Pharisees came to Jesus and said, "Go away from here! Herod wants to kill you!"

[32]Jesus said to them, "Go tell that fox Herod, 'Today and tomorrow I am forcing demons out and healing people. Then, on the third day, I will reach my goal.' [33]Yet I must be on my way today and tomorrow and the next day. Surely it cannot be right for a prophet to be killed anywhere except in Jerusalem.

[34]"Jerusalem, Jerusalem! You kill the prophets and stone to death those who are sent to you. Many times I wanted to gather your people as a hen gathers her chicks under her wings, but you would not let me. [35]Now your house is left completely empty. I tell you, you will not see me until that time when you will say, 'God bless the One who comes in the name of the Lord.' "[n]

Q: Does God still speak to us today?

A: Yes, he does. God created humans for a relationship with himself, so it follows that he would still communicate with people today. God speaks primarily through his Word, but also through other people and through his Holy Spirit within us (Hebrews 3:7, 15).

Healing on the Sabbath

14 [1]On a Sabbath day, when Jesus went to eat at the home of a leading Pharisee, the people were watching Jesus very closely. [2]And in front of him was a man with dropsy.[n] [3]Jesus said to the Pharisees and experts on the law, "Is it right or wrong to heal on the Sabbath day?" [4]But they would not answer his question. So Jesus took the man, healed him, and sent him away. [5]Jesus said to the Pharisees and teachers of the law, "If your child[n] or ox falls into a well on the Sabbath day, will you not pull him out quickly?" [6]And they could not answer him.

Don't Make Yourself Important

[7]When Jesus noticed that some of the guests were choosing the best places to sit, he told this story: [8]"When someone invites you to a wedding feast, don't take the most important seat, because

Change >> Your WORLD

COMPASSION INTERNATIONAL

Using the slogan, "Releasing children from poverty in Jesus' name," Compassion International is working in more than twenty countries with 655,000 children. The ministry began in 1952 to help Korean War orphans with food, shelter, education, and health care, as well as Christian training. For as little as thirty-two dollars a month, you can sponsor a child in the part of the world that you select or touch the greatest need at that particular moment. More than physical help, Compassion provides the Good News about Jesus. Its site includes lots of ways to get involved.

To change your world, visit www.compassion.com.

someone more important than you may have been invited. [9]The host, who invited both of you, will come to you and say, 'Give this person your seat.' Then you will be embarrassed and will have to move to the last place. [10]So when you are invited, go sit in a seat that is not important. When the host comes to you, he may say, 'Friend, move up here to a more important place.' Then all the other guests will respect you. [11]All who make themselves great will be made humble, but those who make themselves humble will be made great."

You Will Be Rewarded

[12]Then Jesus said to the man who had invited him, "When you give a lunch or a dinner, don't invite only your friends, your family, your other relatives, and your rich neighbors. At another time they will invite you to eat with them, and you will be repaid. [13]Instead, when you give a feast, invite the poor, the crippled, the lame, and the blind. [14]Then you will be blessed, because they have nothing and cannot pay you back. But you will be repaid when the good people rise from the dead."

>> **13:35** 'God ... Lord.' Quotation from Psalm 118:26.   **14:2 dropsy** A sickness that causes the body to swell larger and larger.   **14:5 child** Some Greek copies read "donkey."

A Story About a Big Banquet

¹⁵One of those at the table with Jesus heard these things and said to him, "Blessed are the people who will share in the meal in God's kingdom."

¹⁶Jesus said to him, "A man gave a big banquet and invited many people. ¹⁷When it was time to eat, the man sent his servant to tell the guests, 'Come. Everything is ready.'

¹⁸"But all the guests made excuses. The first one said, 'I have just bought a field, and I must go look at it. Please excuse me.' ¹⁹Another said, 'I have just bought five pairs of oxen; I must go and try them. Please excuse me.' ²⁰A third person said, 'I just got married; I can't come.' ²¹So the servant returned and told his master what had happened. Then the master became angry and said, 'Go at once into the streets and alleys of the town, and bring in the poor, the crippled, the blind, and the lame.' ²²Later the servant said to him, 'Master, I did what you commanded, but we still have room.' ²³The master said to the servant, 'Go out to the roads and country lanes, and urge the people there to come so my house will be full. ²⁴I tell you, none of those whom I invited first will eat with me.'"

The Cost of Being Jesus' Follower

²⁵Large crowds were traveling with Jesus, and he turned and said to them, ²⁶"If anyone comes to me but loves his father, mother, wife, children, brothers, or sisters—or even life—more than me, he cannot be my follower. ²⁷Whoever is not willing to carry his cross and follow me cannot be my follower. ²⁸If you want to build a tower, you first sit down and decide how much it will cost, to see if you have enough money to finish the job. ²⁹If you don't, you might lay the foundation, but you would not be able to finish. Then all who would see it would make fun of you, ³⁰saying, 'This person began to build but was not able to finish.'

³¹"If a king is going to fight another king, first he will sit down and plan. He will decide if he and his ten thousand soldiers can defeat the other king who has twenty thousand soldiers. ³²If he can't, then while the other king is still far away, he will send some peo-ple to speak to him and ask for peace. ³³In the same way, you must give up everything you have to be my follower.

Don't Lose Your Influence

³⁴"Salt is good, but if it loses its salty taste, you cannot make it salty again. ³⁵It is no good for the soil or for manure; it is thrown away.

"Let those with ears use them and listen."

A Lost Sheep, a Lost Coin

15 The tax collectors and sinners all came to listen to Jesus. ²But the Pharisees and the teachers of the law began to complain: "Look, this man welcomes sinners and even eats with them."

³Then Jesus told them this story: ⁴"Suppose one of you has a hundred sheep but loses one of them. Then he will leave the other ninety-nine sheep in the open field and go out and look for the lost sheep until he finds it. ⁵And when he finds it, he happily puts it on his shoulders ⁶and goes home. He calls to his friends and neighbors and says, 'Be happy with me because I found my lost sheep.' ⁷In the same way, I tell you there is more joy in heaven over one sinner who changes his heart and life, than over ninety-nine good people who don't need to change.

⁸"Suppose a woman has ten silver coins," but loses one. She will light a lamp, sweep the house, and look carefully for the coin until she finds it. ⁹And when she finds it, she will call her friends and neighbors and say, 'Be happy with me because I have found the coin that I lost.' ¹⁰In the same way, there is joy in the presence of the angels of God when one sinner changes his heart and life."

The Son Who Left Home

¹¹Then Jesus said, "A man had two sons. ¹²The younger son said to his father, 'Give me my share of the property.' So the father divided the property between his two sons. ¹³Then the younger son gathered up all that was his and traveled far away to another country. There he wasted his money in foolish living. ¹⁴After he had spent everything, a time came when there was no food anywhere in the country, and the son was poor and hungry. ¹⁵So he got a job with one of the citizens there who sent the son into the fields to feed pigs. ¹⁶The son was so hungry that he

---

THINK ABOUT IT Luke 14:13–14

THE NEIGHBORS ON THE BLOCK LOOK FORWARD with great anticipation to the time when the couple invites each of them to a party. Although some people offer to bring something to the party, the couple declines and insists on handling each course of the dinner. The couple never hosts their neighbors in hopes of receiving future invitations from them, but simply holds the party using their gift of hospitality.

This is the type of charity Jesus encouraged for his followers. It's easy to invite to a gathering people who will return the favor, but we are to reach outside of ourselves and welcome into our hearts and homes people who can't necessarily bless us in return.

Instead of inviting relatives or family or friends, Jesus encouraged his followers to invite the crippled and the blind and the poor—all people with little or nothing, and who couldn't repay anything. As Jesus said, "You will be repaid when the good people rise from the dead." Our reward for blessing the needy is found in heaven and not on the earth.

▶▶ **15:8 silver coins** Roman denarii. One coin was the average pay for one day's work.

wanted to eat the pods the pigs were eating, but no one gave him anything. [17]When he realized what he was doing, he thought, 'All of my father's servants have plenty of food. But I am here, almost dying with hunger. [18]I will leave and return to my father and say to him, "Father, I have sinned against God and against you. [19]I am no longer worthy to be called your son, but let me be like one of your servants." ' [20]So the son left and went to his father.

"While the son was still a long way off, his father saw him and felt sorry for his son. So the father ran to him and hugged and kissed him. [21]The son said, 'Father, I have sinned against God and against you. I am no longer worthy to be called your son.'" [22]But the father said to his servants, 'Hurry! Bring the best clothes and put them on him. Also, put a ring on his finger and sandals on his feet. [23]And get our fat calf and kill it so we can have a feast and celebrate. [24]My son was dead, but now he is alive again! He was lost, but now he is found!' So they began to celebrate.

[25]"The older son was in the field, and as he came closer to the house, he heard the sound of music and dancing. [26]So he called to one of the servants and asked what all this meant. [27]The servant said, 'Your brother has come back, and your father killed the fat calf, because your brother came home safely.' [28]The older son was angry and would not go in to the feast. So his father went out and begged him to come in. [29]But the older son said to his father, 'I have served you like a slave for many years and have always obeyed your commands. But you never gave me even a young goat to have at a feast with my friends. [30]But your other son, who wasted all your money on prostitutes, comes home, and you kill the fat calf for him!' [31]The father said to him, 'Son, you are always with me, and all that I have is yours. [32]We had to celebrate and be happy because your brother was dead, but now he is alive. He was lost, but now he is found.' "

True Wealth

16 Jesus also said to his followers, "Once there was a rich man who had a manager to take care of his business. This manager was accused of cheating him. [2]So he called the manager in and said to him, 'What is this I hear about you? Give me a report of what you have done with my money, because you can't be my manager any longer.' [3]The manager thought to himself, 'What will I do since my master is taking my job away from me? I am not strong enough to dig ditches, and I am ashamed to beg. [4]I know what I'll do so that when I lose my job people will welcome me into their homes.'

[5]"So the manager called in everyone who owed the master any money. He asked the first one, 'How much do you owe?' [6]He answered, 'Eight hundred gallons of olive oil.' The manager said to him, 'Take your bill, sit down quickly, and write four hundred gallons.' [7]Then the manager asked another one, 'How much do you owe?' He answered, 'One thousand bushels of wheat.' Then the manager said to him, 'Take your bill and write eight hundred bushels.' [8]So, the master praised the dishonest manager for being clever. Yes, worldly people are more clever with their own kind than spiritual people are.

[9]"I tell you, make friends for yourselves using worldly riches so that when those riches are gone, you will be welcomed in those homes that continue forever. [10]Whoever can be trusted with a little can also be trusted with a lot, and whoever is dishonest with a little is dishonest with a lot. [11]If you cannot be trusted with worldly riches, then who will trust you with true riches? [12]And if you cannot be trusted with things that belong to someone else, who will give you things of your own?

[13]"No servant can serve two masters. The servant will hate one master and love the other, or will follow one master and refuse to follow the other. You cannot serve both God and worldly riches."

God's Law Cannot Be Changed

[14]The Pharisees, who loved money, were listening to all these things and made fun of Jesus. [15]He said to them, "You make yourselves look good in front of people, but God knows what is really in your hearts. What is important to people is hateful in God's sight.

[16]"The law of Moses and the writings of the prophets were preached until John[n] came. Since then the Good News about the kingdom of God is being told, and everyone tries to enter it by force. [17]It would be easier for heaven and earth to pass away than for the smallest part of a letter in the law to be changed.

Divorce and Remarriage

[18]"If a man divorces his wife and marries another woman, he is guilty of adultery, and the man who marries a divorced woman is also guilty of adultery."

The Rich Man and Lazarus

[19]Jesus said, "There was a rich man who always dressed in the finest clothes and lived in luxury every day. [20]And a very poor man named Lazarus, whose body was covered with sores, was laid at the rich man's gate. [21]He wanted to eat only the small pieces of food that fell from the rich man's table. And the dogs would come and lick his sores. [22]Later, Lazarus died, and the angels carried him to the arms of Abraham. The rich man died, too, and was buried. [23]In the place of the dead, he was in much pain. The rich man saw Abraham far away

>> live the life

Luke 16:10

The Principle > Be faithful in small things.

Practicing It > Be careful to do your best in all the tasks you are assigned—even those that no one will see or that seem unimportant. Your faithfulness in small tasks matters to God.

>> **15:21 son** Some Greek copies continue, "but let me be like one of your servants" (see verse 19). **16:16 John** John the Baptist, who preached to people about Christ's coming (Matthew 3; Luke 3).

with Lazarus at his side. [24]He called, 'Father Abraham, have mercy on me! Send Lazarus to dip his finger in water and cool my tongue, because I am suffering in this fire!' [25]But Abraham said, 'Child, remember when you were alive you had the good things in life, but bad things happened to Lazarus. Now he is comforted here, and you are suffering. [26]Besides, there is a big pit between you and us, so no one can cross over to you, and no one can leave there and come here.' [27]The rich man said, 'Father, then please send Lazarus to my father's house. [28]I have five brothers, and Lazarus could warn them so that they will not come to this place of pain.' [29]But Abraham said, 'They have the law of Moses and the writings of the prophets; let them learn from them.' [30]The rich man said, 'No, father Abraham! If someone goes to them from the dead, they would believe and change their hearts and lives.' [31]But Abraham said to him, 'If they will not listen to Moses and the prophets, they will not listen to someone who comes back from the dead.' "

Sin and Forgiveness

17 Jesus said to his followers, "Things that cause people to sin will happen, but how terrible for the person who causes them to happen! [2]It would be better for you to be thrown into the sea with a large stone around your neck than to cause one of these little ones to sin. [3]So be careful!

"If another follower sins, warn him, and if he is sorry and stops sinning, forgive him. [4]If he sins against you seven times in one day and says that he is sorry each time, forgive him."

How Big Is Your Faith?

[5]The apostles said to the Lord, "Give us more faith!"

[6]The Lord said, "If your faith were the size of a mustard seed, you could say to this mulberry tree, 'Dig yourself up and plant yourself in the sea,' and it would obey you.

Be Good Servants

[7]"Suppose one of you has a servant who has been plowing the ground or caring for the sheep. When the servant comes in from working in the field, would you say, 'Come in and sit down to eat'? [8]No, you would say to him, 'Prepare something for me to eat. Then get yourself ready and serve me. After I finish eating and drinking, you can eat.' [9]The servant does not get any special thanks for doing what his master commanded. [10]It is the same with you. When you have done everything you are told to do, you should say, 'We are unworthy servants; we have only done the work we should do.' "

Be Thankful

[11]While Jesus was on his way to Jerusalem, he was going through the area between Samaria and Galilee. [12]As he came into a small town, ten men who had a skin disease met him there. They did not come close to Jesus [13]but called to him, "Jesus! Master! Have mercy on us!"

[14]When Jesus saw the men, he said, "Go and show yourselves to the priests."*

As the ten men were going, they were healed. [15]When one of them saw that he was healed, he went back to Jesus, praising God in a loud voice. [16]Then he bowed down at Jesus' feet and thanked him. (And this man was a Samaritan.) [17]Jesus said, "Weren't ten men healed? Where are the other nine? [18]Is this Samaritan the only one who came back to thank God?" [19]Then Jesus said to him, "Stand up and go on your way. You were healed because you believed."

THINK ABOUT IT Luke 16:10

THE NEWSPAPER FREQUENTLY ADVERTISES seminars for learning more about financial management. Whether trying to invest in stocks and bonds or creating a budget to live within one's means, such lessons are valuable for achieving financial success.

Scholars indicate that Jesus talked more about money than any other topic in the New Testament. Perhaps the reason Jesus talked so much about money matters is because, quite frankly, *money matters*. In fact, Jesus said that the level of our responsibility in his eternal kingdom depends on how we manage the resources that God has provided for us in this life. As a result, each of us needs to consider if we are wisely and faithfully managing our money and the material goods entrusted to us.

Jesus understood the fleeting nature of money and worldly riches. He also knew the value of character when he taught, "Whoever can be trusted with a little can also be trusted with a lot, and whoever is dishonest with a little is dishonest with a lot." Wherever you are on the financial spectrum, start being faithful with what you have, and God will be able to entrust you with more.

FACT-OIDS! About 23% of Americans reported owning a laptop or notebook computer in 2003. [Barna.org]

17:14 **show…priests** The Law of Moses said a priest must say when a person with a skin disease became well.

103

FOR
Men Only

ATTENTION One sure-fire way to turn a woman off is to neglect paying attention to her. Whether it is glancing at other women while dining out or listening half-heartedly while channel surfing on the couch, women don't like it when men don't give them the attention they deserve. It doesn't take a genius to realize that when it's the other way around, we don't like being disrespected either. So wise up and tune into the needs of your better half by paying close attention when she's talking. Listening between the lines and learning to anticipate her needs will earn you her respect.

God's Kingdom Is Within You

²⁰Some of the Pharisees asked Jesus, "When will the kingdom of God come?"

Jesus answered, "God's kingdom is coming, but not in a way that you will be able to see with your eyes. ²¹People will not say, 'Look, here it is!' or, 'There it is!' because God's kingdom is within" you."

²²Then Jesus said to his followers, "The time will come when you will want very much to see one of the days of the Son of Man. But you will not see it. ²³People will say to you, 'Look, there he is!' or, 'Look, here he is!' Stay where you are; don't go away and search.

When Jesus Comes Again

²⁴"When the Son of Man comes again, he will shine like lightning, which flashes across the sky and lights it up from one side to the other. ²⁵But first he must suffer many things and be rejected by the people of this time. ²⁶When the Son of Man comes again, it will be as it was when Noah lived. ²⁷People were eating, drinking, marrying, and giving their children to be married until the day Noah entered the boat. Then the flood came and killed them all. ²⁸It will be the same as during the time of Lot. People were eating, drinking, buying, selling, planting, and building. ²⁹But the day Lot left Sodom," fire and sulfur rained down from the sky and killed them all. ³⁰This is how it will be when the Son of Man comes again.

³¹"On that day, a person who is on the roof and whose belongings are in the house should not go inside to get them. A person who is in the field should not go back home. ³²Remember Lot's wife." ³³Those who try to keep their lives will lose them. But those who give up their lives will save them. ³⁴I tell you, on that night two people will be sleeping in one bed; one will be taken and the other will be left. ³⁵There will be two women grinding grain together; one will be taken, and the other will be left. [³⁶Two people will be in the field. One will be taken, and the other will be left.]"

³⁷The followers asked Jesus, "Where will this be, Lord?"

Jesus answered, "Where there is a dead body, there the vultures will gather."

God Will Answer His People

18 Then Jesus used this story to teach his followers that they should always pray and never lose hope. ²"In a certain town there was a judge who did not respect God or care about people. ³In that same town there was a widow who kept coming to this judge, saying, 'Give me my rights against my enemy.' ⁴For a while the judge refused to help her. But afterwards, he thought to himself, 'Even though I don't respect God or care about people, ⁵I will see that she gets her rights. Otherwise she will continue to bother me until I am worn out.' "

⁶The Lord said, "Listen to what the unfair judge said. ⁷God will always give what is right to his people who cry to him night and day, and he will not be slow to answer them. ⁸I tell you, God will help his people quickly. But when the Son of Man comes again, will he find those on earth who believe in him?"

Being Right with God

⁹Jesus told this story to some people who thought they were very good and looked down on everyone else: ¹⁰"A Pharisee and a tax collector both went to the Temple to pray. ¹¹The Pharisee stood alone and prayed, 'God, I thank you that I am not like other people who steal, cheat, or take part in adultery, or even like this tax collector. ¹²I fast" twice a week, and I give one-tenth of everything I get!'

¹³"The tax collector, standing at a distance, would not even look up to heaven. But he beat on his

Q: Does God make mistakes?

A: No. Because God is infinitely perfect in every way, it is impossible for him to make a mistake. God's perfection assures us that we can never go wrong by following God's will for our lives and that we ourselves are part of God's plan for creation (Matthew 5:48).

17:21 **within** Or "among."   17:29 **Sodom** City that God destroyed because the people were so evil.   17:32 **Lot's wife** A story about what happened to Lot's wife is found in Genesis 19:15–17, 26.
17:36 **Two … left.** Some Greek copies do not contain the bracketed text.   18:12 **fast** The people would give up eating for a special time of prayer and worship to God. It was also done to show sadness and disappointment.

chest because he was so sad. He said, 'God, have mercy on me, a sinner.' ¹⁴I tell you, when this man went home, he was right with God, but the Pharisee was not. All who make themselves great will be made humble, but all who make themselves humble will be made great."

Who Will Enter God's Kingdom?

¹⁵Some people brought even their babies to Jesus so he could touch them. When the followers saw this, they told them to stop. ¹⁶But Jesus called for the children, saying, "Let the little children come to me. Don't stop them, because the kingdom of God belongs to people who are like these children. ¹⁷I tell you the truth, you must accept the kingdom of God as if you were a child, or you will never enter it."

A Rich Man's Question

¹⁸A certain leader asked Jesus, "Good Teacher, what must I do to have life forever?"

¹⁹Jesus said to him, "Why do you call me good? Only God is good. ²⁰You know the commands: 'You must not be guilty of adultery. You must not murder anyone. You must not steal. You must not tell lies about your neighbor. Honor your father and mother.' "”

²¹But the leader said, "I have obeyed all these commands since I was a boy."

²²When Jesus heard this, he said to him, "There is still one more thing you need to do. Sell everything you have and give it to the poor, and you will have treasure in heaven. Then come and follow me." ²³But when the man heard this, he became very sad, because he was very rich.

²⁴Jesus looked at him and said, "It is very hard for rich people to enter the kingdom of God. ²⁵It is easier for a camel to go through the eye of a needle than for a rich person to enter the kingdom of God."

Who Can Be Saved?

²⁶When the people heard this, they asked, "Then who can be saved?"

²⁷Jesus answered, "The things impossible for people are possible for God."

²⁸Peter said, "Look, we have left everything and followed you."

²⁹Jesus said, "I tell you the truth, all those who have left houses, wives, brothers, parents, or children for the kingdom of God ³⁰will get much more in this life. And in the age that is coming, they will have life forever."

Jesus Will Rise from the Dead

³¹Then Jesus took the twelve apostles aside and said to them, "We are going to Jerusalem. Everything the prophets wrote about the Son of Man will happen. ³²He will be turned over to those who are evil. They will laugh at him, insult him, spit on him, ³³beat him with whips, and kill him. But on the third day, he will rise to life again." ³⁴The apostles did not understand this; the meaning was hidden from them, and they did not realize what was said.

Jesus Heals a Blind Man

³⁵As Jesus came near the city of Jericho, a blind man was sitting beside the road, begging. ³⁶When he heard the people coming down the road, he asked, "What is happening?"

³⁷They told him, "Jesus, from Nazareth, is going by."

³⁸The blind man cried out, "Jesus, Son of David, have mercy on me!"

³⁹The people leading the group warned the blind man to be quiet. But the blind man shouted even more, "Son of David, have mercy on me!"

⁴⁰Jesus stopped and ordered the blind man to be brought to him. When he came near, Jesus asked him, ⁴¹"What do you want me to do for you?"

He said, "Lord, I want to see."

⁴²Jesus said to him, "Then see. You are healed because you believed."

⁴³At once the man was able to see, and he followed Jesus, thanking God. All the people who saw this praised God.

Zacchaeus Meets Jesus

19 Jesus was going through the city of Jericho. ²A man was there named Zacchaeus, who was a very important tax collector, and he was wealthy. ³He wanted to see who Jesus was, but he was not able because

People
Skills

Healthy Confrontation

When friends or loved ones offend you, it's generally healthy to tell them how you feel. But if you do, then follow a few key guidelines. First, don't blame them for your feelings. "You made me lose my temper" is not a true statement. Nobody but you has control over your emotional responses. Instead, use "I" statements. For example, "When you said that, I got angry." Second, don't generalize a problem by using phrases like "you always" or "you never." Finally, do not pass judgment on the other person's character or the intentions of his or her heart; that is God's job. "What you did was insensitive" is fine. "You don't care about anyone but yourself" is not.

▶▶ 18:20 'You ... mother.' Quotation from Exodus 20:12–16; Deuteronomy 5:16–20.

105

TheFinalScore >>

SUPER BOWL: Champions for Life

WHILE BILLIONS OF PEOPLE WORLDWIDE WATCH on television, millions of dollars worth of merchandise is sold, and advertisements are presented that have commanded astronomical prices, participants say that running onto the field at the Super Bowl is an even bigger thrill.

Players who have played in the big game describe it as the most awesome feeling in all of sports. However, adjusting to life after the glory ends can be tough. Players struggle with depression, drinking, financial losses, and permanent physical injuries.

Within two years of leaving professional football, 78 percent are bankrupt, divorced, or unemployed.

"The biggest challenge many of our players have is looking ahead for the rest of their lives," National Football League Commissioner Paul Tagliabue says.

Former professional players suggest that reinvention of themselves is necessary to move forward after their playing careers end. In other words, instead of trying to salvage their former identity as star athletes, players need to train to become champions for life.

Hebrews 10:36 challenges us to hold on so we can do what God wants and thereby receive what he has promised. Becoming a champion in life is a test lasting long past the glamour and glitz of a game, even one as big as the Super Bowl.

> "Within two years of leaving professional football, 78 percent are bankrupt, divorced, or unemployed."

he was too short to see above the crowd. ⁴He ran ahead to a place where Jesus would come, and he climbed a sycamore tree so he could see him. ⁵When Jesus came to that place, he looked up and said to him, "Zacchaeus, hurry and come down! I must stay at your house today."

⁶Zacchaeus came down quickly and welcomed him gladly. ⁷All the people saw this and began to complain, "Jesus is staying with a sinner!"

⁸But Zacchaeus stood and said to the Lord, "I will give half of my possessions to the poor. And if I have cheated anyone, I will pay back four times more."

⁹Jesus said to him, "Salvation has come to this house today, because this man also belongs to the family of Abraham. ¹⁰The Son of Man came to find lost people and save them."

A Story About Three Servants

¹¹As the people were listening to this, Jesus told them a story because he was near Jerusalem and they thought God's kingdom would appear immediately. ¹²He said: "A very important man went to a country far away to be made a king and then to return home. ¹³So he called ten of his servants and gave a coin to each servant. He said, 'Do business with this money until I get back.' ¹⁴But the people in the kingdom hated the man. So they sent a group to follow him and say, 'We don't want this man to be our king.'

¹⁵"But the man became king. When he returned home, he said, 'Call those servants who have my money so I can know how much they earned with it.'

¹⁶"The first servant came and said, 'Sir, I earned ten coins with the one you gave me.' ¹⁷The king said to the servant, 'Excellent! You are a good servant. Since I can trust you with small things, I will let you rule over ten of my cities.'

¹⁸"The second servant said, 'Sir, I earned five coins with your one.' ¹⁹The king said to this servant, 'You can rule over five cities.'

²⁰"Then another servant came in and said to the king, 'Sir, here is your coin which I wrapped in a piece of cloth and hid. ²¹I was afraid of you, because you are a hard man. You even take money that you didn't earn and gather food that you didn't plant.' ²²Then the king said to the servant, 'I will condemn you by your own words, you evil servant. You knew that I am a hard man, taking money that I didn't earn and gathering food that I didn't plant. ²³Why then didn't you put my money in the bank? Then when I came back, my money would have earned some interest.'

²⁴"The king said to the men who were standing by, 'Take the coin away from this servant and give it to the servant who earned ten coins.' ²⁵They said, 'But sir, that servant already has ten coins.' ²⁶The king said, 'Those who have will be given more, but those who do not have anything will have everything taken away from them. ²⁷Now where are my enemies who didn't want me to be king? Bring them here and kill them before me.' "

Jesus Enters Jerusalem as a King

²⁸After Jesus said this, he went on toward Jerusalem. ²⁹As Jesus came near Bethphage and Bethany, towns near the hill called the Mount of Olives, he sent out two of his followers. ³⁰He said, "Go to the town you can see there. When you enter it, you will find a colt tied there, which no one has ever ridden. Untie it and bring it here to me. ³¹If anyone asks you why you are untying it, say that the Master needs it."

³²The two followers went into town and found the colt just as Jesus had told them. ³³As they were untying it, its owners came out and asked the followers, "Why are you untying our colt?"

³⁴The followers answered, "The Master needs it." ³⁵So they brought it to Jesus, threw their coats on the colt's back, and put Jesus on it. ³⁶As Jesus rode toward Jerusalem, others spread their coats on the road before him.

³⁷As he was coming close to Jerusalem, on the way down the Mount of Olives, the whole crowd of followers began joyfully shouting praise to God for all the miracles they had seen. ³⁸They said,

"God bless the king who comes in the name of the Lord!

Psalm 118:26

There is peace in heaven and glory to God!"

The Bottom Line

Home Equity: Limit Your Borrowing

IF YOU'RE A FIRST-TIME HOMEOWNER, expect to receive appeals to borrow against the equity in your house or condo. While a modest home equity loan may be a source of low-cost funds for a needed improvement, be wary of borrowing against your home just to buy luxury items. If it becomes a habit, you can wind up with a larger debt on your home than your original mortgage. Fail to make the payments, and you will risk losing your largest asset. Don't let the pride of owning many superfluous things deceive you. First John 2:16 indicates that such a desire is not from God.

>> **19:13 coin** A Greek "mina." One mina was enough money to pay a person for working three months.

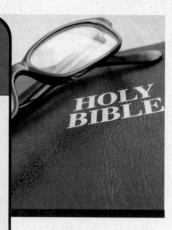

Ten Ways to Grow Spiritually

1. **Read a chapter of the Bible daily.**
2. **Pray for your family and friends.**
3. **Read Bible stories to some children.**
4. **Join a small group or a Bible study class.**
5. **Integrate worship into everyday activities.**
6. **Ask God for wisdom when making decisions.**
7. **Give regularly to your local church.**
8. **Ask people in need how you can pray for them.**
9. **Keep a record of answers to your prayers.**
10. **Ask God for a spiritual mentor in your life.**

[39] Some of the Pharisees in the crowd said to Jesus, "Teacher, tell your followers not to say these things."

[40] But Jesus answered, "I tell you, if my followers didn't say these things, then the stones would cry out."

Jesus Cries for Jerusalem

[41] As Jesus came near Jerusalem, he saw the city and cried for it, [42] saying, "I wish you knew today what would bring you peace. But now it is hidden from you. [43] The time is coming when your enemies will build a wall around you and will hold you in on all sides. [44] They will destroy you and all your people, and not one stone will be left on another. All this will happen because you did not recognize the time when God came to save you."

Jesus Goes to the Temple

[45] Jesus went into the Temple and began to throw out the people who were selling things there. [46] He said, "It is written in the Scriptures, 'My Temple will be a house for prayer.'ⁿ But you have changed it into a 'hideout for robbers'!"ⁿ

[47] Jesus taught in the Temple every day. The leading priests, the experts on the law, and some of the leaders of the people wanted to kill Jesus. [48] But they did not know how they could do it, because all the people were listening closely to him.

Jewish Leaders Question Jesus

20 One day Jesus was in the Temple, teaching the people and telling them the Good News. The leading priests, teachers of the law, and elders came up to talk with him, [2] saying, "Tell us what authority you have to do these things? Who gave you this authority?"

[3] Jesus answered, "I will also ask you a question. Tell me: [4] When John baptized people, was that authority from God or just from other people?"

[5] They argued about this, saying, "If we answer, 'John's baptism was from God,' Jesus will say, 'Then why did you not believe him?' [6] But if we say, 'It was from other people,' all the people will stone us to death, because they believe John was a prophet." [7] So they answered that they didn't know where it came from.

[8] Jesus said to them, "Then I won't tell you what authority I have to do these things."

A Story About God's Son

[9] Then Jesus told the people this story: "A man planted a vineyard and leased it to some farmers. Then he went away for a long time. [10] When it was time for the grapes to be picked, he sent a servant to the farmers to get some of the grapes. But they beat the servant and sent him away empty-handed. [11] Then he sent another servant. They beat this servant also, and showed no respect for him, and sent him away empty-handed. [12] So the man sent a third servant. The farmers wounded him and threw him out. [13] The owner of the vineyard said, 'What will I do now? I will send my son whom I love. Maybe they will respect him.' [14] But when the farmers saw the son, they said to each other, 'This son will inherit the vineyard. If we kill him, it will be ours.' [15] So the farmers threw the son out of the vineyard and killed him.

"What will the owner of this vineyard do to them? [16] He will come and kill those farmers and will give the vineyard to other farmers."

When the people heard this story, they said, "Let this never happen!"

[17] But Jesus looked at them and said, "Then what does this verse mean:

'The stone that the builders rejected
became the cornerstone'? *Psalm 118:22*

[18] Everyone who falls on that stone will be broken, and the person on whom it falls, that person will be crushed!"

[19] The teachers of the law and the leading priests wanted to arrest Jesus at once, because they knew the story was about them. But they were afraid of what the people would do.

Is It Right to Pay Taxes or Not?

[20] So they watched Jesus and sent some spies who acted as if they were sincere. They wanted to trap Jesus in saying something wrong so they could hand him over to the authority and power of the governor. [21] So the spies asked Jesus, "Teacher, we know that what you say and teach is true. You pay no attention to who people are, and you al-

19:46 'My Temple ... prayer.' Quotation from Isaiah 56:7. 19:46 'hideout for robbers' Quotation from Jeremiah 7:11.

108

ways teach the truth about God's way. ²²"Tell us, is it right for us to pay taxes to Caesar or not?"

²³But Jesus, knowing they were trying to trick him, said, ²⁴"Show me a coin. Whose image and name are on it?"

They said, "Caesar's."

²⁵Jesus said to them, "Then give to Caesar the things that are Caesar's, and give to God the things that are God's."

²⁶So they were not able to trap Jesus in anything he said in the presence of the people. And being amazed at his answer, they became silent.

FACT-OIDS!   Sixty-three percent of American men say they follow professional football.   [Harris Interactive]

Some Sadducees Try to Trick Jesus

²⁷Some Sadducees, who believed people would not rise from the dead, came to Jesus. ²⁸They asked, "Teacher, Moses wrote that if a man's brother dies and leaves a wife but no children, then that man must marry the widow and have children for his brother. ²⁹Once there were seven brothers. The first brother married and died, but had no children. ³⁰Then the second brother married the widow, and he died. ³¹And the third brother married the widow, and he died. The same thing happened with all seven brothers; they died and had no children. ³²Finally, the woman died also. ³³Since all seven brothers had married her, whose wife will she be when people rise from the dead?"

³⁴Jesus said to them, "On earth, people marry and are given to someone to marry. ³⁵But those who will be worthy to be raised from the dead and live again will not marry, nor will they be given to someone to marry. ³⁶In that life they are like angels and cannot die. They are children of God, because they have been raised from the dead. ³⁷Even Moses clearly showed that the dead are raised to life. When he wrote about the burning bush, he said that the Lord is 'the God of Abraham, the God of Isaac, and the God

of Jacob.' ³⁸God is the God of the living, not the dead, because all people are alive to him."

³⁹Some of the teachers of the law said, "Teacher, your answer was good." ⁴⁰No one was brave enough to ask him another question.

Is the Christ the Son of David?

⁴¹Then Jesus said, "Why do people say that the Christ is the Son of David? ⁴²In the book of Psalms, David himself says:

'The Lord said to my Lord,
"Sit by me at my right side,
⁴³   until I put your enemies under your
        control." '   *Psalm 110:1*

⁴⁴David calls the Christ 'Lord,' so how can the Christ be his son?"

Jesus Accuses Some Leaders

⁴⁵While all the people were listening, Jesus said to his followers, ⁴⁶"Beware of the teachers of the law. They like to walk around wearing fancy clothes, and they love for people to greet them with respect in the marketplaces. They love to have the most important seats in the synagogues and at feasts. ⁴⁷But they cheat widows and steal their houses and then try to make themselves look good by saying long prayers. They will receive a greater punishment."

True Giving

21 As Jesus looked up, he saw some rich people putting their gifts into the Temple money box. ²Then he saw a poor widow putting two small copper coins into the box. ³He said, "I tell you the truth, this poor widow gave more than all those rich people. ⁴They gave only what they did not need. This woman is very poor, but she gave all she had to live on."

The Temple Will Be Destroyed

⁵Some people were talking about the Temple and how it was decorated with beautiful stones and gifts offered to God.

But Jesus said, ⁶"As for these things you are looking at, the time will come when not one stone will be left on another. Every stone will be thrown down."

⁷They asked Jesus, "Teacher, when will

⊙ Sexcess: GUARDING YOUR THOUGHT LIFE

If you have trouble maintaining purity in your thought life, you are not alone. Men particularly are vulnerable to the sensory barrage of sexual imagery flooding the media landscape. But the good news is that help is available. Scripture reminds us in 2 Corinthians 10:5, "We capture every thought and make it give up and obey Christ." In other words, when an impure thought hits your mind, quit thinking about it by replacing it with a godly thought. Research proves that it is impossible to think two thoughts at the same time. As the old saying goes, "You can't stop birds from flying overhead, but you can keep them from nesting in your hair."

20:37 **burning bush** Read Exodus 3:1–12 in the Old Testament.   20:37 **'the God of … Jacob'** These words are taken from Exodus 3:6.   20:43 **until … control** Literally, "until I make your enemies a footstool for your feet."   21:1 **money box** A special box in the Jewish place of worship where people put their gifts to God.

these things happen? What will be the sign that they are about to take place?"

[8]Jesus said, "Be careful so you are not fooled. Many people will come in my name, saying, 'I am the One' and, 'The time has come!' But don't follow them. [9]When you hear about wars and riots, don't be afraid, because these things must happen first, but the end will come later."

[10]Then he said to them, "Nations will fight against other nations, and kingdoms against other kingdoms. [11]In various places there will be great earthquakes, sicknesses, and a lack of food. Fearful events and great signs will come from heaven.

[12]"But before all these things happen, people will arrest you and treat you cruelly. They will judge you in their synagogues and put you in jail and force you to stand before kings and governors, because you follow me. [13]But this will give you an opportunity to tell about me. [14]Make up your minds not to worry ahead of time about what you will say. [15]I will give you the wisdom to say things that none of your enemies will be able to stand against or prove wrong. [16]Even your parents, brothers, relatives, and friends will turn against you, and they will kill some of you. [17]All people will hate you because you follow me. [18]But none of these things can really harm you. [19]By continuing to have faith you will save your lives.

Jerusalem Will Be Destroyed

[20]"When you see armies all around Jerusalem, you will know it will soon be de-stroyed. [21]At that time, the people in Judea should run away to the mountains. The people in Jerusalem must get out, and those who are near the city should not go in. [22]These are the days of punishment to bring about all that is written in the Scriptures. [23]How terrible it will be for women who are pregnant or have nursing babies! Great trouble will come upon this land, and God will be angry with these people. [24]They will be killed by the sword and taken as prisoners to all nations. Jerusalem will be crushed by non-Jewish people until their time is over.

Don't Fear

[25]"There will be signs in the sun, moon, and stars. On earth, nations will be afraid and confused because of the roar and fury of the sea. [26]People will be so afraid they will faint, wondering what is happening to the world, because the powers of the heavens will be shaken. [27]Then people will see the Son of Man coming in a cloud with power and great glory. [28]When these things begin to happen, look up and hold your heads high, because the time when God will free you is near!"

Jesus' Words Will Live Forever

[29]Then Jesus told this story: "Look at the fig tree and all the other trees. [30]When their

leaves appear, you know that summer is near. [31]In the same way, when you see these things happening, you will know that God's kingdom is near.

[32]"I tell you the truth, all these things will happen while the people of this time are still living. [33]Earth and sky will be destroyed, but the words I have spoken will never be destroyed.

Be Ready All the Time

[34]"Be careful not to spend your time feasting, drinking, or worrying about worldly things. If you do, that day might come on you suddenly, [35]like a trap on all people on earth. [36]So be ready all the time. Pray that you will be strong enough to escape all these things that will happen and that you will be able to stand before the Son of Man."

[37]During the day, Jesus taught the people in the Temple, and at night he went out of the city and stayed on the Mount of Olives. [38]Every morning all the people got up early to go to the Temple to listen to him.

Judas Becomes an Enemy of Jesus

22 It was almost time for the Feast of Unleavened Bread, called the Passover Feast. [2]The leading priests and teachers of the law were trying to find a way to kill Jesus, because they were afraid of the people.

[3]Satan entered Judas Iscariot, one of Jesus' twelve apostles. [4]Judas went to the leading priests and some of the soldiers who guarded the Temple and talked to them about a way to hand Jesus over to them. [5]They were pleased and agreed to give Judas money. [6]He agreed and watched for the best time to hand Jesus over to them when he was away from the crowd.

Jesus Eats the Passover Meal

[7]The Day of Unleavened Bread came when the Passover lambs had to be sacrificed. [8]Jesus said to Peter and John, "Go and prepare the Passover meal for us to eat." [9]They asked, "Where do you want us to prepare it?" [10]Jesus said to them, "After you go into the city, a man carrying a jar of water will meet you. Follow him into the house that he enters, [11]and tell the owner of the

---

{ Deal With It: * Greed

GREED IS AN INSATIABLE YEARNING FOR MORE, a craving that is never satisfied, whether for material goods or other stuff. But Hebrews 13:5 admonishes, "Keep your lives free from the love of money, and be satisfied with what you have." The love of money causes all kinds of evil, but a sense of satisfaction helps keep greed at bay. One way to nip greed in the bud is to cultivate an attitude of gratitude. The more thankful we are for the blessings we enjoy, the less likely we will be to complain about what we feel is lacking in our lives.

Q: How do I receive forgiveness from God?

A: God is always ready and willing to forgive you for any wrong you have done. To receive his forgiveness, you need only to confess your sin and ask him to forgive you. If you do that, you can be confident that you are forgiven (1 John 1:9).

house, 'The Teacher says: "Where is the guest room in which I may eat the Passover meal with my followers?" ' [12]Then he will show you a large, furnished room upstairs. Prepare the Passover meal there."

[13]So Peter and John left and found everything as Jesus had said. And they prepared the Passover meal.

The Lord's Supper

[14]When the time came, Jesus and the apostles were sitting at the table. [15]He said to them, "I wanted very much to eat this Passover meal with you before I suffer. [16]I will not eat another Passover meal until it is given its true meaning in the kingdom of God."

[17]Then Jesus took a cup, gave thanks, and said, "Take this cup and share it among yourselves. [18]I will not drink again from the fruit of the vine" until God's kingdom comes."

[19]Then Jesus took some bread, gave thanks, broke it, and gave it to the apostles, saying, "This is my body," which I am giving for you. Do this to remember me." [20]In the same way, after supper, Jesus took the cup and said, "This cup is the new agreement that God makes with his people. This new agreement begins with my blood which is poured out for you.

Who Will Turn Against Jesus?

[21]"But one of you will turn against me, and his hand is with mine on the table. [22]What God has planned for the Son of Man will happen, but how terrible it will be for that one who turns against the Son of Man."

[23]Then the apostles asked each other which one of them would do that.

Be Like a Servant

[24]The apostles also began to argue about which one of them was the most important. [25]But Jesus said to them, "The kings of the non-Jewish people rule over them, and those who have authority over others like to be called 'friends of the people.' [26]But you must not be like that. Instead, the greatest among you should be like the youngest, and the leader should be like the servant. [27]Who is more important: the one sitting at the table or the one serving? You think the one at the table is more important, but I am like a servant among you.

[28]"You have stayed with me through my struggles. [29]Just as my Fa-

ther has given me a kingdom, I also give you a kingdom [30]so you may eat and drink at my table in my kingdom. And you will sit on thrones, judging the twelve tribes of Israel.

Don't Lose Your Faith!

[31]"Simon, Simon, Satan has asked to test all of you as a farmer sifts his wheat. [32]I have prayed that you will not lose your faith! Help your brothers be stronger when you come back to me."

[33]But Peter said to Jesus, "Lord, I am ready to go with you to prison and even to die with you!"

[34]But Jesus said, "Peter, before the rooster crows this day, you will say three times that you don't know me."

Be Ready for Trouble

[35]Then Jesus said to the apostles, "When I sent you out without a purse, a bag, or sandals, did you need anything?"

They said, "No."

[36]He said to them, "But now if you have a purse or a bag, carry that with you. If you don't have a sword, sell your coat and buy one. [37]The Scripture says, 'He was treated like a criminal,'" and I tell you this scripture must have its full meaning. It was written about me, and it is happening now."

[38]His followers said, "Look, Lord, here are two swords."

He said to them, "That is enough."

▶ Get Aligned

Luke 22:61–62

DENYING JESUS ISN'T ALWAYS AS OVERT as it was for Peter. We deny Jesus whenever we turn our backs on his commands, when we choose to walk off the path he's designed for us, and when we refuse to defend his name before a God-hating world. Denying him can be as simple as falling into a habitual sin, or it can be as complex as taking control over your future rather than offering it to him. The truth is, we've all denied him at times.

Thankfully, there's good news. A closer look at what ultimately happened to Peter displays Christ's redemptive nature. Despite Peter lying about even knowing Jesus, the Lord was quick to forgive. After Jesus' resurrection, the angel at the tomb told the women to "go and tell his followers and Peter" (Mark 16:7).

The Lord knew Peter was hurting, and he wanted to make sure Peter knew he would be all right. In fact, Peter was one of the first to see the risen Christ. The Lord specifically sought out his fallen follower, and he does the same thing for us. If you think you are hopeless, think again. You are forever on God's heart.

22:18 fruit of the vine Product of the grapevine; this may also be translated "wine." **22:19b–20 body** Some Greek copies do not have the rest of verse 19 or verse 20. **22:37 'He…criminal.'** Quotation from Isaiah 53:12.

Jesus Prays Alone

[39]Jesus left the city and went to the Mount of Olives, as he often did, and his followers went with him. [40]When he reached the place, he said to them, "Pray for strength against temptation." [41]Then Jesus went about a stone's throw away from them. He kneeled down and prayed, [42]"Father, if you are willing, take away this cup[n] of suffering. But do what you want, not what I want." [43]Then an angel from heaven appeared to him to strengthen him. [44]Being full of pain, Jesus prayed even harder. His sweat was like drops of blood falling to the ground. [45]When he finished praying, he went to his followers and found them asleep because of their sadness. [46]Jesus said to them, "Why are you sleeping? Get up and pray for strength against temptation."

Jesus Is Arrested

[47]While Jesus was speaking, a crowd came up, and Judas, one of the twelve apostles, was leading them. He came close to Jesus so he could kiss him. [48]But Jesus said to him, "Judas, are you using the kiss to give the Son of Man to his enemies?" [49]When those who were standing around him saw what was happening, they said, "Lord, should we strike them with our swords?" [50]And one of them struck the servant of the high priest and cut off his right ear. [51]Jesus said, "Stop! No more of this." Then he touched the servant's ear and healed him. [52]Those who came to arrest Jesus were the leading priests, the soldiers who guarded the Temple, and the elders. Jesus said to them, "You came out here with swords and clubs as though I were a criminal. [53]I was with you every day in the Temple, and you didn't arrest me there. But this is your time—the time when darkness rules."

Peter Says He Doesn't Know Jesus

[54]They arrested Jesus, and led him away, and brought him into the house of the high priest. Peter followed far behind them. [55]After the soldiers started a fire in the middle of the courtyard and sat together, Peter sat with them. [56]A servant girl saw Peter sitting there in the firelight, and looking closely at him, she said, "This man was also with him." [57]But Peter said this was not true; he said, "Woman, I don't know him." [58]A short time later, another person saw Peter and said, "You are also one of them."

But Peter said, "Man, I am not!"

[59]About an hour later, another man insisted, "Certainly this man was with him, because he is from Galilee, too." [60]But Peter said, "Man, I don't know what you are talking about!"

At once, while Peter was still speaking, a rooster crowed. [61]Then the Lord turned and looked straight at Peter. And Peter remembered what the Lord had said: "Before the rooster crows this day, you will say three times that you don't know me." [62]Then Peter went outside and cried painfully.

The People Make Fun of Jesus

[63]The men who were guarding Jesus began making fun of him and beating him. [64]They blindfolded him and said, "Prove that you are a prophet, and tell us who hit you." [65]They said many cruel things to Jesus.

Jesus Before the Leaders

[66]When day came, the council of the elders of the people, both the leading priests and the teachers of the law, came together and led Jesus to their highest court. [67]They said, "If you are the Christ, tell us."

Jesus said to them, "If I tell you, you will not believe me. [68]And if I ask you, you will not answer. [69]But from now on, the Son of Man will sit at the right hand of the powerful God."

[70]They all said, "Then are you the Son of God?"

Jesus said to them, "You say that I am."

[71]They said, "Why do we need witnesses now? We ourselves heard him say this."

Pilate Questions Jesus

23 Then the whole group stood up and led Jesus to Pilate.[n] [2]They began to accuse Jesus, saying, "We caught this man telling things that mislead our people. He says that we should not pay taxes to Caesar, and he calls himself the Christ, a king."

[3]Pilate asked Jesus, "Are you the king of the Jews?"

Jesus answered, "Those are your words."

[4]Pilate said to the leading priests and the people, "I find nothing against this man."

[5]They were insisting, saying, "But Jesus makes trouble with the people, teaching all around Judea. He began in Galilee, and now he is here."

Pilate Sends Jesus to Herod

[6]Pilate heard this and asked if Jesus was from Galilee. [7]Since Jesus was under Herod's authority, Pilate sent Jesus to Herod, who was in Jerusalem at that time. [8]When Herod saw Jesus, he was very glad, because he had heard about Jesus and had wanted to meet him for a long

Q: Why is the virgin birth of Jesus so important?

A: Jesus was all man and all God. For that to happen, he had to be born of both God and humankind. Without the miraculous virgin birth, Jesus would not have inherited God's holy nature, and, therefore, he could not have redeemed us from our sins (Matthew 1:23).

>> **22:42 cup** Jesus is talking about the painful things that will happen to him. Accepting these things will be hard, like drinking a cup of something bitter. **23:1 Pilate** Pontius Pilate was the Roman governor of Judea from A.D. 26 to A.D. 36.

time. He was hoping to see Jesus work a miracle. ⁹Herod asked Jesus many questions, but Jesus said nothing. ¹⁰The leading priests and teachers of the law were standing there, strongly accusing Jesus. ¹¹After Herod and his soldiers had made fun of Jesus, they dressed him in a kingly robe and sent him back to Pilate. ¹²In the past, Pilate and Herod had always been enemies, but on that day they became friends.

Jesus Must Die

¹³Pilate called the people together with the leading priests and the rulers. ¹⁴He said to them, "You brought this man to me, saying he makes trouble among the people. But I have questioned him before you all, and I have not found him guilty of what you say. ¹⁵Also, Herod found nothing wrong with him; he sent him back to us. Look, he has done nothing for which he should die. ¹⁶So, after I punish him, I will let him go free." [¹⁷Every year at the Passover Feast, Pilate had to release one prisoner to the people.]ⁿ

¹⁸But the people shouted together, "Take this man away! Let Barabbas go free!" ¹⁹(Barabbas was a man who was in prison for his part in a riot in the city and for murder.)

²⁰Pilate wanted to let Jesus go free and told this to the crowd. ²¹But they shouted again, "Crucify him! Crucify him!"

²²A third time Pilate said to them, "Why? What wrong has he done? I can find no reason to kill him. So I will have him punished and set him free."

²³But they continued to shout, demanding that Jesus be crucified. Their yelling became so loud that ²⁴Pilate decided to give them what they wanted. ²⁵He set free the man who was in jail for rioting and murder, and he handed Jesus over to them to do with him as they wished.

Jesus Is Crucified

²⁶As they led Jesus away, Simon, a man from Cyrene, was coming in from the fields. They forced him to carry Jesus' cross and to walk behind him.

²⁷A large crowd of people was following Jesus, including some women who were sad and crying for him. ²⁸But Jesus turned and said to them, "Women of Jerusalem, don't cry for me. Cry for yourselves and for your children. ²⁹The time is coming when people will say, 'Blessed are the women who cannot have children and who have no babies to nurse.' ³⁰Then people will say to the mountains, 'Fall on us!' And they will say to the hills, 'Cover us!' ³¹If they act like this now when life is good, what will happen when bad times come?'"ⁿ

³²There were also two criminals led out with Jesus to be put to death. ³³When they came to a place called the Skull, the soldiers crucified Jesus and the criminals—one on his right and the other on his left. ³⁴Jesus said, "Father, forgive them, because they don't know what they are doing."ⁿ

The soldiers threw lots to decide who would get his clothes. ³⁵The people stood there watching. And the leaders made fun of Jesus, saying, "He saved others. Let him save himself if he is God's Chosen One, the Christ."

³⁶The soldiers also made fun of him, coming to Jesus and offering him some vinegar. ³⁷They said, "If you are the king of the Jews, save yourself!" ³⁸At the top of the cross these words were written: THIS IS THE KING OF THE JEWS.

³⁹One of the criminals on a cross began to shout insults at Jesus: "Aren't you the Christ? Then save yourself and us."

⁴⁰But the other criminal stopped him and said, "You should fear God! You are getting the same punishment he is. ⁴¹We are punished justly, getting what we deserve for what we did. But this man has done nothing wrong." ⁴²Then he said, "Jesus, remember me when you come into your kingdom."

⁴³Jesus said to him, "I tell you the truth, today you will be with me in paradise."ⁿ

Jesus Dies

⁴⁴It was about noon, and the whole land became dark until three o'clock in the afternoon, ⁴⁵because the sun did not shine. The curtain in the Templeⁿ was torn in two. ⁴⁶Jesus cried out in a loud voice, "Father, I give you my life." After Jesus said this, he died.

⁴⁷When the army officer there saw what happened, he praised God, saying, "Surely this was a good man!"

⁴⁸When all the people who had gathered there to watch saw what happened, they returned home, beating their chests because they were so sad. ⁴⁹But those who were close friends of Jesus, including the women who had followed him from Galilee, stood at a distance and watched.

Joseph Takes Jesus' Body

⁵⁰There was a good and religious man named Joseph who was a member of the council. ⁵¹But he had not agreed to the other leaders' plans and actions against Jesus. He was from the town of Arimathea and was waiting for the kingdom of God to come. ⁵²Joseph went to

«TechSupport»

HOME NETWORKING

If you want to share an Internet connection among multiple computers in the same house, it has never been easier. Inexpensive wireless routers can connect several computers to a high-speed network so they can share files and access to the Internet. Configuration can get technical sometimes, but it's nothing a good manual or tech support can't resolve. As a Christian, it is important to connect with other members of the body of Christ and to consult the owner's manual, the Bible.

23:17 *Every . . . people.* Some Greek copies do not contain the bracketed text.   **23:31** *If . . . come?* Literally, "If they do these things in the green tree, what will happen in the dry?"
23:34 *Jesus . . . doing."* Some Greek copies do not have this first part of verse 34.   **23:43** *paradise* Another word for heaven.   **23:45** *curtain in the Temple* A curtain divided the Most Holy Place from the other part of the Temple, the special building in Jerusalem where God commanded the Jewish people to worship him.

113

Pilate to ask for the body of Jesus. [53]He took the body down from the cross, wrapped it in cloth, and put it in a tomb that was cut out of a wall of rock. This tomb had never been used before. [54]This was late on Preparation Day, and when the sun went down, the Sabbath day would begin.

[55]The women who had come from Galilee with Jesus followed Joseph and saw the tomb and how Jesus' body was laid. [56]Then the women left to prepare spices and perfumes.

On the Sabbath day they rested, as the law of Moses commanded.

Jesus Rises from the Dead

24 Very early on the first day of the week, at dawn, the women came to the tomb, bringing the spices they had prepared. [2]They found the stone rolled away from the entrance of the tomb, [3]but when they went in, they did not find the body of the Lord Jesus. [4]While they were wondering about this, two men in shining clothes suddenly stood beside them. [5]The women were very afraid and bowed their heads to the ground. The men said to them, "Why are you looking for a living person in this place for the dead? [6]He is not here; he has risen from the dead. Do you remember what he told you in Galilee? [7]He said the Son of Man must be handed over to sinful people, be crucified, and rise from the dead on the third day." [8]Then the women remembered what Jesus had said.

[9]The women left the tomb and told all these things to the eleven apostles and the other followers. [10]It was Mary Magdalene, Joanna, Mary the mother of James, and some other women who told the apostles everything that had happened at the tomb. [11]But they did not believe the women, because it sounded like nonsense. [12]But Peter got up and ran to the tomb. Bending down and looking in, he saw only the cloth that Jesus' body had been wrapped in. Peter went away to his home, wondering about what had happened.

Jesus on the Road to Emmaus

[13]That same day two of Jesus' followers were going to a town named Emmaus, about seven miles from Jerusalem. [14]They were talking about everything that had happened. [15]While they were talking and discussing, Jesus himself came near and began walking with them, [16]but they were kept from recognizing him. [17]Then he said, "What are these things you are talking about while you walk?"

The two followers stopped, looking very sad. [18]The one named Cleopas answered, "Are you the only visitor in Jerusalem who does not know what just happened there?"

[19]Jesus said to them, "What are you talking about?"

They said, "About Jesus of Nazareth. He was a prophet who said and did many powerful things before God and all the people. [20]Our leaders and the leading priests handed him over to be sentenced to death, and they crucified him. [21]But we were hoping that he would free Israel. Besides this, it is now the third day since this happened. [22]And today some women among us amazed us. Early this morning they went to the tomb, [23]but they did not find his body there. They came and told us that they had seen a vision of angels who said that Jesus was alive! [24]So some of our group went to the tomb, too. They found it just as the women said, but they did not see Jesus."

[25]Then Jesus said to them, "You are foolish and slow to believe everything the prophets said. [26]They said that the Christ must suffer these things before he enters his glory." [27]Then starting with what Moses and all the prophets had said about him, Jesus began to explain everything that had been written about himself in the Scriptures.

[28]They came near the town of Emmaus, and Jesus acted as if he were going farther. [29]But they begged him, "Stay with us, because it is late; it is almost night." So he went in to stay with them.

[30]When Jesus was at the table with them, he

Get Fit

SWIMMING FOR HEALTH   If you're looking for a fun, new way to get into shape, why not try swimming? A terrific low-impact sport, swimming offers an unparalleled cardiovascular workout and does a great job of building strength and stamina in your muscles. If you haven't hit the pool in a while, you might want to sign up for a lesson or two in the basic strokes before launching into a workout routine. But with a little practice, you can soon be lapping your way to a healthier life. Just be sure to use plenty of sunscreen, preferably with a sun protection factor of at least fifteen, if you'll be swimming outdoors. Get more information about swimming by visiting www.swimmingworldmagazine.com.

took some bread, gave thanks, divided it, and gave it to them. [31]And then, they were allowed to recognize Jesus. But when they saw who he was, he disappeared. [32]They said to each other, "It felt like a fire burning in us when Jesus talked to us on the road and explained the Scriptures to us."

[33]So the two followers got up at once and went back to Jerusalem. There they found the eleven apostles and others gathered. [34]They were saying, "The Lord really has risen from the dead! He showed himself to Simon."

sus said to them, "Do you have any food here?" [42]They gave him a piece of broiled fish. [43]While the followers watched, Jesus took the fish and ate it.

[44]He said to them, "Remember when I was with you before? I said that everything written about me must happen—everything in the law of Moses, the books of the prophets, and the Psalms."

[45]Then Jesus opened their minds so they could understand the Scriptures. [46]He said to them, "It is written that the Christ would suffer and rise from the dead on the third day [47]and that a change of

> **❝ I will send you what my Father has promised, but you must stay in Jerusalem until you have received that power from heaven. ❞** LUKE 24:49

[35]Then the two followers told what had happened on the road and how they recognized Jesus when he divided the bread.

Jesus Appears to His Followers

[36]While the two followers were telling this, Jesus himself stood right in the middle of them and said, "Peace be with you."

[37]They were fearful and terrified and thought they were seeing a ghost. [38]But Jesus said, "Why are you troubled? Why do you doubt what you see? [39]Look at my hands and my feet. It is I myself! Touch me and see, because a ghost does not have a living body as you see I have."

[40]After Jesus said this, he showed them his hands and feet. [41]While they still could not believe it because they were amazed and happy, Je-

hearts and lives and forgiveness of sins would be preached in his name to all nations, starting at Jerusalem. [48]You are witnesses of these things. [49]I will send you what my Father has promised, but you must stay in Jerusalem until you have received that power from heaven."

Jesus Goes Back to Heaven

[50]Jesus led his followers as far as Bethany, and he raised his hands and blessed them. [51]While he was blessing them, he was separated from them and carried into heaven. [52]They worshiped him and returned to Jerusalem very happy. [53]They stayed in the Temple all the time, praising God.

THE GOSPEL ACCORDING TO
John

AUTHOR: JOHN
DATE WRITTEN: A.D. 66–98

THE CAMERAS MOVE IN CLOSE FOR AN
intimate chat with a celebrity and the interviewer. The interviewer has researched and delved into the subject's background, so his questions come hard and fast, with the purpose of drawing a distinct picture of the celebrity.

Whereas there were no cameras in his time, the apostle John still was able to reveal a different view of Jesus Christ from any of the other Gospel writers. From the opening words, the stories and the dialogue of this Gospel prove that Jesus is the Son of God and that everyone who believes in him will have eternal life. The deity of Jesus is emphasized through use of his various names, including the Word, Lamb of God, Son of God, Bread of Life, Light, Resurrection, and Vine.

Each chapter reveals a personal and powerful Jesus who is pertinent to our life of faith. This Gospel records Jesus having long conversations with people about his mission and ministry on earth. Also, this Gospel is the only one in which Jesus mentions the promise of the Holy Spirit. John reminds us that, as we welcome the Holy Spirit into our lives, we are empowered to share the message of Jesus with others, so they, too, might experience the eternal life he came to give.

Christ Comes to the World

1 In the beginning there was the Word." The Word was with God, and the Word was God. ²He was with God in the beginning. ³All things were made by him, and nothing was made without him. ⁴In him there was life, and that life was the light of all people. ⁵The Light shines in the darkness, and the darkness has not overpowered" it.

⁶There was a man named John" who was sent by God. ⁷He came to tell people the truth about the Light so that through him all people could hear about the Light and believe. ⁸John was not the Light, but he came to tell people the truth about the Light. ⁹The true Light that gives light to all was coming into the world!

¹⁰The Word was in the world, and the world was made by him, but the world did not know him. ¹¹He came to the world that was his own, but his own people did not accept him. ¹²But to all who did accept him and believe in him he gave the right to become children of God. ¹³They did not become his children in any human way—by any human parents or human desire. They were born of God.

¹⁴The Word became a human and lived among us. We saw his glory—the glory that belongs to the only Son of the Father—and he was full of grace and truth. ¹⁵John tells the truth about him and cries out, saying, "This is the One I told you about: 'The One who comes after me is greater than I am, because he was living before me.' "

¹⁶Because he was full of grace and truth, from him we all received one gift after another. ¹⁷The law was given through Moses, but grace and truth came through Jesus Christ. ¹⁸No one has ever seen God. But God the only Son is very close to the Father," and he has shown us what God is like.

John Tells People About Jesus

¹⁹Here is the truth John" told when the leaders in Jerusalem sent priests and Levites to ask him, "Who are you?"

²⁰John spoke freely and did not refuse to answer. He said, "I am not the Christ."

²¹So they asked him, "Then who are you? Are you Elijah?""

He answered, "No, I am not."

"Are you the Prophet?"" they asked.

He answered, "No."

²²Then they said, "Who are you? Give us an answer to tell those who sent us. What do you say about yourself?"

²³John told them in the words of the prophet Isaiah:

"I am the voice of one
   calling out in the desert:
'Make the road straight for the Lord.' "   *Isaiah 40:3*

²⁴Some Pharisees who had been sent asked John: ²⁵"If you are not the Christ or Elijah or the Prophet, why do you baptize people?"

²⁶John answered, "I baptize with water, but there is one here with you that you don't know about. ²⁷He is the One who comes after me. I am not good enough to untie the strings of his sandals."

²⁸This all happened at Bethany on the other side of the Jordan River, where John was baptizing people.

²⁹The next day John saw Jesus coming toward him. John said, "Look, the Lamb of God," who takes away the sin of the world! ³⁰This is the One I was talking about when I said, 'A man will come after me, but he is greater than I am, because he was living before me.' ³¹Even I did not know who he was, although I came baptizing with water so that the people of Israel would know who he is."

³²⁻³³Then John said, "I saw the Spirit come down from heaven in the form of a dove and rest on him. Until then I did not know who the Christ was. But the God who sent me to baptize with water told me, 'You will see the Spirit come down and rest on a man; he is the One who will baptize with the Holy Spirit.' ³⁴I have seen this happen, and I tell you the truth: This man is the Son of God.""

The First Followers of Jesus

³⁵The next day John" was there again with two of his followers. ³⁶When he saw Jesus walking by, he said, "Look, the Lamb of God!""

³⁷The two followers heard John say this, so they followed Jesus. ³⁸When Jesus turned and saw them following him, he asked, "What are you looking for?"

They said, "Rabbi, where are you staying?" ("Rabbi" means "Teacher.")

³⁹He answered, "Come and see." So the two men went with Jesus and saw where he was staying and stayed there with him that day. It was about four o'clock in the afternoon.

▶Get Aligned

John 1:4–5

THINK ABOUT WHAT HAPPENS WHEN YOU TURN ON THE LIGHT in a room that is pitch black. Obviously, the room lights up. Likewise, when you light a campfire in a forest at night, the same thing occurs. The darkness doesn't overcome the light; the light overcomes the darkness.

We live in dark times. War. Famine. Disease. It would be easy to concede victory to the smothering darkness. But John describes Jesus as the "light of all people." Even better, he declares a truth that too often we forget: "The darkness has not overpowered it."

Satan, the ruler of the realm of darkness, has not overcome the light of Jesus Christ and never will. The Bible gives away the story's ending: light wins, darkness loses. That means that as believers whom Jesus called the light of the world in Matthew 5:14, we are empowered to shine in whatever darkness surrounds us. Wherever we encounter the deprivation and sinfulness that rules this world, we can remember that Jesus has already overcome it and proven that his light will never be extinguished.

1:1 Word The Greek word is "logos," meaning any kind of communication; it could be translated "message." Here, it means Christ, because Christ was the way God told people about himself. **1:5 overpowered** This can also be translated, "understood." **1:6, 19 John** John the Baptist, who preached to people about Christ's coming (Matthew 3, Luke 3). **1:18 But … Father** This could be translated, "But the only God is very close to the Father." Also, some Greek copies read "But the only Son is very close to the Father." (John 1 notes cont. on p. 118.)

⁴⁰One of the two men who followed Jesus after they heard John speak about him was Andrew, Simon Peter's brother. ⁴¹The first thing Andrew did was to find his brother Simon and say to him, "We have found the Messiah." ("Messiah" means "Christ.")

⁴²Then Andrew took Simon to Jesus. Jesus looked at him and said, "You are Simon son of John. You will be called Cephas." ("Cephas" means "Peter."")

⁴³The next day Jesus decided to go to Galilee. He found Philip and said to him, "Follow me."

⁴⁴Philip was from the town of Bethsaida, where Andrew and Peter lived. ⁴⁵Philip found Nathanael and told him, "We have found the man that Moses wrote about in the law, and the prophets also wrote about him. He is Jesus, the son of Joseph, from Nazareth."

⁴⁶But Nathanael said to Philip, "Can anything good come from Nazareth?"

Philip answered, "Come and see."

⁴⁷As Jesus saw Nathanael coming toward him, he said, "Here is truly an Israelite. There is nothing false in him."

⁴⁸Nathanael asked, "How do you know me?"

Jesus answered, "I saw you when you were under the fig tree, before Philip told you about me."

⁴⁹Then Nathanael said to Jesus, "Teacher, you are the Son of God; you are the King of Israel."

⁵⁰Jesus said to Nathanael, "Do you believe simply because I told you I saw you under the fig tree? You will see greater things than that." ⁵¹And Jesus said to them, "I tell you the truth, you will all see heaven open and 'angels of God going up and coming down'" on the Son of Man."

The Wedding at Cana

2 Two days later there was a wedding in the town of Cana in Galilee. Jesus' mother was there, ²and Jesus and his followers were also invited to the wedding. ³When all the wine was gone, Jesus' mother said to him, "They have no more wine."

⁴Jesus answered, "Dear woman, why come to me? My time has not yet come."

⁵His mother said to the servants, "Do whatever he tells you to do."

⁶In that place there were six stone water jars that the Jews used in their washing ceremony." Each jar held about twenty or thirty gallons.

⁷Jesus said to the servants, "Fill the jars with water." So they filled the jars to the top.

⁸Then he said to them, "Now take some out and give it to the master of the feast."

So they took the water to the master. ⁹When he tasted it, the water had become wine. He did not know where the wine came from, but the servants who had brought the water knew. The master of the wedding called the bridegroom ¹⁰and said to him, "People always serve the best wine first. Later, after the guests have been drinking awhile, they serve the cheaper wine. But you have saved the best wine till now."

¹¹So in Cana of Galilee Jesus did his first miracle. There he showed his glory, and his followers believed in him.

Q: Who is the Holy Spirit?

A: The Holy Spirit is God. Often referred to as the Helper, Spirit of God, Holy Ghost, or Spirit of Christ, the Holy Spirit is the presence of God abiding in the hearts of Christians. His primary purpose is to strengthen us and empower us for daily living (John 14:16—17).

Survival Guide

ELECTRICITY: SAVING POWER

The power of God is a good thing, but wasting electrical power is not. You can save electricity with a simple gesture: flicking your wrist. Turn off the lights, radio, television, or computers when you leave a room. If you dislike the hard drive going through frequent boot ups, shut off the monitor, which uses sixty percent of a computer's power. Unplug infrequently used televisions, since many draw juice even when off. Using electric power for heating, for cooking, and for drying clothes is more expensive than gas. And in warm weather, a clothesline is the cheapest option of all.

1:21 Elijah A prophet who spoke for God. He lived hundreds of years before Christ and was expected to return before Christ (Malachi 4:5–6).   **1:21 Prophet** They probably meant the prophet that God told Moses he would send (Deuteronomy 18:15–19).   **1:29 Lamb of God** Name for Jesus. Jesus is like the lambs that were offered for a sacrifice to God.   **1:34 the Son of God** Some Greek copies read "God's Chosen One."   **1:35 John** John the Baptist, who preached to people about Christ's coming (Matthew 3, Luke 3).

Jesus in the Temple

[12]After this, Jesus went to the town of Capernaum with his mother, brothers, and followers. They stayed there for just a few days. [13]When it was almost time for the Jewish Passover Feast, Jesus went to Jerusalem. [14]In the Temple he found people selling cattle, sheep, and doves. He saw others sitting at tables, exchanging different kinds of money. [15]Jesus made a whip out of cords and forced all of them, both the sheep and cattle, to leave the Temple. He turned over the tables and scattered the money of those who were exchanging it. [16]Then he said to those who were selling pigeons, "Take these things out of here! Don't make my Father's house a place for buying and selling!"

[17]When this happened, the followers remembered what was written in the Scriptures: "My strong love for your Temple completely controls me."[n]

[18]Some of his people said to Jesus, "Show us a miracle to prove you have the right to do these things."

[19]Jesus answered them, "Destroy this temple, and I will build it again in three days."

[20]They answered, "It took forty-six years to build this Temple! Do you really believe you can build it again in three days?"

[21](But the temple Jesus meant was his own body. [22]After Jesus was raised from the dead, his followers remembered that Jesus had said this. Then they believed the Scripture and the words Jesus had said.)

[23]When Jesus was in Jerusalem for the Passover Feast, many people believed in him because they saw the miracles he did. [24]But Jesus did not believe in them because he knew them all. [25]He did not need anyone to tell him about people, because he knew what was in people's minds.

Nicodemus Comes to Jesus

3 There was a man named Nicodemus who was one of the Pharisees and an important Jewish leader. [2]One night Nicodemus came to Jesus and said, "Teacher, we know you are a teacher sent from God, because no one can do the miracles you do unless God is with him."

[3]Jesus answered, "I tell you the truth, unless you are born again, you cannot be in God's kingdom."

[4]Nicodemus said, "But if a person is already old, how can he be born again? He cannot enter his mother's womb again. So how can a person be born a second time?"

[5]But Jesus answered, "I tell you the truth, unless you are born from water and the Spirit, you cannot enter God's kingdom. [6]Human life comes from human parents, but spiritual life comes from the Spirit.

Change >> Your WORLD

EVANGELISM EXPLOSION INTERNATIONAL

Dr. D. James Kennedy, the senior pastor of Coral Ridge Presbyterian Church in Fort Lauderdale, Florida, created Evangelism Explosion, and through it, millions of churches have trained their members to be passionate about their relationship with Jesus Christ. You can represent your church by signing up for the leadership training, and you'll receive a complete kit of resources, including teaching notes, an implementation manual, the textbook *Evangelism Explosion* by Dr. Kennedy, and important supplemental booklets. But most importantly, you'll learn to share your faith effectively and help train others to do the same.

To change your world, visit www.eeinternational.org.

Principles: GIVING

Giving is a virtue praised throughout the New Testament. It includes the giving of tithes, or ten percent of one's income, and additional offerings to further the kingdom of God. In Acts 20:35, Luke reminded readers, "It is more blessed to give than to receive." Likewise, Paul encouraged the Corinthian church to be generous, telling it, "God loves the person who gives happily" (2 Corinthians 9:7). In return for our giving, God promises to provide abundant blessings, not only to meet our needs but also to enable us to be a blessing to others.

1:36 **Lamb of God** Name for Jesus. Jesus is like the lambs that were offered for a sacrifice to God. 1:42 **Peter** The Greek name "Peter," like the Aramaic name "Cephas," means "rock." 1:51 **'angels...down'** These words are from Genesis 28:12. 2:6 **washing ceremony** The Jewish people washed themselves in special ways before eating, before worshiping in the Temple, and at other special times. 2:17 **"My...me."** Quotation from Psalm 69:9.

Men of Valor

JAMES THE APOSTLE:
Decisive Follower

James the apostle played a prominent role in Christ's ministry, joining the apostles Peter and John in Christ's inner circle. James was a decisive follower, responding immediately to the call to leave his fishing nets in order to follow Christ (Matthew 4:21–22). However, the New Testament also portrays James as an impetuous man. James was ready to call down fire from heaven on Samaritans who didn't welcome Christ, and he wanted a special place in heaven next to the Lord. Despite his shortcomings, James accompanied Jesus on such key missions as raising a dead girl and praying in the Garden of Gethsemane.

⁷Don't be surprised when I tell you, 'You must all be born again.' ⁸The wind blows where it wants to and you hear the sound of it, but you don't know where the wind comes from or where it is going. It is the same with every person who is born from the Spirit."

⁹Nicodemus asked, "How can this happen?"

¹⁰Jesus said, "You are an important teacher in Israel, and you don't understand these things? ¹¹I tell you the truth, we talk about what we know, and we tell about what we have seen, but you don't accept what we tell you. ¹²I have told you about things here on earth, and you do not believe me. So you will not believe me if I tell you about things of heaven. ¹³The only one who has ever gone up to heaven is the One who came down from heaven—the Son of Man."

¹⁴"Just as Moses lifted up the snake in the desert," the Son of Man must also be lifted up. ¹⁵So that everyone who believes can have eternal life in him.

¹⁶"God loved the world so much that he gave his one and only Son so that whoever believes in him may not be lost, but have eternal life. ¹⁷God did not send his Son into the world to judge the world guilty, but to save the world through him. ¹⁸People who believe in God's Son are not judged guilty. Those who do not believe have already been judged guilty, because they have not believed in God's one and only Son. ¹⁹They are judged by this fact: The Light has come into the world, but they did not want light. They wanted darkness, because they were doing evil things. ²⁰All who do evil hate the light and will not come to the light, because it will show all the evil things they do. ²¹But those who follow the true way come to the light, and it shows that the things they do were done through God."

Jesus and John the Baptist

²²After this, Jesus and his followers went into the area of Judea, where he stayed with his followers and baptized people. ²³John was also baptizing in Aenon, near Salim, because there was plenty of water there. People were going there to be baptized. ²⁴(This was before John was put into prison.)

²⁵Some of John's followers had an argument with a Jew about religious washing." ²⁶So they came to John and said, "Teacher, remember the man who was with you on the other side of the Jordan River, the one you spoke about so much? He is baptizing, and everyone is going to him."

²⁷John answered, "A man can get only what God gives him. ²⁸You yourselves heard me say, 'I am not the Christ, but I am the one sent to prepare the way for him.' ²⁹The bride belongs only to the bridegroom. But the friend who helps the bridegroom stands by and listens to him. He is thrilled that he gets to hear the bridegroom's voice. In the same way, I am really happy. ³⁰He must become greater, and I must become less important.

The One Who Comes from Heaven

³¹"The One who comes from above is greater than all. The one who is from the earth belongs to the earth and talks about things on the earth. But the One who comes from heaven is greater than all. ³²He tells what he has seen and heard, but no one accepts what he says. ³³Whoever accepts what he says has proven that God is true. ³⁴The

{ Book of the Month }

Wild at Heart
by John Eldredge

In this moving work, John Eldredge uses mystery and storytelling to touch the deep wounds that rob men's hearts, minds, and souls of power. Through piercing insights, he inspires men to recapture the true strength God created in them from the beginning. When his wife, Stasi, presents John with a sword symbolic of his love and stewardship of their family, readers will well up with emotions. *Wild at Heart* is refreshingly free of cliché, and contains references to popular culture and films that make the message even more relevant for men seeking truth in a world of relativism.

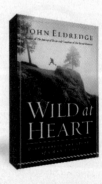

3:13 **the Son of Man** Some Greek copies continue, "who is in heaven." 3:14 **Moses ... desert** When the Israelites were dying from snakebites, God told Moses to put a bronze snake on a pole. The people who looked at the snake were healed (Numbers 21:4–9). 3:25 **religious washing** The Jewish people washed themselves in special ways before eating, before worshiping in the Temple, and at other special times.

>> March

QUOTE OF THE MONTH:
"Discipline is the soul of an army. It makes small numbers formidable, procures success to the weak and esteem to all." —George Washington

1 Pray for a person of influence: Today is director **Ron Howard's** birthday.

2

3

4 Eat some fresh fruit.

5

6 Get a library card.

7

8 Read the Book of **Ephesians** and pray for unity of the church.

9 Head to the gym for a workout.

10

11

12 Pray for a person of influence: Today is musician **James Taylor's** birthday.

13

14

15 Get a physical and thank God for your health.

16

17

18 Plan dinner out with friends.

19 Create a personal web log.

20 Pray for a person of influence: Today is coach **Pat Riley's** birthday.

21

22 Clear the clutter out of your garage.

23

24 Check the oil in the car of a loved one.

25 Pray for a person of influence: Today is musician **Elton John's** birthday.

26 Memorize Acts 20:35.

27

28 Call your mother to say hello.

29

30 Lay off the junk food today.

31 Invite an old friend to coffee.

One whom God sent speaks the words of God, because God gives him the Spirit fully. [35]The Father loves the Son and has given him power over everything. [36]Those who believe in the Son have eternal life, but those who do not obey the Son will never have life. God's anger stays on them."

Jesus and a Samaritan Woman

4 The Pharisees heard that Jesus was making and baptizing more followers than John, [2]although Jesus himself did not baptize people, but his followers did. [3]Jesus knew that the Pharisees had heard about him, so he left Judea and went back to Galilee. [4]But on the way he had to go through the country of Samaria.

[5]In Samaria Jesus came to the town called Sychar, which is near the field Jacob gave to his son Joseph. [6]Jacob's well was there. Jesus was tired from his long trip, so he sat down beside the well. It was about twelve o'clock noon. [7]When a Samaritan woman came to the well to get some water, Jesus said to her, "Please give me a drink." [8](This happened while Jesus' followers were in town buying some food.)

[9]The woman said, "I am surprised that you ask me for a drink, since you are a Jewish man and I am a Samaritan woman." (Jewish people are not friends with Samaritans.")

[10]Jesus said, "If you only knew the free gift of God and who it is that is asking you for water, you would have asked him, and he would have given you living water."

[11]The woman said, "Sir, where will you get this living water? The well is very deep, and you have nothing to get water with. [12]Are you greater than Jacob, our father, who gave us this well and drank from it himself along with his sons and flocks?"

[13]Jesus answered, "Everyone who drinks this water will be thirsty again, [14]but whoever drinks the water I give will never be thirsty. The water I give will become a spring of water gushing up inside that person, giving eternal life."

[15]The woman said to him, "Sir, give me this water so I will never be thirsty again and will not have to come back here to get more water."

[16]Jesus told her, "Go get your husband and come back here."

[17]The woman answered, "I have no husband."

Jesus said to her, "You are right to say you have no husband. [18]Really you have had five husbands, and the man you live with now is not your husband. You told the truth."

[19]The woman said, "Sir, I can see that you are a prophet. [20]Our ancestors worshiped on this mountain, but you say that Jerusalem is the place where people must worship."

[21]Jesus said, "Believe me, woman. The time is coming when neither in Jerusalem nor on this mountain will you actually worship the Father. [22]You Samaritans worship something you don't understand. We understand what we worship, because salvation comes from the Jews. [23]The time is coming when the true worshipers will worship the Father in spirit and truth, and that time is here

Q: What's the difference between a talent and a gift?

A: Talents are natural abilities, such as singing or athletics, that each of us can discover and develop regardless of our connection with God. However, only Christians have spiritual gifts, or unique abilities bestowed by the Spirit to bless others (Romans 12:6—8; 1 Corinthians 12:1—11).

➤ The Bottom Line

Managing Money: Just Do It

MANY PEOPLE LEARN GOOD FINANCIAL MANAGEMENT PRINCIPLES, but simply don't take action. One of the quickest ways to start managing your money is to create a budget and follow it. Place your tax refund in an interest-bearing account rather than spending it. Don't buy what you can't pay for with cash or reasonably pay off with credit. Save at least five percent of your gross income as an investment in your future. Of course, give tithes and offerings to your local church and other ministries. Good stewardship reaps rewards.

➤➤ 4:9 Jewish people … Samaritans. This can also be translated "Jewish people don't use things that Samaritans have used."

already. You see, the Father too is actively seeking such people to worship him. [24]God is spirit, and those who worship him must worship in spirit and truth."

[25]The woman said, "I know that the Messiah is coming." (Messiah is the One called Christ.) "When the Messiah comes, he will explain everything to us."

[26]Then Jesus said, "I am he—I, the one talking to you."

[27]Just then his followers came back from town and were surprised to see him talking with a woman. But none of them asked, "What do you want?" or "Why are you talking with her?"

[28]Then the woman left her water jar and went back to town. She said to the people, [29]"Come and see a man who told me everything I ever did. Do you think he might be the Christ?" [30]So the people left the town and went to see Jesus.

[31]Meanwhile, his followers were begging him, "Teacher, eat something."

[32]But Jesus answered, "I have food to eat that you know nothing about."

[33]So the followers asked themselves, "Did somebody already bring him food?"

[34]Jesus said, "My food is to do what the One who sent me wants me to do and to finish his work. [35]You have a saying, 'Four more months till harvest.' But I tell you, open your eyes and look at the fields ready for harvest now. [36]Already, the one who harvests is being paid and is gathering crops for eternal life. So the one who plants and the one who harvests celebrate at the same time. [37]Here the saying is true, 'One person plants, and another harvests.' [38]I sent you to harvest a crop that you did not work on. Others did the work, and you get to finish up their work."[n]

[39]Many of the Samaritans in that town believed in Jesus because of what the woman said: "He told me everything I ever did." [40]When the Samaritans came to Jesus, they begged him to stay with them, so he stayed there two more days. [41]And many more believed because of the things he said.

[42]They said to the woman, "First we believed in Jesus because of what you said, but now we believe because we heard him ourselves. We know that this man really is the Savior of the world."

Jesus Heals an Officer's Son

[43]Two days later, Jesus left and went to Galilee. [44](Jesus had said before that a prophet is not respected in his own country.) [45]When Jesus arrived in Galilee, the people there welcomed him. They had seen all the things he did at the Passover Feast in Jerusalem, because they had been there, too.

[46]Jesus went again to visit Cana in Galilee where he had changed the water into wine. One of the king's important officers lived in the city of Capernaum, and his son was sick. [47]When he heard that Jesus had come from Judea to Galilee, he went to Jesus and begged him to come to Capernaum and heal his son, because his son was almost dead. [48]Jesus said to him, "You people must see signs and miracles before you will believe in me."

[49]The officer said, "Sir, come before my child dies."

Get Aligned

John 5:17

FROM THE FIRST WORDS OF GENESIS to the final verses of Revelation, God is in motion. The Bible's story begins with him creating the earth, and it ends with the Lord promising to return soon. In between those two points is a blur of events in which God's activity never ceases. He is constantly at work.

Obviously, we are still awaiting Jesus' final coming, which means God is still at work. But for thousands of years that work has sometimes been a mystery to us. Throughout the Old Testament, God's people often doubted his faithfulness when times got tough. Believers in the early church undoubtedly went through periods of questioning God's involvement during times of persecution.

When we're caught in a bleak situation, it's sometimes difficult to see exactly how God is working. Yet the Bible declares throughout its pages that God never stops. Since God is always at work, we are to partner with him in advancing his kingdom. It's not a question of whether God is at work, the question is whether we will join with him or not.

[50]Jesus answered, "Go. Your son will live."

The man believed what Jesus told him and went home. [51]On the way the man's servants came and met him and told him, "Your son is alive."

[52]The man asked, "What time did my son begin to get well?"

They answered, "Yesterday at one o'clock the fever left him."

[53]The father knew that one o'clock was the exact time that Jesus had said, "Your son will live." So the man and all the people who lived in his house believed in Jesus.

[54]That was the second miracle Jesus did after coming from Judea to Galilee.

Jesus Heals a Man at a Pool

5 Later Jesus went to Jerusalem for a special feast. [2]In Jerusalem there is a pool with five covered porches, which is called Bethesda[a] in the Hebrew language.[b] This pool is near the Sheep Gate. [3]Many sick people were lying on the porches beside the pool. Some were blind, some were crippled, and some were paralyzed [, and they waited for the water to move. [4]Sometimes an angel of the Lord came down to the pool and stirred up the water. After the angel did this, the first person to go into the pool was healed from any sickness he had].[c] [5]A man was lying there who had been sick for thirty-eight years. [6]When Jesus saw the man and knew that he had been sick for such a long time, Jesus asked him, "Do you want to be well?"

4:38 I … their work. As a farmer sends workers to harvest grain, Jesus sends his followers out to bring people to God.   5:2 Bethesda Some Greek copies read "Bethzatha" or "Bethsaida," different names for the pool of Bethesda.   5:2 Hebrew language Or Aramaic, the languages of many people in this region in the first century.   5:3–4 and … had Some Greek copies do not contain all or most of the bracketed text.

[7]The sick man answered, "Sir, there is no one to help me get into the pool when the water starts moving. While I am coming to the water, someone else always gets in before me."

[8]Then Jesus said, "Stand up. Pick up your mat and walk." [9]And immediately the man was well; he picked up his mat and began to walk.

The day this happened was a Sabbath day. [10]So the Jews said to the man who had been healed, "Today is the Sabbath. It is against our law for you to carry your mat on the Sabbath day."

[11]But he answered, "The man who made me well told me, 'Pick up your mat and walk.' "

[12]Then they asked him, "Who is the man who told you to pick up your mat and walk?"

[13]But the man who had been healed did not know who it was, because there were many people in that place, and Jesus had left.

[14]Later, Jesus found the man at the Temple and said to him, "See, you are well now. Stop sinning so that something worse does not happen to you."

[15]Then the man left and told his people that Jesus was the one who had made him well.

[16]Because Jesus was doing this on the Sabbath day, some evil people began to persecute him. [17]But Jesus said to them, "My Father never stops working, and so I keep working, too."

[18]This made them try still harder to kill him. They said, "First Jesus was breaking the law about the Sabbath day. Now he says that God is his own Father, making himself equal with God!"

Jesus Has God's Authority

[19]But Jesus said, "I tell you the truth, the Son can do nothing alone. The Son does only what he sees the Father doing, because the Son does whatever the Father does. [20]The Father loves the Son and shows the Son all the things he himself does. But the Father will show the Son even greater things than this so that you can all be amazed. [21]Just as the Father raises the dead and gives them life, so also the Son gives life to those he wants to. [22]In fact, the Father judges no one, but he has given the Son power to do all the judging [23]so that all people will honor the Son as much as they honor the Father. Anyone who does not honor the Son does not honor the Father who sent him.

[24]"I tell you the truth, whoever hears what I say and believes in the One who sent me has eternal life. That person will not be judged guilty but has already left death and entered life. [25]I tell you the truth, the time is coming and is already here when the dead will hear the voice of the Son of God, and those who hear will have life. [26]Life comes from the Father himself, and he has allowed the Son to have life in himself as well. [27]And the Father has given the Son the approval to judge, because he is the Son of Man. [28]Don't be surprised at this: A time is coming when all who are dead and in their graves will hear his voice. [29]Then they will come out of their graves. Those who did good

Q: Is the Bible relevant today?

A: While the Bible was completed a couple of thousand years ago, its accuracy and relevance remain unchanged. The Bible is a repository of great wisdom in addition to being the sole objective source of all the revelation God has given to humanity.

Get Fit

KNOWING YOUR RISKS Just as your relationship with God impacts you spiritually, your family heritage has an impact on the overall health of your body. Likewise, your daily habits, work and home environments, and lifestyle also help to define your health risks. You may be at an increased risk for certain diseases or conditions because of what you do, where you work, how you play, or your family history. Living healthy means you may need to do some homework. Find out about your family history and the unique health risks associated with your job or where you live. Then make smart choices regarding your lifestyle based on what's best for you and your situation.

will rise and have life forever, but those who did evil will rise to be judged guilty.

Jesus Is God's Son

[30] "I can do nothing alone. I judge only the way I am told, so my judgment is fair. I don't try to please myself, but I try to please the One who sent me.

[31] "If only I tell people about myself, what I say is not true. [32] But there is another who tells about me, and I know that the things he says about me are true.

[33] "You have sent people to John, and he has told you the truth. [34] It is not that I need what humans say; I tell you this so you can be saved. [35] John was like a burning and shining lamp, and you were happy to enjoy his light for a while.

[36] "But I have a proof about myself that is greater than that of John. The things I do, which are the things my Father gave me to do, prove that the Father sent me. [37] And the Father himself who sent me has given proof about me. You have never heard his voice or seen what he looks like. [38] His teaching does not live in you, because you don't believe in the One the Father sent. [39] You carefully study the Scriptures because you think they give you eternal life. They do in fact tell about me, [40] but you refuse to come to me to have that life.

[41] "I don't need praise from people. [42] But I know you—I know that you don't have God's love in you. [43] I have come from my Father and speak for him, but you don't accept me. But when another person comes, speaking only for himself, you will accept him. [44] You try to get praise from each other, but you do not try to get the praise that comes from the only God. So how can you believe? [45] Don't think that I will stand before the Father and say you are wrong. The one who says you are wrong is Moses, the one you hoped would save you. [46] If you really believed Moses, you would believe me, because Moses wrote about me. [47] But if you don't believe what Moses wrote, how can you believe what I say?"

More than Five Thousand Fed

6 After this, Jesus went across Lake Galilee (or, Lake Tiberias). [2] Many people followed him because they saw the miracles he did to heal the sick. [3] Jesus went up on a hill and sat down there with his followers. [4] It was almost the time for the Jewish Passover Feast.

[5] When Jesus looked up and saw a large crowd coming toward him, he said to Philip, "Where can we buy enough bread for all these people to eat?" [6] (Jesus asked Philip this question to test him, because Jesus already knew what he planned to do.)

[7] Philip answered, "Someone would have to work almost a year to buy enough bread for each person to have only a little piece."

[8] Another one of his followers, Andrew, Simon Peter's brother, said, [9] "Here is a boy with five loaves of barley bread and two little fish, but that is not enough for so many people."

[10] Jesus said, "Tell the people to sit down." There was plenty of grass there, and about five thousand men sat down there. [11] Then Jesus took the loaves of bread, thanked God for them, and gave them to the peo-

<< TechSupport >>

HIGH-SPEED INTERNET

Dial-up is being left in the dust. Cable and other broadband providers have been gradually increasing bandwidth in preparation for the next generation of content delivery, readying themselves to offer movies and music via their networks. Whereas the Internet is now principally for computer use, soon various devices in the home will utilize the always-on Internet connection to access content from digital libraries on demand. Although the continual access to the Internet makes life more convenient and efficient, don't forget that your real lifeline is your constant connection with God.

ple who were sitting there. He did the same with the fish, giving as much as the people wanted.

[12] When they had all had enough to eat, Jesus said to his followers, "Gather the leftover pieces of fish and bread so that nothing is wasted." [13] So they gathered up the pieces and filled twelve baskets with the pieces left from the five barley loaves.

[14] When the people saw this miracle that Jesus did, they said, "He must truly be the Prophet[n] who is coming into the world."

[15] Jesus knew that the people planned to come and take him by force and make him their king, so he left and went into the hills alone.

Jesus Walks on the Water

[16] That evening Jesus' followers went down to Lake Galilee. [17] It was dark now, and Jesus had not yet come to them. The followers got into a boat and started across the lake to Capernaum. [18] By now a strong wind was blowing, and the waves on the lake were getting bigger. [19] When they had rowed the boat about three or four miles, they saw Jesus walking on the water, coming toward the boat. The followers were afraid, [20] but Jesus said to them, "It is I. Do not be afraid." [21] Then they were glad to take him into the boat. At once the boat came to land at the place where they wanted to go.

The People Seek Jesus

[22] The next day the people who had stayed on the other side of the lake knew that Jesus had not gone in the boat with his followers but that they had left without him. And they knew that only one boat had been there. [23] But then some boats came from Tiberias and landed near the place where the people had eaten the bread after the Lord had given thanks. [24] When the people saw that Jesus and his followers were not there now, they got into boats and went to Capernaum to find Jesus.

>> **6:14 Prophet** They probably meant the prophet that God told Moses he would send (Deuteronomy 18:15–19).

THINK ABOUT IT John 6:35

OUR LIFESTYLE CHOICES DETERMINE a great deal of what happens with our weight. We decide the types of foods and drinks we consume, as well as whether we exercise or not. The results of these choices affect not only our weight but our overall health, also.

Jesus talked with his followers about making similar choices in the spiritual realm. In this passage, Jesus tied his message to topics that every listener knew about: food and drink. He declared that he was the "bread that gives life" and anyone who ate this bread would never be hungry. Jesus also proclaimed, "Whoever believes in me will never be thirsty."

The spiritual nourishment from the Bible can fill our mind, heart, and spirit. Just as we have to consume food and drink for our bodies, we also consistently need to consume the Scriptures and drink from the living water that Jesus promised to give us. If we do that, we will never hunger or thirst again.

Jesus, the Bread of Life

[25]When the people found Jesus on the other side of the lake, they asked him, "Teacher, when did you come here?"

[26]Jesus answered, "I tell you the truth, you aren't looking for me because you saw me do miracles. You are looking for me because you ate the bread and were satisfied. [27]Don't work for the food that spoils. Work for the food that stays good always and gives eternal life. The Son of Man will give you this food, because on him God the Father has put his power."

[28]The people asked Jesus, "What are the things God wants us to do?"

[29]Jesus answered, "The work God wants you to do is this: Believe the One he sent."

[30]So the people asked, "What miracle will you do? If we see a miracle, we will believe you. What will you do? [31]Our ancestors ate the manna in the desert. This is written in the Scriptures: 'He gave them bread from heaven to eat.'"

[32]Jesus said, "I tell you the truth, it was not Moses who gave you bread from heaven; it is my Father who is giving you the true bread from heaven. [33]God's bread is the One who comes down from heaven and gives life to the world."

[34]The people said, "Sir, give us this bread always."

[35]Then Jesus said, "I am the bread that gives life. Whoever comes to me will never be hungry, and whoever believes in me will never be thirsty. [36]But as I told you before, you have seen me and still don't believe. [37]The Father gives me the people who are mine. Every one of them will come to me, and I will always accept them. [38]I came down from heaven to do what God wants me to do, not what I want to do. [39]Here is what the One who sent me wants me to do: I must not lose even one whom God gave me, but I must raise them all on the last day. [40]Those who see the Son and believe in him have eternal life, and I will raise them on the last day. This is what my Father wants."

[41]Some people began to complain about Jesus because he said, "I am the bread that comes down from heaven." [42]They said, "This is Jesus, the son of Joseph. We know his father and mother. How can he say, 'I came down from heaven'?"

[43]But Jesus answered, "Stop complaining to each other. [44]The Father is the One who sent me. No one can come to me unless the Father draws him to me, and I will raise that person up on the last day. [45]It is written in the prophets, 'They will all be taught by God.' Everyone who listens to the Father and learns from him comes to me. [46]No one has seen the Father except the One who is from God; only he has seen the Father. [47]I tell you the truth, whoever believes has eternal life. [48]I am the bread that gives life. [49]Your ancestors ate the manna in the desert, but still they died. [50]Here is the bread that comes down from heaven. Anyone who eats this bread will never die. [51]I am the living bread that came down from heaven. Anyone who eats this bread will live forever. This bread is my flesh, which I will give up so that the world may have life."

[52]Then the evil people began to argue among themselves, saying, "How can this man give us his flesh to eat?"

[53]Jesus said, "I tell you the truth, you must eat the flesh of the Son of Man and drink his blood. Otherwise, you won't have real life in you. [54]Those who eat my flesh and drink my blood have eternal life, and I will raise them up on the last day. [55]My flesh is true food, and my blood is true drink. [56]Those who eat my flesh and drink my blood live in me, and I live in them. [57]The living Father sent me, and I live because of the Father. So whoever eats me will live because of me. [58]I am not like the bread your ancestors ate. They ate that bread and still died. I am the bread that came down from heaven, and whoever eats this bread will live forever." [59]Jesus said all these things while he was teaching in the synagogue in Capernaum.

The Words of Eternal Life

[60]When the followers of Jesus heard this, many of them said, "This teaching is hard. Who can accept it?"

[61]Knowing that his followers were complaining about this, Jesus said, "Does this teaching bother you? [62]Then will it also bother you to see the Son of Man going back

▶▶ 6:31 'He gave … eat.' Quotation from Psalm 78:24.   6:45 'They … God.' Quotation from Isaiah 54:13.

to the place where he came from? ⁶³It is the Spirit that gives life. The flesh doesn't give life. The words I told you are spirit, and they give life. ⁶⁴But some of you don't believe." (Jesus knew from the beginning who did not believe and who would turn against him.) ⁶⁵Jesus said, "That is the reason I said, 'If the Father does not bring a person to me, that one cannot come.' "

⁶⁶After Jesus said this, many of his followers left him and stopped following him.

⁶⁷Jesus asked the twelve followers, "Do you want to leave, too?"

⁶⁸Simon Peter answered him, "Lord, who would we go to? You have the words that give eternal life. ⁶⁹We believe and know that you are the Holy One from God."

⁷⁰Then Jesus answered, "I chose all twelve of you, but one of you is a devil."

⁷¹Jesus was talking about Judas, the son of Simon Iscariot. Judas was one of the twelve, but later he was going to turn against Jesus.

Jesus' Brothers Don't Believe

7After this, Jesus traveled around Galilee. He did not want to travel in Judea, because some evil people there wanted to kill him. ²It was time for the Feast of Shelters. ³So Jesus' brothers said to him, "You should leave here and go to Judea so your followers there can see the miracles you do. ⁴Anyone who wants to be well known does not hide what he does. If you are doing these things, show yourself to the world." ⁵(Even Jesus' brothers did not believe in him.)

⁶Jesus said to his brothers, "The right time for me has not yet come, but any time is right for you. ⁷The world cannot hate you, but it hates me, because I tell it the evil things it does. ⁸So you go to the feast. I will not go yet" to this feast, because the right time for me has not yet come." ⁹After saying this, Jesus stayed in Galilee.

¹⁰But after Jesus' brothers had gone to the feast, Jesus went also. But he did not let people see him. ¹¹At the feast some people were looking for him and saying, "Where is that man?"

¹²Within the large crowd there, many people were whispering to each other about Jesus. Some said, "He is a good man."

Others said, "No, he fools the people." ¹³But no one was brave enough to talk about Jesus openly, because they were afraid of the elders.

Jesus Teaches at the Feast

¹⁴When the feast was about half over, Jesus went to the Temple and began to teach. ¹⁵The people were amazed and said, "This man has never studied in school. How did he learn so much?"

¹⁶Jesus answered, "The things I teach are not my own, but they come from him who sent me. ¹⁷If people choose to do what God wants, they will know that my teaching comes from God and not from me. ¹⁸Those who teach their own ideas are trying to get honor for themselves. But those who try to bring honor to the one who sent them speak the truth, and there is nothing false in them. ¹⁹Moses gave you the law," but none of you obeys that law. Why are you trying to kill me?"

²⁰The people answered, "A demon has come into you. We are not trying to kill you."

²¹Jesus said to them, "I did one miracle, and you are all amazed. ²²Moses gave you the law about circumcision. (But really Moses did not give you circumcision; it came from our ancestors.) And yet you circumcise a baby boy on a Sabbath day. ²³If a baby boy can be circumcised on a Sabbath day to obey the law of Moses, why are you angry at me for healing a person's whole body on the Sabbath day? ²⁴Stop judging by the way things look, but judge by what is really right."

Is Jesus the Christ?

²⁵Then some of the people who lived in Jerusalem said, "This is the man they are trying to kill. ²⁶But he is teaching where everyone can see and hear him, and no one is trying to stop him. Maybe the leaders have decided he really is the Christ. ²⁷But we know where this man is from. Yet when the real Christ comes, no one will know where he comes from."

²⁸Jesus, teaching in the Temple, cried out, "Yes, you know me, and you know where I am from. But I have not come by my own authority. I was sent by the One who is true, whom you don't know. ²⁹But I know him, because I am from him, and he sent me."

Q: What is the church?

A: The church is the living expression of Christ on earth today. The church is God's chosen instrument for accomplishing his purposes in the world. If Christ is the head of the church, then the church is the body of Christ, and it enacts his will on the earth.

>> live the life

John 7:37–38

The Principle > Yearn for more of God.

Practicing It > Set aside an entire afternoon to spend alone with Jesus. Disappear from your regular life and tell only your spouse or a family member where you will be. Spend the day sharing your heart with God, telling him what you yearn for most in your life.

>> **7:8 yet** Some Greek copies do not have this word.   **7:19 law** Moses gave God's people the Law that God gave him on Mount Sinai (Exodus 34:29–32).

People Skills

Conversational Courtesy

Talking is a core aspect of friendship. However, talking between friends requires reciprocity. In a mutually satisfying friendship, both friends talk and listen, usually to an equal degree. Anytime you have been talking for more than a few minutes without participation from the person you are speaking with, you are lecturing or bossing, not conversing. Encourage equal participation in conversations with your friends. Share your thoughts and perspectives without waiting to be asked, but frequently invite your friend to share his perspective, also. Even if your friend is the more reserved type, he'll appreciate the opportunity to express himself and will think more of you as a friend.

[30]When Jesus said this, they tried to seize him. But no one was able to touch him, because it was not yet the right time. [31]But many of the people believed in Jesus. They said, "When the Christ comes, will he do more miracles than this man has done?"

The Leaders Try to Arrest Jesus

[32]The Pharisees heard the crowd whispering these things about Jesus. So the leading priests and the Pharisees sent some Temple guards to arrest him. [33]Jesus said, "I will be with you a little while longer. Then I will go back to the One who sent me. [34]You will look for me, but you will not find me. And you cannot come where I am."

[35]Some people said to each other, "Where will this man go so we cannot find him? Will he go to the Greek cities where our people live and teach the Greek people there? [36]What did he mean when he said, 'You will look for me, but you will not find me,' and 'You cannot come where I am'?"

Jesus Talks About the Spirit

[37]On the last and most important day of the feast Jesus stood up and said in a loud voice, "Let anyone who is thirsty come to me and drink. [38]If anyone believes in me, rivers of living water will flow out from that person's heart, as the Scripture says." [39]Jesus was talk-

Christ will come from David's family and from Bethlehem, the town where David lived." [43]So the people did not agree with each other about Jesus. [44]Some of them wanted to arrest him, but no one was able to touch him.

Some Leaders Won't Believe

[45]The Temple guards went back to the leading priests and the Pharisees, who asked, "Why didn't you bring Jesus?"

[46]The guards answered, "The words he says are greater than the words of any other person who has ever spoken!"

[47]The Pharisees answered, "So Jesus has fooled you also! [48]Have any of the leaders or the Pharisees believed in him? No! [49]But these people, who know nothing about the law, are under God's curse."

[50]Nicodemus, who had gone to see Jesus before, was in that group.[n] He said, [51]"Our law does not judge a person without hearing him and knowing what he has done."

[52]They answered, "Are you from Galilee, too? Study the Scriptures, and you will learn that no prophet comes from Galilee."

Some of the earliest surviving Greek copies do not contain 7:53—8:11.

[[53]And everyone left and went home.

FACT-OIDS!

Fifty-nine percent of adults oppose abolishing the penny and making the nickel the lowest denomination coin. [Harris Interactive]

---

ing about the Holy Spirit. The Spirit had not yet been given, because Jesus had not yet been raised to glory. But later, those who believed in Jesus would receive the Spirit.

The People Argue About Jesus

[40]When the people heard Jesus' words, some of them said, "This man really is the Prophet."[n]

[41]Others said, "He is the Christ."

Still others said, "The Christ will not come from Galilee. [42]The Scripture says that the

The Woman Caught in Adultery

8 Jesus went to the Mount of Olives. [2]But early in the morning he went back to the Temple, and all the people came to him, and he sat and taught them. [3]The teachers of the law and the Pharisees brought a woman who had been caught in adultery. They forced her to stand before the people. [4]They said to Jesus, "Teacher, this woman was caught having sexual relations with a man who is not her husband. [5]The law of Moses commands that we stone to death every woman who

---

 7:40 **Prophet** They probably meant the prophet God told Moses he would send (Deuteronomy 18:15–19). 7:50 **Nicodemus...group.** The story about Nicodemus going and talking to Jesus is in John 3:1–21.

does this. What do you say we should do?" [6]They were asking this to trick Jesus so that they could have some charge against him.

But Jesus bent over and started writing on the ground with his finger. [7]When they continued to ask Jesus their question, he raised up and said, "Anyone here who has never sinned can throw the first stone at her." [8]Then Jesus bent over again and wrote on the ground.

[9]Those who heard Jesus began to leave one by one, first the older men and then the others. Jesus was left there alone with the woman standing before him. [10]Jesus raised up again and asked her, "Woman, where are they? Has no one judged you guilty?"

[11]She answered, "No one, sir."

Then Jesus said, "I also don't judge you guilty. You may go now, but don't sin anymore."]

Jesus Is the Light of the World

[12]Later, Jesus talked to the people again, saying, "I am the light of the world. The person who follows me will never live in darkness but will have the light that gives life."

[13]The Pharisees said to Jesus, "When you talk about yourself, you are the only one to say these things are true. We cannot accept what you say."

[14]Jesus answered, "Yes, I am saying these things about myself, but they are true. I know where I came from and where I am going. But you don't know where I came from or where I am going. [15]You judge by human standards. I am not judging anyone. [16]But when I do judge, I judge truthfully, because I am not alone. The Father who sent me is with me. [17]Your own law says that when two witnesses say the same thing, you must accept what they say. [18]I am one of the witnesses who speaks about myself, and the Father who sent me is the other witness."

[19]They asked, "Where is your father?"

Jesus answered, "You don't know me or my Father. If you knew me, you would know my Father, too." [20]Jesus said these things while he was teaching in the Temple, near where the money is kept. But no one arrested him, because the right time for him had not yet come.

THINK ABOUT IT John 8:12

THE MOONLESS NIGHTS OF THE MONTH always feel a little darker than the other ones. If the sky is crystal clear, the lack of the extra light from the moon makes the stars show more radiantly. Yet the darkness is undeniably heavier on nights without a moon.

If you lived in the New Testament times, before the invention of artificial light sources, the darkness would have felt even blacker. During such dark nights, the only light would have come from a torch or other flame of fire.

Both naturally and spiritually speaking, light dispels the darkness. Fortunately, Jesus promised us a life where we wouldn't have to live in darkness anymore. He said, "I am the light of the world. The person who follows me will never have to live in darkness but will have the light that gives life." It's a promise we can trust in the dark, so we don't need to be scared of the dark anymore.

The People Misunderstand Jesus

[21]Again, Jesus said to the people, "I will leave you, and you will look for me, but you will die in your sins. You cannot come where I am going."

[22]So the Jews asked, "Will he kill himself? Is that why he said, 'You cannot come where I am going'?"

[23]Jesus said, "You people are from here below, but I am from above. You belong to this world, but I don't belong to this world. [24]So I told you that you would die in your sins. Yes, you will die in your sins if you don't believe that I am he."

[25]They asked, "Then who are you?"

Jesus answered, "I am what I have told you from the beginning. [26]I have many things to say and decide about you. But I tell people only the things I have heard from the One who sent me, and he speaks the truth."

[27]The people did not understand that he was talking to them about the Father. [28]So Jesus said to them, "When you lift up the Son of Man, you will know that I am he. You will know that these things I do are not by my own authority but that I say only what the Father has taught me. [29]The One who sent me is with me. I always do what is pleasing to him, so he has not left me alone." [30]While Jesus was saying these things, many people believed in him.

Freedom from Sin

[31]So Jesus said to the Jews who believed in him, "If you continue to obey my teaching, you are truly my followers. [32]Then you will know the truth, and the truth will make you free."

[33]They answered, "We are Abraham's children, and we have never been anyone's slaves. So why do you say we will be free?"

[34]Jesus answered, "I tell you the truth, everyone who lives in sin is a slave to sin. [35]A slave does not stay with a family forever, but a son belongs to the family forever. [36]So if the Son makes you free, you will be truly free. [37]I know you are Abraham's children, but you want to kill me because you don't accept my teaching. [38]I am telling you what my Father has shown me, but you do what your father has told you."

[39]They answered, "Our father is Abraham."

▶Get Aligned

John 8:31–32

SOME FOLKS COMPLAIN ABOUT THE DEMANDS OF JESUS. What many people forget is with whom they have this relationship. Too often we slip into treating Jesus exclusively as a friend and disregard that he is also the Lord of all. As the supreme authority of the universe, he has every right to place conditions on his offer of friendship to us.

The truth is, the Lord is our closest friend. He knows us better than anyone. But in knowing us so intimately as our creator, he also knows what is best for us, even

when we do not. With our best interests forever in mind, he wants us to follow him for our own benefit. As this passage states, it is when we truly follow him that we come to know the truth that sets us free.

Following Jesus, however, requires more than lip service. We are to obey his commands. The Lord prioritizes obedience even higher than sacrifice, and he's looking for followers who comply with action. Many people can talk the talk, but he desires for his followers also to walk the walk.

Jesus said, "If you were really Abraham's children, you would do* the things Abraham did. ⁴⁰I am a man who has told you the truth which I heard from God, but you are trying to kill me. Abraham did nothing like that. ⁴¹So you are doing the things your own father did."

But they said, "We are not like children who never knew who their father was. God is our Father; he is the only Father we have."

⁴²Jesus said to them, "If God were really your Father, you would love me, because I came from God and now I am here. I did not come by my own authority; God sent me. ⁴³You don't understand what I say, because you cannot accept my teaching. ⁴⁴You belong to your father the devil, and you want to do what he wants. He was a murderer from the beginning and was against the truth, because there is no truth in him. When he tells a lie, he shows what he is really like, because he is a liar and the father of lies. ⁴⁵But because I speak the truth, you don't believe me. ⁴⁶Can any of you prove that I am guilty of sin? If I am telling the truth, why don't you believe me? ⁴⁷The person who belongs to God accepts what God says. But you don't accept what God says, because you don't belong to God."

Jesus Is Greater than Abraham

⁴⁸They answered, "We say you are a Samaritan and have a demon in you. Are we not right?"

⁴⁹Jesus answered, "I have no demon in me. I give honor to my Father, but you dishonor me. ⁵⁰I am not trying to get honor for myself.

There is One who wants this honor for me, and he is the judge. ⁵¹I tell you the truth, whoever obeys my teaching will never die."

⁵²They said to Jesus, "Now we know that you have a demon in you! Even Abraham and the prophets died. But you say, 'Whoever obeys my teaching will never die.' ⁵³Do you think you are greater than our father Abraham, who died? And the prophets died, too. Who do you think you are?"

⁵⁴Jesus answered, "If I give honor to myself, that honor is worth nothing. The One who gives me honor is my Father, and you say he is your God. ⁵⁵You don't really know him, but I know him. If I said I did not know him, I would be a liar like you. But I do know him, and I obey what he says. ⁵⁶Your father Abraham was very happy that he would see my day. He saw that day and was glad."

⁵⁷They said to him, "You have never seen Abraham! You are not even fifty years old."

⁵⁸Jesus answered, "I tell you the truth, before Abraham was even born, I am!" ⁵⁹When Jesus said this, the people picked up stones to throw at him. But Jesus hid himself, and then he left the Temple.

Jesus Heals a Man Born Blind

9 As Jesus was walking along, he saw a man who had been born blind. ²His followers asked him, "Teacher, whose sin caused this man to be born blind—his own sin or his parents' sin?"

³Jesus answered, "It is not this man's sin or his parents' sin that made him blind. This man was born blind so that God's power could be shown in him. ⁴While it is daytime, we must continue doing the work of the One who sent me. Night is coming, when no one can work. ⁵While I am in the world, I am the light of the world."

⁶After Jesus said this, he spit on the ground and made some mud with it and put the mud on the man's eyes. ⁷Then he told the man, "Go and wash in the Pool of Siloam." (Siloam means Sent.) So the man went, washed, and came back seeing.

⁸The neighbors and some people who had earlier seen this man begging said, "Isn't this the same man who used to sit and beg?"

⁹Some said, "He is the one," but others said, "No, he only looks like him."

The man himself said, "I am the man."

¹⁰They asked, "How did you get your sight?"

¹¹He answered, "The man

Q: Where did the Bible come from?

A: The books that constitute the Bible were penned by forty different people who lived during a period of fifteen hundred years. The Spirit of God worked through them to record without error his revelation to humankind.

>> 8:39 If…do Some Greek copies read "If you are really Abraham's children, you will do."

130

named Jesus made some mud and put it on my eyes. Then he told me to go to Siloam and wash. So I went and washed, and then I could see."

[12]They asked him, "Where is this man?"

"I don't know," he answered.

Pharisees Question the Healing

[13]Then the people took to the Pharisees the man who had been blind. [14]The day Jesus had made mud and healed his eyes was a Sabbath day. [15]So now the Pharisees asked the man, "How did you get your sight?"

He answered, "He put mud on my eyes, I washed, and now I see."

[16]So some of the Pharisees were saying, "This man does not keep the Sabbath day, so he is not from God."

But others said, "A man who is a sinner can't do miracles like these." So they could not agree with each other.

[17]They asked the man again, "What do you say about him since it was your eyes he opened?"

The man answered, "He is a prophet."

[18]These leaders did not believe that he had been blind and could now see again. So they sent for the man's parents [19]and asked them, "Is this your son who you say was born blind? Then how does he now see?"

[20]His parents answered, "We know that this is our son and that he was born blind. [21]But we don't know how he can now see. We don't know who opened his eyes. Ask him. He is old enough to speak for himself." [22]His parents said this because they were afraid of the elders, who had already decided that anyone who said Jesus was the Christ would be avoided. [23]That is why his parents said, "He is old enough. Ask him."

[24]So for the second time, they called the man who had been blind. They said, "You should give God the glory by telling the truth. We know that this man is a sinner."

[25]He answered, "I don't know if he is a sinner. One thing I do know: I was blind, and now I see."

[26]They asked, "What did he do to you? How did he make you see again?"

[27]He answered, "I already told you, and you didn't listen. Why do you want to hear it again? Do you want to become his followers, too?"

[28]Then they insulted him and said, "You are his follower, but we are followers of Moses. [29]We know that God spoke to Moses, but we don't even know where this man comes from."

[30]The man answered, "This is a very strange thing. You don't know where he comes from, and yet he opened my eyes. [31]We all know that God does not listen to sinners, but he listens to anyone who worships and obeys him. [32]Nobody has ever heard of anyone giving sight to a man born blind. [33]If this man were not from God, he could do nothing."

[34]They answered, "You were born full of sin! Are you trying to teach us?" And they threw him out.

Spiritual Blindness

[35]When Jesus heard that they had thrown him out, Jesus found him and said, "Do you believe in the Son of Man?"

[36]He asked, "Who is the Son of Man, sir, so that I can believe in him?"

[37]Jesus said to him, "You have seen him. The Son of Man is the one talking with you."

[38]He said, "Lord, I believe!" Then the man worshiped Jesus.

[39]Jesus said, "I came into this world so that the world could be judged. I came so that the blind[*] would see and so that those who see will become blind."

[40]Some of the Pharisees who were nearby heard Jesus say this and asked, "Are you saying we are blind, too?"

[41]Jesus said, "If you were blind, you would not be guilty of sin. But since you keep saying you see, your guilt remains."

The Shepherd and His Sheep

10 Jesus said, "I tell you the truth, the person who does not enter the sheepfold by the door, but climbs in some other way, is a thief and a robber. [2]The one who enters by the door is the shepherd of the sheep. [3]The one who guards the door opens it for him. And the sheep listen to the voice of the shepherd. He calls his own sheep by name and leads them out. [4]When he brings all his sheep out, he goes ahead of them, and they follow him because they know his voice. [5]But they will never follow a stranger. They will run away from him because they don't know his voice." [6]Jesus told the people this story, but they did not understand what it meant.

▶ Get Aligned

John 10:18

IT'S EASY TO THINK THAT JESUS WAS KILLED. After all, his face was hardly recognizable from his beatings, his body was bruised, and his hands and feet were nailed to a cross. Obviously, he was murdered, right?

Wrong. He allowed the soldiers who arrested him in the Garden of Gethsemane to capture him. He also permitted the high priests to spit on him, mock him, and beat him. He even granted the Roman soldiers to bruise him, ridicule him, and crucify him.

Every detail of his scourging was by Jesus' own consent. He gave up his life at his own will, not by the hands of his torturers. When the public taunted him with cries to save himself from the cross, the people had no idea about the truth behind their words. He could have saved himself at any moment. He could have called for angels to come to his rescue. In fact, he could have done so prior to experiencing a single scratch on his holy flesh. But he didn't. He chose to die. He chose to embrace the cross. He chose to face the terrible wrath of God, all for you and yours.

▶▶ 9:39 **blind** Jesus is talking about people who are spiritually blind, not physically blind.

FOR Men Only

CHIVALRY If you think that chivalry passed away with the last knight, you are mistaken. Virtually nothing will get a woman's attention quicker than coming to the rescue in her time of need. Whether it is stopping to change a tire for her, walking her home safely, or offering her an umbrella in poor weather, chivalry demonstrates a bravery and strength of spirit that is all too uncommon today. According to the dictionary, chivalry is defined as "gallant and distinguished behavior." It is how a godly guy acts whether or not anyone is watching, for it is a lifestyle based on courage, not convenience.

Jesus Is the Good Shepherd

7So Jesus said again, "I tell you the truth, I am the door for the sheep. 8All the people who came before me were thieves and robbers. The sheep did not listen to them. 9I am the door, and the person who enters through me will be saved and will be able to come in and go out and find pasture. 10A thief comes to steal and kill and destroy, but I came to give life—life in all its fullness.

11"I am the good shepherd. The good shepherd gives his life for the sheep. 12The worker who is paid to keep the sheep is different from the shepherd who owns them. When the worker sees a wolf coming, he runs away and leaves the sheep alone. Then the wolf attacks the sheep and scatters them. 13The man runs away because he is only a paid worker and does not really care about the sheep.

14"I am the good shepherd. I know my sheep, and my sheep know me, 15just as the Father knows me, and I know the Father. I give my life for the sheep. 16I have other sheep that are not in this flock, and I must bring them also. They will listen to my voice, and there will be one flock and one shepherd. 17The Father loves me because I give my life so that I can take it back again. 18No one takes it away from me; I give my own life freely. I have the right to give my life, and I have the right to take it back. This is what my Father commanded me to do."

19Again the leaders did not agree with each other because of these words of Jesus. 20Many of them said, "A demon has come into him and made him crazy. Why listen to him?" 21But others said, "A man who is crazy with a demon does not say things like this. Can a demon open the eyes of the blind?"

Jesus Is Rejected

22The time came for the Feast of Dedication at Jerusalem. It was winter, 23and Jesus was walking in the Temple in Solomon's Porch. 24Some people gathered around him and said, "How long will you make us wonder about you? If you are the Christ, tell us plainly." 25Jesus answered, "I told you already, but you did not believe. The miracles I do in my Father's name show who I am. 26But you don't believe, because you are not my sheep. 27My sheep listen to my voice; I know them, and they follow me. 28I give them eternal life, and they will never die, and no one can steal them out of my hand. 29My Father

Survival Guide

FENCES: LIMITING THE COST

Planning to add a fence to your yard for safety or appearance? While the materials—premade fence, concrete, and screws—may cost several hundred dollars or more (depending on yard size), the labor to have it installed can multiply the bottom-line expense. Instead, consider hiring a professional to set the posts in the ground—generally the most difficult task—then finish the project yourself. Afterward, remember your neighbors on the other side of the fence, since Paul admonishes us in Romans 15:2 to please them.

gave my sheep to me. He is greater than all, and no person can steal my sheep out of my Father's hand. ³⁰The Father and I are one."

³¹Again some of the people picked up stones to kill Jesus. ³²But he said to them, "I have done many good works from the Father. Which of these good works are you killing me for?"

³³They answered, "We are not killing you because of any good work you did, but because you speak against God. You are only a human, but you say you are the same as God!"

³⁴Jesus answered, "It is written in your law that God said, 'I said, you are gods.'ⁿ ³⁵This Scripture called those people gods who received God's message, and Scripture is always true. ³⁶So why do you say that I speak against God because I said, 'I am God's Son'? I am the one God chose and sent into the world. ³⁷If I don't do what my Father does, then don't believe me. ³⁸But if I do what my Father does, even though you don't believe in me, believe what I do. Then you will know and understand that the Father is in me and I am in the Father."

³⁹They tried to take Jesus again, but he escaped from them.

⁴⁰Then he went back across the Jordan River to the place where John had first baptized. Jesus stayed there, ⁴¹and many people came to him and said, "John never did a mir-

THINK ABOUT IT John 10:27–29

UNLESS WE'VE SEEN SHEEP IN A PETTING ZOO or on a farm, most of us aren't very familiar with this well-known biblical animal. Throughout the Bible, God's people are described as sheep. These domesticated animals, generally not the highest in intelligence, need a shepherd to guide them to good pastures and to protect them.

Despite their relatively low intelligence, sheep know how to follow the voice of their shepherd. They depend on their guardian to lead them in the right direction and are highly attuned to the unique sound of his voice.

In the Gospels, Jesus referred to himself as the good shepherd and said his followers knew his voice. As he talked about his flock, Jesus gave this remarkable promise: "I give them eternal life, and they will never die, and no one can steal them out of my hand." No matter what temporary difficulty life throws our direction, we can count on this promise from Jesus for eternal life and security.

acle, but everything John said about this man is true." ⁴²And in that place many believed in Jesus.

The Death of Lazarus

11 A man named Lazarus was sick. He lived in the town of Bethany, where Mary and her sister Martha lived. ²Mary was the woman who later put perfume on the Lord and wiped his feet with her hair. Mary's brother was Lazarus, the man who was now sick. ³So Mary and Martha sent someone to tell Jesus, "Lord, the one you love is sick."

→ The Bottom Line

Financing a Business: Consult Counselors

YOU MAY BE AN INNOVATIVE GENIUS, insightful inventor, or talented artist, yet fail when it comes to balancing your budget. If this is your story and you still hope to establish a business, recognize your need for help. Cash flow, costs of goods sold, and managing accounts receivable may sound like foreign concepts, but they are essential concerns when it comes to running a profitable business. Likewise, so is knowledge of tax laws. This may mean hiring a financial advisor, consulting a CPA, or attending small business seminars to gain more knowledge. Remember Proverbs 15:22, which says that plans "succeed with the advice of many others."

>> 10:34 'I...gods.' Quotation from Psalm 82:6.

[4]"When Jesus heard this, he said, "This sickness will not end in death. It is for the glory of God, to bring glory to the Son of God." [5]Jesus loved Martha and her sister and Lazarus. [6]But when he heard that Lazarus was sick, he stayed where he was for two more days. [7]Then Jesus said to his followers, "Let's go back to Judea."

[8]The followers said, "But Teacher, some people there tried to stone you to death only a short time ago. Now you want to go back there?"

[9]Jesus answered, "Are there not twelve hours in the day? If anyone walks in the daylight, he will not stumble, because he can see by this world's light. [10]But if anyone walks at night, he stumbles because there is no light to help him see."

[11]After Jesus said this, he added, "Our friend Lazarus has fallen asleep, but I am going there to wake him."

[12]The followers said, "But Lord, if he is only asleep, he will be all right."

[13]Jesus meant that Lazarus was dead, but his followers thought he meant Lazarus was really sleeping. [14]So then Jesus said plainly, "Lazarus is dead. [15]And I am glad for your sakes I was not there so that you may believe. But let's go to him now."

[16]Then Thomas (the one called Didymus) said to the other followers, "Let us also go so that we can die with him."

Jesus in Bethany

[17]When Jesus arrived, he learned that Lazarus had already been dead and in the tomb for four days. [18]Bethany was about two miles from Jerusalem. [19]Many of the Jews had come there to comfort Martha and Mary about their brother.

[20]When Martha heard that Jesus was coming, she went out to meet him, but Mary stayed home. [21]Martha said to Jesus, "Lord, if you had been here, my brother would not have died. [22]But I know that even now God will give you anything you ask."

[23]Jesus said, "Your brother will rise and live again."

[24]Martha answered, "I know that he will rise and live again in the resurrection[n] on the last day."

[25]Jesus said to her, "I am the resurrection and the life. Those who believe in me will have life even if they die. [26]And everyone who lives and believes in me will never die. Martha, do you believe this?"

[27]Martha answered, "Yes, Lord. I believe that you are the Christ, the Son of God, the One coming to the world."

Jesus Cries

[28]After Martha said this, she went back and talked to her sister Mary alone. Martha said, "The Teacher is here and he is asking for you." [29]When Mary heard this, she got up quickly and went to Jesus. [30]Jesus had not yet come into the town but was still at the place where Martha had met him. [31]The Jews were with Mary in the house, comforting her. When they saw her stand and leave quickly, they followed her, thinking she was going to the tomb to cry there.

[32]But Mary went to the place where Jesus was. When she saw him, she fell at his feet and said, "Lord, if you had been here, my brother would not have died."

[33]When Jesus saw Mary crying and the Jews who came with her also crying, he was upset and was deeply troubled. [34]He asked, "Where did you bury him?"

"Come and see, Lord," they said.

[35]Jesus cried.

[36]So the Jews said, "See how much he loved him."

[37]But some of them said, "If Jesus opened the eyes of the blind man, why couldn't he keep Lazarus from dying?"

Jesus Raises Lazarus

[38]Again feeling very upset, Jesus came to the tomb. It was a cave with a large stone covering the entrance. [39]Jesus said, "Move the stone away."

Martha, the sister of the dead man, said, "But, Lord, it has been four days since he died. There will be a bad smell."

[40]Then Jesus said to her, "Didn't I tell you that if you believed you would see the glory of God?"

[41]So they moved the stone away from the entrance. Then Jesus looked up and said, "Father, I thank you that you heard me. [42]I know that you always hear me, but I said these things because of the people here around me. I want them to believe that you sent me." [43]After Jesus said this, he cried out in a loud voice, "Lazarus, come out!" [44]The dead man came out, his hands and feet

ⓟ Sexcess:
INTIMATE APPAREL 101

Many an otherwise macho man has wilted at the thought of shopping for lingerie to give his beloved, but with a little planning and forethought, it needn't be intimidating. First and foremost, you need to get her correct size and measurements. If you are trying to surprise her, you can simply check the sizes of the lingerie she has, and go from there. Next, determine what color to get. Black, red, and pink are popular colors, but you need to take her likes and looks into consideration, also. Finally, consider your wife's personality and sensibilities when selecting what type of lingerie to get her, as it needs to flatter her.

 11:24 resurrection Being raised from the dead to live again.

134

Q: What is the Second Coming?

A: The Second Coming refers to a time in the future when Jesus will return to earth for the second time. At the "first coming," Jesus came as a servant to lay down his life for the sins of the world. At the Second Coming, he will return as the conquering king of all.

wrapped with pieces of cloth, and a cloth around his face.

Jesus said to them, "Take the cloth off of him and let him go."

The Plan to Kill Jesus

⁴⁵Many of the people, who had come to visit Mary and saw what Jesus did, believed in him. ⁴⁶But some of them went to the Pharisees and told them what Jesus had done. ⁴⁷Then the leading priests and Pharisees called a meeting of the council. They asked, "What should we do? This man is doing many miracles. ⁴⁸If we let him continue doing these things, everyone will believe in him. Then the Romans will come and take away our Temple and our nation."

⁴⁹One of the men there was Caiaphas, the high priest that year. He said, "You people know nothing! ⁵⁰You don't realize that it is better for one man to die for the people than for the whole nation to be destroyed."

⁵¹Caiaphas did not think of this himself. As high priest that year, he was really prophesying that Jesus would die for their nation ⁵²and for God's scattered children to bring them all together and make them one.

⁵³That day they started planning to kill Jesus. ⁵⁴So Jesus no longer traveled openly among the people. He left there and went to a place near the desert, to a town called Ephraim and stayed there with his followers.

⁵⁵It was almost time for the Passover Feast. Many from the country went up to Jerusalem before the Passover to do the special things to make themselves pure. ⁵⁶The people looked for Jesus and stood in the Temple asking each other, "Is he coming to the Feast? What do you think?" ⁵⁷But the leading priests and the Pharisees had given orders that if anyone knew where Jesus was, he must tell them. Then they could arrest him.

Jesus with Friends in Bethany

12 Six days before the Passover Feast, Jesus went to Bethany, where Lazarus lived. (Lazarus is the man Jesus raised from the dead.) ²There they had a dinner for Jesus. Martha served the food, and Lazarus was one of the people eating with Jesus. ³Mary brought in a pint of very expensive perfume made from pure nard. She poured the perfume on Jesus' feet, and then she wiped his feet with her hair. And the sweet smell from the perfume filled the whole house.

⁴Judas Iscariot, one of Jesus' followers who would later turn against him, was there. Judas said, ⁵"This perfume was worth an entire year's wages. Why wasn't it sold and the money given to the poor?" ⁶But Judas did not really care about the poor; he said this because he was a thief. He was the one who kept the money box, and he often stole from it.

⁷Jesus answered, "Leave her alone. It was right for her to save this perfume for today, the day for me to be prepared for burial. ⁸You will always have the poor with you, but you will not always have me."

The Plot Against Lazarus

⁹A large crowd of people heard that Jesus was in Bethany. So they went there to see not only Jesus but Lazarus, whom Jesus raised from the dead. ¹⁰So the leading priests made plans to kill Lazarus, too. ¹¹Because of Lazarus many of the Jews were leaving them and believing in Jesus.

Jesus Enters Jerusalem

¹²The next day a great crowd who had come to Jerusalem for the Passover Feast heard that Jesus was coming there. ¹³So they took branches of palm trees and went out to meet Jesus, shouting,

▶Get Aligned
John 12:3

Mary understood the meaning of extravagant worship. She modeled how to lavish the Lord with adoration. Too often we give Jesus our half-hearted praise. Some people get more excited cheering at football games than they do worshiping at church.

Mary set the standard for us. This wasn't a cheap bottle of perfume from the local convenience store. It was worth three hundred denarii, which amounted to about a year's worth of salary. On top of that, the alabaster jar holding the perfume was also expensive. Some translations of Mark's Gospel indicate that she broke this to douse the Lord's feet with the liquid. She refused to let money, practicality, and pride to get in the way of giving Jesus the honor he deserved.

Try to recall the last time you extravagantly worshiped Jesus. Forget the typical thirty-minute worship set on Sunday. We're talking extravagant, profuse, even extreme. The kind of worship in which you leave your personal baggage at the door, forget about what you get out of the experience, and simply love your Lord with everything you have. Like Mary, you may have people scoff at your radical expression of love. Nevertheless, it will always be a sweet aroma to the Lord.

Change >> Your WORLD

EVERY HOME FOR CHRIST

It sounds impossible to reach every home for Christ, since there are billions of people in the world. Yet Every Home for Christ intends systematically to make a personal presentation of the Good News of Jesus Christ to every home in the world. Since its beginning, Every Home for Christ, with a full-time staff of more than twelve hundred workers plus fourteen thousand volunteer associates, has distributed more than 2.2 billion Good News messages. More than 35.7 million decision cards have been mailed to the organization's many offices overseas, and the group has established ninety-three thousand village New Testament fellowships called Christ Groups. You can volunteer for long-term or short-term work.

To change your world, visit www.ehc.org.

"Praise" God!
God bless the One who comes in the name of the Lord!
God bless the King of Israel!" *Psalm 118:25–26*

[14]Jesus found a colt and sat on it. This was as the Scripture says,
[15]"Don't be afraid, people of Jerusalem!
Your king is coming,
sitting on the colt of a donkey." *Zechariah 9:9*

[16]The followers of Jesus did not understand this at first. But after Jesus was raised to glory, they remembered that this had been written about him and that they had done these things to him.

People Tell About Jesus

[17]There had been many people with Jesus when he raised Lazarus from the dead and told him to come out of the tomb. Now they were telling others about what Jesus did. [18]Many people went out to meet Jesus, because they had heard about this miracle. [19]So the Pharisees said to each other, "You can see that nothing is going right for us. Look! The whole world is following him."

Jesus Talks About His Death

[20]There were some Greek people, too, who came to Jerusalem to worship at the Passover Feast. [21]They went to Philip, who was from Bethsaida in Galilee, and said, "Sir, we would like to see Jesus." [22]Philip told Andrew, and then Andrew and Philip told Jesus.

[23]Jesus said to them, "The time has come for the Son of Man to receive his glory. [24]I tell you the truth, a grain of wheat must fall to the ground and die to make many seeds. But if it never dies, it remains only a single seed. [25]Those who love their lives will lose them, but those who hate their lives in this world will keep true life forever. [26]Whoever serves me must follow me. Then my servant will be with me everywhere I am. My Father will honor anyone who serves me.

[27]"Now I am very troubled. Should I say, 'Father, save me from this time'? No, I came to this time so I could suffer. [28]Father, bring glory to your name!"

Then a voice came from heaven, "I have brought glory to it, and I will do it again."

[29]The crowd standing there, who heard the voice, said it was thunder. But others said, "An angel has spoken to him."

[30]Jesus said, "That voice was for your sake, not mine. [31]Now is the time for the world to be judged; now the ruler of this world will be thrown down. [32]If I am lifted up from the earth, I will draw all people toward me." [33]Jesus said this to show how he would die.

[34]The crowd said, "We have heard from the law that the Christ will live forever. So why do you say, 'The Son of Man must be lifted up'? Who is this 'Son of Man'?"

[35]Then Jesus said, "The light will be with you for a little longer, so walk while you have the light. Then the darkness will not catch you. If you walk in the darkness, you will not know where you are going. [36]Believe in the light while you still have it so that you will become children of light." When Jesus had said this, he left and hid himself from them.

Some People Won't Believe in Jesus

[37]Though Jesus had done many miracles in front of the people, they still did not believe in him. [38]This was to bring about what Isaiah the prophet had said:

Q: What are demons?

A: Demons are actually fallen angels who rebelled against God and were cast out of heaven along with Lucifer. They are evil beings who serve the will of their master, Satan. Out of hatred for God, they strive to keep people from believing in Jesus Christ.

>> **12:13 Praise** Literally, "Hosanna," a Hebrew word used at first in praying to God for help, but at this time it was probably a shout of joy used in praising God or his Messiah.

"Lord, who believed what we told them?
Who saw the Lord's power in this?" *Isaiah 53:1*

³⁹This is why the people could not believe: Isaiah also had said,

⁴⁰"He has blinded their eyes,
and he has closed their minds.
Otherwise they would see with their eyes
and understand in their minds
and come back to me and be healed." *Isaiah 6:10*

⁴¹Isaiah said this because he saw Jesus' glory and spoke about him.

⁴²But many believed in Jesus, even many of the leaders. But because of the Pharisees, they did not say they believed in him for fear they would be put out of the synagogue. ⁴³They loved praise from people more than praise from God.

⁴⁴Then Jesus cried out, "Whoever believes in me is really believing in the One who sent me. ⁴⁵Whoever sees me sees the One who sent me. ⁴⁶I have come as light into the world so that whoever believes in me would not stay in darkness.

⁴⁷"Anyone who hears my words and does not obey them, I do not judge, because I did not come to judge the world, but to save the world. ⁴⁸There is a judge for those who refuse to believe in me and do not accept my words. The word I have taught will be their judge on the last day. ⁴⁹The things I taught were not from myself. The Father who sent me told me what to say and what to teach. ⁵⁰And I know that eternal life comes from what the Father commands. So whatever I say is what the Father told me to say."

Jesus Washes His Followers' Feet

13 It was almost time for the Passover Feast. Jesus knew that it was time for him to leave this world and go back to the Father. He had always loved those who were his own in the world, and he loved them all the way to the end.

²Jesus and his followers were at the evening meal. The devil had already persuaded Judas Iscariot, the son of Simon, to turn against Jesus. ³Jesus knew that the Father had given him power over everything and that he had come from God and was going back to God. ⁴So during the meal Jesus stood up and took off his outer clothing. Taking a towel, he wrapped it around his waist. ⁵Then he poured water into a bowl and began to wash the followers' feet, drying them with the towel that was wrapped around him.

⁶Jesus came to Simon Peter, who said to him, "Lord, are you going to wash my feet?"

⁷Jesus answered, "You don't understand now what I am doing, but you will understand later."

⁸Peter said, "No, you will never wash my feet."

Jesus answered, "If I don't wash your feet, you are not one of my people."

⁹Simon Peter answered, "Lord, then wash not only my feet, but wash my hands and my head, too!"

¹⁰Jesus said, "After a person has had a bath, his whole body is clean. He needs only to wash his feet. And you men are clean, but not all of you." ¹¹Jesus knew who would turn against him, and that is why he said, "Not all of you are clean."

¹²When he had finished washing their feet, he put on his clothes and sat down again. He asked, "Do you understand what I have just done for you? ¹³You call me 'Teacher' and 'Lord,' and you are right, because that is what I am. ¹⁴If I, your Lord and Teacher, have washed your feet, you also should wash each other's feet. ¹⁵I did this as an example so that you should do as I have done for you. ¹⁶I tell you the truth, a servant is not greater than his master. A messenger is not greater than the one who sent him. ¹⁷If you know these things, you will be blessed if you do them.

¹⁸"I am not talking about all of you. I know those I have chosen. But this is to bring about what the Scripture said: 'The man who ate at my table has turned against me.' ¹⁹I am telling you this now before it happens so that when it happens, you will believe that I am he. ²⁰I tell you the truth, whoever accepts anyone I send also accepts me. And whoever accepts me also accepts the One who sent me."

Jesus Talks About His Death

²¹After Jesus said this, he was very troubled. He said openly, "I tell you the truth, one of you will turn against me."

²²The followers all looked at each other, because they did not know whom Jesus was talking about. ²³One of the followers sitting next to Jesus was the follower Jesus loved. ²⁴Simon Peter motioned to him to ask Jesus whom he was talking about.

²⁵That follower leaned closer to Jesus and asked, "Lord, who is it?"

▶ Get Aligned
John 13:5

HUNDREDS OF BOOKS ARE PUBLISHED EVERY YEAR on how to become a leader. They suggest how to dress for success, to think of shortcuts as means to an end, and to network with others to get to the corner office. In essence, they train people on how to climb the ladder the fastest and claim the prize as king of the hill.

Jesus' version of leadership is completely the opposite. In fact, if he wrote a book on leadership today, it would likely not be very popular. According to our world system, being first in command is about power and authority, not becoming the least of all. Yet that's exactly the secret to true leadership, as Christ exemplified. By washing his followers' feet, he was simply continuing the style of leadership he'd shown throughout his time with them. He led by example, something the world does not teach. But he also led by service that would seem beneath most leaders today.

As the ultimate leader of all life, Jesus was not insecure about his position. He knew his rightful claim as ruler. Still, he was willing to stoop to the lowest level to show what great leadership truly is.

>> **13:18** 'The man...me.' Quotation from Psalm 41:9. **13:23 sitting** Literally, "lying." The people of that time ate lying down and leaning on one arm.

THINK ABOUT IT John 14:2–3

SEVERAL WEEKS BEFORE THE PRESIDENT of the United States arrives anywhere for a visit, an advance team of specialists goes to that destination. This team works with the local authorities to review various details, such as security concerns, transportation needs, and logistical challenges. The President and his team move on a tight schedule, so each possible contingency is carefully considered and handled ahead of his arrival.

Think of Jesus as the advance man who has gone ahead and provided us with the means to live eternally with God in heaven. During the final days of Jesus' life on earth, he knew that soon his life would come to an end and he would be returning to heaven. His apostles were focused on the fact that Jesus would be killed and his life would end, but Jesus looked beyond death to his resurrection and his return to heaven.

As he did, he consoled his followers by promising them that he had prepared a place for them in heaven and left them with these words of hope: "After I go and prepare a place for you, I will come back and take you to be with me so that you may be where I am."

[26]Jesus answered, "I will dip this bread into the dish. The man I give it to is the man who will turn against me." So Jesus took a piece of bread, dipped it, and gave it to Judas Iscariot, the son of Simon. [27]As soon as Judas took the bread, Satan entered him. Jesus said to him, "The thing that you will do—do it quickly." [28]No one at the table understood why Jesus said this to Judas. [29]Since he was the one who kept the money box, some of the followers thought Jesus was telling him to buy what was needed for the feast or to give something to the poor.

[30]Judas took the bread Jesus gave him and immediately went out. It was night.

[31]When Judas was gone, Jesus said, "Now the Son of Man receives his glory, and God receives glory through him. [32]If God receives glory through him,[n] then God will give glory to the Son through himself. And God will give him glory quickly."

[33]Jesus said, "My children, I will be with you only a little longer. You will look for me, and what I told the Jews, I tell you now: Where I am going you cannot come.

[34]"I give you a new command: Love each other. You must love each other as I have loved you. [35]All people will know that you are my followers if you love each other."

Peter Will Say He Doesn't Know Jesus

[36]Simon Peter asked Jesus, "Lord, where are you going?"

Jesus answered, "Where I am going you cannot follow now, but you will follow later."

[37]Peter asked, "Lord, why can't I follow you now? I am ready to die for you!"

[38]Jesus answered, "Are you ready to die for me? I tell you the truth, before the rooster crows, you will say three times that you don't know me."

Jesus Comforts His Followers

14Jesus said, "Don't let your hearts be troubled. Trust in God, and trust in me. [2]There are many rooms in my Father's house; I would not tell you this if it were not true. I am going there to prepare a place for you. [3]After I go and prepare a place for you, I will come back and take you to be with me so that you may be where I am. [4]You know the way to the place where I am going."[n]

[5]Thomas said to Jesus, "Lord, we don't know where you are going. So how can we know the way?"

[6]Jesus answered, "I am the way, and the truth, and the life. The only way to the Father is through me. [7]If you really knew me, you would know my Father, too. But now you do know him, and you have seen him."

[8]Philip said to him, "Lord, show us the Father. That is all we need."

[9]Jesus answered, "I have been with you a long time now. Do you still not know me, Philip? Whoever has seen me has seen the Father. So why do you say, 'Show us the Father'? [10]Don't you believe that I am in the Father and the Father is in me? The words I say to you don't come from me, but the Father lives in me and does his own work. [11]Believe me when I say that I am in the Father and the Father is in me. Or believe because of the miracles I have done. [12]I tell you the truth,

| FACT-OIDS! | Forty-seven million students attend public schools, 7 million attend private schools, and between 1.2 and 2 million are homeschooled. [Harris Interactive] |

whoever believes in me will do the same things that I do. Those who believe will do even greater things than these, because I am going to the Father. [13]And if you ask for anything in my name, I will do it for you so that the Father's glory will be shown through the Son. [14]If you ask me for anything in my name, I will do it.

The Promise of the Holy Spirit

[15]"If you love me, you will obey my commands. [16]I will ask the Father, and he will give

>> **13:32 If . . . him** Some Greek copies do not have this phrase. **14:4 You . . . going.** Some Greek copies read "You know where I am going and the way to the place I am going."

you another Helper[a] to be with you forever— [17]the Spirit of truth. The world cannot accept him, because it does not see him or know him. But you know him, because he lives with you and he will be in you.

[18]"I will not leave you all alone like orphans; I will come back to you. [19]In a little while the world will not see me anymore, but you will see me. Because I live, you will live, too. [20]On that day you will know that I am in my Father, and that you are in me and I am in you. [21]Those who know my commands and obey them are the ones who love me, and my Father will love those who love me. I will love them and will show myself to them."

[22]Then Judas (not Judas Iscariot) said, "But, Lord, why do you plan to show yourself to us and not to the rest of the world?"

[23]Jesus answered, "If people love me, they will obey my teaching. My Father will love them, and we will come to them and make our home with them. [24]Those who do not love me do not obey my teaching. This teaching that you hear is not really mine; it is from my Father, who sent me.

[25]"I have told you all these things while I am with you. [26]But the Helper will teach you everything and will cause you to remember all that I told you. This Helper is the Holy Spirit whom the Father will send in my name.

[27]"I leave you peace; my peace I give you. I do not give it to you as the world does. So don't let your hearts be troubled or afraid. [28]You heard me say to you, 'I am going, but I am coming back to you.' If you loved me, you should be happy that I am going back to the Father, because he is greater than I am. [29]I have told you this now, before it happens, so that when it happens, you will believe. [30]I will not talk with you much longer, because the ruler of this world is coming. He has no power over me, [31]but the world must know that I love the Father, so I do exactly what the Father told me to do.

"Come now, let us go.

Jesus Is Like a Vine

15 "I am the true vine; my Father is the gardener. [2]He cuts off every branch of mine that does not produce fruit. And he trims and cleans every branch that produces fruit so that it will produce even more fruit. [3]You are already clean because of the words I have spoken to you. [4]Remain in me, and I will remain in you. A branch cannot produce fruit alone but must remain in the vine. In the same way, you cannot produce fruit alone but must remain in me.

[5]"I am the vine, and you are the branches. If any remain in me and I remain in them, they produce much fruit. But without me they can do nothing. [6]If any do not remain in me, they are like a branch that is thrown away and then dies. People pick up dead branches, throw them into the fire, and burn them. [7]If you remain in me and follow my teachings, you can ask anything you want, and it will be given to you. [8]You should produce much fruit and show that you are my followers, which brings glory to my Father. [9]I loved you as the Father loved me. Now remain in my love. [10]I have obeyed my Father's commands, and I remain in his love. In the same way, if you obey my commands, you will remain in my love. [11]I have told you these things so that you can have the same joy I have and so that your joy will be the fullest possible joy.

[12]"This is my command: Love each other as I have loved you. [13]The greatest love a person can show is to die for his friends. [14]You are my friends if you do what I command you. [15]I no longer call you servants, because a servant does not know what his master is doing. But I call you friends, because I have made known to you everything I heard from my Father. [16]You did not choose me; I chose you. And I gave you this work: to go and produce fruit, fruit that will last. Then the Father

Q: How can I know God's will for my life?

A: The Bible focuses more on describing the sort of person God wants you to be than on lesser matters like what you do for a living. Focus your efforts on becoming the person whom God wants you to be, and trust him to reveal his specific will for your life in due time.

Principles: GRACE

Grace is the gift of God's unmerited favor. It is demonstrated in God's forgiveness for our mistakes and disobedience of his directions for our lives. We receive grace when we place our faith in Jesus Christ. Grace is good news. It means we can't earn our way to heaven or work hard enough to make God love us more than he already does. All we have to do is accept the gift he freely offers—eternal life through faith in Christ. As Hebrews 13:9 says as encouragement to all believers, "Your hearts should be strengthened by God's grace."

>> **14:16 Helper** "Counselor" or "Comforter." Jesus is talking about the Holy Spirit.

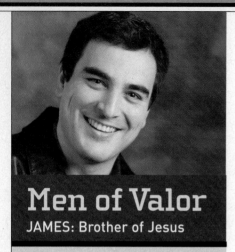

Men of Valor
JAMES: Brother of Jesus

Although the half brother of Christ, initially even James didn't believe in the deity of Jesus. However, after seeing Jesus following his resurrection from the dead (1 Corinthians 15:7), James's outlook changed. He became a leader in the church at Jerusalem and mediated a dispute over whether Gentiles had to be circumcised and follow Jewish customs. According to James, they were to abstain from such things as idol worship and sexual immorality. His conscience awakened, James wrote his namesake book that is every bit as relevant today as when it was written nearly two thousand years ago. In it, James admonishes believers to be doers of God's Word, not just hearers.

will give you anything you ask for in my name. [17]This is my command: Love each other.

Jesus Warns His Followers

[18]"If the world hates you, remember that it hated me first. [19]If you belonged to the world, it would love you as it loves its own. But I have chosen you out of the world, so you don't belong to it. That is why the world hates you. [20]Remember what I told you: A servant is not greater than his master. If peo-

ple did wrong to me, they will do wrong to you, too. And if they obeyed my teaching, they will obey yours, too. [21]They will do all this to you on account of me, because they do not know the One who sent me. [22]If I had not come and spoken to them, they would not be guilty of sin, but now they have no excuse for their sin. [23]Whoever hates me also hates my Father. [24]I did works among them that no one else has ever done. If I had not done these works, they would not be guilty of sin. But now they have seen what I have done, and yet they have hated both me and my Father. [25]But this happened so that what is written in their law would be true: 'They hated me for no reason.'"

[26]"I will send you the Helper" from the Father; he is the Spirit of truth who comes from the Father. When he comes, he will tell about me, [27]and you also must tell people about me, because you have been with me from the beginning.

FACT-OIDS!
Fifty-nine percent of households reported having Internet access at their home in 2003, compared to 50% in 2000. [Barna.org]

16
"I have told you these things to keep you from giving up. [2]People will put you out of their synagogues. Yes, the time is coming when those who kill you will think they are offering service to God. [3]They will do this because they have not known the Father and they have not known me. [4]I have told you these things now so that when the time comes you will remember that I warned you.

The Work of the Holy Spirit

"I did not tell you these things at the beginning, because I was with you then. [5]Now I am going back to the One who sent me. But none of you asks me, 'Where are you going?' [6]Your hearts are filled with sadness because I have told you these things. [7]But I tell you the truth, it is better for you that I go away. When I go away, I will send the Helper" to

you. If I do not go away, the Helper will not come. [8]When the Helper comes, he will prove to the people of the world the truth about sin, about being right with God, and about judgment. [9]He will prove to them that sin is not believing in me. [10]He will prove to them that being right with God comes from my going to the Father and not being seen anymore. [11]And the Helper will prove to them that judgment happened when the ruler of this world was judged.

[12]"I have many more things to say to you, but they are too much for you now. [13]But when the Spirit of truth comes, he will lead you into all truth. He will not speak his own words, but he will speak only what he hears, and he will tell you what is to come. [14]The Spirit of truth will bring glory to me, because he will take what I have to say and tell it to you. [15]All that the Father has is mine. That is why I said that the Spirit will take what I have to say and tell it to you.

Sadness Will Become Happiness

[16]"After a little while you will not see me, and then after a little while you will see me again."

[17]Some of the followers said to each other, "What does Jesus mean when he says, 'After a little while you will not see me, and then after a little while you will see me again'? And what does he mean when he says, 'Because I am going to the Father'?" [18]They also asked, "What does he mean by 'a little while'? We don't understand what he is saying."

[19]Jesus saw that the followers wanted to ask him about this, so he said to them, "Are you asking each other what I meant when I said, 'After a little while you will not see me, and then after a little while you will see me again'? [20]I tell you the truth, you will cry and be sad, but the world will be happy. You will be sad, but your sadness will become joy.

 15:25 'They...reason.' These words could be from Psalm 35:19 or Psalm 69:4.   15:26 Helper "Counselor" or "Comforter." Jesus is talking about the Holy Spirit.   16:7 Helper "Counselor" or "Comforter." Jesus is talking about the Holy Spirit.

140

²¹"When a woman gives birth to a baby, she has pain, because her time has come. But when her baby is born, she forgets the pain, because she is so happy that a child has been born into the world. ²²It is the same with you. Now you are sad, but I will see you again and you will be happy, and no one will take away your joy. ²³In that day you will not ask me for anything. I tell you the truth, my Father will give you anything you ask for in my name. ²⁴Until now you have not asked for anything in my name. Ask and you will receive, so that your joy will be the fullest possible joy.

³³"I told you these things so that you can have peace in me. In this world you will have trouble, but be brave! I have defeated the world."

Jesus Prays for His Followers

17 After Jesus said these things, he looked toward heaven and prayed, "Father, the time has come. Give glory to your Son so that the Son can give glory to you. ²You gave the Son power over all people so that the Son could give eternal life to all those you gave him. ³And this is eternal life: that people know you, the only true

> **"After a little while you will not see me, and then after a little while you will see me again. "**
>
> JOHN 16:16

Victory over the World

²⁵"I have told you these things indirectly in stories. But the time will come when I will not use stories like that to tell you things; I will speak to you in plain words about the Father. ²⁶In that day you will ask the Father for things in my name. I mean, I will not need to ask the Father for you. ²⁷The Father himself loves you. He loves you because you loved me and believed that I came from God. ²⁸I came from the Father into the world. Now I am leaving the world and going back to the Father."

²⁹Then the followers of Jesus said, "You are speaking clearly to us now and are not using stories that are hard to understand. ³⁰We can see now that you know all things. You can answer a person's question even before it is asked. This makes us believe you came from God."

³¹Jesus answered, "So now you believe? ³²Listen to me; a time is coming when you will be scattered, each to your own home. That time is now here. You will leave me alone, but I am never really alone, because the Father is with me.

God, and that they know Jesus Christ, the One you sent. ⁴Having finished the work you gave me to do, I brought you glory on earth. ⁵And now, Father, give me glory with you; give me the glory I had with you before the world was made.

⁶"I showed what you are like to those you gave me from the world. They belonged to you, and you gave them to me, and they have obeyed your teaching. ⁷Now they know that everything you gave me comes from you. ⁸I gave them the teachings you gave me, and they accepted them. They knew that I truly came from you, and they believed that you sent me. ⁹I am praying for them. I am not praying for people in the world but for those you gave me, because they are yours. ¹⁰All I have is yours, and all you have is mine. And my glory is shown through them. ¹¹I am coming to you; I will not stay in the world any longer. But they are still in the world. Holy Father, keep them safe by the power of your name, the name you gave me, so that they will be one, just as you and I are one. ¹²While I was with them, I kept them

The Bottom Line

Gambling: A Bad Habit

SINCE FORTY-EIGHT OF FIFTY STATES have some form of legalized gambling, and Internet scams abound, the temptation to gamble is universal. Before throwing your money away, realize the reason such enterprises are so profitable is because the odds are stacked against you. Gambling is often touted as an alternative to higher taxes, but the social costs of crime, divorce, and other problems related to gambling cost society far more. Gambling also ruins communities via increased prostitution, pawnshops, child abandonment, gambling addiction, and bankruptcy filings. Gambling glitters like fool's gold but is only for fools.

safe by the power of your name, the name you gave me. I protected them, and only one of them, the one worthy of destruction, was lost so that the Scripture would come true.

13 "I am coming to you now. But I pray these things while I am still in the world so that these followers can have all of my joy in them. 14 I have given them your teaching. And the world has hated them, because they don't belong to the world, just as I don't belong to the world. 15 I am not asking you to take them out of the world but to keep them safe from the Evil One. 16 They don't belong to the world, just as I don't belong to the world. 17 Make them ready for your service through your truth; your teaching is truth. 18 I have sent them into the world, just as you sent me into the world. 19 For their sake, I am making myself ready to serve so that they can be ready for their service of the truth.

20 "I pray for these followers, but I am also praying for all those who will believe in me because of their teaching. 21 Father, I pray that they can be one. As you are in me and I am in you, I pray that they can also be one in us. Then the world will believe that you sent me. 22 I have given these people the glory that you gave me so that they can be one, just as you and I are one. 23 I will be in them and you will be in me so that they will be completely one. Then the world will know that you sent me and that you loved them just as much as you loved me.

24 "Father, I want these people that you gave me to be with me where I am. I want them to see my glory, which you gave me because you loved me before the world was made. 25 Father, you are the One who is good. The world does not know you, but I know you, and these people know you sent me. 26 I showed them what you are like, and I will show them again. Then they will have the same love that you have for me, and I will live in them."

Jesus Is Arrested

18 When Jesus finished praying, he went with his followers across the Kidron Valley. On the other side there was a garden, and Jesus and his followers went into it.

2 Judas knew where this place was, because Jesus met there often with his followers. Judas was the one who turned against Jesus. 3 So Judas came there with a group of soldiers and some guards from the leading priests and the Pharisees. They were carrying torches, lanterns, and weapons.

4 Knowing everything that would happen to him, Jesus went out and asked, "Who is it you are looking for?"

5 They answered, "Jesus from Nazareth."

"I am he," Jesus said. (Judas, the one who turned against Jesus, was standing there with them.) 6 When Jesus said, "I am he," they moved back and fell to the ground.

7 Jesus asked them again, "Who is it you are looking for?"

They said, "Jesus of Nazareth."

8 "I told you that I am he," Jesus said. "So if you are looking for me, let the others go." 9 This happened so that the words Jesus said before would come true: "I have not lost any of the ones you gave me."

Q: What does it mean to grow spiritually?

A: When Christians talk about growing spiritually, they're referring to the deepening of their sense of connection with God and the expression of a Christlike character through their lives. The goal of all Christian spiritual growth is to become more like Christ.

Get Fit

PAMPERING YOURSELF Health is not merely the absence of disease; it is a lifestyle. Whether it's getting enough sleep, relaxing after a stressful day, or enjoying a hobby, it's important to take time to be good to yourself. Make it a priority to balance work, home, and play. Give greater energy to those activities and people in your life who matter most to you. And no matter what comes your way, remember to laugh. It says in Proverbs 17:22 that "a happy heart is like good medicine." So find the humor in life. You'll not only be healthier, you'll be happier. And so will those who love you.

¹⁰Simon Peter, who had a sword, pulled it out and struck the servant of the high priest, cutting off his right ear. (The servant's name was Malchus.) ¹¹Jesus said to Peter, "Put your sword back. Shouldn't I drink the cup" the Father gave me?"

Jesus Is Brought Before Annas

¹²Then the soldiers with their commander and the guards arrested Jesus. They tied him ¹³and led him first to Annas, the father-in-law of Caiaphas, the high priest that year. ¹⁴Caiaphas was the one who told the Jews that it would be better if one man died for all the people.

Peter Says He Doesn't Know Jesus

¹⁵Simon Peter and another one of Jesus' followers went along after Jesus. This follower knew the high priest, so he went with Jesus into the high priest's courtyard. ¹⁶But Peter waited outside near the door. The follower who knew the high priest came back outside, spoke to the girl at the door, and brought Peter inside. ¹⁷The girl at the door said to Peter, "Aren't you also one of that man's followers?"

Peter answered, "No, I am not!"

¹⁸It was cold, so the servants and guards had built a fire and were standing around it, warming themselves. Peter also was standing with them, warming himself.

The High Priest Questions Jesus

¹⁹The high priest asked Jesus questions about his followers and his teaching. ²⁰Jesus answered, "I have spoken openly to everyone. I have always taught in synagogues and in the Temple, where all the Jews come together. I never said anything in secret. ²¹So why do you question me? Ask the people who heard my teaching. They know what I said."

²²When Jesus said this, one of the guards standing there hit him. The guard said, "Is that the way you answer the high priest?"

²³Jesus answered him, "If I said something wrong, then show what it was. But if what I said is true, why do you hit me?"

²⁴Then Annas sent Jesus, who was still tied, to Caiaphas the high priest.

Peter Says Again He Doesn't Know Jesus

²⁵As Simon Peter was standing and warming himself, they said to him, "Aren't you one of that man's followers?"

Peter said it was not true; he said, "No, I am not."

²⁶One of the servants of the high priest was there. This servant was a relative of the man whose ear Peter had cut off. The servant said, "Didn't I see you with him in the garden?"

²⁷Again Peter said it wasn't true. At once a rooster crowed.

Jesus Is Brought Before Pilate

²⁸Early in the morning they led Jesus from Caiaphas's house to the Roman governor's palace. They would not go inside the palace, because they did not want to make themselves unclean;" they wanted to eat the Passover meal. ²⁹So Pilate went outside to them and asked, "What charges do you bring against this man?"

³⁰They answered, "If he were not a criminal, we wouldn't have brought him to you."

³¹Pilate said to them, "Take him yourselves and judge him by your own law."

"But we are not allowed to put anyone to death," the Jews answered. ³²(This happened so that what Jesus said about how he would die would come true.)

³³Then Pilate went back inside the palace and called Jesus to him and asked, "Are you the king of the Jews?"

³⁴Jesus said, "Is that your own question, or did others tell you about me?"

³⁵Pilate answered, "I am not one of you. It was your own people and their leading priests who handed you over to me. What have you done wrong?"

³⁶Jesus answered, "My kingdom does not belong to this world. If it belonged to this world, my servants would have fought to keep me from being given over to the Jewish leaders. But my kingdom is from another place."

³⁷Pilate said, "So you are a king!"

Jesus answered, "You are the one saying I am a king. This is why I was born and came into the world: to tell people the truth. And everyone who belongs to the truth listens to me."

People Skills

Conflict Resolution

Conflict is a normal part of any healthy relationship. That is why it's important to learn how to move through conflict in a healthy way. A day or two after resolving a conflict, come back together for a post-conflict debriefing. Ask your partner how she's feeling, not about the subject of the fight, but about the fight itself. Did she feel like it was a fair discussion? Did you feel heard and understood? Did either of you feel personally attacked? After sharing your experiences, decide together how you will approach conflict differently next time so that you both will feel honored and valued through the process. Pray for each other, also.

18:11 cup Jesus is talking about the painful things that will happen to him. Accepting these things will be very hard, like drinking a cup of something bitter.   18:28 unclean Going into the Roman palace would make them unfit to eat the Passover Feast, according to their Law.

HARLEM GLOBETROTTERS: Goodwill Ambassadors

DESPITE THEIR IDENTIFICATION WITH NEW YORK, the Harlem Globetrotters arose from the South Side of Chicago in 1926, thanks to the clever promotion and coaching of Abe Saperstein. The Globetrotters would go on to become the world's most recognized basketball team. Inducted into the Basketball Hall of Fame in 2002, they have performed for more than 120 million people in 117 countries.

Anyone who has watched this squad knows its comedic genius is as vital as its on-court skills. And though such familiar names as Marques Haynes, Goose Tatum, Meadowlark Lemon, and Curly Neal have long since retired, a new crop of players keeps the show going. As part of their enduring legacy, the Globetrotters are a shining example of how humor and talent can create goodwill ambassadors.

Organized in an era when segregation meant blacks had no chance to play professionally, the "clown princes of basketball" crossed numerous racial boundaries. Even today, with black attendance at Globetrotters' games more than doubling in the past decade, U.S. audiences are still 70 percent white.

In addition, as they reached racially mixed audiences in their early days, this talented collection of players inspired minorities, whose access to society's upper rungs was nearly nonexistent. Finally, they became so big that the Globetrotters' experience opened bigger doors.

Former player Meadowlark Lemon discovered this when he parlayed his visibility into opportunities to publicly discuss his relationship with Christ. No matter what the profession, letting your light shine may place you on a platform of eternal significance. As Matthew 5:16 states, "Live so that they will see the good things you do and will praise your Father in heaven."

> **"...[these] players inspired minorities, whose access to society's upper rungs was nearly nonexistent."**

[38]Pilate said, "What is truth?" After he said this, he went out to the crowd again and said to them, "I find nothing against this man. [39]But it is your custom that I free one prisoner to you at Passover time. Do you want me to free the 'king of the Jews'?"

[40]They shouted back, "No, not him! Let Barabbas go free!" (Barabbas was a robber.)

19 Then Pilate ordered that Jesus be taken away and whipped. [2]The soldiers made a crown from some thorny branches and put it on Jesus' head and put a purple robe around him. [3]Then they came to him many times and said, "Hail, King of the Jews!" and hit him in the face.

[4]Again Pilate came out and said to them, "Look, I am bringing Jesus out to you. I want you to know that I find nothing against him." [5]So Jesus came out, wearing the crown of thorns and the purple robe. Pilate said to them, "Here is the man!"

[6]When the leading priests and the guards saw Jesus, they shouted, "Crucify him! Crucify him!"

But Pilate answered, "Crucify him yourselves, because I find nothing against him."

[7]The leaders answered, "We have a law that says he should die, because he said he is the Son of God."

[8]When Pilate heard this, he was even more afraid. [9]He went back inside the palace and asked Jesus, "Where do you come from?" But Jesus did not answer him. [10]Pilate said, "You refuse to speak to me? Don't you know I have power to set you free and power to have you crucified?"

[11]Jesus answered, "The only power you have over me is the power given to you by God. The man who turned me in to you is guilty of a greater sin."

[12]After this, Pilate tried to let Jesus go. But some in the crowd cried out, "Anyone who makes himself king is against Caesar. If you let this man go, you are no friend of Caesar."

[13]When Pilate heard what they were saying, he brought Jesus out and sat down on the judge's seat at the place called The Stone Pavement. (In the Hebrew language" the name is Gabbatha.) [14]It was about noon on Preparation Day of Passover week. Pilate said to the crowd, "Here is your king!"

[15]They shouted, "Take him away! Take him away! Crucify him!"

Pilate asked them, "Do you want me to crucify your king?"

The leading priests answered, "The only king we have is Caesar."

[16]So Pilate handed Jesus over to them to be crucified.

Jesus Is Crucified

The soldiers took charge of Jesus. [17]Carrying his own cross, Jesus went out to a place called The Place of the Skull, which in the Hebrew language" is called Golgotha. [18]There they crucified Jesus. They also crucified two other men, one on each side, with Jesus in the middle. [19]Pilate wrote a sign and put it on the cross. It read: JESUS OF NAZARETH, THE KING OF THE JEWS. [20]The sign was written in Hebrew, in Latin, and in Greek. Many of the people read the sign, because the place where Jesus was crucified was near the city. [21]The leading priests said to Pilate, "Don't write, 'The King of the Jews.' But write, 'This man said, "I am the King of the Jews." ' "

Q: Why does God allow us to go through trials and tribulations?

A: The Bible actually instructs us to rejoice when we encounter trials because we know God will use the trial to strengthen our faith, develop our character, and deepen our overall capacity to experience God's love (James 1:2–4).

 ## Survival Guide

EXTINGUISHING FIRES: DO YOUR HOMEWORK

Home fires cause nearly $6 billion in damages annually. To be safe, check your fire extinguisher's rating. Class A extinguishers put out fires in combustibles such as wood and paper, while Class B extinguishers handle fires involving flammable liquids like grease and oil. Class C extinguishers are designed for electrical fires, and Class D extinguishers combat those started by flammable metals. The best option is a multi-purpose fire extinguisher designed to fight several types of fires.

 19:13 **Hebrew language** Or Aramaic, the languages of many people in this region in the first century.   19:17 **Hebrew language** Or Aramaic, the languages of many people in this region in the first century.

Ten Ways to Share Your Faith

1. Ask God for divine appointments.

2. Speak the truth from your heart.

3. Remind others of the goodness of God.

4. Answer questions people are asking.

5. Share your testimony with colleagues.

6. Learn to listen between the lines.

7. Be approachable about spiritual issues.

8. Trust the Lord for opportune moments.

9. Seek wisdom about the needs of people.

10. Live a godly life before others.

²²Pilate answered, "What I have written, I have written."

²³After the soldiers crucified Jesus, they took his clothes and divided them into four parts, with each soldier getting one part. They also took his long shirt, which was all one piece of cloth, woven from top to bottom. ²⁴So the soldiers said to each other, "We should not tear this into parts. Let's throw lots to see who will get it." This happened so that this Scripture would come true:

"They divided my clothes among them,
and they threw lots for my clothing."   Psalm 22:18

So the soldiers did this.

²⁵Standing near his cross were Jesus' mother, his mother's sister, Mary the wife of Clopas, and Mary Magdalene. ²⁶When Jesus saw his mother and the follower he loved standing nearby, he said to his mother, "Dear woman, here is your son." ²⁷Then he said to the follower, "Here is your mother." From that time on, the follower took her to live in his home.

Jesus Dies

²⁸After this, Jesus knew that everything had been done. So that the Scripture would come true, he said, "I am thirsty."ⁿ ²⁹There was a jar full of vinegar there, so the soldiers soaked a sponge in it, put the sponge on a branch of a hyssop plant, and lifted it to Jesus' mouth. ³⁰When Jesus tasted the vinegar, he said, "It is finished." Then he bowed his head and died.

³¹This day was Preparation Day, and the next day was a special Sabbath day. Since the religious leaders did not want the bodies to stay on the cross on the Sabbath day, they asked Pilate to order that the legs of the men be brokenⁿ and the bodies be taken away. ³²So the soldiers came and broke the legs of the first man on the cross beside Jesus. Then they broke the legs of the man on the other cross beside Jesus. ³³But when the soldiers came to Jesus and saw that he was already dead, they did not break his legs. ³⁴But one of the soldiers stuck his spear into Jesus' side, and at once blood and water came out. ³⁵(The one who saw this happen is the one who told us this, and whatever he says is true. And he knows that he tells the truth, and he tells it so that you might believe.) ³⁶These things happened to make the Scripture come true: "Not one of his bones will be broken."ⁿ ³⁷And another Scripture says, "They will look at the one they stabbed."ⁿ

Jesus Is Buried

³⁸Later, Joseph from Arimathea asked Pilate if he could take the body of Jesus. (Joseph was a secret follower of Jesus, because he was afraid of some of the leaders.) Pilate gave his permission, so Joseph came and took Jesus' body away. ³⁹Nicodemus, who earlier had come to Jesus at night, went with Joseph. He brought about seventy-five pounds of myrrh and aloes. ⁴⁰These two men took Jesus' body and wrapped it with the spices in pieces of linen cloth, which is how they bury the dead. ⁴¹In the place where Jesus was crucified, there was a garden. In the garden was a new tomb that had never been used before. ⁴²The men laid Jesus in that tomb because it was nearby, and they were preparing to start their Sabbath day.

Jesus' Tomb Is Empty

20 Early on the first day of the week, Mary Magdalene went to the tomb while it was still dark. When she saw that the large stone had been moved away from the tomb, ²she ran to Simon Peter

≪TechSupport≫

ONLINE AUCTIONS

Perhaps it's time to try your hand at online auctions. Although eBay is the most well-known auction site, there are others that also let you choose the auction length and starting price for your item. Sellers with great photographs of their items get better results, so shoot multiple photos from different angles. Whether you're unloading last year's wardrobe or locating rare antiques, remember that things wear out and become obsolete over time. That's why Matthew 6:20 instructs believers to "store your treasures in heaven."

≫ 19:28 **"I am thirsty."** Read Psalms 22:15; 69:21.   19:31 **broken** The breaking of their bones would make them die sooner.   19:36 **"Not one . . . broken."** Quotation from Psalm 34:20. The idea is from Exodus 12:46; Numbers 9:12.   19:37 **"They . . . stabbed."** Quotation from Zechariah 12:10.

146

and the follower whom Jesus loved. Mary said, "They have taken the Lord out of the tomb, and we don't know where they have put him."

³So Peter and the other follower started for the tomb. ⁴They were both running, but the other follower ran faster than Peter and reached the tomb first. ⁵He bent down and looked in and saw the strips of linen cloth lying there, but he did not go in. ⁶Then following him, Simon Peter arrived and went into the tomb and saw the strips of linen lying there. ⁷He also saw the cloth that had been around Jesus' head, which was folded up and laid in a different place from the strips of linen. ⁸Then the other follower, who had reached the tomb first, also went in. He saw and believed. ⁹(They did not yet understand from the Scriptures that Jesus must rise from the dead.)

Jesus Appears to Mary Magdalene

¹⁰Then the followers went back home. ¹¹But Mary stood outside the tomb, crying. As she was crying, she bent down and looked inside the tomb. ¹²She saw two angels dressed in white, sitting where Jesus' body had been, one at the head and one at the feet.

¹³They asked her, "Woman, why are you crying?"

She answered, "They have taken away my Lord, and I don't know where they have put him." ¹⁴When Mary said this, she turned around and saw Jesus standing there, but she did not know it was Jesus.

¹⁵Jesus asked her, "Woman, why are you crying? Whom are you looking for?"

Thinking he was the gardener, she said to him, "Did you take him away, sir? Tell me where you put him, and I will get him."

¹⁶Jesus said to her, "Mary."

Mary turned toward Jesus and said in the Hebrew language," "Rabboni." (This means "Teacher.")

¹⁷Jesus said to her, "Don't hold on to me, because I have not yet gone up to the Father. But go to my brothers and tell them, 'I am going back to my Father and your Father, to my God and your God.'"

¹⁸Mary Magdalene went and said to the fol-lowers, "I saw the Lord!" And she told them what Jesus had said to her.

Jesus Appears to His Followers

¹⁹When it was evening on the first day of the week, Jesus' followers were together. The doors were locked, because they were afraid of the elders. Then Jesus came and stood right in the middle of them and said, "Peace be with you." ²⁰After he said this, he showed them his hands and his side. His followers were thrilled when they saw the Lord.

²¹Then Jesus said again, "Peace be with you. As the Father sent me, I now send you." ²²After he said this, he breathed on them and said, "Receive the Holy Spirit. ²³If you forgive anyone his sins, they are forgiven. If you don't forgive them, they are not forgiven."

Jesus Appears to Thomas

²⁴Thomas (called Didymus), who was one of the twelve, was not with them when Jesus came. ²⁵The other followers kept telling Thomas, "We saw the Lord."

But Thomas said, "I will not believe it until I see the nail marks in his hands and put my finger where the nails were and put my hand into his side."

²⁶A week later the followers were in the house again, and Thomas was with them. The doors were locked, but Jesus came in and stood right in the middle of them. He said, "Peace be with you." ²⁷Then he said to Thomas, "Put your finger here, and look at my hands. Put your hand here in my side. Stop being an unbeliever and believe."

²⁸Thomas said to him, "My Lord and my God!"

²⁹Then Jesus told him, "You believe because you see me. Those who believe without seeing me will be truly blessed."

Why John Wrote This Book

³⁰Jesus did many other miracles in the presence of his followers that are not written in this book. ³¹But these are written so that you may believe that Jesus is the Christ, the Son of God. Then, by believing, you may have life through his name.

Jesus Appears to Seven Followers

21 Later, Jesus showed himself to his followers again—this time at Lake Galilee." This is how he showed himself: ²Some of the followers were together: Simon Peter, Thomas (called Didymus), Nathanael from Cana in Galilee, the two sons of Zebedee, and two other followers. ³Simon Peter said, "I am going out to fish."

The others said, "We will go with you." So they went out and got into the boat. They fished that night but caught nothing.

⁴Early the next morning Jesus stood on the shore, but the followers did not know it was Jesus. ⁵Then he said to them, "Friends, did you catch any fish?"

{ Deal With It: *Pride

PRIDE IS THE SIN THAT CHANGED THE ARCHANGEL LUCIFER into the archenemy of God, and Satan has been fomenting rebellion ever since. Yet, James 4:6 states, "God is against the proud, but he gives grace to the humble." Lucifer's fall from grace proves it is a losing proposi-tion to oppose God. On the other hand, humility is the hallmark of a follower of Christ, who modeled humility while embodying humanity. If our desire is to become more like Christ, then we must humble ourselves as he did, or else risk the pain and humiliation that come as the result of pride.

▶▶ **20:16 Hebrew language** Or Aramaic, the languages of many people in this region in the first century. **21:1 Lake Galilee** Literally, "Sea of Tiberias."

147

Change >> Your WORLD

FOCUS ON THE FAMILY

The institution of the family is under constant attack from our culture. A major force to counteract these attacks has been Focus on the Family, a ministry that began in 1977 with a book on child discipline and a twenty-five-minute radio broadcast. From these humble beginnings, Focus on the Family has grown into a wide array of services, ministries, projects, and outreach groups. The two major pillars of the ministry are (1) marriage and family and (2) a commitment to reach individuals at various stages of life (teens, parents, mid-life, and seniors). There are numerous ways to pray and be actively involved.

To change your world, visit www.family.org.

shore, they saw a fire of hot coals. There were fish on the fire, and there was bread.

[10] Then Jesus said, "Bring some of the fish you just caught."

[11] Simon Peter went into the boat and pulled the net to the shore. It was full of big fish, one hundred fifty-three in all, but even though there were so many, the net did not tear. [12] Jesus said to them, "Come and eat." None of the followers dared ask him, "Who are you?" because they knew it was the Lord. [13] Jesus came and took the bread and gave it to them, along with the fish.

[14] This was now the third time Jesus showed himself to his followers after he was raised from the dead.

Jesus Talks to Peter

[15] When they finished eating, Jesus said to Simon Peter, "Simon son of John, do you love me more than these?"

He answered, "Yes, Lord, you know that I love you."

Jesus said, "Feed my lambs."

[16] Again Jesus said, "Simon son of John, do you love me?"

He answered, "Yes, Lord, you know that I love you."

Jesus said, "Take care of my sheep."

[17] A third time he said, "Simon son of John, do you love me?"

Peter was hurt because Jesus asked him the third time, "Do you love me?" Peter said, "Lord, you know everything; you know that I love you!"

He said to him, "Feed my sheep. [18] I tell you the truth, when you were younger, you tied your own belt and went where you wanted. But when you are old, you will put out your hands and someone else will tie you and take you where you don't want to go." [19] (Jesus said this to show how Peter would die to give glory to God.) Then Jesus said to Peter, "Follow me!"

[20] Peter turned and saw that the follower Jesus loved was walking behind them. (This was the follower who had leaned against Jesus at the supper and had said, "Lord, who will turn against you?") [21] When Peter saw him behind them, he asked Jesus, "Lord, what about him?"

[22] Jesus answered, "If I want him to live until I come back, that is not your business. You follow me."

[23] So a story spread among the followers that this one would not die. But Jesus did not say he would not die. He only said, "If I want him to live until I come back, that is not your business."

[24] That follower is the one who is telling these things and who has now written them down. We know that what he says is true.

[25] There are many other things Jesus did. If every one of them were written down, I suppose the whole world would not be big enough for all the books that would be written.

They answered, "No."

[6] He said, "Throw your net on the right side of the boat, and you will find some." So they did, and they caught so many fish they could not pull the net back into the boat.

[7] The follower whom Jesus loved said to Peter, "It is the Lord!" When Peter heard him say this, he wrapped his coat around himself. (Peter had taken his clothes off.) Then he jumped into the water. [8] The other followers went to shore in the boat, dragging the net full of fish. They were not very far from shore, only about a hundred yards. [9] When the followers stepped out of the boat and onto the

Notes

THE Acts OF THE APOSTLES

AUTHOR: LUKE
DATE WRITTEN: A.D. 63

RADIO PERSONALITY PAUL HARVEY HAS drawn listeners for years with his cliffhanger feature called "The Rest of the Story." He shares unknown details about a person or his or her actions without revealing the full picture; then, after the commercial, he finishes it with the last line, "And now you know the rest of the story."

Almost like one of those popular radio broadcasts, the Book of Acts continues Luke's writing to Theophilus, revealing the rest of the story. Without missing a beat, the Gentile physician continues the story of his Gospel account to provide an accurate record of the birth and growth of the Christian church. Like the ripples caused by a rock thrown into the water, the church starts in Jerusalem but soon expands throughout Judea, Samaria, and to the ends of the earth.

In Acts, you will meet the apostle Paul, who is the most prolific author in the New Testament. When Paul, then known as Saul, meets Jesus on the road to Damascus, his life is transformed and he begins a series of missionary journeys to spread the Good News. As you read about the early church and the lives of new believers, ask God for the power of the Holy Spirit to fill your life so you can continue the story of Acts in today's world.

Luke Writes Another Book

1 To Theophilus.

The first book I wrote was about everything Jesus began to do and teach [2]until the day he was taken up into heaven. Before this, with the help of the Holy Spirit, Jesus told the apostles he had chosen what they should do. [3]After his death, he showed himself to them and proved in many ways that he was alive. The apostles saw Jesus during the forty days after he was raised from the dead, and he spoke to them about the kingdom of God. [4]Once when he was eating with them, he told them not to leave Jerusalem. He said, "Wait here to receive the promise from the Father which I told you about. [5]John baptized people with water, but in a few days you will be baptized with the Holy Spirit."

Jesus Is Taken Up into Heaven

[6]When the apostles were all together, they asked Jesus, "Lord, are you now going to give the kingdom back to Israel?"

[7]Jesus said to them, "The Father is the only One who has the authority to decide dates and times. These things are not for you to know. [8]But when the Holy Spirit comes to you, you will receive power. You will be my witnesses—in Jerusalem, in all of Judea, in Samaria, and in every part of the world."

[9]After he said this, as they were watching, he was lifted up, and a cloud hid him from their sight. [10]As he was going, they were looking into the sky. Suddenly, two men wearing white clothes stood beside them. [11]They said, "Men of Galilee, why are you standing here looking into the sky? Jesus, whom you saw taken up from you into heaven, will come back in the same way you saw him go."

THINK ABOUT IT Acts 1:11

TELEVISION WEATHERCASTERS ARE CAPABLE of miscalculations from time to time. Sometimes they predict a blizzard and nothing happens. Other times they predict no rain and a deluge falls from the sky. However, these forecasters generally know how to study the weather patterns and predict the next day's weather. It's important to be aware of potential changes in the weather, but there is no need to watch the sky continually.

In the opening pages of Acts, Jesus ascended to heaven, and right after the eleven apostles watched the Lord go into the clouds, two men in white appeared and asked, "Why are you standing here looking into the sky? Jesus, whom you saw taken up from you into heaven, will come back in the same way you saw him go."

These men were gazing with their eyes toward the sky, hoping that Jesus would instantly return. Today, we have no need to watch the sky continually for Jesus' return, as it is a prediction with certainty. We can depend on the inevitable return of Jesus Christ.

A New Apostle Is Chosen

[12]Then they went back to Jerusalem from the Mount of Olives. (This mountain is about half a mile from Jerusalem.) [13]When they entered the city, they went to the upstairs room where they were staying. Peter, John, James, Andrew, Philip, Thomas, Bartholomew, Matthew, James son of Alphaeus, Simon (known as the Zealot), and Judas son of James were there. [14]They all continued praying together with some women, including Mary the mother of Jesus, and Jesus' brothers.

[15]During this time there was a meeting of the believers (about one hundred twenty of them). Peter stood up and said, [16-17]"Brothers and sisters, in the Scriptures the Holy Spirit said through David something that must happen involving Judas. He was one of our own group and served together with us. He led those who arrested Jesus." [18](Judas bought a field with the money he got for his evil act. But he fell to his death, his body burst open, and all his intestines poured out. [19]Everyone in Jerusalem learned about this so they named this place Akeldama. In their language Akeldama means "Field of Blood.") [20]"In the Book of Psalms," Peter said, "this is written:

'May his place be empty;
leave no one to live in it.'   *Psalm 69:25*

And it is also written:

'Let another man replace him as leader.'
Psalm 109:8

[21-22]"So now a man must become a witness with us of Jesus' being raised from the dead. He must be one of the men who were part of our group during all the time the Lord Jesus was among us—from the time John was baptizing people until the day Jesus was taken up from us to heaven."

[23]They put the names of two men before the group. One was Joseph Barsabbas, who was also called Justus. The other was Matthias. [24-25]The apostles prayed, "Lord, you know the thoughts of everyone. Show us which one of these two you have chosen to do this work. Show us who should be an apostle in place of Judas, who turned away and went where

FACT-OIDS!

Spam has grown from 8% of e-mail during the 20th century to 58% of e-mail as of December 2003.

[Focus on the Family]

he belongs." ²⁶Then they used lots to choose between them, and the lots showed that Matthias was the one. So he became an apostle with the other eleven.

The Coming of the Holy Spirit

2 When the day of Pentecost came, they were all together in one place. ²Suddenly a noise like a strong, blowing wind came from heaven and filled the whole house where they were sitting. ³They saw something like flames of fire that were separated and stood over each person there. ⁴They were all filled with the Holy Spirit, and they began to speak different languages" by the power the Holy Spirit was giving them.

⁵There were some religious Jews staying in Jerusalem who were from every country in the world. ⁶When they heard this noise, a crowd came together. They were all surprised, because each one heard them speaking in his own language. ⁷They were completely amazed at this. They said, "Look! Aren't all these people that we hear speaking from Galilee? ⁸Then how is it possible that we each hear them in our own languages? We are from different places: ⁹Parthia, Media, Elam, Mesopotamia, Judea, Cappadocia, Pontus, Asia, ¹⁰Phrygia, Pamphylia, Egypt, the areas of Libya near Cyrene, Rome ¹¹(both Jews and those who had become Jews), Crete, and Arabia. But we hear them telling in our own languages about the great things God has done!" ¹²They were all amazed and confused, asking each other, "What does this mean?"

¹³But others were making fun of them, saying, "They have had too much wine."

Peter Speaks to the People

¹⁴But Peter stood up with the eleven apostles, and in a loud voice he spoke to the crowd: "My fellow Jews, and all of you who are in Jerusalem, listen to me. Pay attention to what I have to say. ¹⁵These people are not drunk, as you think; it is only nine o'clock in the morning! ¹⁶But Joel the prophet wrote about what is happening here today:

¹⁷'God says: In the last days
    I will pour out my Spirit on
        all kinds of people.
    Your sons and daughters will
        prophesy.
    Your young men will see
        visions,
    and your old men will
        dream dreams.
¹⁸At that time I will pour out my
        Spirit
    also on my male slaves and female slaves,
    and they will prophesy.
¹⁹I will show miracles
    in the sky and on the earth:
    blood, fire, and thick smoke.
²⁰The sun will become dark,
    the moon red as blood,
    before the overwhelming and glorious day of the Lord will
        come.
²¹Then anyone who calls on the Lord will be saved.'   *Joel 2:28–32*

²²"People of Israel, listen to these words: Jesus from Nazareth was a very special man. God clearly showed this to you by the miracles, wonders, and signs he did through Jesus. You all know this, because it happened right here among you. ²³Jesus was given to you, and with the help of those who don't know the law, you put him to death by nailing him to a cross. But this was God's plan which he had made long ago; he knew all this would happen. ²⁴God raised Jesus from the dead and set him free from the pain of death, because death could not hold him. ²⁵For David said this about him:

'I keep the Lord before me always.

Q: What is prayer?

A: Prayer is simply talking with God. You don't have to be in a church or use special language to talk with God. He is always with you everywhere you go, so you can talk to him just as you would speak with a trusted friend. Ask questions and expect answers.

FOR Men Only

SECURITY Near the top of a woman's list of preferred qualities in a relationship is security, and not just the financial type either. Regardless of a woman's financial status, most will admit the need to feel a sense of security, both in tangible and intangible ways. Security speaks to the desire of a woman to be cherished and nurtured in spirit, soul, and body. One of the most important ways a guy can communicate security to his sweetheart is by loving her unconditionally. If a woman knows that she is valued and adored for who she is and not just what she does, she will feel secure.

LISTEN

>> 2:4 languages This can also be translated "tongues."

>> live the life

Acts 1:8

The Principle > Share your faith with power.

Practicing It > All Christians are called to share the message of Christ with others. However, God doesn't expect you to do it in your own strength. As you share the message of God's love, rely on the power of the Holy Spirit to help you.

Because he is close by my side,
I will not be hurt.
26 So I am glad, and I rejoice.
Even my body has hope,
27 because you will not leave me in the grave.
You will not let your Holy One rot.
28 You will teach me how to live a holy life.
Being with you will fill me with joy.'   *Psalm 16:8–11*

29 "Brothers and sisters, I can tell you truly that David, our ancestor, died and was buried. His grave is still here with us today. 30 He was a prophet and knew God had promised him that he would make a person from David's family a king just as he was." 31 Knowing this before it happened, David talked about the Christ rising from the dead. He said:
'He was not left in the grave.
His body did not rot.'
32 So Jesus is the One whom God raised from the dead. And we are all witnesses to this. 33 Jesus was lifted up to heaven and is now at God's right side. The Father has given the Holy Spirit to Jesus as he promised. So Jesus has poured out that Spirit, and this is what you now see and hear. 34 David was not the one who was lifted up to heaven, but he said:
'The Lord said to my Lord,
"Sit by me at my right side,
35   until I put your enemies under your control." '"   *Psalm 110:1*
36 "So, all the people of Israel should know this truly: God has made Jesus—the man you nailed to the cross—both Lord and Christ."

37 When the people heard this, they felt guilty and asked Peter and the other apostles, "What shall we do?"

38 Peter said to them, "Change your hearts and lives and be baptized, each one of you, in the name of Jesus Christ for the forgiveness of your sins. And you will receive the gift of the Holy Spirit. 39 This promise is for you, for your children, and for all who are far away. It is for everyone the Lord our God calls to himself."

40 Peter warned them with many other words. He begged them, "Save yourselves from the evil of today's people!" 41 Then those people who accepted what Peter said were baptized. About three thousand people were added to the number of believers that day. 42 They spent their time learning the apostles' teaching, sharing, breaking bread," and praying together.

The Believers Share

43 The apostles were doing many miracles and signs, and everyone felt great respect for God. 44 All the believers were together and shared everything. 45 They would sell their land and the things they owned and then divide the money and give it to anyone who needed it. 46 The believers met together in the Temple every day. They ate together in their homes, happy to share their food with joyful hearts. 47 They praised God and were liked by all the people. Every day the Lord added those who were being saved to the group of believers.

Peter Heals a Crippled Man

3 One day Peter and John went to the Temple at three o'clock, the time set each day for the afternoon prayer service. 2 There, at the Temple gate called Beautiful Gate, was a man who had been crippled all his life. Every day he was carried to this gate to beg for money from the people going into the Temple. 3 The man saw Peter and John going into the Temple and asked them for money. 4 Peter and John looked straight at him and said, "Look at us!" 5 The man looked at them, thinking they were going to give him some money. 6 But Peter said, "I don't have any silver or gold, but I do have something else I

⊙ Get Aligned

Acts 3:7

PARENTS ARE QUICK TO LEARN the difference between giving their children what they want and what they need. Part of parenthood is understanding that despite your child's rantings and ravings, your job is to bring about what's best for him or her.

The same is true when we minister to someone. Often a person's wants and needs are not aligned. The crippled man at the Temple gate had one thing in mind: money. He had probably been crippled so long that the thought of walking never crossed his mind. His livelihood was determined by the generosity of others, so his focus wasn't on being healed but on how many coins Peter and John might give him.

Instead of offering this man what he wanted, Peter gave him what he needed: a new lease on life. He offered the man a future he probably stopped hoping for years before. As believers who are empowered by the same Holy Spirit as Peter, we are to carry Peter's vision of ministry. Rather than pacifying the expressed desires of hurting people, ask God for the grace to meet their real needs.

>> 2:30 God...was See 2 Samuel 7:13; Psalm 132:11. 2:35 until...control Literally, "until I make your enemies a footstool for your feet." 2:42 breaking bread This may mean a meal as in verse 46, or the Lord's Supper, the special meal Jesus told his followers to eat to remember him (Luke 22:14–20).

can give you. By the power of Jesus Christ from Nazareth, stand up and walk!" [7]Then Peter took the man's right hand and lifted him up. Immediately the man's feet and ankles became strong. [8]He jumped up, stood on his feet, and began to walk. He went into the Temple with them, walking and jumping and praising God. [9-10]All the people recognized him as the crippled man who always sat by the Beautiful Gate begging for money. Now they saw this same man walking and praising God, and they were amazed. They wondered how this could happen.

Peter Speaks to the People

[11]While the man was holding on to Peter and John, all the people were amazed and ran to them at Solomon's Porch. [12]When Peter saw this, he said to them, "People of Israel, why are you surprised? You are looking at us as if it were our own power or goodness that made this man walk. [13]The God of Abraham, Isaac, and Jacob, the God of our ancestors, gave glory to Jesus, his servant. But you handed him over to be killed. Pilate decided to let him go free, but you told Pilate you did not want Jesus. [14]You did not want the One who is holy and good but asked Pilate to give you a murderer[n] instead. [15]And so you killed the One who gives life, but God raised him from the dead. We are witnesses to this. [16]It was faith in Jesus that made this crippled man well. You can see this man, and you know him. He was made completely well because of trust in Jesus, and you all saw it happen!

[17]"Brothers and sisters, I know you did those things to Jesus because neither you nor your leaders understood what you were doing. [18]God said through the prophets that his Christ would suffer and die. And now God has made these things come true in this way. [19]So you must change your hearts and lives! Come back to God, and he will forgive your sins. Then the Lord will send the time of rest. [20]And he will send Jesus, the One he chose to be the Christ. [21]But Jesus must stay in heaven until the time comes when all things will be made right again. God told about this time long ago when he spoke through his holy prophets. [22]Moses said, 'The Lord your God will give you a prophet like me, who is one of your own people. You must listen to everything he tells you. [23]Anyone who does not listen to that prophet will die, cut off from God's people.'[n] [24]Samuel, and all the other prophets who spoke for God after Samuel, told about this time now. [25]You are descendants of the prophets. You have received the agreement God made with your ancestors. He said to your father Abraham, 'Through your descendants all the nations on the earth will be blessed.'[n] [26]God has raised up his servant Jesus and sent him to you first to bless you by turning each of you away from doing evil."

Peter and John at the Council

[4]While Peter and John were speaking to the people, priests, the captain of the soldiers that guarded the Temple, and Sadducees came up to them. [2]They were upset because the two apostles were teaching the people and were preaching that people will rise from the dead through the power of Jesus. [3]The older leaders grabbed Peter and John and put them in jail. Since it was already night, they kept them in jail until the next day. [4]But many of those who had

Q: What's the difference between being attracted to a woman and lusting after her?

A: As men, we are designed by God to be drawn to a woman's beauty, and there is nothing wrong with admiring the beauty of a woman. However, lust goes beyond innocent admiration, for it involves the selfish desire to use a woman for your own pleasure.

➡ The Bottom Line

Energy Conservation: Saving Resources

AMERICANS' LOVE AFFAIR WITH CARS IS LEGENDARY. However, with gasoline prices rising to historic highs, conservation is a smart move. Rather than driving a couple of blocks to the convenience store, try walking instead. Not only will it be healthier for you, but those steps also will save gas. So will measures such as tuning up your engine, keeping tires properly inflated, driving the speed limit, and car-pooling with others. God commends living in such thrifty ways. As Jesus asked in Luke 16:11, "If you cannot be trusted with worldly riches, then who will trust you with true riches?"

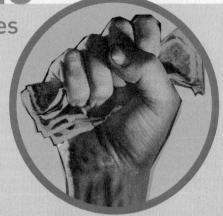

 3:14 murderer Barabbas, the man the crowd asked Pilate to set free instead of Jesus (Luke 23:18).   **3:22—23 'The Lord … people.'** Quotation from Deuteronomy 18:15, 19.   **3:25 'Through … blessed.'** Quotation from Genesis 22:18; 26:4.

154

heard Peter and John preach believed the things they said. There were now about five thousand in the group of believers.

⁵The next day the rulers, the elders, and the teachers of the law met in Jerusalem. ⁶Annas the high priest, Caiaphas, John, and Alexander were there, as well as everyone from the high priest's family. ⁷They made Peter and John stand before them and then asked them, "By what power or authority did you do this?"

⁸Then Peter, filled with the Holy Spirit, said to them, "Rulers of the people and you elders, ⁹are you questioning us about a good thing that was done to a crippled man? Are you asking us who made him well? ¹⁰We want all of you and all the people to know that this man was made well by the power of Jesus Christ from Nazareth. You crucified him, but God raised him from the dead. This man was crippled, but he is now well and able to stand here before you because of the power of Jesus. ¹¹Jesus is

> 'the stone" that you builders rejected,
> which has become the cornerstone.'   *Psalm 118:22*

¹²Jesus is the only One who can save people. No one else in the world is able to save us."

¹³The leaders saw that Peter and John were not afraid to speak, and they understood that these men had no special training or education. So they were amazed. Then they realized that Peter and John had been with Jesus. ¹⁴Because they saw the healed man standing there beside the two apostles, they could say nothing against them. ¹⁵After the leaders ordered them to leave the meeting, they began to talk to each other. ¹⁶They said, "What shall we do with these men? Everyone in Jerusalem knows they have done a great miracle, and we cannot say it is not true. ¹⁷But to keep it from spreading among the people, we must warn them not to talk to people anymore using that name."

¹⁸So they called Peter and John in again and told them not to speak or to teach at all in the name of Jesus. ¹⁹But Peter and John answered them, "You decide what God would want. Should we obey you or God? ²⁰We cannot keep quiet. We must speak about what we have seen and heard." ²¹The leaders warned the apostles again and let

▶ Get Aligned

Acts 4:20

WHEN IS THE LAST TIME you couldn't keep quiet about the Good News of Jesus Christ?

That's a question that hits most believers hard. We often get more excited about our football team winning a close game than what God has done in our lives. But there needs to be some passion in our witness as well.

Peter and John were facing death here, square in the face. They stood in front of a group of the most important religious figures of the day, all of whom wanted them silenced, if not killed. Yet Peter was unapologetic about what he had seen. He couldn't keep quiet about Jesus.

Sure, he may not have been as madly expressive as fans at a ballgame, but he had an even deeper passion that fueled his soul's fire. And his only motivation was to tell others about Christ. If you find yourself needing to be rekindled with this same passion, ask God to stoke the fire. Let him remind you of the depths to which Jesus has gone to save you.

them go free. They could not find a way to punish them, because all the people were praising God for what had been done. ²²The man who received the miracle of healing was more than forty years old.

The Believers Pray

²³After Peter and John left the meeting of leaders, they went to their own group and told them everything the leading priests and the elders had said to them. ²⁴When the believers heard this, they prayed to God together, "Lord, you are the One who made the sky, the earth, the sea, and everything in them. ²⁵By the Holy Spirit, through our father David your servant, you said:

> 'Why are the nations so angry?
> Why are the people making useless plans?
> ²⁶The kings of the earth prepare to fight,
> and their leaders make plans together
> against the Lord
> and his Christ.'   *Psalm 2:1–2*

²⁷These things really happened when Herod, Pontius Pilate, and some Jews and non-Jews all came together against Jesus here in Jerusalem. Jesus is your holy servant, the One you made to be the Christ. ²⁸These people made your plan happen because of your power and your will. ²⁹And now, Lord, listen to their threats. Lord, help us, your servants, to speak your word without fear. ³⁰Show us your power to heal. Give proofs and make miracles happen by the power of Jesus, your holy servant."

▶▶ live the life

Acts 4:31

The Principle > Live without fear.

Practicing It > Think of some courageous action you could take this month to spread the message of Christ. Make a list of three positive things you could do that would take you out of your comfort zone, and then choose to do one starting this week.

▶▶ 4:11 stone A symbol meaning Jesus.

>> live the life

Acts 4:32

The Principle > **Build strong relationships.**

Practicing It > **Commit to getting involved with the community at your church. Attend regularly and start spending time outside the weekly service with the people you meet there.**

[31]After they had prayed, the place where they were meeting was shaken. They were all filled with the Holy Spirit, and they spoke God's word without fear.

The Believers Share

[32]The group of believers were united in their hearts and spirit. All those in the group acted as though their private property belonged to everyone in the group. In fact, they shared everything. [33]With great power the apostles were telling people that the Lord Jesus was truly raised from the dead. And God blessed all the believers very much. [34]There were no needy people among them. From time to time those who owned fields or houses sold them, brought the money, [35]and gave it to the apostles. Then the money was given to anyone who needed it.

[36]One of the believers was named Joseph, a Levite born in Cyprus. The apostles called him Barnabas (which means "one who encourages"). [37]Joseph owned a field, sold it, brought the money, and gave it to the apostles.

Ananias and Sapphira Die

5 But a man named Ananias and his wife Sapphira sold some land. [2]He kept back part of the money for himself; his wife knew about this and agreed to it. But he brought the rest of the money and gave it to the apostles. [3]Peter said, "Ananias, why did you let Satan rule your thoughts to lie to the Holy Spirit and to keep for yourself part of the money you received for the land? [4]Before you sold the land, it belonged to you. And even after you sold it, you could have used the money any way you wanted. Why did you think of doing this? You lied to God, not to us!" [5-6]When Ananias heard this, he fell down and died. Some young men came in, wrapped up his body, carried it out, and buried it. And everyone who heard about this was filled with fear.

[7]About three hours later his wife came in, but she did not know what had happened. [8]Peter said to her, "Tell me, was the money you got for your field this much?"

Sapphira answered, "Yes, that was the price."

[9]Peter said to her, "Why did you and your husband agree to test the Spirit of the Lord? Look! The men who buried your husband are at the door, and they will carry you out." [10]At that moment Sapphira fell down by his feet and died. When the young men came in and saw that she was dead, they carried her out and buried her beside her husband. [11]The whole church and all the others who heard about these things were filled with fear.

The Apostles Heal Many

[12]The apostles did many signs and miracles among the people. And they would all meet together on Solomon's Porch. [13]None of the others dared to join them, but all the people respected them. [14]More and more men and women believed in the Lord and were added to the group of believers. [15]The people placed their sick on beds and mats in the streets, hoping that when Peter passed by at least his shadow

Get Fit

SKIING CROSS COUNTRY   Cross-country skiing has long been touted as one of the best cardiovascular activities in the world, and for good reason. Just about every body part gets engaged in the sport, including the legs, arms, torso, and back. But for all the effort involved, it's actually one of the easiest sports to learn. With just one short lesson, you'll be on your way to exploring snow-draped terrain. It is the stunning scenery, after all, that is the real joy of cross-country skiing. Unlike downhill skiing, cross-country skiing is a pristinely quiet and reflective sport. It can bring great benefits to your body and also to your spirit. Find out how to get started at www.cross-countryski.com.

might fall on them. [16]Crowds came from all the towns around Jerusalem, bringing their sick and those who were bothered by evil spirits, and all of them were healed.

Leaders Try to Stop the Apostles

[17]The high priest and all his friends (a group called the Sadducees) became very jealous. [18]They took the apostles and put them in jail. [19]But during the night, an angel of the Lord opened the doors of the jail and led the apostles outside. The angel said, [20]"Go stand in the Temple and tell the people everything about this new life." [21]When the apostles heard this, they obeyed and went into the Temple early in the morning and continued teaching.

When the high priest and his friends arrived, they called a meeting of the leaders and all the important elders. They sent some men to the jail to bring the apostles to them. [22]But, upon arriving, the officers could not find the apostles. So they went back and reported to the leaders. [23]They said, "The jail was closed and locked, and the guards were standing at the doors. But when we opened the doors, the jail was empty!" [24]Hearing this, the captain of the Temple guards and the leading priests were confused and wondered what was happening.

[25]Then someone came and told them, "Listen! The men you put in jail are standing in the Temple teaching the people." [26]Then the captain and his men went out and brought the apostles back. But the soldiers did not use force, because they were afraid the people would stone them to death.

[27]The soldiers brought the apostles to the meeting and made them stand before the leaders. The high priest questioned them, [28]saying, "We gave you strict orders not to continue teaching in that name. But look, you have filled Jerusalem with your teaching and are trying to make us responsible for this man's death."

[29]Peter and the other apostles answered, "We must obey God, not human authority! [30]You killed Jesus by hanging him on a cross. But God, the God of our ancestors, raised Jesus up from the dead! [31]Jesus is the One whom God raised to be on his right side, as Leader and Savior. Through him, all people could change their hearts and lives and have their sins forgiven. [32]We saw all these things happen. The Holy Spirit, whom God has given to all who obey him, also proves these things are true."

[33]When the leaders heard this, they became angry and wanted to kill them. [34]But a Pharisee named Gamaliel stood up in the meeting.

Q: Will there be marriage in heaven?

A: While there is clear reason to believe that we will recognize and know each other in heaven, Jesus made it clear that the marriage agreement does not carry over into the heavenly realm (Luke 20:34–35).

▶ Get Aligned
Acts 5:38–39

GOD'S WILL IS UNSTOPPABLE. That may be hard to believe when around you are nothing but signs of darkness, yet it is still true. The Bible says in Romans 8:28, "In everything God works for the good of those who love him." He is sovereign over both good and evil in this world.

When we accept that God's will always wins out, our purpose in life becomes redefined. In fact, we might as well throw away our own agenda. Because when we resign to God's rightful supremacy in our lives, our role is simply to get in line with his plan.

Unfortunately, many Christians struggle to do this. They wrestle with finding the will of God, wanting to know their assignment all at once as if they could download an instruction manual for life. While there's nothing wrong with desiring the Lord's guidance in our affairs, the life of faith by definition always requires a level of trust. God does not tease us by not laying out our life's game plan with every detail. His concern is our willingness to stick by him each step of the way. When we do that, his will continues to be unstoppable, with us walking perfectly in step with it.

He was a teacher of the law, and all the people respected him. He ordered the apostles to leave the meeting for a little while. [35]Then he said, "People of Israel, be careful what you are planning to do to these men. [36]Remember when Theudas appeared? He said he was a great man, and about four hundred men joined him. But he was killed, and all his followers were scattered; they were able to do nothing. [37]Later, a man named Judas came from Galilee at the time of the registration.[b] He also led a group of followers and was killed, and all his followers were scattered. [38]And so now I tell you: Stay away from these men, and leave them alone. If their plan comes from human authority, it will fail. [39]But if it is from God, you will not be able to stop them. You might even be fighting against God himself!"

The leaders agreed with what Gamaliel said. [40]They called the apostles in, beat them, and told them not to speak in the name of Jesus again. Then they let them go free. [41]The apostles left the meeting full of joy because they were given the honor of suffering disgrace for Jesus. [42]Every day in the Temple and in people's homes they continued teaching the people and telling the Good News—that Jesus is the Christ.

Seven Leaders Are Chosen

6 The number of followers was growing. But during this same time, the Greek-speaking followers had an argument with the

---

» 5:37 registration Census. A counting of all the people and the things they own.

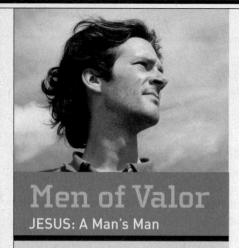

Men of Valor
JESUS: A Man's Man

Jesus lived a sinless life as a man and died on the cross for our sins. Christ's perfection is a principal truth of Scripture, for without it we would be left with just another flawed human being. Contrary to popular belief, he was not immune to emotions. Jesus wept, and while he was a compassionate man, he also brimmed with strength and conviction. When profiteers focused on the Temple as a moneymaking operation instead of a place of worship, Jesus chased them out with a whip. In Revelation 1:12–16, John's description of Christ paints a picture of supreme power. Shining like the sun, eyes flaming like fire, and a two-edged sword coming out of his mouth, Jesus remains a man's man.

other followers. The Greek-speaking widows were not getting their share of the food that was given out every day. ²The twelve apostles called the whole group of followers together and said, "It is not right for us to stop our work of teaching God's word in order to serve tables. ³So, brothers and sisters, choose seven of your own men who are good, full of the Spirit and full of wisdom. We will put them in charge of this work. ⁴Then we can continue to pray and to teach the word of God."

⁵The whole group liked the idea, so they chose these seven men: Stephen (a man with great faith and full of the Holy Spirit), Philip," Procorus, Nicanor, Timon, Parmenas, and Nicolas (a man from Antioch who had become a follower of the Jewish religion). ⁶Then they put these men before the apostles, who prayed and laid their hands" on them.

⁷The word of God was continuing to spread. The group of followers in Jerusalem increased, and a great number of the Jewish priests believed and obeyed.

Stephen Is Accused

⁸Stephen was richly blessed by God who gave him the power to do great miracles and signs among the people. ⁹But some people were against him. They belonged to the synagogue of Free Men" (as it was called), which included people from Cyrene, Alexandria, Cilicia, and Asia. They all came and argued with Stephen.

¹⁰But the Spirit was helping him to speak with wisdom, and his words were so strong that they could not argue with him. ¹¹So they secretly urged some men to say, "We heard Stephen speak against Moses and against God."

¹²This upset the people, the elders, and the teachers of the law. They came and grabbed Stephen and brought him to a meeting of the leaders. ¹³They brought in some people to tell lies about Stephen, saying, "This man is always speaking against this holy place and the law of Moses. ¹⁴We heard him say that Jesus from Nazareth will destroy this place and that Jesus will change the customs Moses gave us." ¹⁵All the people in the meeting were watching Stephen closely and saw that his face looked like the face of an angel.

Stephen's Speech

7 The high priest said to Stephen, "Are these things true?"

²Stephen answered, "Brothers and fathers, listen to me. Our glorious God appeared to Abraham, our ancestor, in Mesopotamia before he lived in Haran. ³God said to Abraham, 'Leave your country and your relatives, and go to the land I will show you.'" ⁴So Abraham left the country of Chaldea and went to live in Haran. After Abraham's father died, God sent him to this place where you now live. ⁵God did not give Abraham any of this land, not even a foot of it. But God promised that he would give this land to him and his descendants, even before Abraham had a child. ⁶This is what God said to him: 'Your descendants will be strangers in a land they don't own. The people there will make them slaves and will mistreat them for four hundred years. ⁷But I will punish the nation where they are slaves. Then your descendants will leave that land and will worship me in this place.'" ⁸God made an agreement with Abraham, the sign of which was circumcision. And so when Abraham had his son Isaac, Abraham circumcised him when he was eight days old. Isaac also circumcised his son Jacob, and Jacob did the same for his sons, the twelve ancestors" of our people.

⁹"Jacob's sons became jealous of Joseph and sold him to be a slave in Egypt. But God was with him ¹⁰and saved him from all his troubles. The king of Egypt liked Joseph and respected him because of the wisdom God gave him. The king made him governor of Egypt and put him in charge of all the people in his palace.

¹¹"Then all the land of Egypt and Canaan became so dry that nothing would grow, and the people suffered very much. Jacob's sons, our ancestors, could not find anything to eat. ¹²But when Jacob heard there was grain

---

FACT-OIDS! About 36 million Americans, or 27% of Internet users, have downloaded music or video files from the Internet.
[Pew Internet and American Life Project]

 6:5 Philip Not the apostle named Philip.   **6:6 laid their hands** The laying on of hands had many purposes, including the giving of a blessing, power, or authority.   **6:9 Free Men** Jewish people who had been slaves or whose fathers had been slaves, but were now free.   **7:3 'Leave…you.'** Quotation from Genesis 12:1.   **7:6–7 'Your descendants…place.'** Quotation from Genesis 15:13–14 and Exodus 3:12.   **7:8 twelve ancestors** Important ancestors of the people of Israel; the leaders of the twelve tribes of Israel.

in Egypt, he sent his sons there. This was their first trip to Egypt. [13]When they went there a second time, Joseph told his brothers who he was, and the king learned about Joseph's family. [14]Then Joseph sent messengers to invite Jacob, his father, to come to Egypt along with all his relatives (seventy-five persons altogether). [15]So Jacob went down to Egypt, where he and his sons died. [16]Later their bodies were moved to Shechem and put in a grave there. (It was the same grave Abraham had bought for a sum of money from the sons of Hamor in Shechem.)

[17]"The promise God made to Abraham was soon to come true, and the number of people in Egypt grew large. [18]Then a new king, who did not know who Joseph was, began to rule Egypt. [19]This king tricked our people and was cruel to our ancestors, forcing them to leave their babies outside to die. [20]At this time Moses was born, and he was very beautiful. For three months Moses was cared for in his father's house. [21]When they put Moses outside, the king's daughter adopted him and raised him as if he were her own son. [22]The Egyptians taught Moses everything they knew, and he was a powerful man in what he said and did.

[23]"When Moses was about forty years old, he thought it would be good to visit his own people, the people of Israel. [24]Moses saw an Egyptian mistreating one of his people, so he defended the Israelite and punished the Egyptian by killing him. [25]Moses thought his own people would understand that God was using him to save them, but they did not. [26]The next day when Moses saw two men of Israel fighting, he tried to make peace between them. He said, 'Men, you are brothers. Why are you hurting each other?' [27]The man who was hurting the other pushed Moses away and said, 'Who made you our ruler and judge? [28]Are you going to kill me as you killed the Egyptian yesterday?' [29]When Moses heard him say this, he left Egypt and went to live in the land of Midian where he was a stranger. While Moses lived in Midian, he had two sons.

[30]"Forty years later an angel appeared to Moses in the flames of a burning bush as he was in the desert near Mount Sinai. [31]When Moses saw this, he was amazed and went near to look closer. Moses heard the Lord's voice say, [32]'I am the God of your ancestors, the God of Abraham, Isaac, and Jacob.' Moses began to shake with fear and was afraid to look. [33]The Lord said to him, 'Take off your sandals, be-

<<TechSupport>>

VIRUS PROTECTION

With hoaxes, Trojan horses, and worms, the Internet is crawling with malicious codes that can infect your computer. Most damaging viruses require an unsuspecting user to open an attachment or click a link. So use discernment about the kinds of files you open and the sites you visit. Don't open an attachment you didn't ask for, and always keep your firewall and antivirus protection software up to date. Like protection software, we are given the armor of God to ward off attacks (see Ephesians 6:10–18).

cause you are standing on holy ground. [34]I have seen the troubles my people have suffered in Egypt. I have heard their cries and have come down to save them. And now, Moses, I am sending you back to Egypt.'

[35]"This Moses was the same man the two men of Israel rejected, saying, 'Who made you a ruler and judge?' Moses is the same man God sent to be a ruler and savior, with the help of the angel that Moses saw in the burning bush. [36]So Moses led the people out of Egypt. He worked miracles and signs in Egypt, at the Red Sea, and then in the desert for forty years. [37]This is the same Moses that said to the people of Israel, 'God will give you a prophet like me, who is one of your own people.' [38]This is the Moses who was with the gathering of the Israelites in the desert. He was with the angel that spoke to him at Mount Sinai, and he was with our ancestors. He received commands from God that give life, and he gave those commands to us.

[39]"But our ancestors did not want to obey Moses. They rejected him and wanted to go back to Egypt. [40]They said to Aaron, 'Make us gods who will lead us. Moses led us out of Egypt, but we don't know what

Principles: HEAVEN

Heaven is the destination of everyone who believes in Jesus and confesses him as Lord. The glimpses of heaven are wonderful. In Revelation 7:9, John wrote of seeing people from every nation and language there, praising the Lord throughout eternity. Elsewhere in the Book of Revelation, heaven is described as a city of pure gold and, yes, pearly gates. The best news of all, however, is that Christ promised he was going there to prepare a place for us as his followers.

7:27–28 'Who...yesterday?' Quotation from Exodus 2:14. 7:32 'I am...Jacob.' Quotation from Exodus 3:6. 7:33–34 'Take...Egypt.' Quotation from Exodus 3:5–10. 7:35 'Who...judge?' Quotation from Exodus 2:14. 7:37 'God...people.' Quotation from Deuteronomy 18:15.

has happened to him.'" ⁴¹So the people made an idol that looked like a calf. Then they brought sacrifices to it and were proud of what they had made with their own hands. ⁴²But God turned against them and did not try to stop them from worshiping the sun, moon, and stars. This is what is written in the book of the prophets: God says,

'People of Israel, you did not bring me sacrifices and offerings
    while you traveled in the desert for forty years.
⁴³You have carried with you
    the tent to worship Molech
    and the idols of the star god Rephan that you made to
        worship.
So I will send you away beyond Babylon.'   *Amos 5:25–27*

⁴⁴"The Holy Tent where God spoke to our ancestors was with them in the desert. God told Moses how to make this Tent, and he made it like the plan God showed him. ⁴⁵Later, Joshua led our ancestors to capture the lands of the other nations. Our people went in, and God forced the other people out. When our people went into this new land, they took with them this same Tent they had received from their ancestors. They kept it until the time of David, ⁴⁶who pleased God and asked God to let him build a house for him, the God of Jacob." ⁴⁷But Solomon was the one who built the Temple.

⁴⁸"But the Most High does not live in houses that people build with their hands. As the prophet says:
⁴⁹'Heaven is my throne,
    and the earth is my footstool.
So do you think you can build a house for me? says the Lord.
    Do I need a place to rest?
⁵⁰Remember, my hand made all these things!' "   *Isaiah 66:1–2*

⁵¹Stephen continued speaking: "You stubborn people! You have not given your hearts to God, nor will you listen to him! You are always against what the Holy Spirit is trying to tell you, just as your ances-tors were. ⁵²Your ancestors tried to hurt every prophet who ever lived. Those prophets said long ago that the One who is good would come, but your ancestors killed them. And now you have turned against and killed the One who is good. ⁵³You received the law of Moses, which God gave you through his angels, but you haven't obeyed it."

Stephen Is Killed

⁵⁴When the leaders heard this, they became furious. They were so mad they were grinding their teeth at Stephen. ⁵⁵But Stephen was full of the Holy Spirit. He looked up to heaven and saw the glory of God and Jesus standing at God's right side. ⁵⁶He said, "Look! I see heaven open and the Son of Man standing at God's right side."

⁵⁷Then they shouted loudly and covered their ears and all ran at Stephen. ⁵⁸They took him out of the city and began to throw stones at him to kill him. And those who told lies against Stephen left their coats with a young man named Saul. ⁵⁹While they were throwing stones, Stephen prayed, "Lord Jesus, receive my spirit." ⁶⁰He fell on his knees and cried in a loud voice, "Lord, do not hold this sin against them." After Stephen said this, he died.

Q: Is it all right to become wealthy?

A: What matters is that whether you are wealthy or not, your heart is fully committed to following God's will for your life. It is all right to become wealthy, but don't let riches turn your heart away from God.

→ The Bottom Line

Health Savings Accounts: Affordable Insurance

IF YOU STRUGGLE TO KEEP UP with rising medical insurance premiums, check out a Health Savings Account (HSA). This alternative to traditional coverage enables you to pay current bills while saving for future expenses. To qualify, you must carry a high-deductible health plan, known as catastrophic coverage. These plans are cheaper than traditional insurance, allowing you to deposit the difference in a tax-free medical savings account. Sign-up can be handled through a bank, credit union, insurance company, or possibly an employer. Such planning is wise; as James 4:14 points out: "You do not know what will happen tomorrow!"

>> **7:40** 'Make … him.' Quotation from Exodus 32:1.   **7:46 Jacob** Some Greek copies read "the house of Jacob." This means the people of Israel.

8 Saul agreed that the killing of Stephen was good.

Troubles for the Believers

On that day the church of Jerusalem began to be persecuted, and all the believers, except the apostles, were scattered throughout Judea and Samaria. [2]And some religious people buried Stephen and cried loudly for him. [3]Saul was also trying to destroy the church, going from house to house, dragging out men and women and putting them in jail. [4]And wherever they were scattered, they told people the Good News.

Philip Preaches in Samaria

[5]Philip went to the city of Samaria and preached about the Christ. [6]When the people there heard Philip and saw the miracles he was doing, they all listened carefully to what he said. [7]Many of these people had evil spirits in them, but Philip made the evil spirits leave. The spirits made a loud noise when they came out. Philip also healed many weak and crippled people there. [8]So the people in that city were very happy.

[9]But there was a man named Simon in that city. Before Philip came there, Simon had practiced magic and amazed all the people of Samaria. He bragged and called himself a great man. [10]All the people—the least important and the most important—paid attention to Simon, saying, "This man has the power of God, called 'the Great Power'!" [11]Simon had amazed them with his magic so long that the people became his followers. [12]But when Philip told them the Good News about the kingdom of God and the power of Jesus Christ, men and women believed Philip and were baptized. [13]Simon himself believed, and after he was baptized, he stayed very close to Philip. When he saw the miracles and the powerful things Philip did, Simon was amazed.

[14]When the apostles who were still in Jerusalem heard that the people of Samaria had accepted the word of God, they sent Peter and John to them. [15]When Peter and John arrived, they prayed that the Samaritan believers might receive the Holy Spirit. [16]These people had been baptized in the name of the Lord Jesus, but the Holy Spirit had not yet come upon any of them. [17]Then, when the two apostles began laying their hands on the people, they received the Holy Spirit.

[18]Simon saw that the Spirit was given to people when the apostles laid their hands on them. So he offered the apostles money, [19]saying, "Give me also this power so that anyone on whom I lay my hands will receive the Holy Spirit."

[20]Peter said to him, "You and your money should both be destroyed, because you thought you could buy God's gift with money. [21]You cannot share with us in this work since your heart is not right before God. [22]Change your heart! Turn away from this evil thing you have done, and pray to the Lord. Maybe he will forgive you for thinking this. [23]I see that you are full of bitter jealousy and ruled by sin."

[24]Simon answered, "Both of you pray for me to the Lord so the things you have said will not happen to me."

[25]After Peter and John told the people what they had seen Jesus do and after they had spoken the message of the Lord, they went back to Jerusalem. On the way, they went through many Samaritan towns and preached the Good News to the people.

Philip Teaches an Ethiopian

[26]An angel of the Lord said to Philip, "Get ready and go south to the road that leads down to Gaza from Jerusalem—the desert road." [27]So Philip got ready and went. On the road he saw a man from Ethiopia, a eunuch. He was an important officer in the service of Candace, the queen of the Ethiopians; he was responsible for taking care of all her money. He had gone to Jerusalem to worship. [28]Now, as he was on his way home, he was sitting in his chariot reading from the Book of Isaiah, the prophet. [29]The Spirit said to Philip, "Go to that chariot and stay near it."

[30]So when Philip ran toward the chariot, he heard the man reading from Isaiah the prophet. Philip asked, "Do you understand what you are reading?"

[31]He answered, "How can I understand unless someone explains it to me?" Then he invited Philip to climb in and sit with him. [32]The portion of Scripture he was reading was this:

"He was like a sheep being led to be killed.
He was quiet, as a lamb is quiet while its wool is being cut;
he never opened his mouth.

Get Aligned
Acts 8:18–19

IF SIMON WERE ALIVE TODAY, he'd likely be selling one of those "As Seen on TV" items on a late-night infomercial. He was a get-rich-quick kind of guy who thought money first, morals later. So when he saw God working through the early apostles, he wanted what they had and was willing to pay anything for it.

Not only was Simon missing the point of the miracles, he was trying to buy God's power with earthly riches. The Holy Spirit wasn't working among these people to make an extra buck or even to expand his fame on earth. He was interested in these people's hearts and lives, and his power was what changed them forever. Simon didn't understand that, and when he offered the apostles money for this "magical power," he got more than a no. Peter said he should be destroyed along with his money. Ouch!

Unfortunately, Christians can use the same mentality when dealing with the Holy Spirit. Though we may not offer him money, we often approach his gifts as if they were commodities. Remember, the Holy Spirit is not a service, but a person who cannot be bought or sold. To those who have been truly changed by his power, he is priceless.

People
Skills

Avoiding Denial

Avoidance and denial undermine honesty in any relationship and eventually lead to unspoken judgments and resentment. In the relationships with your family, don't settle for false harmony. False harmony occurs when two people pretend a conflict doesn't exist and go to any length to avoid it. Instead, commit to paying attention to it and to resolving conflict in a mutually beneficial way. Conflict is part of life, so acknowledge it, anticipate it, and develop healthy ways to move through it. Albert Einstein summed it up beautifully: "In the middle of difficulty lies opportunity." Instead of viewing family conflict as something to avoid, think of it as an opportunity to grow closer.

33
He was shamed and was treated
unfairly.
He died without children to continue his
family.
His life on earth has ended."

Isaiah 53:7–8

34 The officer said to Philip, "Please tell me, who is the prophet talking about—himself or someone else?" 35 Philip began to speak, and starting with this same Scripture, he told the man the Good News about Jesus.

36 While they were traveling down the road, they came to some water. The officer said, "Look, here is water. What is stopping me from being baptized?" [37 Philip answered, "If you believe with all your heart, you can." The officer said, "I believe that Jesus Christ is the Son of God."]n 38 Then the officer commanded the chariot to stop. Both Philip and the officer went down into the water, and Philip baptized him. 39 When they came up out of the water, the Spirit of the Lord took Philip away; the officer never saw him again. And the officer continued on his way home, full of joy. 40 But Philip appeared in a city called Azotus and preached the Good News in all the towns on the way from Azotus to Caesarea.

Saul Is Converted

9 In Jerusalem Saul was still threatening the followers of the Lord by saying he would kill them. So he went to the high priest 2 and asked him to write letters to the synagogues in the city of Damascus. Then if Saul found any followers of Christ's Way, men or women, he would arrest them and bring them back to Jerusalem.

3 So Saul headed toward Damascus. As he came near the city, a bright light from heaven suddenly flashed around him. 4 Saul fell to the ground and heard a voice saying to him, "Saul, Saul! Why are you persecuting me?"

5 Saul said, "Who are you, Lord?"

The voice answered, "I am Jesus, whom you are persecuting. 6 Get up now and go into the city. Someone there will tell you what you must do."

7 The people traveling with Saul stood there but said nothing. They heard the voice, but they saw no one. 8 Saul got up from the ground and opened his eyes, but he could not see. So those with Saul took his hand and led him into Damascus. 9 For three days Saul could not see and did not eat or drink.

10 There was a follower of Jesus in Damascus named Ananias. The Lord spoke to Ananias in a vision, "Ananias!"

Ananias answered, "Here I am, Lord."

11 The Lord said to him, "Get up and go to Straight Street. Find the house of Judas,n and ask for a man named Saul from the city of Tarsus. He is there now, praying. 12 Saul has seen a vision in which a man named Ananias comes to him and lays his hands on him. Then he is able to see again."

13 But Ananias answered, "Lord, many people have told me about this man and the

{ Book of the Month }

The Total Money Makeover
by Dave Ramsey

Personal finance is 80 percent behavior and 20 percent knowledge, popular radio host Dave Ramsey writes. So *The Total Money Makeover* is more than sample budgets and admonishments about tithing. Ramsey gets straight to the heart of the money matter: It is the love of money, not money itself, that is the root of evil. He encourages men to possess riches for the glory of God and to rid themselves of the weight of debt around their necks. His advice: Pay living expenses first, then creditors. Live by a budget and know where every dollar is going. As Ramsey would say, "Do it now."

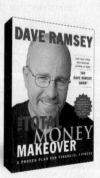

 8:37 Philip...God." Some Greek copies do not contain the bracketed text.   9:11 Judas This is not either of the apostles named Judas.

162

>>April

QUOTE OF THE MONTH:
"It's what you learn after you know it all that counts." —John Wooden

1
Celebrate **April Fools' Day** by playing a harmless practical joke.

2
Buy a stranger a soft drink.

3

4
Martin Luther King Jr. was assassinated in Memphis, Tennessee, on this day in 1968.

5

6

7
Pray for a person of influence: Today is director **Francis Ford Coppola's** birthday.

8

9

10
Pray for a person of influence: Today is sportscaster **John Madden's** birthday.

11

12

13
Memorize James 1:22.

14
Pray for the peace of **Jerusalem**.

15
Taxes are due.

16

17

18
Read the **Book of Romans** and apply what you learn at work.

19

20
Make a donation to your favorite charity.

21

22
Pray for a person of influence: Today is producer **Aaron Spelling's** birthday.

23

24
Volunteer to mow your neighbor's lawn.

25

26
Drink the recommended daily serving of water.

27

28
Play Frisbee in the park.

29
Pray for a person of influence: Today is comedian **Jerry Seinfeld's** birthday.

30
Smile for photographs.

terrible things he did to your holy people in Jerusalem. [14]Now he has come here to Damascus, and the leading priests have given him the power to arrest everyone who worships you."

[15]But the Lord said to Ananias, "Go! I have chosen Saul for an important work. He must tell about me to those who are not Jews, to kings, and to the people of Israel. [16]I will show him how much he must suffer for my name."

[17]So Ananias went to the house of Judas. He laid his hands on Saul and said, "Brother Saul, the Lord Jesus sent me. He is the one you saw on the road on your way here. He sent me so that you can see again and be filled with the Holy Spirit." [18]Immediately, something that looked like fish scales fell from Saul's eyes, and he was able to see again! Then Saul got up and was baptized. [19]After he ate some food, his strength returned.

Saul Preaches in Damascus

Saul stayed with the followers of Jesus in Damascus for a few days. [20]Soon he began to preach about Jesus in the synagogues, saying, "Jesus is the Son of God."

[21]All the people who heard him were amazed. They said, "This is the man who was in Jerusalem trying to destroy those who trust in this name! He came here to arrest the followers of Jesus and take them back to the leading priests."

[22]But Saul grew more powerful. His proofs that Jesus is the Christ were so strong that his own people in Damascus could not argue with him.

[23]After many days, they made plans to kill Saul. [24]They were watching the city gates day and night, but Saul learned about their plan. [25]One night some followers of Saul helped him leave the city by lowering him in a basket through an opening in the city wall.

Saul Preaches in Jerusalem

[26]When Saul went to Jerusalem, he tried to join the group of followers, but they were all afraid of him. They did not believe he was really a follower. [27]But Barnabas accepted Saul and took him to the apostles. Barnabas explained to them that Saul had seen the Lord on the road and the Lord had spoken to Saul. Then he told them how boldly Saul had preached in the name of Jesus in Damascus.

[28]And so Saul stayed with the followers, going everywhere in Jerusalem, preaching boldly in the name of the Lord. [29]He would often talk and argue with the Jewish people who spoke Greek, but they were trying to kill him. [30]When the followers learned about this, they took Saul to Caesarea and from there sent him to Tarsus.

[31]The church everywhere in Judea, Galilee, and Samaria had a time of peace and became stronger. Respecting the Lord by the way they lived, and being encouraged by the Holy Spirit, the group of believers continued to grow.

Peter Heals Aeneas

[32]As Peter was traveling through all the area, he visited God's people who lived in Lydda. [33]There he met a man named Aeneas, who was paralyzed and had not been able to leave his bed for the past eight years. [34]Peter said to him, "Aeneas, Je-

Q: Do all religions teach the same things?

A: Jesus came as God in human form. He said salvation comes only through faith in him. Such truths are irreconcilable with the teachings of all other major religions, which are equally at odds with one another. Other faiths are not equal with Christianity.

Survival Guide

FIXING A FLAT: HOW TO'S

If you think changing a flat tire means calling a AAA wrecker, it's worth learning how to change one yourself in case you get stranded in the middle of nowhere. Most vehicle manuals describe where to find the jack, lug wrench, and spare. Practice on a level spot, since you should never change a tire on an incline. Loosen the lug nuts on the wheel, jack up the car, and change the tire. If this sounds like Greek to you, ask a friend for assistance. Christian community means finding help when you need it.

sus Christ heals you. Stand up and make your bed." Aeneas stood up immediately. ³⁵All the people living in Lydda and on the Plain of Sharon saw him and turned to the Lord.

Peter Heals Tabitha

³⁶In the city of Joppa there was a follower named Tabitha (whose Greek name was Dorcas). She was always doing good deeds and kind acts. ³⁷While Peter was in Lydda, Tabitha became sick and died. Her body was washed and put in a room upstairs. ³⁸Since Lydda is near Joppa and the followers in Joppa heard that Peter was in Lydda, they sent two messengers to Peter. They begged him, "Hurry, please come to us!" ³⁹So Peter got ready and went with them. When he arrived, they took him to the upstairs room where all the widows stood around Peter, crying. They showed him the shirts and coats Tabitha had made when she was still alive. ⁴⁰Peter sent everyone out of the room and kneeled and prayed. Then he turned to the body and said, "Tabitha, stand up." She opened her eyes, and when she saw Peter, she sat up. ⁴¹He gave her his hand and helped her up. Then he called the saints and the widows into the room and showed them that Tabitha was alive. ⁴²People everywhere in Joppa learned about this, and many believed in the Lord. ⁴³Peter stayed in Joppa for many days with a man named Simon who was a tanner.

Peter Teaches Cornelius

10 At Caesarea there was a man named Cornelius, an officer in the Italian group of the Roman army. ²Cornelius was a religious man. He and all the other people who lived in his house worshiped the true God. He gave much of his money to the poor and prayed to God often. ³One afternoon about three o'clock, Cornelius clearly saw a vision. An angel of God came to him and said, "Cornelius!"

⁴Cornelius stared at the angel. He became afraid and said, "What do you want, Lord?"

The angel said, "God has heard your prayers. He has seen that you give to the poor, and he remembers you. ⁵Send some men now to Joppa to bring back a man named Simon who is also called Peter. ⁶He is staying with a man, also named Simon, who is a tanner and has a house beside the sea." ⁷When the angel who spoke to Cornelius left, Cornelius called two of his servants and a soldier, a religious man who worked for him. ⁸Cornelius explained everything to them and sent them to Joppa.

⁹About noon the next day as they came near Joppa, Peter was going up to the roofⁿ to pray. ¹⁰He was hungry and wanted to eat, but while the food was being prepared, he had a vision. ¹¹He saw heaven opened and something coming down that looked like a big sheet being lowered to earth by its four corners. ¹²In it were all kinds of animals, reptiles, and birds. ¹³Then a voice said to Peter, "Get up, Peter; kill and eat."

¹⁴But Peter said, "No, Lord! I have never eaten food that is unholy or unclean."

¹⁵But the voice said to him again, "God has made these things clean, so don't call them 'unholy'!" ¹⁶This happened three times, and at once the sheet was taken back to heaven.

¹⁷While Peter was wondering what this vision meant, the men Cornelius sent had found Simon's house and were standing at the gate. ¹⁸They asked, "Is Simon Peter staying here?"

¹⁹While Peter was still thinking about the vision, the Spirit said to him, "Listen, three men are looking for you. ²⁰Get up and go downstairs. Go with them without doubting, because I have sent them to you."

²¹So Peter went down to the men and said, "I am the one you are looking for. Why did you come here?"

²²They said, "A holy angel spoke to Cornelius, an army officer and a good man; he worships God. All the people respect him. The angel told Cornelius to ask you to come to his house so that he can hear what you have to say." ²³So Peter asked the men to come in and spend the night.

The next day Peter got ready and went with them, and some of the followers from Joppa joined him. ²⁴On the following day they came to Caesarea. Cornelius was waiting for them and had called together his relatives and close friends. ²⁵When Peter entered, Cornelius met him, fell at his feet, and worshiped him. ²⁶But Peter helped him up, saying, "Stand up. I too am only a human." ²⁷As he talked with Cornelius, Peter went inside where he saw many people gathered. ²⁸He said, "You people understand that it is against our law for Jewish people to associate with or visit anyone who is not Jewish.

⏵ Sexcess:
SPEAKING OF SEX

Whether or not your dad had the "sex talk" with you, chances are your sexual training left something to be desired. The truth is, most boys continue to get what little preparation they do get from school, friends, or the media. But there is still no substitute for sitting down with your son and explaining about both the delights and the dangers of sexuality. The trap that some men fall into is the sense of inadequacy at such a task, but your son is living proof that you know more than he does. And the time and attention you give him will speak volumes about your love for him.

 10:9 roof In Bible times houses were built with flat roofs. The roof was used for drying things such as flax and fruit. And it was used as an extra room, as a place for worship, and as a cool place to sleep in the summer.

>> live the life

Acts 11:23—24

The Principle > Encourage fellow believers.

Practicing It > In your relationships with other men, share your strength as well as your weakness. You need men in your life whom you can lean on when you feel discouraged. Likewise, they need to know that they can lean on you for encouragement.

But God has shown me that I should not call any person 'unholy' or 'unclean.' ²⁹That is why I did not argue when I was asked to come here. Now, please tell me why you sent for me."

³⁰Cornelius said, "Four days ago, I was praying in my house at this same time—three o'clock in the afternoon. Suddenly, there was a man standing before me wearing shining clothes. ³¹He said, 'Cornelius, God has heard your prayer and has seen that you give to the poor and remembers you. ³²So send some men to Joppa and ask Simon Peter to come. Peter is staying in the house of a man, also named Simon, who is a tanner and has a house beside the sea.' ³³So I sent for you immediately, and it was very good of you to come. Now we are all here before God to hear everything the Lord has commanded you to tell us."

³⁴Peter began to speak: "I really understand now that to God every person is the same. ³⁵In every country God accepts anyone who worships him and does what is right. ³⁶You know the message that God has sent to the people of Israel is the Good News that peace has come through Jesus Christ. Jesus is the Lord of all people! ³⁷You know what has happened all over Judea, beginning in Galilee after John* preached to the people about baptism. ³⁸You know about Jesus from Nazareth, that God gave him the Holy Spirit and power. You know how Jesus went everywhere doing good and healing those who were ruled by the devil, because God was with him. ³⁹We saw what Jesus did in Judea and in Jerusalem, but the Jews in Jerusalem killed him by hanging him on a cross. ⁴⁰Yet, on the third day, God raised Jesus to life and caused him to be seen, ⁴¹not by all the people, but only by the witnesses God had already chosen. And we are those witnesses who ate and drank with him after he was raised from the dead. ⁴²He told us to preach to the people and to tell them that he is the one whom God chose to be the judge of the living and the dead. ⁴³All the prophets say it is true that all who believe in Jesus will be forgiven of their sins through Jesus' name."

⁴⁴While Peter was still saying this, the Holy Spirit came down on all those who were listening. ⁴⁵The Jewish believers who came with Peter were amazed that the gift of the Holy Spirit had been given even to the nations. ⁴⁶These believers heard them speaking in different languages* and praising God. Then Peter said, ⁴⁷"Can anyone keep these people from being baptized with water? They have received the Holy Spirit just as we did!" ⁴⁸So Peter ordered that they be baptized in the name of Jesus Christ. Then they asked Peter to stay with them for a few days.

Peter Returns to Jerusalem

11 The apostles and the believers in Judea heard that some who were not Jewish had accepted God's teaching too. ²But when Peter came to Jerusalem, some people argued with him. ³They said, "You went into the homes of people who are not circumcised and ate with them!"

⁴So Peter explained the whole story to them. ⁵He said, "I was in the city of Joppa, and while I was praying, I had a vision. I saw something that looked like a big sheet being lowered from heaven by its four corners. It came very close to me. ⁶I looked inside it and saw animals, wild beasts, reptiles, and birds. ⁷I heard a voice say to me, 'Get up, Peter. Kill and eat.' ⁸But I said, 'No, Lord! I have never eaten anything that is unholy or unclean.' ⁹But the voice from heaven spoke again, 'God has made these things clean, so don't call them unholy.' ¹⁰This happened three times. Then the whole thing was taken back to heaven. ¹¹Right then three men who were sent to me from Caesarea came to the house where I was staying. ¹²The Spirit told me to go with them without doubting. These six believers here also went with me, and we entered the house of Cornelius. ¹³He told us about the angel he saw standing in his house. The angel said to him, 'Send some men to Joppa and invite Simon Peter to come. ¹⁴By the words he will say to you, you and all your family will be saved.' ¹⁵When I began my speech, the Holy Spirit came on them just as he came on us at the beginning. ¹⁶Then I remembered the words of the Lord. He said, 'John baptized with water, but you will be baptized with the Holy Spirit.' ¹⁷Since God gave them the same gift he gave us who believed in the Lord Jesus Christ, how could I stop the work of God?"

¹⁸When the believers heard this, they stopped arguing. They praised God and said, "So God is allowing even other nations to turn to him and live."

The Good News Comes to Antioch

¹⁹Many of the believers were scattered when they were persecuted after Stephen was killed. Some of them went as far as Phoenicia, Cyprus, and Antioch telling the message to others, but only to Jews. ²⁰Some of these believers were people from Cyprus and Cyrene. When they came to Antioch, they spoke also to Greeks,* telling them the Good News about the Lord Jesus. ²¹The Lord was helping the believers, and a large group of people believed and turned to the Lord.

²²The church in Jerusalem heard about all of this, so they sent Barnabas to Antioch. ²³⁻²⁴Barnabas was a good man, full of the Holy Spirit and full of faith. When he reached Antioch and saw how God had blessed the people, he was glad. He encouraged all the believers in Antioch always to obey the Lord with all their hearts, and many people became followers of the Lord.

 10:37 John John the Baptist, who preached to people about Christ's coming (Luke 3). **10:46 languages** This can also be translated "tongues." **11:20 Greeks** Some Greek copies read "Hellenists," non-Greeks who spoke Greek.

Q: What is a disciple?

A: "Disciple" is another word for student; the word literally means "one who learns." The disciples in the Bible are those who followed Jesus, learned from him, and obeyed his teachings. The term also refers to all who believe in Jesus and strive to do his will (John 8:31–32).

[25]Then Barnabas went to the city of Tarsus to look for Saul, [26]and when he found Saul, he brought him to Antioch. For a whole year Saul and Barnabas met with the church and taught many people there. In Antioch the followers were called Christians for the first time.

[27]About that time some prophets came from Jerusalem to Antioch. [28]One of them, named Agabus, stood up and spoke with the help of the Holy Spirit. He said, "A very hard time is coming to the whole world. There will be no food to eat." (This happened when Claudius ruled.) [29]The followers all decided to help the believers who lived in Judea, as much as each one could. [30]They gathered the money and gave it to Barnabas and Saul, who brought it to the elders in Judea.

Herod Agrippa Hurts the Church

12 During that same time King Herod began to mistreat some who belonged to the church. [2]He ordered James, the brother of John, to be killed by the sword. [3]Herod saw that some of the people liked this, so he decided to arrest Peter, too. (This happened during the time of the Feast of Unleavened Bread.)

[4]After Herod arrested Peter, he put him in jail and handed him over to be guarded by sixteen soldiers. Herod planned to bring Peter before the people for trial after the Passover Feast. [5]So Peter was kept in jail, but the church prayed earnestly to God for him.

Peter Leaves the Jail

[6]The night before Herod was to bring him to trial, Peter was sleeping between two soldiers, bound with two chains. Other soldiers were guarding the door of the jail. [7]Suddenly, an angel of the Lord stood there, and a light shined in the cell. The angel struck Peter on the side and woke him up. "Hurry! Get up!" the angel said. And the chains fell off Peter's hands. [8]Then the angel told him, "Get dressed and put on your sandals." And Peter did. Then the angel said, "Put on your coat and follow me." [9]So Peter followed him out, but he did not know if what the angel was doing was real; he thought he might be seeing a vision. [10]They went past the first and second guards and came to the iron gate that separated them from the city. The gate opened by itself for them, and they went through it. When they had walked down one street, the angel suddenly left him.

[11]Then Peter realized what had happened. He thought, "Now I know that the Lord really sent his angel to me. He rescued me from Herod and from all the things the people thought would happen."

[12]When he considered this, he went to the home of Mary, the mother of John Mark. Many people were gathered there, praying. [13]Peter knocked on the outside door, and a servant girl named Rhoda came to answer it. [14]When she recognized Peter's voice, she was so happy she forgot to open the door. Instead, she ran inside and told the group, "Peter is at the door!"

[15]They said to her, "You are crazy!" But she kept on saying it was true, so they said, "It must be Peter's angel."

Get Fit

GETTING YOUR SLEEP   Getting a good night's sleep is as essential to our health as diet and exercise. Yet we are one of the most sleep-deprived cultures in the world. To help you get the sleep you need for a healthy life, you'll need to follow some simple tips. Maintain a regular sleep schedule, and sleep as much as you need each night to feel refreshed. Avoid eating a heavy meal or exercising right before bed. Use your bed exclusively for sleeping, instead of trying to read or watch television in bed. If you can't sleep, don't lie in bed awake; instead, get up and pray or read the Bible until you are ready to go back to sleep.

Change >> Your WORLD

HABITAT FOR HUMANITY

Millard and Linda Fuller started Habitat for Humanity with a radical step of faith. They sold their marketing business, gave away the money, and founded the organization with the goal to eliminate unsafe housing and homelessness. Habitat has built more than 175,000 homes in more than one hundred countries to date. The homes are sold to partner families at cost and are financed with affordable, no-interest loans. Far from a give-away program, Habitat requires homeowners to invest hundreds of hours of sweat equity toward building their homes. You can volunteer to help build a home, donate needed materials, or give a monetary donation.

To change your world, visit www.habitat.org.

¹⁶Peter continued to knock, and when they opened the door, they saw him and were amazed. ¹⁷Peter made a sign with his hand to tell them to be quiet. He explained how the Lord led him out of the jail, and he said, "Tell James and the other believers what happened." Then he left to go to another place.

¹⁸The next day the soldiers were very upset and wondered what had happened to Peter. ¹⁹Herod looked everywhere for him but could not find him. So he questioned the guards and ordered that they be killed.

The Death of Herod Agrippa

Later Herod moved from Judea and went to the city of Caesarea, where he stayed. ²⁰Herod was very angry with the people of Tyre and Sidon, but the people of those cities all came in a group to him. After convincing Blastus, the king's personal servant, to be on their side, they asked Herod for peace, because their country got its food from his country.

²¹On a chosen day Herod put on his royal robes, sat on his throne, and made a speech to the people. ²²They shouted, "This is the voice of a god, not a human!" ²³Because Herod did not give the glory to God, an angel of the Lord immediately caused him to become sick, and he was eaten by worms and died.

²⁴God's message continued to spread and reach people.

²⁵After Barnabas and Saul finished their task in Jerusalem, they returned to Antioch, taking John Mark with them.

Barnabas and Saul Are Chosen

13 In the church at Antioch there were these prophets and teachers: Barnabas, Simeon (also called Niger), Lucius (from the city of Cyrene), Manaen (who had grown up with Herod, the ruler), and Saul. ²They were all worshiping the Lord and fasting° for a certain time. During this time the Holy Spirit said to them, "Set apart for me Barnabas and Saul to do a special work for which I have chosen them."

³So after they fasted and prayed, they laid their hands on° Barnabas and Saul and sent them out.

Barnabas and Saul in Cyprus

⁴Barnabas and Saul, sent out by the Holy Spirit, went to the city of Seleucia. From there they sailed to the island of Cyprus. ⁵When they came to Salamis, they preached the Good News of God in the synagogues. John Mark was with them to help.

⁶They went across the whole island to Paphos where they met a magician named Bar-Jesus. He was a false prophet ⁷who always stayed close to Sergius Paulus, the governor and a smart man. He asked Barnabas and Saul to come to him, because he wanted to hear the message of God. ⁸But Elymas, the magician, was against them. (Elymas is the name for Bar-Jesus in the Greek language.) He tried to stop the governor from believing in Jesus. ⁹But Saul, who was also called Paul, was filled with the Holy Spirit. He looked straight at Elymas ¹⁰and said, "You son of the devil! You are an enemy of everything that is right! You are full of evil tricks and lies, always trying to change the Lord's truths into lies. ¹¹Now the Lord will touch you, and you will be blind. For a time you will not be able to see anything— not even the light from the sun."

Then everything became dark for Elymas, and he walked around, trying to find someone to lead him by the hand. ¹²When the governor saw this, he believed because he was amazed at the teaching about the Lord.

Paul and Barnabas Leave Cyprus

¹³Paul and those with him sailed from Paphos and came to Perga, in Pamphylia. There John Mark left them to return to Jerusalem. ¹⁴They continued their trip from Perga and went to Antioch, a city in Pisidia. On the Sabbath day they went into the synagogue and sat down. ¹⁵After the law of Moses and the writings of the prophets were read, the leaders of the synagogue sent a message to Paul and Barnabas: "Brothers, if you have any message that will encourage the people, please speak."

>> **13:2 fasting** The people would give up eating for a special time of prayer and worship to God. It was also done sometimes to show sadness and disappointment. **13:3 laid their hands on** The laying on of hands had many purposes, including the giving of a blessing, power, or authority.

[16]Paul stood up, raised his hand, and said, "You Israelites and you who worship God, please listen! [17]The God of the Israelites chose our ancestors. He made the people great during the time they lived in Egypt, and he brought them out of that country with great power. [18]And he was patient with them[n] for forty years in the desert. [19]God destroyed seven nations in the land of Canaan and gave the land to his people. [20]All this happened in about four hundred fifty years.

"After this, God gave them judges until the time of Samuel the prophet. [21]Then the people asked for a king, so God gave them Saul son of Kish. Saul was from the tribe of Benjamin and was king for forty years. [22]After God took him away, God made David their king. God said about him: 'I have found in David son of Jesse the kind of man I want. He will do all I want him to do.' [23]So God has brought Jesus, one of David's descendants, to Israel to be its Savior, as he promised. [24]Before Jesus came, John[n] preached to all the people of Israel about a baptism of changed hearts and lives. [25]When he was finishing his work, he said, 'Who do you think I am? I am not the Christ. He is coming later, and I am not worthy to untie his sandals.'

[26]"Brothers, sons of the family of Abraham, and others who worship God, listen! The news about this salvation has been sent to us. [27]Those who live in Jerusalem and their leaders did not realize that Jesus was the Savior. They did not understand the words that the prophets wrote, which are read every Sabbath day. But they made them come true when they said Jesus was guilty. [28]They could not find any real reason for Jesus to be put to death, but they asked Pilate to have him killed. [29]When they had done to him all that the Scriptures had said, they took him down from the cross and laid him in a tomb. [30]But God raised him up from the dead! [31]After this, for many days, those who had gone with Jesus from Galilee to Jerusalem saw him. They are now his witnesses to the people. [32]We tell you the Good News about the promise God made to our ancestors. [33]God has made this promise come true for us, his children, by raising Jesus from the dead. We read about this also in Psalm 2:

'You are my Son.
  Today I have become your Father.'

  Psalm 2:7

[34]God raised Jesus from the dead, and he will never go back to the grave and become dust. So God said:

'I will give you the holy and sure blessings
  that I promised to David.'   *Isaiah 55:3*

[35]But in another place God says:

'You will not let your Holy One rot.'

  Psalm 16:10

[36]David did God's will during his lifetime. Then he died and was buried beside his ancestors, and his body did rot in the grave. [37]But the One God raised from the dead did not rot in the grave. [38-39]Brothers, understand what we are telling you: You can have forgiveness of your sins through Jesus. The law of Moses could not free you from your sins. But through Jesus everyone who believes is free from all sins. [40]Be careful! Don't let what the prophets said happen to you:

[41]'Listen, you people who doubt!
  You can wonder, and then die.
  I will do something in your lifetime
    that you won't believe even when
      you are told about it!' "

  Habakkuk 1:5

[42]While Paul and Barnabas were leaving the synagogue, the people asked them to tell

must speak the message of God to you first. But you refuse to listen. You are judging yourselves not worthy of having eternal life! So we will now go to the people of other nations. [47]This is what the Lord told us to do, saying:

'I have made you a light for the nations;
  you will show people all over the world
    the way to be saved.' "

  Isaiah 49:6

[48]When those who were not Jewish heard Paul say this, they were happy and gave honor to the message of the Lord. And the people who were chosen to have life forever believed the message.

[49]So the message of the Lord was spreading through the whole country. [50]But the Jewish people stirred up some of the important religious women and the leaders of the city. They started trouble against Paul and Barnabas and forced them out of their area. [51]So Paul and Barnabas shook the dust off their feet[n] and went to Iconium. [52]But the followers were filled with joy and the Holy Spirit.

Paul and Barnabas in Iconium

14 In Iconium, Paul and Barnabas went as usual to the synagogue. They spoke so well that a great many Jews and Greeks believed. [2]But some people who did not believe excited the others and turned

> **FACT-OIDS!** **Sixty-seven percent of e-mail users said spam made being online unpleasant or annoying.**
> [Pew Internet and American Life Project]

them more about these things on the next Sabbath. [43]When the meeting was over, many people with those who had changed to worship God followed Paul and Barnabas from that place. Paul and Barnabas were persuading them to continue trusting in God's grace.

[44]On the next Sabbath day, almost everyone in the city came to hear the word of the Lord. [45]Seeing the crowd, the Jewish people became very jealous and said insulting things and argued against what Paul said. [46]But Paul and Barnabas spoke very boldly, saying, "We

them against the believers. [3]Paul and Barnabas stayed in Iconium a long time and spoke bravely for the Lord. He showed that their message about his grace was true by giving them the power to work miracles and signs. [4]But the city was divided. Some of the people agreed with the Jews, and others believed the apostles.

[5]Some who were not Jews, some Jews, and some of their rulers wanted to mistreat Paul and Barnabas and to stone them to death. [6]When Paul and Barnabas learned about

---

>> 13:18 And...them Some Greek copies read "And he cared for them."   13:24 John John the Baptist, who preached to people about Christ's coming (Luke 3).   13:51 shook...feet A warning. It showed that they had rejected these people.

169

this, they ran away to Lystra and Derbe, cities in Lycaonia, and to the areas around those cities. [7]They announced the Good News there, too.

Paul in Lystra and Derbe

[8]In Lystra there sat a man who had been born crippled; he had never walked. [9]As this man was listening to Paul speak, Paul looked straight at him and saw that he believed God could heal him. [10]So he cried out, "Stand up on your feet!" The man jumped up and began walking around. [11]When the crowds saw what Paul did, they shouted in the Lycaonian language, "The gods have become like humans and have come down to us!" [12]Then the people began to call Barnabas "Zeus"[n] and Paul "Hermes,"[n] because he was the main speaker. [13]The priest in the temple of Zeus, which was near the city, brought some bulls and flowers to the city gates. He and the people wanted to offer a sacrifice to Paul and Barnabas. [14]But when the apostles, Barnabas and Paul, heard about it, they tore their clothes. They ran in among the people, shouting, [15]"Friends, why are you doing these things? We are only human beings like you. We are bringing you the Good News and are telling you to turn away from these worthless things and turn to the living God. He is the One who made the sky, the earth, the sea, and everything in them. [16]In the past, God let all the nations do what they wanted. [17]Yet he proved he is real by showing kindness, by giving you rain from heaven and crops at the right times, by giving you food and filling your hearts with joy." [18]Even with these words, they were barely able to keep the crowd from offering sacrifices to them.

[19]Then some evil people came from Antioch and Iconium and persuaded the people to turn against Paul. So they threw stones at him and dragged him out of town, thinking they had killed him. [20]But the followers gathered around him, and he got up and went back into the town. The next day he and Barnabas left and went to the city of Derbe.

The Return to Antioch in Syria

[21]Paul and Barnabas told the Good News in Derbe, and many became followers. Paul and Barnabas returned to Lystra, Iconium, and Antioch, [22]making the followers of Jesus stronger and helping them stay in the faith. They said, "We must suffer many things to enter God's kingdom." [23]They chose elders for each church, by praying and fasting[n] for a certain time. These elders had trusted the Lord, so Paul and Barnabas put them in the Lord's care.

[24]Then they went through Pisidia and came to Pamphylia. [25]When they had preached the message in Perga, they went down to Attalia. [26]And from there they sailed away to Antioch where the believers had put them into God's care and had sent them out to do this work. Now they had finished.

[27]When they arrived in Antioch, Paul and Barnabas gathered the church together. They told the church all about what God had done with them and how God had made it possible for those who were not Jewish to believe. [28]And they stayed there a long time with the followers.

The Meeting at Jerusalem

15 Then some people came to Antioch from Judea and began teaching the non-Jewish believers: "You cannot be saved if you are not circumcised as Moses taught us." [2]Paul and Barnabas were against this teaching and argued with them about it. So the church decided to send Paul, Barnabas, and some others to Jerusalem where they could talk more about this with the apostles and elders. [3]The church helped them leave on the trip, and they went through the countries of Phoenicia and Samaria, telling all about

▶Get Aligned

Acts 14:9—10

EXAMINE THE HEALING MINISTRY OF JESUS, and you'll discover a common denominator among those he healed. They all had a degree of faith in Jesus' ability to do what seemed impossible. Some believed Christ more than others, and he commended those people publicly. But the miraculous always occurred when faith—even a mustard seed–sized faith—intersected with God's power.

In this passage of Scripture, Paul perceived that the man in need of healing had faith for it, so he instructed the man to act on his faith by standing up and moving around. As the story illustrates, faith is simply believing in God and trusting him for the outcome. Faith paves the way for the power of God to influence a result. It is the fertile soil God uses to change people's lives around.

If you are waiting for a miracle in your own life, start by taking God at his word. Remember that faith is simple and childlike. God is God, and you are not. You are responsible for exercising faith, and he is responsible for the results.

Q: What is idolatry?

A: Idolatry is the act of worshiping any god other than God. Anything that supplants God's rightful place of authority in our lives can be considered an idol. Common idols in our society today include money, fame, and pleasure (Exodus 20:3).

>> **14:12 "Zeus"** The Greeks believed in many false gods, of whom Zeus was most important. **14:12 "Hermes"** The Greeks believed he was a messenger for the other gods. **14:23 fasting** The people would give up eating for a special time of prayer and worship to God. It was also done sometimes to show sadness and disappointment.

FOR Men Only

COMMITMENT In the no-fault, blame-shifting, litigious society in which we live, a woman wants to know whether or not a man is committed to the relationship long-term. So whether you are married, engaged, or dating, one of the prime ways to show your love is to stay committed to the person you are in relationship with. If love is anything, it is a commitment. As traditional marriage vows affirm, love is a commitment through good times and bad times, regardless of the circumstances. As many will attest, prenuptial agreements are a poor substitute for commitment from the heart. Commit to your love, and it will grow stronger in turn.

how the other nations had turned to God. This made all the believers very happy. ⁴When they arrived in Jerusalem, they were welcomed by the apostles, the elders, and the church. Paul, Barnabas, and the others told about everything God had done with them. ⁵But some of the believers who belonged to the Pharisee group came forward and said, "The non-Jewish believers must be circumcised. They must be told to obey the law of Moses."

⁶The apostles and the elders gathered to consider this problem. ⁷After a long debate, Peter stood up and said to them, "Brothers, you know that in the early days God chose me from among you to preach the Good News to the nations. They heard the Good News from me, and they believed. ⁸God, who knows the thoughts of everyone, accepted them. He showed this to us by giving them the Holy Spirit, just as he did to us. ⁹To God, those people are not different from us. When they believed, he made their hearts pure. ¹⁰So now why are you testing God by putting a heavy load around the necks of the non-Jewish believers? It is a load that neither we nor our ancestors were able to carry. ¹¹But we believe that we and they too will be saved by the grace of the Lord Jesus."

¹²Then the whole group became quiet. They listened to Paul and Barnabas tell about all the miracles and signs that God did through them among the people. ¹³After they finished speaking, James said, "Brothers, listen to me. ¹⁴Simon has told us how God showed his love

for those people. For the first time he is accepting from among them a people to be his own. ¹⁵The words of the prophets agree with this too:

¹⁶'After these things I will return.
    The kingdom of David is like a fallen tent.
But I will rebuild its ruins,
    and I will set it up.
¹⁷Then those people who are left alive may ask the Lord for help,
    and the other nations that belong to me,
says the Lord,
    who will make it happen.
¹⁸And these things have been known for a long time.'

Amos 9:11–12

¹⁹"So I think we should not bother the other people who are turning to God. ²⁰Instead, we should write a letter to them telling them these things: Stay away from food that has been offered to idols (which makes it unclean), any kind of sexual sin, eating animals that have been strangled, and blood. ²¹They should do these things, because for a long time in every city the law of Moses has been taught. And it is still read in the synagogue every Sabbath day."

Letter to Non-Jewish Believers

²²The apostles, the elders, and the whole church decided to send some of their men with Paul and Barnabas to Antioch. They chose Judas Barsabbas and Silas, who were respected by the believers. ²³They sent the following letter with them:

From the apostles and elders, your brothers.
To all the non-Jewish believers in Antioch, Syria, and Cilicia: Greetings!

<<TechSupport>>

SPAM CONTROL

Rare is the inbox that hasn't been bombarded with unsolicited, unwanted e-mail, also known as spam. Although Congress passed legislation that helped reduce the quantity of spam, it remains a problem since the law didn't prohibit the sending of messages, but merely required senders to include a way to "opt out" from future mailings. For your own good, look for e-mail software that lets you customize the settings so that valid messages will get through and junk e-mails won't. Spiritually speaking, it is important to filter out the influx of messages into our lives that contradict God's truth.

24We have heard that some of our group have come to you and said things that trouble and upset you. But we did not tell them to do this. 25We have all agreed to choose some messengers and send them to you with our dear friends Barnabas and Paul— 26people who have given their lives to serve our Lord Jesus Christ. 27So we are sending Judas and Silas, who will tell you the same things. 28It has pleased the Holy Spirit that you should not have a heavy load to carry, and we agree. You need to do only these things: 29Stay away from any food that has been offered to idols, eating any animals that have been strangled, and blood, and any kind of sexual sin. If you stay away from these things, you will do well.

Good-bye.

30So they left Jerusalem and went to Antioch where they gathered the church and gave them the letter. 31When they read it, they were very happy because of the encouraging message. 32Judas and Silas, who were also prophets, said many things to encourage the believers and make them stronger. 33After some time Judas and Silas were sent off in peace by the believers, and they went back to those who had sent them [, 34but Silas decided to remain there]."

35But Paul and Barnabas stayed in Antioch and, along with many others, preached the Good News and taught the people the message of the Lord.

Paul and Barnabas Separate

36After some time, Paul said to Barnabas, "We should go back to all those towns where we preached the message of the Lord. Let's visit the believers and see how they are doing."

37Barnabas wanted to take John Mark with them, 38but he had left them at Pamphylia; he did not continue with them in the work. So Paul did not think it was a good idea to take him. 39Paul and Barnabas had such a serious argument about this that they separated and went different ways. Barnabas took Mark and sailed to Cyprus, 40but Paul chose Silas and left. The believers in Antioch put Paul into the Lord's care, 41and he went through Syria and Cilicia, giving strength to the churches.

Timothy Goes with Paul

16 Paul came to Derbe and Lystra, where a follower named Timothy lived. Timothy's mother was Jewish and a believer, but his father was a Greek. 2The believers in Lystra and Iconium respected Timothy and said good things about him. 3Paul wanted Timothy to travel with him, but all the people living in that area knew that Timothy's father was Greek. So Paul circumcised Timothy to please his mother's people. 4Paul and those with him traveled from town to town and gave the decisions made by the apostles and elders in Jerusalem for the people to obey. 5So the churches became stronger in the faith and grew larger every day.

Paul Is Called Out of Asia

6Paul and those with him went through the areas of Phrygia and Galatia since the Holy Spirit did not let them preach the Good News

Q: What are the Gospels?

A: The Gospels are the first four books of the New Testament: Matthew, Mark, Luke, and John. They are called the Gospels (which means "good news") because they are each first-hand accounts of the life and ministry of Jesus Christ.

→ The Bottom Line

Identity Theft: Taking Precautions

EVEN HIGH-PROFILE PEOPLE CAN FALL VICTIM TO IDENTITY THEFT. While there is no foolproof prevention method, authorities suggest certain precautions. Rarely disclose your Social Security number or other personal information via phone, mail, or Internet. Shred mail containing your name or any account numbers. Carry a minimal number of credit cards and memorize PIN numbers and passwords. Be wary of transacting personal business in Internet cafés, where prying eyes can be at work. Also, check annually with a credit bureau to verify information on your report.

➤➤ 15:34 but...there Some Greek copies do not contain the bracketed text.

in Asia. [7]When they came near the country of Mysia, they tried to go into Bithynia, but the Spirit of Jesus did not let them. [8]So they passed by Mysia and went to Troas. [9]That night Paul saw in a vision a man from Macedonia. The man stood and begged, "Come over to Macedonia and help us." [10]After Paul had seen the vision, we immediately prepared to leave for Macedonia, understanding that God had called us to tell the Good News to those people.

Lydia Becomes a Christian

[11]We left Troas and sailed straight to the island of Samothrace. The next day we sailed to Neapolis.[n] [12]Then we went by land to Philippi, a Roman colony[n] and the leading city in that part of Macedonia. We stayed there for several days.

[13]On the Sabbath day we went outside the city gate to the river where we thought we would find a special place for prayer. Some women had gathered there, so we sat down and talked with them. [14]One of the listeners was a woman named Lydia from the city of Thyatira whose job was selling purple cloth. She worshiped God, and he opened her mind to pay attention to what Paul was saying. [15]She and all the people in her house were baptized. Then she invited us to her home, saying, "If you think I am truly a believer in the Lord, then come stay in my house." And she persuaded us to stay with her.

Paul and Silas in Jail

[16]Once, while we were going to the place for prayer, a servant girl met us. She had a special spirit[n] in her, and she earned a lot of money for her owners by telling fortunes. [17]This girl followed Paul and us, shouting, "These men are servants of the Most High God. They are telling you how you can be saved."

[18]She kept this up for many days. This bothered Paul, so he turned and said to the spirit, "By the power of Jesus Christ, I command you to come out of her!" Immediately, the spirit came out.

[19]When the owners of the servant girl saw this, they knew that now they could not use

her to make money. So they grabbed Paul and Silas and dragged them before the city rulers in the marketplace. [20]They brought Paul and Silas to the Roman rulers and said, "These men are Jews and are making trouble in our city. [21]They are teaching things that are not right for us as Romans to do."

[22]The crowd joined the attack against them. The Roman officers tore the clothes of Paul and Silas and had them beaten with rods. [23]Then Paul and Silas were thrown into jail, and the jailer was ordered to guard them carefully. [24]When he heard this order, he put them far inside the jail and pinned their feet down between large blocks of wood.

[25]About midnight Paul and Silas were praying and singing songs to God as the other prisoners listened. [26]Suddenly, there was a strong earthquake that shook the foundation of the jail. Then all the doors of the jail broke open, and all the prisoners were freed from their chains. [27]The jailer woke up and saw that the jail doors were open. Thinking that the prisoners had already escaped, he got his sword and was about to kill himself.[n] [28]But Paul shouted, "Don't hurt yourself! We are all here."

[29]The jailer told someone to bring a light. Then he ran inside and, shaking with fear, fell down before Paul and Silas. [30]He brought them outside and said, "Men, what must I do to be saved?"

[31]They said to him, "Believe in the Lord Jesus and you will be saved—you and all the people in your house." [32]So Paul and Silas told the message of the Lord to the jailer and all the people in his house. [33]At that hour of the night the jailer took Paul and Silas and washed their wounds. Then he and all his people were baptized immediately. [34]After this the jailer took Paul and Silas home and gave them food. He and his family were very happy because they now believed in God.

[35]The next morning, the Roman officers sent the police to tell the jailer, "Let these men go free."

[36]The jailer said to Paul, "The officers have sent an order to let you go free. You can leave now. Go in peace."

[37]But Paul said to the police, "They beat us in public without a trial, even though we are

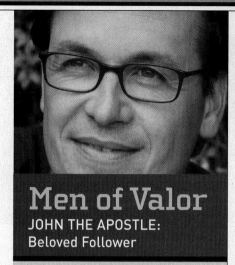

Men of Valor
JOHN THE APOSTLE:
Beloved Follower

John was one of Jesus' dozen apostles. A fisherman, John left his nets to follow Christ and became a strong example of faithfulness to the Lord. Author of the Gospel of John, he later would write the Book of Revelation, a book so rich in imagery and deep in meaning that people still debate its interpretation. John was a devoted follower and part of Christ's inner circle. He accompanied Jesus to the mountain where Christ was transformed, and John reclined next to Christ at the Last Supper. As Jesus hung on the cross, he saw Mary and told John, "Here is your mother" (John 19:27). Obviously, this was a man whom Christ loved.

Roman citizens.[n] And they threw us in jail. Now they want to make us go away quietly. No! Let them come themselves and bring us out."

[38]The police told the Roman officers what Paul said. When the officers heard that Paul and Silas were Roman citizens, they were afraid. [39]So they came and told Paul and Silas they were sorry and took them out of jail and asked them to leave the city. [40]So when they came out of the jail, they went to Lydia's

16:11 Neapolis City in Macedonia. It was the first city Paul visited on the continent of Europe.   16:12 Roman colony A town begun by Romans with Roman laws, customs, and privileges.   16:16 spirit This was a spirit from the devil, which caused her to say she had special knowledge.   16:27 kill himself He thought the leaders would kill him for letting the prisoners escape.   16:37 Roman citizens Roman law said that Roman citizens must not be beaten before they had a trial.

173

+ Ten Ways to Escape Busyness

1. Plan a weeklong media fast.

2. Play golf on a links course.

3. Take the kids tent camping.

4. Enjoy a wilderness canoe trip.

5. Walk along the beach alone.

6. Hike through the woods.

7. Plant a vegetable garden.

8. Wean yourself off caffeine.

9. Research a dream vacation.

10. Go on a mission trip.

house where they saw some of the believers and encouraged them. Then they left.

Paul and Silas in Thessalonica

17 Paul and Silas traveled through Amphipolis and Apollonia and came to Thessalonica where there was a synagogue. [2]Paul went into the synagogue as he always did, and on each Sabbath day for three weeks, he talked with his fellow Jews about the Scriptures. [3]He explained and proved that the Christ must die and then rise from the dead. He said, "This Jesus I am telling you about is the Christ."

[4]Some of them were convinced and joined Paul and Silas, along with many of the Greeks who worshiped God and many of the important women.

[5]But some others became jealous. So they got some evil men from the marketplace, formed a mob, and started a riot. They ran to Jason's house, looking for Paul and Silas, wanting to bring them out to the people. [6]But when they did not find them, they dragged Jason and some other believers to the leaders of the city. The people were yelling, "These people have made trouble everywhere in the world, and now they have come here too! [7]Jason is keeping them in his house. All of them do things against the laws of Caesar, saying there is another king, called Jesus."

[8]When the people and the leaders of the city heard these things, they became very upset. [9]They made Jason and the others put up a sum of money. Then they let the believers go free.

Paul and Silas Go to Berea

[10]That same night the believers sent Paul and Silas to Berea where they went to the synagogue. [11]These people were more willing to listen than the people in Thessalonica. The Bereans were eager to hear what Paul and Silas said and studied the Scriptures every day to find out if these things were true. [12]So, many of them believed, as well as many important Greek women and men. [13]But the people in Thessalonica learned that Paul was preaching the word of God in Berea, too. So they came there, upsetting the people and making trouble. [14]The believers quickly sent Paul away to the coast, but Silas and Timothy stayed in Berea. [15]The people leading Paul went with him to Athens. Then they carried a message from Paul back to Silas and Timothy for them to come to him as soon as they could.

Paul Preaches in Athens

[16]While Paul was waiting for Silas and Timothy in Athens, he was troubled because he saw that the city was full of idols. [17]In the syna-

Survival Guide

REFRIGERATORS: KEEPING COOL

Like other devices that heat and cool, refrigerators are major energy users. To keep yours running economically, turn on its energy-saver switch. Set the refrigerator's thermometer around thirty-seven degrees and the freezer between three and five. Keep your fridge away from heat sources like ovens, dishwashers, and heating ducts. Use a brush or vacuum regularly to clean the condenser coils in the back or on the bottom of the refrigerator to maximize its efficiency and performance.

gogue, he talked with the Jews and the Greeks who worshiped God. He also talked every day with people in the marketplace.

[18]Some of the Epicurean and Stoic philosophers[a] argued with him, saying, "This man doesn't know what he is talking about. What is he trying to say?" Others said, "He seems to be telling us about some other gods," because Paul was telling them about Jesus and his rising from the dead. [19]They got Paul and took him to a meeting of the Areopagus,[b] where they said, "Please explain to us this new idea you have been teaching. [20]The things you are saying are new to us, and we want to know what this teaching means." [21](All the people of Athens and those from other countries who lived there always used their time to talk about the newest ideas.)

[22]Then Paul stood before the meeting of the Areopagus and said, "People of Athens, I can see you are very religious in all things. [23]As I was going through your city, I saw the objects you worship. I found an altar that had these words written on it: TO A GOD WHO IS NOT KNOWN. You worship a god that you don't know, and this is the God I am telling you about! [24]The God who made the whole world and everything in it is the Lord of the land and the sky. He does not live in temples built by human hands. [25]This God is the One who gives life, breath, and everything else to people. He does not need any help from them; he has everything he needs. [26]God began by making one person, and from him came all the different people who live everywhere in the world. God decided exactly when and where they must live. [27]God wanted them to look for him and perhaps search all around for him and find him, though he is not far from any of us: [28]'By his power we live and move and exist.' Some of your own poets have said: 'For we are his children.' [29]Since we are God's children, you must not think that God is like something that people imagine or make from gold, silver, or rock. [30]In the past, people did not understand God, and he ignored this. But now, God tells all people in the world to change their hearts and lives. [31]God has set a day that he will judge all the world with fairness, by the man he chose long ago. And God has proved this to everyone by raising that man from the dead!"

[32]When the people heard about Jesus being raised from the dead, some of them laughed. But others said, "We will hear more about this from you later." [33]So Paul went away from them. [34]But some of the people believed Paul and joined him. Among those who believed was Dionysius, a member of the Areopagus, a woman named Damaris, and some others.

Paul in Corinth

18 Later Paul left Athens and went to Corinth. [2]Here he met a Jew named Aquila who had been born in the country of Pontus. But Aquila and his wife, Priscilla, had recently moved to Corinth from Italy, because Claudius[c] commanded that all Jews must leave Rome. Paul went to visit Aquila and Priscilla. [3]Because they were tentmakers, just as he was, he stayed with them and worked with them. [4]Every Sabbath day he talked with the Jews and Greeks in the synagogue, trying to persuade them to believe in Jesus.

[5]Silas and Timothy came from Macedonia and joined Paul in

Corinth. After this, Paul spent all his time telling people the Good News, showing them that Jesus is the Christ. [6]But they would not accept Paul's teaching and said some evil things. So he shook off the dust from his clothes[d] and said to them, "If you are not saved, it will be your own fault! I have done all I can do! After this, I will go to other nations." [7]Paul left the synagogue and moved into the home of Titius Justus, next to the synagogue. This man worshiped God. [8]Crispus was the leader of that synagogue, and he and all the people living in his house believed in the Lord. Many others in Corinth also listened to Paul and believed and were baptized.

[9]During the night, the Lord told Paul in a vision: "Don't be afraid. Continue talking to people and don't be quiet. [10]I am with you, and no one will hurt you because many of my people are in this city." [11]Paul stayed there for a year and a half, teaching God's word to the people.

Paul Is Brought Before Gallio

[12]When Gallio was the governor of the country of Southern Greece, some people came together against Paul and took him to the court. [13]They said, "This man is teaching people to worship God in a way that is against our law."

[14]Paul was about to say something, but Gallio spoke, saying, "I would listen to you if you were complaining about a crime or

Get Aligned
Acts 18:6

ONE OF THE HARDEST LESSONS A PASSIONATE CHRISTIAN must learn is that he cannot save the world. Nor can he save a single person. With the best of intentions, many believers do all the right things in sharing the Good News of Jesus Christ with others. They explain the truth. They live godly lives. They love others sacrificially. Yet they are still rejected.

The truth is, only Jesus saves. We do not—despite all our honorable, well-intended actions. By God's account, each person must decide for himself whether to believe in Jesus or not. No matter how much we do, we cannot make that ultimate decision for someone else.

So what are believers to do when they're rejected? Sometimes those we've witnessed to simply need more time to reach their decision, in which case we can persevere in prayer. In Paul's case, his listeners weren't just unaccepting, they were rude. They mocked him and his beliefs, and in return he harshly, yet truthfully, said their demise would be their own fault. Whereas we may not have to be so blunt, the key is being able to say, like Paul, that we have done all we could do to help influence others for good.

17:18 **Epicurean and Stoic philosophers** Philosophers were those who searched for truth. Epicureans believed that pleasures, especially pleasures of the mind, were the goal of life. Stoics believed that life should be without feelings of joy or grief. 17:19 **Areopagus** A council or group of important leaders in Athens. They were like judges. 18:2 **Claudius** The emperor (ruler) of Rome, A.D. 41–54. 18:6 **shook...clothes** This was a warning to show that Paul was finished talking to the people in that city.

Q: Is it wrong to judge others?

A: Yes. God is the only one with the authority to pass judgment on the human heart. However, while it is wrong to try to judge a person's heart, it is not wrong to judge whether their actions are good or bad, right or wrong (Matthew 7:1–2; Romans 2:1–2).

some wrong. ¹⁵But the things you are saying are only questions about words and names—arguments about your own law. So you must solve this problem yourselves. I don't want to be a judge of these things." ¹⁶And Gallio made them leave the court.

¹⁷Then they all grabbed Sosthenes, the leader of the synagogue, and beat him there before the court. But this did not bother Gallio.

Paul Returns to Antioch

¹⁸Paul stayed with the believers for many more days. Then he left and sailed for Syria, with Priscilla and Aquila. At Cenchrea Paul cut off his hair," because he had made a promise to God. ¹⁹Then they went to Ephesus, where Paul left Priscilla and Aquila. While Paul was there, he went into the synagogue and talked with the people. ²⁰When they asked him to stay with them longer, he refused. ²¹But as he left, he said, "I will come back to you again if God wants me to." And so he sailed away from Ephesus.

²²When Paul landed at Caesarea, he went and gave greetings to the church in Jerusalem. After that, Paul went to Antioch. ²³He stayed there for a while and then left and went through the regions of Galatia and Phrygia. He traveled from town to town in these regions, giving strength to all the followers.

Apollos in Ephesus and Corinth

²⁴A Jew named Apollos came to Ephesus. He was born in the city of Alexandria and was a good speaker who knew the Scriptures well. ²⁵He had been taught about the way of the Lord and was always very excited when he spoke and taught the truth about Jesus. But the only baptism Apollos knew about was the baptism that John" taught. ²⁶Apollos began to speak very boldly in the synagogue, and when Priscilla and Aquila heard him, they took him to their home and helped him better understand the way of God. ²⁷Now Apollos wanted to go to the country of Southern Greece. So the believers helped him and wrote a letter to the followers there, asking them to accept him. These followers had believed in Jesus because of God's grace, and when Apollos arrived, he helped them very much. ²⁸He argued very strongly with the Jews before all the people, clearly proving with the Scriptures that Jesus is the Christ.

Paul in Ephesus

19 While Apollos was in Corinth, Paul was visiting some places on the way to Ephesus. There he found some followers ²and asked them, "Did you receive the Holy Spirit when you believed?"

They said, "We have never even heard of a Holy Spirit."

³So he asked, "What kind of baptism did you have?"

They said, "It was the baptism that John taught."

⁴Paul said, "John's baptism was a baptism of changed hearts and lives. He told people to believe in the one who would come after him, and that one is Jesus."

⁵When they heard this, they were baptized in the name of the Lord

Get Fit {

HITTING THE ROAD   For a truly adventurous approach to fitness, consider giving mountain biking a try. Few sports will stretch your cardiovascular system to its limits like the slow churn-and-burn of pedaling up a steep hillside trail, but the inspirational view at the top serves as more than enough reward for the effort. And that may not even be the biggest reward of all because there is also the thrill of the ride back down. Mountain biking is great exercise and a fun way to experience the beauty of God's creation. Once you learn what trails are available in your area, strap on your helmet and go cruising. }

➤➤   **18:18 cut … hair** Jews did this to show that the time of a special promise to God was finished.   **18:25 John** John the Baptist, who preached to people about Christ's coming (Luke 3).

Jesus. ⁶Then Paul laid his hands on them,ⁿ and the Holy Spirit came upon them. They began speaking different languagesⁿ and prophesying. ⁷There were about twelve people in this group.

⁸Paul went into the synagogue and spoke out boldly for three months. He talked with the people and persuaded them to accept the things he said about the kingdom of God. ⁹But some of them became stubborn. They refused to believe and said evil things about the Way of Jesus before all the people. So Paul left them, and taking the followers with him, he went to the school of a man named Tyrannus. There Paul talked with people every day ¹⁰for two years. Because of his work, every Jew and Greek in Asia heard the word of the Lord.

The Sons of Sceva

¹¹God used Paul to do some very special miracles. ¹²Some people took handkerchiefs and clothes that Paul had used and put them on the sick. When they did this, the sick were healed and evil spirits left them.

¹³But some people also were traveling around and making evil spirits go out of people. They tried to use the name of the Lord Jesus to force the evil spirits out. They would say, "By the same Jesus that Paul talks about, I order you to come out!" ¹⁴Seven sons of Sceva, a leading priest, were doing this.

¹⁵But one time an evil spirit said to them, "I know Jesus, and I know about Paul, but who are you?"

¹⁶Then the man who had the evil spirit jumped on them. Because he was so much stronger than all of them, they ran away from the house naked and hurt. ¹⁷All the people in Ephesus—Jews and Greeks—learned about this and were filled with fear and gave great honor to the Lord Jesus. ¹⁸Many of the believers began to confess openly and tell all the evil things they had done. ¹⁹Some of them who had used magic brought their magic books and burned them before everyone. Those books were worth about fifty thousand silver coins.ⁿ

²⁰So in a powerful way the word of the Lord kept spreading and growing.

²¹After these things, Paul decided to go to Jerusalem, planning to go through the countries of Macedonia and Southern Greece and then on to Jerusalem. He said, "After I have been to Jerusalem, I must also visit Rome." ²²Paul sent Timothy and Erastus, two of his helpers, ahead to Macedonia, but he himself stayed in Asia for a while.

Trouble in Ephesus

²³And during that time, there was some serious trouble in Ephesus about the Way of Jesus. ²⁴A man named Demetrius, who worked with silver, made little silver models that looked like the temple of the goddess Artemis.ⁿ Those who did this work made much money. ²⁵Demetrius had a meeting with them and some others who did the same kind of work. He told them, "Men, you know that we make a lot of money from our business. ²⁶But look at what this man Paul is doing. He has convinced and turned away many people in Ephesus and in almost all of Asia! He says the gods made by human hands are not real. ²⁷There is a danger that our business will lose its good name, but there is also another danger: People will begin to think that the temple of the great goddess Artemis is not important. Her greatness will be destroyed, and Artemis is the goddess that everyone in Asia and the whole world worships."

²⁸When the others heard this, they became very angry and shouted, "Artemis, the goddess of Ephesus, is great!" ²⁹The whole city became confused. The people grabbed Gaius and Aristarchus, who were from Macedonia and were traveling with Paul, and ran to the theater. ³⁰Paul wanted to go in and talk to the crowd, but the followers did not let him. ³¹Also, some leaders of Asia who were friends of Paul sent him a message, begging him not to go into the theater. ³²Some people were shouting one thing, and some were shouting another. The meeting was completely confused; most of them did not know why they had come together. ³³They put a man named Alexander in front of the people, and some of them told him what to do. Alexander waved his hand so he could explain things to the people. ³⁴But when they saw that Alexander was a Jew, they all shouted the same thing for two hours: "Great is Artemis of Ephesus!"

³⁵Then the city clerk made the crowd be quiet. He said, "People of Ephesus, everyone knows that Ephesus is the city that keeps the temple of the great goddess Artemis and her holy stoneⁿ that fell from heaven. ³⁶Since no one can say this is not true, you should be quiet. Stop and think before you do anything. ³⁷You brought these men here, but they have not said anything evil against our goddess or stolen anything from her temple. ³⁸If Demetrius and those who work with him have a charge against anyone they should go to the courts and judges where they can argue with each other. ³⁹If there is something else you want to talk about, it can be decided at the regular town meeting of the people. ⁴⁰I say this because some people might see this trouble today and say that we are rioting. We could not explain this, because there is no real reason for this meeting." ⁴¹After the city clerk said these things, he told the people to go home.

Paul in Macedonia and Greece

20 When the trouble stopped, Paul sent for the followers to come to him. After he encouraged them and then told them good-bye, he left and went to the country of Macedonia. ²He said many things to strengthen the followers in the different places on his way through Macedonia. Then he went to Greece, ³where he stayed for three months. He was ready to sail for Syria, but

FACT-OIDS! **Fifty-four percent of parents of teens currently use Internet filters, up from 41% in 2000.** [Pew Internet and American Life Project]

19:6 **laid his hands on them** The laying on of hands had many purposes, including the giving of a blessing, power, or authority. 19:6 **languages** This can also be translated "tongues."
 19:19 **fifty thousand silver coins** Probably drachmas. One coin was enough to pay a worker for one day's labor. 19:24 **Artemis** A Greek goddess that the people of Asia Minor worshiped. 19:35 **holy stone** Probably a meteorite or stone that the people thought looked like Artemis.

some evil people were planning something against him. So Paul decided to go back through Macedonia to Syria. ⁴The men who went with him were Sopater son of Pyrrhus, from the city of Berea; Aristarchus and Secundus, from the city of Thessalonica; Gaius, from Derbe; Timothy; and Tychicus and Trophimus, two men from Asia. ⁵These men went on ahead and waited for us at Troas. ⁶We sailed from Philippi after the Feast of Unleavened Bread. Five days later we met them in Troas, where we stayed for seven days.

Paul's Last Visit to Troas

⁷On the first day of the week," we all met together to break bread," and Paul spoke to the group. Because he was planning to leave the next day, he kept on talking until midnight. ⁸We were all together in a room upstairs, and there were many lamps in the room. ⁹A young man named Eutychus was sitting in the window. As Paul continued talking, Eutychus was falling into a deep sleep. Finally, he went sound asleep and fell to the ground from the third floor. When they picked him up, he was dead. ¹⁰Paul went down to Eutychus, knelt down, and put his arms around him. He said, "Don't worry. He is alive now." ¹¹Then Paul went upstairs again, broke bread, and ate. He spoke to them a long time, until it was early morning, and then he left. ¹²They took the young man home alive and were greatly comforted.

The Trip from Troas to Miletus

¹³We went on ahead of Paul and sailed for the city of Assos, where he wanted to join us on the ship. Paul planned it this way because he wanted to go to Assos by land. ¹⁴When he met us there, we took him aboard and went to Mitylene. ¹⁵We sailed from Mitylene and the next day came to a place near Kios. The following day we sailed to Samos, and the next day we reached Miletus. ¹⁶Paul had already decided not to stop at Ephesus, because he did not want to stay too long in Asia. He was hurrying to be in Jerusalem on the day of Pentecost, if that were possible.

The Elders from Ephesus

¹⁷Now from Miletus Paul sent to Ephesus and called for the elders of the church. ¹⁸When they came to him, he said, "You know about my life from the first day I came to Asia. You know the way I lived all the time I was with you. ¹⁹The evil people made plans against me, which troubled me very much. But you know I always served the Lord unselfishly, and I often cried. ²⁰You know I preached to you and did not hold back anything that would help you. You know that I taught you in public and in your homes. ²¹I warned both Jews and Greeks to change their lives and turn to God and believe in our Lord Jesus. ²²But now I must obey the Holy Spirit and go to Jerusalem. I don't know what will happen to me there. ²³I know only that in every city the Holy Spirit tells me that troubles and even jail wait for me. ²⁴I don't care about my own life. The most important thing is that I complete my mission, the work that the Lord Jesus gave me—to tell people the Good News about God's grace.

²⁵"And now, I know that none of you among whom I was preaching the kingdom of God will ever see me again. ²⁶So today I tell you that if any of you should be lost, I am not responsible, ²⁷because I have told you everything God wants you to know. ²⁸Be careful for yourselves and for all the people the Holy Spirit has given to you to oversee. You must be like shepherds to the church of God," which he bought with the death of his own son. ²⁹I know that after I leave, some people will come like wild wolves and try to destroy the flock. ³⁰Also, some from your own group will rise up and twist the truth and will lead away followers after them. ³¹So be careful! Always remember that for three years, day and night, I never stopped warning each of you, and I often cried over you.

Q: How can I be sure God loves me?

A: God has shown us how much he loves us through Jesus' sacrifice on the cross. And his Word assures us that his love is as unconditional as it is infinite. There is nothing you can do to make God stop loving you (John 3:16; Romans 5:8).

Principles: HOLY SPIRIT

The Holy Spirit, also called the Holy Ghost, is referred to throughout the New Testament as our Comforter, Helper, and Counselor. The Holy Spirit is not some mysterious being floating through space. He is the third person of the Trinity, along with God the Father and God the Son, Jesus Christ. Before departing from this earth, Jesus promised his followers that God the Father would send the Holy Spirit to teach all believers and remind them of what Jesus had said. The Holy Spirit lives in all who follow Jesus as Lord, and he empowers believers to live for Christ.

>> **20:7 first day of the week** Sunday, which for Jews began at sunset on our Saturday. But if in this part of Asia a different system of time was used, then the meeting was on our Sunday night. **20:7 break bread** Probably the Lord's Supper, the special meal that Jesus told his followers to eat to remember him (Luke 22:14–20). **20:28 of God** Some Greek copies read "of the Lord."

³²"Now I am putting you in the care of God and the message about his grace. It is able to give you strength, and it will give you the blessings God has for all his holy people. ³³When I was with you, I never wanted anyone's money or fine clothes. ³⁴You know I always worked to take care of my own needs and the needs of those who were with me. ³⁵I showed you in all things that you should work as I did and help the weak. I taught you to remember the words Jesus said: 'It is more blessed to give than to receive.' "

³⁶When Paul had said this, he knelt down with all of them and prayed. ³⁷⁻³⁸And they all cried because Paul had said they would never see him again. They put their arms around him and kissed him. Then they went with him to the ship.

Paul Goes to Jerusalem

21 After we all said good-bye to them, we sailed straight to the island of Cos. The next day we reached Rhodes, and from there we went to Patara. ²There we found a ship going to Phoenicia, so we went aboard and sailed away. ³We sailed near the island of Cyprus, seeing it to the north, but we sailed on to Syria. We stopped at Tyre because the ship needed to unload its cargo there. ⁴We found some followers in Tyre and stayed with them for seven days. Through the Holy Spirit they warned Paul not to go to Jerusalem. ⁵When we finished our visit, we left and continued our trip. All the followers, even the women and children, came outside the city with us. After we all knelt on the beach and prayed, ⁶we said good-bye and got on the ship, and the followers went back home.

⁷We continued our trip from Tyre and arrived at Ptolemais, where we greeted the believers and stayed with them for a day. ⁸The next day we left Ptolemais and went to the city of Caesarea. There we went into the home of Philip the preacher, one of the seven helpers," and stayed with him. ⁹He had four unmarried daughters who had the gift of prophesying. ¹⁰After we had been there for some time, a prophet named Agabus arrived from Judea. ¹¹He came to us and borrowed Paul's belt and used it to tie his own hands and feet. He said, "The Holy Spirit says, 'This is how evil people in Jerusalem will tie up the man who wears this belt. Then they will give him to the older leaders.' "

¹²When we all heard this, we and the people there begged Paul not to go to Jerusalem. ¹³But he said, "Why are you crying and making me so sad? I am not only ready to be tied up in Jerusalem, I am ready to die for the Lord Jesus!"

¹⁴We could not persuade him to stay away from Jerusalem. So we stopped begging him and said, "We pray that what the Lord wants will be done."

¹⁵After this, we got ready and started on our way to Jerusalem. ¹⁶Some of the followers from Caesarea went with us and took us to the home of Mnason, where we would stay. He was from Cyprus and was one of the first followers.

Paul Visits James

¹⁷In Jerusalem the believers were glad to see us. ¹⁸The next day Paul went with us to visit James, and all the elders were there. ¹⁹Paul greeted them and told them everything God had done among the other nations through him. ²⁰When they heard this, they praised God. Then they said to Paul, "Brother, you can see that many thousands of our people have become believers. And they think it is very important to obey the law of Moses. ²¹They have heard about your teaching, that you tell our people who live among the nations to leave the law of Moses. They have heard that you tell them not to circumcise their children and not to obey customs. ²²What should we do? They will learn that you have come. ²³So we will tell you what to do: Four of our men have made a promise to God. ²⁴Take these men with you and share in their cleansing ceremony." Pay their expenses so they can shave their heads." Then it will prove to everyone that what

The Bottom Line

Income Taxes: Reducing Your Refund

EVERY SPRING, MANY PEOPLE GO ON SPENDING SPREES, thanks to their income tax refund. However, a large tax refund is a sign of poor planning. Instead of letting Uncle Sam use your money without paying you for the privilege, you could be earning interest on it throughout the year. If you have a large refund, ask your employer what the effect would be of adding an exemption to withholding taxes. Then, each pay period, save the difference. Next year, you will have more money than the government's lump sum. As Proverbs 13:11 says, "Money that is gathered little by little will grow."

>> **21:8 helpers** The seven men chosen for a special work described in Acts 6:1–6. Sometimes they are called "deacons." **21:24 cleansing ceremony** The special things Jews did to end the Nazirite promise. **21:24 shave their heads** Jews did this to show that their promise was finished.

179

they have heard about you is not true and that you follow the law of Moses in your own life. ²⁵We have already sent a letter to the non-Jewish believers. The letter said: 'Do not eat food that has been offered to idols, or blood, or animals that have been strangled. Do not take part in sexual sin.' "

²⁶The next day Paul took the four men and shared in the cleansing ceremony with them. Then he went to the Temple and announced the time when the days of the cleansing ceremony would be finished. On the last day an offering would be given for each of the men.

²⁷When the seven days were almost over, some of his people from Asia saw Paul at the Temple. They caused all the people to be upset and grabbed Paul. ²⁸They shouted, "People of Israel, help us! This is the man who goes everywhere teaching against the law of Moses, against our people, and against this Temple. Now he has brought some Greeks into the Temple and has made this holy place unclean!" ²⁹(They said this because they had seen Trophimus, a man from Ephesus, with Paul in Jerusalem. They thought that Paul had brought him into the Temple.)

³⁰All the people in Jerusalem became upset. Together they ran, took Paul, and dragged him out of the Temple. The Temple doors were closed immediately. ³¹While they were trying to kill Paul, the commander of the Roman army in Jerusalem learned that there was trouble in the whole city. ³²Immediately he took some officers and soldiers and ran to the place where the crowd was gathered. When the people saw them, they stopped

beating Paul. ³³The commander went to Paul and arrested him. He told his soldiers to tie Paul with two chains. Then he asked who he was and what he had done wrong. ³⁴Some in the crowd were yelling one thing, and some were yelling another. Because of all this confusion and shouting, the commander could not learn what had happened. So he ordered the soldiers to take Paul to the army building. ³⁵When Paul came to the steps, the soldiers had to carry him because the people were ready to hurt him. ³⁶The whole mob was following them, shouting, "Kill him!"

³⁷As the soldiers were about to take Paul into the army building, he spoke to the commander, "May I say something to you?"

The commander said, "Do you speak Greek? ³⁸I thought you were the Egyptian who started some trouble against the government not long ago and led four thousand killers out to the desert."

³⁹Paul said, "No, I am a Jew from Tarsus in the country of Cilicia. I am a citizen of that important city. Please, let me speak to the people."

⁴⁰The commander gave permission, so Paul stood on the steps and waved his hand to quiet the people. When there was silence, he spoke to them in the Hebrew language.

Paul Speaks to the People

22 Paul said, "Brothers and fathers, listen to my defense to you." ²When they heard him speaking the Hebrew language," they became very quiet. Paul said, ³"I am a Jew, born in Tarsus in the country of Cilicia, but I grew up in this city. I was a student of Gamaliel," who carefully taught me everything about the law of our ancestors. I was very serious about serving God, just as are all of you here today. ⁴I persecuted the people who followed the Way of Jesus, and some of them were even killed. I arrested men and women and put them in jail. ⁵The high priest and the whole council of elders can tell you this is true. They gave me letters to the brothers in Damascus. So I was going there to arrest these people and bring them back to Jerusalem to be punished.

⁶"About noon when I came near Damascus, a bright light from heaven suddenly flashed all around me. ⁷I fell to the ground and heard a voice saying, 'Saul, Saul, why are you persecuting me?' ⁸I asked, 'Who are you, Lord?' The voice said, 'I am Jesus from Nazareth whom you are persecuting.' ⁹Those who were with me did not understand the voice, but they saw the light. ¹⁰I said, 'What shall I do, Lord?' The Lord answered, 'Get up and go to Damascus. There you will be told about all the things I have planned for you to do.' ¹¹I could not see, because the bright light had made me blind. So my companions led me into Damascus.

¹²"There a man named Ananias came to me. He was a religious man; he obeyed the law of Moses, and all the Jews who lived there respected him. ¹³He stood by me and said, 'Brother Saul, see again!' Immediately I was able to see him. ¹⁴He said, 'The God of our ancestors chose you long ago to know his plan, to see the Righteous One, and to hear words from him. ¹⁵You will be his witness to all people, telling them about what you have seen and heard. ¹⁶Now, why wait any longer? Get up, be baptized, and wash your sins away, trusting in him to save you.'

¹⁷"Later, when I returned to Jerusalem, I was praying in the Temple, and I saw a vision. ¹⁸I saw the Lord saying to me, 'Hurry!

{ Deal With It:
*Appetites

A MAN'S APPETITES TYPICALLY RANGE FROM SEX TO FOOD TO SEX. Whereas God created us with natural appetites, it is up to us to discipline ourselves so that our appetites don't control us. In our modern age of excesses and excuses, moderation has become a foreign concept. Still, if we are to experience a healthy, abundant life, we must learn to keep our desires in check. One way to do that is to limit our exposure to stimuli that feed our craving for more. Whether it is cutting our time in the buffet line or turning our heads from alluring ads, the challenge is to sanctify our senses.

>> **22:2 Hebrew language** Or Aramaic, the languages of many people in this region in the first century.   **22:3 Gamaliel** A very important teacher of the Pharisees, a Jewish religious group (Acts 5:34).

Q: What is a parable?

A: A parable is a truth wrapped in a story. Unlike an allegory, in which every element of the story has a direct symbolic meaning, a parable is a more like a morality tale that is designed to emphasize one key truth or principle.

Leave Jerusalem now! The people here will not accept the truth about me.' [19]But I said, 'Lord, they know that in every synagogue I put the believers in jail and beat them. [20]They also know I was there when Stephen, your witness, was killed. I stood there agreeing and holding the coats of those who were killing him!' [21]But the Lord said to me, 'Leave now. I will send you far away to the other nations.' "

[22]The crowd listened to Paul until he said this. Then they began shouting, "Get rid of him! He doesn't deserve to live!" [23]They shouted, threw off their coats," and threw dust into the air."

[24]Then the commander ordered the soldiers to take Paul into the army building and beat him. He wanted to make Paul tell why the people were shouting against him like this. [25]But as the soldiers were tying him up, preparing to beat him, Paul said to an officer nearby, "Do you have the right to beat a Roman citizen" who has not been proven guilty?"

[26]When the officer heard this, he went to the commander and reported it. The officer said, "Do you know what you are doing? This man is a Roman citizen."

[27]The commander came to Paul and said, "Tell me, are you really a Roman citizen?"

He answered, "Yes."

[28]The commander said, "I paid a lot of money to become a Roman citizen."

But Paul said, "I was born a citizen."

[29]The men who were preparing to question Paul moved away from him immediately. The commander was frightened because he had already tied Paul, and Paul was a Roman citizen.

Paul Speaks to Leaders

[30]The next day the commander decided to learn why the Jews were accusing Paul. So he ordered the leading priests and the council to meet. The commander took Paul's chains off. Then he brought Paul out and stood him before their meeting.

23 Paul looked at the council and said, "Brothers, I have lived my life without guilt feelings before God up to this day." [2]Ananias," the high priest, heard this and told the men who were standing near Paul to hit him on the mouth. [3]Paul said to Ananias, "God will hit you, too! You are like a wall that has been painted white. You sit there and judge me, using the law of Moses, but you are telling them to hit me, and that is against the law."

[4]The men standing near Paul said to him, "You cannot insult God's high priest like that!"

[5]Paul said, "Brothers, I did not know this man was the high priest. It is written in the Scriptures, 'You must not curse a leader of your people.' ""

[6]Some of the men in the meeting were Sadducees, and others were Pharisees. Knowing this, Paul shouted to them, "My brothers, I am a Pharisee, and my father was a Pharisee. I am on trial here because I believe that people will rise from the dead."

[7]When Paul said this, there was an argument between the Pharisees and the Sadducees, and the group was divided. [8](The Sadducees do not believe in angels or spirits or that people will rise from the dead. But the Pharisees believe in them all.) [9]So there was a great uproar. Some of the teachers of the law, who were Pharisees, stood up and argued, "We find nothing wrong with this man. Maybe an angel or a spirit did speak to him."

[10]The argument was beginning to turn into such a fight that the commander was afraid some evil people would tear Paul to pieces. So he told the soldiers to go down and take Paul away and put him in the army building.

[11]The next night the Lord came and stood by Paul. He said, "Be brave! You have told people in Jerusalem about me. You must do the same in Rome."

[12]In the morning some evil people made a plan to kill Paul, and they took an oath not to eat or drink anything until they had killed him. [13]There were more than forty men who made this plan. [14]They went to the leading priests and the elders and said, "We have taken an oath

«TechSupport»

FREE LONG DISTANCE

If you have high-speed Internet, odds are good that your connection provides far more bandwidth than you really need. A new kind of phone service uses all this spare network capacity to allow digital voice data to travel over the same fiber optic cables that serve up e-mail, digital downloads, and Web pages to your home.

"Voice over Internet Protocol" (VoIP) phone service is extremely affordable, with no per-minute or long-distance charges in the United States, and it works with your existing phone equipment. However, when you experience trouble in life, remember to call on God for help.

22:23 threw off their coats This showed that the people were very angry with Paul. **22:23 threw dust into the air** This showed even greater anger. **22:25 Roman citizen** Roman law said that Roman citizens must not be beaten before they had a trial. **23:2 Ananias** This is not the same man named Ananias in Acts 22:12. **23:5 'You … people.'** Quotation from Exodus 22:28.

People
Skills

Defusing Arguments

When you feel a conversation quickly escalating into an argument, it's often a good idea to ask for some time to collect your thoughts. Taking a break can give you time to release the tension that may be getting in the way of honest communication. During the break, take a step back from the conflict and clarify your position. Determine what the real issue is and what needs changing. It also helps to determine what part of the issue is your responsibility and what part is not. Dealing with such details ahead of time allows you to discuss difficult issues with greater clarity and less emotion. It also doesn't hurt to pray for the other party.

not to eat or drink until we have killed Paul. [15]So this is what we want you to do: Send a message to the commander to bring Paul out to you as though you want to ask him more questions. We will be waiting to kill him while he is on the way here."

[16]But Paul's nephew heard about this plan and went to the army building and told Paul. [17]Then Paul called one of the officers and said, "Take this young man to the commander. He has a message for him."

[18]So the officer brought Paul's nephew to the commander and said, "The prisoner, Paul, asked me to bring this young man to you. He wants to tell you something."

[19]The commander took the young man's hand and led him to a place where they could be alone. He asked, "What do you want to tell me?"

[20]The young man said, "The Jews have decided to ask you to bring Paul down to their council meeting tomorrow. They want you to think they are going to ask him more questions. [21]But don't believe them! More than forty men are hiding and waiting to kill Paul. They have all taken an oath not to eat or drink until they have killed him. Now they are waiting for you to agree."

[22]The commander sent the young man away, ordering him, "Don't tell anyone that you have told me about their plan."

Paul Is Sent to Caesarea

[23]Then the commander called two officers and said, "I need some men to go to Caesarea. Get two hundred soldiers, seventy horsemen, and two hundred men with spears ready to leave at nine o'clock tonight. [24]Get some horses for Paul to ride so he can be taken to Governor Felix safely." [25]And he wrote a letter that said:

[26]From Claudius Lysias.

To the Most Excellent Governor Felix:

Greetings.

[27]Some of the Jews had taken this man and planned to kill him. But I learned that he is a Roman citizen, so I went with my soldiers and saved him. [28]I wanted to know why they were accusing him, so I brought him before their council meeting. [29]I learned that these people said Paul did some things that were wrong by their own laws, but no charge was worthy of jail or death. [30]When I was told that some of them were planning to kill Paul, I sent him to

▶ Sexcess:
COMMUNICATION CLUES

One of the secrets to a better love life is right under our noses: our mouths. Like it or not, women love to talk and be talked to. So rather than fight a losing battle, we're better off simply learning how to become better communicators. The good news for us guys is that communication draws a couple closer, not only emotionally, but also physically. Simple things like asking your sweetie how her day was, and then listening closely to her as she shares, will do wonders for your relationship. Women are wired for sound more than sight, but as you meet her needs, you'll see yours met, also.

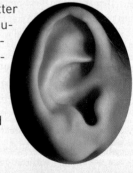

you at once. I also told them to tell you what they have against him.

[31]So the soldiers did what they were told and took Paul and brought him to the city of Antipatris that night. [32]The next day the horsemen went with Paul to Caesarea, but the other soldiers went back to the army building in Jerusalem. [33]When the horsemen came to Caesarea and gave the letter to the governor, they turned Paul over to him. [34]The governor read the letter and asked Paul, "What area are you from?" When he learned that Paul was from Cilicia, [35]he said, "I will hear your case when those who are against you come here, too." Then the governor gave orders for Paul to be kept under guard in Herod's palace.

Paul Is Accused

24 Five days later Ananias, the high priest, went to the city of Caesarea with some of the elders and a lawyer named Tertullus. They had come to make charges against Paul before the governor. [2]Paul was called into the meeting, and Tertullus began to accuse him, saying, "Most Excellent Felix! Our people enjoy much peace because of you, and many wrong things in our country are being made right through your wise help. [3]We accept these things always and in every place, and we are thankful for them. [4]But not wanting to take any more of your time, I beg you to be kind and listen to our few words. [5]We have found this man to be a troublemaker, stirring up his people everywhere in the world. He is a leader of the Nazarene group. [6]Also, he was trying to make the Temple unclean, but we stopped him. [And we wanted to judge him by our own law. [7]But the officer Lysias came and used much force to take him from us. [8]And Lysias commanded those who wanted to accuse Paul to come to you.]" By asking him questions yourself, you can decide if all these things are true." [9]The others agreed and said that all of this was true.

[10]When the governor made a sign for Paul to speak, Paul said, "Governor Felix, I know you have been a judge over this nation for a long time. So I am happy to defend myself before you. [11]You can learn for yourself that I went to worship in Jerusalem only twelve days ago. [12]Those who are accusing me did not find me arguing with anyone in the Temple or stirring up the people in the synagogues or in the city. [13]They cannot prove the things they are saying against me now. [14]But I will tell you this: I worship the God of our ancestors as a follower of the Way of Jesus. The others say that the Way of Jesus is not the right way. But I believe everything that is taught in the law of Moses and that is written in the books of the Prophets. [15]I have the same hope in God that they have—the hope that all people, good and bad, will surely be raised from the dead. [16]This is why I always try to do what I believe is right before God and people.

[17]"After being away from Jerusalem for several years, I went back to bring money to my people and to offer sacrifices. [18]I was doing this when they found me in the Temple. I had finished the cleansing ceremony and had not made any trouble; no people were gathering around me. [19]But there were some people from Asia who should be here, standing before you. If I have really done anything wrong, they

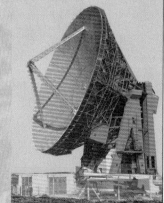

Change >> Your WORLD

HCJB WORLD RADIO

The world's first missionary broadcast organization has been touching lives around the globe for almost seventy years. Started in Ecuador, HCJB (Heralding Christ Jesus' Blessings) broadcasts in more than one hundred different languages and dialects to more than ninety countries with the passion to communicate the Good News of Jesus Christ. Besides the radio, the organization ministers through health care and training. Nationals are trained as missionaries, pastors, and health care workers to show the love of Jesus in practical ways around the globe. The radio ministry invites others to become involved through praying, going, or giving.

To change your world, visit www.hcjb.org.

are the ones who should accuse me. [20]Or ask these people here if they found any wrong in me when I stood before the council in Jerusalem. [21]But I did shout one thing when I stood before them: 'You are judging me today because I believe that people will rise from the dead!' "

[22]Felix already understood much about the Way of Jesus. He stopped the trial and said, "When commander Lysias comes here, I will decide your case." [23]Felix told the officer to keep Paul guarded but to give him some freedom and to let his friends bring what he needed.

Paul Speaks to Felix and His Wife

[24]After some days Felix came with his wife, Drusilla, who was Jewish, and asked for Paul to be brought to him. He listened to Paul talk about believing in Christ Jesus. [25]But Felix became afraid when Paul spoke about living right, self-control, and the time when God will judge the world. He said, "Go away now. When I have more time, I will call for you." [26]At the same time Felix hoped that Paul would give him some money, so he often sent for Paul and talked with him.

>> 24:6—8 **And...you.** Some Greek copies do not contain the bracketed text.

BASEBALL: Celebrating Family Fun

AMID UNFOLDING DRUG SCANDALS, GRUMBLINGS about overpaid professional players, and complaints the game is too slow, baseball has taken it on the chin lately. Yet, don't allow naysayers to overshadow the reality that baseball can still make its case as America's favorite pastime.

No other popular sport can claim origins dating to 1834, the first organized league in 1857, more than 70,000 books written about it, and so many statistics that *Baseball Almanac's* interactive encyclopedia has more than 110,000 pages.

Also, there are the numerous colorful characters, such as the renowned New York Yankee player and manager Yogi Berra, asking in his inimitable way,

"If people don't want to come out to the ballpark, how are you going to stop them?"

Baseball has family ties, too. More than 350 sets of brothers have made it to the major leagues. More importantly, the sport is a source of wholesome enjoyment at countless summer picnics, family reunions, parent-child outings, and weekend getaways.

Fans of baseball would do well to heed Paul's advice in Philippians 4:8: "Think about the things that are true and honorable and right and pure...." With the game of baseball, don't allow negative headlines to distract from enjoying its family-oriented fun.

> **"Baseball has family ties, too. More than 350 sets of brothers have made it to the major leagues."**

³²"Now I am putting you in the care of God and the message about his grace. It is able to give you strength, and it will give you the blessings God has for all his holy people. ³³When I was with you, I never wanted anyone's money or fine clothes. ³⁴You know I always worked to take care of my own needs and the needs of those who were with me. ³⁵I showed you in all things that you should work as I did and help the weak. I taught you to remember the words Jesus said: 'It is more blessed to give than to receive.' "

³⁶When Paul had said this, he knelt down with all of them and prayed. ³⁷⁻³⁸And they all cried because Paul had said they would never see him again. They put their arms around him and kissed him. Then they went with him to the ship.

Paul Goes to Jerusalem

21 After we all said good-bye to them, we sailed straight to the island of Cos. The next day we reached Rhodes, and from there we went to Patara. ²There we found a ship going to Phoenicia, so we went aboard and sailed away. ³We sailed near the island of Cyprus, seeing it to the north, but we sailed on to Syria. We stopped at Tyre because the ship needed to unload its cargo there. ⁴We found some followers in Tyre and stayed with them for seven days. Through the Holy Spirit they warned Paul not to go to Jerusalem. ⁵When we finished our visit, we left and continued our trip. All the followers, even the women and children, came outside the city with us. After we all knelt on the beach and prayed, ⁶we said good-bye and got on the ship, and the followers went back home.

⁷We continued our trip from Tyre and arrived at Ptolemais, where we greeted the believers and stayed with them for a day. ⁸The next day we left Ptolemais and went to the city of Caesarea. There we went into the home of Philip the preacher, one of the seven helpers," and stayed with him. ⁹He had four unmarried daughters who had the gift of prophesying. ¹⁰After we had been there for some time, a prophet named Agabus arrived from Judea. ¹¹He came to us and borrowed Paul's belt and used it to tie his own hands and feet. He said, "The Holy Spirit says, 'This is how evil people in Jerusalem will tie up the man who wears this belt. Then they will give him to the older leaders.' "

¹²When we all heard this, we and the people there begged Paul not to go to Jerusalem. ¹³But he said, "Why are you crying and making me so sad? I am not only ready to be tied up in Jerusalem, I am ready to die for the Lord Jesus!"

¹⁴We could not persuade him to stay away from Jerusalem. So we stopped begging him and said, "We pray that what the Lord wants will be done."

¹⁵After this, we got ready and started on our way to Jerusalem. ¹⁶Some of the followers from Caesarea went with us and took us to the home of Mnason, where we would stay. He was from Cyprus and was one of the first followers.

Paul Visits James

¹⁷In Jerusalem the believers were glad to see us. ¹⁸The next day Paul went with us to visit James, and all the elders were there. ¹⁹Paul greeted them and told them everything God had done among the other nations through him. ²⁰When they heard this, they praised God. Then they said to Paul, "Brother, you can see that many thousands of our people have become believers. And they think it is very important to obey the law of Moses. ²¹They have heard about your teaching, that you tell our people who live among the nations to leave the law of Moses. They have heard that you tell them not to circumcise their children and not to obey customs. ²²What should we do? They will learn that you have come. ²³So we will tell you what to do: Four of our men have made a promise to God. ²⁴Take these men with you and share in their cleansing ceremony." Pay their expenses so they can shave their heads." Then it will prove to everyone that what

The Bottom Line

Income Taxes: Reducing Your Refund

EVERY SPRING, MANY PEOPLE GO ON SPENDING SPREES, thanks to their income tax refund. However, a large tax refund is a sign of poor planning. Instead of letting Uncle Sam use your money without paying you for the privilege, you could be earning interest on it throughout the year. If you have a large refund, ask your employer what the effect would be of adding an exemption to withholding taxes. Then, each pay period, save the difference. Next year, you will have more money than the government's lump sum. As Proverbs 13:11 says, "Money that is gathered little by little will grow."

21:8 helpers The seven men chosen for a special work described in Acts 6:1–6. Sometimes they are called "deacons." **21:24 cleansing ceremony** The special things Jews did to end the Nazirite promise.   **21:24 shave their heads** Jews did this to show that their promise was finished.

they have heard about you is not true and that you follow the law of Moses in your own life. [25]We have already sent a letter to the non-Jewish believers. The letter said: 'Do not eat food that has been offered to idols, or blood, or animals that have been strangled. Do not take part in sexual sin.' "

[26]The next day Paul took the four men and shared in the cleansing ceremony with them. Then he went to the Temple and announced the time when the days of the cleansing ceremony would be finished. On the last day an offering would be given for each of the men.

[27]When the seven days were almost over, some of his people from Asia saw Paul at the Temple. They caused all the people to be upset and grabbed Paul. [28]They shouted, "People of Israel, help us! This is the man who goes everywhere teaching against the law of Moses, against our people, and against this Temple. Now he has brought some Greeks into the Temple and has made this holy place unclean!" [29](They said this because they had seen Trophimus, a man from Ephesus, with Paul in Jerusalem. They thought that Paul had brought him into the Temple.)

[30]All the people in Jerusalem became upset. Together they ran, took Paul, and dragged him out of the Temple. The Temple doors were closed immediately. [31]While they were trying to kill Paul, the commander of the Roman army in Jerusalem learned that there was trouble in the whole city. [32]Immediately he took some officers and soldiers and ran to the place where the crowd was gathered. When the people saw them, they stopped

beating Paul. [33]The commander went to Paul and arrested him. He told his soldiers to tie Paul with two chains. Then he asked who he was and what he had done wrong. [34]Some in the crowd were yelling one thing, and some were yelling another. Because of all this confusion and shouting, the commander could not learn what had happened. So he ordered the soldiers to take Paul to the army building. [35]When Paul came to the steps, the soldiers had to carry him because the people were ready to hurt him. [36]The whole mob was following them, shouting, "Kill him!"

[37]As the soldiers were about to take Paul into the army building, he spoke to the commander, "May I say something to you?"

The commander said, "Do you speak Greek? [38]I thought you were the Egyptian who started some trouble against the government not long ago and led four thousand killers out to the desert."

[39]Paul said, "No, I am a Jew from Tarsus in the country of Cilicia. I am a citizen of that important city. Please, let me speak to the people."

[40]The commander gave permission, so Paul stood on the steps and waved his hand to quiet the people. When there was silence, he spoke to them in the Hebrew language.

Paul Speaks to the People

22 Paul said, "Brothers and fathers, listen to my defense to you." [2]When they heard him speaking the Hebrew language, they became very quiet. Paul said, [3]"I am a Jew, born in Tarsus in the country of Cilicia, but I grew up in this city. I was a student of Gamaliel, who carefully taught me everything about the law of our ancestors. I was very serious about serving God, just as are all of you here today. [4]I persecuted the people who followed the Way of Jesus, and some of them were even killed. I arrested men and women and put them in jail. [5]The high priest and the whole council of elders can tell you this is true. They gave me letters to the brothers in Damascus. So I was going there to arrest these people and bring them back to Jerusalem to be punished.

[6]"About noon when I came near Damascus, a bright light from heaven suddenly flashed all around me. [7]I fell to the ground and heard a voice saying, 'Saul, Saul, why are you persecuting me?' [8]I asked, 'Who are you, Lord?' The voice said, 'I am Jesus from Nazareth whom you are persecuting.' [9]Those who were with me did not understand the voice, but they saw the light. [10]I said, 'What shall I do, Lord?' The Lord answered, 'Get up and go to Damascus. There you will be told about all the things I have planned for you to do.' [11]I could not see, because the bright light had made me blind. So my companions led me into Damascus.

[12]"There a man named Ananias came to me. He was a religious man; he obeyed the law of Moses, and all the Jews who lived there respected him. [13]He stood by me and said, 'Brother Saul, see again!' Immediately I was able to see him. [14]He said, 'The God of our ancestors chose you long ago to know his plan, to see the Righteous One, and to hear words from him. [15]You will be his witness to all people, telling them about what you have seen and heard. [16]Now, why wait any longer? Get up, be baptized, and wash your sins away, trusting in him to save you.'

[17]"Later, when I returned to Jerusalem, I was praying in the Temple, and I saw a vision. [18]I saw the Lord saying to me, 'Hurry!

{ Deal With It: *Appetites

A MAN'S APPETITES TYPICALLY RANGE FROM SEX TO FOOD TO SEX. Whereas God created us with natural appetites, it is up to us to discipline ourselves so that our appetites don't control us. In our modern age of excesses and excuses, moderation has become a foreign concept. Still, if we are to experience a healthy, abundant life, we must learn to keep our desires in check. One way to do that is to limit our exposure to stimuli that feed our craving for more. Whether it is cutting our time in the buffet line or turning our heads from alluring ads, the challenge is to sanctify our senses.

22:2 Hebrew language Or Aramaic, the languages of many people in this region in the first century.   **22:3 Gamaliel** A very important teacher of the Pharisees, a Jewish religious group (Acts 5:34).

Q: What is a parable?

A: A parable is a truth wrapped in a story. Unlike an allegory, in which every element of the story has a direct symbolic meaning, a parable is a more like a morality tale that is designed to emphasize one key truth or principle.

Leave Jerusalem now! The people here will not accept the truth about me.' ¹⁹But I said, 'Lord, they know that in every synagogue I put the believers in jail and beat them. ²⁰They also know I was there when Stephen, your witness, was killed. I stood there agreeing and holding the coats of those who were killing him!' ²¹But the Lord said to me, 'Leave now. I will send you far away to the other nations.' "

²²The crowd listened to Paul until he said this. Then they began shouting, "Get rid of him! He doesn't deserve to live!" ²³They shouted, threw off their coats," and threw dust into the air."

²⁴Then the commander ordered the soldiers to take Paul into the army building and beat him. He wanted to make Paul tell why the people were shouting against him like this. ²⁵But as the soldiers were tying him up, preparing to beat him, Paul said to an officer nearby, "Do you have the right to beat a Roman citizen" who has not been proven guilty?"

²⁶When the officer heard this, he went to the commander and reported it. The officer said, "Do you know what you are doing? This man is a Roman citizen."

²⁷The commander came to Paul and said, "Tell me, are you really a Roman citizen?"

He answered, "Yes."

²⁸The commander said, "I paid a lot of money to become a Roman citizen."

But Paul said, "I was born a citizen."

²⁹The men who were preparing to question Paul moved away from him immediately. The commander was frightened because he had already tied Paul, and Paul was a Roman citizen.

Paul Speaks to Leaders

³⁰The next day the commander decided to learn why the Jews were accusing Paul. So he ordered the leading priests and the council to meet. The commander took Paul's chains off. Then he brought Paul out and stood him before their meeting.

23 Paul looked at the council and said, "Brothers, I have lived my life without guilt feelings before God up to this day." ²Ananias," the high priest, heard this and told the men who were

standing near Paul to hit him on the mouth. ³Paul said to Ananias, "God will hit you, too! You are like a wall that has been painted white. You sit there and judge me, using the law of Moses, but you are telling them to hit me, and that is against the law."

⁴The men standing near Paul said to him, "You cannot insult God's high priest like that!"

⁵Paul said, "Brothers, I did not know this man was the high priest. It is written in the Scriptures, 'You must not curse a leader of your people.' ""

⁶Some of the men in the meeting were Sadducees, and others were Pharisees. Knowing this, Paul shouted to them, "My brothers, I am a Pharisee, and my father was a Pharisee. I am on trial here because I believe that people will rise from the dead."

⁷When Paul said this, there was an argument between the Pharisees and the Sadducees, and the group was divided. ⁸(The Sadducees do not believe in angels or spirits or that people will rise from the dead. But the Pharisees believe in them all.) ⁹So there was a great uproar. Some of the teachers of the law, who were Pharisees, stood up and argued, "We find nothing wrong with this man. Maybe an angel or a spirit did speak to him."

¹⁰The argument was beginning to turn into such a fight that the commander was afraid some evil people would tear Paul to pieces. So he told the soldiers to go down and take Paul away and put him in the army building.

¹¹The next night the Lord came and stood by Paul. He said, "Be brave! You have told people in Jerusalem about me. You must do the same in Rome."

¹²In the morning some evil people made a plan to kill Paul, and they took an oath not to eat or drink anything until they had killed him. ¹³There were more than forty men who made this plan. ¹⁴They went to the leading priests and the elders and said, "We have taken an oath

‹‹TechSupport››

FREE LONG DISTANCE

If you have high-speed Internet, odds are good that your connection provides far more bandwidth than you really need. A new kind of phone service uses all this spare network capacity to allow digital voice data to travel over the same fiber optic cables that serve up e-mail, digital downloads, and Web pages to your home.

"Voice over Internet Protocol" (VoIP) phone service is extremely affordable, with no per-minute or long-distance charges in the United States, and it works with your existing phone equipment. However, when you experience trouble in life, remember to call on God for help.

>> **22:23 threw off their coats** This showed that the people were very angry with Paul. **22:23 threw dust into the air** This showed even greater anger. **22:25 Roman citizen** Roman law said that Roman citizens must not be beaten before they had a trial. **23:2 Ananias** This is not the same man named Ananias in Acts 22:12. **23:5 'You...people.'** Quotation from Exodus 22:28.

People Skills

Defusing Arguments

When you feel a conversation quickly escalating into an argument, it's often a good idea to ask for some time to collect your thoughts. Taking a break can give you time to release the tension that may be getting in the way of honest communication. During the break, take a step back from the conflict and clarify your position. Determine what the real issue is and what needs changing. It also helps to determine what part of the issue is your responsibility and what part is not. Dealing with such details ahead of time allows you to discuss difficult issues with greater clarity and less emotion. It also doesn't hurt to pray for the other party.

not to eat or drink until we have killed Paul. [15]So this is what we want you to do: Send a message to the commander to bring Paul out to you as though you want to ask him more questions. We will be waiting to kill him while he is on the way here."

[16]But Paul's nephew heard about this plan and went to the army building and told Paul. [17]Then Paul called one of the officers and said, "Take this young man to the commander. He has a message for him."

[18]So the officer brought Paul's nephew to the commander and said, "The prisoner, Paul, asked me to bring this young man to you. He wants to tell you something."

[19]The commander took the young man's hand and led him to a place where they could be alone. He asked, "What do you want to tell me?"

[20]The young man said, "The Jews have decided to ask you to bring Paul down to their council meeting tomorrow. They want you to think they are going to ask him more questions. [21]But don't believe them! More than forty men are hiding and waiting to kill Paul. They have all taken an oath not to eat or drink until they have killed him. Now they are waiting for you to agree."

[22]The commander sent the young man away, ordering him, "Don't tell anyone that you have told me about their plan."

Paul Is Sent to Caesarea

[23]Then the commander called two officers and said, "I need some men to go to Caesarea. Get two hundred soldiers, seventy horsemen, and two hundred men with spears ready to leave at nine o'clock tonight. [24]Get some horses for Paul to ride so he can be taken to Governor Felix safely." [25]And he wrote a letter that said:

[26]From Claudius Lysias.

To the Most Excellent Governor Felix:

Greetings.

[27]Some of the Jews had taken this man and planned to kill him. But I learned that he is a Roman citizen, so I went with my soldiers and saved him. [28]I wanted to know why they were accusing him, so I brought him before their council meeting. [29]I learned that these people said Paul did some things that were wrong by their own laws, but no charge was worthy of jail or death. [30]When I was told that some of them were planning to kill Paul, I sent him to

⊙ Sexcess:
COMMUNICATION CLUES

One of the secrets to a better love life is right under our noses: our mouths. Like it or not, women love to talk and be talked to. So rather than fight a losing battle, we're better off simply learning how to become better communicators. The good news for us guys is that communication draws a couple closer, not only emotionally, but also physically. Simple things like asking your sweetie how her day was, and then listening closely to her as she shares, will do wonders for your relationship. Women are wired for sound more than sight, but as you meet her needs, you'll see yours met, also.

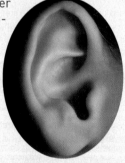

you at once. I also told them to tell you what they have against him.

[31]So the soldiers did what they were told and took Paul and brought him to the city of Antipatris that night. [32]The next day the horsemen went with Paul to Caesarea, but the other soldiers went back to the army building in Jerusalem. [33]When the horsemen came to Caesarea and gave the letter to the governor, they turned Paul over to him. [34]The governor read the letter and asked Paul, "What area are you from?" When he learned that Paul was from Cilicia, [35]he said, "I will hear your case when those who are against you come here, too." Then the governor gave orders for Paul to be kept under guard in Herod's palace.

Paul Is Accused

24 Five days later Ananias, the high priest, went to the city of Caesarea with some of the elders and a lawyer named Tertullus. They had come to make charges against Paul before the governor. [2]Paul was called into the meeting, and Tertullus began to accuse him, saying, "Most Excellent Felix! Our people enjoy much peace because of you, and many wrong things in our country are being made right through your wise help. [3]We accept these things always and in every place, and we are thankful for them. [4]But not wanting to take any more of your time, I beg you to be kind and listen to our few words. [5]We have found this man to be a troublemaker, stirring up his people everywhere in the world. He is a leader of the Nazarene group. [6]Also, he was trying to make the Temple unclean, but we stopped him. [And we wanted to judge him by our own law. [7]But the officer Lysias came and used much force to take him from us. [8]And Lysias commanded those who wanted to accuse Paul to come to you.]* By asking him questions yourself, you can decide if all these things are true." [9]The others agreed and said that all of this was true.

[10]When the governor made a sign for Paul to speak, Paul said, "Governor Felix, I know you have been a judge over this nation for a long time. So I am happy to defend myself before you. [11]You can learn for yourself that I went to worship in Jerusalem only twelve days ago. [12]Those who are accusing me did not find me arguing with anyone in the Temple or stirring up the people in the synagogues or in the city. [13]They cannot prove the things they are saying against me now. [14]But I will tell you this: I worship the God of our ancestors as a follower of the Way of Jesus. The others say that the Way of Jesus is not the right way. But I believe everything that is taught in the law of Moses and that is written in the books of the Prophets. [15]I have the same hope in God that they have—the hope that all people, good and bad, will surely be raised from the dead. [16]This is why I always try to do what I believe is right before God and people.

[17]"After being away from Jerusalem for several years, I went back to bring money to my people and to offer sacrifices. [18]I was doing this when they found me in the Temple. I had finished the cleansing ceremony and had not made any trouble; no people were gathering around me. [19]But there were some people from Asia who should be here, standing before you. If I have really done anything wrong, they

Change >> Your WORLD

HCJB WORLD RADIO

The world's first missionary broadcast organization has been touching lives around the globe for almost seventy years. Started in Ecuador, HCJB (Heralding Christ Jesus' Blessings) broadcasts in more than one hundred different languages and dialects to more than ninety countries with the passion to communicate the Good News of Jesus Christ. Besides the radio, the organization ministers through health care and training. Nationals are trained as missionaries, pastors, and health care workers to show the love of Jesus in practical ways around the globe. The radio ministry invites others to become involved through praying, going, or giving.

To change your world, visit www.hcjb.org.

are the ones who should accuse me. [20]Or ask these people here if they found any wrong in me when I stood before the council in Jerusalem. [21]But I did shout one thing when I stood before them: 'You are judging me today because I believe that people will rise from the dead!'"

[22]Felix already understood much about the Way of Jesus. He stopped the trial and said, "When commander Lysias comes here, I will decide your case." [23]Felix told the officer to keep Paul guarded but to give him some freedom and to let his friends bring what he needed.

Paul Speaks to Felix and His Wife

[24]After some days Felix came with his wife, Drusilla, who was Jewish, and asked for Paul to be brought to him. He listened to Paul talk about believing in Christ Jesus. [25]But Felix became afraid when Paul spoke about living right, self-control, and the time when God will judge the world. He said, "Go away now. When I have more time, I will call for you." [26]At the same time Felix hoped that Paul would give him some money, so he often sent for Paul and talked with him.

>> 24:6–8 **And…you.** Some Greek copies do not contain the bracketed text.

TheFinalScore >>

BASEBALL: Celebrating Family Fun

AMID UNFOLDING DRUG SCANDALS, GRUMBLINGS about overpaid professional players, and complaints the game is too slow, baseball has taken it on the chin lately. Yet, don't allow naysayers to overshadow the reality that baseball can still make its case as America's favorite pastime.

No other popular sport can claim origins dating to 1834, the first organized league in 1857, more than 70,000 books written about it, and so many statistics that *Baseball Almanac*'s interactive encyclopedia has more than 110,000 pages.

Also, there are the numerous colorful characters, such as the renowned New York Yankee player and manager Yogi Berra, asking in his inimitable way,

"If people don't want to come out to the ballpark, how are you going to stop them?"

Baseball has family ties, too. More than 350 sets of brothers have made it to the major leagues. More importantly, the sport is a source of wholesome enjoyment at countless summer picnics, family reunions, parent-child outings, and weekend getaways.

Fans of baseball would do well to heed Paul's advice in Philippians 4:8: "Think about the things that are true and honorable and right and pure...." With the game of baseball, don't allow negative headlines to distract from enjoying its family-oriented fun.

> **"Baseball has family ties, too. More than 350 sets of brothers have made it to the major leagues."**

27But after two years, Felix was replaced by Porcius Festus as governor. But Felix had left Paul in prison to please the Jews.

Paul Asks to See Caesar

25 Three days after Festus became governor, he went from Caesarea to Jerusalem. 2There the leading priests and the important leaders made charges against Paul before Festus. 3They asked Festus to do them a favor. They wanted him to send Paul back to Jerusalem, because they had a plan to kill him on the way. 4But Festus answered that Paul would be kept in Caesarea and that he himself was returning there soon. 5He said, "Some of your leaders should go with me. They can accuse the man there in Caesarea, if he has really done something wrong."

6Festus stayed in Jerusalem another eight or ten days and then went back to Caesarea. The next day he told the soldiers to bring Paul before him. Festus was seated on the judge's seat 7when Paul came into the room. The people who had come from Jerusalem stood around him, making serious charges against him, which they could not prove. 8This is what Paul said to defend himself: "I have done nothing wrong against the law, against the Temple, or against Caesar."

9But Festus wanted to please the people. So he asked Paul, "Do you want to go to Jerusalem for me to judge you there on these charges?"

10Paul said, "I am standing at Caesar's judgment seat now, where I should be judged. I have done nothing wrong to them; you know this is true. 11If I have done something wrong and the law says I must die, I do not ask to be saved from death. But if these charges are not true, then no one can give me to them. I want Caesar to hear my case!"

12Festus talked about this with his advisers. Then he said, "You have asked to see Caesar, so you will go to Caesar!"

Paul Before King Agrippa

13A few days later King Agrippa and Bernice came to Caesarea to visit Festus. 14They stayed there for some time, and Festus told the king about Paul's case. Festus said, "There is a man that Felix left in prison. 15When I went to Jerusalem, the leading priests and the elders there made charges against him, asking me to sentence him to death. 16But I answered, 'When a man is accused of a crime, Romans do not hand him over until he has been allowed to face his accusers and defend himself against their charges.' 17So when these people came here to Caesarea for the trial, I did not waste time. The next day I sat on the judge's seat and commanded that the man be brought in. 18They stood up and accused him, but not of any serious crime as I thought they would. 19The things they said were about their own religion and about a man named Jesus who died. But Paul said that he is still alive. 20Not knowing how to find out about these questions, I asked Paul, 'Do you want to go to Jerusalem and be judged there?' 21But he asked to be kept in Caesarea. He wants a decision from the emperor.* So I ordered that he be held until I could send him to Caesar."

22Agrippa said to Festus, "I would also like to hear this man myself."

Q: Will God really answer my prayers?

A: Yes. If your request is aligned with the promises of Scripture, then the answer is "yes." If not, then the answer is "no." If it is a request that is not covered by Scripture, then you can trust that God will act with your best interest at heart (2 Corinthians 1:20).

The Bottom Line

Investing: Select What You Know

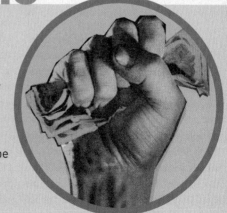

WHEN OIL PRICES SKYROCKET, OIL STOCKS ATTRACT INVESTORS' ATTENTION. At other times, it is real estate, gold, or inventions promising to conserve energy or revolutionize modern lifestyles. Be careful before investing in anything you don't understand. A company may be involved in a multi-billion-dollar industry, but that doesn't mean that particular firm will be profitable. Remember, if it sounds too good to be true, chances are it is. In the parable found in Luke 19:11–27, Jesus commended servants who used their master's money wisely. You, too, should be careful when putting money to work.

>> **25:21 emperor** The ruler of the Roman Empire, which was almost all the known world.

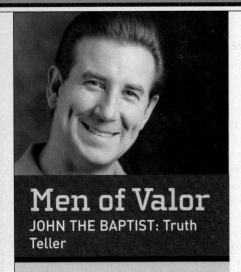

Men of Valor

JOHN THE BAPTIST: Truth Teller

John the Baptist earned his name for baptizing people, but his primary role was proclaiming Christ's coming before Jesus' public ministry began. John said Jesus would baptize people with the Holy Spirit and fire. In modern terms, John is best described as a nonconformist: living in the desert, clothed in camel's hair and a leather belt, eating locusts and honey. Ultimately, John was beheaded after telling King Herod he was wrong for taking his brother's wife as a bride. Telling the truth can be costly when it offends the rich and powerful, but John is renowned to this day for his courage.

Festus said, "Tomorrow you will hear him." ²³The next day Agrippa and Bernice appeared with great show, acting like very important people. They went into the judgment room with the army leaders and the important men of Caesarea. Then Festus ordered the soldiers to bring Paul in. ²⁴Festus said, "King Agrippa and all who are gathered here with us, you see this man. All the people, here and in Jerusalem, have complained to me about him, shouting that he should not live any longer. ²⁵When I judged him, I found no

reason to order his death. But since he asked to be judged by Caesar, I decided to send him. ²⁶But I have nothing definite to write the emperor about him. So I have brought him before all of you—especially you, King Agrippa. I hope you can question him and give me something to write. ²⁷I think it is foolish to send a prisoner to Caesar without telling what charges are against him."

Paul Defends Himself

26 Agrippa said to Paul, "You may now speak to defend yourself."

Then Paul raised his hand and began to speak. ²He said, "King Agrippa, I am very blessed to stand before you and will answer all the charges the evil people make against me. ³You know so much about all the customs and the things they argue about, so please listen to me patiently.

⁴"All my people know about my whole life, how I lived from the beginning in my own country and later in Jerusalem. ⁵They have known me for a long time. If they want to, they can tell you that I was a good Pharisee. And the Pharisees obey the laws of my tradition more carefully than any other group. ⁶Now I am on trial because I hope for the promise that God made to our ancestors. ⁷This is the promise that the twelve tribes of our people hope to receive as they serve God day and night. My king, they have accused me because I hope for this same promise! ⁸Why do any of you people think it is impossible for God to raise people from the dead?

⁹"I, too, thought I ought to do many things against Jesus from Nazareth. ¹⁰And that is what I did in Jerusalem. The leading priests gave me the power to put many of God's people in jail, and when they were being killed, I agreed it was a good thing. ¹¹In every synagogue, I often punished them and tried to make them speak against Jesus. I was so angry against them I even went to other cities to find them and punish them.

¹²"One time the leading priests gave me permission and the power to go to Damascus. ¹³On the way there, at noon, I saw a light from heaven. It was brighter than the sun and flashed all around me and those who were traveling with me. ¹⁴We all fell to the

ground. Then I heard a voice speaking to me in the Hebrew language," saying, 'Saul, Saul, why are you persecuting me? You are only hurting yourself by fighting me.' ¹⁵I said, 'Who are you, Lord?' The Lord said, 'I am Jesus, the one you are persecuting. ¹⁶Stand up! I have chosen you to be my servant and my witness—you will tell people the things that you have seen and the things that I will show you. This is why I have come to you today. ¹⁷I will keep you safe from your own people and also from the others. I am sending you to them ¹⁸to open their eyes so that they may turn away from darkness to the light, away from the power of Satan and to God. Then their sins can be forgiven, and they can have a place with those people who have been made holy by believing in me.'

¹⁹"King Agrippa, after I had this vision from heaven, I obeyed it. ²⁰I began telling people that they should change their hearts and lives and turn to God and do things to show they really had changed. I told this first to those in Damascus, then in Jerusalem, and in every part of Judea, and also to the other people. ²¹This is why the Jews took me and were trying to kill me in the Temple. ²²But God has helped me, and so I stand here today, telling all people, small and great, what I have seen. But I am saying only what Moses and the prophets said would happen—²³that the Christ would die, and as the first to rise from the dead, he would bring light to all people."

Paul Tries to Persuade Agrippa

²⁴While Paul was saying these things to defend himself, Festus said loudly, "Paul, you are out of your mind! Too much study has driven you crazy!"

²⁵Paul said, "Most excellent Festus, I am not crazy. My words are true and sensible. ²⁶King Agrippa knows about these things, and I can speak freely to him. I know he has heard about all of these things, because they did not happen off in a corner. ²⁷King Agrippa, do you believe what the prophets wrote? I know you believe."

²⁸King Agrippa said to Paul, "Do you think you can persuade me to become a Christian in such a short time?"

>> 26:14 **Hebrew language** Or Aramaic, the languages of many people in this region in the first century.

²⁹Paul said, "Whether it is a short or a long time, I pray to God that not only you but every person listening to me today would be saved and be like me—except for these chains I have."

³⁰Then King Agrippa, Governor Festus, Bernice, and all the people sitting with them stood up ³¹and left the room. Talking to each other, they said, "There is no reason why this man should die or be put in jail." ³²And Agrippa said to Festus, "We could let this man go free, but he has asked Caesar to hear his case."

Paul Sails for Rome

27 It was decided that we would sail for Italy. An officer named Julius, who served in the emperor's* army, guarded Paul and some other prisoners. ²We got on a ship that was from the city of Adramyttium and was about to sail to different ports in Asia. Aristarchus, a man from the city of Thessalonica in Macedonia, went with us. ³The next day we came to Sidon. Julius was very good to Paul and gave him freedom to go visit his friends, who took care of his needs. ⁴We left Sidon and sailed close to the island of Cyprus, because the wind was blowing against us. ⁵We went across the sea by Cilicia and Pamphylia and landed at the city of Myra, in Lycia. ⁶There the officer found a ship from Alexandria that was going to Italy, so he put us on it.

⁷We sailed slowly for many days. We had a hard time reaching Cnidus because the wind was blowing against us, and we could not go any farther. So we sailed by the south side of the island of Crete near Salmone. ⁸Sailing past it was hard. Then we came to a place called Fair Havens, near the city of Lasea.

⁹We had lost much time, and it was now dangerous to sail, because it was already after the Day of Cleansing.* So Paul warned them, ¹⁰"Men, I can see there will be a lot of trouble on this trip. The ship, the cargo, and even our lives may be lost." ¹¹But the captain and the owner of the ship did not agree with Paul, and the officer believed what the captain and owner of the ship said. ¹²Since that harbor was not a good place for the ship to stay for the winter, most of the men decided that the ship should leave. They hoped we could go to Phoenix and stay there for the winter. Phoenix, a city on the island of Crete, had a harbor which faced southwest and northwest.

The Storm

¹³When a good wind began to blow from the south, the men on the ship thought, "This is the wind we wanted, and now we have it." So they pulled up the anchor, and we sailed very close to the island of Crete. ¹⁴But then a very strong wind named the "northeaster" came from the island. ¹⁵The ship was caught in it and could not sail against it. So we stopped trying and let the wind carry us. ¹⁶When we went below a small island named Cauda, we were barely able to bring in the lifeboat. ¹⁷After the men took the lifeboat in, they tied ropes around the ship to hold it together. The men were afraid that the ship would hit the sandbanks of

Q: What does God think of divorce?

A: God hates divorce. Nevertheless, even though divorce runs counter to his desire for people due to the pain it causes, the Bible does specify that divorce is permitted in the case of marital unfaithfulness (Malachi 2:16; Matthew 19:3–9).

Get Fit

MONITORING BLOOD PRESSURE You may think high blood pressure is only a problem for the elderly, but you're wrong. Most men who develop the condition get it in their mid-30s. Unlike other dangerous physical conditions, high blood pressure has almost no symptoms at all—until it's too late. To ensure that you're not at risk, have your blood pressure checked several times every year, even if it means doing it for free at the local drugstore. If your blood pressure rate repeatedly comes back higher than 120/80, consider seeing your family physician. Regardless of the reading, work to lower your blood pressure by taking good care of yourself. And don't forget to pray about it.

>> **27:1 emperor** The ruler of the Roman Empire, which was almost all the known world. **27:9 Day of Cleansing** An important Jewish holy day in the fall of the year. This was the time of year that bad storms arose on the sea.

FOR Men Only

FAITHFULNESS Faithfulness is the cornerstone of any relationship, but it is particularly important when it comes to marriage. The entire marital bond is predicated on mutual trust and commitment to faithfulness. It is as much a matter of the heart as it is of actions. As Jesus said in Matthew 5:28, "If anyone looks at a woman and wants to sin sexually with her, in his mind he has already done that sin with the woman." Remaining faithful in word, thought, and deed is no small task in today's sex-saturated society, but through the grace and help of God, it is an achievable one.

LISTEN

Syrtis," so they lowered the sail and let the wind carry the ship. ¹⁸The next day the storm was blowing us so hard that the men threw out some of the cargo. ¹⁹A day later with their own hands they threw out the ship's equipment. ²⁰When we could not see the sun or the stars for many days, and the storm was very bad, we lost all hope of being saved.

²¹After the men had gone without food for a long time, Paul stood up before them and said, "Men, you should have listened to me. You should not have sailed from Crete. Then you would not have all this trouble and loss. ²²But now I tell you to cheer up because none of you will die. Only the ship will be lost. ²³Last night an angel came to me from the God I belong to and worship. ²⁴The angel said, 'Paul, do not be afraid. You must stand before Caesar. And God has promised you that he will save the lives of everyone sailing with you.' ²⁵So men, have courage. I trust in God that everything will happen as his angel told me. ²⁶But we will crash on an island."

²⁷On the fourteenth night we were still being carried around in the Adriatic Sea." About midnight the sailors thought we were close to land, ²⁸so they lowered a rope with a weight on the end of it into the water. They found that the water was one hundred twenty feet deep. They went a little farther and lowered the rope again. It was ninety feet deep. ²⁹The sailors were afraid that we would hit the rocks, so they threw four anchors into the water and prayed for daylight to come. ³⁰Some of the sailors wanted to leave the ship, and they lowered the lifeboat, pretending they were throwing more anchors from

the front of the ship. ³¹But Paul told the officer and the other soldiers, "If these men do not stay in the ship, your lives cannot be saved." ³²So the soldiers cut the ropes and let the lifeboat fall into the water.

³³Just before dawn Paul began persuading all the people to eat something. He said, "For the past fourteen days you have been waiting and watching and not eating. ³⁴Now I beg you to eat something. You need it to stay alive. None of you will lose even one hair off your heads." ³⁵After he said this, Paul took some bread and thanked God for it before all of them. He broke off a piece and began eating. ³⁶They all felt better and started eating, too. ³⁷There were two hundred seventy-six people on the ship. ³⁸When they had eaten all they wanted, they began making the ship lighter by throwing the grain into the sea.

The Ship Is Destroyed

³⁹When daylight came, the sailors saw land. They did not know what land it was, but they saw a bay with a beach and wanted to sail the ship to the beach if they could. ⁴⁰So they cut the ropes to the anchors and left the anchors in the sea. At the same time, they untied the ropes that were holding the rudders. Then they raised the front sail into the wind and sailed toward the beach. ⁴¹But the ship hit a sandbank. The front of the ship stuck there and could not move, but the back of the ship began to break up from the big waves.

⁴²The soldiers decided to kill the prisoners so none of them could swim away and escape. ⁴³But Julius, the officer, wanted to let Paul live and did not allow the soldiers to kill the prisoners. Instead he ordered everyone who could swim to jump into the water first and swim to land. ⁴⁴The rest were to follow using wooden boards or pieces of the ship. And this is how all the people made it safely to land.

Paul on the Island of Malta

28 When we were safe on land, we learned that the island was called Malta. ²The people who lived there were very good to us. Because it was raining and very cold, they made a fire and welcomed all of us. ³Paul gathered a pile of sticks and was putting them on the fire when a poisonous snake came out because of the heat and bit him on the hand. ⁴The people living on the island saw the snake hanging from Paul's hand and said to each other, "This man must be a murderer! He did not die in the sea, but Justice" does not want him to live." ⁵But Paul shook the snake off into the fire and was not hurt. ⁶The people thought that Paul would swell up or fall down dead. They waited and watched him for a long time, but nothing bad happened to him. So they changed their minds and said, "He is a god!"

⁷There were some fields around there owned by Publius, an important man on the island. He welcomed us into his home and was very good to us for three days. ⁸Publius' father was sick with a fever and dysentery." Paul went to him, prayed, and put his hands on the man and healed him. ⁹After this, all the other sick people on the island came to Paul, and he healed them, too. ¹⁰⁻¹¹The people on the island

>> **27:17 Syrtis** Shallow area in the sea near the Libyan coast.   **27:27 Adriatic Sea** The sea between Greece and Italy, including the central Mediterranean.   **28:4 Justice** The people thought there was a god named Justice who would punish bad people.   **28:8 dysentery** A sickness like diarrhea.

gave us many honors. When we were ready to leave, three months later, they gave us the things we needed.

Paul Goes to Rome

We got on a ship from Alexandria that had stayed on the island during the winter. On the front of the ship was the sign of the twin gods." ¹²We stopped at Syracuse for three days. ¹³From there we sailed to Rhegium. The next day a wind began to blow from the south, and a day later we came to Puteoli. ¹⁴We found some believers there who asked us to stay with them for a week. Finally, we came to Rome. ¹⁵The believers in Rome heard that we were there and came out as far as the Market of Appius" and the Three Inns" to meet us. When Paul saw them, he was encouraged and thanked God.

Paul in Rome

¹⁶When we arrived at Rome, Paul was allowed to live alone, with the soldier who guarded him.

¹⁷Three days later Paul sent for the leaders there. When they came together, he said, "Brothers, I have done nothing against our people or the customs of our ancestors. But I was arrested in Jerusalem and given to the Romans. ¹⁸After they asked me many questions, they could find no reason why I should be killed. They wanted to let me go free, ¹⁹but the evil people there argued against that. So I had to ask to come to Rome to have my trial before Caesar. But I have no charge to bring against my own people. ²⁰That is why I wanted to see you and talk with you. I am bound with this chain because I believe in the hope of Israel."

²¹They answered Paul, "We have received no letters from Judea about you. None of our Jewish brothers who have come from there brought news or told us anything bad about you. ²²But we want to hear your ideas, because we know that people everywhere are speaking against this religious group."

²³Paul and the people chose a day for a meeting and on that day many more of the Jews met with Paul at the place he was staying. He spoke to them all day long. Using the law of Moses and the prophets' writings, he explained the kingdom of God, and he tried to persuade them to believe these things about Jesus. ²⁴Some believed what Paul said, but others did not. ²⁵So they argued and began leaving after Paul said one more thing to them: "The Holy Spirit spoke the truth to your ancestors through Isaiah the prophet, saying,

²⁶'Go to this people and say:
You will listen and listen, but you will not understand.
    You will look and look, but you will not learn,
²⁷because these people have become stubborn.
    They don't hear with their ears,
    and they have closed their eyes.
Otherwise, they might really understand
    what they see with their eyes
    and hear with their ears.
They might really understand in their minds
    and come back to me and be healed.'   *Isaiah 6:9–10*

²⁸"I want you to know that God has also sent his salvation to all nations, and they will listen!" [²⁹After Paul said this, the Jews left. They were arguing very much with each other.]"

³⁰Paul stayed two full years in his own rented house and welcomed all people who came to visit him. ³¹He boldly preached about the kingdom of God and taught about the Lord Jesus Christ, and no one stopped him.

Survival Guide

GARDENS: REAPING REWARDS

The Bible has numerous references to planting and reaping. Planting a garden will help you understand those references while yielding tasty vegetables. Starting one isn't difficult; all you need is a well-drained plot of ground. Many states have agricultural agencies that will test your soil and advise you about how to fertilize it. Seeds can be purchased at a garden supply store. Even apartment dwellers can use planting boxes for such crops as tomatoes, beans, or peppers. Watching plants develop over time will help you appreciate how God nurtures us spiritually.

 28:10–11 twin gods Statues of Castor and Pollux, gods in old Greek tales.   **28:15 Market of Appius** A town about twenty-seven miles from Rome.   **28:15 Three Inns** A town about thirty miles from Rome.   **28:29 After . . . other.** Some Greek copies do not contain the bracketed text.

THE **LETTER** OF PAUL THE APOSTLE TO THE
Romans

AUTHOR: ROMANS
DATE WRITTEN: A.D. 57

IMAGINE YOU ARE DRIVING INTO UNFAMILIAR

territory and you make a wrong turn. It looks like the right exit off the highway, but it turns out to be a wrong move. Everyone makes wrong moves in some area of life. In his letter to the Romans, the apostle Paul writes to the Christians of Rome about the consequences of making such moves.

Paul presents a convincing case that everyone has sinned and fallen short of God's course for life. As he points out, it is because of God's amazing grace, coupled with simple faith in the redeeming work of Jesus Christ's sacrifice, that the church has been set on the right path. Paul shows that through following God's map, the Roman road to salvation, believers are able to gain freedom over the power of sin.

The majority of this letter presents the Roman Christians with a compelling argument for following Jesus. The final chapters of Paul's letter turn to practical matters for the growing church, including his thoughts on spiritual gifts, good citizenship, and church government.

1 From Paul, a servant of Christ Jesus. God called me to be an apostle and chose me to tell the Good News.

[2]God promised this Good News long ago through his prophets, as it is written in the Holy Scriptures. [3-4]The Good News is about God's Son, Jesus Christ our Lord. As a man, he was born from the family of David. But through the Spirit of holiness he was declared to be God's Son with great power by rising from the dead. [5]Through Christ, God gave me the special work of an apostle, which was to lead people of all nations to believe and obey. I do this work for him. [6]And you who are in Rome are also called to belong to Jesus Christ.

[7]To all of you in Rome whom God loves and has called to be his holy people:

Grace and peace to you from God our Father and the Lord Jesus Christ.

A Prayer of Thanks

[8]First I want to say that I thank my God through Jesus Christ for all of you, because people everywhere in the world are talking about your faith. [9]God, whom I serve with my whole heart by telling the Good News about his Son, knows that I always mention you [10]every time I pray. I pray that I will be allowed to come to you, and this will happen if God wants it. [11]I want very much to see you, to give you some spiritual gift to make you strong. [12]I mean that I want us to help each other with the faith we have. Your faith will help me, and my faith will help you. [13]Brothers and sisters, I want you to know that I planned many times to come to you, but this has not been possible. I wanted to come so that I could help you grow spiritually as I have helped the other non-Jewish people.

[14]I have a duty to all people—Greeks and those who are not Greeks, the wise and the foolish. [15]That is why I want so much to preach the Good News to you in Rome.

[16]I am not ashamed of the Good News, because it is the power God uses to save everyone who believes—to save the Jews first, and then to save non-Jews. [17]The Good News shows how God makes people right with himself—that it begins and ends with faith. As the Scripture says, "But those who are right with God will live by faith."[n]

>> live the life

Romans 1:16–17

The Principle > Share your faith boldly.

Practicing It > Invite your friends to attend church with you. After the service, share lunch and ask them to tell you about their thoughts about your church and about God. Afterward, tell them about your own relationship with God.

<<TechSupport>>

ONLINE JOURNALS

There is a better way than e-mail to stay in touch with family, and friends—your own on-line journal. Services like Xanga.com and LiveJournal.com make it free and easy to get started. Send out an e-mail containing your new Web site address, and ask your family members and friends to bookmark it. The rest is up to you. Travel logs, diaries, and hobby advice make great content for an online journal. You might even use one to document your journey as a follower of Jesus Christ and share your insights as a believer with others.

All People Have Done Wrong

[18]God's anger is shown from heaven against all the evil and wrong things people do. By their own evil lives they hide the truth. [19]God shows his anger because some knowledge of him has been made clear to them. Yes, God has shown himself to them. [20]There are things about him that people cannot see—his eternal power and all the things that make him God. But since the beginning of the world those things have been easy to understand by what God has made. So people have no excuse for the bad things they do. [21]They knew God, but they did not give glory to God or thank him. Their thinking became useless. Their foolish minds were filled with darkness. [22]They said they were wise, but they became fools. [23]They traded the glory of God who lives forever for the worship of idols made to look like earthly people, birds, animals, and snakes.

[24]Because they did these things, God left them and let them go their sinful way, wanting only to do evil. As a result, they became full of sexual sin, using their bodies wrongly with each other. [25]They traded the truth of God for a lie. They worshiped and served what had been created instead of the God who created those things, who should be praised forever. Amen.

[26]Because people did those things, God left them and let them do the shameful things they wanted to do. Women stopped having natural sex and started having sex with other women. [27]In the same way, men stopped having natural sex and began wanting each other. Men did shameful things with other men, and in their bodies they received the punishment for those wrongs.

[28]People did not think it was important to have a true knowledge of God. So God left them and allowed them to have their own worthless thinking and to do things they should not do. [29]They are filled with every kind of sin, evil, selfishness, and hatred. They are full of jealousy, murder, fighting, lying, and thinking the worst about each

>> 1:17 "But those ... faith." Quotation from Habakkuk 2:4.

other. They gossip [30]and say evil things about each other. They hate God. They are rude and conceited and brag about themselves. They invent ways of doing evil. They do not obey their parents. [31]They are foolish, they do not keep their promises, and they show no kindness or mercy to others. [32]They know God's law says that those who live like this should die. But they themselves not only continue to do these evil things, they applaud others who do them.

You People Also Are Sinful

2 If you think you can judge others, you are wrong. When you judge them, you are really judging yourself guilty, because you do the same things they do. [2]God judges those who do wrong things, and we know that his judging is right. [3]You judge those who do wrong, but you do wrong yourselves. Do you think you will be able to escape the judgment of God? [4]He has been very kind and patient, waiting for you to change, but you think nothing of his kindness. Perhaps you do not understand that God is kind to you so you will change your hearts and lives. [5]But you are stubborn and refuse to change, so you are making your own punishment even greater on the day he shows his anger. On that day everyone will see God's right judgments. [6]God will reward or punish every person for what that person has done. [7]Some people, by always continuing to do good, live for God's glory, for honor, and for life that has no end. God will give them life forever. [8]But other people are selfish. They refuse to follow

truth and, instead, follow evil. God will give them his punishment and anger. [9]He will give trouble and suffering to everyone who does evil—to the Jews first and also to those who are not Jews. [10]But he will give glory, honor, and peace to everyone who does good—to the Jews first and also to those who are not Jews. [11]For God judges all people in the same way.

[12]People who do not have the law and who are sinners will be lost, although they do not have the law. And, in the same way, those who have the law and are sinners will be judged by the law. [13]Hearing the law does not make people right with God. It is those who obey the law who will be right with him. [14](Those who are not Jews do not have the law, but when they freely do what the law commands, they are the law for themselves. This is true even though they do not have the law. [15]They show that in their hearts they know what is right and wrong, just as the law commands. And they show this by their consciences. Sometimes their thoughts tell them they did wrong, and sometimes their thoughts tell them they did right.) [16]All these things will happen on the day when God, through Christ Jesus, will judge people's secret thoughts. The Good News that I preach says this.

The Jews and the Law

[17]What about you? You call yourself a Jew. You trust in the law of Moses and brag that you are close to God. [18]You know what he wants you to do and what is important, because you have learned the law. [19]You think you are a guide for the blind and a light for those who are in darkness. [20]You think you can show foolish people what is right and teach those who know nothing. You have the law; so you think you know everything and have all truth. [21]You teach others, so why don't you teach yourself? You tell others not to steal, but you steal. [22]You say that others must not take part in adultery, but you are guilty of that sin. You hate idols, but you steal from temples. [23]You brag about having God's law, but you bring shame to God by breaking his law, [24]just as the Scriptures say: "Those who are not Jews speak against God's name because of you."

Q: What is the Trinity?

A: The word "trinity" refers to the three persons of the Godhead—God the Father, God the Son, and God the Holy Spirit. Although there is one God, he has chosen to reveal himself to us through these three distinct but unified personal expressions of his being.

▶ Get Aligned

Romans 2:13

THE BIBLE SPEAKS REPEATEDLY ABOUT ACTING UPON GOD'S WORD. From the Lord declaring his desire for obedience above sacrifice in the Old Testament to the parables of Jesus in the New Testament, the message is clear: following God is not just about hearing; it's about doing.

So why is that message repeated so often throughout the Bible? Because long before Jesus came to this earth, we made following God a religion. We turned his relationship with us into a rite that excused us from sin. In Paul's time, he dealt with Jews—those who

were God's chosen people, but who had rejected his only Son. They believed that simply by being Jewish they were right with God.

Today we deal with the same attitude of inherited faith. Neither having familial relationships nor sitting in a church building will get you into heaven. Only believing in Jesus will enable that to happen. That confession of faith leads to a living, active faith, which by nature requires doing. Even though we are free from a works-related faith, truly following God will always require action on our part.

▶▶ 2:24 "Those...you." Quotation from Isaiah 52:5; Ezekiel 36:20.

²⁵If you follow the law, your circumcision has meaning. But if you break the law, it is as if you were never circumcised. ²⁶People who are not Jews are not circumcised, but if they do what the law says, it is as if they were circumcised. ²⁷You Jews have the written law and circumcision, but you break the law. So those who are not circumcised in their bodies, but still obey the law, will show that you are guilty. ²⁸They can do this because a person is not a true Jew if he is only a Jew in his physical body; true circumcision is not only on the outside of the body. ²⁹A person is a Jew only if he is a Jew inside; true circumcision is done in the heart by the Spirit, not by the written law. Such a person gets praise from God rather than from people.

3 So, do Jews have anything that other people do not have? Is there anything special about being circumcised? ²Yes, of course, there is in every way. The most important thing is this: God trusted the Jews with his teachings. ³If some Jews were not faithful to him, will that stop God from doing what he promised? ⁴No! God will continue to be true even when every person is false. As the Scriptures say:

"So you will be shown to be right when you speak,
and you will win your case." *Psalm 51:4*

⁵When we do wrong, that shows more clearly that God is right. So can we say that God is wrong to punish us? (I am talking as people might talk.) ⁶No! If God could not punish us, he could not judge the world.

⁷A person might say, "When I lie, it really gives him glory, because my lie shows God's truth. So why am I judged a sinner?" ⁸It would be the same to say, "We should do evil so that good will come." Some people find fault with us and say we teach this, but they are wrong and deserve the punishment they will receive.

All People Are Guilty

⁹So are we Jews better than others? No! We have already said that Jews and those who are not Jews are all guilty of sin. ¹⁰As the Scriptures say:

"There is no one who always does what is right,
not even one.
¹¹There is no one who understands.
There is no one who looks to God for help.
¹²All have turned away.
Together, everyone has become useless.
There is no one who does anything good;
there is not even one." *Psalm 14:1–3*
¹³"Their throats are like open graves;
they use their tongues for telling lies." *Psalm 5:9*
"Their words are like snake poison." *Psalm 140:3*
¹⁴ "Their mouths are full of cursing and hate." *Psalm 10:7*
¹⁵"They are always ready to kill people.
¹⁶ Everywhere they go they cause ruin and misery.
¹⁷They don't know how to live in peace." *Isaiah 59:7–8*
¹⁸ "They have no fear of God." *Psalm 36:1*

¹⁹We know that the law's commands are for those who have the law. This stops all excuses and brings the whole world under God's judgment, ²⁰because no one can be made right with God by following the law. The law only shows us our sin.

How God Makes People Right

²¹But God has a way to make people right with him without the law, and he has now shown us that way which the law and the prophets told us about. ²²God makes people right with himself through their faith in Jesus Christ. This is true for all who believe in Christ, because all people are the same: ²³Everyone has sinned and fallen short of God's glorious standard, ²⁴and all need to be made right with God by his grace, which is a free gift. They need to be made free from sin through Jesus Christ. ²⁵God sent him to die in our place to take away our sins. We receive forgiveness through faith in the blood of Jesus' death. This showed that God always does what is right and fair, as in the past when he was patient and did not punish people for their sins. ²⁶And God gave Jesus to show today that he does what is right. God did this so he could judge rightly and so he could make right any person who has faith in Jesus.

²⁷So do we have a reason to brag about ourselves? No! And why not? It is the way of faith that stops all bragging, not the way of trying to obey the law. ²⁸A person is made right with God through faith, not through obeying the law. ²⁹Is God only the God of the Jews? Is he not also the God of those who are not Jews? ³⁰Of course he is, because

▶Get Aligned
Romans 3:22

BEING RIGHT WITH GOD IS HAVING THE ABILITY TO BE IN RELATIONSHIP WITH HIM. Before Christ, only a high priest could walk into God's presence once a year. People experienced God from afar because their sinfulness disqualified them from intimacy with him. Now, we're free to commune with the God of the universe.

But have you ever thought about what it really took to make you right with God? In Old Testament times, a payment was required to make amends for a sin. That price was an unblemished lamb. Sacrificing the animal paid off the debt of people's sin and settled their account with God. But paying off the ultimate debt—the sinfulness of all people for all time—called for a remarkable price: the perfect, spotless Lamb of God, Jesus Christ. Only his blood could cancel the punishment for our sinfulness, which was death and separation from God.

When Christ offered himself to be slaughtered, he took on the wrath of God toward all sin. He faced every ounce of God's just fury and experienced anguish we cannot fathom. Yet he settled the score. In order for us to join him in relationship with the Father, Jesus made us right before God.

there is only one God. He will make Jews right with him by their faith, and he will also make those who are not Jews right with him through their faith. ³¹So do we destroy the law by following the way of faith? No! Faith causes us to be what the law truly wants.

FACT-OIDS! Forty-four percent of American Internet users say they use online banking. [Pew Internet and American Life Project]

The Example of Abraham

4 So what can we say that Abraham,ⁿ the father of our people, learned about faith? ²If Abraham was made right by the things he did, he had a reason to brag. But this is not God's view, ³because the Scripture says, "Abraham believed God, and God accepted Abraham's faith, and that faith made him right with God."ⁿ

⁴When people work, their pay is not given as a gift, but as something earned. ⁵But people cannot do any work that will make them right with God. So they must trust in him, who makes even evil people right in his sight. Then God accepts their faith, and that makes them right with him. ⁶David said the same thing. He said that people are truly blessed when God, without paying attention to their deeds, makes people right with himself.

⁷"Blessed are they
  whose sins are forgiven,
  whose wrongs are pardoned.
⁸Blessed is the person
  whom the Lord does not consider
  guilty."   *Psalm 32:1–2*

⁹Is this blessing only for those who are circumcised or also for those who are not circumcised? We have already said that God accepted Abraham's faith and that faith made him right with God. ¹⁰So how did this happen? Did God accept Abraham before or after he was circumcised? It was before his circumcision. ¹¹Abraham was circumcised to show that he was right with God through faith before he was circumcised. So Abraham is the father of all those who believe but are not circumcised; he is the father of all believers who are accepted as being right with God. ¹²And Abraham is also the father of those who have been circumcised and who live following the faith that our father Abraham had before he was circumcised.

God Keeps His Promise

¹³Abrahamⁿ and his descendants received the promise that they would get the whole world. He did not receive that promise through the law, but through being right with God by his faith. ¹⁴If people could receive what God promised by following the law, then faith is worthless. And God's promise to Abraham is worthless, ¹⁵because the law can only bring God's anger. But if there is no law, there is nothing to disobey.

¹⁶So people receive God's promise by having faith. This happens so the promise can be a free gift. Then all of Abraham's children can have that promise. It is not only for those who live under the law of Moses but for anyone who lives with faith like that of Abraham, who is the father of us all. ¹⁷As it is written in the Scriptures: "I am making you a father of many nations."ⁿ This is true before God, the God Abraham believed, the God who gives life to the dead and who creates something out of nothing.

¹⁸There was no hope that Abraham would have children. But Abraham believed God and continued hoping, and so he became the father of many nations. As God told him, "Your descendants also will be too many to count."ⁿ ¹⁹Abraham was almost a hundred years old, much past the age for having children, and Sarah could not have children. Abraham thought about all this, but his faith in God did not become weak. ²⁰He never doubted that God would keep his promise, and he never stopped believing. He grew stronger in his faith and gave praise to God. ²¹Abraham felt sure that God was able to do what he had promised. ²²So, "God accepted Abraham's faith, and that faith made him right with God."ⁿ ²³Those words ("God accepted Abraham's faith") were written not only for Abraham ²⁴but also for us. God will accept us also because we believe in the One who raised Jesus our Lord from the dead. ²⁵Jesus was given to die for our sins, and he was raised from the dead to make us right with God.

Right with God

5 Since we have been made right with God by our faith, we haveⁿ peace with God. This happened through our Lord Jesus Christ, ²who through our faithⁿ has brought

{Book of the Month}

Good to Great
by Jim Collins

Former Stanford Business School professor Jim Collins started with a simple question: Why do so few companies make the leap from good to great? What followed was an exhaustive quantitative study of Fortune 500 companies by Collins and his team of student researchers. After defining the terms "good" and "great," Collins then offered the key factors that led to the move to the next level. *Good to Great* is a useful template for transforming any good organization into a great one. Collins, while popular with business leaders, also has a lot to say about personal effectiveness, family leadership, and non-profit/church stewardship.

GOOD TO GREAT JIM COLLINS

4:1, 13 Abraham Most respected ancestor of the Jews. Every Jew hoped to see Abraham.   **4:3 "Abraham … God."** Quotation from Genesis 15:6.   **4:17 "I … nations."** Quotation from Genesis 17:5.   **4:18 "Your … count."** Quotation from Genesis 15:5.   **4:22 "God … God."** Quotation from Genesis 15:6.   **5:1 we have** Some Greek copies read "let us have."   **5:2 through our faith** Some Greek copies do not have this phrase.

>>May

QUOTE OF THE MONTH:
"Everything that can be counted doesn't necessarily count; everything that counts can't necessarily be counted."
—Albert Einstein

1 Change your home's air filter.

2

3

4 Volunteer to coach a Little League team.

5 Pray for your family and close friends.

6

7

8 Memorize Philippians 4:8.

9 Pray for a person of influence: Today is musician **Billy Joel's** birthday.

10 Clean the grill as preparation for **Memorial Day** cookouts.

11

12

13 Tune up your bike and hit the road with a buddy for the day.

14 Pray for a person of influence: Today is director **George Lucas's** birthday.

15

16 Learn to change the oil in your car.

17 Write a thank-you note to someone you are thankful for.

18

19

20 Celebrate **Armed Forces Day** by praying for families separated by war.

21

22 Return any overdue movie rentals.

23 Pray for a person of influence: Today is comedian **Drew Carey's** birthday.

24 Plan to celebrate **Memorial Day** with loved ones.

25

26

27

28 Read the **Book of James** and then act on it.

29

30 Fly the American flag with pride.

31 Pray for a person of influence: Today is director **Clint Eastwood's** birthday.

>> live the life

Romans 5:1–2

The Principle > Enjoy peace with God.

Practicing It > God is always ready to forgive us, but sometimes we are not as willing to forgive ourselves. If you are still condemning yourself for some mistake you've made in the past, make the decision to let it go.

us into that blessing of God's grace that we now enjoy. And we are happy because of the hope we have of sharing God's glory. ³We also have joy with our troubles, because we know that these troubles produce patience. ⁴And patience produces character, and character produces hope. ⁵And this hope will never disappoint us, because God has poured out his love to fill our hearts. He gave us his love through the Holy Spirit, whom God has given to us.

⁶When we were unable to help ourselves, at the right time, Christ died for us, although we were living against God. ⁷Very few people will die to save the life of someone else. Although perhaps for a good person someone might possibly die. ⁸But God shows his great love for us in this way: Christ died for us while we were still sinners.

⁹So through Christ we will surely be saved from God's anger, because we have been made right with God by the blood of Christ's death. ¹⁰While we were God's enemies, he made us his friends through the death of his Son. Surely, now that we are his friends, he will save us through his Son's life. ¹¹And not only that, but now we are also very happy in God through our Lord Jesus Christ. Through him we are now God's friends again.

Adam and Christ Compared

¹²Sin came into the world because of what one man did, and with sin came death. This is why everyone must die—because everyone sinned. ¹³Sin was in the world before the law of Moses, but sin is not counted against us as breaking a command when there is no law. ¹⁴But from the time of Adam to the time of Moses, everyone had to die, even those who had not sinned by breaking a command, as Adam had.

Adam was like the One who was coming in the future. ¹⁵But God's free gift is not like Adam's sin. Many people died because of the sin of that one man. But the grace from God was much greater; many people received God's gift of life by the grace of the one man, Jesus Christ. ¹⁶After Adam sinned once, he was judged guilty. But the gift of God is different. God's free gift came after many sins, and it makes people right with God. ¹⁷One man sinned, and so death ruled all people because of that one man. But now those people who accept God's full grace and the great gift of being made right with him will surely have true life and rule through the one man, Jesus Christ.

¹⁸So as one sin of Adam brought the punishment of death to all people, one good act that Christ did makes all people right with God. And that brings true life for all. ¹⁹One man disobeyed God, and many became sinners. In the same way, one man obeyed God, and many will be made right. ²⁰The law came to make sin worse. But when sin grew worse, God's grace increased. ²¹Sin once used death to rule us, but God gave people more of his grace so that grace could rule by making people right with him. And this brings life forever through Jesus Christ our Lord.

Dead to Sin but Alive in Christ

6 So do you think we should continue sinning so that God will give us even more grace? ²No! We died to our old sinful lives, so how can we continue living with sin? ³Did you forget that all of us became part of Christ when we were baptized? We shared his death in our baptism. ⁴When we were baptized, we were buried with Christ and shared his death. So, just as Christ was raised from the dead by the wonderful power of the Father, we also can live a new life.

⁵Christ died, and we have been joined with him by dying too. So we will also be joined with him by rising from the dead as he did. ⁶We know that our old life died with Christ on the cross so that our sinful selves would have no power over us and we would not be slaves to sin. ⁷Anyone who has died is made free from sin's control.

Principles: HOPE

Hope is the confident expectation of good. In Hebrews 6:19 it says, "We have this hope as an anchor for the soul, sure and strong." Hope serves as the basis of faith, for without it, one would have little reason to believe. Paul wrote in Romans 5:5, "And this hope will never disappoint us, because God has poured out his love to fill our hearts." Paul also exhorted believers always to be prepared to explain why they have hope. Faith in Jesus Christ gives believers hope that far exceeds a faint wish that things merely will get better one day.

Q: Why is homosexuality a sin?

A: God designed sexual intimacy as an expression of love and commitment between a man and a woman in the context of marriage. Sexual relations between members of the same gender are outside the boundaries of God's expressed will (Romans 1:26–27).

[8]If we died with Christ, we know we will also live with him. [9]Christ was raised from the dead, and we know that he cannot die again. Death has no power over him now. [10]Yes, when Christ died, he died to defeat the power of sin one time—enough for all time. He now has a new life, and his new life is with God. [11]In the same way, you should see yourselves as being dead to the power of sin and alive with God through Christ Jesus.

[12]So, do not let sin control your life here on earth so that you do what your sinful self wants to do. [13]Do not offer the parts of your body to serve sin, as things to be used in doing evil. Instead, offer yourselves to God as people who have died and now live. Offer the parts of your body to God to be used in doing good. [14]Sin will not be your master, because you are not under law but under God's grace.

Be Slaves of Righteousness

[15]So what should we do? Should we sin because we are under grace and not under law? No! [16]Surely you know that when you give yourselves like slaves to obey someone, then you are really slaves of that person. The person you obey is your master. You can follow sin, which brings spiritual death, or you can obey God, which makes you right with him. [17]In the past you were slaves to sin—sin controlled you. But thank God, you fully obeyed the things that you were taught. [18]You were made free from sin, and now you are slaves to goodness. [19]I use this example because this is hard for you to understand. In the past you offered the parts of your body to be slaves to sin and evil; you lived only for evil. In the same way now you must give yourselves to be slaves of goodness. Then you will live only for God.

[20]In the past you were slaves to sin, and goodness did not control you. [21]You did evil things, and now you are ashamed of them. Those things only bring death. [22]But now you are free from sin and have become slaves of God. This brings you a life that is only for God, and this gives you life forever. [23]The payment for sin is death. But God gives us the free gift of life forever in Christ Jesus our Lord.

An Example from Marriage

7 Brothers and sisters, all of you understand the law of Moses. So surely you know that the law rules over people only while they are alive. [2]For example, a woman must stay married to her husband as long as he is alive. But if her husband dies, she is free from the law of marriage. [3]But if she marries another man while her husband is still alive, the law says she is guilty of adultery. But if her husband dies, she is free from the law of marriage. Then if she marries another man, she is not guilty of adultery.

[4]In the same way, my brothers and sisters, your old selves died, and you became free from the law through the body of Christ. This happened so that you might belong to someone else—the One who was raised from the dead—and so that we might be used in service to God. [5]In the past, we were ruled by our sinful selves. The law made us want to do sinful things that controlled our bodies, so the things we did were bringing us death. [6]In the past, the law held us like prisoners, but our old selves died, and we were made free from the law. So now

<<TechSupport>>

ELECTRONIC BANKING

If you want to save money on postage stamps and checks, electronic banking is a convenient way to pay your monthly bills with less stress. All you need to do is set up an account with your bank and you'll be ready to go. You can also use electronic banking to budget and prioritize your gifts to God. Simply set up a recurring monthly payment through your online checking account, and your bank will draft payments automatically. Instead of giving God what's left over or forgetting altogether, you'll be offering him the firstfruits of the abundance he's blessed you with.

>> live the life

Romans 5:3–5

The Principle > Persevere under trial.

Practicing It > Select a short collection of Bible passages that encourage you to persevere under trial, and commit them to memory. When tough times come, meditate on these verses to shore up your faith.

THINK ABOUT IT Romans 6:23

USUALLY AT AN EARLY AGE, we learn the value of working and then receiving payment for that work. Recall your first job for someone outside of your family. Possibly you worked in the summer or after school. You were hired for a certain hourly fee, then worked a set number of hours. It seemed like you would never receive any money for the hours of effort you put into the job. But then payday arrived, and your anticipation grew as you waited to receive the first check.

Maybe you were planning to purchase something special with the funds from your first check. You slipped away to a quiet spot away from anyone's prying eyes and tore open the envelope. Disappointment rushed across your face as you saw the extra fees and taxes that were removed before your payment. But, ultimately, you felt good because you had worked and earned a check.

The apostle Paul uses this metaphor of payment in relation to sin. Each of us has sinned, and as this passage of Scripture reminds us, "The payment for sin is death." Wow! Now notice the promise: "But God gives us the free gift of life forever in Christ Jesus our Lord." Celebrate God's free gift through Christ today!

we serve God in a new way with the Spirit, and not in the old way with written rules.

Our Fight Against Sin

⁷You might think I am saying that sin and the law are the same thing. That is not true. But the law was the only way I could learn what sin meant. I would never have known what it means to want to take something belonging to someone else if the law had not said, "You must not want to take your neighbor's things."ⁿ ⁸And sin found a way to use that command and cause me to want all kinds of things I should not want. But without the law, sin has no power. ⁹I was alive before I knew the law. But when the law's command came to me, then sin began to live, ¹⁰and I died. The command was meant to bring life, but for me it brought death. ¹¹Sin found a way to fool me by using the command to make me die.

¹²So the law is holy, and the command is holy and right and good. ¹³Does this mean that something that is good brought death to me? No! Sin used something that is good to bring death to me. This happened so that I could see what sin is really like; the command was used to show that sin is very evil.

The War Within Us

¹⁴We know that the law is spiritual, but I am not spiritual since sin rules me as if I were its slave. ¹⁵I do not understand the things I do. I do not do what I want to do, and I do the things I hate. ¹⁶And if I do not want to do the hated things I do, that means I agree that the law is good. ¹⁷But I am not really the one who is doing these hated things; it is sin living in me that does them. ¹⁸Yes, I know that nothing good lives in me—I mean nothing good lives in the part of me that is earthly and sinful. I want to do the things that are good, but I do not do them. ¹⁹I do not do the good things I want to

→ The Bottom Line

Irregular Expenses: Paying Them Monthly

NOTHING CAN CREATE HAVOC WITH MONTHLY SPENDING PLANS like expenses that only come due every six months or a year, such as car insurance or life insurance. Without planning, sizable bills will leave you scrambling for funds. Instead, treat them as a monthly expense. If a $450 bill comes due twice a year, set aside $75 each month in a savings or money market account. When the bill arrives, the money you set aside will cover it. As recorded in 1 Corinthians 16:1–2, this is the principle that Paul advised the Galatian churches to follow in funding God's work.

do, but I do the bad things I do not want to do. ²⁰So if I do things I do not want to do, then I am not the one doing them. It is sin living in me that does those things.

²¹So I have learned this rule: When I want to do good, evil is there with me. ²²In my mind, I am happy with God's law. ²³But I see another law working in my body, which makes war against the law that my mind accepts. That other law working in my body is the law of sin, and it makes me its prisoner. ²⁴What a miserable man I am! Who will save me from this body that brings me death? ²⁵I thank God for saving me through Jesus Christ our Lord!

So in my mind I am a slave to God's law, but in my sinful self I am a slave to the law of sin.

are against God, because they refuse to obey God's law and really are not even able to obey God's law. ⁸Those people who are ruled by their sinful selves cannot please God.

⁹But you are not ruled by your sinful selves. You are ruled by the Spirit, if that Spirit of God really lives in you. But the person who does not have the Spirit of Christ does not belong to Christ. ¹⁰Your body will always be dead because of sin. But if Christ is in you, then the Spirit gives you life, because Christ made you right with God. ¹¹God raised Jesus from the dead, and if God's Spirit is living in you, he will also give life to your bodies that die. God is the One who raised Christ from the dead, and he will give life through" his Spirit that lives in you.

¹²So, my brothers and sisters, we must not

People
Skills

Confronting Anger

When your kids confront you with anger or frustration, try not to take their actions personally, even if they lash out at you in what seems a personal manner. Instead, realize that their behavior is more likely about their own fear or insecurity than it is about you as an individual. Instead of reacting, take a deep breath and give your child the space to communicate what is on his or her mind. Try to uncover their concerns and frustrations. Responding to anger in a calm and nondefensive way opens the door for honest communication and provides a great model for your kids to follow in their other relationships.

FACT-OIDS! Five million Americans post or share information daily on the Internet using personal Web logs.

[Pew Internet and American Life Project]

Be Ruled by the Spirit

8 So now, those who are in Christ Jesus are not judged guilty." ²Through Christ Jesus the law of the Spirit that brings life made you" free from the law that brings sin and death. ³The law was without power, because the law was made weak by our sinful selves. But God did what the law could not do. He sent his own Son to earth with the same human life that others use for sin. By sending his Son to be an offering for sin, God used a human life to destroy sin. ⁴He did this so that we could be the kind of people the law correctly wants us to be. Now we do not live following our sinful selves, but we live following the Spirit.

⁵Those who live following their sinful selves think only about things that their sinful selves want. But those who live following the Spirit are thinking about the things the Spirit wants them to do. ⁶If people's thinking is controlled by the sinful self, there is death. But if their thinking is controlled by the Spirit, there is life and peace. ⁷When people's thinking is controlled by the sinful self, they

be ruled by our sinful selves or live the way our sinful selves want. ¹³If you use your lives to do the wrong things your sinful selves want, you will die spiritually. But if you use the Spirit's help to stop doing the wrong things you do with your body, you will have true life.

¹⁴The true children of God are those who let God's Spirit lead them. ¹⁵The Spirit we received does not make us slaves again to fear; it makes us children of God. With that Spirit we cry out, "Father."" ¹⁶And the Spirit himself joins with our spirits to say we are God's children. ¹⁷If we are God's children, we will receive blessings from God together with Christ. But we must suffer as Christ suffered so that we will have glory as Christ has glory.

Our Future Glory

¹⁸The sufferings we have now are nothing compared to the great glory that will be shown to us. ¹⁹Everything God made is waiting with excitement for God to show his children's glory completely. ²⁰Everything God made was changed to become useless, not by

---

▶▶ **8:1 guilty** Some Greek copies continue, "those who do not live in the power of their sinful selves, but in the power of the Spirit." **8:2 you** Some Greek copies read "me." **8:11 through** Some Greek copies read "because of." **8:15 "Father"** Literally, "Abba, Father." Jewish children called their fathers "Abba."

>> live the life

Romans 8:6

The Principle > Positive thinking promotes peace.

Practicing It > Allow your thoughts to focus on the positive, uplifting things of the Spirit as you go through the day. Nurture your awareness of his presence, and follow his leading. This is the key to walking in peace.

its own wish but because God wanted it and because all along there was this hope: ²¹that everything God made would be set free from ruin to have the freedom and glory that belong to God's children.

²²We know that everything God made has been waiting until now in pain, like a woman ready to give birth. ²³Not only the world, but we also have been waiting with pain inside us. We have the Spirit as the first part of God's promise. So we are waiting for God to finish making us his own children, which means our bodies will be made free.

⊙ Get Aligned

Romans 8:28

"GOD WORKS FOR THE GOOD OF THOSE WHO LOVE HIM." Before mentally casting off this oft-quoted verse as Christianese, consider the powerful truth it contains. Its message to believers is essentially that God can transform the bleakest of situations into glorious reflections of himself.

Consider how many times you have seen that in your own life. If you're on the verge of doubting whether this verse applies to you any longer, think again. Revisit your walk with God. Recount the most difficult periods of your past.

Recall the times when he has rescued you.

The truth is that unlike people, God cannot break his promise. He is the definition of truth and, therefore, is eternally true to his word. So when the Bible declares he is working for your good in everything, it's safe to say that means all things. Life may include circumstances that get your attention solely fixed on him, but whatever happens you can be assured that as his child, he is always at work to bring about the best for your life.

²⁴We were saved, and we have this hope. If we see what we are waiting for, that is not really hope. People do not hope for something they already have. ²⁵But we are hoping for something we do not have yet, and we are waiting for it patiently.

²⁶Also, the Spirit helps us with our weakness. We do not know how to pray as we should. But the Spirit himself speaks to God for us, even begs God for us with deep feelings that words cannot explain. ²⁷God can see what is in people's hearts. And he knows what is in the mind of the Spirit, because the Spirit speaks to God for his people in the way God wants.

²⁸We know that in everything God works for the good of those who love him." They are the people he called, because that was his plan. ²⁹God knew them before he made the world, and he chose them to be like his Son so that Jesus would be the firstborn" of many brothers and sisters. ³⁰God planned for them to be like his Son; and those he planned to be like his Son, he also called; and those he called, he also made right with him; and those he made right, he also glorified.

God's Love in Christ Jesus

³¹So what should we say about this? If God is for us, no one can defeat us. ³²He did not spare his own Son but gave him for us all. So with Jesus, God will surely give us all things. ³³Who can accuse the people God has chosen? No one, because God is the One who makes them right. ³⁴Who can say God's people are guilty? No one, because Christ Jesus died, but he was also raised from the dead, and now he is on God's right side, appealing to God for us. ³⁵Can anything separate us from the love Christ has for us? Can troubles or problems or sufferings or hunger or nakedness or danger or violent death? ³⁶As it is written in the Scriptures:

"For you we are in danger of death all the time.
    People think we are worth no more than sheep to be killed."

Psalm 44:22

³⁷But in all these things we are completely victorious through God who showed his love for us. ³⁸Yes, I am sure that neither death, nor life, nor angels, nor ruling spirits, nothing now, nothing in the future, no powers, ³⁹nothing above us, nothing below us, nor anything

Q: Are we living in the Last Days?

A: Yes. But that doesn't necessarily mean the world will end anytime soon. When the Bible talks about the Last Days, it's referring to the span of time following the ascension of Christ and ending with his return, and no one knows when that will be (1 John 2:18).

 8:28 We . . . him. Some Greek copies read "We know that everything works together for good for those who love God." **8:29 firstborn** Here this probably means that Christ was the first in God's family to share God's glory.

else in the whole world will ever be able to separate us from the love of God that is in Christ Jesus our Lord.

God and the Jewish People

9 I am in Christ, and I am telling you the truth; I do not lie. My conscience is ruled by the Holy Spirit, and it tells me I am not lying. [2]I have great sorrow and always feel much sadness. [3]I wish I could help my Jewish brothers and sisters, my people. I would even wish that I were cursed and cut off from Christ if that would help them. [4]They are the people of Israel, God's chosen children. They have seen the glory of God, and they have the agreements that God made between himself and his people. God gave them the law of Moses and the right way of worship and his promises. [5]They are the descendants of our great ancestors, and they are the earthly family into which Christ was born, who is God over all. Praise him forever![n] Amen.

[6]It is not that God failed to keep his promise to them. But only some of the people of Israel are truly God's people,[n] [7]and only some of Abraham's[n] descendants are true children of Abraham. But God said to Abraham: "The descendants I promised you will be from Isaac."[n] [8]This means that not all of Abraham's descendants are God's true children. Abraham's true children are those who become God's children because of the promise God made to Abraham. [9]God's promise to Abraham was this: "At the right time I will return, and Sarah will have a son."[n] [10]And that is not all. Rebekah's sons

own plan. He was chosen because he was the one God wanted to call, not because of anything he did. [13]As the Scripture says, "I loved Jacob, but I hated Esau."[n]

[14]So what should we say about this? Is God unfair? In no way. [15]God said to Moses, "I will show kindness to anyone to whom I want to show kindness, and I will show mercy to anyone to whom I want to show mercy."[n] [16]So God will choose the one to whom he decides to show mercy; his choice does not depend on what people want or try to do. [17]The Scripture says to the king of Egypt: "I made you king for this reason: to show my power in you so that my name will be talked about in all the earth."[n] [18]So God shows mercy where he wants to show mercy, and he makes stubborn the people he wants to make stubborn.

[19]So one of you will ask me: "Then why does God blame us for our sins? Who can fight his will?" [20]You are only human, and human beings have no right to question God. An object should not ask the person who made it, "Why did you make me like this?" [21]The potter can make anything he wants to make. He can use the same clay to make one thing for special use and another thing for daily use.

[22]It is the same way with God. He wanted to show his anger and to let people see his power. But he patiently stayed with those people he was angry with—people who were made ready to be destroyed. [23]He waited with patience so that he could make known his rich glory to the people who receive his mercy. He has prepared these people to have

Men of Valor
JOSEPH: Follower of Dreams

Although Mary earned acclaim as the mother of Jesus, little is said about Christ's human father. Yet Joseph also played a key role in biblical history, listening to God whenever the Lord spoke to him through dreams. Initially, after learning that Mary was pregnant by the Holy Spirit, Joseph planned to divorce her secretly. But Joseph obeyed when an angel told him to take Mary as his wife. Joseph also fled from Herod, went to Egypt, and returned to Israel at God's direction. When his young family reached Israel, he settled in Galilee after being warned in a dream to avoid Judea. The life of Joseph shows that we should trust God more than ourselves, for following godly mandates yields eternal rewards.

FACT-OIDS! About 68% of the 100 million homes in the United States already have at least one personal computer. [Creative Strategies]

had the same father, our father Isaac. [11-12]But before the two boys were born, God told Rebekah, "The older will serve the younger."[n] This was before the boys had done anything good or bad. God said this so that the one chosen would be chosen because of God's

his glory, [24]and we are those people whom God called. He called us not from the Jews only but also from those who are not Jews. [25]As the Scripture says in Hosea:

"I will say, 'You are my people'
    to those I had called 'not my people.'

And I will show my love
    to those people I did not love."
                                Hosea 2:1, 23
[26]"They were called,
    'You are not my people,'
but later they will be called
    'children of the living God.'" *Hosea 1:10*
[27]And Isaiah cries out about Israel:
"The people of Israel are many,
    like the grains of sand by the sea.
But only a few of them will be saved,

9:5 born…forever! This can also mean "born. May God, who rules over all things, be praised forever!" 9:6 God's people Literally, "Israel," the people God chose to bring his blessings to the world. 9:7 Abraham Most respected ancestor of the Jews. Every Jew hoped to see Abraham. 9:7 "The descendants…Isaac." Quotation from Genesis 21:12. 9:9 "At…son." Quotation from Genesis 18:10, 14. 9:11–12 "The older…younger." Quotation from Genesis 25:23. 9:13 "I…Esau." Quotation from Malachi 1:2–3. (Romans 9 notes cont. on p. 202.)

Ten Ways to Be a Good Steward

1. Reduce waste by reusing plastic bags.

2. Monitor the thermostat setting.

3. Eat fresh fruits and vegetables.

4. Recycle metal cans and glass bottles.

5. Replace incandescent bulbs with fluorescent ones.

6. Keep cash reserves for emergencies.

7. Check your local library for movies to borrow.

8. Clean your closets and donate clothes to charity.

9. Dine out only on special occasions.

10. Live within your means by limiting debt.

²⁸ because the Lord will quickly and completely punish the people on the earth."

Isaiah 10:22–23

²⁹It is as Isaiah said:

"The Lord All-Powerful allowed a few of our descendants to live. Otherwise we would have been completely destroyed like the cities of Sodom and Gomorrah."ⁿ *Isaiah 1:9*

³⁰So what does all this mean? Those who are not Jews were not trying to make themselves right with God, but they were made right with God because of their faith. ³¹The people of Israel tried to follow a law to make themselves right with God. But they did not succeed, ³²because they tried to make themselves right by the things they did instead of trusting in God to make them right. They stumbled over the stone that causes people to stumble. ³³As it is written in the Scripture:

"I will put in Jerusalem a stone that causes people to stumble, a rock that makes them fall. Anyone who trusts in him will never be disappointed."

Isaiah 8:14; 28:16

10 Brothers and sisters, the thing I want most is for all the Jews to be saved. That is my prayer to God. ²I can say this about them: They really try to follow God, but they do not know the right way. ³Because they did not know the way that God makes people right with him, they tried to make themselves right in their own way. So they did not accept God's way of making people right.

⁴Christ ended the law so that everyone who believes in him may be right with God.

⁵Moses writes about being made right by following the law. He says, "A person who obeys these things will live because of them."ⁿ ⁶But this is what the Scripture says about being made right through faith: "Don't say to yourself, 'Who will go up into heaven?' " (That means, "Who will go up to heaven and bring Christ down to earth?") ⁷"And do not say, 'Who will go down into the world below?' " (That means, "Who will go down and bring Christ up from the dead?") ⁸This is what the Scripture says: "The word is near you; it is in your mouth and in your heart."ⁿ That is the teaching of faith that we are telling. ⁹If you declare with your mouth, "Jesus is Lord," and if you believe in your heart that God raised Jesus from the dead, you will be saved. ¹⁰We believe with our hearts, and so we are made right with God. And we declare with our mouths that we believe, and so we are saved. ¹¹As the Scripture says, "Anyone who trusts in him will never be disappointed."ⁿ ¹²That Scripture says "anyone" because there is no difference between those who are Jews and those who are not. The same Lord is the Lord of all and gives many blessings to all who trust in him, ¹³as the Scripture says, "Anyone who calls on the Lord will be saved."ⁿ

¹⁴But before people can ask the Lord for help, they must believe in him; and before they can believe in him, they must hear about him; and for them to hear about the Lord, someone must tell them; ¹⁵and before someone can go and tell them, that person must be sent. It is written, "How beautiful is the person who comes to bring good news."ⁿ ¹⁶But not all the Jews accepted the good news. Isaiah said, "Lord, who believed what we told them?"ⁿ ¹⁷So faith comes from hearing the Good News, and people hear the Good News when someone tells them about Christ.

¹⁸But I ask: Didn't people hear the Good News? Yes, they heard—as the Scripture says:

"Their message went out through all the world; their words go everywhere on earth." *Psalm 19:4*

¹⁹Again I ask: Didn't the people of Israel understand? Yes, they did understand. First, Moses says:

Q: What is grace?

A: When the Bible speaks of grace, it's referring to a blessing of power that God extends to all Christians in their efforts to follow him. Often defined as "God's unmerited favor," grace is the ability God gives us to carry out his will in our lives (1 Corinthians 15:10).

9:15 "I … mercy." Quotation from Exodus 33:19.   9:17 "I … earth." Quotation from Exodus 9:16.   9:29 **Sodom and Gomorrah** Two cities that God destroyed because the people were so evil.   10:5 "A person … them." Quotation from Leviticus 18:5.   10:6–8 But … heart." Quotations from Deuteronomy 9:4; 30:12–14; Psalm 107:26.   10:11 "Anyone … disappointed." Quotation from Isaiah 28:16.   10:13 "Anyone … saved." Quotation from Joel 2:32.   10:15 "How … news." Quotation from Isaiah 52:7.   10:16 "Lord, … them?" Quotation from Isaiah 53:1.

202

FOR Men Only

HUMILITY

The hallmark of the Christian life is the often forgotten quality of humility. Personified by none other than Jesus Christ, humility is the missing ingredient in many a person's relationship recipe. Too many times, women are left yearning for the men in their lives to simply admit fault. Pity the poor fool who can't even stop and ask for directions! A man's pride often keeps him from owning up to even the slightest of errors. Yet humility is simply the acknowledgment of reality: we don't know it all, and we need help. The good news is that the Holy Spirit is our helper.

"I will use those who are not a nation to make you jealous.
  I will use a nation that does not understand to make you
    angry."
Deuteronomy 32:21

²⁰Then Isaiah is bold enough to say:
"I was found by those who were not asking me for help.
  I made myself known to people who were not looking for me."
Isaiah 65:1

²¹But about Israel God says,
"All day long I stood ready to accept
  people who disobey and are stubborn."
Isaiah 65:2

God Shows Mercy to All People

11 So I ask: Did God throw out his people? No! I myself am an Israelite from the family of Abraham, from the tribe of Benjamin. ²God chose the Israelites to be his people before they were born, and he has not thrown his people out. Surely you know what the Scripture says about Elijah, how he prayed to God against the people of Israel. ³"Lord," he said, "they have killed your prophets, and they have destroyed your altars. I am the only prophet left, and now they are trying to kill me, too.'" ⁴But what answer did God give Elijah? He said, "But I have left seven thousand people in Israel who have never bowed down before Baal.'" ⁵It is the same now. There are a few people that God has chosen by his grace. ⁶And if he chose them by grace, it is not for the things they have done. If they could be made God's people by what they did, God's gift of grace would not really be a gift.

⁷So this is what has happened: Although the Israelites tried to be right with God, they did not succeed, but the ones God chose did become right with him. The others were made stubborn and refused to listen to God. ⁸As it is written in the Scriptures:
"God gave the people a dull mind so they could not understand."
Isaiah 29:10

"He closed their eyes so they could not see
  and their ears so they could not hear.
This continues until today."
Deuteronomy 29:4

⁹And David says:
"Let their own feasts trap them and cause their ruin;
  let their feasts cause them to stumble and be paid back.

▶ Survival Guide

GAZEBOS: ENJOYING THE OUTDOORS

Gazebos are a tradition thousands of years old. Going through cycles in the U.S., they returned to popularity in the 1980s. If you add one to your property, choose a site that will offer a 360-degree view of the surroundings. As with decks, gazebos can be purchased in kits that can offer savings over building one from scratch. Advanced carpentry skills are suggested if you want to tackle the job from start to finish. A gazebo is a great place for relaxation and fellowship with family and friends, as well as quiet talks with God.

▶▶ 11:3 "they…too" Quotation from 1 Kings 19:10, 14.   11:4 "But…Baal." Quotation from 1 Kings 19:18.

Get Fit

PACKING HEALTHY SNACKS Use these tips to help you eat healthy at work: Make your own snacks by packing little bags or containers of ready-to-eat vegetables or pretzels to keep in your briefcase or car. Likewise, stash packets of instant oatmeal and some juice boxes in your desk at work. Eat small amounts every few hours to stave off hunger and keep your metabolism humming. When you have to eat out, take the time to scout out restaurants near your workplace that offer healthy alternatives. You don't have to count every calorie, carbohydrate, or fat gram to stay healthy. Just keep your focus on what is healthy for your body—as well as your spirit—and you'll do fine.

[10]"Let their eyes be closed so they cannot see
and their backs be forever weak from troubles." *Psalm 69:22–23*

[11]So I ask: When the Jews fell, did that fall destroy them? No! But their failure brought salvation to those who are not Jews, in order to make the Jews jealous. [12]The Jews' failure brought rich blessings for the world, and the Jews' loss brought rich blessings for the non-Jewish people. So surely the world will receive much richer blessings when enough Jews become the kind of people God wants.

[13]Now I am speaking to you who are not Jews. I am an apostle to those who are not Jews, and since I have that work, I will make the most of it. [14]I hope I can make my own people jealous and, in that way, help some of them to be saved. [15]When God turned away from the Jews, he became friends with other people in the world. So when God accepts the Jews, surely that will bring them life after death.

Deal With It: *Overload

BETWEEN UPLOADS AND DOWN-LOADS, MANY OF US TEETER on the brink of technology overload. While technology has its advantages, its availability has made it more important than ever that we pull away and unplug occasionally. From cell phones to laptops, the opportunities abound for exchanging e-mails, handling calls, and doing other tasks on the go and around the clock. But if our multimedia gadgetry causes us to lose the focus on our loved ones, then we need to put the high-tech tools on hold and tune into some high-touch activity instead. God designed us to function in actual reality, not virtual reality.

[16]If the first piece of bread is offered to God, then the whole loaf is made holy. If the roots of a tree are holy, then the tree's branches are holy too.

[17]It is as if some of the branches from an olive tree have been broken off. You non-Jewish people are like the branch of a wild olive tree that has been joined to that first tree. You now share the strength and life of the first tree, the Jews. [18]So do not brag about those branches that were broken off. If you brag, remember that you do not support the root, but the root supports you. [19]You will say, "Branches were broken off so that I could be joined to their tree." [20]That is true. But those branches were broken off because they did not believe, and you continue to be part of the tree only because you believe. Do not be proud, but be afraid. [21]If God did not let the natural branches of that tree stay, then he will not let you stay if you don't believe.

[22]So you see that God is kind and also very strict. He punishes those who stop following him. But God is kind to you, if you continue following in his kindness. If you do not, you will be cut off from the tree. [23]And if the Jews will believe in God again, he will accept them back. God is able to put them back where they were. [24]It is not natural for a wild branch to be part of a good tree. And you who are

Q: What is heaven like?

A: There is a lot we don't know about heaven. We do know that it is a place of unparalleled beauty and glory, where there is no suffering, decay, or death. In heaven, we will see God face-to-face and spend eternity in his presence (Revelation 4:1–11).

not Jews are like a branch cut from a wild olive tree and joined to a good olive tree. But since those Jews are like a branch that grew from the good tree, surely they can be joined to their own tree again.

²⁵I want you to understand this secret, brothers and sisters, so you will understand that you do not know everything: Part of Israel has been made stubborn, but that will change when many who are not Jews have come to God. ²⁶And that is how all Israel will be saved. It is written in the Scriptures:

"The Savior will come from
   Jerusalem;
he will take away all evil from
   the family of Jacob."
²⁷And I will make this agreement
   with those people
when I take away their sins."

Isaiah 59:20–21; 27:9

²⁸The Jews refuse to accept the Good News, so they are God's enemies. This has happened to help you who are not Jews. But the Jews are still God's chosen people, and he loves them very much because of the promises he made to their ancestors. ²⁹God never changes his mind about the people he calls and the things he gives them. ³⁰At one time you refused to obey God. But now you have received mercy, because those people refused to obey. ³¹And now the Jews refuse to obey, because God showed mercy to you. But this happened so that they also can" receive mercy from him. ³²God has given all people over to their stubborn ways so that he can show mercy to all.

▶ Get Aligned
Romans 12:1

It is heard at the Super Bowl, Oscars, Grammys, and virtually every major entertainment event. From "I'd like to thank God" to "This is for the Holocaust survivors," actors, artists, and athletes all dedicate their performances to someone or something significant to them.

If you had to dedicate each day to someone or something, who or what would it be? Paul says we are to dedicate our lives each day to God. But there's a major difference between giving oral thanks to God and living sacrificially for him. Sacrifices require something. In fact, most require a lot. To offer our entire life as a living sacrifice to God means daily giving up everything we are. It means placing all our dreams, talents, possessions, motives, and thoughts on the altar in worship of him every day.

Consider whether you are willing to sacrifice that much that often. It's easy to say we are willing to do so when we're in the limelight. Around others, it sounds great to dedicate our lives to God as if we were giving an acceptance speech. But the question is how much we offer to him in private. Living a life of sacrifice happens moment by moment, day by day.

Praise to God

³³Yes, God's riches are very great, and his wisdom and knowledge have no end! No one can explain the things God decides or understand his ways. ³⁴As the Scripture says,

"Who has known the mind of the Lord,
   or who has been able to give him advice?"   *Isaiah 40:13*
³⁵"No one has ever given God anything
   that he must pay back."   *Job 41:11*
³⁶Yes, God made all things, and everything continues through him and for him. To him be the glory forever! Amen.

Give Your Lives to God

12 So brothers and sisters, since God has shown us great mercy, I beg you to offer your lives as a living sacrifice to him. Your offering must be only for God and pleasing to him, which is the spiritual way for you to worship. ²Do not be shaped by this world; instead be changed within by a new way of thinking. Then you will be able to decide what God wants for you; you will know what is good

«Tech Support»

INSTANT MESSAGING

Instant messaging is a great way to stay in touch, but you can easily lose track of time. Control how much time you spend instant messaging by turning off the automatic sign-on feature that is built into most instant messaging software. When you do get online to send and receive instant messages, observe common courtesy. While most instant messages are casual and conversational, it's polite to begin with a short "hello" so you don't catch someone off guard. Additionally, remember to sign off graciously.

» 11:26 Jacob Father of the twelve family groups of Israel, the people God chose to be his people.   11:31 can Some Greek copies read "can now."

205

>> live the life

Romans 12:1

The Principle > **Worship God with your life.**

Practicing It > **Offer your life to God as a living sacrifice. List two or three things that change about your life as a result of you committing it fully to God, then choose one as a goal to move toward in the coming weeks.**

and pleasing to him and what is perfect. [3]Because God has given me a special gift, I have something to say to everyone among you. Do not think you are better than you are. You must decide what you really are by the amount of faith God has given you. [4]Each one of us has a body with many parts, and these parts all have different uses. [5]In the same way, we are many, but in Christ we are all one body. Each one is a part of that body, and each part belongs to all the other parts. [6]We all have different gifts, each of which came because of the grace God gave us. The person who has the gift of prophecy should use that gift in agreement with the faith. [7]Anyone who has the gift of serving should serve. Anyone who has the gift of teaching should teach. [8]Whoever has the gift of encouraging others should encourage. Whoever has the gift of giving to others should give freely. Anyone who has the gift of being a leader should try hard when he leads. Whoever has the gift of showing mercy to others should do so with joy.

[9]Your love must be real. Hate what is evil, and hold on to what is good. [10]Love each other like brothers and sisters. Give each other more honor than you want for yourselves. [11]Do not be lazy but work hard, serving the Lord with all your heart. [12]Be joyful because you

Change >> Your WORLD

INTERVARSITY CHRISTIAN FELLOWSHIP

For many college students, this time of life involves intellectual searching. Since they are away from home, they find the freedom of choice. InterVarsity Christian Fellowship/USA provides these students with a rich tradition of campus witness, thoughtful discipleship, and a concern for world missions. The organization serves more than thirty-five thousand students at more than 560 colleges and universities nationwide. Every three years, InterVarsity organizes Urbana, a student mission conference where more than eighteen thousand students explore short-term and vocational missions. Also, more than nineteen thousand people attend InterVarsity's four training centers each year to focus on God and become equipped for service.

To change your world, visit www.intervarsity.org.

>> live the life

Romans 12:10–11

The Principle > **Serve others with diligence.**

Practicing It > **Go to each of your friends and family members and ask him or her for ideas on how you can serve each person better. Doing this will not only demonstrate how much you care, but the answers they give you may take your relationship to a whole new level.**

have hope. Be patient when trouble comes, and pray at all times. [13]Share with God's people who need help. Bring strangers in need into your homes.

[14]Wish good for those who harm you; wish them well and do not curse them. [15]Be happy with those who are happy, and be sad with those who are sad. [16]Live in peace with each other. Do not be proud, but make friends with those who seem unimportant. Do not think how smart you are.

[17]If someone does wrong to you, do not pay him back by doing wrong to him. Try to do what everyone thinks is right. [18]Do your best to live in peace with everyone. [19]My friends, do not try to punish others when they wrong you, but wait for God to punish them with his anger. It is written: "I will punish those who do wrong; I will repay them,"[n] says the Lord. [20]But you should do this:

>> 12:19 "I . . . them." Quotation from Deuteronomy 32:35.

>> live the life

Romans 12:18

The Principle > Live in peace with others.

Practicing It > When you find yourself in conflict with a friend or even an acquaintance, do all you can within reason to make peace with that person. Don't wait for him or her to come to you. Take the first step yourself.

"If your enemy is hungry, feed him;
    if he is thirsty, give him a drink.
Doing this will be like pouring burning coals on his head."

Proverbs 25:21–22

²¹Do not let evil defeat you, but defeat evil by doing good.

Christians Should Obey the Law

13 All of you must yield to the government rulers. No one rules unless God has given him the power to rule, and no one rules now without that power from God. ²So those who are against the government are really against what God has commanded. And they will bring punishment on themselves. ³Those who do right do not have to fear the rulers; only those who do wrong fear them. Do you want to be unafraid of the rulers? Then do what is right, and they will praise you. ⁴The ruler is God's servant to help you. But if you do wrong, then be afraid. He has the power to punish; he is God's ser-vant to punish those who do wrong. ⁵So you must yield to the government, not only because you might be punished, but because you know it is right.

⁶This is also why you pay taxes. Rulers are working for God and give their time to their work. ⁷Pay everyone, then, what you owe. If you owe any kind of tax, pay it. Show respect and honor to them all.

Loving Others

⁸Do not owe people anything, except always owe love to each other, because the person who loves others has obeyed all the law. ⁹The law says, "You must not be guilty of adultery. You must not murder anyone. You must not steal. You must not want to take your neighbor's things."ⁿ All these commands and all others are really only one rule: "Love your neighbor as you love your-self."ⁿ ¹⁰Love never hurts a neigh-bor, so loving is obeying all the law.

¹¹Do this because we live in an important time. It is now time for you to wake up from your sleep, be-cause our salvation is nearer now than when we first believed. ¹²The

Q: Was Jesus re-ally sinless?

A: Yes. He never disobeyed God in any way. Still, that doesn't mean he didn't struggle with temptation. The Bible says that Jesus was tempted in every way that we are, yet he did not sin. So even though he was sinless, he can still relate to us (Hebrews 4:15).

→ The Bottom Line

Kids: Teaching Them Values

CHILDREN ARE BECOMING SHOPPERS AT AN EARLY AGE. According to one study, kids between six and twelve shop two to three times a week. More youngsters go shopping than attend church, participate in youth groups, play outdoors, or engage in household conversation. Nearly half of youngsters in adolescence daydream about being rich, spurred on by advertisers who dangle fantasies in front of their televi-sion-saturated eyes. Yet Christ said in Luke 12:23, "Life is more than food, and the body is more than clothes." If you have children, teach them that the things that last in life can't be found at the mall.

>> 13:9 "You ... things." Quotation from Exodus 20:13–15, 17.   13:9 "Love ... yourself." Quotation from Leviticus 19:18.

207

"night"" is almost finished, and the "day"" is almost here. So we should stop doing things that belong to darkness and take up the weapons used for fighting in the light. [13]Let us live in a right way, like people who belong to the day. We should not have wild parties or get drunk. There should be no sexual sins of any kind, no fighting or jealousy. [14]But clothe yourselves with the Lord Jesus Christ and forget about satisfying your sinful self.

Do Not Criticize Other People

14 Accept into your group someone who is weak in faith, and do not argue about opinions. [2]One person believes it is right to eat all kinds of food." But another, who is weak, believes it is right to eat only vegetables. [3]The one who knows that it is right to eat any kind of food must not reject the one who eats only vegetables. And the person who eats only vegetables must not think that the one who eats all foods is wrong, because God has accepted that person. [4]You cannot judge another person's servant. The master decides if the servant is doing well or not. And the Lord's servant will do well because the Lord helps him do well.

[5]Some think that one day is more important than another, and others think that every day is the same. Let all be sure in their own mind. [6]Those who think one day is more important than other days are doing that for the Lord. And those who eat all kinds of food are doing that for the Lord, and they give thanks to God. Others who refuse to eat some foods do that for the Lord, and they give thanks to God. [7]We do not live or die for ourselves. [8]If we live, we are living for the Lord, and if we die, we are dying for the Lord. So living or dying, we belong to the Lord.

[9]The reason Christ died and rose from the dead to live again was so he would be Lord over both the dead and the living. [10]So why do you judge your brothers or sisters in Christ? And why do you think you are better than they are? We will all stand before God to be judged, [11]because it is written in the Scriptures:

" 'As surely as I live,' says the Lord,
   'Everyone will bow before me;
   everyone will say that I am
     God.' "

Isaiah 45:23

[12]So each of us will have to answer to God.

Do Not Cause Others to Sin

[13]For that reason we should stop judging each other. We must make up our minds not to do anything that will make another Christian sin. [14]I am in the Lord Jesus, and I know that there is no food that is wrong to eat. But if a person believes something is wrong, that thing is wrong for him. [15]If you hurt your brother's or sister's faith because of something you eat, you are not really following the way of love. Do not destroy someone's faith by eating food he thinks is wrong, because Christ died for him. [16]Do not allow what you think is good to become what others say is evil. [17]In the kingdom of God, eating and drinking are not important. The important things are living right with God, peace, and joy in the Holy Spirit. [18]Anyone who serves Christ by living this way is pleasing God and will be accepted by other people.

[19]So let us try to do what makes peace and helps one another. [20]Do not let the eating of food destroy the work of God. All foods are all right to eat, but it is wrong to eat food that causes someone else to sin. [21]It is better not to eat meat or drink wine or do anything that will cause your brother or sister to sin.

[22]Your beliefs about these things should be kept secret between you and God. People are happy if they can do what they think is right without feeling guilty. [23]But those who eat something without being sure it is right are wrong because they did not believe it was right. Anything that is done without believing it is right is a sin.

15 We who are strong in faith should help the weak with their weaknesses, and not please only ourselves. [2]Let each of us please our neighbors for their good, to help them be stronger in faith. [3]Even Christ did not live to please himself. It was as the Scriptures said: "When people insult you, it hurts me."" [4]Everything that was written in the past was written to teach us. The Scriptures give us patience and encouragement so that we can have hope. [5]May the patience and encouragement

Q: Why did God give us free will?

A: For our love to be genuine, it must be something we freely choose to give. Love that is demanded or forced is not really love. God created us with free will because he wanted to share in a love relationship with human beings who freely choose to love him in return.

>> live the life

Romans 14:4

The Principle > Walk in integrity regarding others.

Practicing It > Do your best to live out your beliefs with integrity and a clear conscience. At the same time, beware of casting judgment on another Christian when his beliefs do not precisely match your own. Don't let your integrity turn into a reason to judge others.

13:12 **"night"** This is used as a symbol of the sinful world we live in. This world will soon end.   13:12 **"day"** This is used as a symbol of the good time that is coming, when we will be with God.

 14:2 **all ... food** The Jewish law said there were some foods Jews should not eat. When Jews became Christians, some of them did not understand they could now eat all foods.   15:3 **"When ... me."** Quotation from Psalm 69:9.

that come from God allow you to live in harmony with each other the way Christ Jesus wants. [6]Then you will all be joined together, and you will give glory to God the Father of our Lord Jesus Christ. [7]Christ accepted you, so you should accept each other, which will bring glory to God. [8]I tell you that Christ became a servant of the Jews to show that God's promises to the Jewish ancestors are true. [9]And he also did this so that those who are not Jews could give glory to God for the mercy he gives to them. It is written in the Scriptures:

"So I will praise you among the non-Jewish people.
I will sing praises to your name."   *Psalm 18:49*

[10]The Scripture also says,

"Be happy, you who are not Jews, together with his people."
                                                       Deuteronomy 32:43

[11]Again the Scripture says,

"All you who are not Jews, praise the Lord.
All you people, sing praises to him."   *Psalm 117:1*

[12]And Isaiah says,

"A new king will come from the family of Jesse."
He will come to rule over the non-Jewish people,
and they will have hope because of him."   *Isaiah 11:10*

[13]I pray that the God who gives hope will fill you with much joy and peace while you trust in him. Then your hope will overflow by the power of the Holy Spirit.

Paul Talks About His Work

[14]My brothers and sisters, I am sure that you are full of goodness. I know that you have all the knowledge you need and that you are able to teach each other. [15]But I have written to you very openly about some things I wanted you to remember. I did this because God gave me this special gift: [16]to be a minister of Christ Jesus to those who are not Jews. I served God by teaching his Good News, so that the non-Jewish people could be an offering that God would accept—an offering made holy by the Holy Spirit.

[17]So I am proud of what I have done for God in Christ Jesus. [18]I will not talk about anything except what Christ has done through me in leading those who are not Jews to obey God. They have obeyed God because of what I have said and done, [19]because of the power of mir-

>> live the life

Romans 15:13

The Principle > Live in hope daily.

Practicing It > Make it a part of your regular prayer time to ask God to fill you with his peace and joy and to give you the strength to trust in him fully. He will answer that prayer, and your life will become rich in hope.

acles and the great things they saw, and because of the power of the Holy Spirit. I preached the Good News from Jerusalem all the way around to Illyricum, and so I have finished that part of my work. [20]I always want to preach the Good News in places where people have never heard of Christ, because I do not want to build on the work someone else has already started. [21]But it is written in the Scriptures:

"Those who were not told about him will see,
and those who have not heard about him will understand."
                                                       Isaiah 52:15

Paul's Plan to Visit Rome

[22]This is the reason I was stopped many times from coming to you. [23]Now I have finished my work here. Since for many years I have wanted to come to you, [24]I hope to visit you on my way to Spain. After I enjoy being with you for a while, I hope you can help me on my trip. [25]Now I am going to Jerusalem to help God's people. [26]The believers in Macedonia and Southern Greece were happy to give their money to help the poor among God's people at Jerusalem. [27]They were happy to do this, and really they owe it to them. These who are not Jews have shared in the Jews' spiritual blessings, so they should use their material possessions to help the Jews. [28]After I am sure the poor in Jerusalem get the money that has been given for them, I will

Principles: LORD'S SUPPER

The Lord's Supper commemorates Christ's last meal before he was taken captive and crucified. During this meal, Jesus took a cup of wine, thanked God for it, and told his apostles to drink from it. Next, he broke bread and distributed it, telling them it represented his body, which he would give up for them on the cross. Afterward, Christ said the cup illustrated a new relationship with God: "This cup is the new agreement that God makes with his people" (Luke 22:20). Also called communion, Christians observe the Lord's Supper in obedience to Christ's command to remember him by it.

>> 15:12 **Jesse** Jesse was the father of David, king of Israel. Jesus was from their family.

People
Skills

Offering Apologies

Everyone makes mistakes, and sometimes those errors in judgment can hurt those close to us. When that happens, we need to be quick to apologize as soon as we make an error. Suffice it to say, you should never lie simply to avoid saying you are sorry or that you made a mistake. When you've made an error, take a deep breath and admit it, apologizing for your actions or behaviors. Not only will it lift any looming sense of guilt and stress, the apology will help repair any damage done. Also, your timely admission and apology will demonstrate strength of character and show your resolve to avoid the error in the future.

leave for Spain and stop and visit you. ²⁹I know that when I come to you I will bring Christ's full blessing.

³⁰Brothers and sisters, I beg you to help me in my work by praying to God for me. Do this because of our Lord Jesus and the love that the Holy Spirit gives us. ³¹Pray that I will be saved from the nonbelievers in Judea and that this help I bring to Jerusalem will please God's people there. ³²Then, if God wants me to, I will come to you with joy, and together you and I will have a time of rest. ³³The God who gives peace be with you all. Amen.

Greetings to the Christians

16 I recommend to you our sister Phoebe, who is a helper" in the church in Cenchrea. ²I ask you to accept her in the Lord in the way God's people should. Help her with anything she needs, because she has helped me and many other people also.

³Give my greetings to Priscilla and Aquila, who work together with me in Christ Jesus ⁴and who risked their own lives to save my life. I am thankful to them, and all the non-Jewish churches are thankful as well. ⁵Also, greet for me the church that meets at their house.

Greetings to my dear friend Epenetus, who was the first person in Asia to follow Christ. ⁶Greetings to Mary, who worked very hard for you. ⁷Greetings to Andronicus and Junia, my relatives, who were in prison with me. They are very important apostles. They were believers in Christ before I was. ⁸Greetings to Ampliatus, my dear friend in the Lord. ⁹Greetings to Urbanus, a worker together with me for Christ. And greetings to my dear friend Stachys. ¹⁰Greetings to Apelles, who was tested and proved that he truly loves Christ. Greetings to all those who are in the family of Aristobulus. ¹¹Greetings to Herodion, my fellow citizen. Greetings to all those in the family of Narcissus who belong to the Lord. ¹²Greetings to Tryphena and Tryphosa, women who work very hard for the Lord. Greetings to my dear friend Persis, who also has worked very hard for the Lord. ¹³Greetings to Rufus, who is a special person in the Lord, and to his mother, who has been like a mother to me also. ¹⁴Greetings to Asyncritus, Phlegon, Hermes, Patrobas, Hermas, and all the brothers and sisters who are with them. ¹⁵Greetings to Philologus and Julia, Nereus and his sister, and Olympas, and to all God's people with them. ¹⁶Greet each other with a holy kiss. All of Christ's churches send greetings to you.

⊙ Sexcess:
HARNESSING OUR HORMONES

Suffice it to say that men are wired very differently from women. Our sex drive is typically calibrated at a much higher level than our mate's. So the challenge becomes how to keep our raging hormones in check, aside from getting castrated. The secret lies in where we choose to focus our attention. Admittedly, we live in a sex-saturated society where quick fixes are just a mouse click away. But despite all the distractions, life continues to be a series of decisions about whether we will be driven by our fleshly desires or by our better selves. As Galatians 5:16 says, "Live by following the Spirit. Then you will not do what your sinful selves want."

▶▶ 16:1 **helper** Literally, "deaconess." This might mean the same as one of the special women helpers in 1 Timothy 3:11.

¹⁷Brothers and sisters, I ask you to look out for those who cause people to be against each other and who upset other people's faith. They are against the true teaching you learned, so stay away from them. ¹⁸Such people are not serving our Lord Christ but are only doing what pleases themselves. They use fancy talk and fine words to fool the minds of those who do not know about evil. ¹⁹All the believers have heard that you obey, so I am very happy because of you. But I want you to be wise in what is good and innocent in what is evil.

²⁰The God who brings peace will soon defeat Satan and give you power over him.

The grace of our Lord Jesus be with you.

²¹Timothy, a worker together with me, sends greetings, as well as Lucius, Jason, and Sosipater, my relatives.

²²I am Tertius, and I am writing this letter from Paul. I send greetings to you in the Lord.

²³Gaius is letting me and the whole church here use his home. He also sends greetings to you, as do Erastus, the city treasurer, and our brother Quartus. [²⁴The grace of our Lord Jesus Christ be with all of you. Amen.]ⁿ

²⁵Glory to God who can make you strong in faith by the Good News that I tell people and by the message about Jesus Christ. The message about Christ is the secret that was hidden for long ages past but is now made known. ²⁶It has been made clear through the writings of the prophets. And by the command of the eternal God it is made known to all nations that they might believe and obey.

²⁷To the only wise God be glory forever through Jesus Christ! Amen.

FACT-OIDS! The population of the United States is about 300 million people. [Census.gov]

16:24 **The ... Amen.** Some Greek copies do not contain the bracketed text.

THE **FIRST** LETTER OF PAUL THE APOSTLE TO THE
Corinthians

AUTHOR: PAUL
DATE WRITTEN: A.D. 56–57

WHEN YOU HEAR ABOUT A PROBLEM, you are probably quick to suggest a solution to the difficulty. Whereas women like to talk thoroughly through a situation, men generally like to move immediately to a resolution. A man's man, Paul heard from several different sources about the struggles of the church in Corinth, a Greek city with at least a dozen pagan temples, and he acted to address them.

The most famous temple in Corinth was erected to Aphrodite, the goddess of love, where worshipers had practiced prostitution as part of their religious observances. Sexual immorality had crept into the Corinthian church, plaguing the city's Christians practically from the beginning. Besides tackling the sex sins, Paul also addresses such issues as believers suing each other in court, abusing the Lord's Supper, and following false teaching about the Resurrection.

As Paul confronts the Corinthians about their shortcomings, he calls on them to stand apart from the sinners around them by rejecting their hedonistic values and lifestyles. With specific instruction, Paul provides practical suggestions for following Jesus in the midst of a corrupt society. The letter concludes by admonishing the Corinthian church to stand firm in its faith, to give itself fully to the work of the Lord, and to let love guide its every action.

1

From Paul. God called me to be an apostle of Christ Jesus because that is what God wanted. Also from Sosthenes, our brother in Christ.

²To the church of God in Corinth, to you who have been made holy in Christ Jesus. You were called to be God's holy people with all people everywhere who pray in the name of the Lord Jesus Christ—their Lord and ours:

³Grace and peace to you from God our Father and the Lord Jesus Christ.

Paul Gives Thanks to God

⁴I always thank my God for you because of the grace God has given you in Christ Jesus. ⁵I thank God because in Christ you have been made rich in every way, in all your speaking and in all your knowledge. ⁶Just as our witness about Christ has been guaranteed to you, ⁷so you have every gift from God while you wait for our Lord Jesus Christ to come again. ⁸Jesus will keep you strong until the end so that there will be no wrong in you on the day our Lord Jesus Christ comes again. ⁹God, who has called you into fellowship with his Son, Jesus Christ our Lord, is faithful.

Problems in the Church

¹⁰I beg you, brothers and sisters, by the name of our Lord Jesus Christ that all of you agree with each other and not be split into groups. I beg that you be completely joined together by having the same kind of thinking and the same purpose. ¹¹My brothers and sisters, some people from Chloe's family have told me quite plainly that there are quarrels among you. ¹²This is what I mean: One of you says, "I follow Paul"; another says, "I follow Apollos"; another says, "I follow Peter"; and another says, "I follow Christ." ¹³Christ has been divided up into different groups! Did Paul die on the cross for you? No! Were you baptized in the name of Paul? No! ¹⁴I thank God I did not

baptize any of you except Crispus and Gaius ¹⁵so that now no one can say you were baptized in my name. ¹⁶(I also baptized the family of Stephanas, but I do not remember that I baptized anyone else.)

▶ Get Aligned
1 Corinthians 1:18

WHAT KIND OF GOD WOULD SAC-RIFICE HIS SON? Better yet, what kind of supreme being would allow himself to be publicly humiliated in the most degrading, ungodly way possible? Jesus' death on the cross has seemed foolish to the world for more than two thousand years.

Yet the cross involves much more than just our Savior's death. It is life to every sinner reaching for hope. Were it not for Jesus' sacrifice, we would have no chance of ever being right with God. Even if we followed every religious ritual exactly, our very nature of sinfulness would make it impossible for us to be in God's presence.

Through Christ's crucifixion, the Son of God became the spotless sacrifice that God required to make amends. The payment for sin was death. The payment for all of humanity's sin for all time was slaughtering the only possible perfect sacrifice: the Son of God himself. Yet because of his love for us, Jesus endured every moment of the cross while fulfilling dozens of thousand-year-old prophecies. Best of all, he emerged victorious over death. The cross is anything but foolish. Whereas our Lord suffered much upon it, his sacrifice is our very life, strength, and hope.

Get Fit

GOING THE DISTANCE One way to motivate yourself toward greater physical health is to set a goal that challenges you to stretch beyond your perceived physical limitations. For many, that goal takes on the form of a marathon. Admittedly, finishing a marathon is not the sort of goal that attracts everyone, but it may be exactly the kind of big challenge you need to propel your health to the next level. At www.coolrunning.com, you can learn all there is to know about what it takes to run a marathon—from training schedules to nutrition guides to tips for navigating the crowds on race day. And remember, life is a lot like a marathon, so pace yourself to go the distance.

TheFinalScore »

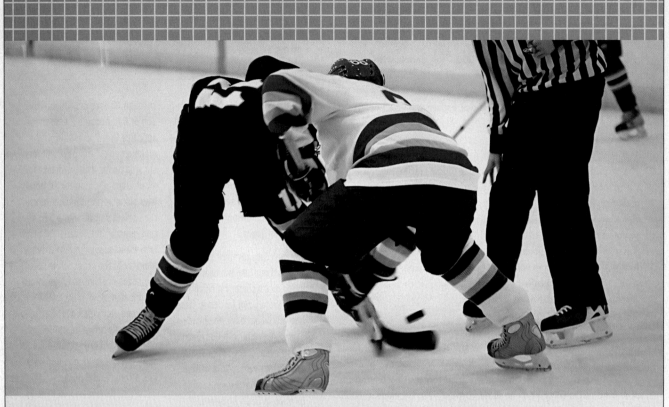

HOCKEY: Actions Have Consequences

THE FASTEST MOVING OF ALL SPORTS, HOCKEY is a game better suited for viewing in person than on television. Seats in the arena provide a much better appreciation for the skills involved in hurtling a puck across the rink at lightning-fast speed.

Its roots go back thousands of years, but it wasn't until the mid-1850s that British soldiers stationed in Canada devised ice hockey. Formal rules followed in 1879 and they have been an integral part of hockey ever since. Breaking them means a setback for the offender; and, if serious enough, it may include expulsion from the game.

Minor penalties, such as tripping, illegal use of the stick, or intentionally delaying the game, send a player to the penalty box for two minutes. Major penalties, such as fighting, sit a player down for five minutes. Engage in misconduct, such as showing a lack of respect for an official or head-butting, and a player will sit for twice as long.

Because each side only fields six players, and one must constantly defend the net, the loss of even one person can spell the difference between victory and defeat. Likewise, in the Bible God spells out rules that explain how to live in harmony with each other.

First John 3:4 says that sinning is living against God's law. The results of ignoring that law can be serious: guilt, broken relationships, dysfunctional homes, and destroyed lives. In life, as in hockey, actions have consequences.

> **"Likewise, in the Bible God spells out rules that explain how to live in harmony with each other."**

Q: What does it mean to envy?

A: Envy means desiring to be like another person. It results in bitterness that comes from comparing ourselves to others. We might envy someone who we see as being more attractive, more athletic, or more loved by others, but God calls it a sin (Titus 3:3).

[17]Christ did not send me to baptize people but to preach the Good News. And he sent me to preach the Good News without using words of human wisdom so that the cross* of Christ would not lose its power.

Christ Is God's Power and Wisdom

[18]The teaching about the cross is foolishness to those who are being lost, but to us who are being saved it is the power of God. [19]It is written in the Scriptures:

"I will cause the wise to lose
their wisdom;
I will make the wise unable
to understand." *Isaiah 29:14*

[20]Where is the wise person? Where is the educated person? Where is the skilled talker of this world? God has made the wisdom of the world foolish. [21]In the wisdom of God the world did not know God through its own wisdom. So God chose to use the message that sounds foolish to save those who believe. [22]The Jews ask for miracles, and the Greeks want wisdom. [23]But we preach a crucified Christ. This causes the Jews to stumble and is foolishness to non-Jews. [24]But Christ is the power of God and the wisdom of God to those people God has called—Jews and Greeks. [25]Even the foolishness of God is wiser than human wisdom, and the weakness of God is stronger than human strength.

[26]Brothers and sisters, look at what you were when God called you. Not many of you were wise in the way the world judges wisdom. Not many of you had great influence. Not many of you came from important families. [27]But God chose the foolish things of the world to shame the wise, and he chose the weak things of the world to shame the strong. [28]He chose what the world thinks is unimportant and what the world looks down on and thinks is nothing in order to destroy what the world thinks is important. [29]God did this so that no one can brag in his presence. [30]Because of God you are in Christ Jesus, who has become for us wisdom from God. In Christ we are put right with God, and have been made holy, and have been set free from sin. [31]So, as the Scripture says, "If people want to brag, they should brag only about the Lord."*

The Message of Christ's Death

2 Dear brothers and sisters, when I came to you, I did not come preaching God's secret* with fancy words or a show of human wisdom. [2]I decided that while I was with you I would forget about everything except Jesus Christ and his death on the cross. [3]So when I came to you, I was weak and fearful and trembling. [4]My teaching and preaching were not with words of human wisdom that persuade people but with proof of the power that the Spirit gives. [5]This was so that your faith would be in God's power and not in human wisdom.

God's Wisdom

[6]However, I speak a wisdom to those who are mature. But this wisdom is not from this world or from the rulers of this world, who are losing their power. [7]I speak God's secret wisdom, which he has kept hidden. Before the world began, God planned this wisdom for our glory. [8]None of the rulers of this world understood it. If they had, they would not have crucified the Lord of glory. [9]But as it is written in the Scriptures:

"No one has ever seen this,
and no one has ever heard about it.
No one has ever imagined
what God has prepared for those who love him." *Isaiah 64:4*

[10]But God has shown us these things through the Spirit.

The Spirit searches out all things, even the deep secrets of God. [11]Who knows the thoughts that another person has? Only a person's spirit that lives within him knows his thoughts. It is the same with God. No one knows the thoughts of God except the Spirit of God. [12]Now we did not receive the spirit of the world, but we received the Spirit that is from God so that we can know all that God has given us. [13]And we speak about these things, not with words taught us by human wisdom but with words taught us by the Spirit. And so we explain spiritual truths to spiritual people. [14]A person who does not have the Spirit does not accept the truths that come from the Spirit of God. That person thinks they are foolish and cannot understand them, because they can only be judged to be true by the Spirit. [15]The spiritual person is able to judge all things, but no one can judge him. The Scripture says:

>> live the life

1 Corinthians 2:2–5

The Principle > Share your faith with others.

Practicing It > Volunteer to be a mentor in the life of a young person. As you get to know each other better, invite your friend to share with you any questions he may have about God. As the opportunity arises, share your faith.

>> 1:17 **cross** Paul uses the cross as a picture of the Good News, the story of Christ's death and rising from the dead for people's sins. The cross, or Christ's death, was God's way to save people. 1:31 **"If…Lord."** Quotation from Jeremiah 9:24. 2:1 **God's secret** Some Greek copies read "God's message."

Men of Valor
LAZARUS: Friend of Jesus

Like Christ, Lazarus is one of the few people mentioned in the Bible to have risen from the dead. Although Jesus heard that his friend Lazarus was ill, he insisted the sickness would not end in death. When Jesus arrived, Lazarus had been dead for four days. After weeping and praying, Jesus called for him to come out of the grave. The rest is history. Jesus returned to Bethany and was the guest of honor at a dinner that Lazarus attended. A large crowd gathered to see both men, which infuriated the leading priests. Already plotting to kill Christ, they planned to kill Lazarus, also. Getting too close to Christ can bring persecution, but even death can't separate someone from the love of God.

¹⁶"Who has known the mind of the Lord?
    Who has been able to teach him?"

Isaiah 40:13

But we have the mind of Christ.

Following People Is Wrong

3 Brothers and sisters, in the past I could not talk to you as I talk to spiritual people. I had to talk to you as I would to people without the Spirit—babies in Christ. ²The teaching I gave you was like milk, not solid food, because you were not able to take solid food. And even now you are not ready. ³You are still not spiritual, because there is jealousy and quarreling among you, and this shows that you are not spiritual. You are acting like people of the world. ⁴One of you says, "I belong to Paul," and another says, "I belong to Apollos." When you say things like this, you are acting like people of the world.

⁵Is Apollos important? No! Is Paul important? No! We are only servants of God who helped you believe. Each one of us did the work God gave us to do. ⁶I planted the seed, and Apollos watered it. But God is the One who made it grow. ⁷So the one who plants is not important, and the one who waters is not important. Only God, who makes things grow, is important. ⁸The one who plants and the one who waters have the same purpose, and each will be rewarded for his own work. ⁹We are God's workers, working together; you are like God's farm, God's house.

¹⁰Using the gift God gave me, I laid the foundation of that house like an expert builder. Others are building on that foundation, but all people should be careful how they build on it. ¹¹The foundation that has already been laid is Jesus Christ, and no one can lay down any other foundation. ¹²But if people build on that foundation, using gold, silver, jewels, wood, grass, or straw, ¹³their work will be clearly seen, because the Day of Judgment* will make it visible. That Day will appear with fire, and the fire will test everyone's work to show what sort of work it was. ¹⁴If the building that has been put on the foundation still stands, the builder will get a reward. ¹⁵But if the building is burned up, the builder will suffer loss. The builder will be saved, but it will be as one who escaped from a fire.

¹⁶Don't you know that you are God's temple and that God's Spirit lives in you? ¹⁷If anyone destroys God's temple, God will destroy that person, because God's temple is holy and you are that temple.

¹⁸Do not fool yourselves. If you think you are wise in this world, you should become a fool so that you can become truly wise, ¹⁹because the wisdom of this world is foolishness with God. It is written in the Scriptures, "He catches those who are wise in their own clever traps."* ²⁰It is also written in the Scriptures, "The Lord knows what wise people think. He knows their thoughts are just a puff of wind."* ²¹So you should not brag about human leaders. All things belong to you: ²²Paul, Apollos, and Peter; the world, life, death, the present, and the future—all these belong to you. ²³And you belong to Christ, and Christ belongs to God.

Apostles Are Servants of Christ

4 People should think of us as servants of Christ, the ones God has trusted with

{Book of the Month}

The Barbarian Way
by Erwin McManus

In pastor Erwin McManus's insightful book, he offers hope to men who long for a powerful and personal relationship with Jesus Christ by encouraging them to return to a barbaric and pure practice of the faith. He calls men to a dangerous, rugged life of following Jesus as Lord, saying, "Jesus is lost in a religion bearing his name." McManus teaches from life experiences and an observer's eye for spiritual lessons in contemporary culture. To McManus, being a Christian means acknowledging the presence of a kingdom of darkness that wants to steal men's hopes and dreams—and parachuting behind enemy lines anyway.

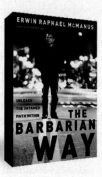

3:13 Day of Judgment The day Christ will come to judge all people and take his people home to live with him.   **3:19 "He...traps."** Quotation from Job 5:13.   **3:20 "The Lord...wind."** Quotation from Psalm 94:11.

>>June

QUOTE OF THE MONTH:
"I have been driven many times upon my knees by the overwhelming conviction that I had nowhere else to go."
—Abraham Lincoln

1 Pray for a person of influence: Today is singer **Pat Boone's** birthday.

2 Check the batteries in your smoke detectors.

3

4 Go for an evening stroll with someone you love.

5 Donate your old cell phone to a worthy cause.

6

7

8 Update your resume.

9 Pray for a person of influence: Today is actor **Johnny Depp's** birthday.

10

11 Memorize Psalm 91:1.

12

13

14 Pray for a person of influence: Today is businessman **Donald Trump's** birthday.

15 Make a play list of your favorite tunes.

16

17

18 Pray for a person of influence: Today is musician **Paul McCartney's** birthday.

19

20 Call your dad to say thanks.

21

22 Check your progress on the goals you set in January.

23 Pray for troops serving overseas.

24

25 Donate your spare change to charity.

26

27 Forgive someone who doesn't deserve it.

28

29 Fly a kite with friends.

30

Change >> Your WORLD

JEWS FOR JESUS

Many Jewish people tend to dismiss the evangelistic methods and materials couched in Christian jargon. For more than three decades, Jews for Jesus has been sharing the Good News on campuses and streets across the country and around the world. Started in the San Francisco Bay area with a handful of people, today Jews for Jesus is an international ministry with a staff of 214 in more than eleven countries and twenty cities. They have a unique focus on the Jewish people and use creative means, such as drama and music combined with provocative newspaper advertising and street witnessing.

To change your world, visit www.jewsforjesus.org.

his secrets. [2]Now in this way those who are trusted with something valuable must show they are worthy of that trust. [3]As for myself, I do not care if I am judged by you or by any human court. I do not even judge myself. [4]I know of no wrong I have done, but this does not make me right before the Lord. The Lord is the One who judges me. [5]So do not judge before the right time; wait until the Lord comes. He will bring to light things that are now hidden in darkness, and will make known the secret purposes of people's hearts. Then God will praise each one of them.

[6]Brothers and sisters, I have used Apollos and myself as examples so you could learn through us the meaning of the saying, "Follow only what is written in the Scriptures." Then you will not be more proud of one person than another. [7]Who says you are better than others? What do you have that was not given to you? And if it was given to you, why do you brag as if you did not receive it as a gift?

[8]You think you already have everything you need. You think you are rich. You think you have become kings without us. I wish you really were kings so we could be kings together with you. [9]But it seems to me that God has put us apostles in last place, like those sentenced to die. We are like a show for the whole world to see—angels and people. [10]We are fools for Christ's sake, but you are very wise in Christ. We are weak, but you are strong. You receive honor, but we are shamed. [11]Even to this very hour we do not have enough to eat or drink or to wear. We are often beaten, and we have no homes in which to live. [12]We work hard with our own hands for our food. When people curse us, we bless them. When they hurt us, we put up with it. [13]When they tell evil lies about us, we speak nice words about them. Even today, we are treated as though we were the garbage of the world—the filth of the earth.

[14]I am not trying to make you feel ashamed. I am writing this to give you a warning as my own dear children. [15]For though you may have ten thousand teachers in Christ, you do not have many fathers. Through the Good News I became your father in Christ Jesus, [16]so I

 # Survival Guide

GRASS: SEEDING VERSUS SODDING

Lush, green lawns add value to a home's overall appearance. If you need to improve your lawn's appearance, think about planting seed, which is much more economical than sod. Use high-quality seed; cheap mixes may have too many weed seeds and inert matter. If you don't have a spreader, sprinkle seed by hand and cover it with hay, mulch or burlap to keep it moist and protect it from birds. Water it often and be patient. Grass takes awhile to get rooted, just as God's Word needs time to grow in your heart.

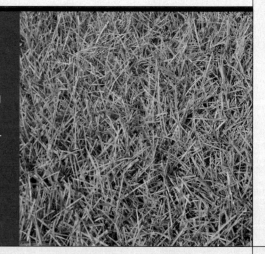

beg you, please follow my example. [17]That is why I am sending to you Timothy, my son in the Lord. I love Timothy, and he is faithful. He will help you remember my way of life in Christ Jesus, just as I teach it in all the churches everywhere.

[18]Some of you have become proud, thinking that I will not come to you again. [19]But I will come to you very soon if the Lord wishes. Then I will know what the proud ones do, not what they say, [20]because the kingdom of God is present not in talk but in power. [21]Which do you want: that I come to you with punishment or with love and gentleness?

Wickedness in the Church

5 It is actually being said that there is sexual sin among you. And it is a kind that does not happen even among people who do not know God. A man there has his father's wife. [2]And you are proud! You should have been filled with sadness so that the man who did this should be put out of your group. [3]I am not there with you in person, but I am with you in spirit. And I have already judged the man who did that sin as if I were really there. [4]When you meet together in the name of our Lord Jesus, and I meet with you in spirit with the power of our Lord Jesus, [5]then hand this man over to Satan. So his sinful self[6] will be destroyed, and his spirit will be saved on the day of the Lord.

[6]Your bragging is not good. You know the saying, "Just a little yeast makes the whole batch of dough rise." [7]Take out all the old yeast so that you will be a new batch of dough without yeast, which you really are. For Christ, our Passover lamb, has been sacrificed. [8]So let us celebrate this feast, but not with the bread that has the old yeast—the yeast of sin and wickedness. Let us celebrate this feast with the bread that has no yeast—the bread of goodness and truth.

[9]I wrote you in my earlier letter not to associate with those who sin sexually. [10]But I did not mean you should not associate with those of this world who sin sexually, or with the greedy, or robbers, or those who worship idols. To get away from them you would have to leave this world. [11]I am writing to tell you that you must not associate with those who call themselves believers in Christ but who sin sexually, or are greedy, or worship idols, or abuse others with words, or get drunk, or cheat people. Do not even eat with people like that.

[12-13]It is not my business to judge those who are not part of the church. God will judge them. But you must judge the people who are part of the church. The Scripture says, "You must get rid of the evil person among you."[]

Judging Problems Among Christians

6 When you have something against another Christian, how can you bring yourself to go before judges who are not right with God? Why do you not let God's people decide who is right? [2]Surely you know that God's people will judge the world. So if you are to judge the world, are you not able to judge small cases as well? [3]You know that in the future we will

Q: Does someone who commits suicide go to heaven?

A: The Bible says very little about suicide. It does talk, however, about our commitment to Jesus being for eternity. If a person who has decided to trust Jesus Christ for salvation later commits suicide, it is not unreasonable to believe that person will go to heaven.

➜ The Bottom Line

Life Insurance: Protecting Loved Ones

WHEREAS FEW PEOPLE LIKE TO THINK OF DYING, EVERYONE DIES, AND SOME AT A YOUNG AGE. Yes, the odds are against that happening. However, if you have a spouse or children who depend on your earnings, leave them with an adequate sum that can generate income to replace your loss. The amount you should carry and what kind of insurance varies with circumstances; just don't buy so much it puts a strain on your budget. A financial planner or other consultant can offer guidance. Providing for loved ones in case of tragedy shows the spirit of love spelled out in 1 Corinthians 13:1–13.

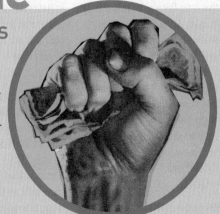

>> **5:5 sinful self** Literally, "flesh." This could also mean his body.   **5:12–13 "You . . . you."** Quotation from Deuteronomy 17:7; 19:19; 22:21, 24; 24:7.

judge angels, so surely we can judge the ordinary things of this life. [4]If you have ordinary cases that must be judged, are you going to appoint people as judges who mean nothing to the church? [5]I say this to shame you. Surely there is someone among you wise enough to judge a complaint between believers. [6]But now one believer goes to court against another believer—and you do this in front of unbelievers!

[7]The fact that you have lawsuits against each other shows that you are already defeated. Why not let yourselves be wronged? Why not let yourselves be cheated? [8]But you yourselves do wrong and cheat, and you do this to other believers!

[9-10]Surely you know that the people who do wrong will not inherit God's kingdom. Do not be fooled. Those who sin sexually, worship idols, take part in adultery, those who are male prostitutes, or men who have sexual relations with other men, those who steal, are greedy, get drunk, lie about others, or rob—these people will not inherit God's kingdom. [11]In the past, some of you were like that, but you were washed clean. You were made holy, and you were made right with God in the name of the Lord Jesus Christ and in the Spirit of our God.

Use Your Bodies for God's Glory

[12]"I am allowed to do all things," but not all things are good for me to do. "I am allowed to do all things," but I will not let anything make me its slave. [13]"Food is for the stomach, and the stomach for food," but God will destroy them both. The body is not for sexual sin but for the Lord, and the Lord is for the body. [14]By his power God has raised the Lord from the dead and will also raise us from the dead. [15]Surely you know that your bodies are parts of Christ himself. So I must never take the parts of Christ and join them to a prostitute! [16]It is written in the Scriptures, "The two will become one body."[n] So you should know that anyone who joins with a prostitute becomes one body with the prostitute. [17]But the one who joins with the Lord is one spirit with the Lord.

[18]So run away from sexual sin. Every other sin people do is outside their bodies, but those who sin sexually sin against their own bodies. [19]You should know that your body is a temple for the Holy Spirit who is in you. You have received the Holy Spirit from God. So you do not belong to yourselves, [20]because you were bought by God for a price. So honor God with your bodies.

About Marriage

7 Now I will discuss the things you wrote me about. It is good for a man not to have sexual relations with a woman. [2]But because sexual sin is a danger, each man should have his own wife, and each woman should have her own husband. [3]The husband should give his wife all that he owes her as his wife. And the wife should give her husband all that she owes him as her husband. [4]The wife does not have full rights over her own body; her husband shares them. And the husband does not have full rights over his own body; his wife shares them. [5]Do not refuse to give your bodies to each other, unless you both agree to stay away from sexual relations for a time so you can give your time to prayer. Then come together again so Satan cannot tempt you because of a lack of self-control. [6]I say this to give you permission to stay away from sexual relations for a time. It is not a command to do so. [7]I wish that everyone were like me, but each person has his own gift from God. One has one gift, another has another gift.

[8]Now for those who are not married and for the widows I say this: It is good for them to stay unmarried as I am. [9]But if they cannot con-

▶Get Aligned
1 Corinthians 6:18

When you hang around a house that is on fire, you're bound to get burned. It's no different when dealing with sexual sin. Paul is explicit in his instructions on what to do when facing sexual temptation: run from it! The problem is that many Christian men like to linger. We take a second glance at the woman wearing a revealing top. Or we click on the link in the X-rated junk e-mail we somehow received.

Keeping ourselves away from such situations begins with guarding our eyes and our minds. Jesus called it as he saw it when he said in Matthew 5:28, "If anyone looks at a woman and wants to sin sexually with her, in his mind he has already done that sin with the woman."

So, how do we avoid letting a lustful thought grow? We flee from it. When our eyes catch the billboard with the bikini models, we turn away and begin to pray. When a woman at work unwittingly shows some skin, we turn away and pray. In any situation that hints of temptation, no matter how seemingly harmless, we are to turn and run.

Q: Is it really wrong for a Christian to marry a non-Christian?

A: Yes. The Bible states that it is against God's will for a Christian to marry a non-Christian. However, it also states that if you are already married and you become a follower of Christ but your spouse does not, that is not an adequate reason to divorce her (1 Corinthians 7:12–13; 2 Corinthians 6:14).

>> 6:16 "The two ... body." Quotation from Genesis 2:24.

People Skills

trol themselves, they should marry. It is better to marry than to burn with sexual desire.

¹⁰Now I give this command for the married people. (The command is not from me; it is from the Lord.) A wife should not leave her husband. ¹¹But if she does leave, she must not marry again, or she should make up with her husband. Also the husband should not divorce his wife.

¹²For all the others I say this (I am saying this, not the Lord): If a Christian man has a wife who is not a believer, and she is happy to live with him, he must not divorce her. ¹³And if a Christian woman has a husband who is not a believer, and he is happy to live with her, she must not divorce him. ¹⁴The husband who is not a believer is made holy through his believing wife. And the wife who

called you. ²¹If you were a slave when God called you, do not let that bother you. But if you can be free, then make good use of your freedom. ²²Those who were slaves when the Lord called them are free persons who belong to the Lord. In the same way, those who were free when they were called are now Christ's slaves. ²³You all were bought at a great price, so do not become slaves of people. ²⁴Brothers and sisters, each of you should stay as you were when you were called, and stay there with God.

Questions About Getting Married

²⁵Now I write about people who are not married. I have no command from the Lord about this; I give my opinion. But I can be trusted, because the Lord has shown me mercy. ²⁶The

FACT-OIDS! There are 4,802 AM radio stations and 8,648 FM radio stations in the United States. [Infoplease.com]

is not a believer is made holy through her believing husband. If this were not true, your children would not be clean, but now your children are holy.

¹⁵But if those who are not believers decide to leave, let them leave. When this happens, the Christian man or woman is free. But God called us⁰ to live in peace. ¹⁶Wife, you don't know; maybe you will save your husband. And husband, you don't know; maybe you will save your wife.

Live as God Called You

¹⁷But in any case each one of you should continue to live the way God has given you to live—the way you were when God called you. This is a rule I make in all the churches. ¹⁸If a man was already circumcised when he was called, he should not undo his circumcision. If a man was without circumcision when he was called, he should not be circumcised. ¹⁹It is not important if a man is circumcised or not. The important thing is obeying God's commands. ²⁰Each one of you should stay the way you were when God

present time is a time of trouble, so I think it is good for you to stay the way you are. ²⁷If you have a wife, do not try to become free from her. If you are not married, do not try to find a wife. ²⁸But if you decide to marry, you have not sinned. And if a girl who has never married decides to marry, she has not sinned. But those who marry will have trouble in this life, and I want you to be free from trouble.

²⁹Brothers and sisters, this is what I mean: We do not have much time left. So starting now, those who have wives should live as if they had no wives. ³⁰Those who are crying should live as if they were not crying. Those who are happy should live as if they were not happy. Those who buy things should live as if they own nothing. ³¹Those who use the things of the world should live as if they were not using them, because this world in its present form will soon be gone.

³²I want you to be free from worry. A man who is not married is busy with the Lord's work, trying to please the Lord. ³³But a man who is married is busy with things of the world, trying to please his wife. ³⁴He must

Speaking Effectively

How you say something is just as important as the words you choose. Just think of the variety of ways a simple phrase like "thank you" can be spoken. Depending on how the words are emphasized, the phrase can convey a full spectrum of meanings, from authentic gratitude to sarcasm. Or think about the phrase, "Come here." How would you say it to a misbehaving child? How might it differ from the tone you use with your wife? It isn't just what you say that matters; it's also *how* you say it! Matching your intonation and inflection to the message you intend to convey will increase your effectiveness when you communicate with others.

Ten Ways to Exercise Leadership

1. Pray for wisdom in leading others.
2. Lead by example in word and deed.
3. Encourage and reward teamwork.
4. Meet with your group regularly.
5. Measure progress and address needs.
6. Discuss individual and corporate goals.
7. Solicit feedback from team members.
8. Praise people publicly for achieving results.
9. Offer correction in the form of coaching.
10. Give thanks to God for the opportunity to lead.

think about two things—pleasing his wife and pleasing the Lord. A woman who is not married or a girl who has never married is busy with the Lord's work. She wants to be holy in body and spirit. But a married woman is busy with things of the world, as to how she can please her husband. ³⁵I am saying this to help you, not to limit you. But I want you to live in the right way, to give yourselves fully to the Lord without concern for other things.

³⁶If a man thinks he is not doing the right thing with the girl he is engaged to, if she is almost past the best age to marry and he feels he should marry her, he should do what he wants. They should get married. It is no sin. ³⁷But if a man is sure in his mind that there is no need for marriage, and has his own desires under control, and has decided not to marry the one to whom he is engaged, he is doing the right thing. ³⁸So the man who marries his girl does right, but the man who does not marry will do better.

³⁹A woman must stay with her husband as long as he lives. But if her husband dies, she is free to marry any man she wants, but she must marry another believer. ⁴⁰The woman is happier if she does not marry again. This is my opinion, but I believe I also have God's Spirit.

About Food Offered to Idols

8 Now I will write about meat that is sacrificed to idols. We know that "we all have knowledge." Knowledge puffs you up with pride, but love builds up. ²If you think you know something, you do not yet know anything as you should. ³But if any person loves God, that person is known by God.

⁴So this is what I say about eating meat sacrificed to idols: We know that an idol is really nothing in the world, and we know there is only one God. ⁵Even though there are things called gods, in heaven or on earth (and there are many "gods" and "lords"), ⁶for us there is only one God—our Father. All things came from him, and we live for him. And there is only one Lord—Jesus Christ. All things were made through him, and we also were made through him.

⁷But not all people know this. Some people are still so used to idols that when they eat meat, they still think of it as being sacrificed to an idol. Because their conscience is weak, when they eat it, they feel guilty. ⁸But food will not bring us closer to God. Refusing to eat does not make us less pleasing to God, and eating does not make us better in God's sight.

⁹But be careful that your freedom does not cause those who are weak in faith to fall into sin. ¹⁰Suppose one of you who has knowl-

Q: What is the Sabbath?

A: God commands us to set aside one day a week as a Sabbath to rest and to worship him, and that day for many is typically Sunday. God thinks so highly of the Sabbath that he made it one of the Ten Commandments, and he rested after creation (Exodus 31:12–17).

<<TechSupport>>

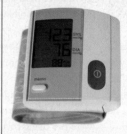

HEALTH AND FITNESS

Amateur athletes and the health-conscious alike can take advantage of technology to fine-tune their performance and keep track of vital statistics. Heart-rate monitors and pedometers keep pace to help you get the most from your workouts. Recording your vital signs is a good way to track your exercise progress, and checking your spiritual pulse is also important. Whenever you pray and study Scripture, take a moment to jot down any insights you gain from your devotions and record answers to prayer.

FOR Men Only

COURTSHIP Whereas courtship may seem like an outdated ritual to some men, the thought of dating your mate appeals to many women, particularly those for whom the romance of relationship has all but evaporated. Courtship as defined here is simply the art of restoring romance to a relationship through random acts of kindness and other reminders of affection. All that is necessary is some creative forethought. For example, instead of driving yourselves on a date, consider getting a chauffer-driven limousine or even horse drawn carriage to whisk the two of you away. Memories of the good time you enjoy together will last long afterthoughts of the added expense.

edge eats in an idol's temple." Someone who is weak in faith might see you eating there and be encouraged to eat meat sacrificed to idols while thinking it is wrong to do so. [11]This weak believer for whom Christ died is ruined because of your "knowledge." [12]When you sin against your brothers and sisters in Christ like this and cause them to do what they feel is wrong, you are also sinning against Christ. [13]So if the food I eat causes them to fall into sin, I will never eat meat again so that I will not cause any of them to sin.

Paul Is like the Other Apostles

9 I am a free man. I am an apostle. I have seen Jesus our Lord. You people are all an example of my work in the Lord. [2]If others do not accept me as an apostle, surely you do, because you are proof that I am an apostle in the Lord.

[3]This is the answer I give people who want to judge me: [4]Do we not have the right to eat and drink? [5]Do we not have the right to bring a believing wife with us when we travel as do the other apostles and the Lord's brothers and Peter? [6]Are Barnabas and I the only ones who must work to earn our living? [7]No soldier ever serves in the army and pays his own salary. No one ever plants a vineyard without eating some of the grapes. No person takes care of a flock without drinking some of the milk.

[8]I do not say this by human authority; God's law also says the same thing. [9]It is written in the law of Moses: "When an ox is working in the grain, do not cover its mouth to keep it from eating."[n] When God said this, was he thinking only about oxen? No. [10]He was really talking about us. Yes, that Scripture was written for us, because it goes on to say: "The one who plows and the one who works in the grain should hope to get some of the grain for their work." [11]Since we planted spiritual seed among you, is it too much if we should harvest material things? [12]If others have the right to get something from you, surely we have this right, too. But we do not use it. No, we put up with everything ourselves so that we will not keep anyone from believing

Get Fit

PROTECTING YOUR SMILE Taking good care of your teeth not only gives you a winning smile, it encourages you toward a healthier lifestyle in general. So what are the essentials for healthy mouth maintenance? First, use a soft-bristled toothbrush and avoid brushing so hard that you damage your gums. Second, floss every day. And most importantly, use a toothpaste with fluoride, which will significantly lower your risk of tooth decay. As you care for your teeth, remember to keep a close watch on what comes out of your mouth, as well. As Proverbs 13:3 suggests, those who are careful about what they say do more than protect their health, they protect their very lives.

>> 8:10 **idol's temple** Building where a god is worshiped.   9:9 **"When an ox … eating."** Quotation from Deuteronomy 25:4.

<<TechSupport>>

WIRELESS CONNECTIONS

Now you can connect personal computers to the Internet without all the multiple wires necessary to network your computers and telephones. New wireless technology is as fast as the wired version, and it is costing less and less. If you've got high-speed Internet at home, a wireless router makes it easy to connect your computers to the Web without making your house look like a corporate communications center. Going wireless is great, but be sure not to "unplug" from the important relationships in your life. Nothing is more important than your relationship with God, so keep the communication flowing!

the Good News of Christ. ¹³Surely you know that those who work at the Temple get their food from the Temple, and those who serve at the altar get part of what is offered at the altar. ¹⁴In the same way, the Lord has commanded that those who tell the Good News should get their living from this work.

¹⁵But I have not used any of these rights. And I am not writing this now to get anything from you. I would rather die than to have my reason for bragging taken away. ¹⁶Telling the Good News does not give me any reason for bragging. Telling the Good News is my duty—something I must do. And how terrible it will be for me if I do not tell the Good News. ¹⁷If I preach because it is my own choice, I have a re-

ward. But if I preach and it is not my choice to do so, I am only doing the duty that was given to me. ¹⁸So what reward do I get? This is my reward: that when I tell the Good News I can offer it freely. I do not use my full rights in my work of preaching the Good News.

¹⁹I am free and belong to no one. But I make myself a slave to all people to win as many as I can. ²⁰To the Jews I became like a Jew to win the Jews. I myself am not ruled by the law. But to those who are ruled by the law I became like a person who is ruled by the law. I did this to win those who are ruled by the law. ²¹To those who are without the law I became like a person who is without the law. I did this to win those people who are without the law. (But really, I am not without God's law—I am ruled by Christ's law.) ²²To those who are weak, I became weak so I could win the weak. I have become all things to all people so I

could save some of them in any way possible. ²³I do all this because of the Good News and so I can share in its blessings.

²⁴You know that in a race all the runners run, but only one gets the prize. So run to win! ²⁵All those who compete in the games use self-control so they can win a crown. That crown is an earthly thing that

Q: Why did Jesus curse the fig tree?

A: Many scholars believe this incident was a symbolic act on Jesus' part. The fig tree, representing Israel, was full of leaves but had no fruit—in much the same way that people in Israel made a public show of loving God, but lacked spiritual fruit (Matthew 21:18–19).

Survival Guide

HAMMERS: NAILING WITH ACCURACY

A hammer is indispensable for driving nails and other assorted uses at home. To get better performance, experts advise not to hold yours too tightly. Grip it in the middle for better control and closer to the end for more power. Start by tapping the nail lightly, and then use the center of the face to drive it home with firm blows. Keep your elbow straight to increase power. Aim to make your nailing straight and true, just like your life overall.

lasts only a short time, but our crown will never be destroyed. [26]So I do not run without a goal. I fight like a boxer who is hitting something—not just the air. [27]I treat my body hard and make it my slave so that I myself will not be disqualified after I have preached to others.

Warnings from Israel's Past

10 Brothers and sisters, I want you to know what happened to our ancestors who followed Moses. They were all under the cloud and all went through the sea. [2]They were all baptized as followers of Moses in the cloud and in the sea. [3]They all ate the same spiritual food, [4]and all drank the same spiritual drink. They drank from that spiritual rock that followed them, and that rock was Christ. [5]But God was not pleased with most of them, so they died in the desert.

[6]And these things happened as examples for us, to stop us from wanting evil things as those people did. [7]Do not worship idols, as some of them did. Just as it is written in the Scriptures: "They sat down to eat and drink, and then they got up and sinned sexually."[n] [8]We must not take part in sexual sins, as some of them did. In one day twenty-three thousand of them died because of their sins. [9]We must not test Christ as some of them did; they were killed by snakes. [10]Do not complain as some of them did; they were killed by the angel that destroys.

[11]The things that happened to those people are examples. They were written down to teach us, because we live in a time when all these things of the past have reached their goal. [12]If you think you are strong, you should be careful not to fall. [13]The only temptation that has come to you is that which everyone has. But you can trust God, who will not permit you to be tempted more than you can stand. But when you are tempted, he will also give you a way to escape so that you will be able to stand it.

[14]So, my dear friends, run away from the worship of idols. [15]I am speaking to you as to reasonable people; judge for yourselves what I say. [16]We give thanks for the cup of blessing,[n] which is a sharing in the blood of Christ. And the bread that we break is a sharing in the body of Christ. [17]Because there is one loaf of bread, we who are many are one body, because we all share that one loaf.

[18]Think about the Israelites: Do not those who eat the sacrifices

▶ Get Aligned
1 Corinthians 10:23–24

AS IT SAYS IN THE GOSPELS, "Love your neighbor as you love yourself" (Matthew 22:39). That kind of selflessness doesn't come easily. Our selfish nature gets in the way. When our favorite team is playing on television and the phone rings with a needy neighbor on the other end asking for yet another favor, our natural selfish attitude is easily provoked.

But Paul elevates the "love your neighbor" factor from simple kindness to pure love. It is one thing to be nice to others; it is another to do what is truly best for them. Whether that love comes easy or tough, true Christlike love is meeting others' needs rather than just their wants.

God has given us the freedom to do what we want within the boundaries of his commands. But he also challenges us to walk as Jesus did, continuously searching for ways to serve others. That includes being mindful of how our actions impact others, whether negatively or positively. We must avoid the habit of acting first and thinking later, and, instead, begin to consider our every action as a way to help others.

share in the altar? [19]I do not mean that the food sacrificed to an idol is important. I do not mean that an idol is anything at all. [20]But I say that what is sacrificed to idols is offered to demons, not to God. And I do not want you to share anything with demons. [21]You cannot drink the cup of the Lord and the cup of demons also. You cannot share in the Lord's table and the table of demons. [22]Are we trying to make the Lord jealous? We are not stronger than he is, are we?

How to Use Christian Freedom

[23]"We are allowed to do all things," but not all things are good for us to do. "We are allowed to do all things," but not all things help others grow stronger. [24]Do not look out only for yourselves. Look out for the good of others also.

[25]Eat any meat that is sold in the meat market. Do not ask questions about it. [26]You may eat it, "because the earth belongs to the Lord, and everything in it."[n] [27]Those who are not believers may invite you to eat with them. If you want to go, eat anything that is put before you. Do not ask questions about it. [28]But if anyone says to you, "That food was offered to idols," do not eat it. Do not eat it because of that person who told you and because eating it might be thought to be wrong. [29]I don't mean you think it is wrong, but the other person might. But why, you ask, should my freedom be judged by someone else's conscience? [30]If I eat

▶▶ live the life

1 Corinthians 10:13

The Principle > Grow in godliness.

Practicing It > Temptations can sometimes feel overwhelming. Nevertheless, with God's help, you always have the power to say no. When you feel weak, ask God to show you the way out of the temptation.

▶▶ 10:7 **"They … sexually."** Quotation from Exodus 32:6. **10:16 cup of blessing** The cup of the fruit of the vine that Christians thank God for and drink at the Lord's Supper. **10:26 "because … it"** Quotation from Psalms 24:1; 50:12; 89:11.

Principles: LOVE

The word "love" often gets defined by worldly terms. However, the biblical description of love is about being selfless rather than selfish. True love means looking out for another person's interests ahead of one's own. The love of God serves as the ultimate example for daily living and is personified by the sacrificial love that Jesus showed by dying in our place. Whereas the Old Testament presented the Ten Commandments, in the New Testament, Christ defined the two greatest commandments as loving God and our neighbors (Matthew 22:37–39). Through selfless acts of love toward others, the world witnesses the true meaning of love.

the meal with thankfulness, why am I criticized because of something for which I thank God?

³¹The answer is, if you eat or drink, or if you do anything, do it all for the glory of God. ³²Never do anything that might hurt others—Jews, Greeks, or God's church— ³³just as I, also, try to please everybody in every way. I am not trying to do what is good for me but what is good for most people so they can be saved.

11 Follow my example, as I follow the example of Christ.

Being Under Authority

²I praise you because you remember me in everything, and you follow closely the teachings just as I gave them to you. ³But I want you to understand this: The head of every man is Christ, the head of a woman is the man," and the head of Christ is God. ⁴Every man who prays or prophesies with his head covered brings shame to his head. ⁵But every woman who prays or prophesies with her head uncovered brings shame to her head. She is the same as a woman who has her head shaved. ⁶If a woman does not cover her head, she should have her hair cut off. But since it is shameful for a woman to cut off her hair or to shave her head, she should cover her head. ⁷But a man should not cover his head, because he is the likeness and glory of God. But woman is man's glory. ⁸Man did not come from woman, but woman came from man. ⁹And man was not made for woman, but woman was made for man. ¹⁰So that is why a woman should have a symbol of authority on her head, because of the angels.

¹¹But in the Lord women are not independent of men, and men are not independent of women. ¹²This is true because woman came from man, but also man is born from woman. But everything comes from God. ¹³Decide this for yourselves: Is it right for a woman to pray to God with her head uncovered? ¹⁴Even nature itself teaches you that wearing long hair is shameful for a man. ¹⁵But long hair is a woman's glory. Long hair is given to her as a covering. ¹⁶Some people may still want to argue about this, but I would add that neither we nor the churches of God have any other practice.

→ The Bottom Line

Living Wills: Specify Your Wishes

HIGHLY PUBLICIZED "RIGHT TO DIE" CASES EMPHASIZE THE NEED TO PREPARE A LIVING WILL. While you are healthy, spell out the medical care you desire in the event you should be seriously injured or struck by disease. You don't have to be old for this to happen, as car wrecks, airplane crashes, and serious illnesses affect people of all ages. As part of this process, you also need a medical power of attorney, appointing someone to make health care decisions if you are unconscious or incapacitated. As Luke 16:15 reminds, only God knows your heart, so don't leave loved ones trying to guess what you want.

>> 11:3 **the man** This could also mean "her husband."

The Lord's Supper

¹⁷In the things I tell you now I do not praise you, because when you come together you do more harm than good. ¹⁸First, I hear that when you meet together as a church you are divided, and I believe some of this. ¹⁹(It is necessary to have differences among you so that it may be clear which of you really have God's approval.) ²⁰When you come together, you are not really eating the Lord's Supper.ᵇ ²¹This is because when you eat, each person eats without waiting for the others. Some people do not get enough to eat, while others have too much to drink. ²²You can eat and drink in your own homes! You seem to think God's church is not important, and you embarrass those who are poor. What should I tell you? Should I praise you? I do not praise you for doing this.

²³The teaching I gave you is the same teaching I received from the Lord: On the night when the Lord Jesus was handed over to be killed, he took bread ²⁴and gave thanks for it. Then he broke the bread and said, "This is my body; it isᵇ for you. Do this to remember me." ²⁵In the same way, after they ate, Jesus took the cup. He said, "This cup is the new agreement that is sealed with the blood of my death. When you drink this, do it to re-member me." ²⁶Every time you eat this bread and drink this cup you are telling others about the Lord's death until he comes.

²⁷So a person who eats the bread or drinks the cup of the Lord in a way that is not worthy of it will be guilty of sinning against the body and the blood of the Lord. ²⁸Look into your own hearts before you eat the bread and drink the cup, ²⁹because all who eat the bread and drink the cup without recognizing the body eat and drink judgment against themselves. ³⁰That is why many in your group are sick and weak, and some of you have died. ³¹But if we judged ourselves in the right way, God would not judge us. ³²But when the Lord judges us, he disciplines us so that we will not be destroyed along with the world.

³³So my brothers and sisters, when you come together to eat, wait for each other. ³⁴Anyone who is too hungry should eat at home so that in meeting together you will not bring God's judgment on yourselves. I will tell you what to do about the other things when I come.

Gifts from the Holy Spirit

12 Now, brothers and sisters, I want you to understand about spiritual gifts. ²You know the way you lived before you were believers. You let yourselves be influenced and led away to worship idols—things that could not speak. ³So I want you to understand that no one who is speaking with the help of God's Spirit says, "Jesus be cursed." And no one can say, "Jesus is Lord," without the help of the Holy Spirit.

⁴There are different kinds of gifts, but they are all from the same Spirit. ⁵There are different ways to serve but the same Lord to serve.

Men of Valor
LUKE: Doctor of Discipleship

Luke was a physician who faithfully followed Christ. Despite being the author of the Gospel of Luke and the Book of Acts, his name appears only a few times in the New Testament. Still, Luke played a major role in biblical history. His account of the church's growth after Christ's resurrection showed how the Holy Spirit worked to overcome such hindrances as religious discrimination, division, and prejudice. Luke accompanied Paul on his missionary journeys, too. Commenting on people who had deserted him, Paul noted in 2 Timothy 4:11, "Luke is the only one still with me." Paul also listed Luke in Philemon 24 as a fellow worker. Luke was as dependable as the sunrise and was an active maker of followers.

⏵ Sexcess:
CELEBRATING THE OPPOSITE SEX

If you are single, whether by choice or circumstance, you are called to abstinence, and rest assured that the grace of God is sufficient for you. The sex drive is a God-given one, but it must never become an all-consuming one, no matter what the circumstances. Whereas it may seem easier said than done, celibacy need never prevent you from enjoying the opposite sex in particular, or life in general. Seeking to form platonic relationships with women now will stand you in good stead throughout life. Despite what the world suggests, sex is not, nor was it meant to be, the end-all of our earthly existence.

>> **11:20 Lord's Supper** The meal Jesus told his followers to eat to remember him (Luke 22:14–20).   **11:24 it is** Some Greek copies read "it is broken."

▶Get Aligned

1 Corinthians 12:18—19

GOD DESIGNED EACH UNIQUE BELIEVER TO FIT HIS BODY, the church. Whereas we are all to aim for Christlikeness, how that comes to fruition is as wonderfully distinctive as the variance shown in a million sunsets. You were made exactly the way God intended, quirks and all. The church was never designed to be uniform. Paul's illustration of the physical body perfectly displays the individuality of each part and how those parts form a fully operational and living organism.

The challenge for most believers, however, is finding their place in the body. Some approach this search as they do life in general;

they passively wait to see what will unfold. Others are so aggressive they push themselves into roles incongruent to their natural abilities and disposition. One thing is certain: the body needs you.

If you are unsure how you can uniquely contribute to the body, consider taking a spiritual gifts test. Volunteer for ministries that pique your interest. Discover your passions, talents, and natural abilities, and then use them for the benefit of the church. Whatever you do, become a part of the body, not someone apart from it. It's one of the main purposes for which God created you.

¹⁴The human body has many parts. ¹⁵The foot might say, "Because I am not a hand, I am not part of the body." But saying this would not stop the foot from being a part of the body. ¹⁶The ear might say, "Because I am not an eye, I am not part of the body." But saying this would not stop the ear from being a part of the body. ¹⁷If the whole body were an eye, it would not be able to hear. If the whole body were an ear, it would not be able to smell. ¹⁸⁻¹⁹If each part of the body were the same part, there would be no body. But truly God put all the parts, each one of them, in the body as he wanted them. ²⁰So then there are many parts, but only one body.

²¹The eye cannot say to the hand, "I don't need you!" And the head cannot say to the foot, "I don't need you!" ²²No! Those parts of the body that seem to be the weaker are really necessary. ²³And the parts of the body we think are less deserving are the parts to which we give the most honor. We give special respect to the parts we want to hide. ²⁴The more respectable parts of our body need no special care. But God put the body together and gave more honor to the parts that need it ²⁵so our body would not be divided. God wanted the different parts to care the same for each other. ²⁶If one part of the body suffers, all the other parts suffer with it. Or if one part of our body is honored, all the other parts share its honor.

²⁷Together you are the body of Christ, and each one of you is a part of that body. ²⁸In the church God has given a place first to apostles, second to prophets, and third to teachers. Then God has given a place to those who do miracles, those who have gifts of healing, those who can help others, those who are able to govern, and those who can speak in different languages." ²⁹Not all are apostles. Not all are prophets. Not all are teachers. Not all do miracles. ³⁰Not all have gifts of healing. Not all speak in different languages. Not all interpret those languages. ³¹But you should truly want to have the greater gifts.

Love Is the Greatest Gift

And now I will show you the best way of all.

13 I may speak in different languages" of people or even angels. But if I do not have love, I am only a noisy bell or a crashing

⁶And there are different ways that God works through people but the same God. God works in all of us in everything we do. ⁷Something from the Spirit can be seen in each person, for the common good. ⁸The Spirit gives one person the ability to speak with wisdom, and the same Spirit gives another the ability to speak with knowledge. ⁹The same Spirit gives faith to one person. And, to another, that one Spirit gives gifts of healing. ¹⁰The Spirit gives to another person the power to do miracles, to another the ability to prophesy. And he gives to another the ability to know the difference between good and evil spirits. The Spirit gives one person the ability to speak in different kinds of languages" and to another the ability to interpret those languages. ¹¹One Spirit, the same Spirit, does all these things, and the Spirit decides what to give each person.

The Body of Christ Works Together

¹²A person's body is one thing, but it has many parts. Though there are many parts to a body, all those parts make only one body. Christ is like that also. ¹³Some of us are Jews, and some are Greeks. Some of us are slaves, and some are free. But we were all baptized into one body through one Spirit. And we were all made to share in the one Spirit.

≫ live the life

1 Corinthians 12:25—26

The Principle > Care for others.

Practicing It > People often come to church lonely, suffering, and in need of love. Look for opportunities to extend compassion toward the hurting people in your church. There are lots of ways to show compassion if you look for them.

≫ **12:10 languages** This can also be translated "tongues."   **12:28 languages** This can also be translated "tongues."   **13:1 languages** This can also be translated "tongues."

Q: Who were the Pharisees?

A: The Pharisees were members of a devout sect of Judaism that strictly followed the written Law of Moses, as well as the religious regulations handed down by oral tradition. They lived supremely disciplined lives, but placed more faith in their duty than in devotion to God.

cymbal. ²I may have the gift of prophecy. I may understand all the secret things of God and have all knowledge, and I may have faith so great I can move mountains. But even with all these things, if I do not have love, then I am nothing. ³I may give away everything I have, and I may even give my body as an offering to be burned." But I gain nothing if I do not have love.

⁴Love is patient and kind. Love is not jealous, it does not brag, and it is not proud. ⁵Love is not rude, is not selfish, and does not get upset with others. Love does not count up wrongs that have been done. ⁶Love takes no pleasure in evil but rejoices over the truth. ⁷Love patiently accepts all things. It always trusts, always hopes, and always endures.

⁸Love never ends. There are gifts of prophecy, but they will be ended. There are gifts of speaking in different languages, but those gifts will stop. There is the gift of knowledge, but it will come to an end. ⁹The reason is that our knowledge and our ability to prophesy are not perfect. ¹⁰But when perfection comes, the things that are not perfect will end. ¹¹When I was a child, I talked like a child, I thought like a child, I reasoned like a child. When I became a man, I stopped those childish ways. ¹²It is the same with us. Now we see a dim reflection, as if we were looking into a mirror, but then we shall see clearly. Now I know only a part, but then I will know fully, as God has known me. ¹³So these three things continue forever: faith, hope, and love. And the greatest of these is love.

Desire Spiritual Gifts

14 You should seek after love, and you should truly want to have the spiritual gifts, especially the gift of prophecy. ²I will explain why. Those who have the gift of speaking in different languages" are not speaking to people; they are speaking to God. No one understands them; they are speaking secret things through the Spirit. ³But those who prophesy are speaking to people to give them strength, encouragement, and comfort. ⁴The ones who speak in different languages are helping only themselves, but those who prophesy are helping the whole church. ⁵I wish all of you had the gift of speaking in different kinds of languages, but more, I wish you would prophesy. Those who prophesy are greater than those who

can only speak in different languages—unless someone is there who can explain what is said so that the whole church can be helped.

⁶Brothers and sisters, will it help you if I come to you speaking in different languages? No! It will help you only if I bring you a new truth or some new knowledge, or prophecy, or teaching. ⁷It is the same as with lifeless things that make sounds—like a flute or a harp. If they do not make clear musical notes, you will not know what is being played. ⁸And in a war, if the trumpet does not give a clear sound, who will prepare for battle? ⁹It is the same with you. Unless you speak clearly with your tongue, no one can understand what you are saying. You will be talking into the air! ¹⁰It may be true that there are all kinds of sounds in the world, and none is without meaning. ¹¹But unless I understand the meaning of what someone says to me, we will be like foreigners to each other. ¹²It is the same with you. Since you want spiritual gifts very much, seek most of all to have the gifts that help the church grow stronger.

¹³The one who has the gift of speaking in a different language should pray for the gift to interpret what is spoken. ¹⁴If I pray in a different language, my spirit is praying, but my mind does nothing. ¹⁵So what should I do? I will pray with my spirit, but I will also pray with my mind. I will sing with my spirit, but I will also sing with my mind. ¹⁶If you praise God with your spirit, those persons there without understanding cannot say amen" to your prayer of thanks, because they do

▶ Get Aligned
1 Corinthians 13:1–3

LOOK UP THE WORD "LOVE" IN A DICTIONARY, and you will find a long list of various definitions. You'll even discover almost a page's worth of variations and derivations of the word. Yet none of those descriptions and explanations of love captures the true state. Some may scratch the surface in relating the emotional feelings connected with love, but none will grasp the element in its entirety.

Love must be lived out from within. Some of us go through our entire life without ever experiencing this. We do the things Paul lists in this poetic passage, the outward motions and abilities that can easily be mistaken for love. While his examples are directly related to the church, they are just as applicable to marriages, friendships, and any other relationships. The underlying point is that, void of love, none of our extravagant deeds matter.

The only way our actions can hold meaning is by having love, which comes directly from God. It is his gift to humanity that ceaselessly proves his glory to believers and nonbelievers alike. Our divine purpose as Christians is to pour out that love to others—unconditionally, actively, and purely.

13:3 give...burned Other Greek copies read "hand over my body in order that I may brag." 14:2 languages This can also be translated "tongues." 14:16 amen To say amen means to agree with the things that were said.

229

not know what you are saying. [17]You may be thanking God in a good way, but the other person is not helped.

[18]I thank God that I speak in different kinds of languages more than all of you. [19]But in the church meetings I would rather speak five words I understand in order to teach others than thousands of words in a different language.

[20]Brothers and sisters, do not think like children. In evil things be like babies, but in your thinking you should be like adults. [21]It is written in the Scriptures:

"With people who use strange words and foreign languages
    I will speak to these people.
But even then they will not listen to me,"   *Isaiah 28:11–12*
says the Lord.

[22]So the gift of speaking in different kinds of languages is a sign for those who do not believe, not for those who do believe. And prophecy is for people who believe, not for those who do not believe. [23]Suppose the whole church meets together and everyone speaks in different languages. If some people come in who do not understand or do not believe, they will say you are crazy. [24]But suppose everyone is prophesying and some people come in who do not believe or do not understand. If everyone is prophesying, their sin will be shown to them, and they will be judged by all that they hear. [25]The secret things in their hearts will be made known. So they will bow down and worship God saying, "Truly, God is with you."

Meetings Should Help the Church

[26]So, brothers and sisters, what should you do? When you meet together, one person has a song, and another has a teaching. Another has a new truth from God. Another speaks in a different language," and another person interprets that language. The purpose of all these things should be to help the church grow strong. [27]When you meet together, if anyone speaks in a different language, it should be only two, or not more than three, who speak. They should speak one after the other, and someone should interpret. [28]But if there is no interpreter, then those who speak in a different language should be quiet in the church meeting. They should speak only to themselves and to God.

[29]Only two or three prophets should speak, and the others should judge what they say. [30]If a message from God comes to another person who is sitting, the first speaker should stop. [31]You can all prophesy one after the other. In this way all the people can be taught and encouraged. [32]The spirits of prophets are under the control of the prophets themselves. [33]God is not a God of confusion but a God of peace.

As is true in all the churches of God's people, [34]women should keep quiet in the church meetings. They are not allowed to speak, but they must yield to this rule as the law says. [35]If they want to learn something, they should ask their own husbands at home. It is shameful for a woman to speak in the church meeting. [36]Did God's teaching come from you? Or are you the only ones to whom it has come?

[37]Those who think they are prophets or spiritual persons should un-

Q: Who were the Sadducees?

A: The Sadducees were members of a devout sect of Judaism that strictly followed the written Law of Moses. Unlike the Pharisees, the Sadducees did not adhere to the rules of tradition, nor did they believe in an afterlife.

Get Fit

BENEFITING FROM PETS   It doesn't matter what it is—dog or cat, ferret or parrot—having a pet can definitely improve your outlook on life and even your physical health. The unconditional love we receive from pets is priceless. In a curious way, it reminds us of the unconditional love we receive from God. Spending time with your pet, even if it's only a few minutes each day, can reduce the levels of stress in your life and help shore up your immune system to fight off disease. So get a pet and enjoy its love. And don't forget to thank God for his love in your life, as well.

▶▶ 14:26 **language** This can also be translated "tongue."

derstand that what I am writing to you is the Lord's command. [38]Those who ignore this will be ignored by God."

[39]So my brothers and sisters, you should truly want to prophesy. But do not stop people from using the gift of speaking in different kinds of languages. [40]But let everything be done in a right and orderly way.

The Good News About Christ

15 Now, brothers and sisters, I want you to remember the Good News I brought to you. You received this Good News

> " Do not be fooled: 'Bad friends will ruin good habits.' Come back to your right way of thinking and stop sinning. "
> 1 CORINTHIANS 15:33–34

and continue strong in it. [2]And you are being saved by it if you continue believing what I told you. If you do not, then you believed for nothing.

[3]I passed on to you what I received, of which this was most important: that Christ died for our sins, as the Scriptures say; [4]that he was buried and was raised to life on the third day as the Scriptures say; [5]and that he was seen by Peter and then by the twelve apostles. [6]After that, Jesus was seen by more than five hundred of the believers at the same time. Most of them are still living today, but some have died. [7]Then he was seen by James and later by all the apostles. [8]Last of all he was seen by me—as by a person not born at the normal time. [9]All the other apostles are greater than I am. I am not even good enough to be called an apostle, because I persecuted the church of God. [10]But God's grace has made me what I am, and his grace to me was not wasted. I worked harder than all the other apostles. (But it was not I really; it was God's grace that was with me.) [11]So if I preached to you or the other apostles preached to you, we all preach the same thing, and this is what you believed.

We Will Be Raised from the Dead

[12]Now since we preached that Christ was raised from the dead, why do some of you say that people will not be raised from the dead? [13]If no one is ever raised from the dead, then Christ has not been raised. [14]And if Christ has not been raised, then our preaching is worth nothing, and your faith is worth nothing. [15]And also, we are guilty of lying about God, because we testified of him that he raised Christ from the dead. But if people are not raised from the dead, then God never raised Christ. [16]If the dead are not raised, Christ has not been raised either. [17]And if Christ has not been raised, then your faith has nothing to it; you are still guilty of your sins. [18]And those in Christ who have already died are lost. [19]If our hope in Christ is for this life only, we should be pitied more than anyone else in the world.

[20]But Christ has truly been raised from the dead—the first one and proof that those who sleep in death will also be raised. [21]Death has come because of what one man did, but the rising from death also

comes because of one man. [22]In Adam all of us die. In the same way, in Christ all of us will be made alive again. [23]But everyone will be raised to life in the right order. Christ was first to be raised. When Christ comes again, those who belong to him will be raised to life, [24]and then the end will come. At that time Christ will destroy all rulers, authorities, and powers, and he will hand over the kingdom to God the Father. [25]Christ must rule until he puts all enemies under his control. [26]The last enemy to be destroyed will be death. [27]The Scripture says that God put all things under his control." When it says "all things" are under him, it is clear this does not include God himself. God is the One who put everything under his control. [28]After everything has been put under the Son, then he will put himself under God, who had put all things under him. Then God will be the complete ruler over everything.

[29]If the dead are never raised, what will people do who are being baptized for the dead? If the dead are not raised at all, why are people being baptized for them?

[30]And what about us? Why do we put ourselves in danger every hour? [31]I die every day. That is true, brothers and sisters, just as it is true that I brag about you in Christ Jesus our Lord. [32]If I fought wild animals in Ephesus only with human hopes, I have gained nothing. If the dead are not raised, "Let us eat and drink, because tomorrow we will die."

[33]Do not be fooled: "Bad friends will ruin good habits." [34]Come back to your right way of thinking and stop sinning. Some of you do not know God—I say this to shame you.

What Kind of Body Will We Have?

[35]But someone may ask, "How are the dead raised? What kind of body will they have?" [36]Foolish person! When you sow a seed, it must die in the ground before it

Q: Who were the Essenes?

A: The Essenes were members of a devout sect of Judaism that strictly adhered to the written Law of Moses. The Essenes most likely branched off from the Pharisees sometime before Christ and were typically separatists, living in communal environments apart from society.

>> 14:38 Those...God. Some Greek copies read "Those who are ignorant of this will stay ignorant." 15:27 God put...control. From Psalm 8:6. 15:32 "Let us...die." Quotation from Isaiah 22:13; 56:12.

People
Skills

Evaluating Relationships

At least once a year, prayerfully set aside time to clarify your goals in your relationships with those closest to you. How has the relationship changed during the past year? It helps to determine where it is presently and where you want it to be in the future. What will it take to move you in that direction? Relationships take work and attentive care, but they don't have to be a burden so long as you take regular time to dream together about what you want your relationship to look like. Then let that vision serve as your motivation to move forward together.

can live and grow. ³⁷And when you sow it, it does not have the same "body" it will have later. What you sow is only a bare seed, maybe wheat or something else. ³⁸But God gives it a body that he has planned for it, and God gives each kind of seed its own body. ³⁹All things made of flesh are not the same: People have one kind of flesh, animals have another, birds have another, and fish have another. ⁴⁰Also there are heavenly bodies and earthly bodies. But the beauty of the heavenly bodies is one kind, and the beauty of the earthly bodies is another. ⁴¹The sun has one kind of beauty, the moon has another beauty, and the stars have another. And each star is different in its beauty.

⁴²It is the same with the dead who are raised to life. The body that is "planted" will ruin and decay, but it is raised to a life that cannot be destroyed. ⁴³When the body is "planted," it is without honor, but it is raised in glory. When the body is "planted," it is weak, but when it is raised, it is powerful. ⁴⁴The body that is "planted" is a physical body. When it is raised, it is a spiritual body.

There is a physical body, and there is also a spiritual body. ⁴⁵It is written in the Scriptures: "The first man, Adam, became a living person."ⁿ But the last Adam became a spirit that gives life. ⁴⁶The spiritual did not come first, but the physical and then the spiritual. ⁴⁷The first man came from the dust of the earth. The second man came from heaven. ⁴⁸People who belong to the earth are like the first man of earth. But those people who belong to heaven are like the man of heaven. ⁴⁹Just as we were made like the man of earth, so we willⁿ also be made like the man of heaven.

⁵⁰I tell you this, brothers and sisters: Flesh and blood cannot have a part in the kingdom of God. Something that will ruin cannot have a part in something that never ruins. ⁵¹But look! I tell you this secret: We will not all sleep in death, but we will all be changed. ⁵²It will take only a second—as quickly as an eye blinks—when the last trumpet sounds. The trumpet will sound, and those who have died will be raised to live forever, and we will all be changed. ⁵³This body that can be destroyed must clothe itself with something that can never be destroyed. And this body that dies must clothe itself with something that can never die. ⁵⁴So this body that can be destroyed

---

THINK ABOUT IT 1 Corinthians 15:58

PEOPLE ARE CALLED UPON TO STAND STRONG against a variety of pressures and one of the most familiar is the pressure of negotiation. The activity of negotiating is called a variety of names: haggling, bargaining, bartering, or wrangling. Whether you are working on a contract for your company, bidding on something on eBay, or haggling with a car salesman over a new vehicle, you are actively engaged in trying to get the best deal possible.

If the process is typical, you determine a point where you will stand firm and not lower your price. Then if the other party tries to move you lower, it is a deal-breaker and the negotiation is ended. You pick a point, stand firm, and walk away from the negotiations.

In the spiritual realm, the apostle Paul wrote about the necessity to "stand strong" against life's pressures and "not let anything move you." Don't hold anything back, but firmly engage in God's work. By getting fully involved in kingdom business, you will receive the promise of this verse, "Your work in the Lord is never wasted."

⏩ 15:45 "The first … person." Quotation from Genesis 2:7. 15:49 **so we will** Some Greek copies read "so let us."

232

will clothe itself with that which can never be destroyed, and this body that dies will clothe itself with that which can never die. When this happens, this Scripture will be made true:

"Death is destroyed forever in victory."   *Isaiah 25:8*
⁵⁵"Death, where is your victory?

Death, where is your pain?"   *Hosea 13:14*
⁵⁶Death's power to hurt is sin, and the power of sin is the law. ⁵⁷But we thank God! He gives us the victory through our Lord Jesus Christ.

⁵⁸So my dear brothers and sisters, stand strong. Do not let anything move you. Always give yourselves fully to the work of the Lord, because you know that your work in the Lord is never wasted.

The Gift for Other Believers

16 Now I will write about the collection of money for God's people. Do the same thing I told the Galatian churches to do: ²On the first day of every week, each one of you should put aside money as you have been blessed. Save it up so you will not have to collect money after I come. ³When I arrive, I will send whomever you approve to take your gift to Jerusalem. I will send them with letters of introduction, ⁴and if it seems good for me to go also, they will go along with me.

Paul's Plans

⁵I plan to go through Macedonia, so I will come to you after I go through there. ⁶Perhaps I will stay with you for a time or even all winter. Then you can help me on my trip, wherever I go. ⁷I do not want to see you now just in passing. I hope to stay a longer time with you if the Lord allows it. ⁸But I will stay at Ephesus until Pentecost, ⁹because a good opportunity for a great and growing work has been given to me now. And there are many people working against me.

¹⁰If Timothy comes to you, see to it that he has nothing to fear with you, because he is working for the Lord just as I am. ¹¹So none of you should treat Timothy as unimportant, but help him on his trip in peace so that he can come back to me. I am expecting him to come with the brothers.

¹²Now about our brother Apollos: I strongly encouraged him to visit you with the other brothers. He did not at all want to come now; he will come when he has the opportunity.

>> live the life

1 Corinthians 16:13

The Principle > Remain strong in the faith.

Practicing It > Don't be surprised when your faith is tested. Instead, commit yourself to stand firm in your faith no matter what happens. Ask God for courage when your strength grows faint, and he will sustain you.

Paul Ends His Letter

¹³Be alert. Continue strong in the faith. Have courage, and be strong. ¹⁴Do everything in love.

¹⁵You know that the family of Stephanas were the first believers in Southern Greece and that they have given themselves to the service of God's people. I ask you, brothers and sisters, ¹⁶to follow the leading of people like these and anyone else who works and serves with them.

¹⁷I am happy that Stephanas, Fortunatus, and Achaicus have come. You are not here, but they have filled your place. ¹⁸They have refreshed my spirit and yours. You should recognize the value of people like these.

¹⁹The churches in Asia send greetings to you. Aquila and Priscilla greet you in the Lord, as does the church that meets in their house. ²⁰All the brothers and sisters here send greetings. Give each other a holy kiss when you meet.

²¹I, Paul, am writing this greeting with my own hand.

²²If anyone does not love the Lord, let him be separated from God—lost forever!

Come, O Lord!

²³The grace of the Lord Jesus be with you.

²⁴My love be with all of you in Christ Jesus."

>> 16:24 **My...Jesus.** Some Greek copies add "Amen."

THE **SECOND** LETTER OF PAUL THE APOSTLE TO THE
Corinthians

AUTHOR: PAUL
DATE WRITTEN: A.D. 56–57

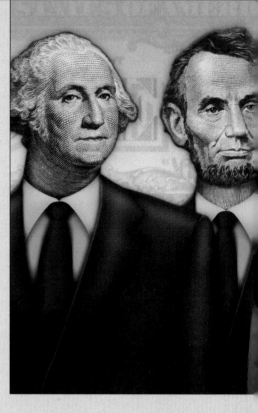

BANK TELLERS ARE TRAINED TO RECOGNIZE
a counterfeit bill. The paper looks different and some of
the features of the authentic currency are absent. It is a
false representation of the real deal. Sometimes counterfeit or false teachers infiltrate the church. In Corinth,
these false teachers challenged the apostle Paul's integrity
and questioned whether he was a legitimate apostle of Jesus Christ.

At the opening of this second letter to the Corinthian
church, Paul reminds the believers of his proven honesty,
his straightforward teaching, his plans to visit them
again, and of his previous letter to them. Then he con-
fronts the false teachers and exhorts the true believers not to turn away from
the Good News.

Paul also challenges the Christians in Corinth to give generously to the
poorer Christians in Jerusalem, while the final portion of the letter provides a
stirring defense of Paul's credentials as a genuine apostle. With real compassion
and straight talk, Paul encourages the Corinthians to recognize false teaching,
to remain committed to God's truth, and to influence their culture for good.

1 From Paul, an apostle of Christ Jesus. I am an apostle because that is what God wanted. Also from Timothy our brother in Christ.

To the church of God in Corinth, and to all of God's people everywhere in Southern Greece:

²Grace and peace to you from God our Father and the Lord Jesus Christ.

Paul Gives Thanks to God

³Praise be to the God and Father of our Lord Jesus Christ. God is the Father who is full of mercy and all comfort. ⁴He comforts us every time we have trouble, so when others have trouble, we can comfort them with the same comfort God gives us. ⁵We share in the many sufferings of Christ. In the same way, much comfort comes to us through Christ. ⁶If we have troubles, it is for your comfort and salvation, and if we have comfort, you also have comfort. This helps you to accept patiently the same sufferings we have. ⁷Our hope for you is strong, knowing that you share in our sufferings and also in the comfort we receive.

⁸Brothers and sisters, we want you to know about the trouble we suffered in Asia. We had great burdens there that were beyond our own strength. We even gave up hope of living. ⁹Truly, in our own hearts we believed we would die. But this happened so we would not trust in ourselves but in God, who raises people from the dead. ¹⁰God saved us from these great dangers of death, and he will continue to save us. We have put our hope in him, and he will save us again. ¹¹And you can help us with your prayers. Then many people will give thanks for us—that God blessed us because of their many prayers.

The Change in Paul's Plans

¹²This is what we are proud of, and I can say it with a clear conscience: In everything we have done in the world, and especially with you, we have had an honest[b] and sincere heart from God. We did this by God's grace, not by the kind of wisdom the world has. ¹³⁻¹⁴We write to you only what you can read and understand. And I hope that as you have understood some things about us, you may come to know everything about us. Then you can be proud of us, as we will be proud of you on the day our Lord Jesus Christ comes again.

¹⁵I was so sure of all this that I made plans to visit you first so you could be blessed twice. ¹⁶I planned to visit you on my way to Macedonia and again on my way back. I wanted to get help from you for my trip to Judea. ¹⁷Do you think that I made these plans without really meaning it? Or maybe you think I make plans as the world does, so that I say yes, yes and at the same time no, no.

¹⁸But since you can believe God, you can believe that what we tell you is never both yes and no. ¹⁹The Son of God, Jesus Christ, that Silas and Timothy and I preached to you, was not yes and no. In Christ it has always been yes. ²⁰The yes to all of God's promises is in Christ, and through Christ we say yes to the glory of God. ²¹Remember, God is the One who makes you and us strong in Christ. God made us his chosen people. ²²He put his mark on us to show that

Q: Who were the Zealots?

A: The Zealots were Jews who fiercely opposed the Roman occupation of their country. They often refused to pay taxes to Caesar, frequently proclaimed that God would drive the Romans from Israel, and held fierce loyalty to the Jewish traditions.

➡ The Bottom Line

Giving: Check Your Motives

PROBLEMS ARISE WHEN PEOPLE EXPECT MIRACULOUS RETURNS AFTER GIVING TO A CHURCH. Instead, they ought to be expecting God to bless them through their work. Rather than expecting windfalls like winning the lottery, the Bible closely connects work with God's blessing. It points to the success Jesus' followers had when Jesus told them where to fish in John 21:3–6. If you're looking for success, ask God to bless the work of your hands.

FACT-OIDS!

In 2002, Americans made 110.2 million visits to hospital emergency rooms, about one for every three people.

[National Center for Health Statistics]

we are his, and he put his Spirit in our hearts to be a guarantee for all he has promised.

[23]I tell you this, and I ask God to be my witness that this is true: The reason I did not come back to Corinth was to keep you from being punished or hurt. [24]We are not trying to control your faith. You are strong in faith. But we are workers with you for your own joy.

2 So I decided that my next visit to you would not be another one to make you sad. [2]If I make you sad, who will make me glad? Only you can make me glad—particularly the person whom I made sad. [3]I wrote you a letter for this reason: that when I came to you I would not be made sad by the people who should make me happy. I felt sure of all of you, that you would share my joy. [4]When I wrote to you before, I was very troubled and unhappy in my heart, and I wrote with many tears. I did not write to make you sad, but to let you know how much I love you.

Forgive the Sinner

[5]Someone there among you has caused sadness, not to me, but to all of you. I mean he caused sadness to all in some way. (I do not want to make it sound worse than it really is.) [6]The punishment that most of you gave him is enough for him. [7]But now you should forgive him and comfort him to keep him from having too much sadness and giving up completely. [8]So I beg you to show that you love him. [9]I wrote you to test you and to see if you obey in everything. [10]If you forgive someone, I also forgive him. And what I have forgiven—if I had anything to forgive—I forgave it for you, as if Christ were with me. [11]I did this so that Satan would not win anything from us, because we know very well what Satan's plans are.

Paul's Concern in Troas

[12]When I came to Troas to preach the Good News of Christ, the Lord gave me a good opportunity there. [13]But I had no peace, because I did not find my brother Titus. So I said good-bye to them at Troas and went to Macedonia.

Victory Through Christ

[14]But thanks be to God, who always leads us as captives in Christ's victory parade. God uses us to spread his knowledge everywhere like a sweet-smelling perfume. [15]Our offering to God is this: We are the sweet smell of Christ among those who are being saved and among those who are being lost. [16]To those who are lost, we are the smell of death that brings death, but to those who are being saved, we are the smell of life that brings life. So who is able to do this work? [17]We do not sell the word of God for a profit as many other people do. But in Christ we speak the truth before God, as messengers of God.

{ Book of the Month }

Failing Forward
by John Maxwell

Best-selling author John Maxwell packs this book with stories of ordinary people who overcame momentary failures to achieve extraordinary results. The common thread running through all their lives is how they dealt with failure. For example, Maxwell tells the story of S. Truett Cathy, who returned from World War II to start a restaurant. His two brothers (and business partners) were killed in a plane crash, and his second restaurant later burned to the ground. However, those failures further strengthened Cathy's resolve, and he persevered to found Chick-fil-A, the largest privately held chicken fast-food chain in the United States, a business worth nearly $1 billion today.

JOHN C. Maxwell
Failing Forward

{ Deal With It: *Drugs

THE ILLICIT USE OF DRUGS CAN COVER THE RANGE OF ADDICTIONS from over-the-counter medications to alcohol to illegal narcotics. While often used as an escape mechanism, drugs instead deliver the double boomerang effect: the inevitable lows after the temporary high *and* the corresponding pain drug addiction causes in the lives of loved ones. To compound the problem of drug abuse, especially as it relates to alcohol, it is often generational in scope. But by the grace of God, the curse can be reversed. Addicts are trying to fill a God-sized void that only God can fit, and the prescription for it is becoming dependent on Christ.

>>July

QUOTE OF THE MONTH:
"I've had a lot of worries in my life, most of which never happened." —Mark Twain

1 Share some ice cream with someone you love.

2

3

4 Celebrate **Independence Day** by thanking God for the gift of liberty.

5 Start a recycling system for your household.

6

7

8 Help someone change a flat tire.

9 Pray for a person of influence: Today is actor **Tom Hanks's** birthday.

10

11 Memorize Matthew 6:33.

12

13 Pray for a person of influence: Today is actor **Harrison Ford's** birthday.

14

15

16 Ask for forgiveness from a friend.

17

18 Contact your favorite high school teacher and thank them for their influence.

19 Say a prayer for your next-door neighbor.

20

21 Neil Armstrong became the first man to walk on the moon on this day in 1969.

22 Pray for a person of influence: Today is announcer **Alex Trebek's** birthday.

23 Go berry picking with a friend.

24

25

26 Rent a convertible and go cruising with the top down.

27 Take a moonlit stroll with your significant other.

28

29

30 Forgive someone a debt they owe you.

31 Pray for a person of influence: Today is author **Joanne Rowling's** birthday.

<<TechSupport>>

TiVo

TiVo is like a VCR that never runs out of space. Blending the worlds of television and personal computers, TiVo is a hard-drive-based device that connects to your television set and allows you to record and pause live television, as well as tape and catalog hours of programs while you're away. Best of all, you can tape an entire season of a favorite program and zip through commercials with the press of a button. With all the time you're saving by not watching commercials, you can invest more time in building relationships.

Servants of the New Agreement

3 Are we starting to brag about ourselves again? Do we need letters of introduction to you or from you, like some other people? ²You yourselves are our letter, written on our hearts, known and read by everyone. ³You show that you are a letter from Christ sent through us. This letter is not written with ink but with the Spirit of the living God. It is not written on stone tablets* but on human hearts.

⁴We can say this, because through Christ we feel certain before God. ⁵We are not saying that we can do this work ourselves. It is God who makes us able to do all that we do. ⁶He made us able to be servants of a new agreement from himself to his people. This new agreement is not a written law, but it is of the Spirit. The written law brings death, but the Spirit gives life.

⁷The law that brought death was written in words on stone. It came with God's glory, which made Moses' face so bright that the Israelites could not continue to look at it. But that glory later disappeared. ⁸So surely the new way that brings the Spirit has even more glory. ⁹If the law that judged people guilty of sin had glory, surely the new way that makes people right with God has much greater glory. ¹⁰That old law had glory, but it really loses its glory when it is compared to the much greater glory of this new way. ¹¹If that law which disappeared came with glory, then this new way which continues forever has much greater glory.

¹²We have this hope, so we are very bold. ¹³We are not like Moses, who put a covering over his face so the Israelites would not see it. The glory was disappearing, and Moses did not want them to see it end. ¹⁴But their minds were closed, and even today that same covering hides the meaning when they read the old agreement. That covering is taken away only through Christ. ¹⁵Even today, when they read the law of

Q: Why did the Pharisees and Sadducees hate Jesus so much?

A: By the time of Jesus, both sects of religious leaders had become powerful political forces in Israel and ruled in a theocratic system that became corrupt. Jesus openly challenged their authority, so they sought to have him condemned and killed.

▶ Survival Guide

INSULATION: PROTECTING YOUR INVESTMENT

Just as you wear a coat to keep warm, insulation helps to reduce heat flow. That keeps heat inside your home in cold weather and outside in the summer. A well-insulated home means lower utility costs, increased comfort, and better sound absorption. If you have an attic that serves only as a storage area, check it first to see if additional insulation is warranted. It may also be needed in outside walls, basement walls, floors over unheated garages, and between interior walls. Insulation helps protect your biggest investment.

>> **3:3 stone tablets** Meaning the Law of Moses that was written on stone tablets (Exodus 24:12; 25:16).

▶ Get Aligned
2 Corinthians 4:16

Everyone knows that our bodies don't stay young forever. Our hair begins to thin. We acquire that spare tire. Our knees, back, and shoulders hurt from doing things that once came so easily. To stall the aging process, we take care of our health by watching what we eat and staying active.

And we need to give the same attention to our spiritual health. It's possible to find our soul suffering from the same process as a result of neglect. We can find ourselves coasting on spiritual cruise control, never feeding or strengthening our spiritual muscles. Or we can become spiritually obese,

loaded with the knowledge of the Bible but never acting upon what resides in our head.

Without a steady diet of spiritual food and exercise, our spirit will never grow. It will atrophy like an unused muscle that over time becomes almost impossible to revive. Whereas we should never forsake taking care of our bodies, Jesus made it clear that our spirit is what matters eternally. When we realize we've been spending more time strengthening our body than our spirit, it is time to align our priorities with what God says matters most.

Spiritual Treasure in Clay Jars

[7]We have this treasure from God, but we are like clay jars that hold the treasure. This shows that the great power is from God, not from us. [8]We have troubles all around us, but we are not defeated. We do not know what to do, but we do not give up the hope of living. [9]We are persecuted, but God does not leave us. We are hurt sometimes, but we are not destroyed. [10]We carry the death of Jesus in our own bodies so that the life of Jesus can also be seen in our bodies. [11]We are alive, but for Jesus we are always in danger of death so that the life of Jesus can be seen in our bodies that die. [12]So death is working in us, but life is working in you.

[13]It is written in the Scriptures, "I believed, so I spoke."[n] Our faith is like this, too. We believe, and so we speak. [14]God raised the Lord Jesus from the dead, and we know that God will also raise us with Jesus. God will bring us together with you, and we will stand before him. [15]All these things are for you. And so the grace of God that is being given

Change >> Your WORLD

OFFICERS' CHRISTIAN FELLOWSHIP

Military leaders sometimes wonder if they are alone in their faith and following Jesus. With the desire to establish a godly military, Officers' Christian Fellowship (OCF) serves those men and women who are serving their country. The OCF works with active duty officers, enlisted personnel, guard and reserve members, academy and ROTC cadets/midshipmen, international military personnel, retirees, and widows. Through its small group fellowship and outreach, combined with prayer and conference centers, OCF is making an impact on the military. It provides a number of resources to help the members of the military grow in their faith.

To change your world, visit www.ocfusa.org.

Moses, there is a covering over their minds. [16]But when a person changes and follows the Lord, that covering is taken away. [17]The Lord is the Spirit, and where the Spirit of the Lord is, there is freedom. [18]Our faces, then, are not covered. We all show the Lord's glory, and we are being changed to be like him. This change in us brings ever greater glory, which comes from the Lord, who is the Spirit.

Preaching the Good News

4 God, with his mercy, gave us this work to do, so we don't give up. [2]But we have turned away from secret and shameful ways. We use no trickery, and we do not change the teaching of God. We teach the truth plainly, showing everyone who we are. Then they can know in their hearts what kind of people we are in God's sight. [3]If the Good News that we preach is hidden, it is hidden only to those who are lost. [4]The devil who rules this world has blinded the minds of those who do not believe. They cannot see the light of the Good News—the Good News about the glory of Christ, who is exactly like God. [5]We do not preach about ourselves, but we preach that Jesus Christ is Lord and that we are your servants for Jesus. [6]God once said, "Let the light shine out of the darkness!" This is the same God who made his light shine in our hearts by letting us know the glory of God that is in the face of Christ.

>> 4:13 "I ... spoke." Quotation from Psalm 116:10.

TheFinalScore »

THE OLYMPICS: Hope of Peace

THROUGHOUT HISTORY, ATHLETICS HAVE ACTED as a common world language, as seen by the apostle Paul's references to races and boxing in 1 Corinthians 9:24–27. Although there is no biblical evidence, it isn't hard to imagine that Paul was exposed to the ancient Olympics on his travels through Greece.

Dating back at least eight centuries before Christ, the games were so popular that Greece declared an international truce a month before to allow athletes to travel safely to Olympia. Despite its noble intentions, a glance at Olympic history uncovers examples of false religions and political conflicts.

The original games took place during a religious festival to honor Zeus, king of the Greek gods. It included the sacrifice of 100 oxen, while athletes prayed to the gods for victory. Political alliances were also announced at Olympia. After a military conquest in 365 B.C., the invaders presided over the 104th Olympiad. When the original rulers regained control, they declared those Olympics invalid.

Despite themes of peace and international brotherhood espoused by the modern Olympic movement, religion and politics still play a role in the games. Additionally, there is the threat of terrorism, which makes intense security precautions a fact of modern life.

So, thousands of years after they began, the Olympics have failed to fulfill the dreams of world peace. This isn't surprising, since Luke 2:14 assures us that the only peace on earth is "among the people who please God."

"So, thousands of years after they began, the Olympics have failed to fulfill the dreams of world peace."

FOR Men Only

GENEROSITY As someone once said, "You make a living by what you get, but you make a life by what you give." Just as getting is an acquired behavior, so is giving. A fellow learns to be generous with his finances by exercising faith through the giving of tithes and offerings. When a woman witnesses your giving spirit and generosity toward others, it will build a belief in her that you will take good care of her, also. If you are generous with your goods, then you are more likely to be a good steward of what money cannot buy, including love.

LISTEN

to more and more people will bring increasing thanks to God for his glory.

Living by Faith

[16] So we do not give up. Our physical body is becoming older and weaker, but our spirit inside us is made new every day. [17] We have small troubles for a while now, but they are helping us gain an eternal glory that is much greater than the troubles. [18] We set our eyes not on what we see but on what we cannot see. What we see will last only a short time, but what we cannot see will last forever.

5 We know that our body—the tent we live in here on earth—will be destroyed. But when that happens, God will have a house for us. It will not be a house made by human hands; instead, it will be a home in heaven that will last forever. [2] But now we groan in this tent. We want God to give us our heavenly home, [3] because it will clothe us so we will not be naked. [4] While we live in this body, we have burdens, and we groan. We do not want to be naked, but we want to be clothed with our heavenly home. Then this body that dies will be fully covered with life. [5] This is what God made us for, and he has given us the Spirit to be a guarantee for this new life.

[6] So we always have courage. We know that while we live in this body, we are away from the Lord. [7] We live by what we believe, not by what we can see. [8] So I say that we have courage. We really want to be away from this body and be at home with the Lord. [9] Our only goal is to please God whether we live here or there, [10] because we must all stand before Christ to be judged. Each of us will receive what we should get—good or bad—for the things we did in the earthly body.

Becoming Friends with God

[11] Since we know what it means to fear the Lord, we try to help people accept the truth about us. God knows what we really are, and I hope that in your hearts you know, too. [12] We are not trying to prove ourselves to you again, but we are telling you about ourselves so you will be proud of us. Then you will have an answer for those who are proud about things that can be seen rather than what is in the heart. [13] If we are out of our minds, it is for God. If we have our right minds, it is for you. [14] The love of Christ controls us, because we know that One died for all, so all have died. [15] Christ died for all so that those who live would not continue to live for themselves. He died for them and was raised from the dead so that they would live for him.

[16] From this time on we do not think of anyone as the world does. In the past we thought of Christ as the world thinks, but we no longer think of him in that way. [17] If anyone belongs to Christ, there is a new creation. The old things have gone; everything is made new! [18] All this

Q: What's so important about the Great Commission?

A: The Great Commission was the final set of instructions Jesus gave to his followers before his ascension. His command to "make followers of all people in the world" quickly became the chief focus of the church (Matthew 28:18—20).

>> live the life

2 Corinthians 5:20

The Principle > **Point others toward God.**

Practicing It > **Be alert for ways God may use you to draw people to himself. If you are willing, God will provide opportunities for you to share his message of love with people who need to hear it.**

Ten Ways to Become a Good Friend

1. Encourage people in their walk with God.

2. Ask others for their regular prayer support.

3. Be observant and offer your help when needed.

4. Take the high road and forgive an offense.

5. Pray for healthy relationships in life.

6. Practice exercising patience toward others.

7. Remember how it feels to be a newcomer.

8. Learn to serve others with a good attitude.

9. Attend special occasions when invited.

10. Offer to house sit for neighbors.

is from God. Through Christ, God made peace between us and himself, and God gave us the work of telling everyone about the peace we can have with him. [19]God was in Christ, making peace between the world and himself. In Christ, God did not hold the world guilty of its sins. And he gave us this message of peace. [20]So we have been sent to speak for Christ. It is as if God is calling to you through us. We speak for Christ when we beg you to be at peace with God. [21]Christ had no sin, but God made him become sin so that in Christ we could become right with God.

6 We are workers together with God, so we beg you: Do not let the grace that you received from God be for nothing. [2]God says,

"At the right time I heard your prayers.
On the day of salvation I helped you."   *Isaiah 49:8*

I tell you that the "right time" is now, and the "day of salvation" is now.

[3]We do not want anyone to find fault with our work, so nothing we do will be a problem for anyone. [4]But in every way we show we are servants of God: in accepting many hard things, in troubles, in difficulties, and in great problems. [5]We are beaten and thrown into prison. We meet those who become upset with us and start riots. We work hard, and sometimes we get no sleep or food. [6]We show we are servants of God by our pure lives, our understanding, patience, and kindness, by the Holy Spirit, by true love, [7]by speaking the truth, and by God's power. We use our right living to defend ourselves against

everything. [8]Some people honor us, but others blame us. Some people say evil things about us, but others say good things. Some people say we are liars, but we speak the truth. [9]We are not known, but we are well known. We seem to be dying, but we continue to live. We are punished, but we are not killed. [10]We have much sadness, but we are always rejoicing. We are poor, but we are making many people rich in faith. We have nothing, but really we have everything.

[11]We have spoken freely to you in Corinth and have opened our hearts to you. [12]Our feelings of love for you have not stopped, but you have stopped your feelings of love for us. [13]I speak to you as if you were my children. Do to us as we have done—open your hearts to us.

Warning About Non-Christians

[14]You are not the same as those who do not believe. So do not join yourselves to them. Good and bad do not belong together. Light and darkness cannot share together. [15]How can Christ and Belial, the devil, have any agreement? What can a believer have together with a nonbeliever? [16]The temple of God cannot have any agreement with idols, and we are the temple of the living God. As God said: "I will live with them and walk with them. And I will be their God, and they will be my people."[n]

[17]"Leave those people,
    and be separate, says the Lord.
Touch nothing that is unclean,
    and I will accept you."   *Isaiah 52:11; Ezekiel 20:34, 41*

[18]"I will be your father,
    and you will be my sons and daughters,
    says the Lord Almighty."   *2 Samuel 7:14*

7 Dear friends, we have these promises from God, so we should make ourselves pure—free from anything that makes body or soul unclean. We should try to become holy in the way we live, because we respect God.

Paul's Joy

[2]Open your hearts to us. We have not done wrong to anyone, we have not ruined the faith of anyone, and we have not cheated anyone.

Q: Can demons really possess people?

A: Yes. The Bible is replete with examples of demon possession. Jesus himself encountered many demon-possessed people during his ministry, and he treated the demonic influence on people's lives as a factual reality (Matthew 8:16).

>> 6:16 "I . . . people." Quotation from Leviticus 26:11–12; Jeremiah 32:38; Ezekiel 37:27.

[3]I do not say this to blame you. I told you before that we love you so much we would live or die with you. [4]I feel very sure of you and am very proud of you. You give me much comfort, and in all of our troubles I have great joy.

[5]When we came into Macedonia, we had no rest. We found trouble all around us. We had fighting on the outside and fear on the inside. [6]But God, who comforts those who are troubled, comforted us when Titus came. [7]We were comforted, not only by his coming but also by the comfort you gave him. Titus told us about your wish to see me and that you are very sorry for what you did. He also told me about your great care for me, and when I heard this, I was much happier.

[8]Even if my letter made you sad, I am not sorry I wrote it. At first I was sorry, because it made you sad, but you were sad only for a short time. [9]Now I am happy, not because you were made sad, but because your sorrow made you change your lives. You became sad in the way God wanted you to, so you were not hurt by us in any way. [10]The kind of sorrow God wants makes people change their hearts and lives. This leads to salvation, and you cannot be sorry for that. But the kind of sorrow the world has brings death. [11]See

what this sorrow—the sorrow God wanted you to have—has done to you: It has made you very serious. It made you want to restore yourselves. It made you angry and afraid. It made you want to see me. It made you care. It made you want to do the right thing. In every way you have regained your innocence. [12]I wrote that letter, not because of the one who did the wrong or because of the person who was hurt. I wrote the letter so you could see, before God, the great care you have for us. [13]That is why we were comforted.

Not only were we very comforted, we were even happier to see that Titus was so happy. All of you made him feel much better. [14]I bragged to Titus about you, and you showed that I was right. Everything we said to you was true, and you have proved that what we bragged about to Titus is true. [15]And his love for you is stronger when he remembers that you were all ready to obey. You welcomed him with respect and fear. [16]I am very happy that I can trust you fully.

Christian Giving

8 And now, brothers and sisters, we want you to know about the grace God gave the churches in Macedonia. [2]They have been tested by great troubles, and they are very

People Skills

Paying Attention

The hours you spend at work can get hectic, but that is no excuse for treating colleagues like unwanted interruptions in your schedule. Instead, give your peers your full attention anytime you interact with them. Maintain eye contact when someone else is talking. Resist the urge to look over the person's shoulder, down at the paperwork in your hand, or, worst of all, at your watch. Keep your gaze and your attention focused on the other person's eyes. It is an easy but effective way to ensure that others always will feel valued and respected when dealing with you. Besides, you never know who might put in a good word for you.

▶ Sexcess:
THE DATING DILEMMA

Dating has become a minefield for many, but some tried and true tips will help guide the way for the wary. First, consider the dating process an audition for your affection. You are only setting yourself up for hurt and heartache if you lower your standards by dating the type of person you would not marry. Second, plan your date ahead of time and limit the amount of time you'll be alone privately. Whether that means going out with other couples or only visiting in public places, the temptations to lust and sin will be curbed. With the proper preparation, the dating ritual doesn't need to be cause for concern.

▶Get Aligned
2 Corinthians 8:14

AS STEWARDS OF WHAT GOD HAS GIVEN US IN THE FINANCIAL REALM, we are to handle our money wisely. But unknown to many, God has also shared the secret to having a successful portfolio. It has nothing to do with the stock market, home equity, or retirement plans. The secret is giving.

Plain and simple, the way to financial security is through giving to those in need. It sounds crazy, yet it's a universal principle established by a generous God. In Proverbs 28:27, the Lord promises that those who give to the poor will not lack. In Proverbs 19:17, he even defines giving to

the poor as lending to him. God's heart is stirred for the poor, and as good stewards, giving to those in need should be automatic on our part.

No matter what tax bracket we fall in or what financial trial we're facing, we can always give to those less fortunate. When we have no money to give, we can offer our time, talents, or simply encouragement. There's no better place to do this than the church, which is called to be an extension of God's kindness and mercy. By maintaining a lifestyle of giving, we'll discover that God truly does provide everything we need.

a way we did not expect: They first gave themselves to the Lord and to us. This is what God wants. ⁶So we asked Titus to help you finish this special work of grace since he is the one who started it. ⁷You are rich in everything—in faith, in speaking, in knowledge, in truly wanting to help, and in the love you learned from us.ᵃ In the same way, be strong also in the grace of giving.

⁸I am not commanding you to give. But I want to see if your love is true by comparing you with others that really want to help. ⁹You know the grace of our Lord Jesus Christ. You know that Christ was rich, but for you he became poor so that by his becoming poor you might become rich.

¹⁰This is what I think you should do: Last year you were the first to want to give, and you were the first who gave. ¹¹So now finish the work you started. Then your "doing" will be equal to your "wanting to do." Give from what you have. ¹²If you want to give, your gift will be accepted. It will be judged by what you have, not by what you do not have. ¹³We do not want you to have troubles while other people are at ease, but we want everything to be equal. ¹⁴At this time you have plenty. What you have can help others who are in need. Then later, when they have plenty, they can help you when you are in need, and all will be equal. ¹⁵As it is written in the Scriptures, "The person who gathered more did not have too much, nor did the person who gathered less have too little."ᵇ

Titus and His Companions Help

¹⁶I thank God because he gave Titus the same love for you that I have. ¹⁷Titus accepted what we asked him to do. He wanted very much to go to you, and this was his own idea. ¹⁸We are sending with him the brother who is praised by all the churches because of his service in preaching the Good News. ¹⁹Also, this brother was chosen by the churches to go with us when we deliver this gift of money. We are doing this service to bring glory to the Lord and to show that we really want to help.

poor. But they gave much because of their great joy. ³I can tell you that they gave as much as they were able and even more than they could afford. No one told them to do it. ⁴But they begged and pleaded with us to let them share in this service for God's people. ⁵And they gave in

➡ **The Bottom Line**
Mortgages: Avoid Chasing Rates

IF YOU'RE TAKING THE PLUNGE INTO HOME BUYING, that typically means obtaining a mortgage loan. However, don't fret about interest rates. What's more important are such issues as the down payment and whether or not the payments fit your budget. You can also see if you qualify for a lower-cost, subsidized loan. Timing a purchase to interest rates is like following the stock market. Like stocks, interest rates go up and down, and nobody knows where they're going at any given time. Your decision should include prayer. James 1:5 promises God will give us wisdom if we simply ask.

 8:7 in...us Some Greek copies read "in your love for us." 8:15 "The person...little." Quotation from Exodus 16:18.

Get Fit

GOING ROCK CLIMBING   The physical benefits of rock climbing are truly impressive. It builds muscle strength, produces amazing stamina, and does wonders for your balance. But any climber will tell you that the real challenge of the sport is in your head. Rock climbing requires extreme strategic focus, and those who practice it often speak of the amazing calming effects that that level of concentration has on the mind. It also takes strong faith, a belief that surmounting the rock face is doable and that reaching the summit is probable. Why not try this faith- and body-stretching sport for yourself? You can learn more about it at www.rockclimbing.com.

²⁰We are being careful so that no one will criticize us for the way we are handling this large gift. ²¹We are trying hard to do what the Lord accepts as right and also what people think is right.

²²Also, we are sending with them our brother, who is always ready to help. He has proved this to us in many ways, and he wants to help even more now, because he has much faith in you. ²³Now about Titus—he is my partner who is working with me to help you. And about the other brothers—they are sent from the churches, and they bring glory to Christ. ²⁴So show these men the proof of your love and the reason we are proud of you. Then all the churches can see it.

Help for Fellow Christians

9 I really do not need to write you about this help for God's people. ²I know you want to help. I have been bragging about this to the people in Macedonia, telling them that you in Southern Greece have been ready to give since last year. And your desire to give has made most of them ready to give also. ³But I am sending the brothers to you so that our bragging about you in this will not be empty words. I want you to be ready, as I said you would be. ⁴If any of the people from Macedonia come with me and find that you are not ready, we will be ashamed that we were so sure of you. (And you will be ashamed, too!) ⁵So I thought I should ask these brothers to go to you before we do. They will finish getting in order the generous gift you promised so it will be ready when we come. And it will be a generous gift—not one that you did not want to give.

⁶Remember this: The person who plants a little will have a small harvest, but the person who plants a lot will have a big harvest. ⁷Each of you should give as you have decided in your heart to give. You should not be sad when you give, and you should not give because you feel forced to give. God loves the person who gives happily. ⁸And

God can give you more blessings than you need. Then you will always have plenty of everything—enough to give to every good work. ⁹It is written in the Scriptures:

"He gives freely to the poor.
     The things he does are right and will continue forever."

Psalm 112:9

¹⁰God is the One who gives seed to the farmer and bread for food. He will give you all the seed you need and make it grow so there will be a great harvest from your goodness. ¹¹He will make you rich in every way so that you can always give freely. And your giving through us will cause many to give thanks to God. ¹²This service you do not only helps the needs of God's people, it also brings many more thanks to God. ¹³It is a proof of your faith. Many people will praise God because you obey the Good News of Christ—the gospel you say you believe—and because you freely share with them and with all others. ¹⁴And when they pray, they will wish they could be with you because

>> live the life

2 Corinthians 9:7

The Principle > Give from your heart.

Practicing It > If you aren't already giving ten percent, or a tithe, of your income to the church, make a commitment to start now. When you give, offer your donation cheerfully and with no strings attached.

Men of Valor
MARK: Redeemed from Running

Author of the second Gospel, Mark is something of a mystery. Mark 14:51–52 described a young man who followed Christ after his arrest, but fled when some men grabbed his garment. Bible scholars speculate the young man was Mark. Running reflected his character. Although Mark accompanied Paul and Barnabas on a missionary journey, he then deserted Paul in Pamphylia. Later, when Barnabas wanted to take Mark on a visit to various towns, Paul disagreed so vehemently that he and Barnabas parted company. Yet there was reconciliation. Paul told Timothy to bring Mark along on a visit "because he can help me in my work here" (2 Timothy 4:11). Mark stumbled, but recovered and found forgiveness.

of the great grace that God has given you. ¹⁵Thanks be to God for his gift that is too wonderful for words.

Paul Defends His Ministry

10 I, Paul, am begging you with the gentleness and the kindness of Christ. Some people say that I am easy on you when I am with you and bold when I am away. ²They think we live in a worldly way, and I plan to be very bold with them when I come. I beg you that when I come I will not need to use that same boldness with you. ³We do live in the world, but we do not fight in the same way the world fights. ⁴We fight with weapons that are different from those the world uses. Our weapons have power from God that can destroy the enemy's strong places. We destroy people's arguments ⁵and every proud thing that raises itself against the knowledge of God. We capture every thought and make it give up and obey Christ. ⁶We are ready to punish anyone there who does not obey, but first we want you to obey fully.

⁷You must look at the facts before you. If you feel sure that you belong to Christ, you must remember that we belong to Christ just as you do. ⁸It is true that we brag freely about the authority the Lord gave us. But this authority is to build you up, not to tear you down. So I will not be ashamed. ⁹I do not want you to think I am trying to scare you with my letters. ¹⁰Some people say, "Paul's letters are powerful and sound important, but when he is with us, he is weak. And his speaking is nothing." ¹¹They should know this: We are not there with you now, so we say these things in letters. But when we are there with you, we will show the same authority that we show in our letters.

¹²We do not dare to compare ourselves with those who think they are very important. They use themselves to measure themselves, and they judge themselves by what they themselves are. This shows that they know nothing. ¹³But we will not brag about things outside the work that was given us to do. We will limit our bragging to the work that God gave us, and this includes our work with you. ¹⁴We are not bragging too much, as we would be if we had not already come to you. But we have come to you with the Good News of Christ. ¹⁵We limit our bragging to the work that is ours, not what others have done. We hope that as your faith continues to grow, you will help our work to grow much larger.

THINK ABOUT IT 2 Corinthians 10:4–5

MANY OF US PLAYED IMAGINARY GAMES as children. Perhaps we invaded a corner of our bedroom and turned it into a fort. Maybe we climbed a tree and called it a castle that was only for a special group of friends. We fought imaginary villains and staved off their attacks. Now as adults, there are still forts and castles to defend, but they are in the spiritual realm.

Paul wrote about strongholds and used language that recalled the rock forts that protected the coast. Ultimately, the Romans pulled down these forts or strongholds when they battled against the pirates. Think about what strongholds are holding you back in life. It might be an anger problem or a struggle against pornography or a selfish spirit that looks for your personal gain at every turn.

As we engage in this battle against the strongholds of our life, Paul reminds us that in God we will be victorious. "Our weapons have power from God that can destroy the enemy's strong places," he wrote. Take a few moments to pause and thank God for his power against the strongholds of your life.

>> live the life

2 Corinthians 10:12

The Principle > Quit comparing yourself to others.

Practicing It > You are a unique creation in Christ with your own gifts, talents, and abilities. Instead of wasting energy trying to be like somebody else, strive to make the most of what God has given you.

[16]We want to tell the Good News in the areas beyond your city. We do not want to brag about work that has already been done in another person's area. [17]But, "If people want to brag, they should brag only about the Lord."[n] [18]It is not those who say they are good who are accepted but those the Lord thinks are good.

Paul and the False Apostles

11 I wish you would be patient with me even when I am a little foolish, but you are already doing that. [2]I am jealous over you with a jealousy that comes from God. I promised to give you to Christ, as your only husband. I want to give you as his pure bride. [3]But I am afraid that your minds will be led away from your true and pure following of Christ just as Eve was tricked by the snake with his evil ways. [4]You are very patient with anyone who comes to you and preaches a different Jesus from the one we preached. You are very willing to accept a spirit or gospel that is different from the Spirit and Good News you received from us.

[5]I do not think that those "great apostles" are any better than I am. [6]I may not be a trained speaker, but I do have knowledge. We have shown this to you clearly in every way.

[7]I preached God's Good News to you without pay. I made myself unimportant to make you important. Do you think that was wrong?

[8]I accepted pay from other churches, taking their money so I could serve you. [9]If I needed something when I was with you, I did not trouble any of you. The brothers who came from Macedonia gave me all that I needed. I did not allow myself to depend on you in any way, and I will never depend on you. [10]No one in Southern Greece will stop me from bragging about that. I say this with the truth of Christ in me. [11]And why do I not depend on you? Do you think it is because I do not love you? God knows that I love you.

[12]And I will continue doing what I am doing now, because I want to stop those people from having a reason to brag. They would like to say that the work they brag about is the same as ours. [13]Such men are not true apostles but are workers who lie. They change themselves to look like apostles of Christ. [14]This does not surprise us. Even Satan changes himself to look like an angel of light.[n] [15]So it does not surprise us if Satan's servants also make themselves look like servants who work for what is right. But in the end they will be punished for what they do.

Paul Tells About His Sufferings

[16]I tell you again: No one should think I am a fool. But if you think so, accept me as you would accept a fool. Then I can brag a little, too. [17]When I brag because I feel sure of myself, I am not talking as the Lord would talk but as a fool. [18]Many people are bragging about their

Q: Why did Jesus have to die?

A: When Adam and Eve first sinned, they introduced death and division into creation. Because God loves humanity, he sought to repair the breech. God sent Jesus, who was sinless, to act as a perfect sacrifice for us by dying in our place (Ephesians 2:13–19).

Principles: PEACE

Peace is the overall sense that no matter what happens, things will turn out all right. Jesus died and rose from the dead so that we could be at peace with ourselves, others, and God. As it declares in 2 Corinthians 5:18, "Through Christ, God made peace between us and himself, and God gave us the work of telling everyone about the peace we can have with him." The type of peace that God gives is a peace that our minds can't fathom. We don't find this peace through what we do, but through a personal relationship with Jesus.

>> **10:17** "If . . . Lord." Quotation from Jeremiah 9:24. **11:14 angel of light** Messenger from God. The devil fools people so that they think he is from God.

lives in the world. So I will brag too. [19]You are wise, so you will gladly be patient with fools! [20]You are even patient with those who order you around, or use you, or trick you, or think they are better than you, or hit you in the face. [21]It is shameful to me to say this, but we were too "weak" to do those things to you!

But if anyone else is brave enough to brag, then I also will be brave and brag. (I am talking as a fool.) [22]Are they Hebrews?" So am I. Are they Israelites? So am I. Are they from Abraham's family? So am I. [23]Are they serving Christ? I am serving him more. (I am crazy to talk like this.) I have worked much harder than they. I have been in prison more often. I have been hurt more in beatings. I have been near death many times. [24]Five times the Jews have given me their punishment of thirty-nine lashes with a whip. [25]Three different times I was beaten with rods. One time I was almost stoned to death. Three times I was in ships that wrecked, and one of those times I spent a night and a day in the sea. [26]I have gone on many travels and have been in danger from rivers, thieves, my own people, the Jews, and those who are not Jews. I have been in danger in cities, in places where no one lives, and on the sea. And I have been in danger with false Christians. [27]I have done hard and tiring work, and many times I did not sleep. I have been hungry and thirsty, and many times I have been without food. I have been cold and without clothes. [28]Besides all this, there is on me every day the load of my concern for all the churches. [29]I feel weak every time someone is weak, and I feel upset every time someone is led into sin.

[30]If I must brag, I will brag about the things that show I am weak. [31]God knows I am not lying. He is the God and Father of the Lord Jesus Christ, and he is to be praised forever. [32]When I was in Damascus, the governor under King Aretas wanted to arrest me, so he put guards around the city. [33]But my friends lowered me in a basket through a hole in the city wall. So I escaped from the governor.

A Special Blessing in Paul's Life

12 I must continue to brag. It will do no good, but I will talk now about visions and revelations" from the Lord. [2]I know a man in Christ who was taken up to the third heaven fourteen years ago. I do not know whether the man was in his body or out of his body, but God knows. [3-4]And I know that this man was taken up to paradise." I don't know if he was in his body or away from his body, but God knows. He heard things he is not able to explain, things that no human is allowed to tell. [5]I will brag about a man like that, but I will not brag about myself, except about my weaknesses. [6]But if I wanted to brag about myself, I would not be a fool, because I would be telling the truth. But I will not brag about myself. I do not want people to think more of me than what they see me do or hear me say.

[7]So that I would not become too proud of the wonderful things that were shown to me, a painful physical problem" was given to me. This problem was a messenger from Satan, sent to beat me and keep me

Q: What is the cost of being a follower of Christ?

A: The choice to follow Jesus is not one to be taken lightly. Following Christ means consistently laying down our will in favor of his, as well as enduring such struggles as persecution, suffering, and trials for the sake of the kingdom of God (Luke 14:26—33).

Survival Guide

LAUNDRY: PRESERVING RESOURCES

Even if you have a spouse who does your laundry, remember that ninety percent of a washer's energy goes to heating water. Most clothes can be washed in warm or cold water; the latter rinses fine. Running the washer only when full saves water and energy. With dryers, set the timer carefully so as not to over-dry clothes. Check the lint filter often, since buildup blocks airflow and lengthens drying time. By the way, if this subject makes your eyes glaze over, then rejoice in Proverbs 18:22: "When a man finds a wife, he finds something good."

11:22 **Hebrews** A name for the Jews that some Jews were very proud of.   12:1 **revelations** Revelation is making known a truth that was hidden.   12:3–4 **paradise** Another word for heaven.
12:7 **painful physical problem** Literally, "thorn in the flesh."

from being too proud. ⁸I begged the Lord three times to take this problem away from me. ⁹But he said to me, "My grace is enough for you. When you are weak, my power is made perfect in you." So I am very happy to brag about my weaknesses. Then Christ's power can live in me. ¹⁰For this reason I am happy when I have weaknesses, insults, hard times, sufferings, and all kinds of troubles for Christ. Because when I am weak, then I am truly strong.

Paul's Love for the Christians

¹¹I have been talking like a fool, but you made me do it. You are the ones who should say good things about me. I am worth nothing, but those "great apostles" are not worth any more than I am! ¹²When I was with you, I patiently did the things that prove I am an apostle—signs, wonders, and miracles. ¹³So you received everything that the other churches have received. Only one thing was different: I was not a burden to you. Forgive me for this!

¹⁴I am now ready to visit you the third time, and I will not be a burden to you. I want nothing from you, except you. Children should not have to save up to give to their parents. Parents should save to give to their children. ¹⁵So I am happy to give everything I have for you, even myself. If I love you more, will you love me less?

¹⁶It is clear I was not a burden to you, but you think I was tricky and lied to catch you. ¹⁷Did I cheat you by using any of the messengers I sent to you? No, you know I did not. ¹⁸I asked Titus to go to you, and I sent our brother with him. Titus did not cheat you, did he? No, you know that Titus and I did the same thing and with the same spirit.

¹⁹Do you think we have been defending ourselves to you all this time? We have been speaking in Christ and before God. You are our dear friends, and everything we do is to make you stronger. ²⁰I am afraid that when I come, you will not be what I want you to be, and I will not be what you want me to be. I am afraid that among you there may be arguing, jealousy, anger, selfish fighting, evil talk, gossip, pride, and confusion. ²¹I am afraid that when I come to you again, my God will make me ashamed before you. I may be saddened by many of those who have sinned because they have not changed their hearts or turned from their sexual sins and the shameful things they have done.

Final Warnings and Greetings

13 I will come to you for the third time. "Every case must be proved by two or three witnesses." ²When I was with you the second time, I gave a warning to those who had sinned. Now I am away from you, and I give a warning to all the others. When I come to you again, I will not be easy with them. ³You want proof that Christ is speaking through me. My proof is that he is not weak among you, but he is powerful. ⁴It is true that he was weak when he was killed on the cross, but he lives now by God's power. It is true that we are weak in Christ, but for you we will be alive in Christ by God's power.

⁵Look closely at yourselves. Test yourselves to see if you are living in the faith. You know that Jesus Christ is in you—unless you fail the test. ⁶But I hope you will see that we ourselves have not failed the test.

<<TechSupport>>

DIGITAL MOVIES

If you have a digital video camera and a personal computer, you are missing out if you're not making home movies. Software makes it possible for just about anyone to import and edit raw footage of special events; add still photos, soundtracks, and titles; and burn it all to a CD or DVD so it can be played back over the Internet or on a standard DVD player. Think of all the creative ways you could use your gear to help further the ministry of your local church or favorite charity group.

⁷We pray to God that you will not do anything wrong. It is not important to see that we have passed the test, but it is important that you do what is right, even if it seems we have failed. ⁸We cannot do anything against the truth, but only for the truth. ⁹We are happy to be weak, if you are strong, and we pray that you will become complete. ¹⁰I am writing this while I am away from you so that when I come I will not have to be harsh in my use of authority. The Lord gave me this authority to build you up, not to tear you down.

¹¹Now, brothers and sisters, I say good-bye. Live in harmony. Do what I have asked you to do. Agree with each other, and live in peace. Then the God of love and peace will be with you.

¹²Greet each other with a holy kiss. ¹³All of God's holy people send greetings to you.

¹⁴The grace of the Lord Jesus Christ, the love of God, and the fellowship of the Holy Spirit be with you all.

>> live the life

2 Corinthians 12:10

The Principle > Trade your weakness for strength.

Practicing It > There is no need to pretend to be strong all the time or to try to hide your weaknesses where no one can see them. Lay down your weaknesses before God, and ask him to use them to display his grace and strength through your life.

13:1 "Every . . . witnesses." Quotation from Deuteronomy 19:15.

249

THE **LETTER** OF PAUL THE APOSTLE TO THE

Galatians

AUTHOR: PAUL
DATE WRITTEN: A.D. 55–57

YOU'VE PROBABLY SEEN THAT VACANT
stare—at least on television or the movies. The person is standing behind prison bars and gripping them desperately. It is a natural yearning for freedom. Imagine the elation that person feels when he reaches the day of his release and the doors swing open. Suddenly, he is free to begin a new life.

In his letter to the church at Galatia, Paul celebrates the charter of Christian freedom. This early church was struggling with the teaching from Judaizers, or Jews who insisted that Gentile believers obey Jewish laws in addition to trusting Christ for salvation. Paul reminded them that the laws from the Old Testament removed any freedoms from these Christians and locked them in bondage. As a missionary to the Gentiles, Paul repeatedly faced this issue from such false teachers.

Even today many people want us to believe we can earn God's favor through a set of rules or rituals. The Book of Galatians celebrates the reality of liberty in Christ—our freedom from the law and the power of sin. By grace through faith alone, we have been justified, and with faith alone we can discover a new life of freedom in the Spirit.

1 From Paul, an apostle. I was not chosen to be an apostle by human beings, nor was I sent from human beings. I was made an apostle through Jesus Christ and God the Father who raised Jesus from the dead. [2]This letter is also from all those of God's family[n] who are with me.

To the churches in Galatia:[n]

[3]Grace and peace to you from God our Father and the Lord Jesus Christ. [4]Jesus gave himself for our sins to free us from this evil world we live in, as God the Father planned. [5]The glory belongs to God forever and ever. Amen.

The Only Good News

[6]God, by his grace through Christ, called you to become his people. So I am amazed that you are turning away so quickly and believing something different than the Good News. [7]Really, there is no other Good News. But some people are confusing you; they want to change the Good News of Christ. [8]We preached to you the Good News. So if we ourselves, or even an angel from heaven, should preach to you something different, we should be judged guilty! [9]I said this before, and now I say it again: You have already accepted the Good News. If anyone is preaching something different to you, let that person be judged guilty!

[10]Do you think I am trying to make people accept me? No, God is the One I am trying to please. Am I trying to please people? If I still wanted to please people, I would not be a servant of Christ.

Paul's Authority Is from God

[11]Brothers and sisters, I want you to know that the Good News I preached to you was not made up by human beings. [12]I did not get it from humans, nor did anyone teach it to me, but Jesus Christ showed it to me.

[13]You have heard about my past life in the Jewish religion. I attacked the church of God and tried to destroy it. [14]I was becoming a leader in the Jewish religion, doing better than most other Jews of my age. I tried harder than anyone else to follow the teachings handed down by our ancestors.

[15]But God had special plans for me and set me apart for his work

▶ Get Aligned
Galatians 1:15

IT'S HARD TO BELIEVE GOD HAS A SPECIAL PLAN FOR YOU when your life feels about as unique as the latest pop song. If status quo is all you've ever known, uniqueness may not be part of your vocabulary. But despite your feelings, your knowledge, and your experience, this verse remains true. As cheesy or foreign as it may sound, you are special, and God has plans specifically designed for you that involve a future filled with peace and hope.

The obvious follow-up question is, how do you find those plans? In Matthew 6:33, Jesus said,

"Seek first God's kingdom and what God wants. Then all your other needs will be met as well." When you go after the things of God first, the rest takes care of itself. And the rest includes God's overall plan for your life.

The point isn't to acquire a roadmap for life so you can know how everything is supposed to turn out. The point is simply to follow God today. Seek his will. Abide in him. Get his direction for today, not for next year. He is a proven, faithful God, and you can be assured that his plans are secure.

➡ **The Bottom Line**

Oil Changes: Scheduling Preventative Maintenance

MANY AUTOMOBILE MANUFACTURERS RECOMMEND CHANGING OIL every three thousand to thirty-five hundred miles, but unless you do a lot of driving in stop-and-go traffic, it may not be necessary to change it that often. Car-care experts recommend every five thousand miles, and a motorist driving relatively short distances on rural roads may go seventy-five hundred miles between changes. As with other maintenance, if your car is under warranty, check to see whether oil changes are required at certain intervals. If in doubt, changing oil frequently won't hurt your engine. And a smooth running engine will lengthen the life of your car.

 1:2 those ... family The Greek text says "brothers." **1:2 Galatia** Probably the same country where Paul preached and began churches on his first missionary trip. Read the Book of Acts, chapters 13 and 14.

FOR Men Only

GODLINESS The best way to attract a godly woman is to be a godly man. Many men want a woman who is serious about her faith, yet they don't realize that to appeal to that type of woman, they need to be that type of man. If your goal is to marry a woman with high moral standards and strong convictions, then you need to be a man with high moral standards and strong convictions. Otherwise, she won't be interested in you. If you are living a godly life, don't get duped into compromising your standards to appease a woman who may not share the same goals.

LISTEN

even before I was born. He called me through his grace [16]and showed his son to me so that I might tell the Good News about him to those who are not Jewish. When God called me, I did not get advice or help from any person. [17]I did not go to Jerusalem to see those who were apostles before I was. But, without waiting, I went away to Arabia and later went back to Damascus.

[18]After three years I went to Jerusalem to meet Peter and stayed with him for fifteen days. [19]I met no other apostles, except James, the brother of the Lord. [20]God knows that these things I write are not lies. [21]Later, I went to the areas of Syria and Cilicia.

>> live the life

Galatians 1:24

The Principle > **Inspire other believers.**

Practicing It > **Strive to live the sort of life that inspires others to worship God. Don't make yourself the star of your own story; instead, make Christ the star of all that you do. Give glory to him, and encourage others to do the same.**

[22]In Judea the churches in Christ had never met me. [23]They had only heard it said, "This man who was attacking us is now preaching the same faith that he once tried to destroy." [24]And these believers praised God because of me.

Other Apostles Accepted Paul

2 After fourteen years I went to Jerusalem again, this time with Barnabas. I also took Titus with me. [2]I went because God showed me I should go. I met with the believers there, and in private I told their leaders the Good News that I preach to the non-Jewish people. I did not want my past work and the work I am now doing to be wasted. [3]Titus was with me, but he was not forced to be circumcised, even though he was a Greek. [4]We talked about this problem because some false believers had come into our group secretly. They came in like spies to overturn the freedom we have in Christ Jesus. They wanted to make us slaves. [5]But we did not give in to those false believers for a minute. We wanted the truth of the Good News to continue for you.

[6]Those leaders who seemed to be important did not change the Good News that I preach. (It doesn't matter to me if they were "important" or not. To God everyone is the same.) [7]But these leaders saw that I had been given the work of telling the Good News to those who are not Jewish, just as Peter had the work of telling the Jews. [8]God gave Peter the power to work as an apostle for the Jewish people. But he also gave me the power to work as an apostle for those who are not Jews. [9]James, Peter, and John, who seemed to be the leaders, understood that God had given me this special grace, so they accepted Barnabas and me. They agreed that they would go to the Jewish people and that we should go to those who are not Jewish. [10]The only thing they asked us was to remember to help the poor—something I really wanted to do.

Paul Shows that Peter Was Wrong

[11]When Peter came to Antioch, I challenged him to his face, because he was wrong. [12]Peter ate with the non-Jewish people until

Q: Why did Judas betray Jesus?

A: Some scholars believe he did it in a vain attempt to force Jesus into the role of political revolutionary. Others think that Judas became corrupted by greed and had grown disillusioned with the message of sacrifice and service that Christ taught (Luke 22:3–6).

>> live the life

Galatians 2:20

The Principle > Live by faith.

Practicing It > Christianity is not a system of laws or a philosophy; it's a relationship between you and Jesus. Only as you come to know him on a deeper level will you really be able to trust him with your whole life.

some Jewish people sent from James came to Antioch. When they arrived, Peter stopped eating with those who weren't Jewish, and he separated himself from them. He was afraid of the Jews. 13 So Peter was a hypocrite, as were the other Jewish believers who joined with him. Even Barnabas was influenced by what these Jewish believers did. 14 When I saw they were not following the truth of the Good News, I spoke to Peter in front of them all. I said, "Peter, you are a Jew, but you are not living like a Jew. You are living like those who are not Jewish. So why do you now try to force those who are not Jewish to live like Jews?"

15 We were not born as non-Jewish "sinners," but as Jews. 16 Yet we know that a person is made right with God not by following the law, but by trusting in Jesus Christ. So we, too, have put our faith in Christ Jesus, that we might be made right with God because we trusted in Christ. It is not because we followed the law, because no one can be made right with God by following the law.

17 We Jews came to Christ, trying to be made right with God, and it became clear that we are sinners, too. Does this mean that Christ encourages sin? No! 18 But I would really be wrong to begin teaching again those things that I gave up. 19 It was the law that put me to death, and I died to the law so that I can now live for God. 20 I was put to death on the cross with Christ, and I do not live anymore—it is Christ who lives in me. I still live in my body, but I live by faith in the Son of God who loved me and gave himself to save me. 21 By saying these things I am not going against God's grace. Just the opposite, if the law could make us right with God, then Christ's death would be useless.

Blessing Comes Through Faith

3 You people in Galatia were told very clearly about the death of Jesus Christ on the cross. But you were foolish; you let someone trick you. 2 Tell me this one thing: How did you receive the Holy Spirit? Did you receive the Spirit by following the law? No, you received the Spirit because you heard the Good News and believed it. 3 You began your life in Christ by the Spirit. Now are you trying to make it complete by your own power? That is foolish. 4 Were all your experiences wasted? I hope not! 5 Does God give you the Spirit and work miracles among you because you follow the law? No, he does these things because you heard the Good News and believed it.

6 The Scriptures say the same thing about Abraham: "Abraham believed God, and God accepted Abraham's faith, and that faith made him right with God."[n] 7 So you should know that the true children of Abraham are those who have faith. 8 The Scriptures, telling what would happen in the future, said that God would make the non-Jewish people right through their faith. This Good News was told to Abraham beforehand, as the Scripture says: "All nations will be blessed through you."[n] 9 So all who believe as Abraham believed are blessed just as Abraham was. 10 But those who depend on following the law to make them right are under a curse, because the Scriptures say, "Anyone will be cursed who does not always obey what is written in the Book of the Law."[n] 11 Now it is clear that no one can be made right with God by the law, because the Scriptures say, "Those who are right with God

Change>> Your WORLD

OPEN DOORS

In 1955, a young Dutch missionary discovered that Christians behind the Iron Curtain desperately needed copies of the Bible and other Good News literature. As a result, Brother Andrew distributed a suitcase full of Christian literature and began a ministry later called Open Doors. Brother Andrew became known as "God's Smuggler," and an international best-selling book telling his story was widely distributed. Today, Open Doors works in more than sixty countries, and in the past year, the organization delivered more than four million adult Bibles, children's Bibles, study Bibles, and other biblical books to persecuted Christians.

To change your world, visit www.opendoorsusa.org.

>> 3:6 "Abraham ... God." Quotation from Genesis 15:6. 3:8 "All ... you." Quotation from Genesis 12:3 and 18:18. 3:10 "Anyone ... Law." Quotation from Deuteronomy 27:26.

Men of Valor
NICODEMUS: Pharisee to Follower

While biblical details about Nicodemus are sketchy, they still show a man touched deeply by Christ's teaching. A Pharisee, Nicodemus took a great risk when he approached Jesus one evening to ask about his teachings. Jesus said that to enter God's kingdom, one must be born again from water and the Spirit (John 3:5). While John does not record Nicodemus's immediate response, later the Pharisee defended Christ. When an angry mob wanted to seize him, Nicodemus calmed the situation by saying, "Our law does not judge a person without hearing him and knowing what he has done" (John 7:51). After Christ's crucifixion, Nicodemus helped prepare his body for burial. Obviously, he wasn't like the other Pharisees who wanted to see Jesus killed.

will live by faith."[n] [12]The law is not based on faith. It says, "A person who obeys these things will live because of them."[n] [13]Christ took away the curse the law put on us. He changed places with us and put himself under that curse. It is written in

FACT-OIDS!
The top-grossing film of all time was *Titanic*, earning more than $600 million domestically.
[Exhibitor Relations Co.]

the Scriptures, "Anyone whose body is displayed on a tree" is cursed." [14]Christ did this so that God's blessing promised to Abraham might come through Jesus Christ to those who are not Jews. Jesus died so that by our believing we could receive the Spirit that God promised.

The Law and the Promise

[15]Brothers and sisters, let us think in human terms: Even an agreement made between two persons is firm. After that agreement is accepted by both people, no one can stop it or add anything to it. [16]God made promises both to Abraham and to his descendant. God did not say, "and to your descendants." That would mean many people. But God said, "and to your descendant." That means only one person; that person is Christ. [17]This is what I mean: God had an agreement with Abraham and promised to keep it. The law, which came four hundred thirty years later, cannot change that agreement and so destroy God's promise to Abraham. [18]If the law could give us Abraham's blessing, then the promise would not be necessary. But that is not possible, because God freely gave his blessings to Abraham through the promise he had made.

[19]So what was the law for? It was given to show that the wrong things people do are against God's will. And it continued until the special descendant, who had been promised, came. The law was given through angels who used Moses for a mediator" to give the law to people. [20]But a mediator is not needed when there is only one side, and God is only one.

The Purpose of the Law of Moses

[21]Does this mean that the law is against God's promises? Never! That would be true only if the law could make us right with God. But God did not give a law that can bring life. [22]Instead, the Scriptures showed that the

whole world is bound by sin. This was so the promise would be given through faith to people who believe in Jesus Christ.

[23]Before this faith came, we were all held prisoners by the law. We had no freedom until God showed us the way of faith that was coming. [24]In other words, the law was our guardian leading us to Christ so that we

{Book of the Month}

Why Men Hate Going to Church
by David Murrow

If church ever bores you to tears, you're not alone, says author David Murrow. Men are the largest unchurched people group in the United States, according to Murrow. While women fill the majority of the pews, he says men would rather be in the garage, the wilderness, or the workplace. So, he asks, what's wrong with church that it doesn't appeal to men? The answer: the church emphasizes safety over risk, stability over change, preservation over expansion, and predictability over adventure. Murrow's plan for change: Offer great male leadership. Men want fun, friendly competition, physical activity, and a place to find spiritual mentorship and a band of brothers.

3:11 "Those...faith." Quotation from Habakkuk 2:4. 3:12 "A person...them." Quotation from Leviticus 18:5. 3:13 displayed on a tree Deuteronomy 21:22–23 says that when a person was killed for doing wrong, the body was hung on a tree to show shame. Paul means that the cross of Jesus was like that. 3:19 mediator A person who helps one person talk to or give something to another person.

>>August

QUOTE OF THE MONTH:
"It is our attitude at the beginning of a difficult task which, more than anything else, will affect its successful outcome."
—William James

1 Make sure your family has all its shots.

2

3 Pray for a person of influence: Today is entrepreneur **Martha Stewart's** birthday.

4

5 Wash and wax the family car.

6 Call an old friend you've lost touch with.

7

8

9 Get your dry cleaning done.

10

11 Pray for a person of influence: Today is wrestler **Hulk Hogan's** birthday.

12 Send a note to a loved one.

13

14 Memorize Hebrews 4:12.

15

16 **Elvis Presley** died on this day in 1977.

17

18 Pray for a person of influence: Today is actor **Robert Redford's** birthday.

19

20 Read the **Book of Colossians** to learn more about the person of Jesus Christ.

21

22 Stow a first aid kit in your car.

23

24 Learn how to do CPR.

25 Pray for a person of influence: Today is entertainer **Regis Philbin's** birthday.

26

27 Catch a matinee to escape the summer heat.

28

29

30 Feed a stranger's parking meter.

31 Offer to help someone move.

THINK ABOUT IT Galatians 4:6–7

A RECENT COMMERCIAL HAS THE FAMILY gathered in a lawyer's office to watch a video of a loved one's last will and testament. The deceased woman's face fills the television screen and begins to recount a story about one of the family members. Suddenly, one man reaches for the control and fast-forwards the tape. He never wanted to hear this information when she was alive—much less now that she's gone.

The family is gathered because as direct descendants, they have the right to inherit something. It's one of the blessings of being a child in that particular family. This possibility of inheritance isn't open to just anyone. If people outside of the family tried to get inside, they would be barred from the meeting.

The same is true in the spiritual realm of life. Because we have made a personal commitment to a relationship with God through Jesus Christ, we have become children of God. As Paul wrote, "God sent the Spirit of his Son into your hearts." Then we are given the rich promise, "God will give you the blessing he promised, because you are his child." We can live in expectancy of God's blessing as one of his children.

could be made right with God through faith. ²⁵Now the way of faith has come, and we no longer live under a guardian.

²⁶⁻²⁷You were all baptized into Christ, and so you were all clothed with Christ. This means that you are all children of God through faith in Christ Jesus. ²⁸In Christ, there is no difference between Jew and Greek, slave and free person, male and female. You are all the same in Christ Jesus. ²⁹You belong to Christ, so you are Abraham's descendants. You will inherit all of God's blessings because of the promise God made to Abraham.

4 I want to tell you this: While those who will inherit their fathers' property are still children, they are no different from slaves. It does not matter that the children own everything. ²While they are children, they must obey those who are chosen to care for them. But when the children reach the age set by their fathers, they are free. ³It is the same for us. We were once like children, slaves to the useless rules of this world. ⁴But when the right time came, God sent his Son who was born of a woman and lived under the law. ⁵God did this so he could buy freedom for those who were under the law and so we could become his children.

⁶Since you are God's children, God sent the Spirit of his Son into your hearts, and the Spirit cries out, "Father."ⁿ ⁷So now you are not a slave; you are God's child, and God will give you the blessing he promised, because you are his child.

Paul's Love for the Christians

⁸In the past you did not know God. You were slaves to gods that were not real. ⁹But now you know the true God. Really, it is God who knows you. So why do you turn back to those weak and useless rules you followed before? Do you want to be slaves to those things again? ¹⁰You still follow teachings about special days, months, seasons,

Get Fit

PARTNERING FOR PROGRESS   In your quest to get into shape, you don't have to go it alone. In fact, statistics show that it's better if you don't. The accountability that comes from exercising with a partner consistently produces better results—and besides that, it's more fun. Whether your exercise of choice is running, biking, or even walking, inviting a friend to join your journey will hold you to your goals and bring the results you want more quickly. As Ecclesiastes 4:9 reminds us, "Two people are better than one, because they get more done by working together." And to make the partnership even more meaningful, why not pray together before every workout?

➤➤ 4:6 "Father" Literally, "Abba, Father." Jewish children called their fathers "Abba."

and years. ¹¹I am afraid for you, that my work for you has been wasted.

¹²Brothers and sisters, I became like you, so I beg you to become like me. You were very good to me before. ¹³You remember that it was because of an illness that I came to you the first time, preaching the Good News. ¹⁴Though my sickness was a trouble for you, you did not hate me or make me leave. But you welcomed me as an angel from God, as if I were Jesus Christ himself! ¹⁵You were very happy then, but where is that joy now? I am ready to testify that you would have taken out your eyes and given them to me if that were possible. ¹⁶Now am I your enemy because I tell you the truth?

¹⁷Those people* are working hard to persuade you, but this is not good for you. They want to persuade you to turn against us and follow only them. ¹⁸It is good for people to show interest in you, but only if their purpose is good. This is always true, not just when I am with you. ¹⁹My little children, again I feel the pain of childbirth for you until you truly become like Christ. ²⁰I wish I could be with you now and could change the way I am talking to you, because I do not know what to think about you.

The Example of Hagar and Sarah

²¹Some of you still want to be under the law. Tell me, do you know what the law says? ²²The Scriptures say that Abraham had two sons. The mother of one son was a slave woman, and the mother of the other son was a free woman. ²³Abraham's son from the slave woman was born in the normal human way. But the son from the free woman was born because of the promise God made to Abraham.

²⁴This story teaches something else: The two women are like the two agreements between God and his people. One agreement is the law that God made on Mount Sinai,* and the people who are under this agreement are like slaves. The mother named Hagar is like that agreement. ²⁵She is like Mount Sinai in Arabia and is a picture of the earthly city of Jerusalem. This city and its people are slaves to the law. ²⁶But the heavenly Jerusalem, which is above, is like the free woman. She is our mother. ²⁷It is written in the Scriptures:

"Be happy, Jerusalem.
   You are like a woman who never gave birth to children.
   Start singing and shout for joy.
   You never felt the pain of giving birth,
but you will have more children
   than the woman who has a husband."   *Isaiah 54:1*

²⁸My brothers and sisters, you are God's children because of his promise, as Isaac was then. ²⁹The son who was born in the normal way treated the other son badly. It is the same today. ³⁰But what does the Scripture say? "Throw out the slave woman and her son. The son of the slave woman should not inherit anything. The son of the free woman should receive it all."* ³¹So, my brothers and sisters, we are not children of the slave woman, but of the free woman.

Keep Your Freedom

5 We have freedom now, because Christ made us free. So stand strong. Do not change and go back into the slavery of the law. ²Listen, I Paul tell you that if you go back to the law by being circumcised, Christ does you no good. ³Again, I warn every man: If you allow yourselves to be circumcised, you must follow all the law. ⁴If you try to be made right with God through the law, your life with Christ is over—you have left God's grace. ⁵But we have the true hope that comes from being made right with God, and by the Spirit we wait eagerly for this hope. ⁶When we are in Christ Jesus, it is not important if we are circumcised or not. The important thing is faith—the kind of faith that works through love.

⁷You were running a good race. Who stopped you from following

▶Get Aligned
Galatians 5:16–18

ITS UNOFFICIAL NAME COULD BE "SPIRITUAL SPLIT-PERSONALITY DISORDER." As Christians, we all suffer from it. In fact, it has been around since the beginning of human history, afflicting men from Adam to Solomon to you. On one hand, we want to please God. Our deep desire is to follow Christ, to emulate his holy walk through humanity. Of course, that is our better side.

But then, on the other hand, there is our natural inclination. Blame it on the fallen state that we inherited from Adam. Just as we strive to please God, many times we end up facedown in the mud, having succumbed to yet another temptation. For many men, it is a gripping cycle.

If you're stuck in the sin rut, this passage from Galatians offers the way out: follow the Holy Spirit. When we adhere to the Spirit's way rather than our own bent, we remain in God's intended path for our lives, which doesn't revolve around whatever pleases us. Under the Spirit's guidance, we are no longer caught in that vicious cycle of sin.

>> live the life

Galatians 5:1

The Principle > Stand strong in faith.

Practicing It > As you grow in your faith, don't let yourself get caught up in religious rules and regulations that have nothing to do with true godliness. Jesus came to set you free, and you no longer have anything to prove to anyone because he has accepted you.

4:17 Those people They are the false teachers who were bothering the believers in Galatia (Galatians 1:7).   **4:24 Mount Sinai** Mountain in Arabia where God gave his Law to Moses (Exodus 19 and 20).   **4:30 "Throw...all."** Quotation from Genesis 21:10.

the true way? ⁸This change did not come from the One who chose you. ⁹Be careful! "Just a little yeast makes the whole batch of dough rise." ¹⁰But I trust in the Lord that you will not believe those different ideas. Whoever is confusing you with such ideas will be punished.

¹¹My brothers and sisters, I do not teach that a man must be circumcised. If I teach circumcision, why am I still being attacked? If I still taught circumcision, my preaching about the cross would not be a problem. ¹²I wish the people who are bothering you would castrate" themselves!

> ❝My brothers and sisters, God called you to be free, but do not use your freedom as an excuse to do what pleases your sinful self. Serve each other with love.❞
>
> GALATIANS 5:13

¹³My brothers and sisters, God called you to be free, but do not use your freedom as an excuse to do what pleases your sinful self. Serve each other with love. ¹⁴The whole law is made complete in this one command: "Love your neighbor as you love yourself."" ¹⁵If you go on hurting each other and tearing each other apart, be careful, or you will completely destroy each other.

The Spirit and Human Nature

¹⁶So I tell you: Live by following the Spirit. Then you will not do what your sinful selves want. ¹⁷Our sinful selves want what is against the Spirit, and the Spirit wants what is against our sinful selves. The two are against each other, so you cannot do just what you please. ¹⁸But if the Spirit is leading you, you are not under the law. ¹⁹The wrong things the sinful self does are clear: being sexually unfaithful, not being pure, taking part in sexual sins, ²⁰worshiping gods, doing witchcraft, hating, making trouble, being jealous, being angry, being selfish, making people angry with each other, causing divisions

among people, ²¹feeling envy, being drunk, having wild and wasteful parties, and doing other things like these. I warn you now as I warned you before: Those who do these things will not inherit God's kingdom. ²²But the Spirit produces the fruit of love, joy, peace, patience, kindness, goodness, faithfulness, ²³gentleness, self-control. There is no law that says these things are wrong. ²⁴Those who belong to Christ Jesus have crucified their own sinful selves. They have given up their old selfish feelings and the evil things they wanted to do. ²⁵We get our new life from the Spirit, so we should follow the Spirit. ²⁶We must not be proud or make trouble with each other or be jealous of each other.

Help Each Other

6 Brothers and sisters, if someone in your group does something wrong, you who are spiritual should go to that person and gently help make him right again. But be careful, because you might be tempted to sin, too. ²By helping each other with your troubles, you truly obey the law of Christ. ³If anyone thinks he is important when he really is not, he is only fooling himself. ⁴Each person should judge his own actions and not compare himself with others. Then he can be proud for what he himself has done. ⁵Each person must be responsible for himself.

⁶Anyone who is learning the teaching of God should share all the good things he has with his teacher.

Life Is like Planting a Field

⁷Do not be fooled: You cannot cheat God. People harvest only what they plant. ⁸If they plant to satisfy their sinful selves, their sinful selves will bring them ruin. But if they plant to please the Spirit, they will receive eternal life from the Spirit. ⁹We must not become tired of doing good. We will receive our harvest of eternal life at the right time if we do not give up. ¹⁰When we have the opportunity to help anyone, we should do it. But we should give special attention to those who are in the family of believers.

Paul Ends His Letter

¹¹See what large letters I use to write this myself. ¹²Some people are trying to force you to be circumcised so the Jews will accept them.

Q: What does it mean to be right with God?

A: In the New Testament sense, being made right with God is less about perfect behavior and more about receiving the free gift of righteousness that God gives to all those who place their faith in Jesus Christ (Romans 5:19).

> >> live the life

Galatians 5:22–23

The Principle > **Exercise some self-control.**

Practicing It > **Tell a close friend or your spouse about an area of your life where you are struggling with self-control. Ask him or her to partner with you in praying for God's Spirit to help you overcome in that area.**

5:12 **castrate** To cut off part of the male sex organ. Paul uses this word because it is similar to "circumcision." Paul wanted to show that he is very upset with the false teachers.
5:14 **"Love...yourself."** Quotation from Leviticus 19:18.

>> live the life

Galatians 6:9

The Principle > **Do not give up.**

Practicing It > **When serving others in the name of Christ, you can't always see the results of your labor right away. However, doing good to others is its own reward, and it brings glory to God. So keep giving even when you don't see immediate change in people's lives.**

They are afraid they will be attacked if they follow only the cross of Christ." [13]Those who are circumcised do not obey the law themselves, but they want you to be circumcised so they can brag about what they forced you to do. [14]I hope I will never brag about things like that. The cross of our Lord Jesus Christ is my only reason for bragging. Through the cross of Jesus my world was crucified, and I died to the world. [15]It is not important if a man is circumcised or uncircumcised. The important thing is being the new people God has made. [16]Peace and mercy to those who follow this rule—and to all of God's people.

[17]So do not give me any more trouble. I have scars on my body that show" I belong to Christ Jesus.

[18]My brothers and sisters, the grace of our Lord Jesus Christ be with your spirit. Amen.

>> 6:12 **cross of Christ** Paul uses the cross as a picture of the Good News, the story of Christ's death and rising from the dead to pay for our sins. The cross, or Christ's death, was God's way to save us.   6:17 **that show** Many times Paul was beaten and whipped by people who were against him because he was teaching about Christ. The scars were from these beatings.

THE **LETTER** OF PAUL THE APOSTLE TO THE
Ephesians

AUTHOR: PAUL
DATE WRITTEN: A.D. 60–63

A GLANCE ACROSS TODAY'S CHURCH

landscape reveals that the body of Christ comes in a variety of sizes, shapes, and experiences. Some churches feature small groups of Christians in a traditional church setting, whereas other churches draw thousands into an auditorium or a school gymnasium. The church of Jesus Christ isn't confined to a particular group or a place. It reaches around the globe.

In this letter, the apostle Paul writes to the church at Ephesus, one of the most important cities in western Asia Minor, which is now Turkey. Instead of addressing a particular error or concern, Paul writes to strengthen believers in their Christian faith, explaining the nature and purpose of the church as the body of Christ. The letter begins with a series of statements about God's blessings, then explains that God's purpose becomes ours when we respond to Christ's love in faith.

Paul celebrates Christ as the center of the church and challenges each individual to work with others for the unity of the body of Christ. Finally, Paul reminds Christians of the constant spiritual battle against the forces of darkness and the necessity to use spiritual weapons, not carnal ones, to combat them.

1 From Paul, an apostle of Christ Jesus. I am an apostle because that is what God wanted.

To God's holy people living in Ephesus,[a] believers in Christ Jesus: ²Grace and peace to you from God our Father and the Lord Jesus Christ.

Spiritual Blessings in Christ

³Praise be to the God and Father of our Lord Jesus Christ. In Christ, God has given us every spiritual blessing in the heavenly world. ⁴That is, in Christ, he chose us before the world was made so that we would be his holy people—people without blame before him. ⁵Because of his love, God had already decided to make us his own children through Jesus Christ. That was what he wanted and what pleased him, ⁶and it brings praise to God because of his wonderful grace. God gave that grace to us freely, in Christ, the One he loves. ⁷In Christ we are set free by the blood of his death, and so we have forgiveness of sins. How rich is God's grace, ⁸which he has given to us so fully and freely. God, with full wisdom and understanding, ⁹let us know his secret purpose. This was what God wanted, and he planned to do it through Christ. ¹⁰His goal was to carry out his plan, when the right time came, that all things in heaven and on earth would be joined together in Christ as the head.

¹¹In Christ we were chosen to be God's people, because from the very beginning God had decided this in keeping with his plan. And he is the One who makes everything agree with what he decides and wants. ¹²We are the first people who hoped in Christ, and we were chosen so that we would bring praise to God's glory. ¹³So it is with you. When you heard the true teaching—the Good News about your salvation—you believed in Christ. And in Christ, God put his special mark of ownership on you by giving you the Holy Spirit that he had promised. ¹⁴That Holy Spirit is the guarantee that we will receive what God promised for his people until God gives full freedom to those who are his—to bring praise to God's glory.

Paul's Prayer

¹⁵That is why since I heard about your faith in the Lord Jesus and your love for all God's people, ¹⁶I have not stopped giving thanks to

▶ Get Aligned
Ephesians 1:13—14

THE HOLY SPIRIT IS THE MOST MISUNDERSTOOD PERSON OF GOD'S TRIUNE BEING. Whereas God the Father and God the Son are familiar to us because of their frequent presence throughout Scripture, God the Holy Spirit seems more mysterious. Yet the more we come to know this unseen comforter and guide, the more we begin to realize how essential he is.

First John 4:14 says that "the Father sent his Son to be the Savior of the world." Jesus' resurrection and ascension to heaven left the Holy Spirit as the only part of the Trinity to remain on earth. He is, as Paul says, God's "special mark of ownership" on us. When we become Christians, the Holy Spirit is the one who instantly enters our lives and signals us for eternity as God's property.

But the Holy Spirit is not just a signature on a divine contract. Neither is he a movement of God that occurred only in the early church. The Holy Spirit is active, alive, and just as present now as ever. To list all his roles would take volumes of books. However, one thing is essential to know: the Holy Spirit is willing and available to help us at every moment of our lives.

God for you. I always remember you in my prayers, ¹⁷asking the God of our Lord Jesus Christ, the glorious Father, to give you a spirit of wisdom and revelation so that you will know him better. ¹⁸I pray also that you will have greater understanding in your heart so you will know the hope to which he has called us and that you will know how rich and glorious are the blessings God has promised his holy people. ¹⁹And you will know that God's power is very great for us who believe. That power is the same as the great strength ²⁰God used to raise Christ from the dead and put him at his right side in the heavenly world. ²¹God has put Christ over all rulers, authorities, powers, and kings, not only in this world but also in the next. ²²God put everything under his power and made him the head over everything for the church, ²³which is Christ's body. The church is filled with Christ, and Christ fills everything in every way.

We Now Have Life

2 In the past you were spiritually dead because of your sins and the things you did against God. ²Yes, in the past you lived the way the world lives, following the ruler of the evil powers that are above the earth. That same spirit is now working in those who refuse to obey God. ³In the past all of us lived like them, trying to please our sinful selves and doing all the things our bodies and minds wanted. We should have suffered God's anger because we were sinful by nature. We were the same as all other people.

▶▶ live the life

Ephesians 1:18

The Principle > **Discover hope for your life.**

Practicing It > **To learn more about the hope to which God has called you, do a study on the topic of hope in the New Testament. Explore every passage in which Christians are encouraged to hope, then apply what you learn about it to your heart and life.**

▶▶ **1:1 in Ephesus** Some Greek copies do not have this phrase.

THINK ABOUT IT Ephesians 2:10

WHEN YOU LOOK INTO A MIRROR, how do you feel about yourself? Some guys hate to look at the mirror and are negligent about their appearance, whereas other guys camp in front of the mirror and strive to enhance their image at all costs. You probably fall somewhere between these two extremes.

It's healthy to pause in the rush of life to consider your self-image. Evaluate your comfort level and where you would like to improve. While no one is perfect, we can celebrate ourselves as God created us. Like the bumper sticker says, "God doesn't make junk."

When writing to the Christians at Ephesus, Paul wanted to remind them about the special nature of God's creation and how it was cause for celebration. He wrote, "God has made us what we are." But more than our self-image, God also planned our steps. "In Christ Jesus, God made us to do good works, which God planned in advance for us to live our lives doing." If you wonder about your future and whether God cares about your life, then rest in knowing that he has plans for you to make a difference.

⁴But God's mercy is great, and he loved us very much. ⁵Though we were spiritually dead because of the things we did against God, he gave us new life with Christ. You have been saved by God's grace. ⁶And he raised us up with Christ and gave us a seat with him in the heavens. He did this for those in Christ Jesus ⁷so that for all future time he could show the very great riches of his grace by being kind to us in Christ Jesus. ⁸I mean that you have been saved by grace through believing. You did not save yourselves; it was a gift from God. ⁹It was not the result of your own efforts, so you cannot brag about it. ¹⁰God has made us what we are. In Christ Jesus, God made us to do good works, which God planned in advance for us to live our lives doing.

One in Christ

¹¹You were not born Jewish. You are the people the Jews call "uncircumcised."* Those who call you "uncircumcised" call themselves "circumcised." (Their circumcision is only something they themselves do on their bodies.) ¹²Remember that in the past you were without Christ. You were not citizens of Israel, and you had no part in the agreements* with the promise that God made to his people. You had no hope, and you did not know God. ¹³But now in Christ Jesus, you who were far away from God are brought near through the blood of Christ's death. ¹⁴Christ himself is our peace. He made both Jewish people and those who are not Jews one people. They were separated as if there were a wall between them, but Christ broke down that wall of hate by giving his own body. ¹⁵The Jewish law had many commands and rules, but Christ ended that law. His purpose was to make the two groups of people become one new people in him and in this way make peace. ¹⁶It was also Christ's purpose to end the hatred between the two groups, to make them into one body, and to bring them back to God. Christ did all this with his death on the cross. ¹⁷Christ came and preached peace to you who were far away from God, and to those who were near to God. ¹⁸Yes, it is through Christ we all have the right to come to the Father in one Spirit.

¹⁹Now you who are not Jewish are not foreigners or strangers any longer, but are citizens together with God's holy people. You belong to God's family. ²⁰You are like a building that was built on the foundation of the apostles and prophets. Christ Jesus himself is the most important stone* in that building, ²¹and that whole building is joined together in Christ. He makes it grow and be-

Principles: PRAYER

Prayer is a foundational exercise for believers. It involves talking to God and expressing our thoughts, feelings, and desires. We not only tell him what we want, we confess our mistakes and praise him for answers to past prayers. We also listen to him speak to us through the Holy Spirit. Jesus took prayer seriously, saying his church should be a house for prayer (Matthew 21:13). Jesus showed his followers how to pray, and they, in turn, relied on prayer in selecting church leaders and making other important decisions. Prayer is to be a part of the daily life of believers.

 2:11 "uncircumcised" People not having the mark of circumcision as the Jews had.   **2:12 agreements** The agreements that God gave to his people in the Old Testament.   **2:20 most important stone** Literally, "cornerstone." The first and most important stone in a building.

Q: What is the Law?

A: The Law of Moses, also called the Torah, is the Jewish Scripture. The Torah also is included in the Christian Bible as the first five books of the Old Testament. The Law of Moses established a religious system that Jesus personally fulfilled (Galatians 4:4–5).

come a holy temple in the Lord. [22]And in Christ you, too, are being built together with the Jews into a place where God lives through the Spirit.

Paul's Work in Telling the Good News

3 So I, Paul, am a prisoner of Christ Jesus for you who are not Jews. [2]Surely you have heard that God gave me this work to tell you about his grace. [3]He let me know his secret by showing it to me. I have already written a little about this. [4]If you read what I wrote then, you can see that I truly understand the secret about the Christ. [5]People who lived in other times were not told that secret. But now, through the Spirit, God has shown that secret to his holy apostles and prophets. [6]This is that secret: that through the Good News those who are not Jews will share with the Jews in God's blessing. They belong to the same body, and they share together in the promise that God made in Christ Jesus.

[7]By God's special gift of grace given to me through his power, I became a servant to tell that Good News. [8]I am the least important of all God's people, but God gave me this gift—to tell those who are not Jews the Good News about the riches of Christ, which are too great to understand fully. [9]And God gave me the work of telling all people about the plan for his secret, which has been hidden in him since the beginning of time. He is the

One who created everything. [10]His purpose was that through the church all the rulers and powers in the heavenly world will now know God's wisdom, which has so many forms. [11]This agrees with the purpose God had since the beginning of time, and he carried out his plan through Christ Jesus our Lord. [12]In Christ we can come before God with freedom and without fear. We can do this through faith in Christ. [13]So I ask you not to become discouraged because of the sufferings I am having for you. My sufferings are for your glory.

The Love of Christ

[14]So I bow in prayer before the Father [15]from whom every family in heaven and on earth gets its true name. [16]I ask the Father in his great glory to give you the power to be strong inwardly through his Spirit. [17]I pray that Christ will live in your hearts by faith and that your life will be strong in love and be built on love. [18]And I pray that you and all God's holy people will have the power to understand the greatness of Christ's love—how wide and how long and how high and how deep that love is. [19]Christ's love is greater than anyone can ever know, but I pray that you will be able to know that love. Then you can be filled with the fullness of God.

[20]With God's power working in us, God can do much, much more than anything we can ask or imagine. [21]To him be glory in the church and in Christ Jesus for all time, forever and ever. Amen.

⊙Get Aligned
Ephesians 4:14

FRANK ABAGNALE JR. BECAME INFAMOUS IN THE 1960S FOR HIS OUTRAGEOUS SCAMS THAT NETTED HIM MILLIONS OF DOLLARS. Between the ages of 16 and 21, he posed as an airline pilot, a college professor, an attorney, and a pediatrician—and fooled experts in the process. Even law officers were allegedly duped once when, after being surrounded with no hope for escape, Abagnale pretended to be one of them and got away.

When it comes to twisting God's truth, some leaders can be just as convincing as Abagnale was in his day. Think of those swindled by corrupt preachers during the past several years. Most donors were earnestly seeking God, trying to obey his commands, yet they fell for the persuasive pleadings of smooth talkers.

It is said that the truth can be deceiving, but often lies are just as tricky to detect, especially for Christians whose first reaction is one of acceptance and love. Paul says we avoid being duped in such a manner by growing mature in the truth. By rooting ourselves in the Word of God, we develop the discernment to tell fact from fiction.

▶▶ live the life

Ephesians 4:1–3

The Principle > Accept others in love.

Practicing It > Reach out to someone in your life whom you find especially difficult to love. It may be a colleague or a friend at church. Spend extra time with this person and ask God to give you his compassion for that person's heart.

>> live the life

Ephesians 4:25

The Principle > **Tell the truth.**

Practicing It > **If there is a secret sin or habit that you are keeping from those close to you, make the decision to come clean. Telling them what's going on will not only deepen your integrity, but also will provide you with the support you will need to break free.**

The Unity of the Body

4 I am in prison because I belong to the Lord. Therefore I urge you who have been chosen by God to live up to the life to which God called you. ²Always be humble, gentle, and patient, accepting each other in love. ³You are joined together with peace through the Spirit, so make every effort to continue together in this way. ⁴There is one body and one Spirit, and God called you to have one hope. ⁵There is one Lord, one faith, and one baptism. ⁶There is one God and Father of everything. He rules everything and is everywhere and is in everything.

⁷Christ gave each one of us the special gift of grace, showing how generous he is. ⁸That is why it says in the Scriptures,

"When he went up to the heights,
he led a parade of captives,
and he gave gifts to people."

Psalm 68:18

⁹When it says, "He went up," what does it mean? It means that he first came down to the earth. ¹⁰So Jesus came down, and he is the same One who went up above all the heaven. Christ did that to fill everything with his presence. ¹¹And Christ gave gifts to people—he made some to be apostles, some to be prophets, some to go and tell the Good News, and some to have the work of caring for and teaching God's people. ¹²Christ gave those gifts to prepare God's holy people for the work of serving, to make the body of Christ stronger. ¹³This work must continue until we are all joined together in the same faith and in the same knowledge of the Son of God. We must become like a mature person, growing until we become like Christ and have his perfection.

¹⁴Then we will no longer be babies. We will not be tossed about like a ship that the waves carry one way and then another. We will not be influenced by every new teaching we hear from people who are trying to fool us. They make plans and try any kind of trick to fool people into following the wrong path. ¹⁵No! Speaking the truth with love, we will grow up in every way into Christ, who is the head. ¹⁶The whole body depends on Christ, and all the parts of the body are joined and held together. Each part does its own work to make the whole body grow and be strong with love.

The Way You Should Live

¹⁷In the Lord's name, I tell you this. Do not continue living like those who do not believe. Their thoughts are worth nothing. ¹⁸They do not understand, and they know nothing, because they refuse to listen. So they cannot have the life that God gives. ¹⁹They have lost all feeling of shame, and they use their lives for doing evil. They continually want to do all kinds of evil. ²⁰But what you learned in Christ was not like this. ²¹I know that you heard about him, and you are in him, so you were taught the truth that is in Jesus. ²²You were taught to leave your old self—to stop living the evil way you lived before. That old self becomes worse, because people are fooled by the evil things they want to do. ²³But you were taught to be made new in your hearts, ²⁴to become a new person. That new person is made to be like God—made to be truly good and holy.

²⁵So you must stop telling lies. Tell each other the truth, because we

Q: Do all Christians have spiritual gifts?

A: The Holy Spirit bestows spiritual gifts on every person who puts his or her faith in Christ. No one has every spiritual gift, but everyone has at least one, and they are all designed to empower Christians to accomplish God's will (Romans 12:6–8; 1 Corinthians 12:1–11).

>> live the life

Ephesians 4:29

The Principle > **Encourage others with words.**

Practicing It > **Avoid gossip or any conversation that degrades another human being. Instead, focus your interactions with others on building them up and encouraging them toward developing a closer relationship with God.**

all belong to each other in the same body." [26]When you are angry, do not sin, and be sure to stop being angry before the end of the day. [27]Do not give the devil a way to defeat you. [28]Those who are stealing must stop stealing and start working. They should earn an honest living for themselves. Then they will have something to share with those who are poor. [29]When you talk, do not say harmful things, but say what people need—words that will help others become stronger. Then what you say will do good to those who listen to you. [30]And do not make the Holy Spirit sad. The Spirit is God's proof that you belong to him. God gave you the Spirit to show that God will make you free when the final day comes. [31]Do not be bitter or angry or mad. Never shout angrily or say things to hurt others. Never do anything evil. [32]Be kind and loving to each other, and forgive each other just as God forgave you in Christ.

Living in the Light

5 You are God's children whom he loves, so try to be like him. [2]Live a life of love just as Christ loved us and gave himself for us as a sweet-smelling offering and sacrifice to God.

[3]But there must be no sexual sin among you, or any kind of evil or greed. Those things are not right for God's holy people. [4]Also, there must be no evil talk among you,

---

THINK ABOUT IT Ephesians 4:29

WOMEN SPEAK AT A RATE OF 250 WORDS per minute, and men speak at 125 words per minute. At that rate, in the course of a day, women on average speak 25,000 words, compared to a man's average of 12,000. By the end of the day, men are talked out, and women still have a day's worth of conversation in them.

Whether you speak a little or a lot, words have immense power to hurt or to heal. In a few words, you can cut off an in-depth conversation or you can send a friend packing. If you speak the truth with authority, it can end a heated argument in moments.

Consider how you use this power daily as you interact with colleagues, family members, friends, and neighbors. The selection process is a conscious choice that each of us makes each time we speak. As Paul wrote, "When you talk, do not say harmful things, but say what people need—words that will help others become stronger." The focus of your words should be on helping others grow stronger. The Bible includes this promise, "Then what you say will do good to those who listen."

---

and you must not speak foolishly or tell evil jokes. These things are not right for you. Instead, you should be giving thanks to God. [5]You can be sure of this: No one will have a place in the kingdom of Christ and of God who sins sexually, or does evil things, or is greedy. Anyone who is greedy is serving a false god.

[6]Do not let anyone fool you by telling you things that are not true, because these things will bring God's anger on those who do not obey him. [7]So have nothing to do with them.

 # Survival Guide

MOWING: THE CUTTING EDGE

Hebrews 4:12 reminds us, "God's word is alive and working and is sharper than a double-edged sword." Likewise, you need a honed instrument to cut your grass. Try the following maintenance tips on your lawnmower and reap the benefits. First, sharpen the blade. A dull blade tears the grass instead of cutting it, making the mower work harder. Next, remember to clean and dry your mower after each use. Instead of putting the mower away wet, wipe off grass, moisture, and debris. Finally, keep it tuned. Change the spark plug annually. Clean the air filter every six months, and replace the oil every three months.

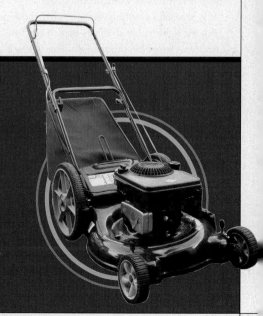

>> **4:25 Tell ... body.** Quotation from Zechariah 8:16.

▶Get Aligned

Ephesians 5:11

GOD SEES ALL. IGNORING HIS OMNIPRESENCE, we try to get away with certain sins, ones that Paul calls the "things done in darkness." These can be anything from a pornography addiction to tax evasion to simply loathing someone in secret. The root issue is rarely the sin itself, though that certainly must be dealt with, but rather the attitude of our heart. We convince ourselves that the fewer people who know about our sin, the more we can get away with it. Yet the very person we're sinning against—God—has been watching us all along.

Paul offers a word of advice on how to avoid this destructive path.

Rather than hang around temptation, we are to have nothing to do with those things that easily pull us into the darkness. If you struggle with pornography, have someone set up blocking software on your computer or television. If it is gambling, have a trusted Christian brother hold you accountable to your finances.

Whatever your secret sin, the key is shedding light on the darkness and divulging it for what it is. Once we expose our sins with a heart of confession, God is faithful to walk us through the process of real repentance and recovery.

[8]In the past you were full of darkness, but now you are full of light in the Lord. So live like children who belong to the light. [9]Light brings every kind of goodness, right living, and truth. [10]Try to learn what pleases the Lord. [11]Have nothing to do with the things done in darkness, which are not worth anything. But show that they are wrong. [12]It is shameful even to talk about what those people do in secret. [13]But the light makes all things easy to see, [14]and everything that is made easy to see can become light. This is why it is said:

>> live the life

Ephesians 5:15–16

The Principle > Live wisely and do good.

Practicing It > The wise man makes the most of his time. Prayerfully consider how you spend your time each day and determine how you could use your time more wisely. Plan your days so that you'll be able to make the most of your time.

"Wake up, sleeper!
 Rise from death,
 and Christ will shine on you."

[15]So be very careful how you live. Do not live like those who are not wise, but live wisely. [16]Use every chance you have for doing good, because these are evil times. [17]So do not be foolish but learn what the Lord wants you to do. [18]Do not be drunk with wine, which will ruin you, but be filled with the Spirit. [19]Speak to each other with psalms, hymns, and spiritual songs, singing and making music in your hearts to the Lord. [20]Always give thanks to God the Father for everything, in the name of our Lord Jesus Christ.

Wives and Husbands

[21]Yield to obey each other as you would to Christ.

[22]Wives, yield to your husbands, as you do to the Lord, [23]because the husband is the head of the wife, as Christ is the head of the church. And he is the Savior of the body, which is the church. [24]As the church yields to Christ, so you wives should yield to your husbands in everything.

[25]Husbands, love your wives as Christ loved the church and gave himself for it [26]to make it belong to God. Christ used the word to make the church clean by washing it with water. [27]He died so that he could give the church to himself like a bride in all her beauty. He died so that the church could be pure and without fault, with no evil or sin or any other wrong thing in it. [28]In the same way, husbands should love their wives as they love their own bodies. The man who loves his

▶Get Aligned

Ephesians 5:25

IN APPROXIMATELY A DOZEN WORDS, PAUL GIVES HUSBANDS THE ASSIGNMENT OF THEIR LIVES: "Love your wife as Christ loved the church." Wow. That is no small feat. Jesus' love for the church compelled him willingly to die for its sake. His compassion was so strong for it that he endured the cross so that his people—even those who would mislead the church, who would betray their fellow believers, and who would misrepresent him—could walk in victory.

Most husbands would die for their wives. We're inherently

willing to forfeit our own life no matter what. But we also need to exhibit the same passion under less extreme measures. The question is how your sacrificial love appears on a daily basis. The answer to that can be seen in your wife's current state of mind.

If she is overcome with worrying about the future, constantly comparing herself to fashion models, or calling for help with rearing the children, you need to communicate your love to her in ways that meet her specific needs. Your wife is your glory, so treat her like it.

>> live the life

Ephesians 5:20

The Principle > Give thanks for all things.

Practicing It > At the end of each day, spend a few minutes writing down what you are thankful for about that day. Think of new things to write each day. Before very long, you'll find yourself walking through the day with a grateful heart.

wife loves himself. [29]No one ever hates his own body, but feeds and takes care of it. And that is what Christ does for the church, [30]because we are parts of his body. [31]The Scripture says, "So a man will leave his father and mother and be united with his wife, and the two will become one body."[n] [32]That secret is very important—I am talking about Christ and the church. [33]But each one of you must love his wife as he loves himself, and a wife must respect her husband.

Children and Parents

6 Children, obey your parents as the Lord wants, because this is the right thing to do. [2]The command says, "Honor your father and mother."[n] This is the first command that has a promise with it— [3]"Then everything will be well with you, and you will have a long life on the earth."[n]

[4]Fathers, do not make your children angry, but raise them with the training and teaching of the Lord.

Slaves and Masters

[5]Slaves, obey your masters here on earth with fear and respect and from a sincere heart, just as you obey Christ. [6]You must do this not only while they are watching you, to please them. With all your heart you must do what God wants as people who are obeying Christ. [7]Do your work with enthusiasm. Work as if you were serving the Lord, not as if you were serving only men and women. [8]Remember that the Lord will give a reward to everyone, slave or free, for doing good.

[9]Masters, in the same way, be good to your slaves. Do not threaten them. Remember that the One who is your Master and their Master is in heaven, and he treats everyone alike.

Wear the Full Armor of God

[10]Finally, be strong in the Lord and in his great power. [11]Put on the full armor of God so that you can fight against the devil's evil tricks.

[12]Our fight is not against people on earth but against the rulers and authorities and the powers of this world's darkness, against the spiritual powers of evil in the heavenly world. [13]That is why you need to put on God's full armor. Then on the day of evil you will be able to stand strong. And when you have finished the whole fight, you will still be standing. [14]So stand strong, with the belt of truth tied around your waist and the protection of right living on your chest. [15]On your feet wear the Good News of peace to help you stand strong. [16]And also use the shield of faith with which you can stop all the burning arrows of the Evil One. [17]Accept God's salvation as your helmet, and take the sword of the Spirit, which is the word of God. [18]Pray in the Spirit at all times with all kinds of prayers, asking for everything you need. To do this you must always be ready and never give up. Always pray for all God's people.

[19]Also pray for me that when I speak, God will give me words so that I can tell the secret of the Good News without fear. [20]I have been sent to preach this Good News, and I am doing that now, here in prison. Pray that when I preach the Good News I will speak without fear, as I should.

Final Greetings

[21]I am sending to you Tychicus, our brother whom we love and a faithful servant of the Lord's work. He will tell you everything that is happening with me. Then you will know how I am and what I am doing. [22]I am sending him to you for this reason—so that you will know how we are, and he can encourage you.

[23]Peace and love with faith to you brothers and sisters from God the Father and the Lord Jesus Christ. [24]Grace to all of you who love our Lord Jesus Christ with love that never ends.

>> live the life

Ephesians 6:18

The Principle > Pray for other people.

Practicing It > Make a commitment to begin praying with your spouse or a close friend regularly. Bring your concerns to God together, taking time to pray for your friends and family and for the work of God in your church and community.

>> 5:31 "So ... body." Quotation from Genesis 2:24.   6:2 "Honor ... mother." Quotation from Exodus 20:12; Deuteronomy 5:16.   6:3 "Then ... earth." Quotation from Exodus 20:12; Deuteronomy 5:16.

267

THE **LETTER** OF PAUL THE APOSTLE TO THE
Philippians

AUTHOR: PAUL
DATE WRITTEN: A.D. 60–63

THINK OF THE WORD "HAPPY" AND YOU
might return to a special birthday or holiday party. Or it may remind you of a walk through a beautiful park holding hands with someone you love. Everyone wants to experience happiness, and many of us spend a lifetime chasing this elusive feeling. On the other hand, think about the word "joy." A quiet confidence, joy comes from the assurance of God's love and his constant workings in our daily life.

The apostle Paul wrote the church at Philippi a short letter that many have called a treatise on joy. Ironically, Paul was in a Roman prison with his hands and feet chained to an army guard when he wrote these words to believers. As Paul writes, joy is not dependent on events but is found as we focus our attention on knowing Christ and obeying him.

According to Paul, the successful Christian life is realized as we mature in Christ and identify with the humility and self-sacrifice that Christ personified. Paul's secret to experiencing joy was grounded in his personal relationship with Jesus Christ, and this letter reminds us that joy doesn't come from outward circumstances but from an inward dependence on Christ's daily strength.

1 From Paul and Timothy, servants of Christ Jesus.

To all of God's holy people in Christ Jesus who live in Philippi, including your overseers and deacons:

²Grace and peace to you from God our Father and the Lord Jesus Christ.

Paul's Prayer

³I thank my God every time I remember you, ⁴always praying with joy for all of you. ⁵I thank God for the help you gave me while I preached the Good News—help you gave from the first day you believed until now. ⁶God began doing a good work in you, and I am sure he will continue it until it is finished when Jesus Christ comes again. ⁷And I know that I am right to think like this about all of you, because I have you in my heart. All of you share in God's grace with me while I am in prison and while I am defending and proving the truth of the Good News. ⁸God knows that I want to see you very much, because I love all of you with the love of Christ Jesus.

⁹This is my prayer for you: that your love will grow more and more; that you will have knowledge and understanding with your love; ¹⁰that you will see the difference between good and bad and will choose the good; that you will be pure and without wrong for the coming of Christ; ¹¹that you will be filled with the good things produced in your life by Christ to bring glory and praise to God.

Paul's Troubles Help the Work

¹²I want you brothers and sisters to know that what has happened to me has helped to spread the Good News. ¹³All the palace guards and everyone else knows that I am in prison because I am a believer in Christ. ¹⁴Because I am in prison, most of the believers have become more bold in Christ and are not afraid to speak the word of God.

¹⁵It is true that some preach about Christ because they are jealous and ambitious, but others preach about Christ because they want to help. ¹⁶They preach because they have love, and they know that God gave me the work of defending the Good News. ¹⁷But the others preach about Christ for selfish and wrong reasons, wanting to make trouble for me in prison.

¹⁸But it doesn't matter. The important thing is that in every way, whether for right or wrong reasons, they are preaching about Christ. So I am happy, and I will continue to be happy. ¹⁹Because you are praying for me and the Spirit of Jesus Christ is helping me, I know this trouble will bring my freedom. ²⁰I expect and hope that I will not fail Christ in anything but that I will have the courage now, as always, to show the greatness of Christ in my life here on earth, whether I live or die. ²¹To me the only important thing about living is Christ, and dying would be profit for me. ²²If I continue living in my body, I will be able to work for the Lord. I do not know what to choose—living or dying. ²³It is hard to choose between the two. I want to leave this life and be with Christ, which is much better, ²⁴but you need me here in my body. ²⁵Since I am sure of this, I know I will stay with you to help you grow and have joy in your faith. ²⁶You will be very happy in Christ Jesus when I am with you again.

²⁷Only one thing concerns me: Be sure that you live in a way that brings honor to the Good News of Christ. Then whether I come and visit you or am away from you, I will hear that you are standing strong with one purpose, that you work together as one for the faith of the Good News, ²⁸and that you are not afraid of those who are against you. All of this is proof that your enemies will be destroyed but that you will be saved by God. ²⁹God gave you the honor not only of believing in Christ but also of suffering for him, both of which bring glory to Christ. ³⁰When I was with you, you saw the struggles I

▶Get Aligned

Philippians 1:29

WHEN IS THE LAST TIME YOUR PASTOR ASKED HOW MUCH YOU HAD SUFFERED FOR CHRIST? Being afflicted for our faith isn't common in a country blessed with religious freedom. Yet our passive view of suffering for God must change if we are to align ourselves with the truth, which calls persecution an honor that brings glory to God. Obviously, no one enjoys the prospect of pain. Jesus wasn't celebrating on his way to the cross. Nevertheless, he understood the glory his anguish would bring to his Father, and so must we.

Persecution gives believers the opportunity to defy the norm. In the face of hatred, violence, and injustice, we can love radically. The world will recognize we are Christians by our love. Glory emerges from believers being mistreated unjustly for their faith. By our unwavering faith, we can show the world true calling and conviction.

Other religions hold martyrdom in high esteem, yet Christians do not suffer to show their diligence or devotion, or even to earn a place in the afterlife. We suffer because our Savior suffered, and, as Paul writes in Philippians 3:10, we know him more when we "share in his sufferings."

≫ live the life

Philippians 1:20

The Principle > Live with courage.

Practicing It > Never shrink from something you know God is calling you to do. Live with courage and step out in faith to obey God's leading, knowing that you can never fail so long as you are walking in obedience to him.

<<TechSupport>>

CAMPING GEAR

Going camping used to mean lugging around heavy equipment to a dark campsite and fiddling with tent poles on an empty stomach. But advances in technology have taken the sting out of the great outdoors. Today's tents pop up automatically and sleeping pads auto-inflate. The best light source is a new generation of krypton headlamps, so you can use your hands for more important things, like building a fire. Later, before calling it a day, look heavenward and admire the handiwork of God.

had, and you hear about the struggles I am having now. You yourselves are having the same kind of struggles.

2 Does your life in Christ give you strength? Does his love comfort you? Do we share together in the spirit? Do you have mercy and kindness? ²If so, make me very happy by having the same thoughts, sharing the same love, and having one mind and purpose. ³When you do things, do not let selfishness or pride be your guide. Instead, be humble and give more honor to others than to yourselves. ⁴Do not be interested only in your own life, but be interested in the lives of others.

Be Unselfish Like Christ

⁵In your lives you must think and act like Christ Jesus.
⁶Christ himself was like God in everything.
But he did not think that being equal with God was something to be used for his own benefit.
⁷But he gave up his place with God and made himself nothing.

>> live the life

Philippians 2:3

The Principle > Be humble and honor others.

Practicing It > Practice putting others' needs ahead of your own—especially within your family or circle of close friends. Don't demand your own way; instead, honor those close to you by giving preference to them.

He was born as a man
and became like a servant.
⁸And when he was living as a man,
he humbled himself and was fully obedient to God,
even when that caused his death—death on a cross.
⁹So God raised him to the highest place.
God made his name greater than every other name
¹⁰so that every knee will bow to the name of Jesus—everyone in heaven, on earth, and under the earth.
¹¹And everyone will confess that Jesus Christ is Lord and bring glory to God the Father.

Be the People God Wants You to Be

¹²My dear friends, you have always obeyed God when I was with you. It is even more important that you obey now while I am away from you. Keep on working to complete your salvation with fear and trembling, ¹³because God is working in you to help you want to do and be able to do what pleases him.

¹⁴Do everything without complaining or arguing. ¹⁵Then you will be innocent and without any wrong. You will be God's children without fault. But you are living with crooked and mean people all around you, among whom you shine like stars in the dark world. ¹⁶You offer the teaching that gives life. So when Christ comes again, I can be happy because my work was not wasted. I ran the race and won.

¹⁷Your faith makes you offer your lives as a sacrifice in serving God. If I have to offer my own blood with your sacrifice, I will be happy and full of joy with all of you. ¹⁸You also should be happy and full of joy with me.

Timothy and Epaphroditus

¹⁹I hope in the Lord Jesus to send Timothy to you soon. I will be happy to learn how you are. ²⁰I have no one else like Timothy, who truly cares for you. ²¹Other people are interested only in their own lives, not in the work of Jesus Christ. ²²You know the kind of person Timothy is. You know he has served with me in telling the Good

Q: Who are the apostles?

A: The word "apostle" means "sent one," and the title is generally given to the original followers upon whom Jesus bestowed the authority to carry his message to the ends of the earth. Paul, though not one of Jesus' original followers, is also considered an apostle.

News, as a son serves his father. ²³I plan to send him to you quickly when I know what will happen to me. ²⁴I am sure that the Lord will help me to come to you soon.

²⁵Epaphroditus, my brother in Christ, works and serves with me in the army of Christ. When I needed help, you sent him to me. I think now that I must send him back to you, ²⁶because he wants very much to see all of you. He is worried because you heard that he was sick. ²⁷Yes, he was sick, and nearly died, but God had mercy on him and me too so that I would not have more sadness. ²⁸I want very much to send him to you so that when you see him you can be happy, and I can stop worrying about you. ²⁹Welcome him in the Lord with much joy. Give honor to people like him, ³⁰because he almost died for the work of Christ. He risked his life to give me the help you could not give in your service to me.

The Importance of Christ

3 My brothers and sisters, be full of joy in the Lord. It is no trouble for me to write the same things to you again, and it will help you to be more ready. ²Watch out for those who do evil, who are like dogs, who demand to cut ⁿ the body. ³We are the ones who are truly circumcised. We worship God through his Spirit, and our pride is in Christ Jesus. We do not put trust in ourselves or anything we can do, ⁴although I might be able to put

trust in myself. If anyone thinks he has a reason to trust in himself, he should know that I have greater reason for trusting in myself. ⁵I was circumcised eight days after my birth. I am from the people of Israel and the tribe of Benjamin. I am a Hebrew, and my parents were Hebrews. I had a strict view of the law,

which is why I became a Pharisee. ⁶I was so enthusiastic I tried to hurt the church. No one could find fault with the way I obeyed the law of Moses. ⁷Those things were important to me, but now I think they are worth nothing because of Christ. ⁸Not only those things, but I think that all things are worth

THINK ABOUT IT Philippians 2:14–15

IT ALMOST ALWAYS HAPPENS when you are in a rush to get somewhere. You get short-changed at the cash register or the workman doesn't complete the job properly, and it needs to be redone or corrected. When you must complain in order to handle the situation, there is a right way and a wrong way to assert your position.

The wrong way is to become loud with the offending person and verbally abuse him or her with your complaint. The right way is to explain gently but persistently your position on the situation and how you would like it to be resolved. There is little need for intimidation techniques, when calm persuasive action will yield results.

This method also will allow you to follow the instruction from the apostle Paul, "Do everything without complaining or arguing." He adds a promise, "Then you will be innocent and without any wrong. You will be God's children without fault." We live in a world that is crooked and at times dishonest, but there is a right way and a wrong way to assert ourselves and correct the situation. Take the high road and address issues calmly.

The Bottom Line

Overdraft Protection: Poor Planning

BANKS SELL OVERDRAFT PROTECTION AS A WAY TO AVOID BOUNCED CHECKS AND ACHIEVE PEACE OF MIND BY NEVER RUNNING SHORT OF FUNDS. But beware: peace comes with a price. Such fees have increased and can be almost as costly as a bounced check. Nor do all banks ask if you want this protection; they just make it part of a standard checking account, ATM card, or debit card. Fall short on several transactions, and the fees quickly add up. Like the ant that stores up food in Proverbs 6:8, better to store up sufficient funds and not spend more than you have than to pay fees for poor planning.

>> 3:2 cut The word in Greek is like the word "circumcise," but it means "to cut completely off."

THINK ABOUT IT Philippians 3:7–14

THINK OF HOW YOU DEFINE THE WORD "SUCCESS." Perhaps it's a moving target from year to year or month to month. If you are in sales, then you have a specific sales quota to meet or beat. If you are in production, then your definition may involve a certain amount of output. Each person devotes energy toward the goal of success and reaching that goal in his mind.

Paul could compare pedigrees with the best of men. He was schooled in one of the best Jewish schools and was a leader among the Pharisees. When Paul met Jesus Christ and became a Christian, his goals and definition for success took a radical change in a new direction.

He talked about the pedigree of his Jewish upbringing and said, "Those things were important to me, but now I think they are worth nothing because of Christ. Not only those things, but I think that all things are worth nothing compared with the greatness of knowing Christ Jesus my Lord." Paul's definition of success was focused on Christ and eternity in heaven. Anything else in the success category pales when compared to knowing Christ.

nothing compared with the greatness of knowing Christ Jesus my Lord. Because of him, I have lost all those things, and now I know they are worthless trash. This allows me to have Christ [9]and to belong to him. Now I am right with God, not because I followed the law, but because I believed in Christ. God uses my faith to make me right with him. [10]I want to know Christ and the power that raised him from the dead. I want to share in his sufferings and become like him in his death. [11]Then I have hope that I myself will be raised from the dead.

Continuing Toward Our Goal

[12]I do not mean that I am already as God wants me to be. I have not yet reached that goal, but I continue trying to reach it and to make it mine. Christ wants me to do that, which is the reason he made me his. [13]Brothers and sisters, I know that I have not yet reached that goal, but there is one thing I always do. Forgetting the past and straining toward what is ahead, [14]I keep trying to reach the goal and get the prize for which God called me through Christ to the life above.

[15]All of us who are spiritually mature should think this way, too. And if there are things you do not agree with, God will make them clear to you. [16]But we should continue following the truth we already have.

[17]Brothers and sisters, all of you should try to follow my example and to copy those who live the way we showed you. [18]Many people live like enemies of the cross of Christ. I have often told you about them, and it makes me cry to tell you about them now. [19]In the end, they will be destroyed. They do whatever their bodies want, they are proud of their shameful acts, and they think only about earthly things. [20]But our homeland is in heaven, and we are waiting for our Savior, the Lord Jesus Christ, to come from heaven. [21]By his power to rule all things, he will change our humble bodies and make them like his own glorious body.

What the Christians Are to Do

4 My dear brothers and sisters, I love you and want to see you. You bring me joy and make me proud of you, so stand strong in the Lord as I have told you.

[2]I ask Euodia and Syntyche to agree in the Lord. [3]And I ask you, my faithful friend, to help these women. They served with me in telling the Good News, together with Clement and others who worked with me, whose names are written in the book of life.

[4]Be full of joy in the Lord always. I will say again, be full of joy.

[5]Let everyone see that you are gentle and kind. The Lord is coming soon. [6]Do not worry about anything, but pray and ask God for everything you need, always giving thanks. [7]And God's peace, which is so great we cannot understand it, will keep your hearts and minds in Christ Jesus.

[8]Brothers and sisters, think about the things that are good and worthy of praise. Think about the things that are true and honorable and right and pure and beautiful and respected. [9]Do what you learned and received from me, what I told you, and what you saw me do. And the God who gives peace will be with you.

Paul Thanks the Christians

[10]I am very happy in the Lord that you have shown your care for me again. You continued to care about me, but there was no way for you to show it. [11]I am not telling you this because I need anything. I have learned to be satisfied with the things I have and with

FACT-OIDS! **About 70 million Americans use the Internet every day.**
[Pew Internet and American Life Project]

>> 4:3 **book of life** God's book that has the names of all God's chosen people (Revelation 3:5; 21:27).

>> live the life

Philippians 4:4

The Principle > **Be full of joy.**

Practicing It > **Make celebration a regular part of your routine. At least once each month, gather a group of friends to enjoy each other and celebrate what God is doing in each of your lives.**

everything that happens. [12]I know how to live when I am poor, and I know how to live when I have plenty. I have learned the secret of being happy at any time in everything that happens, when I have enough to eat and when I go hungry, when I have more than I need and when I do not have enough. [13]I can do all things through Christ, because he gives me strength.

[14]But it was good that you helped me when I needed it. [15]You Philippians remember when I first preached the Good News there. When I left Macedonia, you were the only church that gave me help. [16]Several

>> live the life

Philippians 4:6–7

The Principle > **Do not worry.**

Practicing It > **Don't let anxiety or stress over life's problems rob you of peace. Every day, take a few minutes to give your concerns over to God, and ask him to comfort you with the incredible peace that only he can give.**

> Get Aligned
Philippians 4:12

MEN ARE PROVIDERS, HUNTERS, AND GATHERERS. It is in our blood to supply for our family, and most of us sacrifice so our family can have food on the table and a roof overhead. But in the process of providing, it is easy to buy into the world's version of success. Judging by the ads blitzing us from every angle, happiness is found in the latest home theater system, the fastest sports car, or the biggest house.

You're smart enough to know differently. But ask yourself if you are smart enough to really walk this truth. Question whether you get sidetracked every now and then by the desire to earn more money. Perhaps you've gotten caught in the trap of keeping up with the Joneses.

We'd all like to be rich and not have to worry about money. But Paul challenges us to be content in whatever state we find ourselves, whether that of plenty or want. Material wealth doesn't necessarily equate to happiness, fulfillment, and a meaningful life. In fact, it often can be a major distraction. Pursue things that are eternal rather than temporary, and you'll be rich indeed.

times you sent me things I needed when I was in Thessalonica. [17]Really, it is not that I want to receive gifts from you, but I want you to have the good that comes from giving. [18]And now I have everything, and more. I have all I need, because Epaphroditus brought your gift to me. It is like a sweet-smelling sacrifice offered to God, who accepts that sacrifice and is pleased with it. [19]My God will use his wonderful riches in Christ Jesus to give you everything you need. [20]Glory to our God and Father forever and ever! Amen.

[21]Greet each of God's people in Christ Jesus. Those who are with me send greetings to you. [22]All of God's people greet you, particularly those from the palace of Caesar.

[23]The grace of the Lord Jesus Christ be with you all.

THE **LETTER** OF PAUL THE APOSTLE TO THE

Colossians

AUTHOR: PAUL
DATE WRITTEN: A.D. 60–63

IF YOU MAKE A POT OF COFFEE AND THE filter accidentally gets bent, the grounds fall into the pot of coffee. The first few cups are fine since the grounds drift to the bottom of the pot, but imagine the awful taste of those final cups of coffee. The spilt grounds ruin the otherwise flavorful experience.

In the same way, Paul writes to the church at Colossae about the difficulty when false teaching mixes with the truth about Jesus. At first, the Colossian Christians were content to follow Jesus alone, but then they added ideas from other philosophies and religions, much like people do today. To combat this mixture of religious ideas, Paul emphasizes Christ's deity and his oneness with the Father, along with his sacrificial death on the cross.

In the final part of the letter, Paul turns to practical matters such as dealing with impure thoughts, sexual immorality, and worldly lusts. He exhorts us to take every opportunity to tell others about the Good News and reminds us that as followers of Jesus, connected to Christ through faith, we are able to experience eternal life and the power for daily living.

1

From Paul, an apostle of Christ Jesus. I am an apostle because that is what God wanted. Also from Timothy, our brother. [2]To the holy and faithful brothers and sisters in Christ that live in Colossae:

Grace and peace to you from God our Father.[a]

[3]In our prayers for you we always thank God, the Father of our Lord Jesus Christ, [4]because we have heard about the faith you have in Christ Jesus and the love you have for all of God's people. [5]You have this faith and love because of your hope, and what you hope for is kept safe for you in heaven. You learned about this hope when you heard the message about the truth, the Good News [6]that was told to you. Everywhere in the world that Good News is bringing blessings and is growing. This has happened with you, too, since you heard the Good News and understood the truth about the grace of God. [7]You learned about God's grace from Epaphras, whom we love. He works together with us and is a faithful servant of Christ for us.[b] [8]He also told us about the love you have from the Holy Spirit.

[9]Because of this, since the day we heard about you, we have continued praying for you, asking God that you will know fully what he wants. We pray that you will also have great wisdom and understanding in spiritual things [10]so that you will live the kind of life that honors and pleases the Lord in every way. You will produce fruit in every good work and grow in the knowledge of God. [11]God will strengthen you with his own great power so that you will not give up when troubles come, but you will be patient. [12]And you will joyfully give thanks to the Father who has made you[c] able to have a share in all that he has prepared for his people in the kingdom of light. [13]God has freed us from the power of darkness, and he brought us into the kingdom of his dear Son. [14]The Son paid for our sins,[d] and in him we have forgiveness.

The Importance of Christ

[15]No one can see God, but Jesus Christ is exactly like him. He ranks higher than everything that has been made. [16]Through his power all things were made—things in heaven and on earth, things seen and unseen, all powers, authorities, lords, and rulers. All things were made through Christ and for Christ. [17]He was there before anything

▶ Get Aligned
Colossians 2:11

CIRCUMCISION WAS A BIG DEAL TO THE NATION OF ISRAEL. It was a unique physical sign of God's covenant with them. But the Jews had taken this to the extreme and become prideful of their inherited favor with God. When Christ opened the gates of his Father's kingdom to both Jews and non-Jews, those already circumcised took exception to the new followers who claimed the same spiritual heritage, yet had no physical sign to back such an assertion.

In Galatians 6:15, Paul clears the air by saying, "It is not important if a man is circumcised or uncircumcised. The important thing is being the new people God has made." And here in Colossians, he states that by Christ's death, all are now circumcised where it counts: the heart.

Today, most men in our society don't go around talking about circumcision. The majority of us had the procedure done as a baby to avoid any potential infections in the future. But what is involved—the painful removal of flesh in the most private of areas—is powerfully symbolic to Christ's redemption of our lives. By his death, he cut away the sinful, fleshly nature in our hearts and marked us as his chosen people.

was made, and all things continue because of him. [18]He is the head of the body, which is the church. Everything comes from him. He is the first one who was raised from the dead. So in all things Jesus has first place. [19]God was pleased for all of himself to live in Christ. [20]And through Christ, God has brought all things back to himself again—things on earth and things in heaven. God made peace through the blood of Christ's death on the cross.

[21]At one time you were separated from God. You were his enemies in your minds, and the evil things you did were against God. [22]But now God has made you his friends again. He did this through Christ's death in the body so that he might bring you into God's presence as people who are holy, with no wrong, and with nothing of which God can judge you guilty. [23]This will happen if you continue strong and sure in your faith. You must not be moved away from the hope brought to you by the Good News that you heard. That same Good News has been told to everyone in the world, and I, Paul, help in preaching that Good News.

Paul's Work for the Church

[24]I am happy in my sufferings for you. There are things that Christ must still suffer through his body, the church. I am accepting, in my body, my part of these things that must be suffered. [25]I became a servant of the church because God gave me a special work to do that

▶▶ live the life

Colossians 1:3

The Principle > Cultivate an attitude of gratitude.

Practicing It > Make a list of the dozen people who are closest to you. Beside each name, write two or three things you are thankful for in that person. Next, go to each person and tell him or her what you wrote.

▶▶ 1:2 **Father** Some Greek copies continue, "and the Lord Jesus Christ." 1:7 **for us** Some Greek copies read "for you." 1:12 **you** Some Greek copies read "us." 1:14 **sins** Some Greek copies continue, "with his blood."

Men of Valor
PAUL: Blinded by Light

Paul's Christian conversion was so dramatic that an amazing turnaround is today referred to as a "Damascus Road experience." The former Pharisee, then known as Saul, was pursuing Christ's followers when the Lord struck him with a blinding light and asked, "Why are you persecuting me?" (Acts 9:4). That marked the start of one of the most renowned ministries in biblical history. A tentmaker by trade, Paul wrote thirteen books of the New Testament and took frequent missionary journeys, showing that businessmen can also be spiritual leaders. Paul reminded people that what matters most is not appearance, but heartfelt faith. His instruction on church practices, forging unity through Christ, and embracing God's grace still guides believers.

THINK ABOUT IT Colossians 3:16

MUSIC PREFERENCE IS AN INTIMATE and personal choice. Some of us listen to the oldies radio station, while others tune into jazz, and still others love the majesty of classical music. There are infinite choices in the music categories, but some of the lyrics are more edifying to your spirit than others.

It's something to consider as you make such choices in daily life. If the music has filled your heart and mind, it can be the first thought you have for the day. As the classic hymn says, "When morning gilds the skies my heart awakening cries: May Jesus Christ be praised! Alike at work and prayer, to Jesus I repair: May Jesus Christ be praised."

Allow the words from the following passage of Scripture to burn in your heart as you are tuned to the songs: "Let the teaching of Christ live in you richly. Use all wisdom to teach and instruct each other by singing psalms, hymns, and spiritual songs with thankfulness in your hearts to God." Your music choices can become another means for the teaching and instruction of Christ to dwell in your heart and mind.

helps you, and that work is to tell fully the message of God. ²⁶This message is the secret that was hidden from everyone since the beginning of time, but now it is made known to God's holy people. ²⁷God decided to let his people know this rich and glorious secret which he has for all people. This secret is Christ himself, who is in you. He is our only hope for glory. ²⁸So we continue to preach Christ to each person, using all wisdom to warn and to teach everyone, in order to bring each one into God's presence as a mature person in Christ. ²⁹To do this, I work and struggle, using Christ's great strength that works so powerfully in me.

2 I want you to know how hard I work for you, those in Laodicea, and others who have never seen me. ²I want them to be strengthened and joined together with love so that they may be rich in their understanding. This leads to their knowing fully God's secret, that is, Christ himself. ³In him all the treasures of wisdom and knowledge are safely kept.

⁴I say this so that no one can fool you by arguments that seem good, but are false. ⁵Though I am absent from you in my body, my heart is with you, and I am happy to see your good lives and your strong faith in Christ.

Continue to Live in Christ

⁶As you received Christ Jesus the Lord, so continue to live in him. ⁷Keep your roots deep in him and have your lives built on him. Be strong in the faith, just as you were taught, and always be thankful.

⁸Be sure that no one leads you away with false and empty teaching that is only human, which comes from the ruling spirits of this world, and not from Christ. ⁹All of God lives fully in Christ (even when Christ was on earth), ¹⁰and you have a full and true life in Christ, who is ruler over all rulers and powers.

¹¹Also in Christ you had a different kind of circumcision, a circumcision not done by hands. It was through Christ's circumcision, that is, his death, that you were made free from the power of your sinful self. ¹²When you were baptized, you were buried with Christ, and you were raised up with him through your faith in God's power that was shown when he raised Christ from the dead. ¹³When you were spiritually dead because of your sins and because you were not free from the power of your sinful self, God made you alive with Christ, and he forgave all our sins.

[14]He canceled the debt, which listed all the rules we failed to follow. He took away that record with its rules and nailed it to the cross. [15]God stripped the spiritual rulers and powers of their authority. With the cross, he won the victory and showed the world that they were powerless.

Don't Follow People's Rules

[16]So do not let anyone make rules for you about eating and drinking or about a religious feast, a New Moon Festival, or a Sabbath day. [17]These things were like a shadow of what was to come. But what is true and real has come and is found in Christ. [18]Do not let anyone disqualify you by making you humiliate yourself and worship angels. Such people enter into visions, which fill them with foolish pride because of their human way of thinking. [19]They do not hold tightly to Christ, the head. It is from him that all the parts of the body are cared for and held together. So it grows in the way God wants it to grow.

[20]Since you died with Christ and were made free from the ruling spirits of the world, why do you act as if you still belong to this world by following rules like these: [21]"Don't handle this," "Don't taste that," "Don't even touch that thing"? [22]These rules refer to earthly things that are gone as soon as they are used. They are only human commands and teachings. [23]They seem to be wise, but they are only part of a human religion. They make people pretend not to be proud and make them punish their bodies, but they do not really control the evil desires of the sinful self.

Your New Life in Christ

3 Since you were raised from the dead with Christ, aim at what is in heaven, where Christ is sitting at the right hand of God. [2]Think only about the things in heaven, not the things on earth. [3]Your old sinful self has died, and your new life is kept with Christ in God. [4]Christ is your* life, and when he comes again, you will share in his glory.

[5]So put all evil things out of your life: sexual sinning, doing evil, letting evil thoughts control you, wanting things that are evil, and greed. This is really serving a false god. [6]These things make God angry.* [7]In your past, evil life you also did these things.

[8]But now also put these things out of your life: anger, bad temper, doing or saying things to hurt others, and using evil words when you talk. [9]Do not lie to each other. You have left your old sinful life and the things you did before. [10]You have begun to live the new life, in which you are being made new and are becoming like the One who made you. This new life brings you the true knowledge of God. [11]In the new life there is no difference between Greeks and Jews, those who are circumcised and those who are not circumcised, or people who are foreigners, or Scythians.* There is no difference between slaves and free people. But Christ is in all believers, and Christ is all that is important.

[12]God has chosen you and made you his holy people. He loves you. So you should always clothe yourselves with mercy, kindness, humility, gentleness, and patience. [13]Bear with each other, and forgive each other. If someone does wrong to you, forgive that person because the Lord forgave you. [14]Even more than all this, clothe yourself in love. Love is what holds you all together in perfect unity. [15]Let the peace that Christ gives control your think-

>> live the life

Colossians 3:16

The Principle > **Study the Bible.**

Practicing It > **Practice meditating on a small portion of scripture each morning as you eat breakfast and prepare for work. You might post a passage on your mirror, refrigerator, or dashboard so you can think about it as you go about your routine.**

Q: What reward can we expect to receive in heaven?

A: The Bible says that when we become Christians, we become God's children. As members of God's family, we become joint heirs of the blessings that God has prepared for Christ himself, including ruling and reigning forever (Colossians 3:24; 1 Peter 1:3–4).

>> live the life

Colossians 3:12

The Principle > **Show mercy to others.**

Practicing It > **Determine one way you could demonstrate greater compassion on the job. Give it a try this week, asking God's Spirit to reveal his heart of compassion through you toward others you work with.**

3:4 your Some Greek copies read "our." **3:6 These … angry** Some Greek copies continue, "against the people who do not obey God." **3:11 Scythians** The Scythians were known as very wild and cruel people.

277

▶ Get Aligned

Colossians 3:21

MEN USUALLY ASSOCIATE NAGGING WITH DOMINEERING WIVES, yet Paul chose to link this negative connotation with fathers' treatment of their children. He understood the incredible power dads have in speaking into their children's lives. When we bless our kids and speak words of love, hope, and wisdom over them, they face the future with confidence. Conversely, when we nag them and douse them with negativity, they're more likely to walk in uncertainty and failure.

The problem many of us have is trying to compensate for our own failures by placing high expectations on our children. We don't want to see them make the same mistakes we've made, so we try to force them into success, usually resulting in our kids' outward rebellion or inner resentment. Though it hurts to see your children suffer, wise parenting includes allowing your children to fail on their own so they can learn their own lessons.

The original Greek word Paul used, *erithizo*, means "to stir up or provoke" and can be used both positively or negatively. As fathers, we must commit to be a positive force of influence for our children, guiding our offspring toward a bright future.

ing, because you were all called together in one body° to have peace. Always be thankful. ¹⁶Let the teaching of Christ live in you richly. Use all wisdom to teach and instruct each other by singing psalms, hymns, and spiritual songs with thankfulness in your hearts to God. ¹⁷Everything you do or say should be done to obey Jesus your Lord. And in all you do, give thanks to God the Father through Jesus.

Your New Life with Other People

¹⁸Wives, yield to the authority of your husbands, because this is the right thing to do in the Lord.

¹⁹Husbands, love your wives and be gentle with them.

²⁰Children, obey your parents in all things, because this pleases the Lord.

²¹Fathers, do not nag your children. If you are too hard to please, they may want to stop trying.

²²Slaves, obey your masters in all things. Do not obey just when they are watching you, to gain their favor, but serve them honestly, because you respect the Lord. ²³In all the work you are doing, work the best you can. Work as if you were doing it for the Lord, not for people. ²⁴Remember that you will receive your reward from the Lord, which he promised to his people. You are serving the Lord Christ. ²⁵But remember that anyone who does wrong will be punished for that wrong, and the Lord treats everyone the same.

4 Masters, give what is good and fair to your slaves. Remember that you have a Master in heaven.

What the Christians Are to Do

²Continue praying, keeping alert, and always thanking God. ³Also pray for us that God will give us an opportunity to tell people his message. Pray that we can preach the secret that God has made known about Christ. This is why I am in prison. ⁴Pray that I can speak in a way that will make it clear, as I should.

⁵Be wise in the way you act with people who are not believers, making the most of every opportunity. ⁶When you talk, you should always be kind and pleasant so you will be able to answer everyone in the way you should.

News About the People with Paul

⁷Tychicus is my dear brother in Christ and a faithful minister and servant with me in the Lord. He will tell you all the things that are happening to me. ⁸This is why I am sending him: so you may know how we are° and he may encourage you. ⁹I send him with Onesimus, a faithful and dear brother in Christ, and one of your group. They will tell you all that has happened here.

¹⁰Aristarchus, a prisoner with me, and Mark, the cousin of Barnabas, greet you. (I have already told you what to do about Mark. If he comes, welcome him.) ¹¹Jesus, who is called Justus, also greets you. These are the only Jewish believers who work with me for the kingdom of God, and they have been a comfort to me.

¹²Epaphras, a servant of Jesus Christ, from your group, also greets you. He always prays for you that you will grow to be spiritually mature and have everything God wants for you. ¹³I know he has worked hard for you and the people in Laodicea and in Hierapolis. ¹⁴Demas and our dear friend Luke, the doctor, greet you.

¹⁵Greet the brothers and sisters in Laodicea. And greet Nympha and the church that meets in her house. ¹⁶After this letter is read to you, be sure it is also read to the church in Laodicea. And you read the letter that I wrote to Laodicea. ¹⁷Tell Archippus, "Be sure to finish the work the Lord gave you."

¹⁸I, Paul, greet you and write this with my own hand. Remember me in prison. Grace be with you.

>> live the life

Colossians 4:2

The Principle > Continue in prayer.

Practicing It > Make prayer a central theme in your day. Pray in the morning while preparing for the day. Pray during your breaks and at lunchtime. Pray also in the evening with your family. Saturate your day in prayer.

>> **3:15 body** The spiritual body of Christ, meaning the church or his people.   **4:8 so...are** Some Greek copies read "so he may know how you are."

Notes

THE **FIRST** LETTER OF PAUL THE APOSTLE TO THE
Thessalonians

AUTHOR: PAUL
DATE WRITTEN: A.D. 51–52

AT FIRST THE JOB LOOKS LIKE A PERFECT

fit. Everyone on the team cooperates, and the work flows between the staff and various clients. Then, suddenly, one of the staff members has a family emergency. Another person is lured to a different company by a better job. The bumps in the road arrive and you are left wondering what happened.

During his second missionary journey, the apostle Paul established the church at Thessalonica, but he had to leave the fledgling group, and during his absence some issues arose. His initial letter to the church had a dual purpose. First, Paul exhorted each believer to follow Christ in his or her daily living and to avoid sexual immorality. They were to love each other and live as good citizens in the midst of a corrupt and sinful world.

Second, Paul reminded the Christians of their hope in the Resurrection, for every believer, whether alive or dead, will be united with Christ one day. Finally, he reminded each believer to be prepared for the return of Jesus Christ, as no one knows its timing. Therefore, each day should be lived in preparedness and holiness as unto the Lord.

Get Fit

PADDLING TOWARD FITNESS For a refreshing move to a healthier lifestyle, grab a paddle, life preserver, and water-worthy vessel, and get to the nearest body of open water. Paddle sports, such as canoeing and kayaking (both sea and river), have exploded in popularity in recent decades, and for good reason. Each variation provides its own unique approach to fun and fitness on the water. Paddling or rowing clubs are active near most lakes or coastlines, and they usually provide classes for beginners interested in wading into the sport. To dive in and find out what paddling options are available in your area, you can start by visiting www.paddling.net.

1 From Paul, Silas, and Timothy.
To the church in Thessalonica, the church in God the Father and the Lord Jesus Christ:
Grace and peace to you.

The Faith of the Thessalonians

²We always thank God for all of you and mention you when we pray. ³We continually recall before God our Father the things you have done because of your faith and the work you have done because of your love. And we thank him that you continue to be strong because of your hope in our Lord Jesus Christ.

⁴Brothers and sisters, God loves you, and we know he has chosen you, ⁵because the Good News we brought to you came not only with words, but with power, with the Holy Spirit, and with sure knowledge that it is true. Also you know how we lived when we were with you in order to help you. ⁶And you became like us and like the Lord. You suffered much, but still you accepted the teaching with the joy that comes from the Holy Spirit. ⁷So you became an example to all the believers in Macedonia and Southern Greece. ⁸And the Lord's teaching spread from you not only into Macedonia and Southern Greece, but now your faith in God has become known everywhere. So we do not need to say anything about it. ⁹People everywhere are

→ The Bottom Line

Retirement: Planning for It

THE SOCIAL SECURITY ADMINISTRATION WARNS THAT BY 2042, payroll taxes will only generate seventy-three percent of scheduled benefits. Regardless of what steps Uncle Sam takes in the meantime, this program was never intended to be the sole source of retirement income. Saving for retirement is aided by time, for even small sums of cash invested in an IRA, 401(k), or other pension plan can multiply over several decades. Procrastinating in your 20s and 30s will make saving an adequate amount that much harder by the time you reach your 40s. Pay attention to the words of Proverbs 21:20, which says that "fools waste everything they have."

People Skills

Staying Teachable

Teachability is essential for healthy relationships, and it takes humility to stay teachable. Make a habit of listening to and embracing the messages you hear from your family and friends. Their advice will often help you recognize blind spots and become a more self-aware person. Be open to letting go of personal habits in response to their requests. This might mean watching less television, trying a new activity outside your comfort zone, or taking the initiative more often in your relationships. Simple changes like these can deeply enrich the quality of your relationships, and they will ultimately transform your experience of life itself.

telling about the way you accepted us when we were there with you. They tell how you stopped worshiping idols and began serving the living and true God. ¹⁰And you wait for God's Son, whom God raised from the dead, to come from heaven. He is Jesus, who saves us from God's angry judgment that is sure to come.

Paul's Work in Thessalonica

2 Brothers and sisters, you know our visit to you was not a failure. ²Before we came to you, we suffered in Philippi. People there insulted us, as you know, and many people were against us. But our God helped us to be brave and to tell you his Good News. ³Our appeal does not come from lies or wrong reasons, nor were we trying to trick you. ⁴But we speak the Good News because God tested us and trusted us to do it. When we speak, we are not trying to please people, but God, who tests our hearts. ⁵You know that we never tried to influence you by saying nice things about you. We were not trying to get your money; we had no selfishness to hide from you. God knows that this is true. ⁶We were not looking for human praise, from you or anyone else, ⁷even though as apostles of Christ we could have used our authority over you.

But we were very gentle with you," like a mother caring for her little children. ⁸Because we loved you, we were happy to share not only God's Good News with you, but even our own lives. You had become so dear to us! ⁹Brothers and sisters, I know you remember our hard work and difficulties. We worked night and day so we would not burden any of you while we preached God's Good News to you.

¹⁰When we were with you, we lived in a holy and honest way, without fault. You know this is true, and so does God. ¹¹You know that we treated each of you as a father treats his own children. ¹²We encouraged you, we urged you, and we insisted that you live good lives for God, who calls you to his glorious kingdom.

¹³Also, we always thank God because when you heard his message from us, you accepted it as the word of God, not the words of humans. And it really is God's message which works in you who believe. ¹⁴Brothers and sisters, your experiences have been like those of God's churches in Christ that are in Judea." You suffered from the people of your own

⊙ Sexcess: RESISTING TEMPTATION

Temptations abound for men today, but despite the fierce battles we fight, it is a winnable war. If we'll admit it, many times we personally leave the door open to temptation by not properly guarding the entry points to our souls, namely our eyes and ears. Whether it is tempting song lyrics, music videos, television commercials, or pop-up ads we face, we need to defend ourselves vigilantly against the enemy's onslaughts. Being the visually stimulated creatures we are, our eyes can particularly get us into trouble if we don't watch out. As Proverbs 4:25 reminds us, "Keep your eyes focused on what is right, and look straight ahead to what is good."

2:7 But...you Some Greek copies read "But we were like infants among you."   **2:14 Judea** The Jewish land where Jesus lived and taught and where the church first began.

FOR Men Only

COMPASSION There is a good reason why women are often drawn to men with pets: it typically suggests a certain degree of compassion that they are looking for in a man. But whether or not you own a dog or cat, you can cultivate the quality of compassion in your life. Compassion is simply an inclination toward assisting others, usually those less fortunate than you. It complements the nurturing instincts of a woman when it comes time to rear a family. So work on reaching out to help people in need. If all else fails, visit the local pet store!

country, as they suffered from the Jews [15]who killed both the Lord Jesus and the prophets and forced us to leave that country. They do not please God and are against all people. [16]They try to stop us from teaching those who are not Jews so they may be saved. By doing this, they are increasing their sins to the limit. The anger of God has come to them at last.

<<TechSupport>>

FINANCIAL MANAGEMENT

Personal computers have revolutionized the way we manage personal finances. Software such as Quicken and Money makes it possible to track your bills, expenses, and income over time, empowering you to watch your spending and simplify your tax paperwork. The reports and charts give you a snapshot of your finances in one place, making it easier to manage your money. Track your giving record using the software, and you will gain a visual reminder of the ways God has blessed you and your finances.

Paul Wants to Visit Them Again

[17]Brothers and sisters, though we were separated from you for a short time, our thoughts were still with you. We wanted very much to see you and tried hard to do so. [18]We wanted to come to you. I, Paul, tried to come more than once, but Satan stopped us. [19]You are our hope, our joy, and the crown we will take pride in when our Lord Jesus Christ comes. [20]Truly you are our glory and our joy.

3 When we could not wait any longer, we decided it was best to stay in Athens alone [2]and send Timothy to you. Timothy, our brother, works with us for God and helps us tell people the Good News about Christ. We sent him to strengthen and encourage you in your faith [3]so none of you would be upset by these troubles. You yourselves know that we must face these troubles. [4]Even when we were with you, we told you we all would have to suffer, and you know it has happened. [5]Because of this, when I could wait no longer, I sent Timothy to you so I could learn about your faith. I was afraid the devil had tempted you, and perhaps our hard work would have been wasted.

[6]But Timothy now has come back to us from you and has brought us good news about your faith and love. He told us that you always remember us in a good way and that you want to see us just as much as we want to see you. [7]So, brothers and sisters, while we have much trouble and suffering, we are encouraged about you because of your faith. [8]Our life is really full if you stand strong in the Lord. [9]We have so much joy before our God because of you. We cannot thank him enough for all the joy we feel. [10]Night and day we continue praying with all our heart that we can see you again and give you all the things you need to make your faith strong.

[11]Now may our God and Father himself and our Lord Jesus prepare the way for us to come to you. [12]May the Lord make your love grow more and multiply for each other and for all people so that you will love others as we love you. [13]May your hearts be made strong so that you will be holy and without fault before our God and Father when our Lord Jesus comes with all his holy ones.

Q: Does the spiritual realm really impact my life?

A: Many scriptures in the New Testament stress the reality of the spiritual realm and encourage us to recognize its ongoing impact on our lives. Though we cannot actually see it with our physical eyes, the spiritual realm is a very real place (Ephesians 6:12).

▶Get Aligned

1 Thessalonians 4:7

EVERYONE WRESTLES WITH SIN. WE ARE BORN INTO IT, are surrounded with it from the moment we breathe, and confront it every day of our life. In fact, Romans 3:10 says, "There is no one who always does what is right, not even one." If that is true, why do the Scriptures say that God wants us to be holy?

The answer is through our Savior, Jesus Christ. Not only did his death on the cross allow us to have eternal life with God, it opened up a realm of holiness we could never have entered if not for his ultimate sacrifice. Because of his crucifixion and resurrection, we are clothed in righteousness.

Jesus put a cloak on us that covers what is really underneath—our sinful nature. Without his work at the cross, we wouldn't even have a chance to strive for holiness. But with his covering, God now sees us as holy saints. We may still wrestle with sin because we live in earthly bodies, but our spirits have already been declared holy.

A Life that Pleases God

4 Brothers and sisters, we taught you how to live in a way that will please God, and you are living that way. Now we ask and encourage you in the Lord Jesus to live that way even more. ²You know what we told you to do by the authority of the Lord Jesus. ³God wants you to be holy and to stay away from sexual sins. ⁴He wants each of you to learn to control your own body[b] in a way that is holy and honorable. ⁵Don't use your body for sexual sin like the people who do not know God. ⁶Also, do not wrong or cheat another Christian in this way. The Lord will punish people who do those things as we have already told you and warned you. ⁷God called us to be holy and does not want us to live in sin. ⁸So the person who refuses to obey this teaching is disobeying God, not simply a human teaching. And God is the One who gives us his Holy Spirit.

⁹We do not need to write you about having love for your Christian family, because God has already taught you to love each other. ¹⁰And truly you do love the Christians in all of Macedonia. Brothers and sisters, now we encourage you to love them even more.

¹¹Do all you can to live a peaceful life. Take care of your own business, and do your own work as we have already told you. ¹²If you do, then people who are not believers will respect you, and you will not have to depend on others for what you need.

The Lord's Coming

¹³Brothers and sisters, we want you to know about those Christians who have died so you will not be sad, as others who have no hope.

¹⁴We believe that Jesus died and that he rose again. So, because of him, God will raise with Jesus those who have died. ¹⁵What we tell you now is the Lord's own message. We who are living when the Lord comes again will not go before those who have already died. ¹⁶The Lord himself will come down from heaven with a loud command, with the voice of the archangel,[b] and with the trumpet call of God. And those who have died believing in Christ will rise first. ¹⁷After that, we who are still alive will be gathered up with them in the clouds to meet the Lord in the air. And we will be with the Lord forever. ¹⁸So encourage each other with these words.

Be Ready for the Lord's Coming

5 Now, brothers and sisters, we do not need to write you about times and dates. ²You know very well that the day the Lord comes again will be a surprise, like a thief that comes in the night. ³While people are saying, "We have peace and we are safe," they will be destroyed quickly. It is like pains that come quickly to a woman having a baby. Those people will not escape. ⁴But you, brothers and sisters, are not living in darkness, and so that day will not surprise you like a thief. ⁵You are all people who belong to the light and to the day. We do not belong to the

Q: Does God promise Christians a happy life?

A: Though many Christians seem to think so, the truth is that God has never guaranteed that Christians will have a happy life. However, he does promise always to be present with us and to provide the strength to overcome any trial (John 16:33; James 1:2).

▶▶ live the life

1 Thessalonians 5:11

The Principle > Encourage other people.

Practicing It > The next time you sit down for coffee with a friend, let that person be the focus of the conversation. Ask questions about his life and really take time to listen to what he responds. Ask how you can support him in whatever challenge or opportunity he is facing.

▶▶ **4:4 learn...body** This might also mean "learn to live with your own wife."   **4:16 archangel** The leader among God's angels or messengers.

night or to darkness. [6]So we should not be like other people who are sleeping, but we should be alert and have self-control. [7]Those who sleep, sleep at night. Those who get drunk, get drunk at night. [8]But we belong to the day, so we should control ourselves. We should wear faith and love to protect us, and the hope of salvation should be our helmet. [9]God did not choose us to suffer his anger but to have salvation through our Lord Jesus Christ. [10]Jesus died for us so that we can live together with him, whether we are alive or dead when he comes. [11]So encourage each other and give each other strength, just as you are doing now.

Final Instructions and Greetings

[12]Now, brothers and sisters, we ask you to appreciate those who work hard among you, who lead you in the Lord and teach you. [13]Respect them with a very special love because of the work they do.

Live in peace with each other. [14]We ask you, brothers and sisters, to warn those who do not work. Encourage the people who are afraid. Help those who are weak. Be patient with everyone. [15]Be sure that no one pays back wrong for wrong, but always try to do what is good for each other and for all people.

[16]Always be joyful. [17]Pray continually, [18]and give thanks whatever happens. That is what God wants for you in Christ Jesus.

[19]Do not hold back the work of the Holy Spirit. [20]Do not treat prophecy as if it were unimportant. [21]But test everything. Keep what is good, [22]and stay away from everything that is evil.

THINK ABOUT IT 1 Thessalonians 4:11–12

HECTIC IS THE PACE THAT CHARACTERIZES OUR LIVES. We fling out of bed at the last minute with too little sleep, then gulp down some breakfast and race down the highway to arrive at work for a series of meetings. The electronic gadgets of the world only serve to help us work faster and faster. If we can't keep up the pace, then we are in danger of being left behind.

In our culture, it's a challenge to follow the admonition of Paul to "do all you can to live a peaceful life." It's a wonder anyone can get off the rollercoaster and find that type of peace and quiet. The apostle wasn't objecting to the noise level in our homes or workplace as much as our own pace of life. When the word "hectic" is a part of your vocabulary, it's hard to find time for prayer or meditation.

One practical means for many people to find this type of peace is to cut down on television watching. Notice the promised reward for living a peaceful life: "If you do, then people who are not believers will respect you, and you will not have to depend on others for what you need."

[23]Now may God himself, the God of peace, make you pure, belonging only to him. May your whole self—spirit, soul, and body—be kept safe and without fault when our Lord Jesus Christ comes. [24]You can trust the One who calls you to do that for you.

[25]Brothers and sisters, pray for us. [26]Give each other a holy kiss when you meet. [27]I tell you by the authority of the Lord to read this letter to all the believers.

[28]The grace of our Lord Jesus Christ be with you.

Principles: RESURRECTION

The resurrection refers to the act of God raising Jesus Christ from the dead after having been crucified on the cross. As it states in Acts 2:32, "So Jesus is the One whom God raised from the dead." The resurrection proves the deity of Jesus and gives everyone who believes in him the hope of eternal life. Jesus' resurrection is the most important event in all of human history and is an example of what God promises for us after our physical death. Eventually, we will be raised to live with Jesus and those who have died in faith before us.

THE **SECOND** LETTER OF PAUL THE APOSTLE TO THE

Thessalonians

AUTHOR: PAUL
DATE WRITTEN: A.D. 51–52

COMEDIAN JAY LENO PRESENTS a regular feature of *The Tonight Show* called Headlines. He reads actual headlines such as, "Town officials take stand on manure pile." You can assume these officials took a position on the issue and weren't actually standing on the pile. As the feature illustrates, miscommunication happens despite good intentions.

And it happened even in the letters of Paul. In his first letter to the church at Thessalonica, the apostle encouraged them and affirmed the reality that Jesus could return at any moment. When some of the Christians heard this news, they quit working and began to wait for Jesus. Also the church was continually persecuted and to some who were waiting, it only confirmed the second coming of Christ.

To address these issues, Paul writes this second letter to clarify the misunderstandings. As he reminds his readers, believers shouldn't listen to rumors since a number of events must be fulfilled before Christ will return. In the meantime, Christians should remain steadfast in following Christ's truth and pray for strength and courage to spread the message of hope. To be prepared for the return of Christ means that we will tell others about Jesus, reach out to people in need, and build up the body of Christ.

▶Get Aligned

2 Thessalonians 2:10

IT'S NO SECRET THAT HOLLYWOOD HAS A FASCINATION WITH DARKNESS. It loves to sensationalize mass murderers and serial rapists, showing their every appalling act in graphic detail. We're supposed to root for the good guys, yet this generation of entertainment gives far more airtime to what's evil and grotesque than to positive morals. Whether it's through television, movies, music, or video games, we've become a society enamored more with the dark than the light.

Don't fall victim to believing this is just by chance. As the last days approach, so grows the assault of evil. Although no one knows when Jesus will return, you can't help but look around at the world situation and compare it to the Bible's description of the end times.

The key for believers is not to be fooled by the times. It's obvious this world is on a slippery moral slope. Yet Satan is more concerned about lulling believers into an apathetic existence than he is about capitalizing on the issues themselves. Little harm can come from a church that preaches but never acts. As believers aware of the times in which we live, we must keep watch for Satan's ploys while standing on the truth that Jesus rules.

---

1 From Paul, Silas, and Timothy.
To the church in Thessalonica in God our Father and the Lord Jesus Christ:
²Grace and peace to you from God the Father and the Lord Jesus Christ.

Paul Talks About God's Judgment

³We must always thank God for you, brothers and sisters. This is only right, because your faith is growing more and more, and the love that every one of you has for each other is increasing. ⁴So we brag about you to the other churches of God. We tell them about the way you continue to be strong and have faith even though you are being treated badly and are suffering many troubles.

⁵This is proof that God is right in his judgment. He wants you to be counted worthy of his kingdom for which you are suffering. ⁶God will do what is right. He will give trouble to those who trouble you. ⁷And he will give rest to you who are troubled and to us also when the Lord Jesus appears with burning fire from heaven with his powerful angels. ⁸Then he will punish those who do not know God and who do not obey the Good News about our Lord Jesus Christ. ⁹Those people will be punished with a destruction that continues forever. They will be kept away from the Lord and from his great power. ¹⁰This will hap-

pen on the day when the Lord Jesus comes to receive glory because of his holy people. And all the people who have believed will be amazed at Jesus. You will be in that group, because you believed what we told you.

¹¹That is why we always pray for you, asking our God to help you live the kind of life he called you to live. We pray that with his power God will help you do the good things you want and perform the works that come from your faith. ¹²We pray all this so that the name of our Lord Jesus Christ will have glory in you, and you will have glory in him. That glory comes from the grace of our God and the Lord Jesus Christ.

Evil Things Will Happen

2 Brothers and sisters, we have something to say about the coming of our Lord Jesus Christ and the time when we will meet together with him. ²Do not become easily upset in your thinking or

Change >> Your WORLD

PRISON FELLOWSHIP MINISTRIES

Society often scorns or neglects its prisoners, ex-prisoners, and their families. Prison Fellowship Ministries founder Chuck Colson, who served as special counsel to President Nixon, went to prison in 1975 for Watergate-related crimes. Upon his release, he returned to prison and founded the largest prison ministry in the world, partnering with thousands of churches and tens of thousands of volunteers. From the well-known Angel Tree project, which provides Christmas gifts for children of prisoners, to visiting prisons, and from leading Bible studies or seminars to participating in a pen pal program linking volunteers to prisoners for correspondence, the opportunities abound.

To change your world, visit www.pfm.org.

+ **Ten Ways to Enjoy Life**

1. Get away for a weekend.

2. Enjoy a nice long nap.

3. Walk around the block.

4. Delegate chores to others.

5. Request help when necessary.

6. Ask people to respect limits.

7. Set realistic goals and deadlines.

8. Offer to help someone else.

9. Serve at your local church.

10. Volunteer to tutor a child.

You are saved by the Spirit that makes you holy and by your faith in the truth. ¹⁴God used the Good News that we preached to call you to be saved so you can share in the glory of our Lord Jesus Christ. ¹⁵So, brothers and sisters, stand strong and continue to believe the teachings we gave you in our speaking and in our letter.

¹⁶⁻¹⁷May our Lord Jesus Christ himself and God our Father encourage you and strengthen you in every good thing you do and say. God loved us, and through his grace he gave us a good hope and encouragement that continues forever.

Pray for Us

3 And now, brothers and sisters, pray for us that the Lord's teaching will continue to spread quickly and that people will give honor to that teaching, just as happened with you. ²And pray that we

> **"Do not let anyone fool you in any way. That day of the Lord will not come until the turning away from God happens and the Man of Evil, who is on his way to hell, appears."**
>
> 2 THESSALONIANS 2:3

will be protected from stubborn and evil people, because not all people believe.

³But the Lord is faithful and will give you strength and will protect you from the Evil One. ⁴The Lord makes us feel sure that you are doing and will continue to do the things we told you. ⁵May the Lord lead your hearts into God's love and Christ's patience.

afraid if you hear that the day of the Lord has already come. Someone may have said this in a prophecy or in a message or in a letter as if it came from us. ³Do not let anyone fool you in any way. That day of the Lord will not come until the turning away[*] from God happens and the Man of Evil,[*] who is on his way to hell, appears. ⁴He will be against and put himself above any so-called god or anything that people worship. And that Man of Evil will even go into God's Temple and sit there and say that he is God.

⁵I told you when I was with you that all this would happen. Do you not remember? ⁶And now you know what is stopping that Man of Evil so he will appear at the right time. ⁷The secret power of evil is already working in the world, but there is one who is stopping that power. And he will continue to stop it until he is taken out of the way. ⁸Then that Man of Evil will appear, and the Lord Jesus will kill him with the breath that comes from his mouth and will destroy him with the glory of his coming. ⁹The Man of Evil will come by the power of Satan. He will have great power, and he will do many different false miracles, signs, and wonders. ¹⁰He will use every kind of evil to trick those who are lost. They will die, because they refused to love the truth. (If they loved the truth, they would be saved.) ¹¹For this reason God sends them something powerful that leads them away from the truth so they will believe a lie. ¹²So all those will be judged guilty who did not believe the truth, but enjoyed doing evil.

You Are Chosen for Salvation

¹³Brothers and sisters, whom the Lord loves, God chose you from the beginning[*] to be saved. So we must always thank God for you.

>> **live the life**

2 Thessalonians 3:1

The Principle > **Pray for church leaders.**

Practicing It > **Commit to pray daily for the leaders in your church, as well as other Christians you know who are working in positions of leadership to further the kingdom of God. Pray for their protection and for the will of God to be displayed in their lives.**

 2:3 turning away Or "the rebellion."   **2:3 Man of Evil** Some Greek copies read "Man of Sin."   **2:13 God . . . beginning** Some Greek copies read "God chose you as the firstfruits of the harvest."

FACT-OIDS!

Residents of Hong Kong spend more time online at home than residents of any other nation in the world. [Nielsen-NetRatings]

Men of Valor
PETER: A Solid Rock

Peter betrayed Jesus before Christ's crucifixion, but that isn't the whole story. By the time Peter was in position to deny he knew Christ, all the other followers had fled. And although he cracked under pressure, Peter went on to become a faithful apostle. Even before His death, Jesus called this follower a "rock" and promised to build his church on Peter and all who would confess Christ as Lord. On the day of Pentecost, Peter preached one of Christianity's most important sermons. His faith was so strong that people hauled sick loved ones into the street, hoping Peter's shadow might fall on them and heal them. Martyred later for his faith, Peter gave hope to every man who has ever made mistakes.

The Duty to Work

⁶Brothers and sisters, by the authority of our Lord Jesus Christ we command you to stay away from any believer who refuses to work and does not follow the teaching we gave you. ⁷You yourselves know that you should live as we live. We were not lazy when we were with you. ⁸And when we ate another person's food, we always paid for it. We worked very hard night and day so we would not be an expense to any of you. ⁹We had the right to ask you to help us, but we worked to take care of ourselves so we would be an example for you to follow. ¹⁰When we were with you, we gave you this rule: "Anyone who refuses to work should not eat."

¹¹We hear that some people in your group refuse to work. They do nothing but busy themselves in other people's lives. ¹²We command those people and beg them in the Lord Jesus Christ to work quietly and earn their own food. ¹³But you, brothers and sisters, never become tired of doing good.

¹⁴If some people do not obey what we tell you in this letter, then take note of them. Have nothing to do with them so they will feel ashamed. ¹⁵But do not treat them as enemies. Warn them as fellow believers.

Final Words

¹⁶Now may the Lord of peace give you peace at all times and in every way. The Lord be with all of you.

¹⁷I, Paul, end this letter now in my own handwriting. All my letters have this to show they are from me. This is the way I write. ¹⁸The grace of our Lord Jesus Christ be with you all.

THINK ABOUT IT 2 Thessalonians 2:16–17

EVEN THE MOST OPTIMISTIC and upbeat person can experience times of despair and discouragement in life. The weight of the workplace or a family matter or simply a personal habit that you are trying to change can move you to a new emotional low. The feeling can overwhelm you and cause you to wonder where to turn for encouragement and strength.

As Christians, we have the Holy Spirit living inside us, a spiritual power source that nonbelievers don't possess. Many also have discovered courage and strength from reading the hymnbook of the early church, the Book of Psalms. From being a refugee on the run to becoming the king of Israel, David knew the highs and lows of life very well. His psalms, and those of other candid authors, show that it's okay to communicate honestly with God and lean on him for strength.

Additionally, we always can find encouragement through prayer. As you spend time with God today, focus on the words of this promise, "May our Lord Jesus Christ himself and God our Father encourage you and strengthen you in every good thing you do and say."

THE **FIRST** LETTER OF PAUL THE APOSTLE TO
Timothy

AUTHOR: PAUL
DATE WRITTEN: A.D. 62–66

PICTURE THIS HEARTENING SCENE: A grown man is mowing his yard while his young son follows behind with his plastic lawn mower. The boy thinks that if dad is working, then he wants to be in the middle of the action. As the image illustrates, whether we think about it or not, we are role models for our children.

While the apostle Paul had no biological son, he writes this first letter to Timothy with the affectionate words of a father toward his son. Raised with godly influence, Timothy became Paul's traveling companion and devoted friend. Paul is writing from prison in Rome to one of his closest companions. Timothy had probably served as the leader of the church at Ephesus, and Paul hoped to visit him. Before his visit, Paul wrote his young friend to give Timothy encouragement and practical instruction as a young leader.

This letter is filled with advice, such as the practical qualifications for church leaders, some instruction regarding the characteristics of public worship, and the steps involved in disciplining church leaders, such as pastors. Paul completes this letter with a stirring call to every believer to be actively and lovingly involved in the ministry of the church.

1 From Paul, an apostle of Christ Jesus, by the command of God our Savior and Christ Jesus our hope.

²To Timothy, a true child to me because you believe:

Grace, mercy, and peace from God the Father and Christ Jesus our Lord.

Warning Against False Teaching

³I asked you to stay longer in Ephesus when I went into Macedonia so you could command some people there to stop teaching false things. ⁴Tell them not to spend their time on stories that are not true and on long lists of names in family histories. These things only bring arguments; they do not help God's work, which is done in faith. ⁵The purpose of this command is for people to have love, a love that comes from a pure heart and a good conscience and a true faith. ⁶Some people have missed these things and turned to useless talk. ⁷They want to be teachers of the law, but they do not understand either what they are talking about or what they are sure about.

⁸But we know that the law is good if someone uses it lawfully. ⁹We also know that the law is not made for good people but for those who are against the law and for those who refuse to follow it. It is for people who are against God and are sinful, who are unholy and ungodly, who kill their fathers and mothers, who murder, ¹⁰who take part in sexual sins, who have sexual relations with people of the same sex, who sell slaves, who tell lies, who speak falsely, and who do anything against the true teaching of God. ¹¹That teaching is part of the Good News of the blessed God that he gave me to tell.

Thanks for God's Mercy

¹²I thank Christ Jesus our Lord, who gave me strength, because he trusted me and gave me this work of serving him. ¹³In the past I spoke against Christ and persecuted him and did all kinds of things to hurt him. But God showed me mercy, because I did not know what I was doing. I did not believe. ¹⁴But the grace of our Lord was fully given to me, and with that grace came the faith and love that are in Christ Jesus.

¹⁵What I say is true, and you should fully accept it: Christ Jesus came into the world to save sinners, of whom I am the worst. ¹⁶But I was given mercy so that in me, the worst of all sinners, Christ Jesus could show that he has patience without limit. His patience with me made me an example for those who would believe in him and have life forever. ¹⁷To the King that rules forever, who will never die, who cannot be seen, the only God, be honor and glory forever and ever. Amen.

¹⁸Timothy, my child, I am giving you a command that agrees with the prophecies that were given about you in the past. I tell you this so you can follow them and fight the good fight. ¹⁹Continue to have faith and do what you know is right. Some people have rejected this, and their faith has been shipwrecked. ²⁰Hymenaeus

Q: What does it mean to live holy?

A: To live holy means to be "sanctified" or "set apart" through a manner of living. When the Bible talks about living a holy life, it is referring to the commitment Christians make to separate themselves from acting sinfully or selfishly toward others (1 Corinthians 6:11).

Get Fit

MAINTAINING MOMENTUM Make it a daily challenge to find ways to move your body. Climb stairs if given a choice between that and escalators or elevators. Walk your dog, chase your kids, or mow the lawn. Anything that gets your heart pumping not only qualifies as a fitness activity, it is a stress buster, also. Make it a priority to get active at every opportunity. It doesn't have to be an hour in the gym or a half-hour aerobics class. That's great when you're up to it. But in the meantime, just get moving. And also don't forget that prayer is the lifeblood of a healthy spiritual life.

Sexcess:
THE SANCTITY OF SEX

The attitude of "if it feels good, do it" is propelling our society toward more and more promiscuity and permissiveness. The immorality ranges from the growing acceptance of so-called alternative lifestyles—including homosexuality, bisexuality, and other perversions of heterosexuality—to acts not fit to print. Yet God has called us as men to stand our ground and turn the tide of degradation and decadence. Godly guys realize that passions are powerful, and, as such, need to be placed within the proper confines of the marriage relationship. So the next time you are tempted to relax your standards, realize you are flirting with disaster, and don't.

[15]But she will be saved through having children if she continues in faith, love, and holiness, with self-control.

Elders in the Church

3 What I say is true: Anyone wanting to become an overseer desires a good work. [2]An overseer must not give people a reason to criticize him, and he must have only one wife. He must be self-controlled, wise, respected by others, ready to welcome guests, and able to teach. [3]He must not drink too much wine or like to fight, but rather be gentle and peaceable, not loving money. [4]He must be a good family leader, having children who cooperate with full respect. [5](If

{Book of the Month}

and Alexander have done that, and I have given them to Satan so they will learn not to speak against God.

Some Rules for Men and Women

2 First, I tell you to pray for all people, asking God for what they need and being thankful to him. [2]Pray for rulers and for all who have authority so that we can have quiet and peaceful lives full of worship and respect for God. [3]This is good, and it pleases God our Savior, [4]who wants all people to be saved

apostle. (I am telling the truth; I am not lying.) I was chosen to teach those who are not Jews to believe and to know the truth.

[8]So, I want the men everywhere to pray, lifting up their hands in a holy manner, without anger and arguments.

[9]Also, women should wear proper clothes that show respect and self-control, not using braided hair or gold or pearls or expensive clothes. [10]Instead, they should do good deeds, which is right for women who say they worship God.

FACT-OIDS!

The average American spends two months of every year watching television. [A.C. Nielsen]

and to know the truth. [5]There is one God and one mediator so that human beings can reach God. That way is through Christ Jesus, who is himself human. [6]He gave himself as a payment to free all people. He is proof that came at the right time. [7]That is why I was chosen to tell the Good News and to be an

[11]Let a woman learn by listening quietly and being ready to cooperate in everything. [12]But I do not allow a woman to teach or to have authority over a man, but to listen quietly, [13]because Adam was formed first and then Eve. [14]And Adam was not tricked, but the woman was tricked and became a sinner.

Winning Every Day
by Lou Holtz

Winning every day begins with a solid game plan, says famous coach Lou Holtz, who led Notre Dame to a 1998 national championship. Holtz peppers his 10-point game plan with engaging anecdotes from his own experiences as a coach, husband, and father. One secret to his success: When he lost a coaching job, Holtz wrote a list of 107 goals he wanted to achieve in each dimension of life. To date, he has achieved 99 of them, including dining at the White House and meeting the Pope. Holtz's book helps get you in a winning frame of mind every time you charge onto the field of life.

>>September

QUOTE OF THE MONTH:
"Making the simple complicated is commonplace; making the complicated simple, that's creative." —Charles Mingus

1
Plan to celebrate **Labor Day** by relaxing.

2

3

4
Pray for a person of influence: Today is broadcaster **Paul Harvey's** birthday.

5
Clip some coupons and save.

6
Host neighbors to a barbeque picnic.

7

8

9

10
Sing your favorite song in the shower.

11
Pray for peace among the nations of the world.

12

13
Memorize Proverbs 15:1.

14

15

16
Thank God for your family and friends.

17

18
Pray for a person of influence: Today is cyclist **Lance Armstrong's** birthday.

19

20
Volunteer to serve dinner at a homeless shelter.

21

22

23
Pray for a person of influence: Today is musician **Bruce Springsteen's** birthday.

24
Get involved with local politics.

VOTE

25
Pray for a person of influence: Today is journalist **Barbara Walters's** birthday.

26

27

28
Do a favor for someone at work today.

29
Watch your favorite movie with someone you love.

30
Ask a trusted friend to keep you accountable for living godly.

<<TechSupport>>

WEBLOGS

Weblogs, or blogs for short, are Web sites that allow writers to post news and commentary in a chronological order and syndicate their posts to a community of subscribers. There is a blog for every interest, and it is simple to join the fun. To get started, check out Blogger.com or TypePad.com to register and see a list of sample blogs. Personal blogs are a great way to publish your own insights about faith and life to a waiting world.

someone does not know how to lead the family, how can that person take care of God's church?) ⁶But an elder must not be a new believer, or he might be too proud of himself and be judged guilty just as the devil was. ⁷An elder must also have the respect of people who are not in the church so he will not be criticized by others and caught in the devil's trap.

Deacons in the Church

⁸In the same way, deacons must be respected by others, not saying things they do not mean. They must not drink too much wine or try to get rich by cheating others. ⁹With a clear conscience they must follow the secret of the faith that God made known to us. ¹⁰Test them first. Then let them serve as deacons if you find nothing wrong in them. ¹¹In the same way, women* must be respected by others. They must not speak evil of others. They must be self-controlled and trustworthy in everything. ¹²Deacons must have only one wife and be good leaders of their children and their own families. ¹³Those who serve well as deacons are making an honorable place for themselves, and they will be very bold in their faith in Christ Jesus.

The Secret of Our Life

¹⁴Although I hope I can come to you soon, I am writing these things to you now. ¹⁵Then, even if I am delayed, you will know how to live in the family of God. That family is the church of the living God, the support and foundation of the truth. ¹⁶Without doubt, the secret of our life of worship is great:

He* was shown to us in a human body,
    proved right in spirit,
and seen by angels.
    He was proclaimed to the nations,
believed in by the world,
    and taken up in glory.

A Warning About False Teachers

4 Now the Holy Spirit clearly says that in the later times some people will stop believing the faith. They will follow spirits that lie and teachings of demons. ²Such teachings come from the false words of liars whose consciences are destroyed as if by a hot iron. ³They forbid people to marry and tell them not to eat certain foods which God created to be eaten with thanks by people who believe and know the truth. ⁴Everything God made is good, and nothing should be refused if it is accepted with thanks, ⁵because it is made holy by what God has said and by prayer.

➡ The Bottom Line

Savings: Bank on It

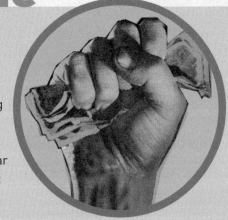

IN 2004, AMERICANS' SAVINGS RATE DROPPED TO THE LOWEST LEVEL IN DECADES—LESS THAN TWO PERCENT OF DISPOSABLE INCOME. Without savings, you are flirting with disaster. If just starting your career, you might think you can't afford to save. However, the truth is you can't afford not to. If your employer offers a savings plan, sign up for it. Or, if you have access to a credit union, deposit a regular amount from each paycheck. Collect spare change, and use it to start a savings account. Just as Proverbs 10:4 reminds us that a hard worker becomes rich, looking for ways to save will pay off handsomely.

>> **3:11 women** This might mean the wives of the deacons, or it might mean women who serve in the same way as deacons.   **3:16 He** Some Greek copies read "God."

>> live the life

1 Timothy 4:16

The Principle > Live and teach rightly.

Practicing It > Watch your speech closely. Whether you realize it or not, your words have great impact on the people around you. Let your conversation be motivated by love and reflect the truth you find in Scripture.

Be a Good Servant of Christ

⁶By telling these things to the brothers and sisters, you will be a good servant of Christ Jesus. You will be made strong by the words of the faith and the good teaching which you have been following. ⁷But do not follow foolish stories that disagree with God's truth, but train yourself to serve God. ⁸Training your body helps you in some ways, but serving God helps you in every way by bringing you blessings in this life and in the future life, too. ⁹What I say is true, and you should fully accept it. ¹⁰This is why we work and struggle:ⁿ We hope in the living God who is the Savior of all people, especially of those who believe.

¹¹Command and teach these things. ¹²Do not let anyone treat you as if you are unimportant because you are young. Instead, be an example to the believers with your words, your actions, your love, your faith, and your pure life. ¹³Until I come, continue to read the Scriptures to the people, strengthen them, and teach them. ¹⁴Use the gift you have, which was given to you through prophecy when the group of elders laid their hands onⁿ you. ¹⁵Continue to do those things; give your life to doing them so your progress may be seen by everyone. ¹⁶Be careful in your life and in your teaching. If you continue to live and teach rightly, you will save both yourself and those who listen to you.

Rules for Living with Others

5 Do not speak angrily to an older man, but plead with him as if he were your father. Treat younger men like brothers, ²older women like mothers, and younger women like sisters. Always treat them in a pure way.

³Take care of widows who are truly widows. ⁴But if a widow has children or grandchildren, let them first learn to do their duty to their own family and to repay their parents or grandparents. That pleases God. ⁵The true widow, who is all alone, puts her hope in God and continues to pray night and day for God's help. ⁶But the widow who uses her life to please herself is really dead while she is alive. ⁷Tell the believers to do these things so that no one can criticize them. ⁸Whoever does not care for his own relatives, especially his own family members, has turned against the faith and

Q: If God knows everything, why pray to him?

A: Prayer isn't so much about informing God about an issue as it is about building a relationship with him. Since God is all-knowing, we can focus our prayers on the things we aren't so clear about, such as God's will for us in a situation (1 Thessalonians 5:17).

Survival Guide

WATER PIPES: PREVENT DAMAGING LEAKS

The water damage from frozen or burst pipes costs homeowners more than fire, high winds, or burglary. Insulation and heating tape are two simple ways to prevent freezing; if a pipe travels through an unheated area, you may want to relocate it. In severe, below-freezing weather, let a pencil-size stream of water run all night to keep pipes open, and leave cabinet doors open under sinks to allow the heat from your home to warm pipes.

>> **4:10 struggle** Some Greek copies read "suffer."   **4:14 laid their hands on** The laying on of hands had many purposes, including the giving of a blessing, power, or authority.

THINK ABOUT IT 1 Timothy 6:6–10

IT IS A CHALLENGE IN OUR CULTURE to balance between our needs and our wants. Everyone has basic needs for food, clothing, and shelter. Yet, overindulgence is pervasive in our society. Just look around at the bulging waistlines and the increases in personal bankruptcy. The television commercials and the radio ads and the print advertisements are like a siren calling to us and saying, "You must buy more."

In this portion of Scripture, Paul warns Timothy about the love of money. It's not that money in itself is evil. Paul doesn't contend money is the problem. Nor does he say that money is at the root of every evil, as it is often misinterpreted. It's the love of money or the greed for money that causes all types of personal difficulties.

This passage provides a different solution to the consumerism trend of our culture. Paul defines contentment as being satisfied with food and clothing. If we have anything above those basic needs, then we can celebrate and live with contentment. As he wrote, "Serving God does make us very rich, if we are satisfied with what we have."

is worse than someone who does not believe in God.

⁹To be on the list of widows, a woman must be at least sixty years old. She must have been faithful to her husband. ¹⁰She must be known for her good works—works such as raising her children, welcoming strangers, washing the feet of God's people, helping those in trouble, and giving her life to do all kinds of good deeds.

¹¹But do not put younger widows on that list. After they give themselves to Christ, they are pulled away from him by their physical desires, and then they want to marry again. ¹²They will be judged for not doing what they first promised to do. ¹³Besides that, they learn to waste their time, going from house to house. And they not only waste their time but also begin to gossip and busy themselves with other people's lives, saying things they should not say. ¹⁴So I want the younger widows to marry, have children, and manage their homes. Then no enemy will have any reason to criticize them. ¹⁵But some have already turned away to follow Satan.

¹⁶If any woman who is a believer has widows in her family, she should care for them herself. The church should not have to care for them. Then it will be able to take care of those who are truly widows.

¹⁷The elders who lead the church well should receive double honor, especially those who work hard by speaking and teaching, ¹⁸because the Scripture says: "When an ox is working in the grain, do not cover its mouth to keep it from eating,"ⁿ and "A worker should be given his pay."ⁿ

¹⁹Do not listen to someone who accuses an elder, without two or three witnesses. ²⁰Tell those who continue sinning that they are wrong. Do this in front of the whole church so that the others will have a warning.

²¹Before God and Christ Jesus and the chosen angels, I command you to do these things without showing favor of any kind to anyone.

²²Think carefully before you lay your hands onⁿ anyone, and don't share in the sins of others. Keep yourself pure.

²³Stop drinking only water, but drink a little wine to help your stomach and your frequent sicknesses.

²⁴The sins of some people are easy to see even before they are judged, but the sins of others are seen only later. ²⁵So also good deeds are easy to see, but even those that are not easily seen cannot stay hidden.

6 All who are slaves under a yoke should show full respect to their masters so no one will speak against God's name and our teaching. ²The slaves whose masters are believers should not show their masters any

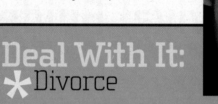

} Deal With It: * Divorce

NEARLY HALF OF ALL MARRIAGES END IN DIVORCE, and the divorce rate is about the same inside the church as it is outside the church. The Bible clearly states in Matthew 5:32, "the only reason for a man to divorce his wife is if she has sexual relations with another man." Even then many couples are able to save their marriages. Divorce has become such a matter of convenience that some states allow couples to dissolve their marriages for a nominal fee and little or no waiting period. God hates divorce, but he loves people. And he is ready, willing, and able to help ease the pain that divorce causes in people's lives.

 5:18 "When…eating." Quotation from Deuteronomy 25:4.   5:18 "A worker…pay." Quotation from Luke 10:7.   5:22 **lay your hands on** The laying on of hands had many purposes, including the giving of a blessing, power, or authority.

less respect because they are believers. They should serve their masters even better, because they are helping believers they love.

You must teach and preach these things.

False Teaching and True Riches

[3]Anyone who has a different teaching does not agree with the true teaching of our Lord Jesus Christ and the teaching that shows the true way to serve God. [4]This person is full of pride and understands nothing, but is sick with a love for arguing and fighting about words. This brings jealousy, fighting, speaking against others, evil mistrust, [5]and constant quarrels from those who have evil minds and have lost the truth. They think that serving God is a way to get rich.

[6]Serving God does make us very rich, if we are satisfied with what we have. [7]We brought nothing into the world, so we can take nothing out. [8]But, if we have food and clothes, we will be satisfied with that. [9]Those who want to become rich bring temptation to themselves and are caught in a trap. They want many foolish and harmful things that ruin and destroy people. [10]The love of money causes all kinds of evil. Some people have left the faith, because they wanted to get more money, but they have caused themselves much sorrow.

Some Things to Remember

[11]But you, man of God, run away from all those things. Instead, live in the right way, serve God, have faith, love, patience, and gentleness. [12]Fight the good fight of faith, grabbing hold of the life that continues forever. You were called to have that life when you confessed the good confession before many witnesses. [13]In the sight of God, who gives life to everything, and of Christ Jesus, I give you a command. Christ Jesus made the good confession when he stood before Pontius

▶Get Aligned
1 Timothy 6:10

THE BIBLE FREQUENTLY TALKS ABOUT MONEY, and not always in a good light. But there's an important thing to note in this passage: money is not the cause of evil, the *love* of money is. Dollars and cents are not inherently wrong; it's how important those dollars and cents are to us.

God requires us to subject all we own to his lordship, which is difficult if we are also worshiping our financial riches. In Matthew 6:33, Christ stated, "Seek first God's kingdom and what God wants. Then all your other needs will be met as well." It's not that God doesn't want us to have things, he simply doesn't want things to have us.

Money fits in that list of things that can get in the way of spiritual growth. Everyone likes being comfortable. It's nice not to have to worry about meeting your mortgage payment or paying for your kids' college tuition. But attaining those things can easily become a passion, a reason for living that's placed far above following God. And that kind of love is what God hates.

Pilate. [14]Do what you were commanded to do without wrong or blame until our Lord Jesus Christ comes again. [15]God will make that happen at the right time. He is the blessed and only Ruler, the King of all kings and the Lord of all lords. [16]He is the only One who never dies. He lives in light so bright no one can go near it. No one has ever seen God, or can see him. May honor and power belong to God forever. Amen.

[17]Command those who are rich with things of this world not to be proud. Tell them to hope in God, not in their uncertain riches. God richly gives us everything to enjoy. [18]Tell the rich people to do good, to be rich in doing good deeds, to be generous and ready to share. [19]By doing that, they will be saving a treasure for themselves as a strong foundation for the future. Then they will be able to have the life that is true life.

[20]Timothy, guard what God has trusted to you. Stay away from foolish, useless talk and from the arguments of what is falsely called "knowledge." [21]By saying they have that "knowledge," some have missed the true faith.

Grace be with you.

>> live the life

1 Timothy 6:10

The Principle > Be content with your life.

Practicing It > Don't get caught up in the allure of monetary success. Having lots of money or possessions might impress some people, but it doesn't impress God. Instead of focusing on becoming a rich man, focus on becoming a great man in Christ.

THE **SECOND** LETTER OF PAUL THE APOSTLE TO
Timothy

AUTHOR: PAUL
DATE WRITTEN: A.D. 66–67

AS THE FAMILY MEMBERS GATHER AT the lawyer's office, their anticipation runs high. The attorney opens his folder and begins to read the document, "The last will and testament of ..." If you've ever created a will, then you have left some of these types of final words for your family.

Cut off from the rest of the world, Paul sat in a cold Roman prison and knew he would soon be executed. He captures his final words of instruction and encouragement to Timothy, the pastor of the church at Ephesus. As he passes the mantle of leadership to his young companion, Paul reminds Timothy of the qualities of a faithful minister of Jesus Christ. He challenges Timothy to hold to sound doctrine, avoid godless chatter, and to keep his life pure.

Next, Paul warns his friend about the terrible times of the last days where self-centered people will attempt to use the church for their own purposes and will teach false doctrines. Prepare for these unfaithful people through your steadfast commitment to the strength and power of the Scriptures, he reminds Timothy. Paul ends with a stirring exhortation to preach the Word and fulfill one's ministry until the end. With his closing words, Paul reveals the loneliness of prison and his profound love for the church of Christ.

▶Get Aligned
2 Timothy 1:5

WHAT WOULD HAPPEN IF YOU INHERITED MILLIONS OF DOLLARS FROM YOUR PARENTS? You'd never have to work again. There would be no more stress over paying bills. Your family could live comfortably. In fact, your children would be secure for their entire lives.

The same concept of inheritance exists in the spiritual realm. Believers can pass down a rich spiritual heritage to their children. Our legacy of faith can continue for generations after us as we model a mature walk with God. By making our lives an example for our children and instilling in them godly values, we can pave the spiritual future for our family.

Maybe you inherited such a legacy. Maybe your parents were godly believers who not only reared you in the truth but also exemplified Christ. If so, build upon this rich heritage for your children and their children. But if you are the first Christian in your family line, or if your parents passed down more burdens than blessings, here's the good news: you can begin a new heritage no matter what your past has been. Commit each day to be a chance to invest eternal matters in your children. As a pioneer for your family, you can pass along a legacy of true riches.

1 From Paul, an apostle of Christ Jesus by the will of God. God sent me to tell about the promise of life that is in Christ Jesus. ²To Timothy, a dear child to me:

Grace, mercy, and peace to you from God the Father and Christ Jesus our Lord.

Encouragement for Timothy

³I thank God as I always mention you in my prayers, day and night. I serve him, doing what I know is right as my ancestors did. ⁴Remembering that you cried for me, I want very much to see you so I can be filled with joy. ⁵I remember your true faith. That faith first lived in your grandmother Lois and in your mother Eunice, and I know you now have that same faith. ⁶This is why I remind you to keep using the gift God gave you when I laid my hands on" you. Now let it grow, as a small flame grows into a fire. ⁷God did not give us a spirit that makes us afraid but a spirit of power and love and self-control.

⁸So do not be ashamed to tell people about our Lord Jesus, and do not be ashamed of me, in prison for the Lord. But suffer with me for the Good News. God, who gives us the strength to do that, ⁹saved us and made us his holy people. That was not because of anything we did ourselves but because of God's purpose and grace. That grace was given to us through Christ Jesus before time began, ¹⁰but it is now shown to us by the coming of our Savior Christ Jesus. He destroyed death, and through the Good News he showed us the way to have life that cannot be destroyed. ¹¹I was chosen to tell that Good News and to be an apostle and a teacher. ¹²I am suffering now because I tell the Good News, but I am not ashamed, because I know Jesus, the One in whom I have believed. And I am sure he is able to protect what he has trusted me with until that day." ¹³Follow the pattern of true teachings that you heard from me in faith and love, which are in Christ Jesus. ¹⁴Protect the truth that you were given; protect it with the help of the Holy Spirit who lives in us.

¹⁵You know that everyone in Asia has left me, even Phygelus and Hermogenes. ¹⁶May the Lord show mercy to the family of Onesiphorus, who has often helped me and was not ashamed that I was in prison. ¹⁷When he came to Rome, he looked eagerly for me until he found me. ¹⁸May the Lord allow him to find mercy from the Lord on that day. You know how many ways he helped me in Ephesus.

Change >> Your WORLD

PROMISE KEEPERS

Millions of men have been discipled as a result of their involvement in Promise Keepers, since Coach Bill McCartney founded the organization in 1990. Centered on seven key promises, through seminars and small accountability groups, Promise Keepers has helped men understand their need for accountability and integrity in our rough and tumble world. As one of its promises states, "A Promise Keeper is committed to practicing spiritual, moral, ethical, and sexual purity." Whether you actively participate in a small group or large conference or gain personal insight from their tapes or resources, you can find help and encouragement when you need it.

To change your world, visit www.promisekeepers.org.

 1:6 laid my hands on The laying on of hands had many purposes, including the giving of a blessing, power, or authority.   **1:12 day** The day Christ will come to judge all people and take his people to live with him.

People
Skills

Handling Jealousy

Jealousy has no place in a friendship. Yet anytime there is a perceived inequality or imbalance in the friendship, the door is open for jealousy to take root. If you have jealous feelings toward a friend, take time to examine your own heart. Determine what is causing you to feel jealous and what your jealousy is telling you about your own life and beliefs. Instead of feeling jealous, decide what the response is that you really want. Remember, you are ultimately responsible for who you are and the life that you create. So instead of choosing jealousy, use the success of your friend as motivation to improve your own life.

THINK ABOUT IT 2 Timothy 1:12

DURING THE GREAT DEPRESSION, there was a run on the banks. People who had deposited money into the banks were unable to withdraw their savings. The loss of their money gave many of these individuals a chronic distrust of the banking system. They changed how they lived from day to day, only operating on a cash basis and often hiding stacks of money in secret places in their homes.

Today, because of banking laws and guarantees from the Federal Reserve System, there is greater trust in the banks. Yet nothing in this physical world is totally secure. Paul himself knew firsthand about the trials of life. He wrote his beloved pupil Timothy from prison and declared, "I am not ashamed, because I know Jesus, the One in whom I have believed. And I am sure he is able to protect what he has trusted me with until that day."

Jesus will return for those who trust him. It's something we can count on happening. There is much uncertainty in the world, and though you can't place all your trust in the banks, you can trust in Jesus.

A Loyal Soldier of Christ Jesus

2 You then, Timothy, my child, be strong in the grace we have in Christ Jesus. [2]You should teach people whom you can trust the things you and many others have heard me say. Then they will be able to teach others. [3]Share in the troubles we have like a good soldier of Christ Jesus. [4]A soldier wants to please the enlisting officer, so no one serving in the army wastes time with everyday matters. [5]Also an athlete who takes part in a contest must obey all the rules in order to win. [6]The farmer who works hard should be the first person to get some of the food that was grown. [7]Think about what I am saying, because the Lord will give you the ability to understand everything.

[8]Remember Jesus Christ, who was raised from the dead, who is from the family of David. This is the Good News I preach, [9]and I am suffering because of it to the point of being bound with chains like a criminal. But God's teaching is not in chains. [10]So I pa-

tiently accept all these troubles so that those whom God has chosen can have the salvation that is in Christ Jesus. With that salvation comes glory that never ends.

[11]This teaching is true:
If we died with him, we will also live with him.
[12]If we accept suffering, we will also rule with him.
If we say we don't know him, he will say he doesn't know us.
[13]If we are not faithful, he will still be faithful,
because he must be true to who he is.

A Worker Pleasing to God

[14]Continue teaching these things, warning people in God's presence not to argue about words. It does not help anyone, and it ruins those who listen. [15]Make every effort to give yourself to God as the kind of person he will approve. Be a worker who is not ashamed and who uses the true teaching in the right

>> live the life

2 Timothy 2:2

The Principle > Train others to teach.

Practicing It > Develop a mentoring program at your church. Spending time with other men who are seeking God is a great way to strengthen one another's faith and to build life-long friendships at the same time.

way. [16]Stay away from foolish, useless talk, because that will lead people further away from God. [17]Their evil teaching will spread like a sickness inside the body. Hymenaeus and Philetus are like that. [18]They have left the true teaching, saying that the rising from the dead has already taken place, and so they are destroying the faith of some people. [19]But God's strong foundation continues to stand. These words are written on the seal: "The Lord knows those who belong to him,"* and "Everyone who wants to belong to the Lord must stop doing wrong."

[20]In a large house there are not only things made of gold and silver, but also things made of wood and clay. Some things are used for special purposes, and others are made for ordinary jobs. [21]All who make themselves clean from evil will be used for special purposes. They will be made holy, useful to the Master, ready to do any good work.

[22]But run away from the evil desires of youth. Try hard to live right and to have faith, love, and peace, together with those who trust in the Lord from pure hearts. [23]Stay away from foolish and stupid arguments, because you know they grow into quarrels. [24]And a servant of the Lord must not quarrel but must be kind to everyone, a good teacher, and patient. [25]The Lord's servant must gently teach those who disagree. Then maybe God will let them change their

>> live the life

2 Timothy 2:15

The Principle > Study to become more knowledgeable.

Practicing It > Choose a book of the Bible you want to learn more about, and then make a commitment to study it in depth. Use a Bible study guide to help you, and ask a friend to join you for the journey.

minds so they can accept the truth. [26]And they may wake up and escape from the trap of the devil, who catches them to do what he wants.

The Last Days

3 Remember this! In the last days there will be many troubles, [2]because people will love themselves, love money, brag, and be proud. They will say evil things against others and will not obey their parents or be thankful or be the kind of people God wants. [3]They will not love others, will refuse to forgive, will gossip, and will not control themselves. They will be cruel, will hate what is good, [4]will turn against their friends, and will do foolish things without thinking. They will be conceited, will love pleasure instead of God, [5]and will act as if they serve God but will not have his power. Stay away from those people. [6]Some of them go into homes and get control of silly women who are full of sin and are led by many evil desires. [7]These women are always learning new teachings, but they are never able to understand the truth fully. [8]Just as Jannes and Jambres were against Moses, these people are against the truth. Their thinking has been ruined, and they have failed in trying to follow the faith. [9]But they will not be successful in what they do, because as with Jannes and Jambres, everyone will see that they are foolish.

(>) Get Aligned

2 Timothy 3:16—17

IT IS ASTOUNDING THE NUMBER OF PEOPLE, CHRISTIANS INCLUDED, WHO TAKE GOD'S WORD FOR GRANTED. Although nine out of ten American adults own a Bible, less than forty percent actually read from it during the week, other than at church. Only sixty percent of all American adults believe the Bible is completely accurate in its teachings. In other words, four out of ten think God's Word has mistakes in it.

Is it any wonder that so many Christians lead ineffective lives with no influence on the world surrounding them? We forget the description of the Bible in Hebrews 4:12: "God's word is alive and working and is sharper than a double-edged sword. It cuts all the way into us, where the soul and the spirit are joined, to the center of our joints and bones. And it judges the thoughts and feelings in our hearts."

The Bible is not outdated or irrelevant, despite what today's culture may say. It has stood through thousands of years of being mocked, burned, and misinterpreted. It remains the plumb line of truth and will not shift according to popular belief or relativism. For believers, it is a continuously open invitation to discover God's heart.

>> 2:19 "The Lord...him." Quotation from Numbers 16:5.

FOR
Men Only

GROOMING   Like it or not, women like well-groomed men. But good grooming doesn't mean you have to become a metrosexual male with an obsession for products like hair mousse and facial cosmetics. All we're talking about here is some simple pointers in addition to the basics like showering, shaving, and shampooing. Start with a good haircut that flatters and complements your features, not just one that's popular. Use deodorant and cologne with subtle scents that aren't so strong they overwhelm. Maintain good oral hygiene by brushing and flossing regularly. Finally, smile! Nothing communicates confidence and sex appeal like a flash of the pearly whites.

LISTEN

you were a child you have known the Holy Scriptures which are able to make you wise. And that wisdom leads to salvation through faith in Christ Jesus. ¹⁶All Scripture is inspired by God and is useful for teaching, for showing people what is wrong in their lives, for correcting faults, and for teaching how to live right. ¹⁷Using the Scriptures, the person who serves God will be capable, having all that is needed to do every good work.

4 I give you a command in the presence of God and Christ Jesus, the One who will judge the living and the dead, and by his coming and his kingdom: ²Preach the Good News. Be ready at all times, and tell people what they need to do. Tell them when they are wrong. Encourage them with great patience and careful teaching, ³because the time will come when people will not listen to the true teaching but will find many more teachers who please them by saying the things they want to hear. ⁴They will stop listening to the truth and will begin to follow false stories. ⁵But you should control yourself at all times, accept troubles, do the work of telling the Good News, and complete all the duties of a servant of God.

⁶My life is being given as an offering to God, and the time has come for me to leave this life. ⁷I have fought the good fight, I have finished the race, I have kept the faith. ⁸Now, a crown is being held for me—a crown for being right with God. The Lord, the judge who judges rightly, will give the crown to me on that day"—not only to me but to all those who have waited with love for him to come again.

Obey the Teachings

¹⁰But you have followed what I teach, the way I live, my goal, faith, patience, and love. You know I never give up. ¹¹You know how I have been hurt and have suffered, as in Antioch, Iconium, and Lystra. I have suffered, but the Lord saved me from all those troubles. ¹²Everyone who wants to live as God desires, in Christ Jesus, will be persecuted. ¹³But people who are evil and cheat others will go from bad to worse. They will fool others, but they will also be fooling themselves.

¹⁴But you should continue following the teachings you learned. You know they are true, because you trust those who taught you. ¹⁵Since

Personal Words

⁹Do your best to come to me as soon as you can, ¹⁰because Demas, who loved this world, left me and went to Thessalonica. Crescens went to Galatia, and Titus went to Dalmatia. ¹¹Luke is the only one still with me. Get Mark and bring him with you when you come, because he can help me in my work here. ¹²I sent Tychicus to Ephesus. ¹³When I was in Troas, I left my coat there with Carpus. So when you come, bring it to me, along with my books, particularly the ones written on parchment."

¹⁴Alexander the metalworker did many harmful things against me. The Lord will punish him for what he did. ¹⁵You also should be careful that he does not hurt you, because he fought strongly against our teaching.

Principles: RIGHTEOUSNESS

Righteousness is right standing with God. It is freedom from guilt or condemnation. Righteousness is a gift from God, and it only comes from trusting in Christ. First Corinthians 1:30 states, "In Christ we are put right with God, and have been made holy, and have been set free from sin." If we could become righteous through our own efforts, there wouldn't have been any reason for Jesus to die. Of course, our right standing with God needs to be reflected in right living, but it is never to be confused with earning our righteousness in Christ.

>> **4:8 day** The day Christ will come to judge all people and take his people to live with him.   **4:13 parchment** A writing paper made from the skins of sheep.

>> live the life

2 Timothy 3:5

The Principle > **Beware of hypocrites.**

Practicing It > **Don't hang out with people who pretend to follow God but really don't. Their example will only bring you down. Instead, surround yourself with others like you who are genuinely striving to know, love, and follow Jesus.**

[16]The first time I defended myself, no one helped me; everyone left me. May they be forgiven. [17]But the Lord stayed with me and gave me strength so I could fully tell the Good News to all those who are not Jews. So I was saved from the lion's mouth. [18]The Lord will save me when anyone tries to hurt me, and he will bring me safely to his heavenly kingdom. Glory forever and ever be the Lord's. Amen.

Final Greetings

[19]Greet Priscilla and Aquila and the family of Onesiphorus. [20]Erastus stayed in Corinth, and I left Trophimus sick in Miletus. [21]Try as hard as you can to come to me before winter.

Eubulus sends greetings to you. Also Pudens, Linus, Claudia, and all the brothers and sisters in Christ greet you.

[22]The Lord be with your spirit. Grace be with you.

THE **LETTER** OF PAUL THE APOSTLE TO
Titus

AUTHOR: PAUL
DATE WRITTEN: A.D. 62–66

THE POPULAR PASTOR DREW LARGE
numbers of people into his ministry. Throughout the
years, the church regularly moved to a larger auditorium.
Finally, one day the minister made a personal decision to
retire from the pulpit, creating a vacuum of leadership.
The apostle Paul addresses this type of change in leadership in his letter to his friend Titus, a likely Greek convert
who was supervising the churches on the island of Crete.

Paul was keenly aware that the local church is not to be
built on a particular personality or minister but on Jesus
Christ. He provides Titus with a list of qualifications for
pastoral leadership, then contrasts the false leaders with
faithful elders. Then Paul urges Titus to live as a mature Christian, teaching
courage and conviction.

Besides identifying key characteristics of a leader, Paul exhorts Titus and the local church to understand the importance of living an upright life, obeying the government, and controlling their speech. He reminds older believers to serve as role
models or examples for younger Christians. In the final portion, the elder apostle
concludes by encouraging all Christians to live peaceably inside the church so that
their faith will provide a living example to the community around them.

Get Fit

DRINKING WATER Nothing improves your health like drinking plenty of water. Water not only fills you up and decreases your appetite, but it also fuels your body to run at top efficiency. Water flushes out your system, rids your body of toxins, and replenishes your skin. Health experts recommend a minimum of sixty-four ounces, or eight glasses, of water each day. But that's just a minimum. When it comes to water, more is typically better. Remember, the extra trips to the restroom qualify as exercise, too. And while you're swigging that refreshing water, don't forget to thank God for the living water he offers us in Christ.

1 From Paul, a servant of God and an apostle of Jesus Christ. I was sent to help the faith of God's chosen people and to help them know the truth that shows people how to serve God. ²That faith and that knowledge come from the hope for life forever, which God promised to us before time began. And God cannot lie. ³At the right time God let the world know about that life through preaching. He trusted me with that work, and I preached by the command of God our Savior.

⁴To Titus, my true child in the faith we share:

Grace and peace from God the Father and Christ Jesus our Savior.

Titus' Work in Crete

⁵I left you in Crete so you could finish doing the things that still needed to be done and so you could appoint elders in every town, as I directed you. ⁶An elder must not be guilty of doing wrong, must have only one wife, and must have believing children. They must not be known as children who are wild and do not cooperate. ⁷As God's managers, overseers must not be guilty of doing wrong, being selfish, or becoming angry quickly. They must not drink too much wine, like to fight, or try to get rich by cheating others. ⁸Overseers must be ready to welcome guests, love what is good, be wise, live right, and be holy and self-controlled. ⁹By holding on to the trustworthy word just as we

→ The Bottom Line

Secured Credit Cards: Understanding Terms

YOU MAY HAVE SEEN ADVERTISEMENTS FOR SECURED CREDIT CARDS. They function like a credit card but are funded by deposits at the bank issuing the card. A secured card can help establish credit, especially if overspending wrecked yours. But understand the terms before signing up for a secured credit card. Many carry high rates of interest and may have annual fees or other conditions. Be wary of those offered by credit-counseling services wanting to fix your credit or any that require calling a 1-900 number. As you work to restore your credit, exercise fiscal discipline to avoid repeating the same mistakes.

▶ Get Aligned

Titus 2:8

WHEN YOU EARN THE REPUTATION OF BEING UNTRUTHFUL, PEOPLE STOP BELIEVING YOU. But speaking the truth keeps you above reproach. When you are known for being honest, people can take your words at face value. By remaining full of integrity, you cannot be criticized. Your lifestyle will convince the critics of the legitimacy of your faith.

There will always be people who try to defy your beliefs. In fact, some will pick at your words just for sport, arguing for argument's sake. Paul even talked about this crowd in Titus 3:9–10: "Stay away from those who have foolish arguments…. Those things are worth nothing and will not help anyone…. Avoid someone who causes arguments."

Paul isn't saying to back down from attacks on your faith. Christians should be prepared to defend their beliefs in season and out of season. But you should be wise with whom you spend your time arguing. Learn to discern whose hearts are eager for the truth and whose aren't. And remember that in the end, the truth will win out, for God said so.

teach it, overseers can help people by using true teaching, and they can show those who are against the true teaching that they are wrong.

[10]There are many people who refuse to cooperate, who talk about worthless things and lead others into the wrong way—mainly those who insist on circumcision to be saved. [11]These people must be stopped, because they are upsetting whole families by teaching things they should not teach, which they do to get rich by cheating people. [12]Even one of their own prophets said, "Cretans are always liars, evil animals, and lazy people who do nothing but eat." [13]The words that prophet said are true. So firmly tell those people they are wrong so they may become strong in the faith, [14]not accepting Jewish false stories and the commands of people who reject the truth. [15]To those who are pure, all things are pure, but to those who are full of sin and do not believe, nothing is pure. Both their minds and their consciences have been ruined. [16]They say they know God, but their actions show they do not accept him. They are hateful people, they refuse to obey, and they are useless for doing anything good.

Following the True Teaching

2 But you must tell everyone what to do to follow the true teaching. [2]Teach older men to be self-controlled, serious, wise, strong in faith, in love, and in patience.

[3]In the same way, teach older women to be holy in their behavior, not speaking against others or enslaved to too much wine, but teach-

ing what is good. [4]Then they can teach the young women to love their husbands, to love their children, [5]to be wise and pure, to be good workers at home, to be kind, and to yield to their husbands. Then no one will be able to criticize the teaching God gave us.

> ❝In every way be an example of doing good deeds.❞ TITUS 2:7

[6]In the same way, encourage young men to be wise. [7]In every way be an example of doing good deeds. When you teach, do it with honesty and seriousness. [8]Speak the truth so that you cannot be criticized. Then those who are against you will be ashamed because there is nothing bad to say about us.

[9]Slaves should yield to their own masters at all times, trying to please them and not arguing with them. [10]They should not steal from them but should show their masters they can be fully trusted so that in everything they do they will make the teaching of God our Savior attractive.

[11]That is the way we should live, because God's grace that can save everyone has come. [12]It teaches us not to live against God nor to do the evil things the world wants to do. Instead, that grace teaches us to live in the present age in a wise and right way and in a way that shows we serve God. [13]We should live like that while we wait for our great hope and the coming of the glory of our great God and Savior Jesus Christ. [14]He gave himself for us so he might pay the price to free us from all evil and to make us pure people who belong only to him— people who are always wanting to do good deeds.

[15]Say these things and encourage the people and tell them what is wrong in their lives, with all authority. Do not let anyone treat you as if you were unimportant.

The Right Way to Live

3 Remind the believers to yield to the authority of rulers and government leaders, to obey them, to be ready to do good, [2]to speak

▶▶ live the life

Titus 3:1–2

The Principle > **Be ready to do good.**

Practicing It > **When someone at the office or at home becomes overly demanding, make the choice not to respond in anger. Think of a way you can extend kindness instead. Doing good can diffuse a conflict quickly and open the door to deeper understanding.**

no evil about anyone, to live in peace, and to be gentle and polite to all people.

³In the past we also were foolish. We did not obey, we were wrong, and we were slaves to many things our bodies wanted and enjoyed. We spent our lives doing evil and being jealous. People hated us, and we hated each other. ⁴But when the kindness and love of God our Savior was shown, ⁵he saved us because of his mercy. It was not because of good deeds we did to be right with him. He saved us through the washing that made us new people through the Holy Spirit. ⁶God poured out richly upon us that Holy Spirit through Jesus Christ our Savior. ⁷Being made right with God by his grace, we could have the hope of receiving the life that never ends.

⁸This teaching is true, and I want you to be sure the people understand these things. Then those who believe in God will be careful to use their lives for doing good. These things are good and will help everyone.

⁹But stay away from those who have foolish arguments and talk about useless family histories and argue and quarrel about the law. Those things are worth nothing and will not help anyone. ¹⁰After a first and second warning, avoid someone who causes arguments. ¹¹You can know that such people are evil and sinful; their own sins prove them wrong.

THINK ABOUT IT Titus 3:5–7

GOOD DEEDS ARE EVERYWHERE. A wealthy man donates a new wing to the local children's hospital amounting to millions of dollars. A man volunteers every Saturday afternoon at the Big Brother organization to spend time with a boy who doesn't have a father. Another man is active in his local Boy Scout troop as an assistant scoutmaster.

If you pause to talk with such individuals, often you will learn that many are good people but are counting on their good deeds to earn their way into heaven. Though they are attempting to win the approval of God, their desire isn't based in reality.

Paul wrote to Titus about this concern and how our entrance into eternity isn't based on our actions, but on God's mercy: "He saved us because of his mercy. It was not because of good needs we did to be right with him. He saved us through the washing that made us new people through the Holy Spirit." The next time you talk with someone about this truth, remind him of the emphasis on God's mercy and not on our actions.

Some Things to Remember

¹²When I send Artemas or Tychicus to you, make every effort to come to me at Nicopolis, because I have decided to stay there this winter. ¹³Do all you can to help Zenas the lawyer and Apollos on their journey so that they have everything they need. ¹⁴Our people must learn to use their lives for doing good deeds to provide what is necessary so that their lives will not be useless.

¹⁵All who are with me greet you. Greet those who love us in the faith.

Grace be with you all.

 # Survival Guide

SAWS: CUTTING WITH CARE

Every weekend handyman needs a saw among his tools. To get better performance, allow the saw to do the work. Start by pulling it toward you, which is easier than pushing forward. Use light force and a downward motion for better leverage. If you need to trim tree branches—the most common use—try a pole saw. Available in lengths of more than twenty feet, these specialty saws allow you to cut high limbs while standing firm on the ground. That's the same kind of footing you'll secure spiritually by studying the Bible.

THE **LETTER** OF PAUL THE APOSTLE TO

Philemon

AUTHOR: PAUL
DATE WRITTEN: A.D. 60–63

WHEN YOU ARE WOUNDED BY A FAMILY

member or close friend, you may struggle to find the grace for forgiveness. In the Book of Philemon, the apostle Paul tackles the delicate subject of forgiveness with diplomacy and even a lighthearted tone. This brief letter is written to Philemon, a wealthy Christian from Colossae.

As he writes, Paul intercedes for Onesimus, one of Philemon's slaves who apparently stole from him and escaped to Rome, where he met with Paul and became a devout follower of Christ. Paul offers to repay the stolen money with personal funds, but moves his appeal beyond the restoration of money. Paul asks Philemon to forgive his slave and welcome Onesimus as a brother in Christ.

Paul doesn't ask for Onesimus's freedom from slavery. Instead, he pleads for Philemon to offer grace in place of justice. First, Paul builds rapport with Philemon, then persuades his mind, and finally appeals to his emotions. Written during Paul's first imprisonment in Rome, his letter to Philemon is an example of how to appeal to another Christian with courtesy and generosity.

[1]From Paul, a prisoner of Christ Jesus, and from Timothy, our brother.

To Philemon, our dear friend and worker with us; [2]to Apphia, our sister; to Archippus, a worker with us; and to the church that meets in your home:

[3]Grace and peace to you from God our Father and the Lord Jesus Christ.

Philemon's Love and Faith

[4]I always thank my God when I mention you in my prayers, [5]because I hear about the love you have for all God's holy people and the faith you have in the Lord Jesus. [6]I pray that the faith you share may make you understand every blessing we have in Christ. [7]I have great joy and comfort, my brother, because the love you have shown to God's people has refreshed them.

Accept Onesimus as a Brother

[8]So, in Christ, I could be bold and order you to do what is right. [9]But because I love you, I am pleading with you instead. I, Paul, an old man now and also a prisoner for Christ Jesus, [10]am pleading with you for my child Onesimus, who became my child while I was in prison. [11]In the past he was useless to you, but now he has become useful for both you and me.

[12]I am sending him back to you, and with him I am sending my own heart. [13]I wanted to keep him with me so that in your place he might help me while I am in prison for the Good News. [14]But I did not want to do anything without asking you first so that any good you do for me will be because you want to do it, not because I forced you. [15]Maybe Onesimus was separated from you for a short time so you could have him back forever— [16]no longer as a slave, but better than a slave, as a loved brother. I love him very much, but you will love him even more, both as a person and as a believer in the Lord.

[17]So if you consider me your partner, welcome Onesimus as you would welcome me. [18]If he has done anything wrong to you or if he owes you anything, charge that to me. [19]I, Paul, am writing this with my own hand. I will pay it back, and I will say nothing about what you owe me for your own life. [20]So, my brother, I ask that you do this for me in the Lord: Refresh my heart in Christ. [21]I write this letter, knowing that you will do what I ask you and even more.

[22]One more thing—prepare a room for me in which to stay, because I hope God will answer your prayers and I will be able to come to you.

Final Greetings

[23]Epaphras, a prisoner with me for Christ Jesus, sends greetings to you. [24]And also Mark, Aristarchus, Demas, and Luke, workers together with me, send greetings.

[25]The grace of our Lord Jesus Christ be with your spirit.

THINK ABOUT IT Philemon 15–16

HINDSIGHT IS USUALLY BETTER than the ability to forecast the future. In the middle of a crisis at work, it is tempting to wonder why you're going through such an experience. Similarly, if an emergency affects your family, you may ponder why you have to deal with it.

Some people feel strongly that we can't know the reasons behind events and that it's not right to question God about such matters. Yet Paul wrote an inquiring letter to his friend Philemon about the runaway-slave-turned-Christian, Onesimus.

The apostle found it valuable to reflect on the lessons from an experience after the fact. He wanted to use hindsight as a tool to grow in his faith, saying, "Maybe Onesimus was separated from you for a short time so you could have him back forever." Paul had a zeal for life and wanted to make sure he learned from every experience so he wouldn't be doomed to repeat those mistakes in the future. The next time you face a crisis, remind yourself to look for the lessons God wants you to learn. Who knows? You may find clarity without the help of hindsight.

THE **LETTER** TO THE

Hebrews

AUTHOR: UNKNOWN
DATE WRITTEN: A.D. 65

MANY PEOPLE LOVE A BARGAIN. THEY will invest hours at garage sales or flea markets hunting for the best value for their money. With the advent of the Internet, shopping for the best value has grown even more competitive. Some bargain hunters make their living wheeling and dealing on sites like eBay, trading one item for another.

This same process of selection is often practiced in the spiritual realm. For example, to get what they thought was the better deal, the New Testament Christians had started to trade one type of religion for another. The early believers had practiced Judaism before converting to Christianity, but they often carried some of their old beliefs with them. Yet, when Christ came, he fulfilled the law, replacing rules with relationships. Now eternal life was freely given to everyone who trusted in Jesus.

The message of Hebrews was written to Jews who were struggling with their new faith. Throughout the letter, the writer shows the superiority of a relationship with Jesus. Christ is shown to be supreme and completely sufficient for salvation. Instead of returning to the legalism of Judaism, believers in Jesus are encouraged to live each day in simple faith.

God Spoke Through His Son

1 In the past God spoke to our ancestors through the prophets many times and in many different ways. ²But now in these last days God has spoken to us through his Son. God has chosen his Son to own all things, and through him he made the world. ³The Son reflects the glory of God and shows exactly what God is like. He holds everything together with his powerful word. When the Son made people clean from their sins, he sat down at the right side of God, the Great One in heaven. ⁴The Son became much greater than the angels, and God gave him a name that is much greater than theirs.

⁵This is because God never said to any of the angels,

"You are my Son.
　Today I have become your Father."　　　*Psalm 2:7*

Nor did God say of any angel,

"I will be his Father,
　and he will be my Son."　　　*2 Samuel 7:14*

⁶And when God brings his firstborn Son into the world, he says,

"Let all God's angels worship him.""　　　*Psalm 97:7*

⁷This is what God said about the angels:

"God makes his angels become like winds.
　He makes his servants become like flames of fire."　*Psalm 104:4*

⁸But God said this about his Son:

"God, your throne will last forever and ever.
　You will rule your kingdom with fairness.
⁹You love right and hate evil,
　so God has chosen you from among your friends;
　he has set you apart with much joy."　　　*Psalm 45:6–7*

¹⁰God also says,

"Lord, in the beginning you made the earth,
　and your hands made the skies.

¹¹They will be destroyed, but you will remain.
　They will all wear out like clothes.
¹²You will fold them like a coat.
　And, like clothes, you will change them.
But you never change,
　and your life will never end."　　　*Psalm 102:25–27*

¹³And God never said this to an angel:

"Sit by me at my right side
　until I put your enemies under your control.""　*Psalm 110:1*

¹⁴All the angels are spirits who serve God and are sent to help those who will receive salvation.

Our Salvation Is Great

2 So we must be more careful to follow what we were taught. Then we will not stray away from the truth. ²The teaching God spoke through angels was shown to be true, and anyone who did not follow it or obey it received the punishment that was earned. ³So surely we also will be punished if we ignore this great salvation. The Lord himself first told about this salvation, and those who heard him testified it was true. ⁴God also testified to the truth of the message by using wonders, great signs, many kinds of miracles, and by giving people gifts through the Holy Spirit, just as he wanted.

▶ Get Aligned
Hebrews 2:10

SINCE THE BEGINNING OF HISTORY, GOD HAS DESIRED TO SHARE HIMSELF WITH OTHERS. He created the earth and all its intricacies so others could enjoy it with him. His original plan was one of peace and harmony among all creatures. Everything was designed to revel in his glory.

Much like the wind, God's glory is not easily described, yet it can be seen all around us. When we witness a breathtaking sunset or an awe-inspiring array of clouds, we get a peek at his glory. The same is true when we become a father and our love for our children is so strong we could cry. Yet the Bible indicates God's glory is also a physical presence. Moses was the only man ever to see God's glory, and he only caught a glimpse of God. Nevertheless, after seeing such magnificence, Moses was never the same.

Such is the impact that God's glory can have on our lives. We would be wise, like Moses, to beg to encounter it, not out of pride but from a desire for greater intimacy. After all, it's what we were created to share with our Lord.

≪TechSupport≫

ELECTRONIC GAMES

Home video games have become so mainstream they're going back to the future. New handheld devices cater to an increasingly mobile culture, bringing high-resolution screens and realistic audio to portable gaming devices and even cell phones. But with all the high-tech portability comes the prospect of losing touch with loved ones engrossed in the latest game. So teach your children healthy boundaries with video games by demonstrating good habits, such as trading time spent playing video games for some interactive events like family Bible study, old-fashioned board games, or putting together a photo album.

>> 1:6 **"Let … him."** These words are found in Deuteronomy 32:43 in the Septuagint, the Greek version of the Old Testament, and in a Hebrew copy among the Dead Sea Scrolls.　1:13 **until … control** Literally, "until I make your enemies a footstool for your feet."

Sexcess:
BEWARE WAYWARD WOMEN

In our so-called sexually liberated society, it is men who more and more frequently are finding themselves the unwitting victims of seduction. Women have become brazen in their willingness to waste careers, marriages, and lives, all for their own selfish pleasures. Of course, it is not an entirely new trend, as the Scriptures have warned men for centuries of wayward women and their wiles. Of the seductress, Proverbs 6:25 says, "Don't desire her because she is beautiful. Don't let her capture you by the way she looks at you." Whether it is the girl next door or a total stranger who flirts with you, ignore it, no matter how flattering.

Christ Became like Humans

⁵God did not choose angels to be the rulers of the new world that was coming, which is what we have been talking about. ⁶It is written in the Scriptures,

"Why are people even important to you?
Why do you take care of human beings?
⁷You made them a little lower than the angels
and crowned them with glory and honor."

⁸You put all things under their control."

Psalm 8:4–6

When God put everything under their control, there was nothing left that they did not rule. Still, we do not yet see them ruling over everything. ⁹But we see Jesus, who for a short time was made lower than the angels. And now he is wearing a crown of glory and honor because he suffered and died. And by God's grace, he died for everyone.

¹⁰God is the One who made all things, and all things are for his glory. He wanted to have many children share his glory, so he made the One who leads people to salvation perfect through suffering.

¹¹Jesus, who makes people holy, and those who are made holy are from the same family. So he is not ashamed to call them his brothers and sisters. ¹²He says,

"Then, I will tell my brothers and sisters about you;
I will praise you in the public meeting." *Psalm 22:22*

¹³He also says,

"I will trust in God." *Isaiah 8:17*

And he also says,

"I am here, and with me are the children God has given me."

Isaiah 8:18

¹⁴Since these children are people with physical bodies, Jesus himself became like them. He did this so that, by dying, he could destroy the one who has the power of death—the devil— ¹⁵and free those who were like slaves all their lives because of their fear of death. ¹⁶Clearly, it is not angels that Jesus helps, but the people who are from Abraham." ¹⁷For this reason Jesus had to be made like his brothers and sisters in every way so he could be their merciful and faithful high priest in service to God. Then Jesus could die in their place to take away their sins. ¹⁸And now he can help those who are tempted, because he himself suffered and was tempted.

Jesus Is Greater than Moses

3 So all of you holy brothers and sisters, who were called by God, think about Jesus, who was sent to us and is the high priest of our faith. ²Jesus was faithful to God as Moses was in God's family. ³Jesus has more honor than Moses, just as the builder of a house has more honor than the house itself. ⁴Every house is built by someone, but the builder of everything is God himself. ⁵Moses was faithful in God's family as a servant, and he told what God would say in the future.

{ ## Deal With It:
*Anger

ANGER ITSELF IS NOT A SIN, BUT IT CAN LEAD TO SINFUL ACTS IF WE ARE NOT CAREFUL. The Bible says it is okay for us to get angry, but we are not to allow anger to control our lives. It is only natural to get angry at times. Jesus displayed anger when he chased the moneychangers out of the Temple.

So the issue to deal with is not *if* we'll experience anger, but what to do *when* we experience it. The important thing to remember about anger is that it is an emotion, and, as such, it can be managed, just as all our other emotions can be managed.

2:7 **You … honor.** Some Greek copies continue, "You put them in charge of everything you made." See Psalm 8:6. 2:16 **Abraham** Most respected ancestor of the Jews. Every Jew hoped to see Abraham.

12

>> live the life

Hebrews 3:13

The Principle > Help others daily.

Practicing It > Think of what daily routines you can develop that will encourage your spouse, your children, or others you love. Simply taking time to listen or enjoy each other's company can deeply encourage the hearts of those you love most.

[6]But Christ is faithful as a Son over God's house. And we are God's house if we confidently maintain our hope.

We Must Continue to Follow God

[7]So it is as the Holy Spirit says:

"Today listen to what he says.
[8]Do not be stubborn as in the past
    when you turned against God,
when you tested God in the desert.
[9]There your ancestors tried me and tested me
    and saw the things I did for forty years.
[10]I was angry with them.
    I said, 'They are not loyal to me
    and have not understood my ways.'
[11]I was angry and made a promise,
    'They will never enter my rest.' ""

Psalm 95:7–11

[12]So brothers and sisters, be careful that none of you has an evil, unbelieving heart that will turn you away from the living God. [13]But encourage each other every day while it is "today.""* Help each other so none of you will become hardened because sin has tricked you. [14]We all share in Christ if we keep till the end the sure faith we had in the beginning. [15]This is what the Scripture says:

"Today listen to what he says.
    Do not be stubborn as in the past
    when you turned against God."

Psalm 95:7–8

[16]Who heard God's voice and was against him? It was all those people Moses led out of Egypt. [17]And with whom was God angry for forty years? He was angry with those who sinned, who died in the desert. [18]And to whom was God talking when he promised that they would never enter his rest? He was talking to those who did not obey him. [19]So we see they were not allowed to enter and have God's rest, because they did not believe.

4 Now, since God has left us the promise that we may enter his rest, let us be very careful so none of you will fail to enter. [2]The Good News was preached to us just as it was to them. But the teaching they heard did not help them, because they heard it but did not accept it with faith." [3]We who have believed are able to enter and have God's rest. As God has said,

"I was angry and made a promise,
    'They will never enter my rest.' "

Psalm 95:11

But God's work was finished from the time he made the world. [4]In the Scriptures he talked about the seventh day of the week: "And on the seventh day God rested from all his works.""* [5]And again in the Scripture God said, "They will never enter my rest."

[6]It is still true that some people will enter God's rest, but those who first heard the way to be saved did not enter, because they did not obey. [7]So God planned another day, called "today." He spoke about that day through David a long time later in the same Scripture used before:

"Today listen to what he says.
    Do not be stubborn."

Psalm 95:7–8

[8]We know that Joshua* did not lead the people into that rest, because God spoke later about another day. [9]This shows that the rest* for God's people is still coming. [10]Anyone who enters God's rest will rest from his work as God did. [11]Let us try as hard as we can to enter God's rest so that no one will fail by following the example of those who refused to obey.

[12]God's word is alive and working and is sharper than a double-edged sword. It cuts all the way into us, where the soul and the spirit

(▶) Get Aligned

Hebrews 4:15–16

MANY MEN STRUGGLE TO BELIEVE JESUS REALLY FACED EVERY TEMPTATION THEY HAVE. They point to pornography, gambling, and drugs and claim there is no way Christ dealt with the same issues. But whereas the setting and parameters may be different two thousand years later, the basic temptations are identical. A sex addiction still deals with lust—the same lust Christ faced. Fudging your tax exemptions is still lying, which Jesus had the chance to do at any moment.

The truth is that Jesus was bombarded with the same opportunities to sin moment by moment.

There were certainly women who flung themselves at him. So-called buddies probably offered to help him get rich quick. At times, he could have drunk his sorrows away. Instead, he chose to resist every temptation. He never once gave in. He finished his earthly life completely sinless.

And because of that, he set the standard for us—not only as God's Son but as someone who walked in our shoes. We have the assurance that no matter what situation we face, he has been there. Better yet, given his godly example that guarantees hope, he offers us the same grace to overcome, too.

3:11 rest A place of rest God promised to give his people.   **3:13 "today"** This word is taken from verse 7. It means that it is important to do these things now.   **4:2 because ... faith** Some Greek copies read "because they did not share the faith of those who heard it."   **4:4 "And ... works."** Quotation from Genesis 2:2.   **4:8 Joshua** After Moses died, Joshua became leader of the Jewish people and led them into the land that God promised to give them.   **4:9 rest** Literally, "sabbath rest," meaning a sharing in the rest that God began after he created the world.

+ Ten Ways to Save a Buck

1. Pay with cash instead of credit.

2. Barter instead of paying for services.

3. Borrow tools from your neighbors.

4. Hire professionals for dreaded chores.

5. Buy the right equipment for the job.

6. Check your credit report regularly.

7. Open some type of savings account.

8. Get rid of unnecessary consumer debt.

9. Drink water instead of soft drinks.

10. Create a budget and stick to it.

are joined, to the center of our joints and bones. And it judges the thoughts and feelings in our hearts. ¹³Nothing in all the world can be hidden from God. Everything is clear and lies open before him, and to him we must explain the way we have lived.

Jesus Is Our High Priest

¹⁴Since we have a great high priest, Jesus the Son of God, who has gone into heaven, let us hold on to the faith we have. ¹⁵For our high priest is able to understand our weaknesses. He was tempted in every way that we are, but he did not sin. ¹⁶Let us, then, feel very sure that we can come before God's throne where there is grace. There we can receive mercy and grace to help us when we need it.

5 Every high priest is chosen from among other people. He is given the work of going before God for them to offer gifts and sacrifices for sins. ²Since he himself is weak, he is able to be gentle with those who do not understand and who are doing wrong things. ³Because he is weak, the high priest must offer sacrifices for his own sins and also for the sins of the people.

⁴To be a high priest is an honor, but no one chooses himself for this work. He must be called by God as Aaron* was. ⁵So also Christ did not choose himself to have the honor of being a high priest, but God chose him. God said to him,

"You are my Son.
  Today I have become your Father." *Psalm 2:7*

⁶And in another Scripture God says,

"You are a priest forever,
  a priest like Melchizedek."*

  Psalm 110:4

⁷While Jesus lived on earth, he prayed to God and asked God for help. He prayed with loud cries and tears to the One who could save him from death, and his prayer was heard because he trusted God. ⁸Even though Jesus was the Son of God, he learned obedience by what he suffered. ⁹And because his obedience was perfect, he was able to give eternal salvation to all who obey him. ¹⁰In this way God made Jesus a high priest, a priest like Melchizedek.

Warning Against Falling Away

¹¹We have much to say about this, but it is hard to explain because you are so slow to understand. ¹²By now you should be teachers, but you need someone to teach you again the first lessons of God's message. You still need the teaching that is like milk. You are not ready for solid food. ¹³Anyone who lives on milk is still a baby and knows nothing about right teaching. ¹⁴But solid food is for those who are grown up. They are mature enough to know the difference between good and evil.

Q: Why is it important to share my faith with non-Christians?

A: Perhaps the most compelling reason to share your faith in Christ is because you've experienced God's love personally and want others to experience it, too. God loves everyone, but the main way others hear about Jesus is through us (Romans 1:16–17).

>> live the life

Hebrews 4:12

The Principle > Read wise writings.

Practicing It > As a part of your regular time with God each day, read one verse or short passage from the Book of Proverbs in the Bible. Spend time meditating on each proverb and considering how you can apply its lesson to your life.

>> **5:4 Aaron** Moses' brother and the first Jewish high priest.   **5:6 Melchizedek** A priest and king who lived in the time of Abraham. (Read Genesis 14:17–24.)

TOUR DE FRANCE: Perseverance Plus

CYCLIST LANCE ARMSTRONG'S RECORD-SETTING performances focused America's attention on the Tour de France. But the world's toughest bicycle race has been popular in Europe for more than a century. Changing courses annually, the tour covers about 2,000 miles and can last up to a month, with only half the entrants finishing.

Run in several stages, it covers everything from flat land to mountains, as each stage emphasizes particular skills. No one person finishes alone since the competition consists of nine-member teams. The team's leader is usually its best all-around cyclist, but members offer support through such tasks as helping him up hills by shielding him from wind.

Armstrong's personal story symbolizes the grit needed for this arduous race. Despite winning a pair of individual stages, he ultimately withdrew from three of four tours from 1993 to 1996. Then came a grueling battle with testicular cancer that spread to his lungs and brain. Not until 1998 did he capture the first of his record six French titles.

Those who follow Christ must embrace similar perseverance. Modern preoccupation with comfort and ease has led to the idea that faith in God is an escape route. Yet, in Romans 5:3–4, the apostle Paul writes about how enduring troubles produces patience, character, and hope.

While it takes determination to win the ultimate bicycle race, succeeding in the tour of life requires even more fortitude. Instead of donning a yellow jersey, believers receive a robe of righteousness and it never fades.

> "Modern preoccupation with comfort and ease has led to the idea that faith in God is an escape route."

Change >> Your WORLD

TEEN CHALLENGE

The lives of thousands of men and women have been shattered from drug and alcohol addiction. Yet for more than forty years, Teen Challenge has maintained the same mission: to help youth, adults, and families find freedom from drug addiction and other life-controlling problems. It is the oldest and largest private agency in America. With the transforming power of Jesus Christ, people have become mentally sound, emotionally balanced, socially adjusted, and physically well. A recent Northwestern University study attests to the success of Teen Challenge, as eighty-six percent of its graduates are living drug-free.

To change your world, visit www.teenchallenge.com.

6 So let us go on to grown-up teaching. Let us not go back over the beginning lessons we learned about Christ. We should not again start teaching about faith in God and about turning away from those acts that lead to death. [2]We should not return to the teaching about baptisms," about laying on of hands," about the raising of the dead and eternal judgment. [3]And we will go on to grown-up teaching if God allows.

[4]Some people cannot be brought back again to a changed life. They were once in God's light, and enjoyed heaven's gift, and shared in the Holy Spirit. [5]They found out how good God's word is, and they received the powers of his new world. [6]But they fell away from Christ. It is impossible to bring them back to a changed life again, because they are nailing the Son of God to a cross again and are shaming him in front of others.

[7]Some people are like land that gets plenty of rain. The land produces a good crop for those who work it, and it receives God's blessings. [8]Other people are like land that grows thorns and weeds and is worthless. It is about to be cursed by God and will be destroyed by fire.

[9]Dear friends, we are saying this to you, but we really expect better things from you that will lead to your salvation. [10]God is fair; he will not forget the work you did and the love you showed for him by helping his people. And he will remember that you are still helping them. [11]We want each of you to go on with the same hard work all your lives so you will surely get what you hope for. [12]We do not want you to become lazy. Be like those who through faith and patience will receive what God has promised.

[13]God made a promise to Abraham. And as there is no one greater than God, he used himself when he swore to Abraham, [14]saying, "I will surely bless you and give you many descendants."[n] [15]Abraham waited patiently for this to happen, and he received what God promised.

[16]People always use the name of someone greater than themselves when they swear. The oath proves that what they say is true, and this ends all arguing. [17]God wanted to prove that his promise was true to those who would get what he promised. And he wanted them to understand clearly that his purposes never change, so he made an oath. [18]These two things cannot change: God cannot lie when he makes a promise, and he cannot lie when he makes an oath. These things encourage us who came to God for safety. They give us strength to hold on to the hope we have been given. [19]We have this hope as an anchor for the soul, sure and strong. It enters behind the curtain in the Most Holy Place in heaven, [20]where Jesus has gone ahead of us and for us. He has become the high priest forever, a priest like Melchizedek."

The Priest Melchizedek

7 Melchizedek[n] was the king of Salem and a priest for God Most High. He met Abraham when Abraham was coming back after defeating the kings. When they met, Melchizedek blessed Abraham, [2]and Abraham gave him a tenth of everything he had brought back from the battle. First, Melchizedek's name means "king of goodness," and he is king of Salem, which means "king of peace." [3]No one knows who Melchizedek's father or mother was," where he came from, when he was born, or when he died. Melchizedek is like the Son of God; he continues being a priest forever.

[4]You can see how great Melchizedek was. Abraham, the great father, gave him a tenth of everything that he won in battle. [5]Now the law says that those in the tribe of Levi who become priests must collect a tenth from the people—their own people—even though the priests and the people are from the family of Abraham. [6]Melchizedek was not from the tribe of Levi, but he collected a tenth from Abraham. And he blessed Abraham, the man who had God's promises. [7]Now everyone knows that the more important person blesses the less important person. [8]Priests receive a tenth, even though they are only men who live and then die. But Melchizedek, who received a tenth from Abraham, continues living, as the Scripture says. [9]We might even say that Levi, who receives a tenth, also paid it when

---

>> 6:2 **baptisms** The word here may refer to Christian baptism, or it may refer to the Jewish ceremonial washings. 6:2 **laying on of hands** The laying on of hands had many purposes, including the giving of a blessing, power, or authority. 6:14 "I…descendants." Quotation from Genesis 22:17. 6:20; 7:1 **Melchizedek** A priest and king who lived in the time of Abraham. (Read Genesis 14:17-24.) 7:3 **No…was** Literally, "Melchizedek was without father, without mother, without genealogy."

Abraham paid Melchizedek a tenth. ¹⁰Levi was not yet born, but he was in the body of his ancestor when Melchizedek met Abraham.

¹¹The people were given the lawⁿ concerning the system of priests from the tribe of Levi, but they could not be made perfect through that system. So there was a need for another priest to come, a priest like Melchizedek, not Aaron. ¹²And when a different kind of priest comes, the law must be changed, too. ¹³We are saying these things about Christ, who belonged to a different tribe. No one from that tribe ever served as a priest at the altar. ¹⁴It is clear that our Lord came from the tribe of Judah, and Moses said nothing about priests belonging to that tribe.

Jesus Is like Melchizedek

¹⁵And this becomes even more clear when we see that another priest comes who is like Melchizedek.ⁿ ¹⁶He was not made a priest by human rules and laws but through the power of his life, which continues forever. ¹⁷It is said about him,

"You are a priest forever,
a priest like Melchizedek." *Psalm 110:4*

¹⁸The old rule is now set aside, because it was weak and useless. ¹⁹The law of Moses could not make anything perfect. But now a better hope has been given to us, and with this hope we can come near to God. ²⁰It is important that God did this with an oath. Others became priests without an oath, ²¹but Christ became a priest with God's oath. God said:

"The Lord has made a promise
and will not change his mind.
'You are a priest forever.' " *Psalm 110:4*

²²This means that Jesus is the guarantee of a better agreementⁿ from God to his people.

²³When one of the other priests died, he could not continue being a priest. So there were many priests. ²⁴But because Jesus lives forever, he will never stop serving as priest. ²⁵So he is able always to save those who come to God through him because he always lives, asking God to help them.

²⁶Jesus is the kind of high priest we need. He is holy, sinless, pure, not influenced by sinners, and he is raised above the heavens. ²⁷He is not like the other priests who had to offer sacrifices every day, first for their own sins, and then for the sins of the people. Christ offered his sacrifice only once and for all time when he offered himself. ²⁸The law chooses high priests who are people with weaknesses, but the word of God's oath came later than the law. It made God's Son to be the high priest, and that Son has been made perfect forever.

Jesus Is Our High Priest

8 Here is the point of what we are saying: We have a high priest who sits on the right side of God's throne in heaven. ²Our high priest serves in the Most Holy Place, the true place of worship that was made by God, not by humans.

³Every high priest has the work of offering gifts and sacrifices to God. So our high priest must also offer something to God. ⁴If our high priest were now living on earth, he would not be a priest, because there are already priests here who follow the law by offering

Q: Why hasn't Jesus already returned?

A: God is patient about the return of Christ because he wants as many as possible to hear the truth and accept Jesus as their personal Savior before he returns. There also are prophecies yet to be fulfilled before Christ returns (2 Peter 3:9).

Survival Guide

HOME SECURITY: ENLISTING YOUR NEIGHBOR

Christ said in Matthew 6:19–20 there will be thieves trying to steal your possessions. While there are many sophisticated devices available to protect against home intruders, a low-cost solution is a good neighbor. Let that person know when you'll be away, and ask him to pick up any flyers or other material that clutters your doorstep. If gone for long, have him pick up your newspapers and mail. And if you have a baby monitor, leave it at the neighbor's with the base unit on at your home.

 7:11 The...law This refers to the people of Israel who were given the Law of Moses.   **7:15 Melchizedek** A priest and king who lived in the time of Abraham. (Read Genesis 14:17–24.)   **7:22 agreement** God gives a contract or agreement to his people. For the Jews, this agreement was the Law of Moses. But now God has given a better agreement to his people through Christ.

Men of Valor
SILAS: Worshiper of God

A teacher and missionary, Silas was alongside the apostle Paul during one of the New Testament's most significant events, recorded in Acts 16:16–34. After a missionary journey to Antioch, Silas traveled to Philippi with Paul. There they encountered a slave girl who could tell fortunes. But she was set free after Paul rebuked the evil spirit in her. Angered by the loss of the girl's profit-making potential, her masters seized Paul and Silas and persuaded the magistrates to jail them. At midnight, as Paul and Silas prayed and sang songs to God, an earthquake shook the jail and opened the doors. Set free, they persuaded the jailer and his family to follow Christ. Silas was a powerful worshiper of God.

gifts to God. ⁵The work they do as priests is only a copy and a shadow of what is in heaven. This is why God warned Moses when he was ready to build the Holy Tent: "Be very careful to make everything by the plan I showed you on the mountain."ⁿ ⁶But the priestly work that has been given to Jesus is much greater than the work that was given to the other priests. In the same way, the new

agreement that Jesus brought from God to his people is much greater than the old one. And the new agreement is based on promises of better things.

⁷If there had been nothing wrong with the first agreement," there would have been no need for a second agreement. ⁸But God found something wrong with his people. He says:"

"Look, the time is coming, says the Lord,
    when I will make a new agreement
with the people of Israel
    and the people of Judah.
⁹It will not be like the agreement
    I made with their ancestors
when I took them by the hand
    to bring them out of Egypt.
But they broke that agreement,
    and I turned away from them, says the Lord.
¹⁰This is the agreement I will make
    with the people of Israel at that time, says the Lord.
I will put my teachings in their minds
    and write them on their hearts.
I will be their God,
    and they will be my people.
¹¹People will no longer have to teach their
    neighbors and relatives
to know the Lord,
because all people will know me,
    from the least to the most important.
¹²I will forgive them for the wicked things they did,
    and I will not remember their sins anymore."
                  Jeremiah 31:31–34

¹³God called this a new agreement, so he has made the first agreement old. And anything that is old and worn out is ready to disappear.

The Old Agreement

9 The first agreement" had rules for worship and a place on earth for worship. ²The Holy Tent was set up for this. The first area in the Tent was called the Holy Place. In it were the lamp and the table with the bread that was made holy for God. ³Behind the second curtain was a room called the Most Holy Place. ⁴In it was a golden altar for burning incense and the Ark covered with gold that

held the old agreement. Inside this Ark was a golden jar of manna, Aaron's rod that once grew leaves, and the stone tablets of the old agreement. ⁵Above the Ark were the creatures that showed God's glory, whose wings reached over the lid. But we cannot tell everything about these things now.

⁶When everything in the Tent was made ready in this way, the priests went into the first room every day to worship. ⁷But only the high priest could go into the second room, and he did that only once a year. He could never enter the inner room without taking blood with him, which he offered to God for himself and for sins the people did without knowing they did them. ⁸The Holy Spirit

{ Book of the Month }

Blue Like Jazz
by Donald Miller

A coffeehouse atmosphere mixed with moody weather permeates *Blue Like Jazz*, a portrait of Christian spirituality in a world where Christianity is labeled an outdated and irrelevant religion. In swift plotlines, author Donald Miller writes of his pursuit of meaningful connections with the unchurched without resorting to preaching. With every word coming from experience and revelation, the writing is relevant, poignant, and bittersweet. In one story, Miller and a handful of students turn a joke about hosting a confession booth during a campus fair into an opportunity for other students to hear the Good News. Such laugh-out-loud moments make the book a memorable one.

>> 8:5 "Be … mountain." Quotation from Exodus 25:40.   8:7; 9:1 first agreement The contract God gave the Jewish people when he gave them the Law of Moses.   8:8 But … says Some Greek copies read "But God found something wrong and says to his people."

318

>>October

QUOTE OF THE MONTH:
"Do not go where the path may lead. Go instead where there is no path and leave a trail." —Ralph Waldo Emerson

1
Treat your pastor to a meal.

2

3

4
Pay the toll for the next person.

5

6

7
Pray for a person of influence: Today is musician **Michael W. Smith's** birthday.

8
Pray for needy and neglected children around the world.

9
Take a different route home from work.

10

11

12
Check your credit report.

13
Clean out the fireplace.

14

15
Pray for a person of influence: Today is chef **Emeril Lagasse's** birthday.

16

17

18
The **Grand Ole Opry** opened on this day in 1925.

19
Rake some leaves for exercise.

20
Play softball with the guys.

21

22

23

24
Surprise your significant other with fresh flowers.

25

26
Pray for a person of influence: Today is politician **Hillary Clinton's** birthday.

27
Memorize Luke 6:31.

28
Pray for a person of influence: Today is businessman **Bill Gates's** birthday.

29

30
Teach an old dog new tricks.

31
Offer kind words to strangers.

<<TechSupport>>

AUDIO BOOKS

In a culture where people often spend an hour or more commuting to work, there is little time to spend reading books for learning or for pleasure. Audio books used to be the domain of dramatized popular fiction or dry self-help lectures. But now the increasing demand for a wider range of books on the go has led to a rise in the number of non-fiction and inspirational audio book titles, including the Bible. Some audio books are also available for download to be used on your computer or digital audio player; so, plug and play today.

uses this to show that the way into the Most Holy Place was not open while the system of the old Holy Tent was still being used. ⁹This is an example for the present time. It shows that the gifts and sacrifices offered cannot make the conscience of the worshiper perfect. ¹⁰These gifts and sacrifices were only about food and drink and special washings. They were rules for the body, to be followed until the time of God's new way.

The New Agreement

¹¹But when Christ came as the high priest of the good things we now have,ᵃ he entered the greater and more perfect tent. It is not made by humans and does not belong to this world. ¹²Christ entered the Most Holy Place only once—and for all time. He did not take with him the blood of goats and calves. His sacrifice was his own blood, and by it he set us free from sin forever. ¹³The blood of goats and bulls and the ashes of a cow are sprinkled on the people who are unclean, and this makes their bodies clean again. ¹⁴How much more is done by the blood of Christ. He offered himself through the eternal Spiritᵇ as a perfect sacrifice to God. His blood will make our consciences pure from useless acts so we may serve the living God.

¹⁵For this reason Christ brings a new agreement from God to his people. Those who are called by God can now receive the blessings he has promised, blessings that will last forever. They can have those things because Christ died so that the people who lived under the first agreement could be set free from sin.

¹⁶When there is a will,ᶜ it must be proven that the one who wrote that will is dead. ¹⁷A will means

Q: What does it mean when the Bible talks about the "world"?

A: When the word "world" is used in the Bible, it is not talking about the world of people or the created world. Rather, it is referring to the world "system" or realm that is controlled by Satan and is openly set against God and his ways (1 John 2:15–17).

Get Fit

Heart Rate Control

CALCULATING HEART RATE Depending on your age, physical condition, and fitness goals, you should train in a particular heart-rate zone. Beginners should try to elevate their heart rate between fifty to sixty percent of their maximum, while intermediate and advanced athletes can shoot for seventy to eighty-five percent of their max. To figure your maximum heart rate, simply subtract your age from 220. For example, if you're thirty years old, your maximum heart rate is 190. To exercise at seventy percent of your maximum heart rate, you would aim for a heart rate of approximately 133 beats per minute. While you're calculating your heart rate, thank God for the gift of life!

>> **9:11 good…have** Some Greek copies read "good things that are to come."   **9:14 Spirit** This refers to the Holy Spirit, to Christ's own spirit, or to the spiritual and eternal nature of his sacrifice.   **9:16 will** A legal document that shows how a person's money and property are to be distributed at the time of death. This is the same word in Greek as "agreement" in verse 15.

nothing while the person is alive; it can be used only after the person dies. [18]This is why even the first agreement could not begin without blood to show death. [19]First, Moses told all the people every command in the law. Next he took the blood of calves and mixed it with water. Then he used red wool and a branch of the hyssop plant to sprinkle it on the book of the law and on all the people. [20]He said, "This is the blood that begins the Agreement that God commanded you to obey." [21]In the same way, Moses sprinkled the blood on the Holy Tent and over all the things used in worship. [22]The law says that almost everything must be made clean by blood, and sins cannot be forgiven without blood to show death.

Christ's Death Takes Away Sins

[23]So the copies of the real things in heaven had to be made clean by animal sacrifices. But the real things in heaven need much better sacrifices. [24]Christ did not go into the Most Holy Place made by humans, which is only a copy of the real one. He went into heaven itself and is there now before God to help us. [25]The high priest enters the Most Holy Place once every year with blood that is not his own. But Christ did not offer himself many times. [26]Then he would have had to suffer many times since the world was made. But Christ came only once and for all time at just the right time to take away all sin by sacrificing himself. [27]Just as everyone must die once and then be judged, [28]so Christ was offered as a sacrifice one time to take away the sins of many people. And he will come a second time, not to offer himself for sin, but to bring salvation to those who are waiting for him.

10 The law is only an unclear picture of the good things coming in the future; it is not the real thing. The people under the law offer the same sacrifices every year, but these sacrifices can never make perfect those who come near to worship God. [2]If the law could make them perfect, the sacrifices would have already stopped. The worshipers would be made clean, and they would no longer have a sense of sin. [3]But these sacrifices remind them of their sins every year, [4]because it is impossible for the blood of bulls and goats to take away sins.

[5]So when Christ came into the world, he said:

People Skills

Keeping Confidences

Good friends never break a confidence. Your friendships will not go very deep unless the people in your life know that they can trust you with their secrets. It doesn't take a genius to recognize that if you gossip about other people with your friends, then you will also talk about your friends when they are not around. On the other hand, honoring your friends' privacy in matters both great and small will open the way for greater intimacy. Trust and loyalty go hand in hand. When we know our friends will be loyal to us, we can trust them to be true to our friendship.

⊙ Sexcess:
DEALING WITH LUST

Interestingly, one definition of the word "lust" is "personal inclination." This definition reinforces the truth presented in James 1:14: "But people are tempted when their own evil desire leads them away and traps them." Contrary to popular belief, we are not outwardly tempted to lust; rather, our evil desires, or personal inclinations, cause us to lust inwardly. In order to tame the beast of lust, we must first identify the part of our lives that is drawn to the object of our lust. Since all of us have issues of one type or the other, it is imperative that we recognize them for what they are and deal with them in order to live free from lust.

⊙⊙ 9:20 "This … obey." Quotation from Exodus 24:8.

321

Principles: SABBATH

The Sabbath is the day of the week set aside by God as a day of rest. God even set a personal example for us by resting after the creation of the world! Remembering the Sabbath was so important to God that he made it one of the Ten Commandments, but Israel's religious leaders turned it into a rigid set of regulations. Jesus often rebuked such leaders for caring more about following the rules than helping others. The key principle behind the Sabbath is that we should rest from our labors one day a week, without turning it into a mere religious ritual.

"You do not want sacrifices and offerings,
   but you have prepared a body for me.
6You do not ask for burnt offerings
   and offerings to take away sins.
7Then I said, 'Look, I have come.
   It is written about me in the book.
   God, I have come to do what you want.' "   *Psalm 40:6–8*
8In this Scripture he first said, "You do not want sacrifices and offerings. You do not ask for burnt offerings and offerings to take away sins." (These are all sacrifices that the law commands.) 9Then he said, "Look, I have come to do what you want." God ends the first system of sacrifices so he can set up the new system. 10And because of this, we are made holy through the sacrifice Christ made in his body once and for all time.

11Every day the priests stand and do their religious service, often offering the same sacrifices. Those sacrifices can never take away sins. 12But after Christ offered one sacrifice for sins, forever, he sat down at the right side of God. 13And now Christ waits there for his enemies to be put under his power. 14With one sacrifice he made perfect forever those who are being made holy.

15The Holy Spirit also tells us about this. First he says:
16"This is the agreement* I will make
   with them at that time, says the Lord.
   I will put my teachings in their hearts
   and write them on their minds."   *Jeremiah 31:33*
17Then he says:
"Their sins and the evil things they do—
   I will not remember anymore."   *Jeremiah 31:34*
18Now when these have been forgiven, there is no more need for a sacrifice for sins.

▶ Get Aligned

Hebrews 10:10

ACCORDING TO JOHN 19:30, JESUS UTTERED THREE SIMPLE WORDS FROM THE CROSS BEFORE DYING: "IT IS FINISHED." Though no one around him understood the power behind those words that day, we are the beneficiaries of their meaning. Christ's death settled the eternal score for us. We never again have to work our way toward God or try to earn righteousness through rituals and sacrifices. Gone are the days of slaughtering a lamb every time we sin. Jesus paid the price.

Yet how often do we disregard Jesus' work on the cross? When we succumb to sin repeatedly, we attempt to make it right by promising God we'll never do it again or by making an extra effort to be more spiritual. We try to worship harder or pray longer or witness more fervently. But none of that makes us any better in God's eyes.

Our holiness is never dependent on what we do. If it were, we'd continue to be in the same state before Jesus came along—on a path to hell. Apart from Jesus, nothing in us is holy. But through him, we are completely spotless, and nothing can separate us from the matchless love of God (see Romans 8:38–39).

≫ live the life

Hebrews 10:24

The Principle > **Do good deeds.**

Practicing It > **As you get to know other Christians, always watch for opportunities to encourage them to grow in love. Invite them to join you in acts of service or in praying for the people in their lives.**

 10:16 agreement God gives a contract or agreement to his people. For the Jews, this agreement was the Law of Moses. But now God has given a better agreement to his people through Christ.

>> live the life

Hebrews 10:25

The Principle > Attend church and Bible studies.

Practicing It > If you are not already a part of a church or small group Bible study, join one. The Christian journey was never meant to be a solo expedition. We cannot grow to maturity in our faith without the encouragement and support of other Christians.

>> live the life

Hebrews 10:35-36

The Principle > Persevere under pressure.

Practicing It > It takes time to develop a Christlike attitude in all areas of your life. Be patient with yourself, and don't give up. Your perseverance in learning what it means to be like Jesus in the midst of your daily struggles will pay off in time.

Continue to Trust God

¹⁹So, brothers and sisters, we are completely free to enter the Most Holy Place without fear because of the blood of Jesus' death. ²⁰We can enter through a new and living way that Jesus opened for us. It leads through the curtain—Christ's body. ²¹And since we have a great priest over God's house, ²²let us come near to God with a sincere heart and a sure faith, because we have been made free from a guilty conscience, and our bodies have been washed with pure water. ²³Let us hold firmly to the hope that we have confessed, because we can trust God to do what he promised.

²⁴Let us think about each other and help each other to show love and do good deeds. ²⁵You should not stay away from the church meetings, as some are doing, but you should meet together and encourage each other. Do this even more as you see the day[n] coming.

²⁶If we decide to go on sinning after we have learned the truth, there is no longer any sacrifice for sins. ²⁷There is nothing but fear in wait-ing for the judgment and the terrible fire that will destroy all those who live against God. ²⁸Anyone who refused to obey the law of Moses was found guilty from the proof given by two or three witnesses. He was put to death without mercy. ²⁹So what do you think should be done to those who do not respect the Son of God, who look at the blood of the agreement that made them holy as no different from others' blood, who insult the Spirit of God's grace? Surely they should have a much worse punishment. ³⁰We know that God said, "I will punish those who do wrong; I will repay them."[n] And he also said, "The Lord will judge his people."[n] ³¹It is a terrible thing to fall into the hands of the living God.

³²Remember those days in the past when you first learned the truth. You had a hard struggle with many sufferings, but you continued strong. ³³Sometimes you were hurt and attacked before crowds of people, and sometimes you shared with those who were being treated that way. ³⁴You helped the prisoners. You even had joy when

→ The Bottom Line

Social Investing: Cash With Conscience

THE FASTEST-GROWING CLASS OF MUTUAL FUNDS IS KNOWN AS "SOCIALLY CONSCIOUS." These funds screen out objectionable invest-ments, such as companies producing alcohol, pornography, or tobacco. Others won't invest in any with links to abortion or anti-family policies, while some focus on supporting firms considered environmentally friendly. Since there are numerous definitions of "socially conscious," investigate a fund carefully to see if its goals match yours. However, some investment advisors see no need for such investing, saying own-ing a relatively small portion of a mutual fund has little impact on a particular company. As Romans 14:5 suggests, determining your in-vestments is a matter of personal conscience.

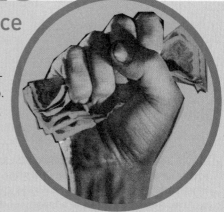

>> **10:25 day** The day Christ will come to judge all people and take his people to live with him. **10:30 "I...them."** Quotation from Deuteronomy 32:35. **10:30 "The Lord...people."** Quotation from Deuteronomy 32:36; Psalm 135:14.

323

FOR Men Only

INTEGRITY

Whereas a man may court a woman with his charm, he'll keep her based on his integrity. Integrity is one of those popular terms used in conversation but rarely defined properly, and even more rarely lived personally. One of its dictionary definitions is "the quality or state of being complete or undivided." The word suggests that one's life is *integrated* as a whole, and one's public self is congruent with one's private self. When a man has integrity, what you see is what you get. There are no hidden agendas or false pretenses. A man with integrity is the same outwardly and inwardly.

all that you owned was taken from you, because you knew you had something better and more lasting.

35So do not lose the courage you had in the past, which has a great reward. 36You must hold on, so you can do what God wants and receive what he has promised. 37For in a very short time,

"The One who is coming will come
and will not be delayed.

38Those who are right with me
will live by faith.

>> live the life

Hebrews 11:1

The Principle > Celebrate your faith.

Practicing It > Recall the unshakeable truths you believe about God. Praise God often for those qualities in him that encourage you to believe. And when times are tough, let those solid truths become the bond to hold you close to God.

But if they turn back with fear,
I will not be pleased with them."   *Habakkuk 2:3–4*

39But we are not those who turn back and are lost. We are people who have faith and are saved.

What Is Faith?

11 Faith means being sure of the things we hope for and knowing that something is real even if we do not see it. 2Faith is the reason we remember great people who lived in the past.

3It is by faith we understand that the whole world was made by God's command so what we see was made by something that cannot be seen.

4It was by faith that Abel offered God a better sacrifice than Cain did. God said he was pleased with the gifts Abel offered and called Abel a good man because of his faith. Abel died, but through his faith he is still speaking.

5It was by faith that Enoch was taken to heaven so he would not die. He could not be found, because God had taken him away. Before he was taken, the Scripture says that he was a man who truly pleased God. 6Without faith no one can please God. Anyone who comes to God must believe that he is real and that he rewards those who truly want to find him.

7It was by faith that Noah heard God's warnings about things he could not yet see. He obeyed God and built a large boat to save his family. By his faith, Noah showed that the world was wrong, and he became one of those who are made right with God through faith.

8It was by faith Abraham obeyed God's call to go to another place God promised to give him. He left his own country, not knowing where he was to go. 9It was by faith that he lived like a foreigner in the country God promised to give him. He lived in tents with Isaac and Jacob, who had received that same promise from God. 10Abraham was waiting for the city" that has real foundations—the city planned and built by God.

11He was too old to have children, and Sarah could not have children. It was by faith that Abraham was made able to become a father, because he trusted God to do what he had promised." 12This man was so old he was almost dead, but from him came as many descendants as there are stars in the sky. Like the sand on the seashore, they could not be counted.

13All these great people died in faith. They did not get the things that God promised his people, but they saw them coming far in the future and were glad. They said they were like visitors and strangers on earth. 14When people say such things, they show they are looking for a country that will be their own. 15If they had been thinking about the country they had left, they could have gone back. 16But they were waiting for a better country—a heavenly country. So God is not ashamed to be called their God, because he has prepared a city for them.

17It was by faith that Abraham, when God tested him, offered his

---

11:10 city The spiritual "city" where God's people live with him. Also called "the heavenly Jerusalem." (See Hebrews 12:22.) **11:11 It … promised.** Some Greek copies refer to Sarah's faith, rather than Abraham's.

son Isaac as a sacrifice. God made the promises to Abraham, but Abraham was ready to offer his own son as a sacrifice. [18]God had said, "The descendants I promised you will be from Isaac."" [19]Abraham believed that God could raise the dead, and really, it was as if Abraham got Isaac back from death.

[20]It was by faith that Isaac blessed the future of Jacob and Esau. [21]It was by faith that Jacob, as he was dying, blessed each one of Joseph's sons. Then he worshiped as he leaned on the top of his walking stick.

[22]It was by faith that Joseph, while he was dying, spoke about the Israelites leaving Egypt and gave instructions about what to do with his body.

> **66 Through their faith they defeated kingdoms. They did what was right, received God's promises, and shut the mouths of lions. 99**   HEBREWS 11:33

[23]It was by faith that Moses' parents hid him for three months after he was born. They saw that Moses was a beautiful baby, and they were not afraid to disobey the king's order.

[24]It was by faith that Moses, when he grew up, refused to be called the son of the king of Egypt's daughter. [25]He chose to suffer with God's people instead of enjoying sin for a short time. [26]He thought it was better to suffer for the Christ than to have all the treasures of Egypt, because he was looking for God's reward. [27]It was by faith that Moses left Egypt and was not afraid of the king's anger. Moses continued strong as if he could see the God that no one can see. [28]It was by faith that Moses prepared the Passover and spread the blood on the doors so the one who brings death would not kill the firstborn sons of Israel.

[29]It was by faith that the people crossed the Red Sea as if it were dry land. But when the Egyptians tried it, they were drowned.

[30]It was by faith that the walls of Jericho fell after the people had marched around them for seven days.

[31]It was by faith that Rahab, the prostitute, welcomed the spies and was not killed with those who refused to obey God.

[32]Do I need to give more examples? I do not have time to tell you about Gideon, Barak, Samson, Jephthah, David, Samuel, and the prophets. [33]Through their faith they defeated kingdoms. They did what was right, received God's promises, and shut the mouths of lions. [34]They stopped great fires and were saved from being killed with swords. They were weak, and yet were made strong. They were powerful in battle and defeated other armies. [35]Women received their dead relatives raised back to life. Others were tortured and refused to accept their freedom so they could be raised from the dead to a better life. [36]Some were laughed at and beaten. Others were put in chains and thrown into prison. [37]They were stoned to death, they were cut in half," and they were killed with swords. Some wore the skins of sheep and goats. They were poor, abused, and treated badly. [38]The world was not good enough for them! They wandered in deserts and mountains, living in caves and holes in the earth.

[39]All these people are known for their faith, but none of them received what God had promised. [40]God planned to give us something better so that they would be made perfect, but only together with us.

Follow Jesus' Example

12 We are surrounded by a great cloud of people whose lives tell us what faith means. So let us run the race that is before us and never give up. We should remove from our lives anything that would get in the way and the sin that so easily holds us back. [2]Let us look only to Jesus, the One who began our faith and who makes it perfect. He suffered death on the cross. But he accepted the shame as if it were nothing because of the joy that God put before him. And now he is sitting at the right side of God's throne. [3]Think about Jesus' example. He held on while wicked people were doing evil things to him. So do not get tired and stop trying.

Q: What will we look like in heaven?

A: All we know is that when we get to heaven, we will be like Jesus, and we will see and know God as he truly is. We also know that at the time of Jesus' return to earth, we will receive a new body that will be something like the resurrected body of Jesus (1 John 3:1–3).

>> live the life

Hebrews 12:1

The Principle > Never give up.

Practicing It > Do a study of the great men of faith in the Bible, with a goal to discover how they embodied a life of faith and perseverance. Start with Enoch and Noah, then move forward chronologically to Abraham, Joseph, Moses, David, and Daniel.

>> 11:18 "The descendants ... Isaac." Quotation from Genesis 21:12.   11:37 **they were cut in half** Some Greek copies also include, "they were tested."

>> live the life

Hebrews 12:12-13

The Principle > Develop your character.

Practicing It > Determine what character quality those folks closest to you would say is a weakness in you. Make it your goal to grow stronger in that area of your life this year. Ask God to guide you in developing a plan for improving that character trait in your life.

God Is like a Father

⁴You are struggling against sin, but your struggles have not yet caused you to be killed. ⁵You have forgotten the encouraging words that call you his children:

"My child, don't think the Lord's discipline is worth nothing,
and don't stop trying when he corrects you.
⁶The Lord disciplines those he loves,
and he punishes everyone he accepts as his child."

Proverbs 3:11–12

⁷So hold on through your sufferings, because they are like a father's discipline. God is treating you as children. All children are disciplined by their fathers. ⁸If you are never disciplined (and every child must be disciplined), you are not true children. ⁹We have all had fathers here on earth who disciplined us, and we respected them. So it is even more important that we accept discipline from the Father of our spirits so we will have life. ¹⁰Our fathers on earth disciplined us for a short time in the way they thought was best. But God disciplines us to help us, so we can become holy as he is. ¹¹We do not enjoy being disciplined. It is painful at the time, but later, after we have learned from it, we have peace, because we start living in the right way.

Be Careful How You Live

¹²You have become weak, so make yourselves strong again. ¹³Keep on the right path, so the weak will not stumble but rather be strengthened.

¹⁴Try to live in peace with all people, and try to live free from sin. Anyone whose life is not holy will never see the Lord. ¹⁵Be careful that no one fails to receive God's grace and begins to cause trouble among you. A person like that can ruin many of you. ¹⁶Be careful that no one takes part in sexual sin or is like Esau and never thinks about God. As the oldest son, Esau would have received everything from his father, but he sold all that for a single meal. ¹⁷You remember that after Esau did this, he wanted to get his father's blessing, but his father refused. Esau could find no way to change what he

had done, even though he wanted the blessing so much that he cried.

¹⁸You have not come to a mountain that can be touched and that is burning with fire. You have not come to darkness, sadness, and storms. ¹⁹You have not come to the noise of a trumpet or to the sound of a voice like the one the people of Israel heard and begged not to hear another word. ²⁰They did not want to hear the command: "If anything, even an animal, touches the mountain, it must be put to death with stones."ⁿ ²¹What they saw was so terrible that Moses said, "I am shaking with fear."ⁿ

²²But you have come to Mount Zion,ⁿ to the city of the living God, the heavenly Jerusalem. You have come to thousands of angels gathered together with joy. ²³You have come to the meeting of God's firstbornⁿ children whose names are written in heaven. You have come to God, the judge of all people, and to the spirits of good people who have been made perfect. ²⁴You have come to Jesus, the One who brought the new agreement from God to his people, and you have come to the sprinkled bloodⁿ that has a better message than the blood of Abel.ⁿ

²⁵So be careful and do not refuse to listen when God speaks. Others refused to listen to him when he warned them on earth, and they did not escape. So it will be worse for us if we refuse to listen to God who warns us from heaven. ²⁶When he spoke before, his voice shook the earth, but now he has promised, "Once again I will shake not only the earth but also the heavens."ⁿ ²⁷The words "once again" clearly show us that everything that was made—things that can be shaken—will be destroyed. Only the things that cannot be shaken will remain.

²⁸So let us be thankful, because we have a kingdom that cannot be shaken. We should worship God in a way that pleases him with respect and fear, ²⁹because our God is like a fire that burns things up.

13 Keep on loving each other as brothers and sisters. ²Remember to welcome strangers, because some who have done this have welcomed angels without knowing it. ³Remember those who are in prison as if you were in prison with them. Remember those who are suffering as if you were suffering with them.

⁴Marriage should be honored by everyone, and husband and wife should keep their marriage pure. God will judge as guilty those who

>> live the life

Hebrews 13:17

The Principle > Respect the authorities.

Practicing It > Part of living in obedience to God is showing the proper respect for those in authority over your life. Out of respect for God, obey those he has placed in authority over you, both at church and elsewhere.

12:20 **"If ... stones."** Quotation from Exodus 19:12–13. 12:21 **"I ... fear."** Quotation from Deuteronomy 9:19. 12:22 **Mount Zion** Another name for Jerusalem, here meaning the spiritual city of God's people. 12:23 **firstborn** The first son born in a Jewish family was given the most important place in the family and received special blessings. All of God's children are like that. 12:24 **sprinkled blood** The blood of Jesus' death. 12:24 **Abel** The son of Adam and Eve, who was killed by his brother Cain (Genesis 4:8). 12:26 **"Once ... heavens."** Quotation from Haggai 2:6, 21.

take part in sexual sins. ⁵Keep your lives free from the love of money, and be satisfied with what you have. God has said,

"I will never leave you;
I will never abandon you."

Deuteronomy 31:6

⁶So we can be sure when we say,

"I will not be afraid, because the Lord is my helper.
People can't do anything to me."

Psalm 118:6

⁷Remember your leaders who taught God's message to you. Remember how they lived and died, and copy their faith. ⁸Jesus Christ is the same yesterday, today, and forever.

⁹Do not let all kinds of strange teachings lead you into the wrong way. Your hearts should be strengthened by God's grace, not by obeying rules about foods, which do not help those who obey them.

¹⁰We have a sacrifice, but the priests who serve in the Holy Tent cannot eat from it. ¹¹The high priest carries the blood of animals into the Most Holy Place where he offers this blood for sins. But the bodies of the animals are burned outside the camp. ¹²So Jesus also suffered outside the city to make his people holy with his own blood. ¹³So let us go to Jesus outside the camp, holding on as he did when we are abused.

¹⁴Here on earth we do not have a city that lasts forever, but we are looking for the city that we will have in the future. ¹⁵So through Jesus let us always offer to God our sacrifice of praise, coming from lips that speak his name. ¹⁶Do not forget to do good to others, and share with them, because such sacrifices please God.

¹⁷Obey your leaders and act under their authority. They are watching over you, because

THINK ABOUT IT Hebrews 13:5–6

ONE DAY YOU ARE WALKING OUTSIDE, and due to some family pressures you are feeling a bit distracted. A honking horn shakes you out of your distraction, and you quickly move back as the car flies past, almost hitting you.

Maybe you've flown on a plane in challenging weather and the pilot had to make an emergency landing. Perhaps you were driving on the highway when you nodded off to sleep and instantly awoke just in time. Depending on the situation, in a flash, we can go from faith to fear in our lives.

As Christians, we place our faith in Christ. We are God's children and can live each day in his care and protection, no matter what threatens us. As God promised in this passage, "I will never leave you; I will never abandon you." Because we can rest in the Lord, we have the ability to face our fears and say, "I will not be afraid because the Lord is my helper. People can't do anything to me."

they are responsible for your souls. Obey them so that they will do this work with joy, not sadness. It will not help you to make their work hard.

¹⁸Pray for us. We are sure that we have a clear conscience, because we always want to do the right thing. ¹⁹I especially beg you to pray so that God will send me back to you soon.

²⁰⁻²¹I pray that the God of peace will give you every good thing you need so you can do what he wants. God raised from the dead our Lord Jesus, the Great Shepherd of the sheep, because of the blood of his death. His

blood began the eternal agreement that God made with his people. I pray that God will do in us what pleases him, through Jesus Christ, and to him be glory forever and ever. Amen.

²²My brothers and sisters, I beg you to listen patiently to this message I have written to encourage you, because it is not very long. ²³I want you to know that our brother Timothy has been let out of prison. If he arrives soon, we will both come to see you.

²⁴Greet all your leaders and all of God's people. Those from Italy send greetings to you. ²⁵Grace be with you all.

THE **LETTER** OF
James

AUTHOR: JAMES
DATE WRITTEN: A.D. 48–50

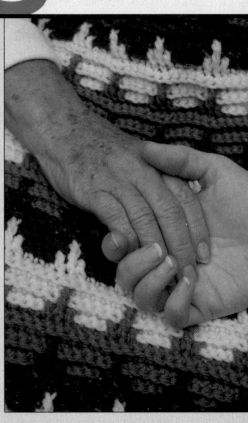

SOME PEOPLE SUGGEST THAT HAVING
faith in Jesus Christ does away with the need for doing
good works. Others elevate the importance of good works
in the spiritual life. James, the brother of Jesus and leader
in the Jerusalem church, knew Christians who made great
claims of faith but often didn't show it in their actions.
While these believers had all the right answers, their daily
living was a complete contradiction to the truth.

As James writes in his letter, it is not enough to talk
about possessing faith, for the proof of faith is a changed
life. Whereas works are not the point of the Christian life,
according to James, a genuine faith in Jesus Christ will
produce good deeds. This letter is loaded with practical teaching about how
to handle life's trials and temptations. James points out that when someone
successfully overcomes a difficulty, it naturally produces strong character and maturity in his or her faith.

James reveals that our salvation is evidenced by the fruit of faith and not by the
keeping of the law. He challenges believers to show love to others by overcoming
selfishness, and he shows that wisdom is demonstrated through thoughtful
speech and sincere service. Faith in action is the message of the Book of James.

1 From James, a servant of God and of the Lord Jesus Christ.

To all of God's people who are scattered everywhere in the world:

Greetings.

Faith and Wisdom

²My brothers and sisters, when you have many kinds of troubles, you should be full of joy, ³because you know that these troubles test your faith, and this will give you patience. ⁴Let your patience show itself perfectly in what you do. Then you will be perfect and complete and will have everything you need. ⁵But if any of you needs wisdom, you should ask God for it. He is generous to everyone and will give you wisdom without criticizing you. ⁶But when you ask God, you must believe and not doubt. Anyone who doubts is like a wave in the sea, blown up and down by the wind. ⁷⁻⁸Such doubters are thinking two different things at the same time, and they cannot decide about anything they do. They should not think they will receive anything from the Lord.

True Riches

⁹Believers who are poor should take pride that God has made them spiritually rich. ¹⁰Those who are rich should take pride that God has shown them that they are spiritually poor. The rich will die like a wild flower in the grass. ¹¹The sun rises with burning heat and dries up the plants. The flower falls off, and its beauty is gone. In the same way the rich will die while they are still taking care of business.

THINK ABOUT IT James 1:17–18

PEOPLE ARE FICKLE. One day you think you have a friendship. Then something gets in the way, whether consciously or not, and that friendship is strained, or in some cases over. Some people are in your life only for a particular season.

Maybe you've grown close to a colleague at work and your relationship is thriving, and then that person has to move away. Perhaps it is the pastor of your local church who gets called to another congregation, and you lose touch with him.

Whereas friendships come and go, there are some constants in our world. For example, the sun comes up each morning and the moon brightens the night sky. James, the brother of Jesus, knew firsthand about the fickleness of human nature, so he chose to focus on the eternal nature of God with this promise, "Every good action and every perfect gift is from God. These good gifts come down from the Creator of the sun, moon, and stars, who does not change like their shifting shadows." We can celebrate God's gracious acts in our life and the good gifts he gives.

Temptation Is Not from God

¹²When people are tempted and still continue strong, they should be happy. After they have proved their faith, God will reward them with life forever. God promised this to

Get Fit

WARMING UP WISELY You shouldn't move from rest into a full-fledged fitness routine without warming up properly. A gradual warm up will help you improve the range of motion in your joints, increase muscle flexibility, and reduce the chance of injury by making your muscles and ligaments more elastic and pliable. To warm up correctly, walk or jog at an easy pace for about ten minutes. Once your muscles are warm and flexible, take some time to stretch each major muscle group, holding each stretch for twenty seconds or more. One way to warm up spiritually is to ask God to show you areas of your life that need stretching.

>> live the life

James 1:2-4

The Principle > Develop joy and patience.

Practicing It > As you go through a difficult time, use the test or trial as an opportunity to grow spiritually by asking God to help you develop greater patience and joy through the struggle.

all those who love him. [13]When people are tempted, they should not say, "God is tempting me." Evil cannot tempt God, and God himself does not tempt anyone. [14]But people are tempted when their own evil desire leads them away and traps them. [15]This desire leads to sin, and then the sin grows and brings death.

[16]My dear brothers and sisters, do not be fooled about this. [17]Every good action and every perfect gift is from God. These good gifts come down from the Creator of the sun, moon, and stars, who does not change like their shifting shadows. [18]God decided to give us life

▶Get Aligned

James 1:22

ACTION. IT'S ALMOST A TABOO WORD IN TODAY'S COME-AS-YOU-ARE CHURCH CULTURE. In our concern with making people comfortable at church, we deliver bite-sized messages, take-home challenges, and volunteer-based discussions. It's possible for a baby Christian to attend church faithfully for a year and not change a single thing about his life.

The Bible is a book of action. It's certainly a book of receiving God's grace, mercy, and love—things that require nothing but an open heart. Yet in today's postmodern society, we tend to emphasize the

"receiving" side of things far more than the "doing" side for fear of treading on works-based territory. To be sure, there is nothing we can do to earn our salvation, for Jesus did it all.

Still, there is a crucial balance that James emphasizes here. In addition to hearing the truth, we are to respond to it. This doesn't mean you have to preach on a street corner or picket an abortion clinic to make a point. It simply means that when God's Word challenges you, the right response is to act. Don't wait for a time when you feel more inclined; act on the Word of God today.

through the word of truth so we might be the most important of all the things he made.

Listening and Obeying

[19]My dear brothers and sisters, always be willing to listen and slow to speak. Do not become angry easily, [20]because anger will not help you live the right kind of life God wants. [21]So put out of your life every evil thing and every kind of wrong. Then in gentleness accept God's teaching that is planted in your hearts, which can save you.

[22]Do what God's teaching says; when you only listen and do nothing, you are fooling yourselves. [23]Those who hear God's teaching and do nothing are like people who look at themselves in a mirror. [24]They see their faces and then go away and quickly forget what they looked like. [25]But the truly happy people are those who carefully study God's perfect law that makes people free, and they continue to study it. They do not forget what they heard, but they obey what God's teaching says. Those who do this will be made happy.

The True Way to Worship God

[26]People who think they are religious but say things they should not say are just fooling themselves. Their "religion" is worth nothing. [27]Religion that God accepts as pure and without fault is this: caring for orphans or widows who need help, and keeping yourself free from the world's evil influence.

Love All People

2 My dear brothers and sisters, as believers in our glorious Lord Jesus Christ, never think some people are more important than others. [2]Suppose someone comes into your church meeting wearing nice clothes and a gold ring. At the same time a poor person comes in wearing old, dirty clothes. [3]You show special attention to the one wearing nice clothes and say, "Please, sit here in this good seat." But you say to the poor person, "Stand over there," or, "Sit on the floor by my feet." [4]What are you doing? You are making some people more important than others, and with evil thoughts you are deciding that one person is better.

[5]Listen, my dear brothers and sisters! God chose the poor in the world to be rich with faith and to receive the kingdom God promised to those who love him. [6]But you show no respect to the poor. The rich are always trying to control your lives. They are the ones who take you to court. [7]And they are the ones who speak against Jesus, who owns you.

[8]This royal law is found in the Scriptures: "Love your neighbor as you love yourself."[n] If you obey this law, you are doing right. [9]But if you treat one person as being more important than another, you are sinning. You are guilty of breaking God's law. [10]A person who follows all of God's law but fails to obey even one command is guilty of breaking all the commands in that law. [11]The same God who said, "You must not be guilty of adultery,"[n] also said, "You must not murder anyone."[n] So if you do not take part in adultery but you murder someone, you are guilty of breaking all of God's law. [12]In everything you say

2:8 "Love...yourself." Quotation from Leviticus 19:18.   **2:11** "You...adultery." Quotation from Exodus 20:14 and Deuteronomy 5:18.   **2:11** "You...anyone." Quotation from Exodus 20:13 and Deuteronomy 5:17.

and do, remember that you will be judged by the law that makes people free. [13]So you must show mercy to others, or God will not show mercy to you when he judges you. But the person who shows mercy can stand without fear at the judgment.

Faith and Good Works

[14]My brothers and sisters, if people say they have faith, but do nothing, their faith is worth nothing. Can faith like that save them? [15]A brother or sister in Christ might need clothes or food. [16]If you say to that person, "God be with you! I hope you stay warm and get plenty to eat," but you do not give what that person needs, your words are worth nothing. [17]In the same way, faith by itself—that does nothing—is dead.

[18]Someone might say, "You have faith, but I have deeds." Show me your faith without doing anything, and I will show you my faith by what I do. [19]You believe there is one God. Good! But the demons believe that, too, and they tremble with fear.

[20]You foolish person! Must you be shown that faith that does nothing is worth nothing? [21]Abraham, our ancestor, was made right with God by what he did when he offered his son Isaac on the altar. [22]So you see that Abraham's faith and the things he did worked together. His faith was made perfect by what he did. [23]This shows the full meaning of the Scripture that says: "Abraham believed God, and God accepted Abraham's faith, and that faith made him right with God."[n] And Abraham was called God's friend.[n] [24]So you see that people are made right with God by what they do, not by faith only.

[25]Another example is Rahab, a prostitute, who was made right with God by something she did. She welcomed the spies into her home and helped them escape by a different road.

[26]Just as a person's body that does not have a spirit is dead, so faith that does nothing is dead!

Controlling the Things We Say

3 My brothers and sisters, not many of you should become teachers, because you know that we who teach will be judged more strictly. [2]We all make many mistakes. If people never said anything wrong, they would be perfect and able to control their entire selves,

<<TechSupport>>

TECH ETIQUETTE

There are voicemails that never seem to end and e-mail that reads like Morse code. These days, the effect of instant and accelerated communication technology has made manners seem inconvenient and outdated. But the truth is, polite and considerate messages stand out among the crowd. Use the "Golden Rule" of communication: keep messages courteous and to the point. If necessary, write a couple of thoughts on paper before you leave a voice message or send an e-mail. As Jesus taught the disciples in Luke 6:31, "Do to others what you would want them to do to you."

too. [3]When we put bits into the mouths of horses to make them obey us, we can control their whole bodies. [4]Also a ship is very big, and it is pushed by strong winds. But a very small rudder controls that big ship, making it go wherever the pilot wants. [5]It is the same with the tongue. It is a small part of the body, but it brags about great things.

A big forest fire can be started with only a little flame. [6]And the tongue is like a fire. It is a whole world of evil among the parts of our bodies. The tongue spreads its evil through the whole body. The tongue is set on fire by hell, and it starts a fire that influences all of life. [7]People can tame every kind of wild animal, bird, reptile, and fish, and they have tamed them, [8]but no one can tame the tongue. It is wild and evil and full of deadly poison. [9]We use our tongues to praise our Lord and Father, but then we curse people, whom God made like himself. [10]Praises and curses come from the same mouth! My brothers and sisters, this should not happen. [11]Do good and bad water flow from the same spring? [12]My brothers and sisters, can a fig tree make olives, or can a grapevine make figs? No! And a well full of salty water cannot give good water.

True Wisdom

[13]Are there those among you who are truly wise and understanding? Then they should show it by living right and doing good things with a gentleness that comes from wisdom. [14]But if you are selfish and have bitter jealousy in your hearts, do not brag. Your bragging is a lie that hides the truth. [15]That kind of "wisdom" does not come from God but from the world. It is not spiritual; it is from the devil. [16]Where jealousy and selfishness are, there will be confusion and every kind of evil. [17]But the wisdom that comes from God is first of all pure, then peaceful, gentle, and easy to please. This wisdom is always

>> live the life

James 1:21

The Principle > Accept the Scriptures.

Practicing It > As you read and study the Bible, recognize it for what it is—the authoritative Word of God. Be teachable and open as you study the Bible, and be willing to apply its commands and wisdom to your life immediately.

>> 2:23 "Abraham ... God." Quotation from Genesis 15:6.   2:23 God's friend These words about Abraham are found in 2 Chronicles 20:7 and Isaiah 41:8.

>> live the life

James 3:13

The Principle > **Do good things.**

Practicing It > **You can recognize true wisdom not by how much somebody knows, but by the way he or she treats other people. As you gain wisdom in your walk with God, demonstrate what you have learned by doing good to others and treating them with kindness.**

ready to help those who are troubled and to do good for others. It is always fair and honest. ¹⁸People who work for peace in a peaceful way plant a good crop of right-living.

Give Yourselves to God

4 Do you know where your fights and arguments come from? They come from the selfish desires that war within you. ²You want things, but you do not have them. So you are ready to kill and are jealous of other people, but you still cannot get what you want. So you argue and fight. You do not get what you want, because you do not ask God. ³Or when you ask, you do not receive because the reason you ask is wrong. You want things so you can use them for your own pleasures.

⁴So, you are not loyal to God! You should know that loving the world is the same as hating God. Anyone who wants to be a friend of the world becomes God's enemy. ⁵Do you think the Scripture means nothing that says, "The Spirit that God made to live in us wants us for himself alone"? ⁶But God gives us even more grace, as the Scripture says,

"God is against the proud,
but he gives grace to the humble."   *Proverbs 3:34*

⁷So give yourselves completely to God. Stand against the devil, and the devil will run from you. ⁸Come near to God, and God will come near to you. You sinners, clean sin out of your lives. You who are trying to follow God and the world at the same time, make your thinking pure. ⁹Be sad, cry, and weep! Change your laughter into crying and your joy into sadness. ¹⁰Humble yourself in the Lord's presence, and he will honor you.

You Are Not the Judge

¹¹Brothers and sisters, do not tell evil lies about each other. If you speak against your fellow believers or judge them, you are judging and speaking against the law they follow. And when you are judging the law, you are no longer a follower of the law. You have become a judge. ¹²God is the only Lawmaker and Judge. He is the only One who can save and destroy. So it is not right for you to judge your neighbor.

Let God Plan Your Life

¹³Some of you say, "Today or tomorrow we will go to some city. We will stay there a year, do business, and make money." ¹⁴But you do not know what will happen tomorrow! Your life is like a mist. You can see it for a short time, but then it goes away. ¹⁵So you should say, "If the Lord wants, we will live and do this or that." ¹⁶But now you are proud and you brag. All of this bragging is wrong. ¹⁷Anyone who knows the right thing to do, but does not do it, is sinning.

⊙ Get Aligned

James 3:5

GUYS ARE KNOWN FOR BRAGGING. IT IS TYPICALLY PART OF THE CAMARADERIE WE SHARE AS MEN, who often define closeness as the ability to pick at each other. From practical jokes to trash talk on the court, we love to talk it up and dish it out in the name of fun and games.

But what about subtler forms of bragging? Bragging isn't always overt boasting; sometimes it's what we don't say rather than what is spoken. We can forget to mention our mistakes in order to make us look better. Or we can take the usual route and talk about ourselves endlessly, painting a near-perfect picture.

Whatever the form, bragging is out of bounds for a believer. In truth, the only thing we have to brag about is Jesus and what he has done in our lives. Sure, we may be talented in certain areas, but all our gifts are from God. The hallmark characteristic of a follower of Christ is humility, which is the opposite of bragging. Ultimately, our verbal praise needs to go to our Lord and not ourselves.

>> live the life

James 4:6

The Principle > **Walk in humility.**

Practicing It > **Consider in which areas of your life you struggle most with pride. Confess your pride to God, and ask him to show you how to develop an attitude of humility in all areas of your life.**

>> 4:5 "The Spirit...alone." These words may be from Exodus 20:5.

A Warning to the Rich

5 You rich people, listen! Cry and be very sad because of the troubles that are coming to you. ²Your riches have rotted, and your clothes have been eaten by moths. ³Your gold and silver have rusted, and that rust will be a proof that you were wrong. It will eat your bodies like fire. You saved your treasure for the last days. ⁴The pay you did not give the workers who mowed your fields cries out against you, and the cries of the workers have been heard by the Lord All-Powerful. ⁵Your life on earth was full of rich living and pleasing yourselves with everything you wanted. You made yourselves fat, like an animal ready to be killed. ⁶You have judged guilty and then murdered innocent people, who were not against you.

Be Patient

⁷Brothers and sisters, be patient until the Lord comes again. A farmer patiently waits for his valuable crop to grow from the earth and for it to receive the autumn and spring rains. ⁸You, too, must be patient. Do not give up hope, because the Lord is coming soon. ⁹Brothers and sisters, do not complain against each other or you will be judged guilty. And the Judge is ready to come! ¹⁰Brothers and sisters, follow the example of the prophets who spoke for the Lord. They suffered many hard things, but they were patient. ¹¹We say they are happy because they did not give up. You have heard about Job's patience, and you know the Lord's purpose for him in the end. You know the Lord is full of mercy and is kind.

Be Careful What You Say

¹²My brothers and sisters, above all, do not use an oath when you make a promise. Don't use the name of heaven, earth, or anything else to prove what you say. When you mean yes, say only yes, and when you mean no, say only no so you will not be judged guilty.

The Power of Prayer

¹³Anyone who is having troubles should pray. Anyone who is happy should sing praises. ¹⁴Anyone who is sick should call church's elders. They should pray for and pour oil on the person" in the name of the Lord. ¹⁵And the prayer that is said with faith will make the sick person well; the Lord will heal that person. And if the person has sinned, the sins will be forgiven. ¹⁶Confess your sins to each other and pray for each other so God can heal you. When a believing person prays, great things happen. ¹⁷Elijah was a human being just like us. He prayed that it would not rain, and it did not rain on the land for three and a half years! ¹⁸Then Elijah prayed again, and the rain came down from the sky, and the land produced crops again.

Saving a Soul

¹⁹My brothers and sisters, if one of you wanders away from the truth, and someone helps that person come back, ²⁰remember this: Anyone who brings a sinner back from the wrong way will save that sinner's soul from death and will cause many sins to be forgiven.

>> live the life

James 5:16

The Principle > Pray with a partner.

Practicing It > Ask your spouse or closest friend to become your prayer partner and pray together regularly. As a part of your prayer time, confess your sins to each other and go before God together to receive his forgiveness.

Survival Guide

TOOLS: KEEPING THEM SHARP

Whether you're trying to trim hedges, saw wood, or cut a piece of paper, nothing makes the job more difficult than dull blades. Sharpening equipment used to mean buying a whetstone or file and grinding on the edges or finding a tool shop or hardware store that handled such chores. However, modern tool, knife, and scissor sharpeners can make short order of this task. Keeping tools sharp and ready for their job is an important part of home maintenance. As Proverbs 27:17 reminds us, "As iron sharpens iron, so people can improve each other."

>> **5:14 pour oil on the person** Oil was used in the name of the Lord as a sign that the person was now set apart for God's special attention and care.

THE **FIRST** LETTER OF
Peter

AUTHOR: PETER
DATE WRITTEN: A.D. 63–64

PERHAPS AT YOUR PLACE OF BUSINESS

others are pressuring you to compromise accounting principles. They suggest that everyone is doing it. You refuse and later you find that you are ostracized from the group. Like it or not, this type of persecution fills our world.

The apostle Peter knew persecution firsthand, but on a much more hostile level. He was often threatened and beaten and even thrown into jail for his faith. This letter is written to other Christians who face persecution. Peter reminds believers about God's gift of salvation and how trials will refine their faith.

The letter also encourages believers to continue striving for a holy life, trusting in God to become more like Jesus Christ. According to Peter, when persecution comes into our lives, we are to consider Jesus as our role model. Peter suggests we follow these three steps when dealing with persecution: expect persecution for Christ's sake, thank God for the privilege of suffering for Christ, and trust God for deliverance. As Peter reveals, Christ is our strength for faithfully enduring such suffering.

1

From Peter, an apostle of Jesus Christ.

To God's chosen people who are away from their homes and are scattered all around Pontus, Galatia, Cappadocia, Asia, and Bithynia. [2]God planned long ago to choose you by making you his holy people, which is the Spirit's work. God wanted you to obey him and to be made clean by the blood of the death of Jesus Christ.

Grace and peace be yours more and more.

We Have a Living Hope

[3]Praise be to the God and Father of our Lord Jesus Christ. In God's great mercy he has caused us to be born again into a living hope, because Jesus Christ rose from the dead. [4]Now we hope for the blessings God has for his children. These blessings, which cannot be destroyed or be spoiled or lose their beauty, are kept in heaven for you. [5]God's power protects you through your faith until salvation is shown to you at the end of time. [6]This makes you very happy, even though now for a short time different kinds of troubles may make you sad. [7]These troubles come to prove that your faith is pure. This purity of faith is worth more than gold, which can be proved to be pure by fire but will ruin. But the purity of your faith will bring you praise and glory and honor when Jesus Christ is shown to you. [8]You have not seen Christ, but still you love him. You cannot see him now, but you believe in him. So you are filled with a joy that cannot be explained, a joy full of glory. [9]And you are receiving the goal of your faith—the salvation of your souls.

[10]The prophets searched carefully and tried to learn about this salvation. They prophesied about the grace that was coming to you. [11]The Spirit of Christ was in the prophets, telling in advance about the sufferings of Christ and about the glory that would follow those sufferings. The prophets tried to learn about what the Spirit was showing them, when those things would happen, and what the world would be like at that time. [12]It was shown them that their service was not for themselves but for you, when they told about the truths you have now heard. Those who preached the Good

Change Your WORLD >>

THE NAVIGATORS

It's admittedly a challenge to navigate the spiritual waters of life. Two of the hallmarks of the ministry of The Navigators are one-to-one relationships and small group studies focused on discipleship. The organization touches lives in everyday settings, such as college campuses, military bases, inner cities, prisons, and youth camps. The Navigators primarily focus in three areas: application of the Bible into everyday life, passing on what they learn to others, and training new believers to reach others. Whether in the boardroom with business people, on the college campus with students, or with soldiers in the military, The Navigators are helping people grow in their faith.

To change your world, visit www.navigators.org.

News to you told you those things with the help of the Holy Spirit who was sent from heaven—things into which angels desire to look.

A Call to Holy Living

[13]So prepare your minds for service and have self-control. All your hope should be for the gift of grace that will be yours when Jesus Christ is shown to you. [14]Now that you are obedient children of God do not live as you did in the past. You did not understand, so you did the evil things you wanted. [15]But be holy in all you do, just as God, the One who called you, is holy. [16]It is written in the Scriptures: "You must be holy, because I am holy."[*]

[17]You pray to God and call him Father, and he judges each person's work equally. So while you are here on earth, you should live with respect for God. [18]You know that in the past you were living in a worthless way, a way passed down from the people who lived before you. But

>> live the life

1 Peter 1:14–16

The Principle > Live a holy life.

Practicing It > God has called us to live a holy life, and that includes saying no to such temptations as lust. The world may suggest that lust is acceptable, but it isn't. Lust goes against God's will for our lives, and, with his help, we have the power not to lust.

>> 1:16 "You must be … holy." Quotation from Leviticus 11:45; 19:2; 20:7.

People Skills

Praising Others

Be liberal with praise in all of your relationships, including children, siblings, parents, friends, and, of course, your spouse. Get in the habit of searching for qualities or behaviors you can genuinely praise in your loved ones. At their best, our closest relationships should be about encouraging each other to become the best version of ourselves. By regularly noticing and calling attention to the positive traits and actions of others, you can have a powerful, transforming impact on their lives. What is more, you will foster an atmosphere of acceptance and encouragement between you, and you'll open the way for them to encourage the best in you.

you were saved from that useless life. You were bought, not with something that ruins like gold or silver, [19]but with the precious blood of Christ, who was like a pure and perfect lamb. [20]Christ was chosen before the world was made, but he was shown to the world in these last times for your sake. [21]Through Christ you believe in God, who raised Christ from the dead and gave him glory. So your faith and your hope are in God.

[22]Now that your obedience to the truth has purified your souls, you can have true love for your Christian brothers and sisters. So love each other deeply with all your heart." [23]You have been born again, and this new life did not come from something that dies, but from something that cannot die. You were born again through God's living message that continues forever. [24]The Scripture says,

"All people are like the grass,
and all their glory is like the flowers of the field.
The grass dies and the flowers fall,
[25] but the word of the Lord will live forever." *Isaiah 40:6–8*

And this is the word that was preached to you.

Jesus Is the Living Stone

2 So then, rid yourselves of all evil, all lying, hypocrisy, jealousy, and evil speech. [2]As newborn babies want milk, you should want the pure and simple teaching. By it you can mature in your salvation, [3]because you have already examined and seen how good the Lord is.

[4]Come to the Lord Jesus, the "stone"[n] that lives. The people of the world did not want this stone, but he was the stone God chose, and he was precious. [5]You also are like living stones, so let yourselves be used to build a spiritual temple—to be holy priests who offer spiritual sacrifices to God. He will accept those sacrifices through Jesus Christ. [6]The Scripture says,

"I will put a stone in the ground in Jerusalem.
Everything will be built on this important and precious rock.
Anyone who trusts in him
will never be disappointed." *Isaiah 28:16*

[7]This stone is worth much to you who believe. But to the people who do not believe,

"the stone that the builders rejected
has become the cornerstone." *Psalm 118:22*

⊙ Sexcess:
EASING TOWARD ECSTASY

Men are typically more motivated than women to experience the physical release that results from sexual activity, so when it comes to foreplay, many wonder what they need to "play for." If it were up to most men, sex would likely become a simple case of "wham, bam, thank you, ma'am." But that is not fair to women, nor is it God's design. Women need the added intimacy of cuddling, hugging, kissing, and caressing, and if we men would learn to accommodate them, we might find that the entire scope of our sex lives would increase and improve. It is a wise man who eases his wife toward ecstasy.

>> **1:22 with all your heart** Some Greek copies read "with a pure heart."   **2:4 "stone"** The most important stone in God's spiritual temple or house (his people).

⁸Also, he is

"a stone that causes people to stumble,
a rock that makes them fall." *Isaiah 8:14*

They stumble because they do not obey what God says, which is what God planned to happen to them.

⁹But you are a chosen people, royal priests, a holy nation, a people for God's own possession. You were chosen to tell about the wonderful acts of God, who called you out of darkness into his wonderful light. ¹⁰At one time you were not a people, but now you are God's people. In the past you had never received mercy, but now you have received God's mercy.

Live for God

¹¹Dear friends, you are like foreigners and strangers in this world. I beg you to avoid the evil things your bodies want to do that fight against your soul. ¹²People who do not believe are living all around you and might say that you are doing wrong. Live such good lives that they will see the good things you do and will give glory to God on the day when Christ comes again.

Yield to Every Human Authority

¹³For the Lord's sake, yield to the people who have authority in this world: the king, who is the highest authority, ¹⁴and the leaders who are sent by him to punish those who do wrong and to praise those who do right. ¹⁵It is God's desire that by doing good you should stop foolish people from saying stupid things about you. ¹⁶Live as free people, but do not use your freedom as an excuse to do evil. Live as servants of God. ¹⁷Show respect for all people: Love the brothers and sisters of God's family, respect God, honor the king.

Follow Christ's Example

¹⁸Slaves, yield to the authority of your masters with all respect, not only those who are good and kind, but also those who are dishonest. ¹⁹A person might have to suffer even when it is unfair, but if he thinks of God and can stand the pain, God is pleased. ²⁰If you are beaten for doing wrong, there is no reason to praise

>> live the life

1 Peter 2:2

The Principle > Desire simple teaching.

Practicing It > Think of a spiritual topic you want to learn more about, then do a word study of that topic by looking up references from Scripture in which that word is used. Focus on the simple, yet profound, meaning of words like grace, love, peace, and trust.

▶ Get Aligned
1 Peter 2:13—14

YOU MAY NOT LIKE YOUR BOSS, YOUR PASTOR, OR YOUR MAYOR. You may disagree with the actions each takes. Maybe you know inside information that makes it hard to respect them. But none of that changes one thing: God allowed him to assume that position. Romans 13:1 says, "No one rules unless God has given him the power to rule, and no one rules now without that power from God."

God knows what he is doing. He didn't make a mistake when he placed someone over you. Does that mean that leader is necessarily godly? Of course not. He may not even know God. In fact, the Bible is full of wicked rulers and leaders who directly opposed God. Undoubtedly, there were godly people who were forced to submit to bad leadership, and they probably wondered what God was doing.

The question is not who's in charge, because we know who ultimately rules; the question is how we submit to the authority God has placed over us. God is interested in our willingness to submit to his will, which may very well include a power-hungry, egotistical boss. In the meantime, we can take comfort in knowing God has the final say-so in the situation.

you for being patient in your punishment. But if you suffer for doing good, and you are patient, then God is pleased. ²¹This is what you were called to do, because Christ suffered for you and gave you an example to follow. So you should do as he did.

²²"He had never sinned,
and he had never lied." *Isaiah 53:9*

²³People insulted Christ, but he did not insult them in return. Christ suffered, but he did not threaten. He let God, the One who judges rightly, take care of him. ²⁴Christ carried our sins in his body on the cross so we would stop living for sin and start living for what is right. And you are healed because of his wounds. ²⁵You were like sheep that wandered away, but now you have come back to the Shepherd and Overseer of your souls.

Wives and Husbands

3 In the same way, you wives should yield to your husbands. Then, if some husbands do not obey God's teaching, they will be persuaded to believe without anyone's saying a word to them. They will be persuaded by the way their wives live. ²Your husbands will see the pure lives you live with your respect for God. ³It is not fancy hair, gold jewelry, or fine clothes that should make you beautiful. ⁴No, your beauty should come from within you—

Men of Valor
STEPHEN: Full of Grace

One of the first deacons chosen to serve the early church, Stephen was a man of wisdom and spiritual maturity. According to Acts, God gave him the power to perform great signs and miracles. Instead of acclaim, that only earned him opposition from some Jews. Unable to contradict his wisdom, they resorted to rumor, accusing him of blaspheming Moses and God. Eventually, they succeeded in dragging him before the religious leaders for a hearing. Instead of cowering, Stephen told the truth: Israel had rejected Jesus, the Messiah. His powerful sermon resulted in his death by stoning. As the weapons flew, he prayed, "Lord, do not hold this sin against them" (Acts 7:60). Stephen's godly example of grace under fire serves yet today as an example for all men.

THINK ABOUT IT 1 Peter 2:9–10

OCCASIONALLY IT HAPPENS. Someone finally convinces a publisher to accept his first book. Through a series of events, the book takes off and captures the attention of the public and becomes a best-seller. Now the author has a potential trap to avoid, sometimes called the sophomore jinx. Because the first book was a best-seller, the publisher and the readers have high expectations for the second book.

The pressure on the author can be tremendous, whether self-inflicted or from society. If the second book turns out to be poorly received, then the result is even worse for the author. Whereas you may not have had any such experience with books, it can happen with almost any type of situation in which disappointment tears at your sense of identity and self-worth.

In this uplifting passage, Peter reminds us of our identity in Christ: "You are a chosen people, royal priests, a holy nation, a people for God's own possession. You were chosen to tell about the wonderful acts of God, who called you out of darkness into his wonderful light."

dren of Sarah if you always do what is right and are not afraid.

[7]In the same way, you husbands should live with your wives in an understanding way, since they are weaker than you. But show them respect, because God gives them the same blessing he gives you—the grace that gives true life. Do this so that nothing will stop your prayers.

Suffering for Doing Right

[8]Finally, all of you should be in agreement, understanding each other, loving each other as family, being kind and humble. [9]Do not do wrong to repay a wrong, and do not insult to repay an insult. But repay with a blessing, because you yourselves were called to do this so that you might receive a blessing. [10]The Scripture says,

"A person must do these things
    to enjoy life and have many happy
        days.
He must not say evil things,
    and he must not tell lies.

[11]He must stop doing evil and do good.
    He must look for peace and work for
        it.
[12]The Lord sees the good people
    and listens to their prayers.
But the Lord is against
    those who do evil."

Psalm 34:12–16

[13]If you are trying hard to do good, no one can really hurt you. [14]But even if you suffer for doing right, you are blessed.

"Don't be afraid of what they fear;
    do not dread those things."

Isaiah 8:12–13

[15]But respect Christ as the holy Lord in your hearts. Always be ready to answer everyone who asks you to explain about the hope you have, [16]but answer in a gentle way and with respect. Keep a clear conscience so that those who speak evil of your good life in Christ will be made ashamed. [17]It is better to suffer for doing good than for doing wrong if that is what God wants. [18]Christ himself suffered for sins once. He was not guilty, but he suf-

the beauty of a gentle and quiet spirit that will never be destroyed and is very precious to God. [5]In this same way the holy women who lived long ago and followed God made themselves beautiful, yielding to their own husbands. [6]Sarah obeyed Abraham, her husband, and called him her master. And you women are true chil-

Q: Why is it important to study the Bible?

A: The Bible is the primary source of divine revelation about the personhood of God and his plan for our lives. Studying and adhering to the truths of Scripture keeps us on the right path in our pursuit of God (2 Timothy 3:16).

fered for those who are guilty to bring you to God. His body was killed, but he was made alive in the spirit. [19]And in the spirit he went and preached to the spirits in prison [20]who refused to obey God long ago in the time of Noah. God was waiting patiently for them while Noah was building the boat. Only a few people—eight in all—were saved by water. [21]And that water is like baptism that now saves you—not the washing of dirt from the body, but the promise made to God from a good conscience. And this is because Jesus Christ was raised from the dead. [22]Now Jesus has gone into heaven and is at God's right side ruling over angels, authorities, and powers.

Change Your Lives

4 Since Christ suffered while he was in his body, strengthen yourselves with the same way of thinking Christ had. The person who has suffered in the body is finished with sin. [2]Strengthen yourselves so that you will live here on earth doing what God wants, not the evil things people want. [3]In the past you wasted too much time doing what nonbelievers enjoy. You

>> live the life

1 Peter 4:10

The Principle > Serve others with your gifts.

Practicing It > Look for a new opportunity to serve others through your church. Ask your pastor for ideas, and then choose to invest your time and energy in an area of service that interests you and uses your gifts.

were guilty of sexual sins, evil desires, drunkenness, wild and drunken parties, and hateful idol worship. [4]Nonbelievers think it is strange that you do not do the many wild and wasteful things they do, so they insult you. [5]But they will have to explain this to God, who is ready to judge the living and the dead. [6]For this reason the Good News was preached to those who are now dead. Even though they were judged like all people, the Good News was preached to them so they could live in the spirit as God lives.

Use God's Gifts Wisely

[7]The time is near when all things will end. So think clearly and control yourselves so you will be able to pray. [8]Most importantly, love each other deeply, because love will cause people to forgive each other for many sins. [9]Open your homes to each other, without

→ The Bottom Line

Tune-Ups: Maintaining Your Vehicle

THE COMPUTERIZATION OF CARS HAS MADE DO-IT-YOURSELF MECHANICS A FADING BREED. But automobiles' complexity may lull you into complacency. Experts warn that computers that work to keep your engine running can camouflage malfunctions. Some tell-tale signs of trouble: excessive fuel consumption, knocking when you accelerate, idling after you turn off the ignition, hard starting, or rough running. If you have a newer car, check the warranty to see if certain maintenance is required for the warranty to remain valid. Finally, develop a good relationship with a local mechanic. Trust is important, especially when car maintenance is so expensive.

+ Ten Ways to Leave a Legacy

1. Teach someone how to read.

2. Open a savings account for a child.

3. Pass along a new skill or hobby.

4. Volunteer your time to serve others.

5. File a last will and testament.

6. Keep a journal of your life.

7. Plan a weekly family activity.

8. Write letters to your loved ones.

9. Plant a tree and nurture it.

10. Treat people with compassion.

complaining. [10]Each of you has received a gift to use to serve others. Be good servants of God's various gifts of grace. [11]Anyone who speaks should speak words from God. Anyone who serves should serve with the strength God gives so that in everything God will be praised through Jesus Christ. Power and glory belong to him forever and ever. Amen.

Suffering as a Christian

[12]My friends, do not be surprised at the terrible trouble which now comes to test you. Do not think that something strange is happening to you. [13]But be happy that you are sharing in Christ's sufferings so that you will be happy and full of joy when Christ comes again in glory. [14]When people insult you because you follow Christ, you are blessed, because the glorious Spirit, the Spirit of God, is with you. [15]Do not suffer for murder, theft, or any other crime, nor because you trouble other people. [16]But if you suffer because you are a Christian, do not be ashamed. Praise God because you wear that name. [17]It is time for judgment to begin with God's family. And if that judging begins with us, what will happen to those people who do not obey the Good News of God?

[18]"If it is very hard for a good person to be saved,
    the wicked person and the sinner will surely be lost!"

[19]So those who suffer as God wants should trust their souls to the faithful Creator as they continue to do what is right.

The Flock of God

5 Now I have something to say to the elders in your group. I also am an elder. I have seen Christ's sufferings, and I will share in the glory that will be shown to us. I beg you to [2]shepherd God's flock, for whom you are responsible. Watch over them because you want to, not because you are forced. That is how God wants it. Do it because you are happy to serve, not because you want money. [3]Do not be like a ruler over people you are responsible for, but be good examples to them. [4]Then when Christ, the Chief Shepherd, comes, you will get a glorious crown that will never lose its beauty.

[5]In the same way, younger people should be willing to be under older people. And all of you should be very humble with each other.

"God is against the proud,
    but he gives grace to the humble."   *Proverbs 3:34*

[6]Be humble under God's powerful hand so he will lift you up when the right time comes. [7]Give all your worries to him, because he cares about you.

[8]Control yourselves and be careful! The devil, your enemy, goes around like a roaring lion looking for someone to eat. [9]Refuse to give in to him, by standing strong in your faith. You know that your Christian family all over the world is having the same kinds of suffering.

[10]And after you suffer for a short time, God, who gives all grace, will make everything right. He will make you strong and support you and keep you from falling. He called you to share in his glory in Christ, a glory that will continue forever. [11]All power is his forever and ever. Amen.

Final Greetings

[12]I wrote this short letter with the help of Silas, who I know is a faithful brother in Christ. I wrote to encourage you and to tell you that this is the true grace of God. Stand strong in that grace.

[13]The church in Babylon, who was chosen like you, sends you greetings. Mark, my son in Christ, also greets you. [14]Give each other a kiss of Christian love when you meet.

Peace to all of you who are in Christ.

>> live the life

1 Peter 5:7

The Principle > **Commit your worries to God.**

Practicing It > **Avoid taking your work home with you. Make a habit of leaving your worries at the office door so that when you come home, your mind and heart will be free to relax and enjoy the evening with family or friends.**

>> 4:18 "If…lost!" Quotation from Proverbs 11:31 in the Septuagint, the Greek version of the Old Testament.

Notes

THE **SECOND** LETTER OF
Peter

AUTHOR: PETER
DATE WRITTEN: A.D. 65–66

WHEN THE AMBULANCE SIREN BLARES

in your ear, you quickly look around and pull to the side of the road. The warning lets you know the vehicle needs to get through the traffic quickly. Most of us move rapidly when we are warned because we want to protect ourselves from the impending danger. When we hear a warning, we quickly evaluate the source and the situation, and we respond appropriately.

This second letter from the apostle Peter sounds a warning to every Christian. One of the closest followers of Jesus, the experienced leader warns the church of several alarming threats to its health, including widespread rejection of the faith. The letter marks Peter's final communication in the New Testament.

Peter begins the letter by encouraging every Christian to listen to his voice and to heed his words of wisdom, because time is limited. With directness and authority, Peter warns of false teachers in the last days who will do anything for money and who will reject the things of God. The letter reminds readers that Christ will return and create a new home where believers will live together with him forever. Finally, Peter exhorts believers to keep their hope in the promises of God.

1

From Simon Peter, a servant and apostle of Jesus Christ.

To you who have received a faith as valuable as ours, because our God and Savior Jesus Christ does what is right. [2]Grace and peace be given to you more and more, because you truly know God and Jesus our Lord.

God Has Given Us Blessings

[3]Jesus has the power of God, by which he has given us everything we need to live and to serve God. We have these things because we know him. Jesus called us by his glory and goodness. [4]Through these he gave us the very great and precious promises. With these gifts you can share in God's nature, and the world will not ruin you with its evil desires.

[5]Because you have these blessings, do your best to add these things to your lives: to your faith, add goodness; and to your goodness, add knowledge; [6]and to your knowledge, add self-control; and to your self-control, add patience; and to your patience, add service for God; [7]and to your service for God, add kindness for your brothers and sisters in Christ; and to this kindness, add love. [8]If all these things are in you and are growing, they will help you to be useful and productive in your knowledge of our Lord Jesus Christ. [9]But anyone who does not have these things cannot see clearly. He is blind and has forgotten that he was made clean from his past sins.

[10]My brothers and sisters, try hard to be certain that you really are called and chosen by God. If you do all these things, you will never fall. [11]And you will be given a very great welcome into the eternal kingdom of our Lord and Savior Jesus Christ.

[12]You know these things, and you are very strong in the truth, but I will always help you remember them. [13]I think it is right for me to help you remember as long as I am in this body. [14]I know I must soon leave this body, as our Lord Jesus Christ has shown me. [15]I will try my best so that you may be able to remember these things even after I am gone.

>> live the life

2 Peter 1:5–8

The Principle > **Grow in character.**

Practicing It > **Set aside time each day for your spiritual growth. Focus on activities that will deepen your relationship with God, such as prayer, Bible study, or reading books designed to help you grow.**

Saw Christ's Glory

[16]When we told you about the powerful coming of our Lord Jesus Christ, we were not telling just clever stories that someone invented. But we saw the greatness of Jesus with our own eyes. [17]Jesus heard the voice of God, the Greatest Glory, when he received honor and glory from God the Father. The voice said, "This is my Son, whom I love, and I am very pleased with him." [18]We heard that voice from heaven while we were with Jesus on the holy mountain.

[19]This makes us more sure about the message the prophets gave. It is good for you to follow closely what they said as you would follow a light shining in a dark place, until the day begins and the morning star rises in your hearts. [20]Most of all, you must understand this: No prophecy in the Scriptures ever comes from the prophet's own interpretation. [21]No prophecy ever came from what a person wanted to say, but people led by the Holy Spirit spoke words from God.

Get Fit

MAINTAINING HEALTHY ARTERIES

Most doctors now agree that it is a good idea for men to take a baby aspirin every day. Unless you are allergic to aspirin or at high risk for gastrointestinal bleeding (both of which are rare), this daily dose of aspirin may be one of the most beneficial things you can do for your health. The aspirin acts to reduce the risk of clot formation in your arteries, thereby reducing the risk of both heart attacks and strokes. It also may act in other beneficial ways we don't yet fully understand. Just as it is important to maintain healthy arteries, we must also keep our spiritual lives free from damaging influences.

THINK ABOUT IT 2 Peter 1:2-4

YOU BOUNCE OUT OF BED AND BEGIN THE DAY. After a little breakfast, you jump into the shower and head off to work. After blasting through a series of meetings, phone calls, and e-mails, you head home to relate to the wife and kids. Then it's off to bed so you can wake up and do it all over again. At times, you may be left wondering if you have what it takes to make it in life.

You do if you believe 2 Peter 1:3, where Peter writes, "Jesus has the power of God, by which he has given us everything we need to live and to serve God." Because of your relationship to Jesus, you have received everything you need to experience abundant life.

So, how do you possess these things? "We have these things because we know him," writes Peter. For God's power to be operational in your daily experience, you must know Jesus. As a reminder of the spiritual resources at your disposal, write this passage of Scripture on a notecard. Pull out the notecard at various idle moments throughout the day and meditate on this awesome promise.

False Teachers

2 There used to be false prophets among God's people, just as you will have some false teachers in your group. They will secretly teach things that are wrong—teachings that will cause people to be lost. They will even refuse to accept the Master, Jesus, who bought their freedom. So they will bring quick ruin on themselves. ²Many will follow their evil ways and say evil things about the way of truth. ³Those false teachers only want your money, so they will use you by telling you lies. Their judgment spoken against them long ago is still coming, and their ruin is certain.

⁴When angels sinned, God did not let them go free without punishment. He sent them to hell and put them in caves" of darkness where they are being held for judgment. ⁵And God punished the world long ago when he brought a flood to the world that was full of people who were against him. But God saved Noah, who preached about being right with God, and seven other people with him. ⁶And God also destroyed the evil cities of Sodom and Gomorrah" by burning them until they were ashes. He made those cities an example of what will happen to those who are against God. ⁷But he saved Lot from those cities. Lot, a good man, was troubled because of the filthy lives of evil people. ⁸(Lot was a good man, but because he lived with evil people every day, his good heart was hurt by the evil things he saw and heard.) ⁹So the Lord knows how to save those who serve him when troubles come. He will hold evil people and punish them, while waiting for the Judgment Day. ¹⁰That punishment is especially for those who live by doing the evil things their sinful selves want and who hate authority.

Survival Guide

JUMPSTARTING A BATTERY: POWER UP

Just as a lack of prayer and Bible study leads to a stale spiritual life, a dead battery can leave your car powerless. However, a jumpstart from a fellow motorist can get you going again. Connect one of the cable's positive clamps to the healthy battery's positive terminal. Attach one of the cable's negative clamps to the good battery's negative terminal. Connect the cable's other positive clamp to the positive terminal of the dead battery. Finally, hook the other end on a metal part of the down car, such as the engine block, which keeps sparks away from potentially dangerous battery gases.

 2:4 caves Some Greek copies read "chains."   **2:6 Sodom and Gomorrah** Two cities God destroyed because the people were so evil.

These false teachers are bold and do anything they want. They are not afraid to speak against the angels. [11]But even the angels, who are much stronger and more powerful than false teachers, do not accuse them with insults before[*] the Lord. [12]But these people speak against things they do not understand. They are like animals that act without thinking, animals born to be caught and killed. And, like animals, these false teachers will be destroyed. [13]They have caused many people to suffer, so they themselves will suffer. That is their pay for what they have done. They take pleasure in openly doing evil, so they are like dirty spots and stains among you. They delight in deceiving you while eating meals with you. [14]Every time they look at a woman they want her, and their desire for sin is never satisfied. They lead weak people into the trap of sin, and they have taught their hearts to be greedy. God will punish them! [15]These false teachers left the right road and lost their way, following the way Balaam went. Balaam was the son of Beor, who loved being paid for doing wrong. [16]But a donkey, which cannot talk, told Balaam he was sinning. It spoke with a man's voice and stopped the prophet's crazy thinking.

[17]Those false teachers are like springs without water and clouds blown by a storm. A place in the blackest darkness has been kept for them. [18]They brag with words that mean nothing. By their evil desires they lead people into the trap of sin—people who are just beginning to escape from others who live in error. [19]They promise them freedom, but they themselves are not free. They are slaves of things that will be destroyed. For people are slaves of anything that controls them. [20]They were made free from the evil in the world by knowing our Lord and Savior Jesus Christ. But if they return to evil things and those things control them, then it is worse for them than it was before. [21]Yes, it would be better for them to have never known the right way than to know it and to turn away from the holy teaching that was given to them. [22]What they did is like this true saying: "A dog goes back to what it has thrown up,"[*] and, "After a pig is washed, it goes back and rolls in the mud."

Jesus Will Come Again

3 My friends, this is the second letter I have written you to help your honest minds remember. [2]I want you to think about the words the holy prophets spoke in the past, and remember the command our Lord and Savior gave us through your apostles. [3]It is most important for you to understand what will happen in the last days. People will laugh at you. They will live doing the evil things they want to do. [4]They will say, "Jesus promised to come again. Where is he? Our fathers have died, but the world continues the way it has been since it was made." [5]But they do not want to remember what happened long ago. By the word of God heaven was made, and the earth was made from water and with water. [6]Then the world was flooded and destroyed with water. [7]And that same word of God is keeping

▶ Get Aligned
2 Peter 2:14

"THEIR DESIRE FOR SIN IS NEVER SATISFIED." Sounds like addiction, doesn't it? If you or someone you know has ever been addicted to something, then you understand the havoc it wreaks. Addictions destroy marriages, families, careers, reputations...and worst of all, they destroy individuals, reducing them to a shell of a person. There is nothing Satan loves more than watching Christians fall victim to vicious, never-ending cycles of sin.

But there is also nothing God wants more than to see his children overcome those addictions. No matter if you're addicted to porn, alcohol, gambling, drugs, or other vices, through Jesus, you can overcome it all. That may sound like a cliché, but it's true. History proves that God has an amazing habit of drawing people out of prison cells of sin and leading them into the light of liberty. As 1 John 5:4 says, "Everyone who is a child of God conquers the world. And this is the victory that conquers the world—our faith."

Your simple faith in Jesus is your ticket to victory. It will take hard work, perseverance, and discipline to escape the snares of addiction. But with the Holy Spirit guiding you toward the light, you can break free from the darkness.

Principles: SALVATION

Salvation means being set free from the power and effects of sin. So why do we need to be saved? Romans 3:23 says everyone has sinned and fallen short of God's standard, and Romans 6:23 says the payment for sin is death. The beauty of it is that God showed us his love by Christ dying for us while we were still sinners. Finally, in Romans 10:9–11, it says if we confess that Jesus is Lord and believe it in our heart, we are made right with God and will never be disappointed.

>> **2:11 before** Some Greek copies read "from." **2:22 "A dog...up."** Quotation from Proverbs 26:11.

<<TechSupport>>

HIGH-DEFINITION TELEVISION

Analog technology is becoming very out of date. New digital offerings are about to shake things up in television. Manufacturers are developing new digital television sets with wide displays capable of showing movies in their original widescreen format and more of the playing field during athletic events. The new sets provide exciting viewing options for movie and sports connoisseurs. But don't let high definition fool you; it's still just television. Every now and then, get off the sofa, turn off the television, and share an old-fashioned analog conversation with someone you love.

heaven and earth that we now have in order to be destroyed by fire. They are being kept for the Judgment Day and the destruction of all who are against God.

⁸But do not forget this one thing, dear friends: To the Lord one day is as a thousand years, and a thousand years is as one day. ⁹The Lord is not slow in doing what he promised—the way some people understand slowness. But God is being patient with you. He does not want anyone to be lost, but he wants all people to change their hearts and lives.

¹⁰But the day of the Lord will come like a thief. The skies will disappear with a loud noise. Everything in them will be destroyed by fire, and the earth and everything in it will be exposed." ¹¹In that way

>> live the life

2 Peter 3:17–18

The Principle > Grow in grace.

Practicing It > Lots of people promote different ideas about what God is like and what it means to grow in grace. It's fine to hear them out, but always keep in mind that the real answers are found in Christ and his Word.

everything will be destroyed. So what kind of people should you be? You should live holy lives and serve God, ¹²as you wait for and look forward to the coming of the day of God. When that day comes, the skies will be destroyed with fire, and everything in them will melt with heat. ¹³But God made a promise to us, and we are waiting for a new heaven and a new earth where goodness lives.

¹⁴Dear friends, since you are waiting for this to happen, do your best to be without sin and without fault. Try to be at peace with God. ¹⁵Remember that we are saved because our Lord is patient. Our dear brother Paul told you the same thing when he wrote to you with the wisdom that God gave him. ¹⁶He writes about this in all his letters. Some things in Paul's letters are hard to understand, and people who are ignorant and weak in faith explain these things falsely. They also falsely explain the other Scriptures, but they are destroying themselves by doing this.

¹⁷Dear friends, since you already know about this, be careful. Do not let those evil people lead you away by the wrong they do. Be careful so you will not fall from your strong faith. ¹⁸But grow in the grace and knowledge of our Lord and Savior Jesus Christ. Glory be to him now and forever! Amen.

>> **3:10 and ... exposed** Some Greek copies read "and everything in it will be burned up."

Notes

THE **FIRST** LETTER OF

John

AUTHOR: JOHN
DATE WRITTEN: A.D. 80–95

ONE OF THE MORE DIFFICULT FEELINGS for men to admit is doubt. Yet, if we are honest, every Christian has doubts from time to time. When those types of feelings rise in you, reach for this first letter from John. Its message will dispel your doubts and fortify your faith.

John wrote it to reassure Christians about their faith in Jesus Christ. John was an eyewitness to Jesus' life on earth, resurrection from death, and ascension into heaven. As one of the closest followers of Jesus, John had fellowship with God in the flesh and enjoyed communion with him all the days of his life. He reports to all believers that there is no denial about the incarnation of Jesus Christ, for John had stood in the empty tomb.

According to John, the truth of God's love for us should be our motivation to live for him. Any false teachers who spread doubt about this awesome love should be rejected. John reminds us that as we rest in the love of God and revel in the light of his Son, we experience the eternal life.

Ten Ways to Discover Your Purpose

1. Make a list of your life goals.
2. Pray for wisdom and insight.
3. Worship God with abandon.
4. Take a gifts discovery class.
5. Ask for opportunities to serve.
6. Cultivate an attitude of gratitude.
7. Travel on an overseas mission trip.
8. Seek more responsibility at work.
9. Study occupations that interest you.
10. Give of your time, talent, and treasure.

1 We write you now about what has always existed, which we have heard, we have seen with our own eyes, we have looked at, and we have touched with our hands. We write to you about the Word[n] that gives life. [2]He who gives life was shown to us. We saw him and can give proof about it. And now we announce to you that he has life that continues forever. He was with God the Father and was shown to us. [3]We announce to you what we have seen and heard, because we want you also to have fellowship with us. Our fellowship is with God the Father and with his Son, Jesus Christ. [4]We write this to you so we may be full of joy.[n]

God Forgives Our Sins

[5]Here is the message we have heard from Christ and now announce to you: God is light,[n] and in him there is no darkness at all. [6]So if we say we have fellowship with God, but we continue living in darkness, we are liars and do not follow the truth. [7]But if we live in the light, as God is in the light, we can share fellowship with each other. Then the blood of Jesus, God's Son, cleanses us from every sin.

[8]If we say we have no sin, we are fooling ourselves, and the truth is not in us. [9]But if we confess our sins, he will forgive our sins, because we can trust God to do what is right. He will cleanse us from all the wrongs we have done. [10]If we say we have not sinned, we make God a liar, and we do not accept God's teaching.

Jesus Is Our Helper

2 My dear children, I write this letter to you so you will not sin. But if anyone does sin, we have a helper in the presence of the Father—Jesus Christ, the One who does what is right. [2]He died in our place to take away our sins, and not only our sins but the sins of all people.

[3]We can be sure that we know God if we obey his commands. [4]Anyone who says, "I know God," but does not obey God's commands is a liar, and the truth is not in that person. [5]But if someone obeys God's teaching, then in that person God's love has truly reached its goal. This is how we can be sure we are living in God: [6]Whoever says that he lives in God must live as Jesus lived.

The Command to Love Others

[7]My dear friends, I am not writing a new command to you but an old command you have had from the beginning. It is the teaching you have already heard. [8]But also I am writing a new command to you, and you can see its truth in Jesus and in you, because the darkness is passing away, and the true light is already shining. [9]Anyone who says, "I am in the light,"[n] but hates a brother or sister, is still in the darkness. [10]Whoever loves a brother or sister lives in the light and will not cause anyone to stumble in his faith. [11]But whoever hates a brother or sister is in darkness, lives in darkness, and does not know where to go, because the darkness has made that person blind.

[12]I write to you, dear children,
because your sins are forgiven through Christ.
[13]I write to you, fathers,
because you know the One who existed from the beginning.
I write to you, young people,
because you have defeated the Evil One.
[14]I write to you, children,
because you know the Father.
I write to you, fathers,
because you know the One who existed from the beginning.
I write to you, young people,

>> live the life

1 John 1:9

The Principle > Confess your sins.

Practicing It > When it comes to confessing your sins to God, it's best to do it as the need arises. Keeping your list short helps you maintain a humble attitude and avoid straying too far from God's will for your life.

 1:1 **Word** The Greek word is "logos," meaning any kind of communication. Here, it means Christ, who was the way God told people about himself. 1:4 **so...joy** Some Greek copies read "so you may be full of joy." 1:5 **light** Here, it is used as a symbol of God's goodness or truth. 2:9 **light** Here, it is used as a symbol of God's goodness or truth.

Men of Valor
THOMAS: Doubter No More

Though this follower has been called "Doubting Thomas" for his initial reservations about Christ's resurrection, the nickname distorts the image of a strong believer. One of the original apostles, Thomas was ready to die with Jesus when he thought the Lord was facing death (John 11:16). The apostle was also present at the Last Supper, asking, "How can we know the way?" (John 14:5). True, Thomas expressed doubt that Jesus had risen, saying he wouldn't believe it until he saw the nail marks in Christ's hands and until he could put his fingers into Jesus' body. But when he did, Thomas responded, "My Lord and my God!" (John 20:28). Thomas, like Peter, eagerly acknowledged Christ's divinity.

because you are strong;
the teaching of God lives in you,
and you have defeated the Evil One.
¹⁵Do not love the world or the things in the world. If you love the world, the love of the Father is not in you. ¹⁶These are the ways of the world: wanting to please our sinful selves, wanting the sinful things we see, and being too proud of what we have. None of these come from the Father, but all of them

FACT-OIDS!

Eighteen percent of Americans consider their cell phone their primary number.

[Cellular Telecommunications & Internet Association]

come from the world. ¹⁷The world and everything that people want in it are passing away, but the person who does what God wants lives forever.

Reject the Enemies of Christ

¹⁸My dear children, these are the last days. You have heard that the enemy of Christ is coming, and now many enemies of Christ are already here. This is how we know that these are the last days. ¹⁹These enemies of Christ were in our fellowship, but they left us. They never really belonged to us; if they had been a part of us, they would have stayed with us. But they left, and this shows that none of them really belonged to us.

²⁰You have the gift⁺ that the Holy One gave you, so you all know the truth.⁺ ²¹I do not write to you because you do not know the truth but because you do know the truth. And you know that no lie comes from the truth.

²²Who is the liar? It is the person who does not accept Jesus as the Christ. This is the enemy of Christ: the person who does not accept the Father and his Son. ²³Whoever does not accept the Son does not have the Father. But whoever confesses the Son has the Father, too.

²⁴Be sure you continue to follow the teaching you heard from the beginning. If you continue to follow what you heard from the beginning, you will stay in the Son and in the Father. ²⁵And this is what the Son promised to us—life forever.

²⁶I am writing this letter about those people who are trying to lead you the wrong way. ²⁷Christ gave you a special gift that is still in you, so you do not need any other teacher. His gift teaches you about everything, and it is true, not false. So continue to live in Christ, as his gift taught you.

²⁸Yes, my dear children, live in him so that when Christ comes back, we can be without

fear and not be ashamed in his presence. ²⁹Since you know that Christ is righteous, you know that all who do right are God's children.

We Are God's Children

3 The Father has loved us so much that we are called children of God. And we really are his children. The reason the people in the world do not know us is that they have not

{ Book of the Month }

God and the Oval Office
by John McCollister

John McCollister, a historian and author of several books, takes the reader on a chronological tour of the faith of all 43 presidents. Though George Washington may be thought of as a deist, the first president added the phrase "So help me God" and kissed the Bible at his inauguration ceremony. We learn that each president approached public professions of faith differently. Lincoln, for example, claimed no denominational affiliation but is recognized as one of the most faithful presidents. More recently, Jimmy Carter and George W. Bush each made their personal faith a central element of their election campaigns, with mixed results.

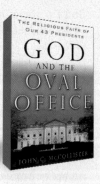

>> **2:20 gift** This might mean the Holy Spirit, or it might mean teaching or truth as in verse 24.   **2:20 you … truth** Some Greek copies read "so you know all things."

>> November

QUOTE OF THE MONTH:

"Character cannot be developed in ease and quiet. Only through experience of trial and suffering can the soul be strengthened, ambition inspired, and success achieved."
—Helen Keller

1
Pray for adoptive families.

2

3

4
Build a fire and read a classic.

5

6

7
Pray for a person of influence: Today is evangelist **Billy Graham's** birthday.

8
Visit the library and check out a book.

9

10

11
Celebrate **Veterans' Day** by praying for the nation's veterans.

12

13

14
Sign up to donate your organs.

15

16

17
Get winter clothes out of storage.

18
Plan an autumn hike with friends.

19
Pray for a person of influence: Today is businessman **Ted Turner's** birthday.

20

21

22
President **John F. Kennedy** was assassinated in Dallas on this day in 1963.

23
Give thanks to God for your blessings.

24

25
Pray for a person of influence: Today is singer **Amy Grant's** birthday.

26
Check the air in your car tires.

27

28
Memorize Romans 10:17.

29
Go get the Christmas tree.

30
Pray for a person of influence: Today is entertainer **Dick Clark's** birthday.

People Skills

Communicating Needs

All of us would like our friends to be so attuned to us that they would know our moods and our needs instinctively. That rarely happens and never happens with any consistency. No one will ever be able to meet your needs if they don't know what your needs are. By voicing your needs, you risk being disappointed if they say "no," but if you are expecting your friends to read your mind and satisfy your needs without your help, you are going to be disappointed without your friends ever knowing why. Tell your friends what you want and what you need. If you don't, you'll be stuck in infantile relationships that can never grow to maturity.

known him. ²Dear friends, now we are children of God, and we have not yet been shown what we will be in the future. But we know that when Christ comes again, we will be like him, because we will see him as he really is. ³Christ is pure, and all who have this hope in Christ keep themselves pure like Christ.

⁴The person who sins breaks God's law. Yes, sin is living against God's law. ⁵You know that Christ came to take away sins and that there is no sin in Christ. ⁶So anyone who lives in Christ does not go on sinning. Anyone who goes on sinning has never really understood Christ and has never known him.

⁷Dear children, do not let anyone lead you the wrong way. Christ is righteous. So to be like Christ a person must do what is right. ⁸The devil has been sinning since the beginning, so anyone who continues to sin belongs to the devil. The Son of God came for this purpose: to destroy the devil's work.

⁹Those who are God's children do not continue sinning, because the new life from God remains in them. They are not able to go on sinning, because they have become children of God. ¹⁰So we can see who God's children are and who the devil's children are: Those who do not do what is right are not God's children, and those who do not love their brothers and sisters are not God's children.

We Must Love Each Other

¹¹This is the teaching you have heard from the beginning: We must love each other. ¹²Do not be like Cain who belonged to the Evil One and killed his brother. And why did he kill him? Because the things Cain did were evil, and the things his brother did were good.

¹³Brothers and sisters, do not be surprised when the people of the world hate you. ¹⁴We know we have left death and have come into life because we love each other. Whoever does not love is still dead. ¹⁵Everyone who hates a brother or sister is a murderer," and you know that no murderers have eternal life in them. ¹⁶This is how we know what real love is: Jesus gave his life for us. So we should give our lives for our brothers and sisters. ¹⁷Suppose someone has enough to live and sees a brother or sister in need, but does not help. Then God's love is not living in that person. ¹⁸My children, we should love people not only with words and talk, but by our actions and true caring.

¹⁹⁻²⁰This is the way we know that we belong

⊙ Sexcess:
ESTABLISHING BOUNDARIES

With the "anything goes" mentality that has become so prevalent today, couples may be tempted to push the envelope in the area of sexuality. But it is the blessed couple that establishes boundaries for its sex life based on mutually agreed upon terms. Suffice it to say that engaging in pornographic stimulation, whether through print or broadcast media, is never an acceptable activity, as it encourages couples to lust after others. Of course, sex involving others outside of the marriage is a strictly forbidden activity. Other than that, each partner needs to communicate his or her own likes and dislikes when it comes to types of sex, sexual positions, and protection.

 3:15 Everyone ... murderer If one person hates a brother or sister, then in the heart that person has killed that brother or sister. Jesus taught about this sin to his followers (Matthew 5:21–26).

TheFinalScore >>

WIMBLEDON: Royal Witnesses

THE WORLD'S PREMIER TENNIS CHAMPIONSHIP, Wimbledon is the only Grand Slam event still played on grass. In 1877, few guessed the original Lawn Tennis Championships would one day attract 450,000 people in attendance and a television audience in the millions.

This two-week event maintains an equally significant air of prestige. The sponsoring All England Lawn & Croquet Club has only 375 full members, plus 100 temporary members and honorary members, such as past Wimbledon singles champions.

Royalty has been associated with Wimbledon for more than a century, stretching back to an 1895 appearance by Crown Princess Stephanie and Prince Batthyány-Strattman of Austria. British royalty followed in 1907 when the Prince of Wales and Princess Mary attended.

The tradition continues, with the club's royal box used to entertain guests from the British royal family. In a concession to modern informality, players now only need to bow or curtsy if the Queen of England or Prince of Wales makes an appearance.

As impressive as Wimbledon may sound, Hebrews 12:1 talks about believers being surrounded by a group of special people whose lives show what faith means. The preceding chapter lists numerous examples of biblical heroes, or royal saints, who performed great feats as champions of the faith and are cheering us on to win the match of our lives.

❝[saints who] performed great feats as champions of the faith and are cheering us on to win the match of our lives.❞

<<TechSupport>>

FREE E-MAIL

Why pay for e-mail when you don't have to? If you can get online, you can get e-mail. It's easy to sign up, and the features of the services are similar. Visit Hotmail.com or Yahoo.com to sign up. Google's Gmail, with its huge storage capacity, is by invitation only, so try asking a techie friend for an invite. Keep in mind that it doesn't hurt to have multiple e-mail accounts for the times that your primary service is out of commission, especially if you operate your own business. You'll never regret being prepared!

to the way of truth. When our hearts make us feel guilty, we can still have peace before God. God is greater than our hearts, and he knows everything. ²¹My dear friends, if our hearts do not make us feel guilty, we can come without fear into God's presence. ²²And God gives us what we ask for because we obey God's commands and do what pleases him. ²³This is what God commands: that we

▶Get Aligned

1 John 3:19–20

WHEN IS LIFE AT ITS BEST? For virtually all of us, it's when we feel good. We avoid feeling bad. When we're feeling lonely, we fix it by interacting with a group of people. When we feel blue, we watch a comedy. Much of what we do is based on our emotions. If we were to take a long, hard look at our daily lives, most of us would discover that we're often ruled by our feelings.

That's why it's so refreshing to know that God will always be greater than our emotions. He will

not waver as we do when we're moody. His truth is constant, as is his character. Even when our hearts tell us we are far from God because of our own sin, we can hold fast to his truth that says he will never leave us or forsake us.

When we don't feel his love, we can return to his Word, which says nothing can separate us from the love of Christ. May God's never-changing character challenge us to become more like him, depending not on our emotions but on his eternal truth.

Change >> YourWORLD

THE SALVATION ARMY

You've seen the red kettles and the bell ringers during the Christmas holidays. For many people, it's practically all they know about the Salvation Army, yet the organization is about much more. Volunteers from the Salvation Army operate facilities to collect used furniture and clothing. When an emergency or national disaster happens, the Salvation Army is present to provide food, clothing, and spiritual encouragement. William Booth founded the movement in 1865, and today the group works with a variety of denominations to motivate them to embrace the salvation provided to them in Christ. The Salvation Army works in more than one hundred countries in 175 languages.

To change your world, visit www.salvationarmy.org.

believe in his Son, Jesus Christ, and that we love each other, just as he commanded. ²⁴The people who obey God's commands live in God, and God lives in them. We know that God lives in us because of the Spirit God gave us.

Warning Against False Teachers

4 My dear friends, many false prophets have gone out into the world. So do not believe every spirit, but test the spirits to see if they are from God. ²This is how you can know God's Spirit: Every spirit who confesses that Jesus Christ came to earth as a human is from God. ³And every spirit who refuses to say this about Jesus is not from God. It is the spirit of the enemy of Christ, which you have heard is coming, and now he is already in the world.

⁴My dear children, you belong to God and have defeated them; because God's Spirit, who is in you, is greater than the devil, who is

FOR Men Only

THOUGHTFULNESS

THOUGHTFULNESS Whereas you might assume that thoughtfulness is a common attribute, it is actually in short supply in most relationships. Although it may be convenient to take your loved ones for granted and to act more thoughtful toward others, it is costly. Making your family and friends settle for leftovers is a menu for disaster. Thoughtfulness may be demonstrated in different ways, but it is most effective when it speaks to a person's love language. For example, if your spouse's love language is acts of service, then helping her with domestic chores like folding the laundry will speak volumes to her about the depth of your love.

LISTEN

in the world. [5]And they belong to the world, so what they say is from the world, and the world listens to them. [6]But we belong to God, and those who know God listen to us. But those who are not from God do not listen to us. That is how we know the Spirit that is true and the spirit that is false.

Love Comes from God

[7]Dear friends, we should love each other, because love comes from God. Everyone who loves has become God's child and knows God. [8]Whoever does not love does not know God, because God is love. [9]This is how God showed his love to us: He sent his one and only Son into the world so that we could have life through him. [10]This is what real love is: It is not our love for God; it is God's love for us. He sent his Son to die in our place to take away our sins.

[11]Dear friends, if God loved us that much we also should love each other. [12]No one has ever seen God, but if we love each other, God lives in us, and his love is made perfect in us.

[13]We know that we live in God and he lives in us, because he gave us his Spirit. [14]We have seen and can testify that the Father sent his Son to be the Savior of the world. [15]Whoever confesses that Jesus is the Son of God has God living inside, and that person lives in God. [16]And so we know the love that God has for us, and we trust that love.

God is love. Those who live in love live in God, and God lives in them. [17]This is how love is made perfect in us: that we can be without fear on the day God judges us, because in this world we are like him. [18]Where God's love is, there is no fear, because God's perfect love drives out fear. It is punishment that makes a person fear, so love is not made perfect in the person who fears.

[19]We love because God first loved us. [20]If people say, "I love God," but hate their brothers or sisters, they are liars. Those who do not love their brothers and sisters, whom they have seen, cannot love God, whom they have never seen. [21]And God gave us this command: Those who love God must also love their brothers and sisters.

➡ The Bottom Line

Extended Warranties: Considering the Downside

BUY A CAR, REFRIGERATOR, LAWNMOWER, OR DOZENS OF OTHER DEVICES, AND YOU WILL BE OFFERED AN EXTENDED WARRANTY. Some service contracts cost almost as much as the purchase, which isn't logical since you can just buy another. The Federal Citizen Information Center warns that extended warranties are rarely worth what you pay for them. Basically, you are insuring against repair expenses. But if nothing breaks down, you don't get a refund. Better to set aside money earmarked for emergencies. This takes discipline, but 2 Timothy 1:7 says God gives us a spirit of self-control.

THINK ABOUT IT 1 John 5:14–15

A STORY IS TOLD ABOUT SATAN calling a number of his demons together into a meeting. He says, "How can we trick the Christians into being discouraged about God?" One demon after another steps forward with a suggestion, but Satan dismisses each idea as ineffective. Finally Satan comes up with an idea of his own: "I'll help convince them their prayers are not heard."

Anyone who believes that story hasn't read the encouragement and truth from this passage about the reality of answered prayer. As John wrote, "If we ask God for anything that agrees with what he wants, he hears us. If we know he hears us every time we ask him, we know we have what we ask from him."

Notice the conditional phrase in this promise: we have to ask God for something that agrees with his desires for us. When we pray and ask God for something that coincides with his will for us, then God hears and answers. It is a solid reassurance for Christians to pray according to God's will.

Faith in the Son of God

5 Everyone who believes that Jesus is the Christ is God's child, and whoever loves the Father also loves the Father's children. ²This is how we know we love God's children: when we love God and obey his commands. ³Loving God means obeying his commands. And God's commands are not too hard for us, ⁴because everyone who is a child of God conquers the world. And this is the victory that conquers the world—our faith. ⁵So the one who conquers the world is the person who believes that Jesus is the Son of God.

⁶Jesus Christ is the One who came by water" and blood." He did not come by water only, but by water and blood. And the Spirit says that this is true, because the Spirit is the truth. ⁷So there are three witnesses:" ⁸the Spirit, the water, and the blood; and these three witnesses agree. ⁹We believe people when they say something is true. But what God says is more important, and he has told us the truth about his own Son. ¹⁰Anyone who believes in the Son of God has the truth that God told us. Anyone who does not believe makes God a liar, because that person does not believe what God told us about his Son. ¹¹This is what God told us: God has given us eternal life, and this life is in his Son. ¹²Whoever has the Son has life, but whoever does not have the Son of God does not have life.

We Have Eternal Life Now

¹³I write this letter to you who believe in the Son of God so you will know you have eternal life. ¹⁴And this is the boldness we have in God's presence: that if we ask God for anything that agrees with what he wants, he hears us. ¹⁵If we know he hears us every time we ask him, we know we have what we ask from him.

¹⁶If anyone sees a brother or sister sinning (sin that does not lead to eternal death), that person should pray, and God will give the sinner life. I am talking about people whose sin does not lead to eternal death. There is sin that leads to death. I do not mean that a person should pray about that sin. ¹⁷Doing wrong is always sin, but there is sin that does not lead to eternal death.

¹⁸We know that those who are God's children do not continue to sin. The Son of God keeps them safe, and the Evil One cannot touch them. ¹⁹We know that we belong to God, but the Evil One controls the whole world. ²⁰We also know that the Son of God has come and has given us understanding so that we can know the True One. And our lives are in the True One and in his Son, Jesus Christ. He is the true God and the eternal life.

²¹So, dear children, keep yourselves away from false gods.

>> **5:6 water** This probably means the water of Jesus' baptism. **5:6 blood** This probably means the blood of Jesus' death. **5:7–8 So . . . witnesses** A few very late Greek copies and the Latin Vulgate continue, "in heaven: the Father, the Word, and the Holy Spirit, and these three witnesses agree. ⁸And there are three witnesses on earth:"

Notes

THE SECOND LETTER OF
John

AUTHOR: JOHN
DATE WRITTEN: A.D. 80–95

TWO WORDS OFTEN APPEAR IN SONGS or greeting cards: "truth" and "love." Yet, the world seldom practices these qualities. In this second letter to the churches, John focuses on these two basic elements of following Jesus Christ. As he reminds his readers, believers need to obey God's truth consistently. John exhorts followers of Jesus to live the truth. It must never be twisted or tweaked to suit our own needs.

A constant theme from this beloved follower of Christ is a focus on that other core element of Christianity—love. Besides living the truth, we are commanded to love God and each other. Truth and love must be connected hand in hand according to John. You can't love at the expense of truth, and you can't neglect the truth for the cause of love. John challenges believers to pursue these two basic characteristics of the faith with a singular focus.

This short letter from John ends by warning believers not even to show hospitality to false teachers. Whereas it may sound harsh and even cruel, John's warning points out serious consequences for those teachers who lead believers away from the truth. As he shows, such teachers harm the people who follow them because they lead them away from eternity with God.

¹From the Elder.ᵇ

To the chosen ladyᵇ and her children:

I love all of you in the truth,ᵇ and all those who know the truth love you. ²We love you because of the truth that lives in us and will be with us forever.

³Grace, mercy, and peace from God the Father and his Son, Jesus Christ, will be with us in truth and love.

⁴I was very happy to learn that some of your children are following the way of truth, as the Father commanded us. ⁵And now, dear lady, this is not a new command but is the same command we have had from the beginning. I ask you that we all love each other. ⁶And love means living the way God commanded us to live. As you have heard from the beginning, his command is this: Live a life of love.

⁷Many false teachers are in the world now who do not confess that Jesus Christ came to earth as a human. Anyone who does not confess this is a false teacher and an enemy of Christ. ⁸Be careful yourselves that you do not lose everything youᵇ have worked for, but that you receive your full reward.

⁹Anyone who goes beyond Christ's teaching and does not continue to follow only his teaching does not have God. But whoever continues to follow the teaching of Christ has both the Father and

>> live the life

2 John 8–9

The Principle > Evaluate your life.

Practicing It > Every so often, take on the role of observer and give yourself a whole-life evaluation. Examine your life at work, at home, at church, and when alone. Determine where you are living out God's truth and what needs to change in your life.

▶Get Aligned

2 John 1–2

WITHIN THE FIRST TWO VERSES OF HIS LETTER, JOHN USES THE WORD *TRUTH* THREE TIMES. It's the first thing he mentions, even before his greeting. Why was he so obsessed with the word? Because his readers were fighting the same battle that rages today.

Truth is supposedly relative in our world. We operate on a "whatever works for you" system that deems any standard of belief valid if it makes you happy, because happiness is the ultimate goal according to many people today.

As Christians, we know better than to base our entire existence on fleeting emotions. We know truth is not relative. Truth is based on God's standards because God *is* truth. And his truth does not shift according to what's trendy and politically correct. This is the truth that resides in us the moment we commit our lives to Jesus Christ. And it's the reason John was so emphatic in encouraging his readers to continue to follow the way of the truth inside them, despite what the world around them said. We, too, can be strengthened in knowing that what we base our beliefs on is not here today and gone tomorrow, for God is forever the truth.

the Son. ¹⁰If someone comes to you and does not bring this teaching, do not welcome or accept that person into your house. ¹¹If you welcome such a person, you share in the evil work.

¹²I have many things to write to you, but I do not want to use paper and ink. Instead, I hope to come to you and talk face to face so we can be full of joy. ¹³The children of your chosen sisterᵇ greet you.

1 Elder "Elder" means an older person. It can also mean a special leader in the church (as in Titus 1:5). 1 lady This might mean a woman, or in this letter it might mean a church. If it is a church, then "her children" would be the people of the church. 1 truth The truth or "Good News" about Jesus Christ that joins all believers together. 8 you Some Greek copies read "we." 13 sister Sister of the "lady" in verse 1. This might be another woman or another church.

359

THE **THIRD** LETTER OF John

AUTHOR: JOHN
DATE WRITTEN: A.D. 80–95

PERHAPS A RELATIVE HAS PAID AN
unannounced visit, derailing your plans to play golf.
Or maybe you've learned that a neighbor has experienced
a death in the family and could use some extra meals. No
matter when it is called for in life, hospitality typically
costs something in terms of our time or expense.

How we react in such situations really tests our true
values and shows whether we care about people or things
in our life. John writes this third letter to a prominent
Christian named Gaius. He affirms Gaius for his Christian lifestyle and commends his hospitality to others.
Then John contrasts this loving behavior from Gaius to
the church leader Diotrephes, who said he followed Christ but whose life didn't reflect Christlike values.

This personal letter provides an opportunity for us to evaluate what we are em-
phasizing in our daily life. As you read it, think about which man's actions are more
like your own. Is your life modeled after Gaius, who generously gave to others
around him? Or are you like Diotrephes, who selfishly looked out for himself and
his possessions?

¹From the Elder."

To my dear friend Gaius, whom I love in the truth:"

²My dear friend, I know your soul is doing fine, and I pray that you are doing well in every way and that your health is good. ³I was very happy when some brothers and sisters came and told me about the truth in your life and how you are following the way of truth. ⁴Nothing gives me greater joy than to hear that my children are following the way of truth.

⁵My dear friend, it is good that you help the brothers and sisters, even those you do not know. ⁶They told the church about your love. Please help them to continue their trip in a way worthy of God. ⁷They started out in service to Christ, and they have been accepting nothing from nonbelievers. ⁸So we should help such people; when we do, we share in their work for the truth.

⁹I wrote something to the church, but Diotrephes, who loves to be their leader, will not listen to us. ¹⁰So if I come, I will talk about what Diotrephes is doing, about how he lies and says evil things about us. But more than that, he refuses to accept the other brothers and sisters; he even stops those who do want to accept them and puts them out of the church.

¹¹My dear friend, do not follow what is bad; follow what is good. The

>> live the life

3 John 8

The Principle > Encourage godly leaders.

Practicing It > Identify the key, godly men who have most profoundly impacted your life. Make a list, then next to each name write one or two ways you can begin to support and encourage those men in the work they do for others.

▶◯Get Aligned

3 John 4

ON HIS FIRST TRIP TO THE PLATE, YOUR SON HITS A HOME RUN. Instead of taking one of her friends, your teenage daughter asks if you'll accompany her to her awards banquet. Your baby's first word is "Dada," and now he can't stop saying it, much to your delight. These are the things that make a father's heart swell with joy. There is little that can compare to the pride a dad has in watching his children excel.

Did you know God feels the same way about watching your journey through life? Nothing gives him greater joy than seeing you walk in his truth, trusting him at every turn of the way, and leaning on him when you cannot travel any farther. Your heavenly Father is a proud father who delights in his children.

Having received the Father's delight, you can impress the same love on your own children. Let them know how proud you are of them. Express your unconditional love for them in both words and action. As they bless you, be reminded of how God feels when you walk in his ways.

one who does good belongs to God. But the one who does evil has never known God.

¹²Everyone says good things about Demetrius, and the truth agrees with what they say. We also speak well of him, and you know what we say is true.

¹³I have many things I want to write you, but I do not want to use pen and ink. ¹⁴I hope to see you soon and talk face to face. ¹⁵Peace to you. The friends here greet you. Please greet each friend there by name.

>> **1 Elder** "Elder" means an older person. It can also mean a special leader in the church (as in Titus 1:5). **1 truth** The truth or "Good News" about Jesus Christ that joins all believers together.

THE **LETTER** OF
Jude

AUTHOR: JUDE
DATE WRITTEN: UNKNOWN

MAYBE YOU'VE SEEN THIS RECENT

commercial on television: A beautiful woman walks into the room and a guy casually leans against the wall trying to look nonchalant. As the man's hand touches the wall, it suddenly crumbles and he falls through it. The termites had eaten through the wall and weakened it. While no one could see it on the surface, the termites had attacked the wall from inside.

Jude, the brother of Jesus and James, writes this short letter to encourage the church to constantly monitor its spiritual health. He warns that false teachers will infiltrate the church, and Christians will face opposition from the culture. Jude encourages believers to be in constant vigilance about their faith and to oppose such falsehoods. He warns that those leaders who guide people away from faith in Christ will be punished in eternity.

This letter also includes a stern warning about believers growing cold in their faith toward Christ. Jude reminds readers that Christians who don't know the truth of the Scriptures will be open to such deception. He closes by exhorting believers to follow the truth that the apostles preached and that was recorded as God's teaching.

¹From Jude, a servant of Jesus Christ and a brother of James.

To all who have been called by God. God the Father loves you, and you have been kept safe in Jesus Christ:

²Mercy, peace, and love be yours richly.

God Will Punish Sinners

³Dear friends, I wanted very much to write you about the salvation we all share. But I felt the need to write you about something else: I want to encourage you to fight hard for the faith that was given the holy people of God once and for all time. ⁴Some people have secretly entered your group. Long ago the prophets wrote about these people who will be judged guilty. They are against God and have changed the grace of our God into a reason for sexual sin. They also refuse to accept Jesus Christ, our only Master and Lord.

⁵I want to remind you of some things you already know: Remember that the Lord" saved his people by bringing them out of the land of Egypt. But later he destroyed all those who did not believe. ⁶And remember the angels who did not keep their place of power but left their proper home. The Lord has kept these angels in darkness, bound with everlasting chains, to be judged on the great day. ⁷Also remember the cities of Sodom and Gomorrah" and the other towns around them. In the same way they were full of sexual sin and people who desired sexual relations that God does not allow. They suffer the punishment of eternal fire, as an example for all to see.

⁸It is the same with these people who have entered your group. They are guided by dreams and make themselves filthy with sin. They reject God's authority and speak against the angels. ⁹Not even the archangel" Michael, when he argued with the devil about who would have the body of Moses, dared to judge the devil guilty. Instead, he said, "The Lord punish you." ¹⁰But these people speak against things they do not understand. And what they do know, by feeling, as dumb animals know things, are the very things that destroy them. ¹¹It will be terrible for them. They have followed the way of Cain, and for money they have given themselves to doing the wrong

that Balaam did. They have fought against God as Korah did, and like Korah, they surely will be destroyed. ¹²They are like dirty spots in your special Christian meals you share. They eat with you and have no fear, caring only for themselves. They are clouds without rain, which the wind blows around. They are autumn trees without fruit that are pulled out of the ground. So they are twice dead. ¹³They are like wild waves of the sea, tossing up their own shameful actions like foam. They are like stars that wander in the sky. A place in the blackest darkness has been kept for them forever.

¹⁴Enoch, the seventh descendant from Adam, said about these people: "Look, the Lord is coming with many thousands of his holy angels to ¹⁵judge every person. He is coming to punish all who are against God for all the evil they have done against him. And he will punish the sinners who are against God for all the evil they have said against him."

¹⁶These people complain and blame others, doing the evil things they want to do. They brag about themselves, and they flatter others to get what they want.

THINK ABOUT IT Jude 25

TAKE A FEW MOMENTS TO CONSIDER your past. Focus on a particular part of your past where you have a positive feeling. Perhaps your family experienced a special time together during a vacation one summer. Possibly there is a shining moment from your career that holds a special place in your life experiences.

Such memories from the past are important, for they serve as touchstones in our lives. Now, recall a particularly low period in your past. Maybe you failed to tell a loved one how much she meant to you before she died. During such low points in your life, whether you knew it or not, Jesus was present. Whether it's a highlight or a low point, Jesus has authority over all of time—past, present, and future.

Jude, the brother of Jesus, calls attention to the fact that Jesus Christ has authority not only over the past, but all of time: "He is the only God, the One who saves us. To him be glory, greatness, power, and authority through Jesus Christ our Lord for all time past, now, and forever."

A Warning and Things to Do

¹⁷Dear friends, remember what the apostles of our Lord Jesus Christ said before. ¹⁸They said to you, "In the last times there will be people who laugh about God, following their own evil desires which are against God." ¹⁹These are the people who divide you, people whose thoughts are only of this world, who do not have the Spirit.

²⁰But dear friends, use your most holy faith to build yourselves up, praying in the Holy Spirit. ²¹Keep yourselves in God's love as you wait for the Lord Jesus Christ with his mercy to give you life forever.

²²Show mercy to some people who have doubts. ²³Take others out of the fire, and save them. Show mercy mixed with fear to others, hating even their clothes which are dirty from sin.

Praise God

²⁴God is strong and can help you not to fall. He can bring you before his glory without any wrong in you and can give you great joy. ²⁵He is the only God, the One who saves us. To him be glory, greatness, power, and authority through Jesus Christ our Lord for all time past, now, and forever. Amen.

---

5 the Lord Some Greek copies read "Jesus."   **7 Sodom and Gomorrah** Two cities God destroyed because they were so evil.   **9 archangel** The leader among God's angels or messengers.

THE
Revelation
OF JESUS CHRIST

AUTHOR: JOHN
DATE WRITTEN: A.D. 90–96

THE STORY IS RIVETING FROM THE
opening scene. The pages of the text fly past in a blur of action and dialogue. While caught up in the drama, it is only natural for readers to wonder about the ending. As with all other books, the Bible has an ending, and the Book of Revelation is it.

The writer of Revelation is John, who was nearing the end of his life in exile on the island of Patmos when he suddenly received a vision from God, which he recorded in this letter to the church. In the early part of Revelation, John writes to seven churches that are in different spiritual conditions concerning their relationship with Christ. It clearly shows the various threats to our faith and our need to guard against them.

The final part of the book provides a revelation to the church of what it will be like to worship God in heaven and of God's judgment on humankind and Satan. The book ends on a hopeful note as John sees the final destination for believers is heaven. For any earthly trial, we are reminded to compare the temporal nature of it to a lifetime in the presence of God.

John Tells About This Book

1 This is the revelation" of Jesus Christ, which God gave to him, to show his servants what must soon happen. And Jesus sent his angel to show it to his servant John, ²who has told everything he has seen. It is the word of God; it is the message from Jesus Christ. ³Blessed is the one who reads the words of God's message, and blessed are the people who hear this message and do what is written in it. The time is near when all of this will happen.

Jesus' Message to the Churches

⁴From John.

To the seven churches in Asia:

Grace and peace to you from the One who is and was and is coming, and from the seven spirits before his throne, ⁵and from Jesus Christ. Jesus is the faithful witness, the first among those raised from the dead. He is the ruler of the kings of the earth.

He is the One who loves us, who made us free from our sins with the blood of his death. ⁶He made us to be a kingdom of priests who serve God his Father. To Jesus Christ be glory and power forever and ever! Amen.

⁷Look, Jesus is coming with the clouds, and everyone will see him, even those who stabbed him. And all peoples of the earth will cry loudly because of him. Yes, this will happen! Amen.

⁸The Lord God says, "I am the Alpha and the Omega." I am the One who is and was and is coming. I am the Almighty."

⁹I, John, am your brother. All of us share with Christ in suffering, in the kingdom, and in patience to continue. I was on the island of Patmos," because I had preached the word of God and the message about Jesus. ¹⁰On the Lord's day I was in the Spirit, and I heard a loud voice behind me that sounded like a trumpet. ¹¹The voice said, "Write what you see in a book and send it to the seven churches: to

Change >> Your WORLD

UNION MISSION MINISTRIES

When they don't know where else to go for help, many needy people have turned to Union Mission Ministries, whose simple mission is "helping hurting people in Jesus' name." Whether people enroll in the Foundations Discipleship Ministries program or the Family Services Ministries or shop in the Union Mission Thrift Store, the Union Mission has been ready, willing, and able to lend a helping hand since 1911. The organization receives no federal, state, or local support of any type, but, instead, depends on donations and volunteers to carry on the work of the ministry.

To change your world, visit www.unionmission.com.

<< TechSupport >>

HYBRID CARS

Auto manufacturers are beginning to introduce hybrid models that may reduce pollution and consumption of fossil fuel. Hybrid engines are battery powered, but use fuel to accelerate. In general, hybrids are surprisingly fuel-efficient cars that operate similarly to their gas-only counterparts. The hybrid typically gains power from braking, as well as from driving, when a motor attached to the wheel engages to charge the battery. So it is in life: we gain strength when we pause and refresh our spirits.

Ephesus, Smyrna, Pergamum, Thyatira, Sardis, Philadelphia, and Laodicea."

¹²I turned to see who was talking to me. When I turned, I saw seven golden lampstands ¹³and someone among the lampstands who was "like a Son of Man."" He was dressed in a long robe and had a gold band around his chest. ¹⁴His head and hair were white like wool, as white as snow, and his eyes were like flames of fire. ¹⁵His feet were like bronze that glows hot in a furnace, and his voice was like the noise of flooding water. ¹⁶He held seven stars in his right hand, and a sharp double-edged sword came out of his mouth. He looked like the sun shining at its brightest time.

¹⁷When I saw him, I fell down at his feet like a dead man. He put his right hand on me and said, "Do not be afraid. I am the First and the Last. ¹⁸I am the One who lives; I was dead, but look, I am alive forever and ever! And I hold the keys to death and to the place of the dead. ¹⁹So write the things you see, what is now and what will happen later. ²⁰Here is the secret of the seven stars that you saw in my right hand

>> 1:1 **revelation** Making known truth that has been hidden.   1:8 **Alpha and the Omega** The first and last letters of the Greek alphabet. This means "the beginning and the end."   1:9 **Patmos** A small island in the Aegean Sea, near the coast of Asia Minor (modern Turkey).   1:13 "**like ... Man**" "Son of Man" is a name Jesus called himself.

365

and the seven golden lampstands: The seven lampstands are the seven churches, and the seven stars are the angels of the seven churches.

To the Church in Ephesus

2 "Write this to the angel of the church in Ephesus:

"The One who holds the seven stars in his right hand and walks among the seven golden lampstands says this: ²I know what you do, how you work hard and never give up. I know you do not put up with the false teachings of evil people. You have tested those who say they are apostles but really are not, and you found they are liars. ³You have patience and have suffered troubles for my name and have not given up.

⁴"But I have this against you: You have left the love you had in the beginning. ⁵So remember where you were before you fell. Change your hearts and do what you did at first. If you do not change, I will come to you and will take away your lampstand from its place. ⁶But there is something you do that is right: You hate what the Nicolaitans" do, as much as I.

⁷"Every person who has ears should listen to what the Spirit says to the churches. To those who win the victory I will give the right to eat the fruit from the tree of life, which is in the garden of God.

To the Church in Smyrna

⁸"Write this to the angel of the church in Smyrna:

"The One who is the First and the Last, who died and came to life again, says this: ⁹I know your troubles and that you are poor, but really you are rich! I know the bad things some people say about you. They say they are Jews, but they are not true Jews. They are a synagogue that belongs to Satan. ¹⁰Do not be afraid of what you are about to suffer. I tell you, the devil will put some of you in prison to test you, and you will suffer for ten days. But be faithful, even if you have to die, and I will give you the crown of life.

¹¹"Everyone who has ears should listen to what the Spirit says to the churches. Those who win the victory will not be hurt by the second death.

To the Church in Pergamum

¹²"Write this to the angel of the church in Pergamum:

"The One who has the sharp, double-edged sword says this: ¹³I know where you live. It is where Satan has his throne. But you are true to me. You did not refuse to tell about your faith in me even during the time of Antipas, my faithful witness who was killed in your city, where Satan lives.

¹⁴"But I have a few things against you: You have some there who follow the teaching of Balaam. He taught Balak how to cause the people of Israel to sin by eating food offered to idols and by taking part in sexual sins. ¹⁵You also have some who follow the teaching of the Nicolaitans." ¹⁶So change your hearts and lives. If you do not, I will come to you quickly and fight against them with the sword that comes out of my mouth.

¹⁷"Everyone who has ears should listen to what the Spirit says to the churches.

"I will give some of the hidden manna to everyone who wins the victory. I will also give to each one who wins the victory a white stone with a new name written on it. No one knows this new name except the one who receives it.

To the Church in Thyatira

¹⁸"Write this to the angel of the church in Thyatira:

"The Son of God, who has eyes that blaze like fire and feet like shining bronze, says this: ¹⁹I know what you do. I know about your love, your faith, your service, and your patience. I know that you are doing more now than you did at first.

²⁰"But I have this against you: You let that woman Jezebel spread false teachings. She says she is a prophetess, but by her teaching she

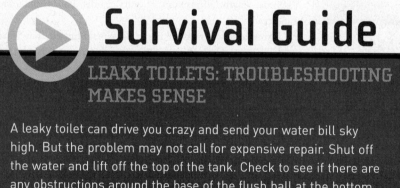

▶ Survival Guide

LEAKY TOILETS: TROUBLESHOOTING MAKES SENSE

A leaky toilet can drive you crazy and send your water bill sky high. But the problem may not call for expensive repair. Shut off the water and lift off the top of the tank. Check to see if there are any obstructions around the base of the flush ball at the bottom of the tank or if something is sticking in the chain. You might also try slightly bending the arm that holds the float ball to lower the water level flushing the tank. As it reminds us in Matthew 11:30, life's solutions aren't always difficult.

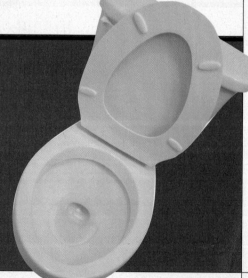

 2:6, 15 Nicolaitans This is the name of a religious group that followed false beliefs and ideas.

FOR Men Only

FRIENDSHIP The foundation of any successful relationship is friendship. Strong friendship is built in countless ways, but one of the primary means is by developing a genuine like for each other by getting to know one another on more than a superficial level. When you hear that couples have grown apart, it usually means that the friendship foundation was on shaky ground. For a marriage to weather the storms of life, a couple needs to lay the necessary groundwork by strengthening their friendship. Whether or not kids are part of the picture, one day you'll be left with each other, and your friendship will help keep the sparks alive.

LISTEN

leads my people to take part in sexual sins and to eat food that is offered to idols. ²¹I have given her time to change her heart and turn away from her sin, but she does not want to change. ²²So I will throw her on a bed of suffering. And all those who take part in adultery with her will suffer greatly if they do not turn away from the wrongs she does. ²³I will also kill her followers. Then all the churches will know I am the One who searches hearts and minds, and I will repay each of you for what you have done.

²⁴"But others of you in Thyatira have not followed her teaching and have not learned what some call Satan's deep secrets. I say to you that I will not put any other load on you. ²⁵Only continue in your loyalty until I come.

²⁶"I will give power over the nations to everyone who wins the victory and continues to be obedient to me until the end.

²⁷'You will rule over them with an iron rod,
   as when pottery is broken into pieces.' *Psalm 2:9*
²⁸This is the same power I received from my Father. I will also give him the morning star. ²⁹Everyone who has ears should listen to what the Spirit says to the churches.

To the Church in Sardis

3 "Write this to the angel of the church in Sardis:
"The One who has the seven spirits and the seven stars says this: I know what you do. People say that you are alive, but really you are dead. ²Wake up! Strengthen what you have left before it dies completely. I have found that what you are doing is less than what my God wants. ³So do not forget what you have received and heard. Obey it, and change your hearts and lives. So you must wake up, or I will come like a thief, and you will not know when I will come to you. ⁴But you have a few there in Sardis who have kept their clothes unstained, so they will walk with me and will wear white clothes, because they are worthy. ⁵Those who win the victory will be dressed in white clothes like them. And I will not erase their names from the book of life, but I will say they belong to me before my Father and before his angels. ⁶Everyone

→ The Bottom Line

Wills: Planning Ahead

THE MAJORITY OF AMERICANS DIE WITHOUT LEAVING A WILL SPECIFYING HOW TO DISTRIBUTE THE PROCEEDS OF THEIR ESTATE. That means the state steps in and divides your assets—and you may not like its decisions. Don't procrastinate, thinking you don't own that much, so it doesn't really matter. As Hebrews 9:27 states, someday you will die. Failing to prepare a will could touch off squabbles over your possessions, sowing the seeds of family division. Someone other than who you would choose may wind up rearing your children. Being a good manager of God's provisions includes wise oversight of them after your death.

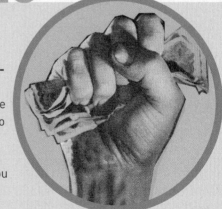

People Skills

Restoring Relationships

Family relationships can be tough. There's a lot of history between you, your siblings, and your parents, and usually a lot of emotional baggage along with it. But if you aren't happy with your family relationships, there is no reason to give up hope. There's always room to renegotiate a relationship that's not working for you. If you could wipe the slate clean, what sort of relationship would you really want to have with your family? Write out a description of the relationship you want and share your desires with your family. By taking this step, you will open the door for your family members to share their desires, also. Then, together, you can restore your relationship.

who has ears should listen to what the Spirit says to the churches.

To the Church in Philadelphia

7"Write this to the angel of the church in Philadelphia:

"This is what the One who is holy and true, who holds the key of David, says. When he opens a door, no one can close it. And when he closes it, no one can open it. 8I know what you do. I have put an open door before you, which no one can close. I know you have little strength, but you have obeyed my teaching and were not afraid to speak my name. 9Those in the synagogue that belongs to Satan say they are Jews, but they are not true Jews; they are liars. I will make them come before you and bow at your feet, and they will know that I have loved you. 10You have obeyed my teaching about not giving up your faith. So I will keep you from the time of trouble that will come to the whole world to test those who live on earth.

11"I am coming soon. Continue strong in your faith so no one will take away your crown. 12I will make those who win the victory pillars in the temple of my God, and they will never have to leave it. I will write on them the name of my God and the name of the city of my God, the new Jerusalem," that comes down out of heaven from my God. I will also write on them my new name. 13Everyone who has ears should listen to what the Spirit says to the churches.

To the Church in Laodicea

14"Write this to the angel of the church in Laodicea:

"The Amen," the faithful and true witness, the ruler of all God has made, says this: 15I know what you do, that you are not hot or cold. I wish that you were hot or cold! 16But because you are lukewarm—neither hot, nor cold—I am ready to spit you out of my mouth. 17You say, 'I am rich, and I have become wealthy and do not need anything.' But you do not know that you are really miserable, pitiful, poor, blind, and naked. 18I advise you to buy from me gold made pure in fire so you can be truly rich. Buy from me white clothes so you can be clothed and so you can cover your shameful nakedness. Buy from me medicine to put on your eyes so you can truly see.

19"I correct and punish those whom I love. So be eager to do right, and change your

▶ Sexcess:
OVERCOMING ADDICTION

Addiction to sex has become rampant in society today, even within the church. In addition to the prevalence and influence of distorted sexual messages, studies suggest that other contributing factors include loneliness, boredom, and anger. Sexual addiction is characterized by an unmanageable escalation in sexual activity, whether real or virtual. At its root is an intimacy deficiency that causes someone to seek counterfeit sexual gratification instead of genuine, God-ordained intimacy. The good news is that the grace of God is available to help anyone struggling with sex addiction to overcome it and live free. The key is to desire freedom more than pleasing the flesh.

 3:12 Jerusalem This name is used to mean the spiritual city God built for his people. See Revelation 21–22.   **3:14 Amen** Used here as a name for Jesus; it means to agree fully that something is true.

hearts and lives. [20]"Here I am! I stand at the door and knock. If you hear my voice and open the door, I will come in and eat with you, and you will eat with me.

[21]"Those who win the victory will sit with me on my throne in the same way that I won the victory and sat down with my Father on his throne. [22]Everyone who has ears should listen to what the Spirit says to the churches."

John Sees Heaven

4 After the vision of these things I looked, and there before me was an open door in heaven. And the same voice that spoke to me before, that sounded like a trumpet, said, "Come up here, and I will show you what must happen after this." [2]Immediately I was in the Spirit, and before me was a throne in heaven, and someone was sitting on it. [3]The One who sat on the throne looked like precious stones, like jasper and carnelian. All around the throne was a rainbow the color of an emerald. [4]Around the throne there were twenty-four other thrones with twenty-four elders sitting on them. They were dressed in white and had golden crowns on their heads. [5]Lightning flashes and noises and thunder came from the throne. Before the throne seven lamps were burning, which are the seven spirits of God. [6]Also before the throne there was something that looked like a sea of glass, clear like crystal.

In the center and around the throne were four living creatures with eyes all over them, in front and in back. [7]The first living creature was like a lion. The second was like a calf. The third had a face like a man. The fourth was like a flying eagle. [8]Each of these four living creatures had six wings and was covered all over with eyes, inside and out. Day and night they never stop saying:

"Holy, holy, holy is the Lord God Almighty.

He was, he is, and he is coming."

[9]These living creatures give glory, honor, and thanks to the One who sits on the throne, who lives forever and ever. [10]Then the twenty-four elders bow down before the One who sits on the throne, and they worship him who lives forever and ever. They put their crowns down before the throne and say:

>> live the life

Revelation 4:10–11

The Principle > Worship the Lord.

Practicing It > Spend at least one hour each week in solitude with God, with no agenda other than to worship him. Sing songs, write stories, or simply tell him what you appreciate about his love.

▶Get Aligned
Revelation 4:8

HOLLYWOOD COULDN'T SCRIPT A MORE BIZARRE SCENE: Winged creatures covered with eyes. A crystal sea. A throne of lightning. John's heavenly vision describes the swirling mysteries of heaven. As strange as his depiction may seem, it gives believers a peek at one awe-inspiring aspect of God: his infiniteness.

The creatures worshiped God in three states—past, present, and future—and yet, in a dimension incomprehensible to our finite brains, all three were applicable at once. The beings witnessed the constant motion of God, his ever-changing glory. With each moment came a new facet of God to be praised, causing them never to stop uttering the words John recites. Their worship never ceases.

And neither should ours. Obviously, we are not in heaven yet. In fact, we have no concept of what it will be like to be overwhelmed perpetually with a sense of newness because nothing on earth is as untainted as God's pure glory. Yet we are given glimpses of it in this world. Clues come through the wonder of nature, through the emotion of a child, through the beauty of a relationship. Even as we yearn for our heavenly home, we can seek the glory of God here on earth.

[11]"You are worthy, our Lord and God,
to receive glory and honor and power,
because you made all things.
Everything existed and was made,
because you wanted it."

5 Then I saw a scroll in the right hand of the One sitting on the throne. The scroll had writing on both sides and was kept closed with seven seals. [2]And I saw a powerful angel calling in a loud voice, "Who is worthy to break the seals and open the scroll?" [3]But there was no one in heaven or on earth or under the earth who could open the scroll or look inside it. [4]I cried bitterly because there was no one who was worthy to open the scroll or look inside. [5]But one of the elders said to me, "Do not cry! The Lion* from the tribe of Judah, David's descendant, has won the victory so that he is able to open the scroll and its seven seals."

[6]Then I saw a Lamb standing in the center of the throne and in the middle of the four living creatures and the elders. The Lamb looked as if he had been killed. He had seven horns and seven eyes, which are the seven spirits of God that were sent into all the world. [7]The Lamb came and took the scroll from the right hand of the One sitting on the throne. [8]When he took the scroll, the four living creatures and the twenty-four elders bowed down before the Lamb. Each one

>> **5:5 Lion** Here refers to Christ.

of them had a harp and golden bowls full of incense, which are the prayers of God's holy people. ⁹And they all sang a new song to the Lamb:

"You are worthy to take the scroll
and to open its seals,
because you were killed,
and with the blood of your death you bought people for God
from every tribe, language, people, and nation.
¹⁰You made them to be a kingdom of priests for our God,
and they will rule on the earth."

¹¹Then I looked, and I heard the voices of many angels around the throne, and the four living creatures, and the elders. There were thousands and thousands of angels, ¹²saying in a loud voice:

"The Lamb who was killed is worthy
to receive power, wealth, wisdom, and strength,
honor, glory, and praise!"

¹³Then I heard all creatures in heaven and on earth and under the earth and in the sea saying:

"To the One who sits on the throne
and to the Lamb
be praise and honor and glory and power
forever and ever."

¹⁴The four living creatures said, "Amen," and the elders bowed down and worshiped.

6 Then I watched while the Lamb opened the first of the seven seals. I heard one of the four living creatures say with a voice like thunder, "Come!" ²I looked, and there before me was a white horse. The rider on the horse held a bow, and he was given a crown, and he rode out, determined to win the victory.

³When the Lamb opened the second seal, I heard the second living creature say, "Come!" ⁴Then another horse came out, a red one. Its rider was given power to take away peace from the earth and to make people kill each other, and he was given a big sword.

⁵When the Lamb opened the third seal, I heard the third living creature say, "Come!" I looked, and there before me was a black horse, and its rider held a pair of scales in his hand. ⁶Then I heard something that sounded like a voice coming from the middle of the four living creatures. The voice said, "A quart of wheat for a day's pay, and three quarts of barley for a day's pay, and do not damage the olive oil and wine!"

⁷When the Lamb opened the fourth seal, I heard the voice of the fourth living creature say, "Come!" ⁸I looked, and there before me was a pale horse. Its rider was named death, and Hades* was following close behind him. They were given power over a fourth of the earth to kill people by war, by starvation, by disease, and by the wild animals of the earth.

⁹When the Lamb opened the fifth seal, I saw under the altar the souls of those who had been killed because they were faithful to the word of God and to the message they had received. ¹⁰These souls

Q: Who was Melchizedek?

A: Melchizedek was the king and high priest of Salem whom Abram encountered in the Old Testament. The writer of the Book of Hebrews likens Melchizedek to Christ because the Scriptures provide no record of his death (Hebrews 7:1–17).

Get Fit

PROTECTING YOUR SKIN Skin cancers are the most common cancers of all by far. Although most varieties of skin cancer are rarely lethal, melanoma presents a serious health risk, especially for men who spend large blocks of time out in the sun. Fortunately, there are a few relatively simple ways to protect yourself. First, do your best to avoid direct sun exposure between the hours of 10 A.M. and 2 P.M., when the sun's rays are at their strongest. Second, anytime you go outside, apply sunscreen to any exposed area of your skin. Finally, see your doctor periodically for a skin check. When it comes to spiritual health, direct exposure to the Son is the best thing for you.

▶▶ 6:8 Hades The unseen world of the dead.

shouted in a loud voice, "Holy and true Lord, how long until you judge the people of the earth and punish them for killing us?" ¹¹Then each one of them was given a white robe and was told to wait a short time longer. There were still some of their fellow servants and brothers and sisters in the service of Christ who must be killed as they were. They had to wait until all of this was finished.

¹²Then I watched while the Lamb opened the sixth seal, and there was a great earthquake. The sun became black like rough black cloth, and the whole moon became red like blood. ¹³And the stars in the sky fell to the earth like figs falling from a fig tree when the wind blows. ¹⁴The sky disappeared as a scroll when it is rolled up, and every mountain and island was moved from its place.

¹⁵Then the kings of the earth, the rulers, the generals, the rich people, the powerful people, the slaves, and the free people hid themselves in caves and in the rocks on the mountains. ¹⁶They called to the mountains and the rocks, "Fall on us. Hide us from the face of the One who sits on the throne and from the anger of the Lamb! ¹⁷The great day for their anger has come, and who can stand against it?"

The 144,000 People of Israel

7 After the vision of these things I saw four angels standing at the four corners of the earth. The angels were holding the four winds of the earth to keep them from blowing on the land or on the sea or on any tree. ²Then I saw another angel coming up from the east who had the seal of the living God. And he called out in a loud voice to the four angels to whom God had given power to harm the earth and the sea. ³He said to them, "Do not harm the land or the sea or the trees until we mark with a sign the foreheads of the people who serve our

Change >> Your WORLD

WORLD VISION

When you consider the issue of world poverty, it's easy to get overwhelmed with the immense task. World Vision assumes that relationships are the starting point, and the end goal of its work is to help transform the lives of the poorest children and families in nearly one hundred countries, including the United States. Through practical demonstration of God's love, such as sponsorship of a child, immunization programs, and HIV/AIDS awareness and prevention, the World Vision staff has focused its work on the root causes of poverty, not just the symptoms, and it daily makes a difference.

To change your world, visit www.worldvision.org.

<< Tech Support >>

GLOBAL POSITIONING SYSTEMS

With global positioning system (GPS) technology, you may never have to fold a map again. Many auto manufacturers are adding in-dash GPS systems that automatically route you from Point A to Point B with the convenience of voice activation. Try it in a rental car, and you may never ask for directions again. GPS systems are even available on golf carts at some courses, indicating the yardage from shot to shot. Just as a GPS system keeps you headed in the right direction, God gave believers the Holy Spirit as an internal compass to help us stay on the right path.

God." ⁴Then I heard how many people were marked with the sign. There were one hundred forty-four thousand from every tribe of the people of Israel.

⁵From the tribe of Judah twelve thousand were marked with the sign,
from the tribe of Reuben twelve thousand,
from the tribe of Gad twelve thousand,
⁶from the tribe of Asher twelve thousand,
from the tribe of Naphtali twelve thousand,
from the tribe of Manasseh twelve thousand,
⁷from the tribe of Simeon twelve thousand,
from the tribe of Levi twelve thousand,
from the tribe of Issachar twelve thousand,
⁸from the tribe of Zebulun twelve thousand,
from the tribe of Joseph twelve thousand,
and from the tribe of Benjamin twelve thousand were marked with the sign.

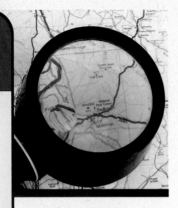

+ Ten Ways to
Plan an Adventure

1. Make a packing list.

2. Stock up on supplies.

3. Use the right equipment.

4. Get a flashlight and batteries.

5. Plan your travel route.

6. Bring plenty of healthy snacks.

7. Pack a water container.

8. Carry bug repellent and a first aid kit.

9. Remember sunscreen and sunglasses.

10. Consult a good map for directions.

The Great Crowd Worships God

⁹After the vision of these things I looked, and there was a great number of people, so many that no one could count them. They were from every nation, tribe, people, and language of the earth. They were all standing before the throne and before the Lamb, wearing white robes and holding palm branches in their hands. ¹⁰They were shouting in a loud voice, "Salvation belongs to our God, who sits on the throne, and to the Lamb." ¹¹All the angels were standing around the throne and the elders and the four living creatures. They all bowed down on their faces before the throne and worshiped God, ¹²saying, "Amen! Praise, glory, wisdom, thanks, honor, power, and strength belong to our God forever and ever. Amen!"

¹³Then one of the elders asked me, "Who are these people dressed in white robes? Where did they come from?"

¹⁴I answered, "You know, sir."

And the elder said to me, "These are the people who have come out of the great distress. They have washed their robes" and made them white in the blood of the Lamb. ¹⁵Because of this, they are before the throne of God. They worship him day and night in his temple. And the One who sits on the throne will be present with them. ¹⁶Those people will never be hungry again, and they will never be thirsty again. The sun will not hurt them, and no heat will burn them, ¹⁷because the Lamb at the center of the throne will be their shepherd. He will lead them to springs of water that give life. And God will wipe away every tear from their eyes."

The Seventh Seal

8 When the Lamb opened the seventh seal, there was silence in heaven for about half an hour. ²And I saw the seven angels who stand before God and to whom were given seven trumpets.

³Another angel came and stood at the altar, holding a golden pan for incense. He was given much incense to offer with the prayers of all God's holy people. The angel put this offering on the golden altar before the throne. ⁴The smoke from the incense went up from the angel's hand to God with the prayers of God's people. ⁵Then the angel filled the incense pan with fire from the altar and threw it on the earth, and there were flashes of lightning, thunder and loud noises, and an earthquake.

The Seven Angels and Trumpets

⁶Then the seven angels who had the seven trumpets prepared to blow them.

⁷The first angel blew his trumpet, and hail and fire mixed with blood were poured down on the earth. And a third of the earth, and all the green grass, and a third of the trees were burned up.

⁸Then the second angel blew his trumpet, and something that looked like a big mountain, burning with fire, was thrown into the sea. And a third of the sea became blood, ⁹a third of the living things in the sea died, and a third of the ships were destroyed.

¹⁰Then the third angel blew his trumpet, and a large star, burning

Principles: SIN

Sin is the natural state of humankind since the fall of Adam and Eve in the Garden of Eden. But the good news is that the death, resurrection, and ascension of Jesus Christ paid the penalty for our sin and redeemed us back into a relationship with God. Whereas our spirits are renewed through faith in Christ, our bodies still desire and do wrong things, or sins. Yet even then, God created a means by which we could receive forgiveness for sins. As 1 John 1:9 states, "But if we confess our sins, he will forgive our sins, because we can trust God to do what is right."

>> 7:14 **washed their robes** This means they believed in Jesus so that their sins could be forgiven by Christ's blood.

People Skills

like a torch, fell from the sky. It fell on a third of the rivers and on the springs of water. [11]The name of the star is Wormwood.º And a third of all the water became bitter, and many people died from drinking the water that was bitter.

[12]Then the fourth angel blew his trumpet, and a third of the sun, and a third of the moon, and a third of the stars were struck. So a third of them became dark, and a third of the day was without light, and also the night.

[13]While I watched, I heard an eagle that was flying high in the air cry out in a loud voice, "Trouble! Trouble! Trouble for those who live on the earth because of the remaining sounds of the trumpets that the other three angels are about to blow!"

9Then the fifth angel blew his trumpet, and I saw a star fall from the sky to the earth. The star was given the key to the deep hole that leads to the bottomless pit. [2]Then it opened up the hole that leads to the bottomless pit, and smoke came up from the hole like smoke from a big furnace. Then the sun and sky became dark because of the smoke from the hole. [3]Then locusts came down to the earth out of the smoke, and they were given the power to sting like scorpions.º [4]They were told not to harm the grass on the earth or any plant or tree. They could harm only the people who did not have the sign of God on their foreheads. [5]These locusts were not given the power to kill anyone, but to cause pain to the people for five months. And the pain they felt was like the pain a scorpion gives when it stings someone. [6]During those days people will look for a way to die, but they will not find it. They will want to die, but death will run away from them.

[7]The locusts looked like horses prepared for battle. On their heads they wore what looked like crowns of gold, and their faces looked like human faces. [8]Their hair was like women's hair, and their teeth were like lions' teeth. [9]Their chests looked like iron breastplates, and the sound of their wings was like the noise of many horses and chariots hurrying into battle. [10]The locusts had tails with stingers like scorpions, and in their tails was their power to hurt people for five months. [11]The locusts had a king who was the angel of the bottomless pit. His name in the Hebrew

Expressing Yourself

Men and women both experience a broad spectrum of feelings during the course of the day. However, many men express difficulty with identifying and sharing their deep feelings, especially with the opposite sex. To develop greater sensitivity in this area, practice going beyond sharing just the facts about your day with the special woman in your life. Instead, tell her what feelings arose for you during the day. Be patient with yourself and pray for emotional clarity. If you stay with it, soon you'll be able to share your heart more deeply and build greater intimacy between you and the one you love.

⊙ Sexcess:
THE PORNOGRAPHY PARADOX

The pervasiveness of pornography distorts society's perceptions of sex and tempts people to yield to their baser sexual instincts. In what is called the "hedonistic paradox," people seek pleasure for its own sake, only to find it has disappeared. For men, the appeal of porn is particularly powerful, and it has been made all the more so by the Internet. What makes Internet pornography so dangerous is its affordability, accessibility, and anonymity. Filter technology helps limit online exposure, but ultimately each man needs to make up his mind to resist the urge to ogle women, whether online or not. As Job 31:1 says, "But I made an agreement with my eyes not to look with desire at a girl."

8:11 **Wormwood** Name of a very bitter plant; used here to give the idea of bitter sorrow.   9:3 **scorpions** A scorpion is an insect that stings with a bad poison.

373

FACT-OIDS! The *Passion of the Christ* DVD sold more than 4.1 million copies in its first day of release. [Exhibitor Relations Co.]

language is Abaddon and in the Greek language is Apollyon."

[12]The first trouble is past; there are still two other troubles that will come.

[13]Then the sixth angel blew his trumpet, and I heard a voice coming from the horns on the golden altar that is before God. [14]The voice said to the sixth angel who had the trumpet, "Free the four angels who are tied at the great river Euphrates." [15]And they let loose the four angels who had been kept ready for this hour and day and month and year so they could kill a third of all people on the earth. [16]I heard how many troops on horses were in their army—two hundred million.

[17]The horses and their riders I saw in the vision looked like this: They had breastplates that were fiery red, dark blue, and yellow like sulfur. The heads of the horses looked like heads of lions, with fire, smoke, and sulfur coming out of their mouths. [18]A third of all the people on earth were killed by these three terrible disasters coming out of the horses' mouths: the fire, the smoke, and the sulfur. [19]The horses' power was in their mouths and in their tails; their tails were like snakes with heads, and with them they hurt people.

[20]The other people who were not killed by these terrible disasters still did not change their hearts and turn away from what they had made with their own hands. They did not stop worshiping demons and idols made of gold, silver, bronze, stone, and wood—things that cannot see or hear or walk. [21]These people did not change their hearts and turn away from murder or evil magic, from their sexual sins or stealing.

The Angel and the Small Scroll

10 Then I saw another powerful angel coming down from heaven dressed in a cloud with a rainbow over his head. His face was like the sun, and his legs were like pillars of fire. [2]The angel was holding a small scroll open in his hand. He put his right foot on the sea and his left foot on the land. [3]Then he shouted loudly like the roaring of a lion. And when he shouted, the voices of seven thunders spoke. [4]When the seven thunders spoke, I started to write. But I heard a voice from heaven say, "Keep hidden what the seven thunders said, and do not write them down."

[5]Then the angel I saw standing on the sea and on the land raised his right hand to heaven, [6]and he made a promise by the power of the One who lives forever and ever. He is the One who made the skies and all that is in them, the earth and all that is in it, and the sea and all that is in it. The angel promised, "There will be no more waiting! [7]In the days when the seventh angel is ready to blow his trumpet, God's secret will be finished. This secret is the Good News God told to his servants, the prophets."

[8]Then I heard the same voice from heaven again, saying to me: "Go and take the open

{ Book of the Month }

Mere Christianity
by C. S. Lewis

In author C. S. Lewis's timeless introduction to the Christian life, he breaks down difficult concepts and questions of faith into simple language that resonates deeply with novice and experienced Christians alike. Lewis doesn't sound like a preacher, for his calling was as a literature teacher, and his trademark English wit and Oxford wisdom enliven every page. The book also serves as a useful handbook for understanding Christian traditions. As an example, why do Christians celebrate communion? Lewis shows that such challenging queries of the faith are answerable, and he addresses them without dampening the mystery or the meaning of walking daily with Christ.

{ Deal With It: *Abuse

IT IS NO SECRET THAT THERE ARE MANY FORMS OF ABUSE, including sexual, physical, and verbal. Yet, the secret to dealing with it, either as a victim or an abuser, is to yield to the lordship of Christ. Victims of abuse often mistakenly feel that they are somehow responsible for the acts perpetrated upon them. Abusers typically come from dysfunctional settings and are, themselves, victims of abuse. Total healing for both is available through the unconditional love and acceptance that comes from a personal relationship with Jesus. The good news is that the vicious cycle of abuse can come to an end.

>> 9:11 **Abaddon, Apollyon** Both names mean "Destroyer."

>>December

{ **QUOTE OF THE MONTH:**
"Reflect upon your present blessings, of which every man has many—not on your past misfortunes, of which all men have some." —Charles Dickens }

1
Pray for a person of influence: Today is director **Woody Allen's** birthday.

2
Fertilize your lawn for winter.

3
Volunteer to help tutor at-risk teens.

4

5
Memorize Galatians 6:10.

6

7

8
Donate your old ties to charity.

9

10
Help decorate the house for the holidays.

11

12

13
Go Christmas caroling with friends.

14

15

16
Pray for a person of influence: Today is journalist **Leslie Stahl's** birthday.

17
Volunteer to help distribute gifts to needy children.

18
Pray for a person of influence: Today is director **Steven Spielberg's** birthday.

19

20

21
Collect canned food for families in need.

22

23
Wish a favorite relative a Merry Christmas.

24
Read the Christmas story aloud from the Book of Luke.

25
Thank God for the gift of his Son.

26

27

28
Celebrate communion with family.

29

30
Pray for a person of influence: Today is golfer **Tiger Woods's** birthday.

31
End the year with prayer and reflection.

Ten Ways to Raise Healthy Kids

1. Encourage trust and honesty.

2. Teach the importance of tithing.

3. Support their gifts and interests.

4. Ask them about their schoolwork.

5. Set goals together as a family.

6. Solicit their ideas and opinions.

7. Invite their friends on outings.

8. Remind them of your love.

9. Cultivate patience and tolerance.

10. Train them how to live godly.

scroll that is in the hand of the angel that is standing on the sea and on the land."

[9]So I went to the angel and told him to give me the small scroll. And he said to me, "Take the scroll and eat it. It will be sour in your stomach, but in your mouth it will be sweet as honey." [10]So I took the small scroll from the angel's hand and ate it. In my mouth it tasted sweet as honey, but after I ate it, it was sour in my stomach. [11]Then I was told, "You must prophesy again about many peoples, nations, languages, and kings."

The Two Witnesses

11 I was given a measuring stick like a rod, and I was told, "Go and measure the temple of God and the altar, and count the people worshiping there. [2]But do not measure the yard outside the temple. Leave it alone, because it has been given to those who are not God's people. And they will trample on the holy city for forty-two months. [3]And I will give power to my two witnesses to prophesy for one thousand two hundred sixty days, and they will be dressed in rough cloth to show their sadness."

[4]These two witnesses are the two olive trees and the two lampstands that stand before the Lord of the earth. [5]And if anyone tries to hurt them, fire comes from their mouths and kills their enemies. And if anyone tries to hurt them in whatever way, in that same way that person will die. [6]These witnesses have the power to stop the sky from raining during the time they are prophesying. And they have power to make the waters become blood, and they have power to send every kind of trouble to the earth as many times as they want.

[7]When the two witnesses have finished telling their message, the beast that comes up from the bottomless pit will fight a war against them. He will defeat them and kill them. [8]The bodies of the two witnesses will lie in the street of the great city where the Lord was killed. This city is named Sodom[n] and Egypt, which has a spiritual meaning. [9]Those from every race of people, tribe, language, and nation will look at the bodies of the two witnesses for three and one-half days, and they will refuse to bury them. [10]People who live on the earth will rejoice and be happy because these two are dead. They will send each other gifts, because these two prophets brought much suffering to those who live on the earth.

[11]But after three and one-half days, God put the breath of life into the two prophets again. They stood on their feet, and everyone who saw them became very afraid. [12]Then the two prophets heard a loud voice from heaven saying, "Come up here!" And they went up into heaven in a cloud as their enemies watched.

[13]In the same hour there was a great earthquake, and a tenth of the city was destroyed. Seven thousand people were killed in the earthquake, and those who did not die were very afraid and gave glory to the God of heaven.

[14]The second trouble is finished. Pay attention: The third trouble is coming soon.

The Seventh Trumpet

[15]Then the seventh angel blew his trumpet. And there were loud voices in heaven, saying:

"The power to rule the world now belongs to our Lord and his Christ,
    and he will rule forever and ever."

[16]Then the twenty-four elders, who sit on their thrones before God, bowed down on their faces and worshiped God. [17]They said:

"We give thanks to you, Lord God Almighty,
    who is and who was,
because you have used your great power
    and have begun to rule!
[18]The people of the world were angry,
    but your anger has come.
The time has come to judge the dead,
    and to reward your servants the prophets
and your holy people,
    all who respect you, great and small.
The time has come to destroy those who destroy the earth!"

[19]Then God's temple in heaven was opened. The Ark that holds the agreement God gave to his people could be seen in his temple. Then there were flashes of lightning, noises, thunder, an earthquake, and a great hailstorm.

The Woman and the Dragon

12 And then a great wonder appeared in heaven: A woman was clothed with the sun, and the moon was under her feet, and a crown of twelve stars was on her head. [2]She was pregnant and cried

---

>> **11:8 Sodom** City that God destroyed because the people were so evil.

out with pain, because she was about to give birth. ³Then another wonder appeared in heaven: There was a giant red dragon with seven heads and seven crowns on each head. He also had ten horns. ⁴His tail swept a third of the stars out of the sky and threw them down to the earth. He stood in front of the woman who was ready to give birth so he could eat her baby as soon as it was born. ⁵Then the woman gave birth to a son who will rule all the nations with an iron rod. And her child was taken up to God and to his throne. ⁶The woman ran away into the desert to a place God prepared for her where she would be taken care of for one thousand two hundred sixty days.

⁷Then there was a war in heaven. Michael* and his angels fought against the dragon, and the dragon and his angels fought back. ⁸But the dragon was not strong enough, and he and his angels lost their place in heaven. ⁹The giant dragon was thrown down out of heaven. (He is that old snake called the devil or Satan, who tricks the whole world.) The dragon with his angels was thrown down to the earth.

¹⁰Then I heard a loud voice in heaven saying:

"The salvation and the power and the kingdom of our God
    and the authority of his Christ have now come.
The accuser of our brothers and sisters,
    who accused them day and night before our God,
    has been thrown down.
¹¹And our brothers and sisters defeated him
    by the blood of the Lamb's death
    and by the message they preached.
They did not love their lives so much
    that they were afraid of death.
¹²So rejoice, you heavens
    and all who live there!
But it will be terrible for the earth and the sea,
    because the devil has come down to you!

Change >> Your WORLD

WYCLIFFE BIBLE TRANSLATORS

Hundreds of people groups don't yet have the Bible in the language of their native tongue. But Wycliffe Bible Translators has completed 611 translations, and the Scriptures are now available to more than seventy-six million people. Wycliffe continues to work in many languages in forty-six countries, as more than 380 million people worldwide still lack the Bible in their own language. At the present rate of translation, they will have to wait another 100 to 150 years and, by anyone's measure, that is too long. The need is great, and the opportunity is urgent for more translation work.

To change your world, visit www.wycliffe.org.

 # Survival Guide

TREES: SHADING YOUR PROPERTY

Shade trees can enhance your property's appearance while reducing heating and cooling bills. The east and west sides are the most important to shade, with the south usually left open so winter sun can warm the house. The type of trees you choose depends on your area of the country, but to prevent root damage to the foundation, don't plant too close to your house. In addition to providing shade, trees also enhance the aesthetic value of your property.

>> **12:7 Michael** The archangel—leader among God's angels or messengers (Jude 9).

FOR Men Only

WISDOM   Many a man insists that his wife submit to him, yet he fails to give her much reason to do so. If there is one quality that breeds confidence in a woman about a man's decision making and, thus, something that will encourage a willingness to submit to him, it is wisdom. The ability to make wise decisions in life is cultivated over time and comes from sound application of under-standing and knowledge. As Proverbs 4:7 states, "Wisdom is the most important thing; so get wisdom." Making the exercise of wisdom a priority in our lives creates an inclination on the part of our mates to listen to us and follow our leading.

He is filled with anger,
  because he knows he does not have much time."
¹³When the dragon saw he had been thrown down to the earth, he hunted for the woman who had given birth to the son. ¹⁴But the woman was given the two wings of a great eagle so she could fly to the place prepared for her in the desert. There she would be taken care of for three and one-half years, away from the snake. ¹⁵Then the snake poured water out of its mouth like a river toward the woman so the flood would carry her away. ¹⁶But the earth helped the woman by opening its mouth and swallowing the river that came from the mouth of the dragon. ¹⁷Then the dragon was very angry at the woman, and he went off to make war against all her other children—those who obey God's commands and who have the message Jesus taught.

¹⁸And the dragon* stood on the seashore.

The Two Beasts

13 Then I saw a beast coming up out of the sea. It had ten horns and seven heads, and there was a crown on each horn. A name against God was written on each head. ²This beast looked like a leopard, with feet like a bear's feet and a mouth like a lion's mouth. And the dragon gave the beast all of his power and his throne and great author-ity. ³One of the heads of the beast looked as if it had been killed by a wound, but this death wound was healed. Then the whole world was amazed and followed the beast. ⁴People worshiped the dragon because he had given his power to the beast. And they also worshiped the beast, asking, "Who is like the beast? Who can make war against it?"

⁵The beast was allowed to say proud words and words against God, and it was allowed to use its power for forty-two months. ⁶It used its mouth to speak against God, against God's name, against the place where God lives, and against all those who live in heaven. ⁷It was given power to make war against God's holy people and to defeat

Get Fit

SIMPLIFYING YOUR LIFE   Most of the stress we experience as men doesn't come from external sources. Much of it comes from things we choose to bring into our lives, such as our possessions. Think of it this way: what you own, you must maintain! When the boat breaks down, the pool stops working, or the grill needs atten-tion, who has to fix it all? And that's a type of stress you may not welcome. You can cut the stress by clearing out those things that you don't actually need to be happy and fulfilled. Jesus said in Luke 12:15 that "life is not measured by how much one owns."

>> 12:18 the dragon Some Greek copies read "I."

them. It was given power over every tribe, people, language, and nation. [8]And all who live on earth will worship the beast—all the people since the beginning of the world whose names are not written in the Lamb's book of life. The Lamb is the One who was killed.

[9]Anyone who has ears should listen:

[10]If you are to be a prisoner,
   then you will be a prisoner.
If you are to be killed with the sword,
   then you will be killed with the sword.
This means that God's holy people must have patience and faith.

[11]Then I saw another beast coming up out of the earth. It had two horns like a lamb, but it spoke like a dragon. [12]This beast stands before the first beast and uses the same power the first beast has. By this power it makes everyone living on earth worship the first beast, who had the death wound that was healed. [13]And the second beast does great miracles so that it even makes fire come down from heaven to earth while people are watching. [14]It fools those who live on earth by the miracles it has been given the power to do. It does these miracles to serve the first beast. The second beast orders people to make an idol to honor the first beast, the one that was wounded by the deadly sword but sprang to life again. [15]The second beast was given power to give life to the idol of the first one so that the idol could speak. And the second beast was given power to command all who will not worship the image of the beast to be killed. [16]The second beast also forced all people, small and great, rich and poor, free and slave, to have a mark on their right hand or on their forehead. [17]No one could buy or sell without this mark, which is the name of the beast or the number of its name. [18]This takes wisdom. Let the one who has understanding find the meaning of the number, which is the number of a person. Its number is 666.*

<< TechSupport >>

PODCASTING

If you grew up pretending you had your own radio show, now's your chance to make it a reality. Inexpensive technology has made it possible to record and distribute customized broadcasts on the Internet to subscribers who sign up for your signal. With these custom "podcasts," subscribers' computers download an audio file from your Web site for later listening. Podcasts cater to the diverse niche interests of those who don't find what they're looking for on traditional radio stations. It also could be a great tool for missionary organizations to use as a way of staying in touch with their supporters.

The Song of the Saved

14 Then I looked, and there before me was the Lamb standing on Mount Zion.* With him were one hundred forty-four thousand people who had his name and his Father's name written on their foreheads. [2]And I heard a sound from heaven like the noise of flooding water and like the sound of loud thunder. The sound I heard was like people playing harps. [3]And they sang a new song before the throne and before the four living creatures and the elders. No one could learn the new song except the one hundred forty-four

→ The Bottom Line
Automatic Withdrawals: A Warning

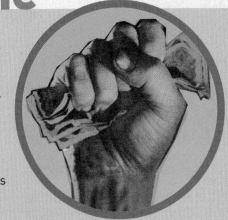

AUTOMATIC CHECKING ACCOUNT WITHDRAWALS CAN BE USED TO PAY EVERYTHING FROM YOUR MORTGAGE TO INSURANCE TO BILLS. However, before granting anyone access to your account, remember that once you give someone such permission, reversing that decision can pose enormous headaches. Forget to deposit adequate funds by the withdrawal date, and you may incur a bounced check fee plus a merchant's penalty. Companies that require monthly bank withdrawals will often allow you to opt out by paying three months in advance. In that case, avoiding problems could outweigh convenience.

>> 13:18 666 Some Greek copies read "616." 14:1 **Mount Zion** Another name for Jerusalem; here meaning the spiritual city of God's people.

People Skills

Selecting Friendships

Enjoying a cadre of close male friendships is vital to a healthy, fulfilling life. But friendship is also a choice. Your friends are some of the most influential people in your life, so it's important that you choose them carefully. If you have friends who consistently bring you down, belittle your dreams, or pull you in directions that aren't good for you, give serious consideration to stepping away from those relationships or even breaking things off altogether. Saying no to friendships that aren't good for you can be tough, but by doing it you will clear the way for other friendships to develop that will genuinely help you become all that you can be.

thousand who had been bought from the earth. ⁴These are the ones who did not do sinful things with women, because they kept themselves pure. They follow the Lamb every place he goes. These one hundred forty-four thousand were bought from among the people of the earth as people to be offered to God and the Lamb. ⁵They were not guilty of telling lies; they are without fault.

The Three Angels

⁶Then I saw another angel flying high in the air. He had the eternal Good News to preach to those who live on earth—to every nation, tribe, language, and people. ⁷He preached in a loud voice, "Fear God and give him praise, because the time has come for God to judge all people. So worship God who made the heavens, and the earth, and the sea, and the springs of water."

⁸Then the second angel followed the first angel and said, "Ruined, ruined is the great city of Babylon! She made all the nations drink the wine of the anger of her adultery."

⁹Then a third angel followed the first two angels, saying in a loud voice: "If anyone worships the beast and his idol and gets the beast's mark on the forehead or on the hand,

¹⁰that one also will drink the wine of God's anger, which is prepared with all its strength in the cup of his anger. And that person will be put in pain with burning sulfur before the holy angels and the Lamb. ¹¹And the smoke from their burning pain will rise forever and ever. There will be no rest, day or night, for those who worship the beast and his idol or who get the mark of his name." ¹²This means God's holy people must be patient. They must obey God's commands and keep their faith in Jesus.

¹³Then I heard a voice from heaven saying, "Write this: Blessed are the dead who die from now on in the Lord."

The Spirit says, "Yes, they will rest from their hard work, and the reward of all they have done stays with them."

The Earth Is Harvested

¹⁴Then I looked, and there before me was a white cloud, and sitting on the white cloud was One who looked like a Son of Man.ⁿ He had a gold crown on his head and a sharp sickleⁿ in his hand. ¹⁵Then another angel came out of the temple and called out in a loud voice to the One who was sitting on the cloud, "Take your sickle and harvest from the

▶ Sexcess: THE MASTURBATION QUESTION

The debate continues over whether or not masturbation is a sin. The simple truth is that the Bible does not specifically address it one way or the other. At the heart of the matter is the matter of the heart. If a man stimulates himself without gazing at images or conjuring them in his mind, then that man must be the judge of whether or not it is acceptable for him. However, that typically is not the issue for the overwhelming majority of men. The trouble for most guys is not that masturbation is used simply as a release, but that it substitutes for sexual maturity and becomes a controlling habit.

>> 14:14 Son of Man "Son of Man" is a name Jesus called himself.   14:14 sickle A farming tool with a curved blade. It was used to harvest grain.

380

TheFinalScore »

THE MASTERS: An Exclusive Club

IN SPORTS, ADMISSION TO THE MASTERS RANKS just behind the Super Bowl and the World Series as the toughest ticket to find. Sold out every year, passes were once rumored to be willed down through generations, although the Augusta National Golf Club insists only a spouse can inherit a deceased mate's pass.

It is small wonder that ticket brokers ask anywhere from $3,000 to $5,000 for four-day admissions to golf's most prestigious event. Winners of the tournament receive a green jacket symbolizing honorary Augusta National membership, automatically thrusting that golfer into the sport's elite circles.

Winning the green jacket is such an honor, it is almost sought ahead of the payout, which in recent years has passed the million-dollar mark. Ironi-

cally, the club's policy only allows champions to keep their jacket for one year before returning it, after which they get to wear it upon visits.

What inspires competitors to strive so hard for such a temporary honor? Prestige, professional achievement, and public acclaim are among the many reasons. But perhaps the most compelling reason of all is the intense drive to belong to such an exclusive group of champions.

Admission to the eternal home that awaits each believer at the end of life is something worth more than worldly trophies. In Luke 10:20, when Christ's followers marveled at the power Jesus had given them, he told them they should be happy "because your names are written in heaven." And entrance into Christ's inner circle lasts for eternity.

"And entrance into Christ's inner circle lasts for eternity."

+ Ten Ways to Build a Strong Marriage

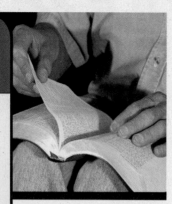

1. Get creative with lovemaking.
2. Celebrate the simple things.
3. Pray for each other regularly.
4. Plan a family vacation.
5. Read the Bible together.
6. Dream about the future.
7. Attend a marriage retreat.
8. Make home a safe haven.
9. Practice the art of forgiveness.
10. Honor your marriage vows.

earth, because the time to harvest has come, and the fruit of the earth is ripe." 16So the One who was sitting on the cloud swung his sickle over the earth, and the earth was harvested.

17Then another angel came out of the temple in heaven, and he also had a sharp sickle. 18And then another angel, who has power over the fire, came from the altar. This angel called to the angel with the sharp sickle, saying, "Take your sharp sickle and gather the bunches of grapes from the earth's vine, because its grapes are ripe." 19Then the angel swung his sickle over the earth. He gathered the earth's grapes and threw them into the great winepress of God's anger. 20They were trampled in the winepress outside the city, and blood flowed out of the winepress as high as horses' bridles for a distance of about one hundred eighty miles.

The Last Troubles

15 Then I saw another wonder in heaven that was great and amazing. There were seven angels bringing seven disasters. These are the last disasters, because after them, God's anger is finished.

2I saw what looked like a sea of glass mixed with fire. All of those who had won the victory over the beast and his idol and over the number of his name were standing by the sea of glass. They had harps that God had given them. 3They sang the song of Moses, the servant of God, and the song of the Lamb:

"You do great and wonderful things,   *Psalm 111:2*
  Lord God Almighty.   *Amos 3:13*

Everything the Lord does is right and true,   *Psalm 145:17*

  King of the nations."
4Everyone will respect you, Lord,   *Jeremiah 10:7*
  and will honor you.
Only you are holy.
All the nations will come
  and worship you,   *Psalm 86:9–10*
because the right things you have done
  are now made known."   *Deuteronomy 32:4*

5After this I saw that the temple (the Tent of the Agreement) in heaven was opened. 6And the seven angels bringing the seven disasters came out of the temple. They were dressed in clean, shining linen and wore golden bands tied around their chests. 7Then one of the four living creatures gave to the seven angels seven golden bowls filled with the anger of God, who lives forever and ever. 8The temple was filled with smoke from the glory and the power of God, and no one could enter the temple until the seven disasters of the seven angels were finished.

The Bowls of God's Anger

16 Then I heard a loud voice from the temple saying to the seven angels, "Go and pour out the seven bowls of God's anger on the earth."

2The first angel left and poured out his bowl on the land. Then ugly and painful sores came upon all those who had the mark of the beast and who worshiped his idol.

3The second angel poured out his bowl on the sea, and it became blood like that of a dead man, and every living thing in the sea died.

4The third angel poured out his bowl on the rivers and the springs of water, and they became blood. 5Then I heard the angel of the waters saying:

"Holy One, you are the One who is and who was.
  You are right to decide to punish these evil people.
6They have poured out the blood of your holy people and your prophets.
So now you have given them blood to drink as they deserve."

Q: Can't a person get into heaven just by living a good life?

A: No. It is impossible to earn our way into heaven by doing good deeds because no matter how good we are, we still will fall short of the standard of absolute holiness and perfection necessary to stand before God and spend eternity in heaven (Ephesians 2:8–9).

>> 15:3 King...nations Some Greek copies read "King of the ages."

7And I heard a voice coming from the altar saying:

"Yes, Lord God Almighty,

the way you punish evil people is right and fair."

8The fourth angel poured out his bowl on the sun, and he was given power to burn the people with fire. 9They were burned by the great heat, and they cursed the name of God, who had control over these disasters. But the people refused to change their hearts and lives and give glory to God.

10The fifth angel poured out his bowl on the throne of the beast, and darkness covered its kingdom. People gnawed their tongues because of the pain. 11They also cursed the God of heaven because of their pain and the sores they had, but they refused to change their hearts and turn away from the evil things they did.

12The sixth angel poured out his bowl on the great river Euphrates so that the water in the river was dried up to prepare the way for the kings from the east to come. 13Then I saw three evil spirits that looked like frogs coming out of the mouth of the dragon, out of the mouth of the beast, and out of the mouth of the false prophet. 14These evil spirits are the spirits of demons, which have power to do miracles. They go out to the kings of the whole world to gather them together for the battle on the great day of God Almighty.

15"Listen! I will come as a thief comes! Blessed are those who stay awake and keep their clothes on so that they will not walk around naked and have people see their shame."

16Then the evil spirits gathered the kings together to the place that is called Armageddon in the Hebrew language.

17The seventh angel poured out his bowl into the air. Then a loud voice came out of the temple from the throne, saying, "It is finished!" 18Then there were flashes of lightning, noises, thunder, and a big earthquake—the worst earthquake that has ever happened since people have been on earth. 19The great city split into three parts, and the cities of the nations were destroyed. And God remembered the sins of Babylon the Great, so he gave that city the cup filled with the wine of his terrible anger. 20Then every island ran away, and mountains disappeared. 21Giant hailstones, each weighing about a hundred pounds, fell from the sky upon people. People cursed God for the disaster of the hail, because this disaster was so terrible.

The Woman on the Animal

17 Then one of the seven angels who had the seven bowls came and spoke to me. He said, "Come, and I will show you the punishment that will be given to the great prostitute, the one sitting over many waters. 2The kings of the earth sinned sexually with her, and the people of the earth became drunk from the wine of her sexual sin."

3Then the angel carried me away by the Spirit to the desert. There I saw a woman sitting on a red beast. It was covered with names against God written on it, and it had seven heads and ten horns. 4The woman was dressed in purple and red and was shining with the gold, precious jewels, and pearls she was wearing. She had a golden cup in her hand, a cup filled with evil things and the uncleanness of her sexual sin. 5On her forehead a title was written that was secret. This is what was written:

THE GREAT BABYLON
MOTHER OF PROSTITUTES
AND OF THE EVIL THINGS OF THE EARTH

6Then I saw that the woman was drunk with the blood of God's holy people and with the blood of those who were killed because of their faith in Jesus.

When I saw the woman, I was very amazed. 7Then the angel said to me, "Why are you amazed? I will tell you the secret of this woman and the beast she rides—the one with seven heads and ten horns. 8The beast you saw was once alive but is not alive now. But soon it will come up out of the bottomless pit and go away to be destroyed. There are people who live on earth whose names have not been written in the book of life since the beginning of the world. They will be amazed when they see the beast, because he was once alive, is not alive now, but will come again.

Change >> YourWORLD

YOUNG LIFE

"It's a sin to bore a kid with the Gospel," said Jim Rayburn, the founder of Young Life. For more than sixty years, Young Life has reached out to teens, with programs in more than eight hundred communities in the United States and Canada, as well as more than forty-five other countries. In excess of one hundred thousand kids are involved in Young Life weekly, with more than a million kids participating in Young Life throughout the year. In addition, Young Life has twenty-four camping properties in the U.S. that involve more than ninety thousand kids for a weekend during the school year or for a week during the summer.

To change your world, visit www.younglife.org.

9"You need a wise mind to understand this. The seven heads on the beast are seven mountains where the woman sits. 10And they are seven kings. Five of the kings have already been destroyed, one of the kings lives now, and another has not yet come. When he comes, he must stay a short time. 11The beast that was once alive, but is not alive now, is also an eighth king. He belongs to the first seven kings, and he will go away to be destroyed.

12"The ten horns you saw are ten kings who have not yet begun to rule, but they will receive power to rule with the beast for one hour. 13All ten of these kings have the same purpose, and they will give their power and authority to the beast. 14They will make war against the Lamb, but the Lamb will defeat them, because he is Lord of lords and King of kings. He will defeat them with his called, chosen, and faithful followers."

15Then the angel said to me, "The waters that you saw, where the prostitute sits, are peoples, races, nations, and languages. 16The ten horns and the beast you saw will hate the prostitute. They will take everything she has and leave her naked. They will eat her body and burn her with fire. 17God made the ten horns want to carry out his purpose by agreeing to give the beast their power to rule, until what God has said comes about. 18The woman you saw is the great city that rules over the kings of the earth."

Babylon Is Destroyed

18After the vision of these things, I saw another angel coming down from heaven. This angel had great power, and his glory made the earth bright. 2He shouted in a powerful voice:

"Ruined, ruined is the great city of Babylon!
She has become a home for demons
and a prison for every evil spirit,
and a prison for every unclean bird
and unclean beast.
3She has been ruined, because all the peoples of the earth
have drunk the wine of the desire of her sexual sin.
She has been ruined also because the kings of the earth
have sinned sexually with her,
and the merchants of the earth
have grown rich from the great wealth of her luxury."

4Then I heard another voice from heaven saying:

"Come out of that city, my people,
so that you will not share in her sins,
so that you will not receive the disasters that will come to her.

5Her sins have piled up as high as the sky,
and God has not forgotten the wrongs she has done.
6Give that city the same as she gave to others.
Pay her back twice as much as she did.
Prepare wine for her that is twice as strong
as the wine she prepared for others.
7She gave herself much glory and rich living.
Give her that much suffering and sadness.
She says to herself, 'I am a queen sitting on my throne.
I am not a widow; I will never be sad.'
8So these disasters will come to her in one day:
death, and crying, and great hunger,
and she will be destroyed by fire,
because the Lord God who judges her is powerful."

9The kings of the earth who sinned sexually with her and shared her wealth will see the smoke from her burning. Then they will cry and be sad because of her death. 10They will be afraid of her suffering and stand far away and say:

"Terrible! How terrible for you, great city, powerful city of Babylon,
because your punishment has come in one hour!"

11And the merchants of the earth will cry and be sad about her, because now there is no one to buy their cargoes— 12cargoes of gold, silver, jewels, pearls, fine linen, purple cloth, silk, red cloth; all kinds of citron wood and all kinds of things made from ivory, expensive wood, bronze, iron, and marble; 13cinnamon, spice, incense, myrrh, frankincense, wine, olive oil, fine flour, wheat, cattle, sheep, horses, carriages, slaves, and human lives.

14The merchants will say,

"Babylon, the good things you wanted are gone from you.
All your rich and fancy things have disappeared.
You will never have them again."

15The merchants who became rich from sell-

Deal With It: Politics

CONTRARY TO POPULAR BELIEF, JESUS ISN'T A MEMBER OF A POLITICAL PARTY. Not that there is anything wrong with supporting one party or the other. We just need to guard against giving politics too large a platform. Although it is important to participate in the political process, we must never do so to the exclusion of prayer and other practices that Christ called even more critical. It is okay for us to vote, petition, lobby, and otherwise get involved in causes we support, but we must remember that the object is to challenge people's hearts about eternal matters, not to change their minds about temporal issues.

Survival Guide

SAVING WATER: CUT THE FLOW

Contrary to popular belief, water is not an endless resource. Three-fourths of home water usage originates in the bathroom, where you can cut the flow with a little effort. Consider installing a low-flush toilet, which uses much less water. Or put something in the tank to reduce water used in flushing, such as a brick or a jug filled with pebbles. Low-flow showerheads can save thousands of gallons a year, as can faucet aerators and pressure-reducing valves. The bottom line is this: cut the flow and save some dough.

ing to her will be afraid of her suffering and will stand far away. They will cry and be sad ¹⁶and say:

"Terrible! How terrible for the great city!

She was dressed in fine linen, purple and red cloth,

and she was shining with gold, precious jewels, and pearls!

¹⁷All these riches have been destroyed in one hour!"

Every sea captain, every passenger, the sailors, and all those who earn their living from the sea stood far away from Babylon. ¹⁸As they saw the smoke from her burning, they cried out loudly, "There was never a city like this great city!" ¹⁹And they threw dust on their heads and cried out, weeping and being sad. They said:

"Terrible! How terrible for the great city!

All the people who had ships on the sea

became rich because of her wealth!

But she has been destroyed in one hour!"

²⁰Be happy because of this, heaven!

Be happy, God's holy people and apostles and prophets!

God has punished her because of what she did to you."

²¹Then a powerful angel picked up a large stone, like one used for grinding grain, and threw it into the sea. He said:

"In the same way, the great city of Babylon will be thrown down,

and it will never be found again.

²²The music of people playing harps and other instruments, flutes,

and trumpets,

will never be heard in you again.

No workman doing any job

will ever be found in you again.

The sound of grinding grain

will never be heard in you again.

²³The light of a lamp

will never shine in you again,

and the voices of a bridegroom and bride

will never be heard in you again.

Your merchants were the world's great people,

and all the nations were tricked by your magic.

²⁴You are guilty of the death of the prophets and God's holy people

and all who have been killed on earth."

People in Heaven Praise God

19 After this vision and announcement I heard what sounded like a great many people in heaven saying:

"Hallelujah!"

Salvation, glory, and power belong to our God,

² because his judgments are true and right.

He has punished the prostitute

who made the earth evil with her sexual sin.

He has paid her back for the death of his servants."

³Again they said:

"Hallelujah!

She is burning, and her smoke will rise forever and ever."

⁴Then the twenty-four elders and the four living creatures bowed down and worshiped God, who sits on the throne. They said:

"Amen, Hallelujah!"

⁵Then a voice came from the throne, saying:

"Praise our God, all you who serve him

and all you who honor him, both small and great!"

⁶Then I heard what sounded like a great many people, like the noise of flooding water, and like the noise of loud thunder. The people were saying:

"Hallelujah!

Our Lord God, the Almighty, rules.

⁷Let us rejoice and be happy

and give God glory,

because the wedding of the Lamb has come,

and the Lamb's bride has made herself ready.

⁸Fine linen, bright and clean, was given to her to wear."

⮞⮞ **19:1 Hallelujah** This means "praise God!"

People Skills

Keeping Promises

We all know it is important to keep our promises. But it is especially true of the promises we make to our kids. All too often, we worry that our clients will fire us if we don't put them first when they ask for more of our time. Yet at the same time, we think that we can make it up to our kids for the times we break promises to them as a result. The reality is that the client typically won't fire you if you set limits, and often he or she will respect you more. On the other hand, your kids will lose faith in you if your break your promises too often, so keep your word.

(The fine linen means the good things done by God's holy people.)

⁹And the angel said to me, "Write this: Blessed are those who have been invited to the wedding meal of the Lamb!" And the angel said, "These are the true words of God."

¹⁰Then I bowed down at the angel's feet to worship him, but he said to me, "Do not worship me! I am a servant like you and your brothers and sisters who have the message of Jesus. Worship God, because the message about Jesus is the spirit that gives all prophecy."

The Rider on the White Horse

¹¹Then I saw heaven opened, and there before me was a white horse. The rider on the horse is called Faithful and True, and he is right when he judges and makes war. ¹²His eyes are like burning fire, and on his head are many crowns. He has a name written on him, which no one but himself knows. ¹³He is dressed in a robe dipped in blood, and his name is the Word of God. ¹⁴The armies of heaven, dressed in fine linen, white and clean, were following him on white horses. ¹⁵Out of the rider's mouth comes a sharp sword that he will use to defeat the nations, and he will rule them with a rod of iron. He will crush out the wine in the winepress of the terrible anger of God the Almighty. ¹⁶On his robe and on his upper leg was written this name: KING OF KINGS AND LORD OF LORDS.

¹⁷Then I saw an angel standing in the sun, and he called with a loud voice to all the birds flying in the sky: "Come and gather together for the great feast of God ¹⁸so that you can eat the bodies of kings, generals, mighty people, horses and their riders, and the bodies of all people—free, slave, small, and great."

¹⁹Then I saw the beast and the kings of the earth. Their armies were gathered together to make war against the rider on the horse and his army. ²⁰But the beast was captured and with him the false prophet who did the miracles for the beast. The false prophet had used these miracles to trick those who had the mark of the beast and worshiped his idol. The false prophet and the beast were thrown alive into the lake of fire that burns with sulfur. ²¹And their armies were killed with the sword that came out of the mouth of the rider on the horse, and all the birds ate the bodies until they were full.

The Thousand Years

20 I saw an angel coming down from heaven. He had the key to the bottomless pit and a large chain in his hand. ²The angel grabbed the dragon, that old snake who is the devil and Satan, and tied him up for a thousand years. ³Then he threw him into the bottomless pit, closed it, and locked it over him. The angel did this so he could not trick the people of the earth anymore until the thousand years were ended. After a thousand years he must be set free for a short time.

⁴Then I saw some thrones and people sitting on them who had been given the power to judge. And I saw the souls of those who had been killed because they were faithful to the message of Jesus and the message from God. They had not worshiped the beast or his idol, and they had not received the mark of the beast on their foreheads or on their hands. They came back to life and ruled with Christ for a thousand years. ⁵(The others that were dead did not live again until the thousand years were ended.) This is the first raising of the dead. ⁶Blessed and holy are those who share in this first raising of the dead. The second death has no power over them. They will be priests for God and for Christ and will rule with him for a thousand years.

⁷When the thousand years are over, Satan will be set free from his prison. ⁸Then he will go out to trick the nations in all the earth—Gog and Magog—to gather them for battle. There are so many people they will be like sand on the seashore. ⁹And Satan's army marched across the earth and gathered around the camp of God's people and the city God loves. But fire came down from heaven and burned them up. ¹⁰And Satan, who tricked them, was thrown into the lake of burning sulfur with the beast and the false prophet. There they will be punished day and night forever and ever.

FOR
Men Only

LOVE
As 1 Corinthians 13:13 states, "And the greatest of these is love." For any relationship to succeed, love must be at its center. Not the so-called love that is subject to feelings, for that is not love at all. Love is not a feeling; it is a commitment. You don't fall in or out of love; you make or break your commitment. Love is often confused with lust, but they couldn't be more different. Love seeks to give, but lust seeks to get. The ultimate example of love is Christ sacrificing his life for us, and, as men, our challenge is to love others as Christ loves us.

People of the World Are Judged

¹¹Then I saw a great white throne and the One who was sitting on it. Earth and sky ran away from him and disappeared. ¹²And I saw the dead, great and small, standing before the throne. Then books were opened, and the book of life was opened. The dead were judged by what they had done, which was written in the books. ¹³The sea gave up the dead who were in it, and Death and Hades" gave up the dead who were in them. Each person was judged by what he had done. ¹⁴And Death and Hades were thrown into the lake of fire. The lake of fire is the second death. ¹⁵And anyone whose name was not found written in the book of life was thrown into the lake of fire.

The New Jerusalem

21 Then I saw a new heaven and a new earth. The first heaven and the first earth had disappeared, and there was no sea anymore. ²And I saw the holy city, the new Jerusalem," coming down out of heaven from God. It was prepared like a bride dressed for her husband. ³And I heard a loud voice from the throne, saying, "Now God's presence is with people, and he will live with them, and they will be his people. God himself will be with them and will be their God." ⁴He will wipe away every tear from their eyes, and there will be no more death, sadness, crying, or pain, because all the old ways are gone."

⁵The One who was sitting on the throne said, "Look! I am making everything new!" Then he said, "Write this, because these words are true and can be trusted."

⁶The One on the throne said to me, "It is finished. I am the Alpha and the Omega," the Beginning and the End. I will give free water from the spring of the water of life to anyone who is thirsty. ⁷Those who win the victory will receive this, and I will be their God, and they will be my children. ⁸But cowards, those who refuse to believe, who do evil things, who kill, who sin sexually, who do evil magic, who worship idols, and who tell lies—all these will have a place in the lake of burning sulfur. This is the second death."

⁹Then one of the seven angels who had the seven bowls full of the seven last troubles came to me, saying, "Come with me, and

Get Fit

SHARING YOUR FEELINGS
Men are notorious for not sharing their feelings, but our habitual stoicism may be doing more than simply frustrating our loved ones—it can also be damaging our health. Studies show that men who regularly share their feelings with their spouses or close friends are generally happier, healthier, and even live longer than men who don't share their feelings. To keep from becoming another one of those statistics, make an effort to share more than just the facts the next time you talk to your wife or best friend. Don't be afraid of telling them how you feel. God never created us to fly solo.

20:13 **Hades** The place of the dead.　21:2 **new Jerusalem** The spiritual city where God's people live with him.　21:3 **and...God** Some Greek copies do not have this phrase.　21:6 **Alpha and the Omega** The first and last letters of the Greek alphabet. This means "the beginning and the end."

<< Tech Support >>

SATELLITE RADIO

There is a television channel for every interest from food to home improvement. The same trend is shaping the future of radio. New satellite technology offers hundreds of channels with a rich sound superior to that of standard radio. The trouble is, you can't listen on existing radio equipment, and, like cell phones, the satellite signal doesn't always work everywhere, so there are trade-offs. Although media is a fixture in our culture, it's important to take a break and unplug now and then. Use those moments to pray and allow the Holy Spirit to speak.

I will show you the bride, the wife of the Lamb." [10]And the angel carried me away by the Spirit to a very large and high mountain. He showed me the holy city, Jerusalem, coming down out of heaven from God. [11]It was shining with the glory of God and was bright like a very expensive jewel, like a jasper, clear as crystal. [12]The city had a great high wall with twelve gates with twelve angels at the gates, and on each gate was written the name of one of the twelve tribes of Israel. [13]There were three gates on the east, three on the north, three on the south, and three on the west. [14]The walls of the city were built on twelve foundation stones, and on the stones were written the names of the twelve apostles of the Lamb.

[15]The angel who talked with me had a measuring rod made of gold to measure the city, its gates, and its wall. [16]The city was built in a square, and its length was equal to its width. The angel measured the city with the rod. The city was 1,500 miles long, 1,500 miles wide, and 1,500 miles high. [17]The angel also measured the wall. It was 216 feet high, by human measurements, which the angel was using. [18]The wall was made of jasper, and the city was made of pure gold, as pure as glass. [19]The foundation stones of the city walls were decorated with every kind of jewel. The first foundation was jasper, the second was sapphire, the third was chalcedony, the fourth was emerald, [20]the fifth was onyx, the sixth was carnelian, the seventh was chrysolite, the eighth was beryl, the ninth was topaz, the tenth was chrysoprase, the eleventh was jacinth, and the twelfth was amethyst. [21]The twelve gates were twelve pearls, each gate having been made from a single pearl. And the street of the city was made of pure gold as clear as glass.

[22]I did not see a temple in the city, because the Lord God Almighty and the Lamb are the city's temple. [23]The city does not need the sun or the moon to shine on it, because the glory of God is its light, and the Lamb is the city's lamp. [24]By its light the people of the world will walk, and the kings of the earth will bring their glory into it. [25]The city's gates will never be shut on any day, because there is no night there. [26]The glory and the honor of the nations will be brought into it. [27]Nothing unclean and no one who does shameful things or tells lies will ever go into it. Only those whose names are written in the Lamb's book of life will enter the city.

22 Then the angel showed me the river of the water of life. It was shining like crystal and was flowing from the throne of God and of the Lamb [2]down the middle of the street of the city. The tree of life was on each side of the river. It produces fruit twelve times a year, once each month. The leaves of the tree are for the healing of all the nations. [3]Nothing that God judges guilty will be in that city. The throne of God and of the Lamb will be there, and God's servants will worship him. [4]They will see his face, and his name will be written on their foreheads. [5]There will never be night again. They will not need the light of a lamp or the light of the sun, because the Lord God will give them light. And they will rule as kings forever and ever.

[6]The angel said to me, "These words can be trusted and are true." The Lord, the God of the spirits of the prophets, sent his angel to

Principles: TEMPTATION

Temptation is the method the devil uses to lure believers into committing sin and, ultimately, to turn believers against God. After Jesus finished preparing for his ministry, Satan tempted him in the desert. Christ overcame his wiles by quoting God's Word, and that is how we must resist as we face temptation ourselves. First Corinthians 10:13 promises that God will always give us a way to escape from sinning. However, it isn't always the devil who tempts us. James 1:14 says that we can be led astray by our own evil desires. Jesus told his followers to pray for strength against temptation, and we should do the same today.

show his servants the things that must happen soon.

[7]"Listen! I am coming soon! Blessed is the one who obeys the words of prophecy in this book."

[8]I, John, am the one who heard and saw these things. When I heard and saw them, I bowed down to worship at the feet of the angel who showed these things to me. [9]But the angel said to me, "Do not worship me! I am a servant like you, your brothers the prophets, and all those who obey the words in this book. Worship God!"

[10]Then the angel told me, "Do not keep secret the words of prophecy in this book, because the time is near for all this to happen. [11]Let whoever is doing evil continue to do evil. Let whoever is unclean continue to be unclean. Let whoever is doing right continue to do right. Let whoever is holy continue to be holy."

[12]"Listen! I am coming soon! I will bring my reward with me, and I will repay each one of you for what you have done. [13]I am the Alpha and the Omega," the First and the Last, the Beginning and the End.

[14]"Blessed are those who wash their robes" so that they will receive the right to eat the fruit from the tree of life and may go through the gates into the city. [15]Outside the city are the evil people, those who do evil magic, who sin sexually, who murder, who worship idols, and who love lies and tell lies.

[16]"I, Jesus, have sent my angel to tell you these things for the churches. I am the de-

THINK ABOUT IT — Revelation 22:17

THE CHORUS IS SUNG AROUND THE WORLD in different languages: "There's a welcome here. There's a welcome here. There's a Christian welcome here." Some people are hesitant to discuss spiritual matters or religion. The saying goes that two topics to avoid with people are religion and politics. In general, these topics are avoided because matters of faith seem forbidding or even scary.

To some people, Christianity is nothing but judgment and condemnation. Yet in the final chapter of Revelation, Jesus offers an open invitation by saying, "Let whoever is thirsty come; whoever wishes may have the water of life as a free gift." His invitation continues to hold the power to draw people to faith today.

You may be confused about many issues when it comes to religion, but listen to God's gracious offer that Christ Jesus wants to forgive you of your sins and welcome you into new life. Accept his invitation to drink the water of eternal life and begin an exciting journey that leads to God.

scendant from the family of David, and I am the bright morning star."

[17]The Spirit and the bride say, "Come!" Let the one who hears this say, "Come!" Let whoever is thirsty come; whoever wishes may have the water of life as a free gift.

[18]I warn everyone who hears the words of the prophecy of this book: If anyone adds anything to these words, God will add to that person the disasters written about in this book. [19]And if anyone takes away from the words of this book of prophecy, God will take away that one's share of the tree of life and of the holy city, which are written about in this book.

[20]Jesus, the One who says these things are true, says, "Yes, I am coming soon."

Amen. Come, Lord Jesus!

[21]The grace of the Lord Jesus be with all. Amen.

22:13 Alpha and the Omega The first and last letters of the Greek alphabet. This means "the beginning and the end." **22:14 wash their robes** This means they believed and obeyed Jesus so that their sins could be forgiven by Christ's blood. The "washing" may refer to baptism (Acts 22:16).

>> 30 Days with Jesus